Praise for the First Edition

"2005 Best Java Book!"

—*Java Developer's Journal*

Hibernate In Action has to be considered the definitive tome on Hibernate. As the authors are intimately involved with the project, the insight on Hibernate that they provide can't be easily duplicated.

—*JavaRanch.com*

"Not only gets you up to speed with Hibernate and its features…It also introduces you to the right way of developing and tuning an industrial-quality Hibernate application. …albeit very technical, it reads astonishingly easy…unfortunately very rare nowadays…[an] excellent piece of work…"

—*JavaLobby.com*

"The first and only full tutorial, reference, and authoritative guide, and one of the most anticipated books of the year for Hibernate users."

—*Dr. Dobb's Journal*

"…the book was beyond my expectations…this book is the ultimate solution."

—*Javalobby.org, (second review, fall 2005)*

"…from none others than the lead developer and the lead documenter, this book is a great introduction and reference documentation to using Hibernate. It is organized in such a way that the concepts are explained in progressive order from very simple to more complex, and the authors take good care of explaining every detail with good examples. …The book not only gets you up to speed with Hibernate and its features (which the documentation does quite well). It also introduces you to the right way of developing and tuning an industrial-quality Hibernate application."

—*Slashdot.org*

"Strongly recommended, because a contemporary and state-of-the-art topic is very well explained, and especially, because the voices come literally from the horses' mouths."

—*C Vu, the Journal of the ACCU*

Java Persistence with Hibernate

REVISED EDITION OF
HIBERNATE IN ACTION

CHRISTIAN BAUER
AND GAVIN KING

M

MANNING

Greenwich
(74° w. long.)

For online information and ordering of this and other Manning books, please visit
www.manning.com. The publisher offers discounts on this book when ordered in quantity.
For more information, please contact:

Special Sales Department
Manning Publications Co.
Cherokee Station
PO Box 20386   Fax: (609) 877-8256
New York, NY 10021   email: orders@manning.com

 Manning Publications Co.   Copyeditor: Tiffany Taylor
209 Bruce Park Avenue   Typesetters: Dottie Marsico
Greenwich, CT 06830   Cover designer: Leslie Haimes

ISBN 1-932394-88-5
Printed in the United States of America

1 2 3 4 5 6 7 8 9 10 – VHG – 10 09 08 07 06

brief contents

contents

vii

PART 3 CONVERSATIONAL OBJECT PROCESSING 381

foreword to the revised edition

When *Hibernate in Action* was published two years ago, it was immediately recognized not only as the definitive book on Hibernate, but also as the definitive work on object/relational mapping.

In the intervening time, the persistence landscape has changed with the release of the Java Persistence API, the new standard for object/relational mapping for Java EE and Java SE which was developed under the Java Community Process as part of the Enterprise JavaBeans 3.0 Specification.

In developing the Java Persistence API, the EJB 3.0 Expert Group benefitted heavily from the experience of the O/R mapping frameworks already in use in the Java community. As one of the leaders among these, Hibernate has had a very significant influence on the technical direction of Java Persistence. This was due not only to the participation of Gavin King and other members of the Hibernate team in the EJB 3.0 standardization effort, but was also due in large part to the direct and pragmatic approach that Hibernate has taken towards O/R mapping and to the simplicity, clarity, and power of its APIs–and their resulting appeal to the Java community.

In addition to their contributions to Java Persistence, the Hibernate developers also have taken major steps forward for Hibernate with the Hibernate 3 release described in this book. Among these are support for operations over large datasets; additional and more sophisticated mapping options, especially for handling legacy databases; data filters; strategies for managing conversations; and integration with Seam, the new framework for web application development with JSF and EJB 3.0.

Java Persistence with Hibernate is therefore considerably more than simply a second edition to *Hibernate in Action*. It provides a comprehensive overview of all the capabilities of the Java Persistence API in addition to those of Hibernate 3, as well as a detailed comparative analysis of the two. It describes how Hibernate has been used to implement the Java Persistence standard, and how to leverage the Hibernate extensions to Java Persistence.

More important, throughout the presentation of Hibernate and Java Persistence, Christian Bauer and Gavin King illustrate and explain the fundamental principles and decisions that need to be taken into account in both the design and use of an object/relational mapping framework. The insights they provide into the underlying issues of ORM give the reader a deep understanding into the effective application of ORM as an enterprise technology.

Java Persistence with Hibernate thus reaches out to a wide range of developers—from newcomers to object/relational mapping to experienced developers—seeking to learn more about cutting-edge technological innovations in the Java community that have occurred and are continuing to emerge as a result of this work.

LINDA DeMICHIEL
Specification Lead
Enterprise JavaBeans 3.0 and Java Persistence
Sun Microsystems

foreword to the first edition

Relational databases are indisputably at the core of the modern enterprise.

While modern programming languages, including Java™, provide an intuitive, object-oriented view of application-level business entities, the enterprise data underlying these entities is heavily relational in nature. Further, the main strength of the relational model—over earlier navigational models as well as over later OODB models—is that by design it is intrinsically agnostic to the programmatic manipulation and application-level view of the data that it serves up.

Many attempts have been made to bridge relational and object-oriented technologies, or to replace one with the other, but the gap between the two is one of the hard facts of enterprise computing today. It is this challenge—to provide a bridge between relational data and Java™ objects—that Hibernate takes on through its object/relational mapping (ORM) approach. Hibernate meets this challenge in a very pragmatic, direct, and realistic way.

As Christian Bauer and Gavin King demonstrate in this book, the effective use of ORM technology in all but the simplest of enterprise environments requires understanding and configuring how the mediation between relational data and objects is performed. This demands that the developer be aware and knowledgeable both of the application and its data requirements, and of the SQL query language, relational storage structures, and the potential for optimization that relational technology offers.

Not only does Hibernate provide a full-function solution that meets these requirements head on, it is also a flexible and configurable architecture. Hibernate's developers designed it with modularity, pluggability, extensibility, and user customization in mind. As a result, in the few years since its initial release, Hibernate has rapidly become one of the leading ORM technologies for enterprise developers—and deservedly so.

This book provides a comprehensive overview of Hibernate. It covers how to use its type mapping capabilities and facilities for modeling associations and inheritance; how to retrieve objects efficiently using the Hibernate query language; how to configure Hibernate for use in both managed and unmanaged environments; and how to use its tools. In addition, throughout the book the authors provide insight into the underlying issues of ORM and into the design choices behind Hibernate. These insights give the reader a deep understanding of the effective use of ORM as an enterprise technology.

Hibernate in Action is the definitive guide to using Hibernate and to object/relational mapping in enterprise computing today.

LINDA DEMICHIEL
Lead Architect, Enterprise JavaBeans
Sun Microsystems

preface to the revised edition

The predecessor of this book, *Hibernate in Action*, started with a quote from Anthony Berglas: "Just because it is possible to push twigs along the ground with one's nose does not necessarily mean that that is the best way to collect firewood." Since then, the Hibernate project and the strategies and concepts software developers rely on to manage information have evolved. However, the fundamental issues are still the same—every company we work with every day still uses SQL databases, and Java is entrenched in the industry as the first choice for enterprise application development.

The tabular representation of data in a relational system is still fundamentally different than the networks of objects used in object-oriented Java applications. We still see the object/relational impedance mismatch, and we frequently see that the importance and cost of this mismatch is underestimated.

On the other hand, we now have a range of tools and solutions available to deal with this problem. We're done collecting firewood, and the pocket lighter has been replaced with a flame thrower.

Hibernate is now available in its third major release; Hibernate 3.2 is the version we describe in this book. Compared to older Hibernate versions, this new major release has twice as many features—and this book is almost double the size of *Hibernate in Action*. Most of these features are ones that you, the developers working with Hibernate every day, have asked for. We've sometimes said that Hibernate is a 90 percent solution for all the problems a Java application developer has to deal with when creating a database application. With the latest Hibernate version, this number is more likely 99 percent.

As Hibernate matured and its user base and community kept growing, the Java standards for data management and database application development were found lacking by many developers. We even told you not to use EJB 2.x entity beans in *Hibernate in Action.*

Enter EJB 3.0 and the new Java Persistence standard. This new industry standard is a major step forward for the Java developer community. It defines a lightweight and simplified programming model and powerful object/relational persistence. Many of the key concepts of the new standard were modeled after Hibernate and other successful object/relational persistence solutions. The latest Hibernate version implements the Java Persistence standard.

So, in addition to the new all-in-one Hibernate for every purpose, you can now use Hibernate like any Java Persistence provider, with or without other EJB 3.0 components and Java EE 5.0 services. This deep integration of Hibernate with such a rich programming model enables you to design and implement application functionality that was difficult to create by hand before.

We wrote this book to give you a complete and accurate guide to both Hibernate and Java Persistence (and also all relevant EJB 3.0 concepts). We hope that you'll enjoy learning Hibernate and that you'll keep this reference bible on your desk for your daily work.

preface to the first edition

Just because it is possible to push twigs along the ground with one's nose does not necessarily mean that that is the best way to collect firewood.

—Anthony Berglas

Today, many software developers work with Enterprise Information Systems (EIS). This kind of application creates, manages, and stores structured information and shares this information between many users in multiple physical locations.

The storage of EIS data involves massive usage of SQL-based database management systems. Every company we've met during our careers uses at least one SQL database; most are completely dependent on relational database technology at the core of their business.

In the past five years, broad adoption of the Java programming language has brought about the ascendancy of the object-oriented paradigm for software development. Developers are now sold on the benefits of object orientation. However, the vast majority of businesses are also tied to long-term investments in expensive relational database systems. Not only are particular vendor products entrenched, but existing legacy data must be made available to (and via) the shiny new object-oriented web applications.

However, the tabular representation of data in a relational system is fundamentally different than the networks of objects used in object-oriented Java applications. This difference has led to the so-called *object/relational paradigm* mismatch.

Traditionally, the importance and cost of this mismatch have been underestimated, and tools for solving the mismatch have been insufficient. Meanwhile, Java developers blame relational technology for the mismatch; data professionals blame object technology.

Object/relational mapping (ORM) is the name given to automated solutions to the mismatch problem. For developers weary of tedious data access code, the good news is that ORM has come of age. Applications built with ORM middleware can be expected to be cheaper, more performant, less vendor-specific, and more able to cope with changes to the internal object or underlying SQL schema. The astonishing thing is that these benefits are now available to Java developers for free.

Gavin King began developing Hibernate in late 2001 when he found that the popular persistence solution at the time—CMP Entity Beans—didn't scale to nontrivial applications with complex data models. Hibernate began life as an independent, noncommercial open source project.

The Hibernate team (including the authors) has learned ORM the hard way—that is, by listening to user requests and implementing what was needed to satisfy those requests. The result, Hibernate, is a practical solution, emphasizing developer productivity and technical leadership. Hibernate has been used by tens of thousands of users and in many thousands of production applications.

When the demands on their time became overwhelming, the Hibernate team concluded that the future success of the project (and Gavin's continued sanity) demanded professional developers dedicated full-time to Hibernate. Hibernate joined jboss.org in late 2003 and now has a commercial aspect; you can purchase commercial support and training from JBoss Inc. But commercial training shouldn't be the only way to learn about Hibernate.

It's obvious that many, perhaps even most, Java projects benefit from the use of an ORM solution like Hibernate—although this wasn't obvious a couple of years ago! As ORM technology becomes increasingly mainstream, product documentation such as Hibernate's free user manual is no longer sufficient. We realized that the Hibernate community and new Hibernate users needed a full-length book, not only to learn about developing software with Hibernate, but also to understand and appreciate the object/relational mismatch and the motivations behind Hibernate's design.

The book you're holding was an enormous effort that occupied most of our spare time for more than a year. It was also the source of many heated disputes and learning experiences. We hope this book is an excellent guide to Hibernate (or, "the Hibernate bible," as one of our reviewers put it) and also the first comprehensive documentation of the object/relational mismatch and ORM in general. We hope you find it helpful and enjoy working with Hibernate.

acknowledgments

This book grew from a small second edition of *Hibernate in Action* into a volume of considerable size. We couldn't have created it without the help of many people.

Emmanuel Bernard did an excellent job as the technical reviewer of this book; thank you for the many hours you spent editing our broken code examples. We'd also like to thank our other reviewers: Patrick Dennis, Jon Skeet, Awais Bajwa, Dan Dobrin, Deiveehan Nallazhagappan, Ryan Daigle, Stuart Caborn, Patrick Peak, TVS Murthy, Bill Fly, David Walend, Dave Dribin, Anjan Bacchu, Gary Udstrand, and Srinivas Nallapati. Special thanks to Linda DeMichiel for agreeing to write the foreword to our book, as she did to the first edition.

Marjan Bace again assembled a great production team at Manning: Sydney Jones edited our crude manuscript and turned it into a real book. Tiffany Taylor, Elizabeth Martin, and Andy Carroll found all our typos and made the book readable. Dottie Marsico was responsible for typesetting and gave this book its great look. Mary Piergies coordinated and organized the production process. We'd like to thank you all for working with us.

about this book

We had three goals when writing this book, so you can read it as

- A tutorial for Hibernate, Java Persistence, and EJB 3.0 that guides you through your first steps with these solutions
- A guide for learning all basic and advanced Hibernate features for object/relational mapping, object processing, querying, performance optimization, and application design
- A reference for whenever you need a complete and technically accurate definition of Hibernate and Java Persistence functionality

Usually, books are either tutorials or reference guides, so this stretch comes at a price. If you're new to Hibernate, we suggest that you start reading the book from the start, with the tutorials in chapters 1 and 2. If you have used an older version of Hibernate, you should read the first two chapters quickly to get an overview and then jump into the middle with chapter 3.

We will, whenever appropriate, tell you if a particular section or subject is optional or reference material that you can safely skip during your first read.

Roadmap

This book is divided into three major parts.

In part 1, we introduce the object/relational paradigm mismatch and explain the fundamentals behind object/relational mapping. We walk through a hands-on tutorial to get you started with your first Hibernate, Java Persistence, or EJB 3.0 project. We look at Java application design for domain models and at the options for creating object/relational mapping metadata.

Mapping Java classes and properties to SQL tables and columns is the focus of part 2. We explore all basic and advanced mapping options in Hibernate and Java Persistence, with XML mapping files and Java annotations. We show you how to deal with inheritance, collections, and complex class associations. Finally, we discuss integration with legacy database schemas and some mapping strategies that are especially tricky.

Part 3 is all about the processing of objects and how you can load and store data with Hibernate and Java Persistence. We introduce the programming interfaces, how to write transactional and conversation-aware applications, and how to write queries. Later, we focus on the correct design and implementation of layered Java applications. We discuss the most common design patterns that are used with Hibernate, such as the Data Access Object (DAO) and EJB Command patterns. You'll see how you can test your Hibernate application easily and what other best practices are relevant if you work an object/relational mapping software.

Finally, we introduce the JBoss Seam framework, which takes many Hibernate concepts to the next level and enables you to create conversational web applications with ease. We promise you'll find this chapter interesting, even if you don't plan to use Seam.

Who should read this book?

Readers of this book should have basic knowledge of object-oriented software development and should have used this knowledge in practice. To understand the application examples, you should be familiar with the Java programming language and the Unified Modeling Language.

Our primary target audience consists of Java developers who work with SQL-based database systems. We'll show you how to substantially increase your productivity by leveraging ORM.

If you're a database developer, the book can be part of your introduction to object-oriented software development.

If you're a database administrator, you'll be interested in how ORM affects performance and how you can tune the performance of the SQL database-management system and persistence layer to achieve performance targets. Because data access is the bottleneck in most Java applications, this book pays close attention to performance issues. Many DBAs are understandably nervous about entrusting performance to tool-generated SQL code; we seek to allay those fears and also to highlight cases where applications shouldn't use tool-managed data access. You may be relieved to discover that we don't claim that ORM is the best solution to every problem.

Code conventions

This book provides copious examples, which include all the Hibernate application artifacts: Java code, Hibernate configuration files, and XML mapping metadata files. Source code in listings or in text is in a `fixed-width font like this` to separate it from ordinary text. Additionally, Java method names, component parameters, object properties, and XML elements and attributes in text are also presented using `fixed-width` font.

Java, HTML, and XML can all be verbose. In many cases, the original source code (available online) has been reformatted; we've added line breaks and reworked indentation to accommodate the available page space in the book. In rare cases, even this was not enough, and listings include line-continuation markers. Additionally, comments in the source code have often been removed from the listings when the code is described in the text.

Code annotations accompany some of the source code listings, highlighting important concepts. In some cases, numbered bullets link to explanations that follow the listing.

Source code downloads

Hibernate is an open source project released under the Lesser GNU Public License. Directions for downloading Hibernate packages, in source or binary form, are available from the Hibernate web site: www.hibernate.org/.

The source code for all Hello World and CaveatEmptor examples in this book is available from http://caveatemptor.hibernate.org/ under a free (BSD-like) license. The CaveatEmptor example application code is available on this web site in different flavors—for example, with a focus on native Hibernate, on Java Persistence, and on JBoss Seam. You can also download the code for the examples in this book from the publisher's website, www.manning.com/bauer2.

About the authors

Christian Bauer is a member of the Hibernate developer team. He works as a trainer, consultant, and product manager for Hibernate, EJB 3.0, and JBoss Seam at JBoss, a division of Red Hat. With Gavin King, Christian wrote *Hibernate in Action.*

Gavin King is the founder of the Hibernate and JBoss Seam projects, and a member of the EJB 3.0 (JSR 220) expert group. He also leads the Web Beans JSR 299, a standardization effort involving Hibernate concepts, JBoss Seam, JSF, and EJB 3.0. Gavin works as a lead developer at JBoss, a division of Red Hat.

Author Online

Your purchase of *Java Persistence with Hibernate* includes free access to a private web forum run by Manning Publications, where you can make comments about the book, ask technical questions, and receive help from the authors and from other users. To access the forum and subscribe to it, point your web browser to www.manning.com/bauer2. This page provides information on how to get onto the forum once you are registered, what kind of help is available, and the rules of conduct on the forum.

Manning's commitment to our readers is to provide a venue where a meaningful dialogue among individual readers and between readers and the authors can take place. It is not a commitment to any specific amount of participation on the part of the author, whose contribution to the AO remains voluntary (and unpaid). We suggest you try asking the authors some challenging questions, lest their interest stray!

The Author Online forum and the archives of previous discussions will be accessible from the publisher's website as long as the book is in print.

about the cover illustration

The illustration on the cover of *Java Persistence with Hibernate* is taken from a collection of costumes of the Ottoman Empire published on January 1, 1802, by William Miller of Old Bond Street, London. The title page is missing from the collection and we have been unable to track it down to date. The book's table of contents identifies the figures in both English and French, and each illustration bears the names of two artists who worked on it, both of whom would no doubt be surprised to find their art gracing the front cover of a computer programming book...two hundred years later.

The collection was purchased by a Manning editor at an antiquarian flea market in the "Garage" on West 26th Street in Manhattan. The seller was an American based in Ankara, Turkey, and the transaction took place just as he was packing up his stand for the day. The Manning editor did not have on his person the substantial amount of cash that was required for the purchase and a credit card and check were both politely turned down. With the seller flying back to Ankara that evening the situation was getting hopeless. What was the solution? It turned out to be nothing more than an old-fashioned verbal agreement sealed with a handshake. The seller simply proposed that the money be transferred to him by wire and the editor walked out with the bank information on a piece of paper and the portfolio of images under his arm. Needless to say, we transferred the funds the next day, and we remain grateful and impressed by this unknown person's trust in one of us. It recalls something that might have happened a long time ago.

The pictures from the Ottoman collection, like the other illustrations that appear on our covers, bring to life the richness and variety of dress customs of two centuries ago. They recall the sense of isolation and distance of that period—and of every other historic period except our own hyperkinetic present.

Dress codes have changed since then and the diversity by region, so rich at the time, has faded away. It is now often hard to tell the inhabitant of one continent from another. Perhaps, trying to view it optimistically, we have traded a cultural and visual diversity for a more varied personal life. Or a more varied and interesting intellectual and technical life.

We at Manning celebrate the inventiveness, the initiative, and, yes, the fun of the computer business with book covers based on the rich diversity of regional life of two centuries ago, brought back to life by the pictures from this collection.

Part 1

Getting started with Hibernate and EJB 3.0

In part 1, we show you why object persistence is such a complex topic and what solutions you can apply in practice. Chapter 1 introduces the object/relational paradigm mismatch and several strategies to deal with it, foremost object/relational mapping (ORM). In chapter 2, we guide you step by step through a tutorial with Hibernate, Java Persistence, and EJB 3.0—you'll implement and test a "Hello World" example in all variations. Thus prepared, in chapter 3 you're ready to learn how to design and implement complex business domain models in Java, and which mapping metadata options you have available.

After reading this part of the book, you'll understand why you need object/relational mapping, and how Hibernate, Java Persistence, and EJB 3.0 work in practice. You'll have written your first small project, and you'll be ready to take on more complex problems. You'll also understand how real-world business entities can be implemented as a Java domain model, and in what format you prefer to work with object/relational mapping metadata.

Understanding object/relational persistence

1

This chapter covers

- Object persistence with SQL databases
- The object/relational paradigm mismatch
- Persistence layers in object-oriented applications
- Object/relational mapping background

The approach to managing persistent data has been a key design decision in every software project we've worked on. Given that persistent data isn't a new or unusual requirement for Java applications, you'd expect to be able to make a simple choice among similar, well-established persistence solutions. Think of web application frameworks (Struts versus WebWork), GUI component frameworks (Swing versus SWT), or template engines (JSP versus Velocity). Each of the competing solutions has various advantages and disadvantages, but they all share the same scope and overall approach. Unfortunately, this isn't yet the case with persistence technologies, where we see some wildly differing solutions to the same problem.

For several years, persistence has been a hot topic of debate in the Java community. Many developers don't even agree on the scope of the problem. Is persistence a problem that is already solved by relational technology and extensions such as stored procedures, or is it a more pervasive problem that must be addressed by special Java component models, such as EJB entity beans? Should we hand-code even the most primitive CRUD (create, read, update, delete) operations in SQL and JDBC, or should this work be automated? How do we achieve portability if every database management system has its own SQL dialect? Should we abandon SQL completely and adopt a different database technology, such as object database systems? Debate continues, but a solution called *object/relational mapping* (ORM) now has wide acceptance. Hibernate is an open source ORM service implementation.

Hibernate is an ambitious project that aims to be a complete solution to the problem of managing persistent data in Java. It mediates the application's interaction with a relational database, leaving the developer free to concentrate on the business problem at hand. Hibernate is a nonintrusive solution. You aren't required to follow many Hibernate-specific rules and design patterns when writing your business logic and persistent classes; thus, Hibernate integrates smoothly with most new and existing applications and doesn't require disruptive changes to the rest of the application.

This book is about Hibernate. We'll cover basic and advanced features and describe some ways to develop new applications using Hibernate. Often, these recommendations won't even be specific to Hibernate. Sometimes they will be our ideas about the *best* ways to do things when working with persistent data, explained in the context of Hibernate. This book is also about Java Persistence, a new standard for persistence that is part of the also updated EJB 3.0 specification. Hibernate implements Java Persistence and supports all the standardized mappings, queries, and APIs. Before we can get started with Hibernate, however, you need to understand the core problems of object persistence and object/relational mapping. This chapter explains why tools like Hibernate and specifications such as Java Persistence and EJB 3.0 are needed.

First, we define persistent data management in the context of object-oriented applications and discuss the relationship of SQL, JDBC, and Java, the underlying technologies and standards that Hibernate is built on. We then discuss the so-called *object/relational paradigm mismatch* and the generic problems we encounter in object-oriented software development with relational databases. These problems make it clear that we need tools and patterns to minimize the time we have to spend on the persistence-related code of our applications. After we look at alternative tools and persistence mechanisms, you'll see that ORM is the best available solution for many scenarios. Our discussion of the advantages and drawbacks of ORM will give you the full background to make the best decision when picking a persistence solution for your own project.

We also take a look at the various Hibernate software modules, and how you can combine them to either work with Hibernate only, or with Java Persistence and EJB 3.0-compliant features.

The best way to learn Hibernate isn't necessarily linear. We understand that you may want to try Hibernate right away. If this is how you'd like to proceed, skip to the second chapter of this book and have a look at the "Hello World" example and set up a project. We recommend that you return here at some point as you circle through the book. That way, you'll be prepared and have all the background concepts you need for the rest of the material.

1.1 What is persistence?

Almost all applications require persistent data. Persistence is one of the fundamental concepts in application development. If an information system didn't preserve data when it was powered off, the system would be of little practical use. When we talk about persistence in Java, we're normally talking about storing data in a relational database using SQL. We'll start by taking a brief look at the technology and how we use it with Java. Armed with that information, we'll then continue our discussion of persistence and how it's implemented in object-oriented applications.

1.1.1 Relational databases

You, like most other developers, have probably worked with a relational database. Most of us use a relational database every day. Relational technology is a known quantity, and this alone is sufficient reason for many organizations to choose it.

But to say only this is to pay less respect than is due. Relational databases are entrenched because they're an incredibly flexible and robust approach to data management. Due to the complete and consistent theoretical foundation of the relational data model, relational databases can effectively guarantee and protect the integrity of the data, among other desirable characteristics. Some people would even say that the last big invention in computing has been the relational concept for data management as first introduced by E.F. Codd (Codd, 1970) more than three decades ago.

Relational database management systems aren't specific to Java, nor is a relational database specific to a particular application. This important principle is known as *data independence.* In other words, and we can't stress this important fact enough, *data lives longer than any application does.* Relational technology provides a way of sharing data among different applications, or among different technologies that form parts of the same application (the transactional engine and the reporting engine, for example). Relational technology is a common denominator of many disparate systems and technology platforms. Hence, the relational data model is often the common enterprise-wide representation of business entities.

Relational database management systems have SQL-based application programming interfaces; hence, we call today's relational database products SQL *database management systems* or, when we're talking about particular systems, SQL *databases.*

Before we go into more detail about the practical aspects of SQL databases, we have to mention an important issue: Although marketed as relational, a database system providing only an SQL data language interface isn't really relational and in many ways isn't even close to the original concept. Naturally, this has led to confusion. SQL practitioners blame the relational data model for shortcomings in the SQL language, and relational data management experts blame the SQL standard for being a weak implementation of the relational model and ideals. Application developers are stuck somewhere in the middle, with the burden to deliver something that works. We'll highlight some important and significant aspects of this issue throughout the book, but generally we'll focus on the practical aspects. If you're interested in more background material, we highly recommend *Practical Issues in Database Management: A Reference for the Thinking Practitioner* by Fabian Pascal (Pascal, 2000).

1.1.2 Understanding SQL

To use Hibernate effectively, a solid understanding of the relational model and SQL is a prerequisite. You need to understand the relational model and topics such as normalization to guarantee the integrity of your data, and you'll need to use your knowledge of SQL to tune the performance of your Hibernate application. Hibernate automates many repetitive coding tasks, but your knowledge of persistence technology must extend beyond Hibernate itself if you want to take advantage of the full power of modern SQL databases. Remember that the underlying goal is robust, efficient management of persistent data.

Let's review some of the SQL terms used in this book. You use SQL as a *data definition language* (DDL) to create a database schema with CREATE and ALTER statements. After creating tables (and indexes, sequences, and so on), you use SQL as a *data manipulation language* (DML) to manipulate and retrieve data. The manipulation operations include *insertions, updates,* and *deletions.* You retrieve data by executing queries with *restrictions, projections,* and *join* operations (including the *Cartesian product*). For efficient reporting, you use SQL to *group, order,* and *aggregate* data as necessary. You can even nest SQL statements inside each other; this technique uses *subselects.*

You've probably used SQL for many years and are familiar with the basic operations and statements written in this language. Still, we know from our own experience that SQL is sometimes hard to remember, and some terms vary in usage. To understand this book, we must use the same terms and concepts, so we advise you to read appendix A if any of the terms we've mentioned are new or unclear.

If you need more details, especially about any performance aspects and how SQL is executed, get a copy of the excellent book *SQL Tuning* by Dan Tow (Tow, 2003). Also read *An Introduction to Database Systems* by Chris Date (Date, 2003) for the theory, concepts, and ideals of (relational) database systems. The latter book is an excellent reference (it's big) for all questions you may possibly have about databases and data management.

Although the relational database is one part of ORM, the other part, of course, consists of the objects in your Java application that need to be persisted to and loaded from the database using SQL.

1.1.3 *Using SQL in Java*

When you work with an SQL database in a Java application, the Java code issues SQL statements to the database via the Java Database Connectivity (JDBC) API. Whether the SQL was written by hand and embedded in the Java code, or generated on the fly by Java code, you use the JDBC API to bind arguments to prepare query parameters, execute the query, scroll through the query result table, retrieve values from the result set, and so on. These are low-level data access tasks; as application developers, we're more interested in the business problem that requires this data access. What we'd really like to write is code that saves and retrieves objects—the instances of our classes—to and from the database, relieving us of this low-level drudgery.

Because the data access tasks are often so tedious, we have to ask: Are the relational data model and (especially) SQL the right choices for persistence in object-oriented applications? We answer this question immediately: Yes! There are many reasons why SQL databases dominate the computing industry—relational database management systems are the only proven data management technology, and they're almost always a *requirement* in any Java project.

However, for the last 15 years, developers have spoken of a *paradigm mismatch*. This mismatch explains why so much effort is expended on persistence-related concerns in every enterprise project. The *paradigms* referred to are object modeling and relational modeling, or perhaps object-oriented programming and SQL.

Let's begin our exploration of the mismatch problem by asking what *persistence* means in the context of object-oriented application development. First we'll widen the simplistic definition of persistence stated at the beginning of this section to a broader, more mature understanding of what is involved in maintaining and using persistent data.

1.1.4   *Persistence in object-oriented applications*

In an object-oriented application, persistence allows an object to outlive the process that created it. The state of the object can be stored to disk, and an object with the same state can be re-created at some point in the future.

This isn't limited to single objects—entire networks of interconnected objects can be made persistent and later re-created in a new process. Most objects aren't persistent; a *transient* object has a limited lifetime that is bounded by the life of the process that instantiated it. Almost all Java applications contain a mix of persistent and transient objects; hence, we need a subsystem that manages our persistent data.

Modern relational databases provide a structured representation of persistent data, enabling the manipulating, sorting, searching, and aggregating of data. Database management systems are responsible for managing concurrency and data integrity; they're responsible for sharing data between multiple users and multiple applications. They guarantee the integrity of the data through integrity rules that have been implemented with constraints. A database management system provides data-level security. When we discuss persistence in this book, we're thinking of all these things:

- Storage, organization, and retrieval of structured data
- Concurrency and data integrity
- Data sharing

And, in particular, we're thinking of these problems in the context of an object-oriented application that uses a domain model.

An application with a domain model doesn't work directly with the tabular representation of the business entities; the application has its own object-oriented model of the business entities. If the database of an online auction system has ITEM and BID tables, for example, the Java application defines Item and Bid classes.

Then, instead of directly working with the rows and columns of an SQL result set, the business logic interacts with this object-oriented domain model and its runtime realization as a network of interconnected objects. Each instance of a Bid has a reference to an auction Item, and each Item may have a collection of references to Bid instances. The business logic isn't executed in the database (as an SQL stored procedure); it's implemented in Java in the application tier. This allows business logic to make use of sophisticated object-oriented concepts such as inheritance and polymorphism. For example, we could use well-known design patterns such as *Strategy, Mediator,* and *Composite* (Gamma and others, 1995), all of which depend on polymorphic method calls.

Now a caveat: Not all Java applications are designed this way, nor should they be. Simple applications may be much better off without a domain model. Complex applications may have to reuse existing stored procedures. SQL and the JDBC API are perfectly serviceable for dealing with pure tabular data, and the JDBC *RowSet* makes CRUD operations even easier. Working with a tabular representation of persistent data is straightforward and well understood.

However, in the case of applications with nontrivial business logic, the domain model approach helps to improve code reuse and maintainability significantly. In practice, *both* strategies are common and needed. Many applications need to execute procedures that modify large sets of data, close to the data. At the same time, other application modules could benefit from an object-oriented domain model that executes regular online transaction processing logic in the application tier. An efficient way to bring persistent data closer to the application code is required.

If we consider SQL and relational databases again, we finally observe the mismatch between the two paradigms. SQL operations such as projection and join always result in a tabular representation of the resulting data. (This is known as *transitive closure*, the result of an operation on relations is always a relation.) This is quite different from the network of interconnected objects used to execute the business logic in a Java application. These are fundamentally different models, not just different ways of visualizing the same model.

With this realization, you can begin to see the problems—some well understood and some less well understood—that must be solved by an application that combines both data representations: an object-oriented domain model and a persistent relational model. Let's take a closer look at this so-called paradigm mismatch.

1.2   *The paradigm mismatch*

The object/relational paradigm mismatch can be broken into several parts, which we'll examine one at a time. Let's start our exploration with a simple example that is problem free. As we build on it, you'll begin to see the mismatch appear.

Suppose you have to design and implement an online e-commerce application. In this application, you need a class to represent information about a user of the system, and another class to represent information about the user's billing details, as shown in figure 1.1.

In this diagram, you can see that a User has many BillingDetails. You can navigate the relationship between the classes in both directions. The classes representing these entities may be extremely simple:

```java
public class User {
    private String username;
    private String name;
    private String address;
    private Set billingDetails;

    // Accessor methods (getter/setter), business methods, etc.
    ...
}
public class BillingDetails {
    private String accountNumber;
    private String accountName;
    private String accountType;
    private User user;

    // Accessor methods (getter/setter), business methods, etc.
    ...
}
```

Figure 1.1
A simple UML class diagram of the
User and BillingDetails entities

Note that we're only interested in the state of the entities with regard to persistence, so we've omitted the implementation of property accessors and business methods (such as getUsername() or billAuction()).

It's easy to come up with a good SQL schema design for this case:

```
create table USERS (
    USERNAME varchar(15) not null primary key,
    NAME varchar(50) not null,
    ADDRESS varchar(100)
)
create table BILLING_DETAILS (
    ACCOUNT_NUMBER varchar(10) not null primary key,
    ACCOUNT_NAME varchar(50) not null,
    ACCOUNT_TYPE varchar(2) not null,
    USERNAME varchar(15) foreign key references user
)
```

The relationship between the two entities is represented as the foreign key, USERNAME, in BILLING_DETAILS. For this simple domain model, the object/relational mismatch is barely in evidence; it's straightforward to write JDBC code to insert, update, and delete information about users and billing details.

Now, let's see what happens when we consider something a little more realistic. The paradigm mismatch will be visible when we add more entities and entity relationships to our application.

The most glaringly obvious problem with our current implementation is that we've designed an address as a simple String value. In most systems, it's necessary to store street, city, state, country, and ZIP code information separately. Of course, we could add these properties directly to the User class, but because it's highly likely that other classes in the system will also carry address information, it makes more sense to create a separate Address class. The updated model is shown in figure 1.2.

Should we also add an ADDRESS table? Not necessarily. It's common to keep address information in the USERS table, in individual columns. This design is likely to perform better, because a table join isn't needed if you want to retrieve the user and address in a single query. The nicest solution may even be to create a user-defined SQL datatype to represent addresses, and to use a single column of that new type in the USERS table instead of several new columns.

Basically, we have the choice of adding either several columns or a single column (of a new SQL datatype). This is clearly a problem of *granularity*.

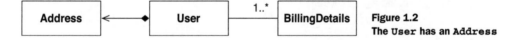

Figure 1.2
The User has an Address

1.2.1 *The problem of granularity*

Granularity refers to the relative size of the types you're working with.

Let's return to our example. Adding a new datatype to our database catalog, to store `Address` Java instances in a single column, sounds like the best approach. A new `Address` type (class) in Java and a new `ADDRESS` SQL datatype should guarantee interoperability. However, you'll find various problems if you check the support for user-defined datatypes (UDT) in today's SQL database management systems.

UDT support is one of a number of so-called *object-relational extensions* to traditional SQL. This term alone is confusing, because it means that the database management system has (or is supposed to support) a sophisticated datatype system—something you take for granted if somebody sells you a system that can handle data in a relational fashion. Unfortunately, UDT support is a somewhat obscure feature of most SQL database management systems and certainly isn't portable between different systems. Furthermore, the SQL standard supports user-defined datatypes, but poorly.

This limitation isn't the fault of the relational data model. You can consider the failure to standardize such an important piece of functionality as fallout from the object-relational database wars between vendors in the mid-1990s. Today, most developers accept that SQL products have limited type systems—no questions asked. However, even with a sophisticated UDT system in our SQL database management system, we would likely still duplicate the type declarations, writing the new type in Java and again in SQL. Attempts to find a solution for the Java space, such as SQLJ, unfortunately, have not had much success.

For these and whatever other reasons, use of UDTs or Java types inside an SQL database isn't common practice in the industry at this time, and it's unlikely that you'll encounter a legacy schema that makes extensive use of UDTs. We therefore can't and won't store instances of our new `Address` class in a single new column that has the same datatype as the Java layer.

Our pragmatic solution for this problem has several columns of built-in vendor-defined SQL types (such as boolean, numeric, and string datatypes). The `USERS` table is usually defined as follows:

```
create table USERS (
    USERNAME varchar(15) not null primary key,
    NAME varchar(50) not null,
    ADDRESS_STREET varchar(50),
    ADDRESS_CITY varchar(15),
    ADDRESS_STATE varchar(15),
```

```
    ADDRESS_ZIPCODE varchar(5),
    ADDRESS_COUNTRY varchar(15)
)
```

Classes in our domain model come in a range of different levels of granularity—from coarse-grained entity classes like `User`, to finer-grained classes like `Address`, down to simple `String`-valued properties such as `zipcode`. In contrast, just two levels of granularity are visible at the level of the SQL database: tables such as `USERS`, and columns such as `ADDRESS_ZIPCODE`.

Many simple persistence mechanisms fail to recognize this mismatch and so end up forcing the less flexible SQL representation upon the object model. We've seen countless `User` classes with properties named `zipcode`!

It turns out that the granularity problem isn't especially difficult to solve. We probably wouldn't even discuss it, were it not for the fact that it's visible in so many existing systems. We describe the solution to this problem in chapter 4, section 4.4, "Fine-grained models and mappings."

A much more difficult and interesting problem arises when we consider domain models that rely on *inheritance*, a feature of object-oriented design we may use to bill the users of our e-commerce application in new and interesting ways.

1.2.2 *The problem of subtypes*

In Java, you implement type inheritance using superclasses and subclasses. To illustrate why this can present a mismatch problem, let's add to our e-commerce application so that we now can accept not only bank account billing, but also credit and debit cards. The most natural way to reflect this change in the model is to use inheritance for the `BillingDetails` class.

We may have an abstract `BillingDetails` superclass, along with several concrete subclasses: `CreditCard`, `BankAccount`, and so on. Each of these subclasses defines slightly different data (and completely different functionality that acts on that data). The UML class diagram in figure 1.3 illustrates this model.

SQL should probably include standard support for *supertables* and *subtables*. This would effectively allow us to create a table that inherits certain columns from

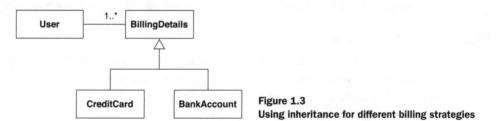

Figure 1.3
Using inheritance for different billing strategies

its parent. However, such a feature would be questionable, because it would introduce a new notion: *virtual columns* in base tables. Traditionally, we expect virtual columns only in virtual tables, which are called *views*. Furthermore, on a theoretical level, the inheritance we applied in Java is *type inheritance*. A table isn't a type, so the notion of supertables and subtables is questionable. In any case, we can take the short route here and observe that SQL database products don't generally implement type or table inheritance, and if they do implement it, they don't follow a standard syntax and usually expose you to data integrity problems (limited integrity rules for updatable views).

In chapter 5, section 5.1, "Mapping class inheritance," we discuss how ORM solutions such as Hibernate solve the problem of persisting a class hierarchy to a database table or tables. This problem is now well understood in the community, and most solutions support approximately the same functionality.

But we aren't finished with inheritance. As soon as we introduce inheritance into the model, we have the possibility of *polymorphism*.

The `User` class has an association to the `BillingDetails` superclass. This is a *polymorphic association*. At runtime, a `User` object may reference an instance of any of the subclasses of `BillingDetails`. Similarly, we want to be able to write *polymorphic queries* that refer to the `BillingDetails` class, and have the query return instances of its subclasses.

SQL databases also lack an obvious way (or at least a standardized way) to represent a polymorphic association. A foreign key constraint refers to exactly one target table; it isn't straightforward to define a foreign key that refers to multiple tables. We'd have to write a procedural constraint to enforce this kind of integrity rule.

The result of this mismatch of subtypes is that the inheritance structure in your model must be persisted in an SQL database that doesn't offer an inheritance strategy. Fortunately, three of the inheritance mapping solutions we show in chapter 5 are designed to accommodate the representation of polymorphic associations and the efficient execution of polymorphic queries.

The next aspect of the object/relational mismatch problem is the issue of *object identity*. You probably noticed that we defined USERNAME as the primary key of our USERS table. Was that a good choice? How do we handle identical objects in Java?

1.2.3   *The problem of identity*

Although the problem of object identity may not be obvious at first, we'll encounter it often in our growing and expanding e-commerce system, such as when we need to check whether two objects are identical. There are three ways to tackle this problem: two in the Java world and one in our SQL database. As expected, they work together only with some help.

Java objects define two different notions of *sameness*:

- Object identity (roughly equivalent to memory location, checked with a==b)
- Equality as determined by the implementation of the equals() method (also called *equality by value*)

On the other hand, the identity of a database row is expressed as the primary key value. As you'll see in chapter 9, section 9.2, "Object identity and equality," neither equals() nor == is naturally equivalent to the primary key value. It's common for several nonidentical objects to simultaneously represent the same row of the database, for example, in concurrently running application threads. Furthermore, some subtle difficulties are involved in implementing equals() correctly for a persistent class.

Let's discuss another problem related to database identity with an example. In our table definition for USERS, we used USERNAME as a primary key. Unfortunately, this decision makes it difficult to change a username; we need to update not only the USERNAME column in USERS, but also the foreign key column in BILLING_DETAILS. To solve this problem, later in the book we'll recommend that you use *surrogate keys* whenever you can't find a good natural key (we'll also discuss what makes a key good). A surrogate key column is a primary key column with no meaning to the user; in other words, a key that isn't presented to the user and is only used for identification of data inside the software system. For example, we may change our table definitions to look like this:

```
create table USERS (
    USER_ID bigint not null primary key,
    USERNAME varchar(15) not null unique,
    NAME varchar(50) not null,
    ...
)
create table BILLING_DETAILS (
    BILLING_DETAILS_ID bigint not null primary key,
    ACCOUNT_NUMBER VARCHAR(10) not null unique,
    ACCOUNT_NAME VARCHAR(50) not null,
    ACCOUNT_TYPE VARCHAR(2) not null,
    USER_ID bigint foreign key references USER
)
```

The USER_ID and BILLING_DETAILS_ID columns contain system-generated values. These columns were introduced purely for the benefit of the data model, so how (if at all) should they be represented in the domain model? We discuss this question in chapter 4, section 4.2, "Mapping entities with identity," and we find a solution with ORM.

In the context of persistence, identity is closely related to how the system handles caching and transactions. Different persistence solutions have chosen different strategies, and this has been an area of confusion. We cover all these interesting topics—and show how they're related—in chapters 10 and 13.

So far, the skeleton e-commerce application we've designed has identified the mismatch problems with mapping granularity, subtypes, and object identity. We're almost ready to move on to other parts of the application, but first we need to discuss the important concept of *associations*: how the relationships between our classes are mapped and handled. Is the foreign key in the database all you need?

1.2.4 *Problems relating to associations*

In our domain model, associations represent the relationships between entities. The User, Address, and BillingDetails classes are all associated; but unlike Address, BillingDetails stands on its own. BillingDetails instances are stored in their own table. Association mapping and the management of entity associations are central concepts in any object persistence solution.

Object-oriented languages represent associations using *object references*; but in the relational world, an association is represented as a *foreign key* column, with copies of key values (and a constraint to guarantee integrity). There are substantial differences between the two representations.

Object references are inherently directional; the association is from one object to the other. They're pointers. If an association between objects should be navigable in both directions, you must define the association *twice*, once in each of the associated classes. You've already seen this in the domain model classes:

```
public class User {
    private Set billingDetails;
    ...
}
public class BillingDetails {
    private User user;
    ...
}
```

On the other hand, foreign key associations aren't by nature directional. *Navigation* has no meaning for a relational data model because you can create arbitrary data associations with *table joins* and *projection*. The challenge is to bridge a completely open data model, which is independent of the application that works with the data, to an application-dependent navigational model, a constrained view of the associations needed by this particular application.

It isn't possible to determine the multiplicity of a unidirectional association by looking only at the Java classes. Java associations can have *many-to-many* multiplicity. For example, the classes could look like this:

```
public class User {
    private Set billingDetails;
    ...
}
public class BillingDetails {
    private Set users;
    ...
}
```

Table associations, on the other hand, are always *one-to-many* or *one-to-one*. You can see the multiplicity immediately by looking at the foreign key definition. The following is a foreign key declaration on the BILLING_DETAILS table for a one-to-many association (or, if read in the other direction, a many-to-one association):

```
USER_ID bigint foreign key references USERS
```

These are one-to-one associations:

```
USER_ID bigint unique foreign key references USERS
BILLING_DETAILS_ID bigint primary key foreign key references USERS
```

If you wish to represent a many-to-many association in a relational database, you must introduce a new table, called a *link table*. This table doesn't appear anywhere in the domain model. For our example, if we consider the relationship between the user and the billing information to be many-to-many, the link table is defined as follows:

```
create table USER_BILLING_DETAILS (
    USER_ID bigint foreign key references USERS,
    BILLING_DETAILS_ID bigint foreign key references BILLING_DETAILS,
    PRIMARY KEY (USER_ID, BILLING_DETAILS_ID)
)
```

We discuss association and collection mappings in great detail in chapters 6 and 7.

So far, the issues we've considered are mainly *structural*. We can see them by considering a purely static view of the system. Perhaps the most difficult problem in object persistence is a *dynamic* problem. It concerns associations, and we've already hinted at it when we drew a distinction between *object network navigation* and *table joins* in section 1.1.4, "Persistence in object-oriented applications." Let's explore this significant mismatch problem in more depth.

1.2.5 *The problem of data navigation*

There is a fundamental difference in the way you access data in Java and in a relational database. In Java, when you access a user's billing information, you call aUser.getBillingDetails().getAccountNumber() or something similar. This is the most natural way to access object-oriented data, and it's often described as walking the object network. You navigate from one object to another, following pointers between instances. Unfortunately, this isn't an efficient way to retrieve data from an SQL database.

The single most important thing you can do to improve the performance of data access code is to *minimize the number of requests to the database.* The most obvious way to do this is to minimize the number of SQL queries. (Of course, there are other more sophisticated ways that follow as a second step.)

Therefore, efficient access to relational data with SQL usually requires joins between the tables of interest. The number of tables included in the join when retrieving data determines the depth of the object network you can navigate in memory. For example, if you need to retrieve a User and aren't interested in the user's billing information, you can write this simple query:

```
select * from USERS u where u.USER_ID = 123
```

On the other hand, if you need to retrieve a User and then subsequently visit each of the associated BillingDetails instances (let's say, to list all the user's credit cards), you write a different query:

```
select *
    from USERS u
    left outer join BILLING_DETAILS bd on bd.USER_ID = u.USER_ID
    where u.USER_ID = 123
```

As you can see, to efficiently use joins you need to know what portion of the object network you plan to access when you retrieve the initial User—this is *before* you start navigating the object network!

On the other hand, any object persistence solution provides functionality for fetching the data of associated objects only when the object is first accessed. However, this piecemeal style of data access is fundamentally inefficient in the context of a relational database, because it requires executing one statement for each node or collection of the object network that is accessed. This is the dreaded *n+1 selects problem.*

This mismatch in the way you access objects in Java and in a relational database is perhaps the single most common source of performance problems in Java applications. There is a natural tension between too many selects and too big selects, which retrieve unnecessary information into memory. Yet, although we've been blessed with innumerable books and magazine articles advising us to use `StringBuffer` for string concatenation, it seems impossible to find any advice about strategies for avoiding the $n+1$ selects problem. Fortunately, Hibernate provides sophisticated features for efficiently and transparently fetching networks of objects from the database to the application accessing them. We discuss these features in chapters 13, 14, and 15.

1.2.6 *The cost of the mismatch*

We now have quite a list of object/relational mismatch problems, and it will be costly (in time and effort) to find solutions, as you may know from experience. This cost is often underestimated, and we think this is a major reason for many failed software projects. In our experience (regularly confirmed by developers we talk to), the main purpose of up to 30 percent of the Java application code written is to handle the tedious SQL/JDBC and manual bridging of the object/relational paradigm mismatch. Despite all this effort, the end result still doesn't feel quite right. We've seen projects nearly sink due to the complexity and inflexibility of their database abstraction layers. We also see Java developers (and DBAs) quickly lose their confidence when design decisions about the persistence strategy for a project have to be made.

One of the major costs is in the area of modeling. The relational and domain models must both encompass the same business entities, but an object-oriented purist will model these entities in a different way than an experienced relational data modeler would. The usual solution to this problem is to bend and twist the domain model and the implemented classes until they match the SQL database schema. (Which, following the principle of data independence, is certainly a safe long-term choice.)

This can be done successfully, but only at the cost of losing some of the advantages of object orientation. Keep in mind that relational modeling is underpinned by relational theory. Object orientation has no such rigorous mathematical definition or body of theoretical work, so we can't look to mathematics to explain how we should bridge the gap between the two paradigms—there is no elegant transformation waiting to be discovered. (Doing away with Java and SQL, and starting from scratch isn't considered elegant.)

The domain modeling mismatch isn't the only source of the inflexibility and the lost productivity that lead to higher costs. A further cause is the JDBC API itself. JDBC and SQL provide a *statement-oriented* (that is, command-oriented) approach to moving data to and from an SQL database. If you want to query or manipulate data, the tables and columns involved must be specified at least three times (insert, update, select), adding to the time required for design and implementation. The distinct dialects for every SQL database management system don't improve the situation.

To round out your understanding of object persistence, and before we approach possible solutions, we need to discuss *application architecture* and the role of a *persistence layer* in typical application design.

1.3 *Persistence layers and alternatives*

In a medium- or large-sized application, it usually makes sense to organize classes by concern. Persistence is one concern; others include presentation, workflow, and business logic.[1] A typical object-oriented architecture includes layers of code that represent the concerns. It's normal and certainly best practice to group all classes and components responsible for persistence into a separate persistence layer in a layered system architecture.

In this section, we first look at the layers of this type of architecture and why we use them. After that, we focus on the layer we're most interested in—the persistence layer—and some of the ways it can be implemented.

1.3.1 *Layered architecture*

A layered architecture defines interfaces between code that implements the various concerns, allowing changes to be made to the way one concern is implemented without significant disruption to code in the other layers. Layering also determines the kinds of interlayer dependencies that occur. The rules are as follows:

- Layers communicate from top to bottom. A layer is dependent only on the layer directly below it.
- Each layer is unaware of any other layers except for the layer just below it.

Different systems group concerns differently, so they define different layers. A typical, proven, high-level application architecture uses three layers: one each for presentation, business logic, and persistence, as shown in figure 1.4.

Let's take a closer look at the layers and elements in the diagram:

---

[1] There are also the so-called *cross-cutting* concerns, which may be implemented generically—by framework code, for example. Typical cross-cutting concerns include logging, authorization, and transaction demarcation.

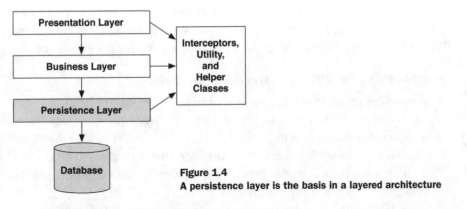

Figure 1.4
A persistence layer is the basis in a layered architecture

- *Presentation layer*—The user interface logic is topmost. Code responsible for the presentation and control of page and screen navigation is in the presentation layer.

- *Business layer*—The exact form of the next layer varies widely between applications. It's generally agreed, however, that the business layer is responsible for implementing any business rules or system requirements that would be understood by users as part of the problem domain. This layer usually includes some kind of controlling component—code that knows when to invoke which business rule. In some systems, this layer has its own internal representation of the business domain entities, and in others it reuses the model defined by the persistence layer. We revisit this issue in chapter 3.

- *Persistence layer*—The persistence layer is a group of classes and components responsible for storing data to, and retrieving it from, one or more data stores. This layer necessarily includes a model of the business domain entities (even if it's only a metadata model).

- *Database*—The database exists outside the Java application itself. It's the actual, persistent representation of the system state. If an SQL database is used, the database includes the relational schema and possibly stored procedures.

- *Helper and utility classes*—Every application has a set of infrastructural helper or utility classes that are used in every layer of the application (such as `Exception` classes for error handling). These infrastructural elements don't form a layer, because they don't obey the rules for interlayer dependency in a layered architecture.

Let's now take a brief look at the various ways the persistence layer can be implemented by Java applications. Don't worry—we'll get to ORM and Hibernate soon. There is much to be learned by looking at other approaches.

1.3.2 *Hand-coding a persistence layer with SQL/JDBC*

The most common approach to Java persistence is for application programmers to work directly with SQL and JDBC. After all, developers are familiar with relational database management systems, they understand SQL, and they know how to work with tables and foreign keys. Moreover, they can always use the well-known and widely used data access object (DAO) pattern to hide complex JDBC code and nonportable SQL from the business logic.

The DAO pattern is a good one—so good that we often recommend its use even with ORM. However, the work involved in manually coding persistence for each domain class is considerable, particularly when multiple SQL dialects are supported. This work usually ends up consuming a large portion of the development effort. Furthermore, when requirements change, a hand-coded solution always requires more attention and maintenance effort.

Why not implement a simple mapping framework to fit the specific requirements of your project? The result of such an effort could even be reused in future projects. Many developers have taken this approach; numerous homegrown object/relational persistence layers are in production systems today. However, we don't recommend this approach. Excellent solutions already exist: not only the (mostly expensive) tools sold by commercial vendors, but also open source projects with free licenses. We're certain you'll be able to find a solution that meets your requirements, both business and technical. It's likely that such a solution will do a great deal more, and do it better, than a solution you could build in a limited time.

Developing a reasonably full-featured ORM may take many developers months. For example, Hibernate is about 80,000 lines of code, some of which is much more difficult than typical application code, along with 25,000 lines of unit test code. This may be more code than is in your application. A great many details can easily be overlooked in such a large project—as both the authors know from experience! Even if an existing tool doesn't fully implement two or three of your more exotic requirements, it's still probably not worth creating your own tool. Any ORM software will handle the tedious common cases—the ones that kill productivity. It's OK if you need to hand-code certain special cases; few applications are composed primarily of special cases.

1.3.3 Using serialization

Java has a built-in persistence mechanism: Serialization provides the ability to write a snapshot of a network of objects (the state of the application) to a byte stream, which may then be persisted to a file or database. Serialization is also used by Java's Remote Method Invocation (RMI) to achieve pass-by value semantics for complex objects. Another use of serialization is to replicate application state across nodes in a cluster of machines.

Why not use serialization for the persistence layer? Unfortunately, a serialized network of interconnected objects can only be accessed as a whole; it's impossible to retrieve any data from the stream without deserializing the entire stream. Thus, the resulting byte stream must be considered unsuitable for arbitrary search or aggregation of large datasets. It isn't even possible to access or update a single object or subset of objects independently. Loading and overwriting an entire object network in each transaction is no option for systems designed to support high concurrency.

Given current technology, serialization is inadequate as a persistence mechanism for high concurrency web and enterprise applications. It has a particular niche as a suitable persistence mechanism for desktop applications.

1.3.4 Object-oriented database systems

Because we work with objects in Java, it would be ideal if there were a way to store those objects in a database without having to bend and twist the object model at all. In the mid-1990s, object-oriented database systems gained attention. They're based on a network data model, which was common before the advent of the relational data model decades ago. The basic idea is to store a network of objects, with all its pointers and nodes, and to re-create the same in-memory graph later on. This can be optimized with various metadata and configuration settings.

An object-oriented database management system (OODBMS) is more like an extension to the application environment than an external data store. An OODBMS usually features a multitiered implementation, with the backend data store, object cache, and client application coupled tightly together and interacting via a proprietary network protocol. Object nodes are kept on pages of memory, which are transported from and to the data store.

Object-oriented database development begins with the top-down definition of host language bindings that add persistence capabilities to the programming language. Hence, object databases offer seamless integration into the object-oriented application environment. This is different from the model used by today's relational databases, where interaction with the database occurs via an intermediate language (SQL) and data independence from a particular application is the major concern.

For background information on object-oriented databases, we recommend the respective chapter in *An Introduction to Database Systems* (Date, 2003).

We won't bother looking too closely into why object-oriented database technology hasn't been more popular; we'll observe that object databases haven't been widely adopted and that it doesn't appear likely that they will be in the near future. We're confident that the overwhelming majority of developers will have far more opportunity to work with relational technology, given the current political realities (predefined deployment environments) and the common requirement for data independence.

1.3.5 *Other options*

Of course, there are other kinds of persistence layers. XML persistence is a variation on the serialization theme; this approach addresses some of the limitations of byte-stream serialization by allowing easy access to the data through a standardized tool interface. However, managing data in XML would expose you to an object/hierarchical mismatch. Furthermore, there is no additional benefit from the XML itself, because it's just another text file format and has no inherent capabilities for data management. You can use stored procedures (even writing them in Java, sometimes) and move the problem into the database tier. So-called object-relational databases have been marketed as a solution, but they offer only a more sophisticated datatype system providing only half the solution to our problems (and further muddling terminology). We're sure there are plenty of other examples, but none of them are likely to become popular in the immediate future.

Political and economic constraints (long-term investments in SQL databases), data independence, and the requirement for access to valuable legacy data call for a different approach. ORM may be the most practical solution to our problems.

1.4 *Object/relational mapping*

Now that we've looked at the alternative techniques for object persistence, it's time to introduce the solution we feel is the best, and the one we use with Hibernate: ORM. Despite its long history (the first research papers were published in the late 1980s), the terms for ORM used by developers vary. Some call it object relational mapping, others prefer the simple object mapping; we exclusively use the term object/relational mapping and its acronym, ORM. The slash stresses the mismatch problem that occurs when the two worlds collide.

In this section, we first look at what ORM is. Then we enumerate the problems that a good ORM solution needs to solve. Finally, we discuss the general benefits that ORM provides and why we recommend this solution.

1.4.1 What is ORM?

In a nutshell, object/relational mapping is the automated (and transparent) persistence of objects in a Java application to the tables in a relational database, using metadata that describes the mapping between the objects and the database.

ORM, in essence, works by (reversibly) transforming data from one representation to another. This implies certain performance penalties. However, if ORM is implemented as middleware, there are many opportunities for optimization that wouldn't exist for a hand-coded persistence layer. The provision and management of metadata that governs the transformation adds to the overhead at development time, but the cost is less than equivalent costs involved in maintaining a hand-coded solution. (And even object databases require significant amounts of metadata.)

> **FAQ** *Isn't ORM a Visio plug-in?* The acronym ORM can also mean *object role modeling*, and this term was invented before object/relational mapping became relevant. It describes a method for information analysis, used in database modeling, and is primarily supported by Microsoft Visio, a graphical modeling tool. Database specialists use it as a replacement or as an addition to the more popular *entity-relationship modeling*. However, if you talk to Java developers about ORM, it's usually in the context of object/relational mapping.

An ORM solution consists of the following four pieces:

- An API for performing basic CRUD operations on objects of persistent classes
- A language or API for specifying queries that refer to classes and properties of classes
- A facility for specifying mapping metadata
- A technique for the ORM implementation to interact with transactional objects to perform dirty checking, lazy association fetching, and other optimization functions

We're using the term *full ORM* to include any persistence layer where SQL is automatically generated from a metadata-based description. We aren't including persistence layers where the object/relational mapping problem is solved manually by developers hand-coding SQL with JDBC. With ORM, the application interacts with the ORM APIs and the domain model classes and is abstracted from the underlying SQL/JDBC. Depending on the features or the particular implementation, the ORM engine may also take on responsibility for issues such as optimistic locking and caching, relieving the application of these concerns entirely.

Let's look at the various ways ORM can be implemented. Mark Fussel (Fussel, 1997), a developer in the field of ORM, defined the following four levels of ORM quality. We have slightly rewritten his descriptions and put them in the context of today's Java application development.

Pure relational

The whole application, including the user interface, is designed around the relational model and SQL-based relational operations. This approach, despite its deficiencies for large systems, can be an excellent solution for simple applications where a low level of code reuse is tolerable. Direct SQL can be fine-tuned in every aspect, but the drawbacks, such as lack of portability and maintainability, are significant, especially in the long run. Applications in this category often make heavy use of stored procedures, shifting some of the work out of the business layer and into the database.

Light object mapping

Entities are represented as classes that are mapped manually to the relational tables. Hand-coded SQL/JDBC is hidden from the business logic using well-known design patterns. This approach is extremely widespread and is successful for applications with a small number of entities, or applications with generic, metadata-driven data models. Stored procedures may have a place in this kind of application.

Medium object mapping

The application is designed around an object model. SQL is generated at build time using a code-generation tool, or at runtime by framework code. Associations between objects are supported by the persistence mechanism, and queries may be specified using an object-oriented expression language. Objects are cached by the persistence layer. A great many ORM products and homegrown persistence layers support at least this level of functionality. It's well suited to medium-sized applications with some complex transactions, particularly when portability between different database products is important. These applications usually don't use stored procedures.

Full object mapping

Full object mapping supports sophisticated object modeling: composition, inheritance, polymorphism, and persistence by reachability. The persistence layer implements transparent persistence; persistent classes do not inherit from any special base class or have to implement a special interface. Efficient fetching strategies (lazy, eager, and prefetching) and caching strategies are implemented transparently to the application. This level of functionality can hardly be achieved by a homegrown persistence layer—it's equivalent to years of development time. A number of commercial and open source Java ORM tools have achieved this level of quality.

This level meets the definition of ORM we're using in this book. Let's look at the problems we expect to be solved by a tool that achieves full object mapping.

1.4.2 Generic ORM problems

The following list of issues, which we'll call the ORM problems, identifies the fundamental questions resolved by a full object/relational mapping tool in a Java environment. Particular ORM tools may provide extra functionality (for example, aggressive caching), but this is a reasonably exhaustive list of the conceptual issues and questions that are specific to object/relational mapping.

1 *What do persistent classes look like?* How *transparent* is the persistence tool? Do we have to adopt a programming model and conventions for classes of the business domain?

2 *How is mapping metadata defined?* Because the object/relational transformation is governed entirely by metadata, the format and definition of this metadata is important. Should an ORM tool provide a GUI interface to manipulate the metadata graphically? Or are there better approaches to metadata definition?

3 *How do object identity and equality relate to database (primary key) identity?* How do we map instances of particular classes to particular table rows?

4 *How should we map class inheritance hierarchies?* There are several standard strategies. What about polymorphic associations, abstract classes, and interfaces?

5 *How does the persistence logic interact at runtime with the objects of the business domain?* This is a problem of generic programming, and there are a number of solutions including source generation, runtime reflection, runtime bytecode generation, and build-time bytecode enhancement. The solution to this problem may affect your build process (but, preferably, shouldn't otherwise affect you as a user).

6 *What is the lifecycle of a persistent object?* Does the lifecycle of some objects depend upon the lifecycle of other associated objects? How do we translate the lifecycle of an object to the lifecycle of a database row?

7 *What facilities are provided for sorting, searching, and aggregating?* The application could do some of these things in memory, but efficient use of relational technology requires that this work often be performed by the database.

8 *How do we efficiently retrieve data with associations?* Efficient access to relational data is usually accomplished via table joins. Object-oriented applications usually access data by navigating an object network. Two data access patterns should be avoided when possible: the *n+1 selects* problem, and its complement, the *Cartesian product* problem (fetching too much data in a single select).

Two additional issues that impose fundamental constraints on the design and architecture of an ORM tool are common to any data access technology:

- Transactions and concurrency
- Cache management (and concurrency)

As you can see, a full object/relational mapping tool needs to address quite a long list of issues. By now, you should be starting to see the value of ORM. In the next section, we look at some of the other benefits you gain when you use an ORM solution.

1.4.3 Why ORM?

An ORM implementation is a complex beast—less complex than an application server, but more complex than a web application framework like Struts or Tapestry. Why should we introduce another complex infrastructural element into our system? Will it be worth it?

It will take us most of this book to provide a complete answer to those questions, but this section provides a quick summary of the most compelling benefits. First, though, let's quickly dispose of a nonbenefit.

A supposed advantage of ORM is that it shields developers from messy SQL. This view holds that object-oriented developers can't be expected to understand SQL or relational databases well, and that they find SQL somehow offensive. On the contrary, we believe that Java developers must have a sufficient level of familiarity with—and appreciation of—relational modeling and SQL in order to work with ORM. ORM is an advanced technique to be used by developers who have already done it the hard way. To use Hibernate effectively, you must be able to view and interpret the SQL statements it issues and understand the implications for performance.

Now, let's look at some of the benefits of ORM and Hibernate.

Productivity

Persistence-related code can be perhaps the most tedious code in a Java application. Hibernate eliminates much of the grunt work (more than you'd expect) and lets you concentrate on the business problem.

No matter which application-development strategy you prefer—top-down, starting with a domain model, or bottom-up, starting with an existing database schema—Hibernate, used together with the appropriate tools, will significantly reduce development time.

Maintainability

Fewer lines of code (LOC) make the system more understandable, because it emphasizes business logic rather than plumbing. Most important, a system with less code is easier to refactor. Automated object/relational persistence substantially reduces LOC. Of course, counting lines of code is a debatable way of measuring application complexity.

However, there are other reasons that a Hibernate application is more maintainable. In systems with hand-coded persistence, an inevitable tension exists between the relational representation and the object model implementing the domain. Changes to one almost always involve changes to the other, and often the design of one representation is compromised to accommodate the existence of the other. (What almost always happens in practice is that the *object model* of the domain is compromised.) ORM provides a buffer between the two models, allowing more elegant use of object orientation on the Java side, and insulating each model from minor changes to the other.

Performance

A common claim is that hand-coded persistence can always be at least as fast, and can often be faster, than automated persistence. This is true in the same sense that it's true that assembly code can always be at least as fast as Java code, or a hand-written parser can always be at least as fast as a parser generated by YACC or ANTLR—in other words, it's beside the point. The unspoken implication of the claim is that hand-coded persistence will perform at least as well in an actual application. But this implication will be true only if the effort required to implement at-least-as-fast hand-coded persistence is similar to the amount of effort involved in utilizing an automated solution. The really interesting question is what happens when we consider time and budget constraints?

Given a persistence task, many optimizations are possible. Some (such as query hints) are much easier to achieve with hand-coded SQL/JDBC. Most optimizations, however, are much easier to achieve with automated ORM. In a project with time constraints, hand-coded persistence usually allows you to make some optimizations. Hibernate allows many more optimizations to be used *all* the time. Furthermore, automated persistence improves developer productivity so much that you can spend more time hand-optimizing the few remaining bottlenecks.

Finally, the people who implemented your ORM software probably had much more time to investigate performance optimizations than you have. Did you know, for instance, that pooling PreparedStatement instances results in a significant performance increase for the DB2 JDBC driver but breaks the InterBase JDBC driver? Did you realize that updating only the changed columns of a table can be significantly faster for some databases but potentially slower for others? In your handcrafted solution, how easy is it to experiment with the impact of these various strategies?

Vendor independence

An ORM abstracts your application away from the underlying SQL database and SQL dialect. If the tool supports a number of different databases (and most do), this confers a certain level of portability on your application. You shouldn't necessarily expect write-once/run-anywhere, because the capabilities of databases differ, and achieving full portability would require sacrificing some of the strength of the more powerful platforms. Nevertheless, it's usually much easier to develop a cross-platform application using ORM. Even if you don't require cross-platform operation, an ORM can still help mitigate some of the risks associated with vendor lock-in.

In addition, database independence helps in development scenarios where developers use a lightweight local database but deploy for production on a different database.

You need to select an ORM product at some point. To make an educated decision, you need a list of the software modules and standards that are available.

1.4.4 *Introducing Hibernate, EJB3, and JPA*

Hibernate is a full object/relational mapping tool that provides all the previously listed ORM benefits. The API you're working with in Hibernate is native and designed by the Hibernate developers. The same is true for the query interfaces and query languages, and for how object/relational mapping metadata is defined.

Before you start your first project with Hibernate, you should consider the EJB 3.0 standard and its subspecification, *Java Persistence*. Let's go back in history and see how this new standard came into existence.

Many Java developers considered EJB 2.1 entity beans as one of the technologies for the implementation of a persistence layer. The whole EJB programming and persistence model has been widely adopted in the industry, and it has been an important factor in the success of J2EE (or, Java EE as it's now called).

However, over the last years, critics of EJB in the developer community became more vocal (especially with regard to entity beans and persistence), and companies realized that the EJB standard should be improved. Sun, as the steering party of J2EE, knew that an overhaul was in order and started a new Java specification request (JSR) with the goal of simplifying EJB in early 2003. This new JSR, Enterprise JavaBeans 3.0 (JSR 220), attracted significant interest. Developers from the Hibernate team joined the expert group early on and helped shape the new specification. Other vendors, including all major and many smaller companies in the Java industry, also contributed to the effort. An important decision made for the new standard was to specify and standardize things that work in practice, taking ideas and concepts from existing successful products and projects. Hibernate, therefore, being a successful data persistence solution, played an important role for the persistence part of the new standard. But what exactly is the relationship between Hibernate and EJB3, and what is Java Persistence?

Understanding the standards

First, it's difficult (if not impossible) to compare a specification and a product. The questions that should be asked are, "Does Hibernate implement the EJB 3.0 specification, and what is the impact on my project? Do I have to use one or the other?"

The new EJB 3.0 specification comes in several parts: The first part defines the new EJB programming model for session beans and message-driven beans, the deployment rules, and so on. The second part of the specification deals with persistence exclusively: entities, object/relational mapping metadata, persistence manager interfaces, and the query language. This second part is called Java Persistence API (JPA), probably because its interfaces are in the package javax.persistence. We'll use this acronym throughout the book.

This separation also exists in EJB 3.0 products; some implement a full EJB 3.0 container that supports all parts of the specification, and other products may implement only the Java Persistence part. Two important principles were designed into the new standard:

- JPA engines should be pluggable, which means you should be able to take out one product and replace it with another if you aren't satisfied—even if you want to stay with the same EJB 3.0 container or Java EE 5.0 application server.

- JPA engines should be able to run outside of an EJB 3.0 (or any other) runtime environment, without a container in plain standard Java.

The consequences of this design are that there are more options for developers and architects, which drives competition and therefore improves overall quality of products. Of course, actual products also offer features that go beyond the specification as vendor-specific extensions (such as for performance tuning, or because the vendor has a focus on a particular vertical problem space).

Hibernate implements Java Persistence, and because a JPA engine must be pluggable, new and interesting combinations of software are possible. You can select from various Hibernate software modules and combine them depending on your project's technical and business requirements.

Hibernate Core

The Hibernate Core is also known as Hibernate 3.2.x, or Hibernate. It's the base service for persistence, with its native API and its mapping metadata stored in XML files. It has a query language called HQL (almost the same as SQL), as well as programmatic query interfaces for Criteria and Example queries. There are hundreds of options and features available for everything, as Hibernate Core is really the foundation and the platform all other modules are built on.

You can use Hibernate Core on its own, independent from any framework or any particular runtime environment with all JDKs. It works in every Java EE/J2EE application server, in Swing applications, in a simple servlet container, and so on. As long as you can configure a data source for Hibernate, it works. Your application code (in your persistence layer) will use Hibernate APIs and queries, and your mapping metadata is written in native Hibernate XML files.

Native Hibernate APIs, queries, and XML mapping files are the primary focus of this book, and they're explained first in all code examples. The reason for that is that Hibernate functionality is a *superset* of all other available options.

Hibernate Annotations

A new way to define application metadata became available with JDK 5.0: type-safe annotations embedded directly in the Java source code. Many Hibernate users are already familiar with this concept, as the XDoclet software supports Javadoc metadata attributes and a preprocessor at compile time (which, for Hibernate, generates XML mapping files).

With the *Hibernate Annotations* package on top of Hibernate Core, you can now use type-safe JDK 5.0 metadata as a replacement or in addition to native Hibernate XML mapping files. You'll find the syntax and semantics of the mapping annotations familiar once you've seen them side-by-side with Hibernate XML mapping files. However, the basic annotations aren't proprietary.

The JPA specification defines object/relational mapping metadata syntax and semantics, with the primary mechanism being JDK 5.0 annotations. (Yes, JDK 5.0 is required for Java EE 5.0 and EJB 3.0.) Naturally, the Hibernate Annotations are a set of basic annotations that implement the JPA standard, and they're also a set of extension annotations you need for more advanced and exotic Hibernate mappings and tuning.

You can use Hibernate Core and Hibernate Annotations to reduce your lines of code for mapping metadata, compared to the native XML files, and you may like the better refactoring capabilities of annotations. You can use only JPA annotations, or you can add a Hibernate extension annotation if complete portability isn't your primary concern. (In practice, you should embrace the product you've chosen instead of denying its existence at all times.)

We'll discuss the impact of annotations on your development process, and how to use them in mappings, throughout this book, along with native Hibernate XML mapping examples.

Hibernate EntityManager

The JPA specification also defines programming interfaces, lifecycle rules for persistent objects, and query features. The Hibernate implementation for this part of JPA is available as Hibernate EntityManager, another optional module you can stack on top of Hibernate Core. You can fall back when a plain Hibernate interface, or even a JDBC Connection is needed. Hibernate's native features are a superset of the JPA persistence features in every respect. (The simple fact is that

Hibernate EntityManager is a small wrapper around Hibernate Core that provides JPA compatibility.)

Working with standardized interfaces and using a standardized query language has the benefit that you can execute your JPA-compatible persistence layer with any EJB 3.0 compliant application server. Or, you can use JPA outside of any particular standardized runtime environment in plain Java (which really means *everywhere* Hibernate Core can be used).

Hibernate Annotations should be considered in combination with Hibernate EntityManager. It's unusual that you'd write your application code against JPA interfaces and with JPA queries, and not create most of your mappings with JPA annotations.

Java EE 5.0 application servers

We don't cover all of EJB 3.0 in this book; our focus is naturally on persistence, and therefore on the JPA part of the specification. (We will, of course, show you many techniques with managed EJB components when we talk about application architecture and design.)

Hibernate is also part of the *JBoss Application Server* (JBoss AS), an implementation of J2EE 1.4 and (soon) Java EE 5.0. A combination of Hibernate Core, Hibernate Annotations, and Hibernate EntityManager forms the persistence engine of this application server. Hence, everything you can use stand-alone, you can also use inside the application server with all the EJB 3.0 benefits, such as session beans, message-driven beans, and other Java EE services.

To complete the picture, you also have to understand that Java EE 5.0 application servers are no longer the monolithic beasts of the J2EE 1.4 era. In fact, the JBoss EJB 3.0 container also comes in an *embeddable* version, which runs *inside* other application servers, and even in Tomcat, or in a unit test, or a Swing application. In the next chapter, you'll prepare a project that utilizes EJB 3.0 components, and you'll install the JBoss server for easy integration testing.

As you can see, native Hibernate features implement significant parts of the specification or are natural vendor extensions, offering additional functionality if required.

Here is a simple trick to see immediately what code you're looking at, whether JPA or native Hibernate. If only the `javax.persistence.*` import is visible, you're working inside the specification; if you also import `org.hibernate.*`, you're using native Hibernate functionality. We'll later show you a few more tricks that will help you cleanly separate portable from vendor-specific code.

FAQ   *What is the future of Hibernate?*   Hibernate Core will be developed independently from and faster than the EJB 3.0 or Java Persistence specifications. It will be the testing ground for new ideas, as it has always been. Any new feature developed for Hibernate Core is immediately and automatically available as an extension for all users of Java Persistence with Hibernate Annotations and Hibernate EntityManager. Over time, if a particular concept has proven its usefulness, Hibernate developers will work with other expert group members on future standardization in an updated EJB or Java Persistence specification. Hence, if you're interested in a quickly evolving standard, we encourage you to use native Hibernate functionality, and to send feedback to the respective expert group. The desire for total portability and the rejection of vendor extensions were major reasons for the stagnation we saw in EJB 1.x and 2.x.

After so much praise of ORM and Hibernate, it's time to look at some actual code. It's time to wrap up the theory and to set up a first project.

1.5   Summary

In this chapter, we've discussed the concept of object persistence and the importance of ORM as an implementation technique.

Object persistence means that individual objects can outlive the application process; they can be saved to a data store and be re-created at a later point in time. The object/relational mismatch comes into play when the data store is an SQL-based relational database management system. For instance, a network of objects can't be saved to a database table; it must be disassembled and persisted to columns of portable SQL datatypes. A good solution for this problem is object/relational mapping (ORM), which is especially helpful if we consider richly typed Java domain models.

A domain model represents the business entities used in a Java application. In a layered system architecture, the domain model is used to execute business logic in the business layer (in Java, not in the database). This business layer communicates with the persistence layer beneath in order to load and store the persistent objects of the domain model. ORM is the middleware in the persistence layer that manages the persistence.

ORM isn't a silver bullet for all persistence tasks; its job is to relieve the developer of 95 percent of object persistence work, such as writing complex SQL statements with many table joins, and copying values from JDBC result sets to objects or graphs of objects. A full-featured ORM middleware solution may provide database portability, certain optimization techniques like caching, and other viable functions that aren't easy to hand-code in a limited time with SQL and JDBC.

It's likely that a better solution than ORM will exist some day. We (and many others) may have to rethink everything we know about SQL, persistence API standards, and application integration. The evolution of today's systems into true relational database systems with seamless object-oriented integration remains pure speculation. But we can't wait, and there is no sign that any of these issues will improve soon (a multibillion dollar industry isn't very agile). ORM is the best solution currently available, and it's a timesaver for developers facing the object/relational mismatch every day. With EJB 3.0, a specification for full object/relational mapping software that is accepted in the Java industry is finally available.

Starting a project

You want to start using Hibernate and Java Persistence, and you want to learn it with a step-by-step example. You want to see both persistence APIs and how you can benefit from native Hibernate or standardized JPA. This is what you'll find in this chapter: a tour through a straightforward "Hello World" application.

However, a good and complete tutorial is already publicly available in the Hibernate reference documentation, so instead of repeating it here, we show you more detailed instructions about Hibernate integration and configuration along the way. If you want to start with a less elaborate tutorial that you can complete in one hour, our advice is to consider the Hibernate reference documentation. It takes you from a simple stand-alone Java application with Hibernate through the most essential mapping concepts and finally demonstrates a Hibernate web application deployed on Tomcat.

In this chapter, you'll learn how to set up a project infrastructure for a plain Java application that integrates Hibernate, and you'll see many more details about how Hibernate can be configured in such an environment. We also discuss configuration and integration of Hibernate in a managed environment—that is, an environment that provides Java EE services.

As a build tool for the "Hello World" project, we introduce Ant and create build scripts that can not only compile and run the project, but also utilize the Hibernate Tools. Depending on your development process, you'll use the Hibernate toolset to export database schemas automatically or even to reverse-engineer a complete application from an existing (legacy) database schema.

Like every good engineer, before you start your first real Hibernate project you should prepare your tools and decide what your development process is going to look like. And, depending on the process you choose, you may naturally prefer different tools. Let's look at this preparation phase and what your options are, and then start a Hibernate project.

2.1   Starting a Hibernate project

In some projects, the development of an application is driven by developers analyzing the business domain in object-oriented terms. In others, it's heavily influenced by an existing relational data model: either a legacy database or a brand-new schema designed by a professional data modeler. There are many choices to be made, and the following questions need to be answered before you can start:

- Can you start from scratch with a clean design of a new business requirement, or is legacy data and/or legacy application code present?

- Can some of the necessary pieces be automatically generated from an existing artifact (for example, Java source from an existing database schema)? Can the database schema be generated from Java code and Hibernate mapping metadata?

- What kind of tool is available to support this work? What about other tools to support the full development cycle?

We'll discuss these questions in the following sections as we set up a basic Hibernate project. This is your road map:

1 Select a development process
2 Set up the project infrastructure
3 Write application code and mappings
4 Configure and start Hibernate
5 Run the application.

After reading the next sections, you'll be prepared for the correct approach in your own project, and you'll also have the background information for more complex scenarios we'll touch on later in this chapter.

2.1.1 Selecting a development process

Let's first get an overview of the available tools, the artifacts they use as source input, and the output that is produced. Figure 2.1 shows various import and

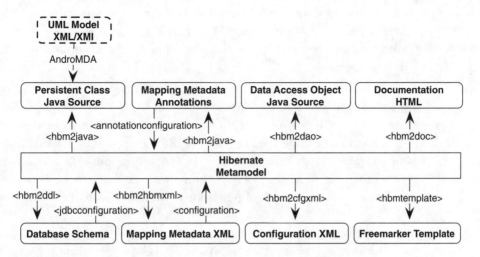

Figure 2.1   Input and output of the tools used for Hibernate development

export tasks for Ant; all the functionality is also available with the Hibernate Tools plug-ins for Eclipse. Refer to this diagram while reading this chapter.[1]

NOTE *Hibernate Tools for Eclipse IDE*—The Hibernate Tools are plug-ins for the *Eclipse IDE* (part of the *JBoss IDE for Eclipse*—a set of wizards, editors, and extra views in Eclipse that help you develop EJB3, Hibernate, JBoss Seam, and other Java applications based on JBoss middleware). The features for forward and reverse engineering are equivalent to the Ant-based tools. The additional *Hibernate Console* view allows you to execute ad hoc Hibernate queries (HQL and `Criteria`) against your database and to browse the result graphically. The Hibernate Tools XML editor supports automatic completion of mapping files, including class, property, and even table and column names. The graphical tools were still in development and available as a beta release during the writing of this book, however, so any screenshots would be obsolete with future releases of the software. The documentation of the Hibernate Tools contains many screenshots and detailed project setup instructions that you can easily adapt to create your first "Hello World" program with the Eclipse IDE.

The following development scenarios are common:

- *Top down*—In *top-down* development, you start with an existing domain model, its implementation in Java, and (ideally) complete freedom with respect to the database schema. You must create mapping metadata—either with XML files or by annotating the Java source—and then optionally let Hibernate's `hbm2ddl` tool generate the database schema. In the absence of an existing database schema, this is the most comfortable development style for most Java developers. You may even use the Hibernate Tools to automatically refresh the database schema on every application restart in development.

- *Bottom up*—Conversely, *bottom-up* development begins with an existing database schema and data model. In this case, the easiest way to proceed is to use the reverse-engineering tools to extract metadata from the database. This metadata can be used to generate XML mapping files, with `hbm2hbmxml` for example. With `hbm2java`, the Hibernate mapping metadata is used to generate Java persistent classes, and even data access objects—in other words, a skeleton for a Java persistence layer. Or, instead of writing to XML

---

[1] Note that AndroMDA, a tool that generates POJO source code from UML diagram files, isn't strictly considered part of the common Hibernate toolset, so it isn't discussed in this chapter. See the community area on the Hibernate website for more information about the Hibernate module for AndroMDA.

mapping files, annotated Java source code (EJB 3.0 entity classes) can be produced directly by the tools. However, not all class association details and Java-specific metainformation can be automatically generated from an SQL database schema with this strategy, so expect some manual work.

- *Middle out*—The Hibernate XML mapping metadata provides sufficient information to completely deduce the database schema and to generate the Java source code for the persistence layer of the application. Furthermore, the XML mapping document isn't too verbose. Hence, some architects and developers prefer *middle-out* development, where they begin with handwritten Hibernate XML mapping files, and then generate the database schema using hbm2ddl and Java classes using hbm2java. The Hibernate XML mapping files are constantly updated during development, and other artifacts are generated from this master definition. Additional business logic or database objects are added through subclassing and auxiliary DDL. This development style can be recommended only for the seasoned Hibernate expert.

- *Meet in the middle*—The most difficult scenario is combining existing Java classes and an existing database schema. In this case, there is little that the Hibernate toolset can do to help. It is, of course, not possible to map arbitrary Java domain models to a given schema, so this scenario usually requires at least some refactoring of the Java classes, database schema, or both. The mapping metadata will almost certainly need to be written by hand and in XML files (though it might be possible to use annotations if there is a close match). This can be an incredibly painful scenario, and it is, fortunately, exceedingly rare.

We now explore the tools and their configuration options in more detail and set up a work environment for typical Hibernate application development. You can follow our instructions step by step and create the same environment, or you can take only the bits and pieces you need, such as the Ant build scripts.

The development process we assume first is top down, and we'll walk through a Hibernate project that doesn't involve any legacy data schemas or Java code. After that, you'll migrate the code to JPA and EJB 3.0, and then you'll start a project bottom up by reverse-engineering from an existing database schema.

2.1.2 Setting up the project

We assume that you've downloaded the latest production release of Hibernate from the Hibernate website at http://www.hibernate.org/ and that you unpacked the archive. You also need *Apache Ant* installed on your development machine.

You should also download a current version of HSQLDB from http://hsqldb.org/ and extract the package; you'll use this database management system for your tests. If you have another database management system already installed, you only need to obtain a JDBC driver for it.

Instead of the sophisticated application you'll develop later in the book, you'll get started with a "Hello World" example. That way, you can focus on the development process without getting distracted by Hibernate details. Let's set up the project directory first.

Creating the work directory

Create a new directory on your system, in any location you like; C:\helloworld is a good choice if you work on Microsoft Windows. We'll refer to this directory as WORKDIR in future examples. Create lib and src subdirectories, and copy all required libraries:

```
WORKDIR
    +lib
      antlr.jar
      asm.jar
      asm-attrs.jars
      c3p0.jar
      cglib.jar
      commons-collections.jar
      commons-logging.jar
      dom4j.jar
      hibernate3.jar
      hsqldb.jar
      jta.jar
    +src
```

The libraries you see in the library directory are from the Hibernate distribution, most of them required for a typical Hibernate project. The hsqldb.jar file is from the HSQLDB distribution; replace it with a different driver JAR if you want to use a different database management system. Keep in mind that some of the libraries you're seeing here may not be required for the particular version of Hibernate you're working with, which is likely a newer release than we used when writing this book. To make sure you have the right set of libraries, always check the lib/README.txt file in the Hibernate distribution package. This file contains an up-to-date list of all required and optional third-party libraries for Hibernate—you only need the libraries listed as required for *runtime*.

In the "Hello World" application, you want to store messages in the database and load them from the database. You need to create the domain model for this business case.

Creating the domain model

Hibernate applications define *persistent classes* that are mapped to database tables. You define these classes based on your analysis of the business domain; hence, they're a model of the domain. The "Hello World" example consists of one class and its mapping. Let's see what a simple persistent class looks like, how the mapping is created, and some of the things you can do with instances of the persistent class in Hibernate.

The objective of this example is to store messages in a database and retrieve them for display. Your application has a simple persistent class, Message, which represents these printable messages. The Message class is shown in listing 2.1.

Listing 2.1 Message.java: a simple persistent class

```java
package hello;

public class Message {              Identifier
    private Long id;          ⤶    attribute
    private String text;        ◁————————  Message text
    private Message nextMessage;   ◁┐  Reference to another
                                    │  Message instance
    Message() {}

    public Message(String text) {
        this.text = text;

    }

    public Long getId() {
        return id;
    }
    private void setId(Long id) {
        this.id = id;
    }

    public String getText() {
        return text;
    }
    public void setText(String text) {
        this.text = text;
    }

    public Message getNextMessage() {
        return nextMessage;
    }
    public void setNextMessage(Message nextMessage) {
        this.nextMessage = nextMessage;
    }
}
```

The Message class has three attributes: the identifier attribute, the text of the message, and a reference to another Message object. The identifier attribute allows the application to access the database identity—the primary key value—of a persistent object. If two instances of Message have the same identifier value, they represent the same row in the database.

This example uses Long for the type of the identifier attribute, but this isn't a requirement. Hibernate allows virtually anything for the identifier type, as you'll see later.

You may have noticed that all attributes of the Message class have JavaBeans-style property accessor methods. The class also has a constructor with no parameters. The persistent classes we show in the examples will almost always look something like this. The no-argument constructor is a requirement (tools like Hibernate use reflection on this constructor to instantiate objects).

Instances of the Message class can be managed (made persistent) by Hibernate, but they don't *have* to be. Because the Message object doesn't implement any Hibernate-specific classes or interfaces, you can use it just like any other Java class:

```
Message message = new Message("Hello World");
    System.out.println( message.getText() );
```

This code fragment does exactly what you've come to expect from "Hello World" applications: It prints *Hello World* to the console. It may look like we're trying to be cute here; in fact, we're demonstrating an important feature that distinguishes Hibernate from some other persistence solutions. The persistent class can be used in any execution context at all—no special container is needed. Note that this is also one of the benefits of the new JPA entities, which are also plain Java objects.

Save the code for the Message class into your source folder, in a directory and package named hello.

Mapping the class to a database schema

To allow the object/relational mapping magic to occur, Hibernate needs some more information about exactly how the Message class should be made persistent. In other words, Hibernate needs to know how instances of that class are supposed to be stored and loaded. This metadata can be written into an *XML mapping document*, which defines, among other things, how properties of the Message class map to columns of a MESSAGES table. Let's look at the mapping document in listing 2.2.

Listing 2.2　A simple Hibernate XML mapping

```xml
<?xml version="1.0"?>
<!DOCTYPE hibernate-mapping PUBLIC
    "-//Hibernate/Hibernate Mapping DTD//EN"
    "http://hibernate.sourceforge.net/hibernate-mapping-3.0.dtd">

<hibernate-mapping>
    <class
        name="hello.Message"
        table="MESSAGES">

        <id
            name="id"
            column="MESSAGE_ID">
            <generator class="increment"/>
        </id>

        <property
            name="text"
            column="MESSAGE_TEXT"/>

        <many-to-one
            name="nextMessage"
            cascade="all"
            column="NEXT_MESSAGE_ID"
            foreign-key="FK_NEXT_MESSAGE"/>

    </class>

</hibernate-mapping>
```

The mapping document tells Hibernate that the Message class is to be persisted to the MESSAGES table, that the identifier property maps to a column named MESSAGE_ID, that the text property maps to a column named MESSAGE_TEXT, and that the property named nextMessage is an association with *many-to-one multiplicity* that maps to a foreign key column named NEXT_MESSAGE_ID. Hibernate also generates the database schema for you and adds a foreign key constraint with the name FK_NEXT_MESSAGE to the database catalog. (Don't worry about the other details for now.)

The XML document isn't difficult to understand. You can easily write and maintain it by hand. Later, we discuss a way of using annotations directly in the source code to define mapping information; but whichever method you choose,

Hibernate has enough information to generate all the SQL statements needed to insert, update, delete, and retrieve instances of the Message class. You no longer need to write these SQL statements by hand.

Create a file named Message.hbm.xml with the content shown in listing 2.2, and place it next to your Message.java file in the source package hello. The *hbm* suffix is a naming convention accepted by the Hibernate community, and most developers prefer to place mapping files next to the source code of their domain classes.

Let's load and store some objects in the main code of the "Hello World" application.

Storing and loading objects

What you really came here to see is Hibernate, so let's save a new Message to the database (see listing 2.3).

Listing 2.3   The "Hello World" main application code

```
package hello;

import java.util.*;

import org.hibernate.*;
import persistence.*;

public class HelloWorld {

    public static void main(String[] args) {

        // First unit of work
        Session session =
            HibernateUtil.getSessionFactory().openSession();
        Transaction tx = session.beginTransaction();

        Message message = new Message("Hello World");
        Long msgId = (Long) session.save(message);

        tx.commit();
        session.close();

        // Second unit of work
        Session newSession =
            HibernateUtil.getSessionFactory().openSession();
        Transaction newTransaction = newSession.beginTransaction();

        List messages =
            newSession.createQuery("from Message m order by
        m.text asc").list();

        System.out.println( messages.size() +
            " message(s) found:" );
```

```
        for ( Iterator iter = messages.iterator();
                iter.hasNext(); ) {
            Message loadedMsg = (Message) iter.next();
            System.out.println( loadedMsg.getText() );
        }

        newTransaction.commit();
        newSession.close();

        // Shutting down the application
        HibernateUtil.shutdown();
    }

}
```

Place this code in the file HelloWorld.java in the source folder of your project, in the `hello` package. Let's walk through the code.

The class has a standard Java `main()` method, and you can call it from the command line directly. Inside the main application code, you execute two separate units of work with Hibernate. The first unit stores a new `Message` object, and the second unit loads all objects and prints their text to the console.

You call the Hibernate `Session`, `Transaction`, and `Query` interfaces to access the database:

- `Session`—A Hibernate `Session` is many things in one. It's a single-threaded nonshared object that represents a particular unit of work with the database. It has the persistence manager API you call to load and store objects. (The `Session` internals consist of a queue of SQL statements that need to be synchronized with the database at some point and a map of managed persistence instances that are monitored by the `Session`.)

- `Transaction`—This Hibernate API can be used to set transaction boundaries programmatically, but it's optional (transaction boundaries aren't). Other choices are JDBC transaction demarcation, the JTA interface, or container-managed transactions with EJBs.

- `Query`—A database query can be written in Hibernate's own object-oriented query language (HQL) or plain SQL. This interface allows you to create queries, bind arguments to placeholders in the query, and execute the query in various ways.

Ignore the line of code that calls `HibernateUtil.getSessionFactory()`—we'll get to it soon.

The first unit of work, if run, results in the execution of something similar to the following SQL:

```
insert into MESSAGES (MESSAGE_ID, MESSAGE_TEXT, NEXT_MESSAGE_ID)
    values (1, 'Hello World', null)
```

Hold on—the MESSAGE_ID column is being initialized to a strange value. You didn't set the id property of message anywhere, so you expect it to be NULL, right? Actually, the id property is special. It's an *identifier property:* It holds a generated unique value. The value is assigned to the Message instance by Hibernate when save() is called. (We'll discuss how the value is generated later.)

Look at the second unit of work. The literal string "from Message m order by m.text asc" is a Hibernate query, expressed in HQL. This query is internally translated into the following SQL when list() is called:

```
select m.MESSAGE_ID, m.MESSAGE_TEXT, m.NEXT_MESSAGE_ID
    from MESSAGES m
    order by m.MESSAGE_TEXT asc
```

If you run this main() method (don't try this now—you still need to configure Hibernate), the output on your console is as follows:

```
1 message(s) found:
    Hello World
```

If you've never used an ORM tool like Hibernate before, you probably expected to see the SQL statements somewhere in the code or mapping metadata, but they aren't there. All SQL is generated at runtime (actually, at startup for all reusable SQL statements).

Your next step would normally be configuring Hibernate. However, if you feel confident, you can add two other Hibernate features—automatic dirty checking and cascading—in a third unit of work by adding the following code to your main application:

```
// Third unit of work
Session thirdSession =
    HibernateUtil.getSessionFactory().openSession();
Transaction thirdTransaction = thirdSession.beginTransaction();

// msgId holds the identifier value of the first message
message = (Message) thirdSession.get( Message.class, msgId );

message.setText( "Greetings Earthling" );
message.setNextMessage(
    new Message( "Take me to your leader (please)" )
);

thirdTransaction.commit();
thirdSession.close();
```

This code calls three SQL statements inside the same database transaction:

```
select m.MESSAGE_ID, m.MESSAGE_TEXT, m.NEXT_MESSAGE_ID
from MESSAGES m
where m.MESSAGE_ID = 1

insert into MESSAGES (MESSAGE_ID, MESSAGE_TEXT, NEXT_MESSAGE_ID)
values (2, 'Take me to your leader (please)', null)

update MESSAGES
set MESSAGE_TEXT = 'Greetings Earthling', NEXT_MESSAGE_ID = 2
where MESSAGE_ID = 1
```

Notice how Hibernate detected the modification to the `text` and `nextMessage` properties of the first message and automatically updated the database—Hibernate did *automatic dirty checking*. This feature saves you the effort of explicitly asking Hibernate to update the database when you modify the state of an object inside a unit of work. Similarly, the new message was made persistent when a reference was created from the first message. This feature is called *cascading save*. It saves you the effort of explicitly making the new object persistent by calling `save()`, as long as it's reachable by an already persistent instance.

Also notice that the ordering of the SQL statements isn't the same as the order in which you set property values. Hibernate uses a sophisticated algorithm to determine an efficient ordering that avoids database foreign key constraint violations but is still sufficiently predictable to the user. This feature is called *transactional write-behind*.

If you ran the application now, you'd get the following output (you'd have to copy the second unit of work after the third to execute the query-display step again):

```
2 message(s) found:
Greetings Earthling
Take me to your leader (please)
```

You now have domain classes, an XML mapping file, and the "Hello World" application code that loads and stores objects. Before you can compile and run this code, you need to create Hibernate's configuration (and resolve the mystery of the `HibernateUtil` class).

2.1.3 *Hibernate configuration and startup*

The regular way of initializing Hibernate is to build a `SessionFactory` object from a `Configuration` object. If you like, you can think of the `Configuration` as an object representation of a configuration file (or a properties file) for Hibernate.

Let's look at some variations before we wrap it up in the `HibernateUtil` class.

Building a SessionFactory

This is an example of a typical Hibernate startup procedure, in one line of code, using automatic configuration file detection:

```
SessionFactory sessionFactory =
    new Configuration().configure().buildSessionFactory();
```

Wait—how did Hibernate know where the configuration file was located and which one to load?

When `new Configuration()` is called, Hibernate searches for a file named `hibernate.properties` in the root of the classpath. If it's found, all `hibernate.*` properties are loaded and added to the `Configuration` object.

When `configure()` is called, Hibernate searches for a file named `hibernate.cfg.xml` in the root of the classpath, and an exception is thrown if it can't be found. You don't have to call this method if you don't have this configuration file, of course. If settings in the XML configuration file are duplicates of properties set earlier, the XML settings override the previous ones.

The location of the `hibernate.properties` configuration file is always the root of the classpath, outside of any package. If you wish to use a different file or to have Hibernate look in a subdirectory of your classpath for the XML configuration file, you must pass a path as an argument of the `configure()` method:

```
SessionFactory sessionFactory = new Configuration()
        .configure("/persistence/auction.cfg.xml")
        .buildSessionFactory();
```

Finally, you can always set additional configuration options or mapping file locations on the `Configuration` object programmatically, before building the `SessionFactory`:

```
SessionFactory sessionFactory = new Configuration()
        .configure("/persistence/auction.cfg.xml")
        .setProperty(Environment.DEFAULT_SCHEMA, "CAVEATEMPTOR")
        .addResource("auction/CreditCard.hbm.xml")
        .buildSessionFactory();
```

Many sources for the configuration are applied here: First the hibernate.properties file in your classpath is read (if present). Next, all settings from /persistence/auction.cfg.xml are added and override any previously applied settings. Finally, an additional configuration property (a default database schema name) is set programmatically, and an additional Hibernate XML mapping metadata file is added to the configuration.

You can, of course, set all options programmatically, or switch between different XML configuration files for different deployment databases. There is effectively no limitation on how you can configure and deploy Hibernate; in the end, you only need to build a `SessionFactory` from a prepared configuration.

NOTE   *Method chaining*—Method chaining is a programming style supported by many Hibernate interfaces. This style is more popular in Smalltalk than in Java and is considered by some people to be less readable and more difficult to debug than the more accepted Java style. However, it's convenient in many cases, such as for the configuration snippets you've seen in this section. Here is how it works: Most Java developers declare setter or adder methods to be of type `void`, meaning they return no value; but in Smalltalk, which has no void type, setter or adder methods usually return the receiving object. We use this Smalltalk style in some code examples, but if you don't like it, you don't need to use it. If you do use this coding style, it's better to write each method invocation on a different line. Otherwise, it may be difficult to step through the code in your debugger.

Now that you know how Hibernate is started and how to build a `SessionFactory`, what to do next? You have to create a configuration file for Hibernate.

Creating an XML configuration file

Let's assume you want to keep things simple, and, like most users, you decide to use a single XML configuration file for Hibernate that contains all the configuration details.

We recommend that you give your new configuration file the default name hibernate.cfg.xml and place it directly in the source directory of your project, outside of any package. That way, it will end up in the root of your classpath after compilation, and Hibernate will find it automatically. Look at the file in listing 2.4.

Listing 2.4   A simple Hibernate XML configuration file

```
<!DOCTYPE hibernate-configuration SYSTEM
"http://hibernate.sourceforge.net/hibernate-configuration-3.0.dtd">

<hibernate-configuration>
  <session-factory>
    <property name="hibernate.connection.driver_class">
        org.hsqldb.jdbcDriver
    </property>
    <property name="hibernate.connection.url">
        jdbc:hsqldb:hsql://localhost
    </property>
    <property name="hibernate.connection.username">
        sa
    </property>
```

```
<property name="hibernate.dialect">
    org.hibernate.dialect.HSQLDialect
</property>

<!-- Use the C3P0 connection pool provider -->
<property name="hibernate.c3p0.min_size">5</property>
<property name="hibernate.c3p0.max_size">20</property>
<property name="hibernate.c3p0.timeout">300</property>
<property name="hibernate.c3p0.max_statements">50</property>
<property name="hibernate.c3p0.idle_test_period">3000</property>

<!-- Show and print nice SQL on stdout -->
<property name="show_sql">true</property>
<property name="format_sql">true</property>

<!-- List of XML mapping files -->
<mapping resource="hello/Message.hbm.xml"/>

    </session-factory>
</hibernate-configuration>
```

The *document type declaration* is used by the XML parser to validate this document against the Hibernate configuration DTD. Note that this isn't the same DTD as the one for Hibernate XML mapping files. Also note that we added some line breaks in the property values to make this more readable—you shouldn't do this in your real configuration file (unless your database username contains a line break).

First in the configuration file are the database connection settings. You need to tell Hibernate which database JDBC driver you're using and how to connect to the database with a URL, a username, and a password (the password here is omitted, because HSQLDB by default doesn't require one). You set a Dialect, so that Hibernate knows which SQL variation it has to generate to talk to your database; dozens of dialects are packaged with Hibernate—look at the Hibernate API documentation to get a list.

In the XML configuration file, Hibernate properties may be specified without the hibernate prefix, so you can write either hibernate.show_sql or just show_sql. Property names and values are otherwise identical to programmatic configuration properties—that is, to the constants as defined in org.hibernate.cfg.Environment. The hibernate.connection.driver_class property, for example, has the constant Environment.DRIVER.

Before we look at some important configuration options, consider the last line in the configuration that names a Hibernate XML mapping file. The Configuration object needs to know about all your XML mapping files before you build the SessionFactory. A SessionFactory is an object that represents a particular

Hibernate configuration for a particular set of mapping metadata. You can either list all your XML mapping files in the Hibernate XML configuration file, or you can set their names and paths programmatically on the `Configuration` object. In any case, if you list them as a *resource*, the path to the mapping files is the relative location on the classpath, with, in this example, `hello` being a package in the root of the classpath.

You also enabled printing of all SQL executed by Hibernate to the console, and you told Hibernate to format it nicely so that you can check what is going on behind the scenes. We'll come back to logging later in this chapter.

Another, sometimes useful, trick is to make configuration options more dynamic with system properties:

```
...
<property name="show_sql">${displaysql}</property>
...
```

You can now specify a system property, such as with `java -displaysql=true`, on the command line when you start your application, and this will automatically be applied to the Hibernate configuration property.

The database connection pool settings deserve extra attention.

The database connection pool

Generally, it isn't advisable to create a connection each time you want to interact with the database. Instead, Java applications should use a *pool* of connections. Each application thread that needs to do work on the database requests a connection from the pool and then returns it to the pool when all SQL operations have been executed. The pool maintains the connections and minimizes the cost of opening and closing connections.

There are three reasons for using a pool:

- Acquiring a new connection is expensive. Some database management systems even start a completely new server process for each connection.

- Maintaining many idle connections is expensive for a database management system, and the pool can optimize the usage of idle connections (or disconnect if there are no requests).

- Creating prepared statements is also expensive for some drivers, and the connection pool can cache statements for a connection across requests.

Figure 2.2 shows the role of a connection pool in an unmanaged application runtime environment (that is, one without any application server).

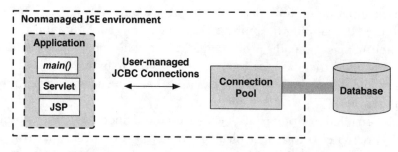

Figure 2.2 JDBC connection pooling in a nonmanaged environment

With no application server to provide a connection pool, an application either implements its own pooling algorithm or relies on a third-party library such as the open source C3P0 connection pooling software. Without Hibernate, the application code calls the connection pool to obtain a JDBC connection and then executes SQL statements with the JDBC programming interface. When the application closes the SQL statements and finally closes the connection, the prepared statements and connection aren't destroyed, but are returned to the pool.

With Hibernate, the picture changes: It acts as a client of the JDBC connection pool, as shown in figure 2.3. The application code uses the Hibernate `Session` and `Query` API for persistence operations, and it manages database transactions (probably) with the Hibernate `Transaction` API.

Hibernate defines a plug-in architecture that allows integration with any connection-pooling software. However, support for C3P0 is built in, and the software comes bundled with Hibernate, so you'll use that (you already copied the c3p0.jar file into your library directory, right?). Hibernate maintains the pool for you, and configuration properties are passed through. How do you configure C3P0 through Hibernate?

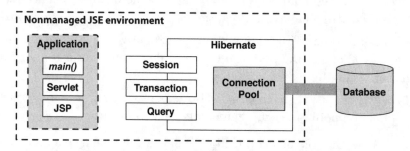

Figure 2.3 Hibernate with a connection pool in a nonmanaged environment

One way to configure the connection pool is to put the settings into your hibernate.cfg.xml configuration file, like you did in the previous section.

Alternatively, you can create a hibernate.properties file in the classpath root of the application. An example of a hibernate.properties file for C3P0 is shown in listing 2.5. Note that this file, with the exception of a list of mapping resources, is equivalent to the configuration shown in listing 2.4.

Listing 2.5 Using hibernate.properties for C3P0 connection pool settings

```
hibernate.connection.driver_class = org.hsqldb.jdbcDriver
hibernate.connection.url = jdbc:hsqldb:hsql://localhost
hibernate.connection.username = sa
hibernate.dialect = org.hibernate.dialect.HSQLDialect

hibernate.c3p0.min_size = 5            ❶  ❷
hibernate.c3p0.max_size = 20           ❷
hibernate.c3p0.timeout = 300           ❸  ❹
hibernate.c3p0.max_statements = 50     ❹
hibernate.c3p0.idle_test_period = 3000
                                       ❺
hibernate.show_sql = true
hibernate.format_sql = true
```

❶ This is the minimum number of JDBC connections that C3P0 keeps ready at all times.

❷ This is the maximum number of connections in the pool. An exception is thrown at runtime if this number is exhausted.

❸ You specify the timeout period (in this case, 300 seconds) after which an idle connection is removed from the pool.

❹ A maximum of 50 prepared statements will be cached. Caching of prepared statements is essential for best performance with Hibernate.

❺ This is the idle time in seconds before a connection is automatically validated.

Specifying properties of the form `hibernate.c3p0.*` selects C3P0 as the connection pool (the `c3p0.max_size` option is needed—you don't need any other switch to enable C3P0 support). C3P0 has more features than shown in the previous example; refer to the properties file in the etc/ subdirectory of the Hibernate distribution to get a comprehensive example you can copy from.

The Javadoc for the class `org.hibernate.cfg.Environment` also documents every Hibernate configuration property. Furthermore, you can find an up-to-date table with all Hibernate configuration options in the Hibernate reference documentation. We'll explain the most important settings throughout the book, however. You already know all you need to get started.

> **FAQ**   *Can I supply my own connections?*   Implement the `org.hibernate.connec-tion.ConnectionProvider` interface, and name your implementation with the `hibernate.connection.provider_class` configuration option. Hibernate will now rely on your custom provider if it needs a database connection.

Now that you've completed the Hibernate configuration file, you can move on and create the `SessionFactory` in your application.

Handling the SessionFactory

In most Hibernate applications, the `SessionFactory` should be instantiated once during application initialization. The single instance should then be used by all code in a particular process, and any `Session` should be created using this single `SessionFactory`. The `SessionFactory` is thread-safe and can be shared; a `Session` is a single-threaded object.

A frequently asked question is where the factory should be stored after creation and how it can be accessed without much hassle. There are more advanced but comfortable options such as JNDI and JMX, but they're usually available only in full Java EE application servers. Instead, we'll introduce a pragmatic and quick solution that solves both the problem of Hibernate startup (the one line of code) and the storing and accessing of the `SessionFactory`: you'll use a static global variable and static initialization.

Both the variable and initialization can be implemented in a single class, which you'll call `HibernateUtil`. This helper class is well known in the Hibernate community—it's a common pattern for Hibernate startup in plain Java applications without Java EE services. A basic implementation is shown in listing 2.6.

Listing 2.6   The `HibernateUtil` class for startup and `SessionFactory` handling

```
package persistence;

import org.hibernate.*;
import org.hibernate.cfg.*;

public class HibernateUtil {

  private static SessionFactory sessionFactory;

  static {
    try {
      sessionFactory=new Configuration()
                        .configure()
```

```
                        .buildSessionFactory();
    } catch (Throwable ex) {
        throw new ExceptionInInitializerError(ex);
    }
}

public static SessionFactory getSessionFactory() {
    // Alternatively, you could look up in JNDI here
    return sessionFactory;
}

public static void shutdown() {
    // Close caches and connection pools
    getSessionFactory().close();
}
}
```

You create a static initializer block to start up Hibernate; this block is executed by the loader of this class exactly once, on initialization when the class is loaded. The first call of `HibernateUtil` in the application loads the class, builds the Session-Factory, and sets the static variable at the same time. If a problem occurs, any `Exception` or `Error` is wrapped and thrown out of the static block (that's why you catch `Throwable`). The wrapping in `ExceptionInInitializerError` is mandatory for static initializers.

You've created this new class in a new package called `persistence`. In a fully featured Hibernate application, you often need such a package—for example, to wrap up your custom persistence layer interceptors and data type converters as part of your infrastructure.

Now, whenever you need access to a Hibernate `Session` in your application, you can get it easily with `HibernateUtil.getSessionFactory().openSession()`, just as you did earlier in the `HelloWorld` main application code.

You're almost ready to run and test the application. But because you certainly want to know what is going on behind the scenes, you'll first enable logging.

Enabling logging and statistics

You've already seen the `hibernate.show_sql` configuration property. You'll need it continually when you develop software with Hibernate; it enables logging of all generated SQL to the console. You'll use it for troubleshooting, for performance tuning, and to see what's going on. If you also enable `hibernate.format_sql`, the output is more readable but takes up more screen space. A third option you haven't set so far is `hibernate.use_sql_comments`—it causes Hibernate to put comments inside all generated SQL statements to hint at their origin. For example, you can then easily see if a particular SQL statement was generated from an explicit query or an on-demand collection initialization.

Enabling the SQL output to stdout is only your first logging option. Hibernate (and many other ORM implementations) execute SQL statements *asynchronously*. An INSERT statement isn't usually executed when the application calls session.save(), nor is an UPDATE immediately issued when the application calls item.setPrice(). Instead, the SQL statements are usually issued at the end of a transaction.

This means that tracing and debugging ORM code is sometimes nontrivial. In theory, it's possible for the application to treat Hibernate as a black box and ignore this behavior. However, when you're troubleshooting a difficult problem, you need to be able to see *exactly* what is going on inside Hibernate. Because Hibernate is open source, you can easily step into the Hibernate code, and occasionally this helps a great deal! Seasoned Hibernate experts debug problems by looking at the Hibernate log and the mapping files only; we encourage you to spend some time with the log output generated by Hibernate and familiarize yourself with the internals.

Hibernate logs all interesting events through *Apache commons-logging*, a thin abstraction layer that directs output to either *Apache Log4j* (if you put log4j.jar in your classpath) or JDK 1.4 logging (if you're running under JDK 1.4 or above and Log4j isn't present). We recommend Log4j because it's more mature, more popular, and under more active development.

To see output from Log4j, you need a file named log4j.properties in your classpath (right next to hibernate.properties or hibernate.cfg.xml). Also, don't forget to copy the log4j.jar library to your lib directory. The Log4j configuration example in listing 2.7 directs all log messages to the console.

Listing 2.7 An example log4j.properties configuration file

```
# Direct log messages to stdout
log4j.appender.stdout=org.apache.log4j.ConsoleAppender
log4j.appender.stdout.Target=System.out
log4j.appender.stdout.layout=org.apache.log4j.PatternLayout
log4j.appender.stdout.layout.ConversionPattern=%d{ABSOLUTE}
    ➥%5p %c{1}:%L - %m%n

# Root logger option
log4j.rootLogger=INFO, stdout

# Hibernate logging options (INFO only shows startup messages)
log4j.logger.org.hibernate=INFO
```

```
# Log JDBC bind parameter runtime arguments
log4j.logger.org.hibernate.type=INFO
```

The last category in this configuration file is especially interesting: It enables the logging of JDBC bind parameters if you set it to DEBUG level, providing information you usually don't see in the ad hoc SQL console log. For a more comprehensive example, check the log4j.properties file bundled in the etc/ directory of the Hibernate distribution, and also look at the Log4j documentation for more information. Note that you should never log anything at DEBUG level in production, because doing so can seriously impact the performance of your application.

You can also monitor Hibernate by enabling live statistics. Without an application server (that is, if you don't have a JMX deployment environment), the easiest way to get statistics out of the Hibernate engine at runtime is the SessionFactory:

```
Statistics stats =
    HibernateUtil.getSessionFactory().getStatistics();

stats.setStatisticsEnabled(true);
...

stats.getSessionOpenCount();
stats.logSummary();

EntityStatistics itemStats =
    stats.getEntityStatistics("auction.model.Item");
itemStats.getFetchCount();
```

The statistics interfaces are Statistics for global information, Entity-Statistics for information about a particular entity, CollectionStatistics for a particular collection role, QueryStatistics for SQL and HQL queries, and SecondLevelCacheStatistics for detailed runtime information about a particular region in the optional second-level data cache. A convenient method is logSummary(), which prints out a complete summary to the console with a single call. If you want to enable the collection of statistics through the configuration, and not programmatically, set the hibernate.generate_statistics configuration property to true. See the API documentation for more information about the various statistics retrieval methods.

Before you run the "Hello World" application, check that your work directory has all the necessary files:

```
WORKDIR
build.xml
+lib
```

```
<all required libraries>
+src
  +hello
    HelloWorld.java
    Message.java
    Message.hbm.xml
  +persistence
    HibernateUtil.java
  hibernate.cfg.xml (or hibernate.properties)
  log4j.properties
```

The first file, build.xml, is the Ant build definition. It contains the Ant targets for building and running the application, which we'll discuss next. You'll also add a target that can generate the database schema automatically.

2.1.4 Running and testing the application

To run the application, you need to compile it first and start the database management system with the right database schema.

Ant is a powerful build system for Java. Typically, you'd write a build.xml file for your project and call the build targets you defined in this file with the Ant command-line tool. You can also call Ant targets from your Java IDE, if that is supported.

Compiling the project with Ant

You'll now add a build.xml file and some targets to the "Hello World" project. The initial content for the build file is shown in listing 2.8—you create this file directly in your WORKDIR.

Listing 2.8   A basic Ant build file for "Hello World"

```
<project name="HelloWorld" default="compile" basedir=".">

    <!-- Name of project and version -->
    <property name="proj.name"      value="HelloWorld"/>
    <property name="proj.version"   value="1.0"/>

    <!-- Global properties for this build -->
    <property name="src.java.dir"   value="src"/>
    <property name="lib.dir"        value="lib"/>
    <property name="build.dir"      value="bin"/>

    <!-- Classpath declaration -->
    <path id="project.classpath">
        <fileset dir="${lib.dir}">
            <include name="**/*.jar"/>
            <include name="**/*.zip"/>
        </fileset>
```

```xml
        </path>

        <!-- Useful shortcuts -->
        <patternset id="meta.files">
            <include name="**/*.xml"/>
            <include name="**/*.properties"/>
        </patternset>

        <!-- Clean up -->
        <target name="clean">
            <delete dir="${build.dir}"/>
            <mkdir dir="${build.dir}"/>
        </target>

        <!-- Compile Java source -->
        <target name="compile" depends="clean">
            <mkdir dir="${build.dir}"/>
            <javac
                srcdir="${src.java.dir}"
                destdir="${build.dir}"
                nowarn="on">
                <classpath refid="project.classpath"/>
            </javac>
        </target>

        <!-- Copy metadata to build classpath -->
        <target name="copymetafiles">
            <copy todir="${build.dir}">
                <fileset dir="${src.java.dir}">
                    <patternset refid="meta.files"/>
                </fileset>
            </copy>
        </target>

        <!-- Run HelloWorld -->
        <target name="run" depends="compile, copymetafiles"
            description="Build and run HelloWorld">
            <java fork="true"
                    classname="hello.HelloWorld"
                    classpathref="project.classpath">
                <classpath path="${build.dir}"/>
            </java>
        </target>

    </project>
```

The first half of this Ant build file contains property settings, such as the project name and global locations of files and directories. You can already see that this build is based on the existing directory layout, your WORKDIR (for Ant, this is the same directory as the basedir). The default target, when this build file is called with no named target, is compile.

Next, a name that can be easily referenced later, `project.classpath`, is defined as a shortcut to all libraries in the library directory of the project. Another shortcut for a pattern that will come in handy is defined as `meta.files`. You need to handle configuration and metadata files separately in the processing of the build, using this filter.

The `clean` target removes all created and compiled files, and cleans the project. The last three targets, `compile`, `copymetafiles`, and `run`, should be self-explanatory. Running the application depends on the compilation of all Java source files, and the copying of all mapping and property configuration files to the build directory.

Now, execute `ant compile` in your WORKDIR to compile the "Hello World" application. You should see no errors (nor any warnings) during compilation and find your compiled class files in the bin directory. Also call `ant copymetafiles` once, and check whether all configuration and mapping files are copied correctly into the bin directory.

Before you run the application, start the database management system and export a fresh database schema.

Starting the HSQL database system

Hibernate supports more than 25 SQL database management systems out of the box, and support for any unknown dialect can be added easily. If you have an existing database, or if you know basic database administration, you can also replace the configuration options (mostly connection and dialect settings) you created earlier with settings for your own preferred system.

To say hello to the world, you need a lightweight, no-frills database system that is easy to install and configure. A good choice is HSQLDB, an open source SQL database management system written in Java. It can run in-process with the main application, but in our experience, running it stand-alone with a TCP port listening for connections is usually more convenient. You've already copied the hsqldb.jar file into the library directory of your WORKDIR—this library includes both the database engine and the JDBC driver required to connect to a running instance.

To start the HSQLDB server, open up a command line, change into your WORKDIR, and run the command shown in figure 2.4. You should see startup messages and finally a help message that tells you how to shut down the database system (it's OK to use Ctrl+C). You'll also find some new files in your WORKDIR, starting with `test`—these are the files used by HSQLDB to store your data. If you want to start with a fresh database, delete the files between restarts of the server.

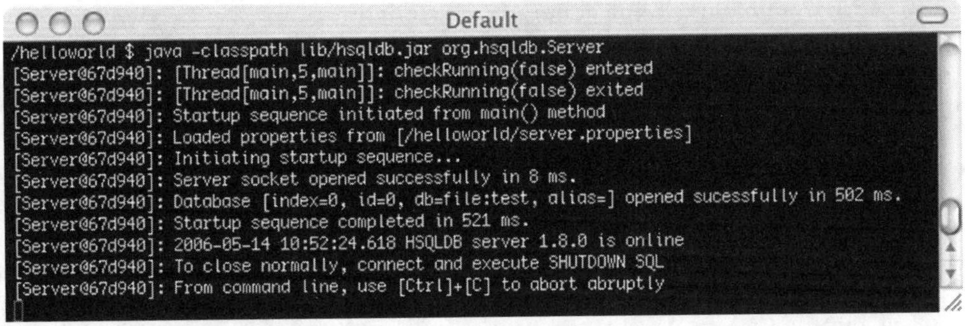

Figure 2.4 Starting the HSQLDB server from the command line

You now have an empty database that has no content, not even a schema. Let's create the schema next.

Exporting the database schema

You can create the database schema by hand by writing SQL DDL with CREATE statements and executing this DDL on your database. Or (and this is much more convenient) you can let Hibernate take care of this and create a default schema for your application. The prerequisite in Hibernate for automatic generation of SQL DDL is always a Hibernate mapping metadata definition, either in XML mapping files or in Java source-code annotations. We assume that you've designed and implemented your domain model classes and written mapping metadata in XML as you followed the previous sections.

The tool used for schema generation is hbm2ddl; its class is org.hibernate. tool.hbm2ddl.SchemaExport, so it's also sometimes called SchemaExport.

There are many ways to run this tool and create a schema:

- You can run <hbm2ddl> in an Ant target in your regular build procedure.

- You can run SchemaExport programmatically in application code, maybe in your HibernateUtil startup class. This isn't common, however, because you rarely need programmatic control over schema generation.

- You can enable automatic export of a schema when your SessionFactory is built by setting the hibernate.hbm2ddl.auto configuration property to create or create-drop. The first setting results in DROP statements followed by CREATE statements when the SessionFactory is built. The second setting adds additional DROP statements when the application is shut down and the SessionFactory is closed—effectively leaving a clean database after every run.

Programmatic schema generation is straightforward:

```
Configuration cfg = new Configuration().configure();
SchemaExport schemaExport = new SchemaExport(cfg);
schemaExport.create(false, true);
```

A new SchemaExport object is created from a Configuration; all settings (such as the database driver, connection URL, and so on) are passed to the SchemaExport constructor. The create(false, true) call triggers the DDL generation process, without any SQL printed to stdout (because of the false setting), but with DDL immediately executed in the database (true). See the SchemaExport API for more information and additional settings.

Your development process determines whether you should enable automatic schema export with the hibernate.hbm2ddl.auto configuration setting. Many new Hibernate users find the automatic dropping and re-creation on Session-Factory build a little confusing. Once you're more familiar with Hibernate, we encourage you to explore this option for fast turnaround times in integration testing.

An additional option for this configuration property, update, can be useful during development: it enables the built-in SchemaUpdate tool, which can make schema evolution easier. If enabled, Hibernate reads the JDBC database metadata on startup and creates new tables and constraints by comparing the old schema with the current mapping metadata. Note that this functionality depends on the quality of the metadata provided by the JDBC driver, an area in which many drivers are lacking. In practice, this feature is therefore less exciting and useful than it sounds.

WARNING   We've seen Hibernate users trying to use SchemaUpdate to update the schema of a production database automatically. This can quickly end in disaster and won't be allowed by your DBA.

You can also run SchemaUpdate programmatically:

```
Configuration cfg = new Configuration().configure();
SchemaUpdate schemaUpdate = new SchemaUpdate(cfg);
schemaUpdate.execute(false);
```

The false setting at the end again disables printing of the SQL DDL to the console and only executes the statements directly on the database. If you export the DDL to the console or a text file, your DBA may be able to use it as a starting point to produce a quality schema-evolution script.

Another hbm2ddl.auto setting useful in development is validate. It enables SchemaValidator to run at startup. This tool can compare your mapping against the JDBC metadata and tell you if the schema and mappings match. You can also run `SchemaValidator` programmatically:

```
Configuration cfg = new Configuration().configure();
new SchemaValidator(cfg).validate();
```

An exception is thrown if a mismatch between the mappings and the database schema is detected.

Because you're basing your build system on Ant, you'll ideally add a schemaexport target to your Ant build that generates and exports a fresh schema for your database whenever you need one (see listing 2.9).

Listing 2.9 Ant target for schema export

```
<taskdef name="hibernatetool"
         classname="org.hibernate.tool.ant.HibernateToolTask"
         classpathref="project.classpath"/>

<target name="schemaexport" depends="compile, copymetafiles"
    description="Exports a generated schema to DB and file">

    <hibernatetool destdir="${basedir}">
        <classpath path="${build.dir}"/>

        <configuration
            configurationfile="${build.dir}/hibernate.cfg.xml"/>

        <hbm2ddl
            drop="true"
            create="true"
            export="true"
            outputfilename="helloworld-ddl.sql"
            delimiter=";"
            format="true"/>

    </hibernatetool>

</target>
```

In this target, you first define a new Ant task that you'd like to use, `Hibernate-ToolTask`. This is a generic task that can do many things—exporting an SQL DDL schema from Hibernate mapping metadata is only one of them. You'll use it throughout this chapter in all Ant builds. Make sure you include all Hibernate libraries, required third-party libraries, and your JDBC driver in the classpath of the task definition. You also need to add the hibernate-tools.jar file, which can be found in the Hibernate Tools download package.

The schemaexport Ant target uses this task, and it also depends on the compiled classes and copied configuration files in the build directory. The basic use of the <hibernatetool> task is always the same: A *configuration* is the starting point for all code artifact generation. The variation shown here, <configuration>, understands Hibernate XML configuration files and reads all Hibernate XML mapping metadata files listed in the given configuration. From that information, an internal Hibernate metadata model (which is what *hbm* stands for everywhere) is produced, and this model data is then processed subsequently by exporters. We discuss tool configurations that can read annotations or a database for reverse engineering later in this chapter.

The other element in the target is a so-called *exporter*. The tool configuration feeds its metadata information to the exporter you selected; in the preceding example, it's the <hbm2ddl> exporter. As you may have guessed, this exporter understands the Hibernate metadata model and produces SQL DDL. You can control the DDL generation with several options:

- The exporter generates SQL, so it's mandatory that you set an SQL dialect in your Hibernate configuration file.

- If drop is set to true, SQL DROP statements will be generated first, and all tables and constraints are removed if they exist. If create is set to true, SQL CREATE statements are generated next, to create all tables and constraints. If you enable both options, you effectively drop and re-create the database schema on every run of the Ant target.

- If export is set to true, all DDL statements are directly executed in the database. The exporter opens a connection to the database using the connection settings found in your configuration file.

- If an outputfilename is present, all DDL statements are written to this file, and the file is saved in the destdir you configured. The delimiter character is appended to all SQL statements written to the file, and if format is enabled, all SQL statements are nicely indented.

You can now generate, print, and directly export the schema to a text file and the database by running ant schemaxport in your WORKDIR. All tables and constraints are dropped and then created again, and you have a fresh database ready. (Ignore any error message that says that a table couldn't be dropped because it didn't exist.)

Check that your database is running and that it has the correct database schema. A useful tool included with HSQLDB is a simple database browser. You can call it with the following Ant target:

```
<target name="dbmanager" description="Start HSQLDB manager">
    <java
        classname="org.hsqldb.util.DatabaseManagerSwing"
        fork="yes"
        classpathref="project.classpath"
        failonerror="true">
        <arg value="-url"/>
        <arg value="jdbc:hsqldb:hsql://localhost/"/>
        <arg value="-driver"/>
        <arg value="org.hsqldb.jdbcDriver"/>
    </java>
</target>
```

You should see the schema shown in figure 2.5 after logging in.

Run your application with ant run, and watch the console for Hibernate log output. You should see your messages being stored, loaded, and printed. Fire an SQL query in the HSQLDB browser to check the content of your database directly.

You now have a working Hibernate infrastructure and Ant project build. You could skip to the next chapter and continue writing and mapping more complex business classes. However, we recommend that you spend some time with the

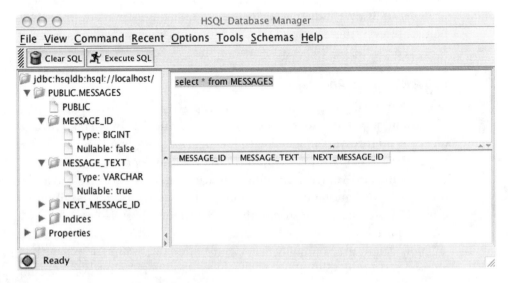

Figure 2.5 The HSQLDB browser and SQL console

"Hello World" application and extend it with more functionality. You can, for example, try different HQL queries or logging options. Don't forget that your database system is still running in the background, and that you have to either export a fresh schema or stop it and delete the database files to get a clean and empty database again.

In the next section, we walk through the "Hello World" example again, with Java Persistence interfaces and EJB 3.0.

2.2   *Starting a Java Persistence project*

In the following sections, we show you some of the advantages of JPA and the new EJB 3.0 standard, and how annotations and the standardized programming interfaces can simplify application development, even when compared with Hibernate. Obviously, designing and linking to standardized interfaces is an advantage if you ever need to port or deploy an application on a different runtime environment. Besides portability, though, there are many good reasons to give JPA a closer look.

We'll now guide you through another "Hello World" example, this time with Hibernate Annotations and Hibernate EntityManager. You'll reuse the basic project infrastructure introduced in the previous section so you can see where JPA differs from Hibernate. After working with annotations and the JPA interfaces, we'll show how an application integrates and interacts with other managed components—EJBs. We'll discuss many more application design examples later in the book; however, this first glimpse will let you decide on a particular approach as soon as possible.

2.2.1   *Using Hibernate Annotations*

Let's first use Hibernate Annotations to replace the Hibernate XML mapping files with inline metadata. You may want to copy your existing "Hello World" project directory before you make the following changes—you'll migrate from native Hibernate to standard JPA mappings (and program code later on).

Copy the Hibernate Annotations libraries to your WORKDIR/lib directory—see the Hibernate Annotations documentation for a list of required libraries. (At the time of writing, hibernate-annotations.jar and the API stubs in ejb3-persistence.jar were required.)

Now delete the src/hello/Message.hbm.xml file. You'll replace this file with annotations in the src/hello/Message.java class source, as shown in listing 2.10.

Listing 2.10 Mapping the Message class with annotations

```java
package hello;

import javax.persistence.*;

@Entity
@Table(name = "MESSAGES")
public class Message {

    @Id @GeneratedValue
    @Column(name = "MESSAGE_ID")
    private Long id;

    @Column(name = "MESSAGE_TEXT")
    private String text;

    @ManyToOne(cascade = CascadeType.ALL)
    @JoinColumn(name = "NEXT_MESSAGE_ID")
    private Message nextMessage;

    private Message() {}

    public Message(String text) {
        this.text = text;
    }

    public Long getId() {
        return id;
    }
    private void setId(Long id) {
        this.id = id;
    }

    public String getText() {
        return text;
    }
    public void setText(String text) {
        this.text = text;
    }

    public Message getNextMessage() {
        return nextMessage;
    }
    public void setNextMessage(Message nextMessage) {
        this.nextMessage = nextMessage;
    }
}
```

The first thing you'll probably notice in this updated business class is the import of the `javax.persistence` interfaces. Inside this package are all the standardized JPA annotations you need to map the `@Entity` class to a database `@Table`. You put annotations on the private fields of the class, starting with `@Id` and `@Generated-Value` for the database identifier mapping. The JPA persistence provider detects that the `@Id` annotation is on a field and assumes that it should access properties on an object directly through fields at runtime. If you placed the `@Id` annotation on the `getId()` method, you'd enable access to properties through getter and setter methods by default. Hence, all other annotations are also placed on either fields or getter methods, following the selected strategy.

Note that the `@Table`, `@Column`, and `@JoinColumn` annotations aren't necessary. All properties of an entity are automatically considered persistent, with default strategies and table/column names. You add them here for clarity and to get the same results as with the XML mapping file. Compare the two mapping metadata strategies now, and you'll see that annotations are much more convenient and reduce the lines of metadata significantly. Annotations are also type-safe, they support autocompletion in your IDE as you type (like any other Java interfaces), and they make refactoring of classes and properties easier.

If you're worried that the import of the JPA interfaces will bind your code to this package, you should know that it's only required on your classpath when the annotations are used by Hibernate at runtime. You can load and execute this class without the JPA interfaces on your classpath as long as you don't want to load and store instances with Hibernate.

A second concern that developers new to annotations sometimes have relates to the inclusion of *configuration metadata* in Java source code. By definition, configuration metadata is metadata that can change for each deployment of the application, such as table names. JPA has a simple solution: You can override or replace all annotated metadata with XML metadata files. Later in the book, we'll show you how this is done.

Let's assume that this is all you want from JPA—annotations instead of XML. You don't want to use the JPA programming interfaces or query language; you'll use Hibernate `Session` and HQL. The only other change you need to make to your project, besides deleting the now obsolete XML mapping file, is a change in the Hibernate configuration, in hibernate.cfg.xml:

```
<!DOCTYPE hibernate-configuration SYSTEM
"http://hibernate.sourceforge.net/hibernate-configuration-3.0.dtd">

<hibernate-configuration>
<session-factory>
    <!-- ... Many property settings ... -->

    <!-- List of annotated classes-->
    <mapping class="hello.Message"/>
```

```
</session-factory>
</hibernate-configuration>
```

The Hibernate configuration file previously had a list of all XML mapping files. This has been replaced with a list of all annotated classes. If you use programmatic configuration of a `SessionFactory`, the `addAnnotatedClass()` method replaces the `addResource()` method:

```
// Load settings from hibernate.properties
AnnotationConfiguration cfg = new AnnotationConfiguration();
// ... set other configuration options programmatically

cfg.addAnnotatedClass(hello.Message.class);

SessionFactory sessionFactory = cfg.buildSessionFactory();
```

Note that you have now used `AnnotationConfiguration` instead of the basic Hibernate `Configuration` interface—this extension understands annotated classes. At a minimum, you also need to change your initializer in `HibernateUtil` to use that interface. If you export the database schema with an Ant target, replace `<configuration>` with `<annotationconfiguration>` in your build.xml file.

This is all you need to change to run the "Hello World" application with annotations. Try running it again, probably with a fresh database.

Annotation metadata can also be global, although you don't need this for the "Hello World" application. Global annotation metadata is placed in a file named package-info.java in a particular package directory. In addition to listing annotated classes, you need to add the packages that contain global metadata to your configuration. For example, in a Hibernate XML configuration file, you need to add the following:

```
<!DOCTYPE hibernate-configuration SYSTEM
"http://hibernate.sourceforge.net/hibernate-configuration-3.0.dtd">

<hibernate-configuration>
<session-factory>
    <!-- ... Many property settings ... -->

    <!-- List of annotated classes-->
    <mapping class="hello.Message"/>

    <!-- List of packages with package-info.java -->
    <mapping package="hello"/>

</session-factory>
</hibernate-configuration>
```

Or you could achieve the same results with programmatic configuration:

```
// Load settings from hibernate.properties
AnnotationConfiguration cfg = new AnnotationConfiguration();
// ... set other configuration options programmatically

cfg.addClass(hello.Message.class);

cfg.addPackage("hello");

SessionFactory sessionFactory = cfg.buildSessionFactory();
```

Let's take this one step further and replace the native Hibernate code that loads and stores messages with code that uses JPA. With Hibernate Annotations *and* Hibernate EntityManager, you can create portable and standards-compliant mappings and data access code.

2.2.2 *Using Hibernate EntityManager*

Hibernate EntityManager is a wrapper around Hibernate Core that provides the JPA programming interfaces, supports the JPA entity instance lifecycle, and allows you to write queries with the standardized Java Persistence query language. Because JPA functionality is a subset of Hibernate's native capabilities, you may wonder why you should use the EntityManager package on top of Hibernate. We'll present a list of advantages later in this section, but you'll see one particular simplification as soon as you configure your project for Hibernate EntityManager: You no longer have to list all annotated classes (or XML mapping files) in your configuration file.

Let's modify the "Hello World" project and prepare it for full JPA compatibility.

Basic JPA configuration

A `SessionFactory` represents a particular logical data-store configuration in a Hibernate application. The `EntityManagerFactory` has the same role in a JPA application, and you configure an `EntityManagerFactory` (EMF) either with configuration files or in application code just as you would configure a `SessionFactory`. The configuration of an EMF, together with a set of mapping metadata (usually annotated classes), is called the *persistence unit.*

The notion of a persistence unit also includes the packaging of the application, but we want to keep this as simple as possible for "Hello World"; we'll assume that you want to start with a standardized JPA configuration and no special packaging. Not only the content, but also the name and location of the JPA configuration file for a persistence unit are standardized.

Create a directory named WORKDIR/etc/META-INF and place the basic configuration file named persistence.xml, shown in listing 2.11, in that directory:

Listing 2.11   Persistence unit configuration file

```
<persistence xmlns="http://java.sun.com/xml/ns/persistence"
    xmlns:xsi="http://www.w3.org/2001/XMLSchema-instance"
    xsi:schemaLocation="http://java.sun.com/xml/ns/persistence
     http://java.sun.com/xml/ns/persistence/persistence_1_0.xsd"
    version="1.0">

    <persistence-unit name="helloworld">
        <properties>
            <property name="hibernate.ejb.cfgfile"
                value="/hibernate.cfg.xml"/>
        </properties>
    </persistence-unit>

</persistence>
```

Every persistence unit needs a name, and in this case it's `helloworld`.

NOTE The XML header in the preceding persistence unit configuration file declares what schema should be used, and it's always the same. We'll omit it in future examples and assume that you'll add it.

A persistence unit is further configured with an arbitrary number of properties, which are all vendor-specific. The property in the previous example, `hibernate.ejb.cfgfile`, acts as a catchall. It refers to a `hibernate.cfg.xml` file (in the root of the classpath) that contains all settings for this persistence unit—you're reusing the existing Hibernate configuration. Later, you'll move all configuration details into the `persistence.xml` file, but for now you're more interested in running "Hello World" with JPA.

The JPA standard says that the persistence.xml file needs to be present in the META-INF directory of a deployed persistence unit. Because you aren't really packaging and deploying the persistence unit, this means that you have to copy persistence.xml into a META-INF directory of the build output directory. Modify your build.xml, and add the following to the `copymetafiles` target:

```
<property name="src.etc.dir" value="etc"/>

<target name="copymetafiles">

    <!-- Copy metadata to build -->
    <copy todir="${build.dir}">
      <fileset dir="${src.java.dir}">
        <patternset refid="meta.files"/>
      </fileset>
    </copy>
```

```
<!-- Copy configuration files from etc/ -->
<copy todir="${build.dir}">
  <fileset dir="${src.etc.dir}">
    <patternset refid="meta.files"/>
  </fileset>
</copy>

</target>
```

Everything found in WORKDIR/etc that matches the `meta.files` pattern is copied to the build output directory, which is part of the classpath at runtime.

Let's rewrite the main application code with JPA.

"Hello World" with JPA

These are your primary programming interfaces in Java Persistence:

- `javax.persistence.Persistence`—A startup class that provides a static method for the creation of an `EntityManagerFactory`.

- `javax.persistence.EntityManagerFactory`—The equivalent to a Hibernate `SessionFactory`. This runtime object represents a particular persistence unit. It's thread-safe, is usually handled as a singleton, and provides methods for the creation of `EntityManager` instances.

- `javax.persistence.EntityManager`—The equivalent to a Hibernate `Session`. This single-threaded, nonshared object represents a particular unit of work for data access. It provides methods to manage the lifecycle of entity instances and to create `Query` instances.

- `javax.persistence.Query`—This is the equivalent to a Hibernate `Query`. An object is a particular JPA query language or native SQL query representation, and it allows safe binding of parameters and provides various methods for the execution of the query.

- `javax.persistence.EntityTransaction`—This is the equivalent to a Hibernate `Transaction`, used in Java SE environments for the demarcation of `RESOURCE_LOCAL` transactions. In Java EE, you rely on the standardized `javax.transaction.UserTransaction` interface of JTA for programmatic transaction demarcation.

To use the JPA interfaces, you need to copy the required libraries to your WORKDIR/lib directory; check the documentation bundled with Hibernate EntityManager for an up-to-date list. You can then rewrite the code in WORKDIR/src/hello/HelloWorld.java and switch from Hibernate to JPA interfaces (see listing 2.12).

Listing 2.12 The "Hello World" main application code with JPA

```java
package hello;

import java.util.*;
import javax.persistence.*;

public class HelloWorld {

    public static void main(String[] args) {

        // Start EntityManagerFactory
        EntityManagerFactory emf =
                Persistence.createEntityManagerFactory("helloworld");

        // First unit of work
        EntityManager em = emf.createEntityManager();
        EntityTransaction tx = em.getTransaction();
        tx.begin();

        Message message = new Message("Hello World");
        em.persist(message);

        tx.commit();
        em.close();

        // Second unit of work
        EntityManager newEm = emf.createEntityManager();
        EntityTransaction newTx = newEm.getTransaction();
        newTx.begin();

        List messages = newEm
            .createQuery("select m from Message m
     order by m.text asc")
            .getResultList();


        System.out.println( messages.size() + " message(s) found" );

        for (Object m : messages) {
            Message loadedMsg = (Message) m;
            System.out.println(loadedMsg.getText());
        }

        newTx.commit();
        newEm.close();

        // Shutting down the application
        emf.close();
    }
}
```

The first thing you probably notice in this code is that there is no Hibernate import anymore, only `javax.peristence.*`. The `EntityManagerFactory` is created with a static call to `Persistence` and the name of the persistence unit. The rest of the code should be self-explanatory—you use JPA just like Hibernate, though there are some minor differences in the API, and methods have slightly different names. Furthermore, you didn't use the `HibernateUtil` class for static initialization of the infrastructure; you can write a `JPAUtil` class and move the creation of an `EntityManagerFactory` there if you want, or you can remove the now unused `WORKDIR/src/persistence` package.

JPA also supports programmatic configuration, with a map of options:

```
Map myProperties = new HashMap();
myProperties.put("hibernate.hbm2ddl.auto", "create-drop");
EntityManagerFactory emf =
  Persistence.createEntityManagerFactory("helloworld", myProperties);
```

Custom programmatic properties override any property you've set in the persistence.xml configuration file.

Try to run the ported `HelloWorld` code with a fresh database. You should see the exact same log output on your screen as you did with native Hibernate—the JPA persistence provider engine is Hibernate.

Automatic detection of metadata

We promised earlier that you won't have to list all your annotated classes or XML mapping files in the configuration, but it's still there, in hibernate.cfg.xml. Let's enable the autodetection feature of JPA.

Run the "Hello World" application again after switching to DEBUG logging for the `org.hibernate` package. Some additional lines should appear in your log:

```
...
Ejb3Configuration:141
   - Trying to find persistence unit: helloworld
Ejb3Configuration:150
   - Analyse of persistence.xml:
       file:/helloworld/build/META-INF/persistence.xml
PersistenceXmlLoader:115
   - Persistent Unit name from persistence.xml: helloworld
Ejb3Configuration:359
   - Detect class: true; detect hbm: true
JarVisitor:178
   - Searching mapped entities in jar/par: file:/helloworld/build
JarVisitor:217
   - Filtering: hello.HelloWorld
JarVisitor:217
   - Filtering: hello.Message
```

```
JarVisitor:255
    - Java element filter matched for hello.Message
Ejb3Configuration:101
    - Creating Factory: helloworld
...
```

On startup, the `Persistence.createEntityManagerFactory()` method tries to locate the persistence unit named `helloworld`. It searches the classpath for all META-INF/persistence.xml files and then configures the EMF if a match is found. The second part of the log shows something you probably didn't expect. The JPA persistence provider tried to find all annotated classes and all Hibernate XML mapping files in the build output directory. The list of annotated classes (or the list of XML mapping files) in hibernate.cfg.xml isn't needed, because `hello.Message`, the annotated entity class, has already been found.

Instead of removing only this single unnecessary option from hibernate.cfg.xml, let's remove the whole file and move all configuration details into persistence.xml (see listing 2.13).

Listing 2.13 Full persistence unit configuration file

```xml
<persistence-unit name="helloworld">

    <provider>org.hibernate.ejb.HibernatePersistence</provider>

    <!-- Not needed, Hibernate supports auto-detection in JSE
        <class>hello.Message</class>
    -->

    <properties>
        <property name="hibernate.archive.autodetection"
            value="class, hbm"/>

        <property name="hibernate.show_sql" value="true"/>
        <property name="hibernate.format_sql" value="true"/>

        <property name="hibernate.connection.driver_class"
                value="org.hsqldb.jdbcDriver"/>
        <property name="hibernate.connection.url"
                value="jdbc:hsqldb:hsql://localhost"/>
        <property name="hibernate.connection.username"
                value="sa"/>

        <property name="hibernate.c3p0.min_size"
                value="5"/>
        <property name="hibernate.c3p0.max_size"
                value="20"/>
        <property name="hibernate.c3p0.timeout"
                value="300"/>
        <property name="hibernate.c3p0.max_statements"
                value="50"/>
```

```
<property name="hibernate.c3p0.idle_test_period"
          value="3000"/>

<property name="hibernate.dialect"
          value="org.hibernate.dialect.HSQLDialect"/>

<property name="hibernate.hbm2ddl.auto" value="create"/>

    </properties>
  </persistence-unit>
```

There are three interesting new elements in this configuration file. First, you set an explicit <provider> that should be used for this persistence unit. This is usually required only if you work with several JPA implementations at the same time, but we hope that Hibernate will, of course, be the only one. Next, the specification requires that you list all annotated classes with <class> elements if you deploy in a non-Java EE environment—Hibernate supports autodetection of mapping metadata everywhere, making this optional. Finally, the Hibernate configuration setting archive.autodetection tells Hibernate what metadata to scan for automatically: annotated classes (class) and/or Hibernate XML mapping files (hbm). By default, Hibernate EntityManager scans for both. The rest of the configuration file contains all options we explained and used earlier in this chapter in the regular hibernate.cfg.xml file.

Automatic detection of annotated classes and XML mapping files is a great feature of JPA. It's usually only available in a Java EE application server; at least, this is what the EJB 3.0 specification guarantees. But Hibernate, as a JPA provider, also implements it in plain Java SE, though you may not be able to use the exact same configuration with any other JPA provider.

You've now created an application that is fully JPA specification-compliant. Your project directory should look like this (note that we also moved log4j.properties to the etc/ directory):

```
WORKDIR
+etc
  log4j.properties
  +META-INF
   persistence.xml
+lib
  <all required libraries>
+src
  +hello
    HelloWorld.java
    Message.java
```

All JPA configuration settings are bundled in persistence.xml, all mapping metadata is included in the Java source code of the Message class, and Hibernate automatically scans and finds the metadata on startup. Compared to pure Hibernate, you now have these benefits:

- Automatic scanning of deployed metadata, an important feature in large projects. Maintaining a list of annotated classes or mapping files becomes difficult if hundreds of entities are developed by a large team.

- Standardized and simplified configuration, with a standard location for the configuration file, and a deployment concept—the persistence unit—that has many more advantages in larger projects that wrap several units (JARs) in an application archive (EAR).

- Standardized data access code, entity instance lifecycle, and queries that are fully portable. There is no proprietary import in your application.

These are only some of the advantages of JPA. You'll see its real power if you combine it with the full EJB 3.0 programming model and other managed components.

2.2.3 *Introducing EJB components*

Java Persistence starts to shine when you also work with EJB 3.0 session beans and message-driven beans (and other Java EE 5.0 standards). The EJB 3.0 specification has been designed to permit the integration of persistence, so you can, for example, get automatic transaction demarcation on bean method boundaries, or a persistence context (think `Session`) that spans the lifecycle of a stateful session EJB.

This section will get you started with EJB 3.0 and JPA in a managed Java EE environment; you'll again modify the "Hello World" application to learn the basics. You need a Java EE environment first—a runtime container that provides Java EE services. There are two ways you can get it:

- You can install a full Java EE 5.0 application server that supports EJB 3.0 and JPA. Several open source (Sun GlassFish, JBoss AS, ObjectWeb EasyBeans) and other proprietary licensed alternatives are on the market at the time of writing, and probably more will be available when you read this book.

- You can install a modular server that provides only the services you need, selected from the full Java EE 5.0 bundle. At a minimum, you probably want an EJB 3.0 container, JTA transaction services, and a JNDI registry. At the time of writing, only JBoss AS provided modular Java EE 5.0 services in an easily customizable package.

To keep things simple and to show you how easy it is to get started with EJB 3.0, you'll install and configure the modular JBoss Application Server and enable only the Java EE 5.0 services you need.

Installing the EJB container

Go to http://jboss.com/products/ejb3, download the modular embeddable server, and unzip the downloaded archive. Copy all libraries that come with the server into your project's WORKDIR/lib directory, and copy all included configuration files to your WORKDIR/src directory. You should now have the following directory layout:

```
WORKDIR
+etc
  default.persistence.properties
  ejb3-interceptors-aop.xml
  embedded-jboss-beans.xml
  jndi.properties
  log4j.properties
  +META-INF
    helloworld-beans.xml
    persistence.xml
+lib
  <all required libraries>
+src
  +hello
    HelloWorld.java
    Message.java
```

The JBoss embeddable server relies on Hibernate for Java Persistence, so the default.persistence.properties file contains default settings for Hibernate that are needed for all deployments (such as JTA integration settings). The ejb3-interceptors-aop.xml and embedded-jboss-beans.xml configuration files contain the services configuration of the server—you can look at these files, but you don't need to modify them now. By default, at the time of writing, the enabled services are JNDI, JCA, JTA, and the EJB 3.0 container—exactly what you need.

To migrate the "Hello World" application, you need a managed datasource, which is a database connection that is handled by the embeddable server. The easiest way to configure a managed datasource is to add a configuration file that deploys the datasource as a managed service. Create the file in listing 2.14 as WORKDIR/etc/META-INF/helloworld-beans.xml.

Listing 2.14 Datasource configuration file for the JBoss server

```
<?xml version="1.0" encoding="UTF-8"?>
<deployment xmlns:xsi="http://www.w3.org/2001/XMLSchema-instance"
  xsi:schemaLocation="urn:jboss:bean-deployer bean-deployer_1_0.xsd"
  xmlns="urn:jboss:bean-deployer:2.0">

  <!-- Enable a JCA datasource available through JNDI -->
  <bean name="helloWorldDatasourceFactory"
```

```
class="org.jboss.resource.adapter.jdbc.local.LocalTxDataSource">

    <property name="jndiName">java:/HelloWorldDS</property>

    <!-- HSQLDB -->
    <property name="driverClass">
        org.hsqldb.jdbcDriver
    </property>
    <property name="connectionURL">
        jdbc:hsqldb:hsql://localhost
    </property>
    <property name="userName">sa</property>

    <property name="minSize">0</property>
    <property name="maxSize">10</property>
    <property name="blockingTimeout">1000</property>
    <property name="idleTimeout">100000</property>

    <property name="transactionManager">
        <inject bean="TransactionManager"/>
    </property>
    <property name="cachedConnectionManager">
        <inject bean="CachedConnectionManager"/>
    </property>
    <property name="initialContextProperties">
        <inject bean="InitialContextProperties"/>
    </property>
</bean>

<bean name="HelloWorldDS" class="java.lang.Object">
    <constructor factoryMethod="getDatasource">
        <factory bean="helloWorldDatasourceFactory"/>
    </constructor>
</bean>

</deployment>
```

Again, the XML header and schema declaration aren't important for this example. You set up two beans: The first is a factory that can produce the second type of bean. The `LocalTxDataSource` is effectively now your database connection pool, and all your connection pool settings are available on this factory. The factory binds a managed datasource under the JNDI name `java:/HelloWorldDS`.

The second bean configuration declares how the registered object named `HelloWorldDS` should be instantiated, if another service looks it up in the JNDI registry. Your "Hello World" application asks for the datasource under this name, and the server calls `getDatasource()` on the `LocalTxDataSource` factory to obtain it.

Also note that we added some line breaks in the property values to make this more readable—you shouldn't do this in your real configuration file (unless your database username contains a line break).

Configuring the persistence unit

Next, you need to change the persistence unit configuration of the "Hello World" application to access a managed JTA datasource, instead of a resource-local connection pool. Change your WORKDIR/etc/META-INF/persistence.xml file as follows:

```
<persistence ...>

    <persistence-unit name="helloworld">
        <jta-data-source>java:/HelloWorldDS</jta-data-source>
        <properties>
            <property name="hibernate.show_sql" value="true"/>
            <property name="hibernate.format_sql" value="true"/>
            <property name="hibernate.dialect"
                      value="org.hibernate.dialect.HSQLDialect"/>
            <property name="hibernate.hbm2ddl.auto" value="create"/>

        </properties>
    </persistence-unit>

</persistence>
```

You removed many Hibernate configuration options that are no longer relevant, such as the connection pool and database connection settings. Instead, you set a `<jta-data-source>` property with the name of the datasource as bound in JNDI. Don't forget that you still need to configure the correct SQL dialect and any other Hibernate options that aren't present in default.persistence.properties.

The installation and configuration of the environment is now complete, (we'll show you the purpose of the jndi.properties files in a moment) and you can rewrite the application code with EJBs.

Writing EJBs

There are many ways to design and create an application with managed components. The "Hello World" application isn't sophisticated enough to show elaborate examples, so we'll introduce only the most basic type of EJB, a *stateless session bean*. (You've already seen entity classes—annotated plain Java classes that can have persistent instances. Note that the term *entity bean* only refers to the old EJB 2.1 entity beans; EJB 3.0 and Java Persistence standardize a lightweight programming model for plain *entity classes*.)

Every EJB session bean needs a *business interface*. This isn't a special interface that needs to implement predefined methods or extend existing ones; it's plain Java. Create the following interface in the WORKDIR/src/hello package:

```
package hello;

public interface MessageHandler {

    public void saveMessages();

    public void showMessages();
}
```

A MessageHandler can save and show messages; it's straightforward. The actual EJB implements this business interface, which is by default considered a local interface (that is, remote EJB clients cannot call it); see listing 2.15.

Listing 2.15 The "Hello World" EJB session bean application code

```
package hello;

import javax.ejb.Stateless;
import javax.persistence.*;
import java.util.List;

@Stateless
public class MessageHandlerBean implements MessageHandler {

    @PersistenceContext
    EntityManager em;

    public void saveMessages() {
        Message message = new Message("Hello World");
        em.persist(message);
    }

    public void showMessages() {
        List messages =
            em.createQuery("select m from Message m
        ➥ order by m.text asc")
                .getResultList();

        System.out.println(messages.size() + " message(s) found:");

        for (Object m : messages) {
            Message loadedMsg = (Message) m;
            System.out.println(loadedMsg.getText());
        }

    }
}
```

There are several interesting things to observe in this implementation. First, it's a plain Java class with no hard dependencies on any other package. It becomes an EJB only with a single metadata annotation, `@Stateless`. EJBs support container-managed services, so you can apply the `@PersistenceContext` annotation, and the server injects a fresh `EntityManager` instance whenever a method on this stateless bean is called. Each method is also assigned a transaction automatically by the container. The transaction starts when the method is called, and commits when the method returns. (It would be rolled back when an exception is thrown inside the method.)

You can now modify the `HelloWorld` main class and delegate all the work of storing and showing messages to the `MessageHandler`.

Running the application

The main class of the "Hello World" application calls the `MessageHandler` stateless session bean after looking it up in the JNDI registry. Obviously, the managed environment and the whole application server, including the JNDI registry, must be booted first. You do all of this in the `main()` method of `HelloWorld.java` (see listing 2.16).

Listing 2.16 "Hello World" main application code, calling EJBs

```
package hello;

import org.jboss.ejb3.embedded.EJB3StandaloneBootstrap;
import javax.naming.InitialContext;

public class HelloWorld {

  public static void main(String[] args) throws Exception {

    // Boot the JBoss Microcontainer with EJB3 settings, automatically
    // loads ejb3-interceptors-aop.xml and embedded-jboss-beans.xml
    EJB3StandaloneBootstrap.boot(null);

    // Deploy custom stateless beans (datasource, mostly)
    EJB3StandaloneBootstrap
       .deployXmlResource("META-INF/helloworld-beans.xml");

    // Deploy all EJBs found on classpath (slow, scans all)
    // EJB3StandaloneBootstrap.scanClasspath();

    // Deploy all EJBs found on classpath (fast, scans build directory)
    // This is a relative location, matching the substring end of one
    // of java.class.path locations. Print out the value of
    // System.getProperty("java.class.path") to see all paths.
    EJB3StandaloneBootstrap.scanClasspath("helloworld-ejb3/bin");

    // Create InitialContext from jndi.properties
```

```
InitialContext initialContext = new InitialContext();

// Look up the stateless MessageHandler EJB
MessageHandler msgHandler = (MessageHandler) initialContext
                        .lookup("MessageHandlerBean/local");

// Call the stateless EJB
msgHandler.saveMessages();
msgHandler.showMessages();

// Shut down EJB container
EJB3StandaloneBootstrap.shutdown();
    }
}
```

The first command in main() boots the server's kernel and deploys the base services found in the service configuration files. Next, the datasource factory configuration you created earlier in helloworld-beans.xml is deployed, and the datasource is bound to JNDI by the container. From that point on, the container is ready to deploy EJBs. The easiest (but often not the fastest) way to deploy all EJBs is to let the container search the whole classpath for any class that has an EJB annotation. To learn about the many other deployment options available, check the JBoss AS documentation bundled in the download.

To look up an EJB, you need an InitialContext, which is your entry point for the JNDI registry. If you instantiate an InitialContext, Java automatically looks for the file jndi.properties on your classpath. You need to create this file in WORKDIR/ etc with settings that match the JBoss server's JNDI registry configuration:

```
java.naming.factory.initial
    ➥ org.jnp.interfaces.LocalOnlyContextFactory
java.naming.factory.url.pkgs org.jboss.naming:org.jnp.interfaces
```

You don't need to know exactly what this configuration means, but it basically points your InitialContext to a JNDI registry running in the local virtual machine (remote EJB client calls would require a JNDI service that supports remote communication).

By default, you look up the MessageHandler bean by the name of an implementation class, with the /local suffix for a local interface. How EJBs are named, how they're bound to JNDI, and how you look them up varies and can be customized. These are the defaults for the JBoss server.

Finally, you call the MessageHandler EJB and let it do all the work automatically in two units—each method call will result in a separate transaction.

This completes our first example with managed EJB components and integrated JPA. You can probably already see how automatic transaction demarcation and `EntityManager` injection can improve the readability of your code. Later, we'll show you how stateful session beans can help you implement sophisticated conversations between the user and the application, with transactional semantics. Furthermore, the EJB components don't contain any unnecessary glue code or infrastructure methods, and they're fully reusable, portable, and executable in any EJB 3.0 container.

> **NOTE** *Packaging of persistence units*—We didn't talk much about the packaging of persistence units—you didn't need to package the "Hello World" example for any of the deployments. However, if you want to use features such as hot redeployment on a full application server, you need to package your application correctly. This includes the usual combination of JARs, WARs, EJB-JARs, and EARs. Deployment and packaging is often also vendor-specific, so you should consult the documentation of your application server for more information. JPA persistence units can be scoped to JARs, WARs, and EJB-JARs, which means that one or several of these archives contains all the annotated classes and a META-INF/persistence.xml configuration file with all settings for this particular unit. You can wrap one or several JARs, WARs, and EJB-JARs in a single enterprise application archive, an EAR. Your application server should correctly detect all persistence units and create the necessary factories automatically. With a unit name attribute on the `@PersistenceContext` annotation, you instruct the container to inject an `EntityManager` from a particular unit.

Full portability of an application isn't often a primary reason to use JPA or EJB 3.0. After all, you made a decision to use Hibernate as your JPA persistence provider. Let's look at how you can fall back and use a Hibernate native feature from time to time.

2.2.4 Switching to Hibernate interfaces

You decided to use Hibernate as a JPA persistence provider for several reasons: First, Hibernate is a good JPA implementation that provides many options that don't affect your code. For example, you can enable the Hibernate second-level data cache in your JPA configuration, and transparently improve the performance and scalability of your application without touching any code.

Second, you can use native Hibernate mappings or APIs when needed. We discuss the mixing of mappings (especially annotations) in chapter 3, section 3.3,

"Object/relational mapping metadata," but here we want to show how you can use a Hibernate API in your JPA application, when needed. Obviously, importing a Hibernate API into your code makes porting the code to a different JPA provider more difficult. Hence, it becomes critically important to isolate these parts of your code properly, or at least to document why and when you used a native Hibernate feature.

You can fall back to Hibernate APIs from their equivalent JPA interfaces and get, for example, a `Configuration`, a `SessionFactory`, and even a `Session` whenever needed.

For example, instead of creating an `EntityManagerFactory` with the `Persistence` static class, you can use a Hibernate `Ejb3Configuration`:

```
Ejb3Configuration cfg = new Ejb3Configuration();
EntityManagerFactory emf =
  cfg.configure("/custom/hibernate.cfg.xml")
     .setProperty("hibernate.show_sql", "false")
     .setInterceptor( new MyInterceptor() )
     .addAnnotatedClass( hello.Message.class )
     .addResource( "/Foo.hbm.xml")
     .buildEntityManagerFactory();

AnnotationConfiguration
        hibCfg = cfg.getHibernateConfiguration();
```

The `Ejb3Configuration` is a new interface that duplicates the regular Hibernate `Configuration` instead of extending it (this is an implementation detail). This means you can get a plain `AnnotationConfiguration` object from an `Ejb3Configuration`, for example, and pass it to a `SchemaExport` instance programmatically.

The `SessionFactory` interface is useful if you need programmatic control over the second-level cache regions. You can get a `SessionFactory` by casting the `EntityManagerFactory` first:

```
HibernateEntityManagerFactory hibEMF =
        (HibernateEntityManagerFactory) emf;
SessionFactory sf = hibEMF.getSessionFactory();
```

The same technique can be applied to get a `Session` from an `EntityManager`:

```
HibernateEntityManager hibEM =
     (HibernateEntityManager) em;
Session session = hibEM.getSession();
```

This isn't the only way to get a native API from the standardized `EntityManager`. The JPA specification supports a `getDelegate()` method that returns the underlying implementation:

```
Session session = (Session) entityManager.getDelegate();
```

Or you can get a `Session` injected into an EJB component (although this only works in the JBoss Application Server):

```
@Stateless
public class MessageHandlerBean implements MessageHandler {

    @PersistenceContext
    Session session;

    ...
}
```

In rare cases, you can fall back to plain JDBC interfaces from the Hibernate `Session`:

```
Connection jdbcConnection = session.connection();
```

This last option comes with some caveats: You aren't allowed to close the JDBC `Connection` you get from Hibernate—this happens automatically. The exception to this rule is that in an environment that relies on aggressive connection releases, which means in a JTA or CMT environment, you *have* to close the returned connection in application code.

A better and safer way to access a JDBC connection directly is through resource injection in a Java EE 5.0. Annotate a field or setter method in an EJB, an EJB listener, a servlet, a servlet filter, or even a JavaServer Faces backing bean, like this:

```
@Resource(mappedName="java:/HelloWorldDS") DataSource ds;
```

So far, we've assumed that you work on a new Hibernate or JPA project that involves no legacy application code or existing database schema. We now switch perspectives and consider a development process that is bottom-up. In such a scenario, you probably want to automatically reverse-engineer artifacts from an existing database schema.

2.3 Reverse engineering a legacy database

Your first step when mapping a legacy database likely involves an automatic reverse-engineering procedure. After all, an entity schema already exists in your database system. To make this easier, Hibernate has a set of tools that can read a schema and produce various artifacts from this metadata, including XML mapping files and Java source code. All of this is template-based, so many customizations are possible.

You can control the reverse-engineering process with tools and tasks in your Ant build. The `HibernateToolTask` you used earlier to export SQL DDL from

Hibernate mapping metadata has many more options, most of which are related to reverse engineering, as to how XML mapping files, Java code, or even whole application skeletons can be generated automatically from an existing database schema.

We'll first show you how to write an Ant target that can load an existing database into a Hibernate metadata model. Next, you'll apply various exporters and produce XML files, Java code, and other useful artifacts from the database tables and columns.

2.3.1 *Creating a database configuration*

Let's assume that you have a new WORKDIR with nothing but the lib directory (and its usual contents) and an empty src directory. To generate mappings and code from an existing database, you first need to create a configuration file that contains your database connection settings:

```
hibernate.dialect = org.hibernate.dialect.HSQLDialect
hibernate.connection.driver_class = org.hsqldb.jdbcDriver
hibernate.connection.url = jdbc:hsqldb:hsql://localhost
hibernate.connection.username = sa
```

Store this file directly in WORKDIR, and name it helloworld.db.properties. The four lines shown here are the minimum that is required to connect to the database and read the metadata of all tables and columns. You could have created a Hibernate XML configuration file instead of hibernate.properties, but there is no reason to make this more complex than necessary.

Write the Ant target next. In a build.xml file in your project, add the following code:

```
<taskdef name="hibernatetool"
    classname="org.hibernate.tool.ant.HibernateToolTask"
    classpathref="project.classpath"/>

<target name="reveng.hbmxml"
        description="Produces XML mapping files in src directory">

    <hibernatetool destdir="${basedir}/src">

        <jdbcconfiguration
            propertyfile="${basedir}/helloworld.db.properties"
            revengfile="${basedir}/helloworld.reveng.xml"/>

        <hbm2hbmxml/> <!-- Export Hibernate XML files -->
        <hbm2cfgxml/> <!-- Export a hibernate.cfg.xml file -->

    </hibernatetool>

</target>
```

The `HibernateToolTask` definition for Ant is the same as before. We assume that you'll reuse most of the build file introduced in previous sections, and that references such as `project.classpath` are the same. The `<hibernatetool>` task is set with WORKDIR/src as the default destination directory for all generated artifacts.

A `<jdbcconfiguration>` is a Hibernate tool configuration that can connect to a database via JDBC and read the JDBC metadata from the database catalog. You usually configure it with two options: database connection settings (the properties file) and an optional reverse-engineering customization file.

The metadata produced by the tool configuration is then fed to exporters. The example Ant target names two such exporters: the `hbm2hbmxml` exporter, as you can guess from its name, takes Hibernate metadata (hbm) from a configuration, and generates Hibernate XML mapping files; the second exporter can prepare a hibernate.cfg.xml file that lists all the generated XML mapping files.

Before we talk about these and various other exporters, let's spend a minute on the reverse-engineering customization file and what you can do with it.

2.3.2 *Customizing reverse engineering*

JDBC metadata—that is, the information you can read from a database about itself via JDBC—often isn't sufficient to create a perfect XML mapping file, let alone Java application code. The opposite may also be true: Your database may contain information that you want to ignore (such as particular tables or columns) or that you wish to transform with nondefault strategies. You can customize the reverse-engineering procedure with a reverse-engineering configuration file, which uses an XML syntax.

Let's assume that you're reverse-engineering the "Hello World" database you created earlier in this chapter, with its single MESSAGES table and only a few columns. With a helloworld.reveng.xml file, as shown in listing 2.17, you can customize this reverse engineering.

Listing 2.17   Configuration for customized reverse engineering

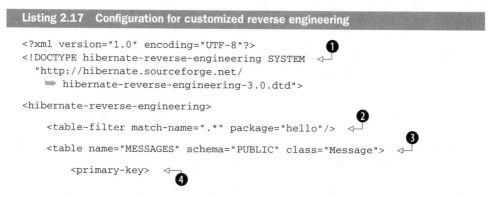

```
<?xml version="1.0" encoding="UTF-8"?>                        ❶
<!DOCTYPE hibernate-reverse-engineering SYSTEM          ↵
  "http://hibernate.sourceforge.net/
    ➥ hibernate-reverse-engineering-3.0.dtd">

<hibernate-reverse-engineering>
                                                          ❷
    <table-filter match-name=".*" package="hello"/>    ↵
                                                              ❸
    <table name="MESSAGES" schema="PUBLIC" class="Message">   ↵

        <primary-key>    ↵
                          ❹
```

```
            <generator class="increment"/>
            <key-column name="MESSAGE_ID" property="id" type="long"/>
        </primary-key>

        <column name="MESSAGE_TEXT" property="text"/>      ⑤

        <foreign-key constraint-name="FK_NEXT_MESSAGE">
            <many-to-one property="nextMessage"/>          ⑥
            <set exclude="true"/>
        </foreign-key>

    </table>

</hibernate-reverse-engineering>
```

❶ This XML file has its own DTD for validation and autocompletion.

❷ A table filter can exclude tables by name with a regular expression. However, in this example, you define a a default package for all classes produced for the tables matching the regular expression.

❸ You can customize individual tables by name. The schema name is usually optional, but HSQLDB assigns the PUBLIC schema to all tables by default so this setting is needed to identify the table when the JDBC metadata is retrieved. You can also set a custom class name for the generated entity here.

❹ The primary key column generates a property named id, the default would be messageId. You also explicitly declare which Hibernate identifier generator should be used.

❺ An individual column can be excluded or, in this case, the name of the generated property can be specified—the default would be messageText.

❻ If the foreign key constraint FK_NEXT_MESSAGE is retrieved from JDBC metadata, a many-to-one association is created by default to the target entity of that class. By matching the foreign key constraint by name, you can specify whether an inverse collection (one-to-many) should also be generated (the example excludes this) and what the name of the many-to-one property should be.

If you now run the Ant target with this customization, it generates a Message.hbm.xml file in the hello package in your source directory. (You need to copy the Freemarker and jTidy JAR files into your library directory first.) The customizations you made result in the same Hibernate mapping file you wrote earlier by hand, shown in listing 2.2.

In addition to the XML mapping file, the Ant target also generates a Hibernate XML configuration file in the source directory:

```
<hibernate-configuration>
  <session-factory>
    <property name="hibernate.connection.driver_class">
        org.hsqldb.jdbcDriver
    </property>
    <property name="hibernate.connection.url">
        jdbc:hsqldb:hsql://localhost
    </property>
    <property name="hibernate.connection.username">
        sa
    </property>
    <property name="hibernate.dialect">
        org.hibernate.dialect.HSQLDialect
    </property>

    <mapping resource="hello/Message.hbm.xml" />

  </session-factory>
</hibernate-configuration>
```

The exporter writes all the database connection settings you used for reverse engineering into this file, assuming that this is the database you want to connect to when you run the application. It also adds all generated XML mapping files to the configuration.

What is your next step? You can start writing the source code for the `Message` Java class. Or you can let the Hibernate Tools generate the classes of the domain model for you.

2.3.3 *Generating Java source code*

Let's assume you have an existing Hibernate XML mapping file for the `Message` class, and you'd like to generate the source for the class. As discussed in chapter 3, a plain Java entity class ideally implements `Serializable`, has a no-arguments constructor, has getters and setters for all properties, and has an encapsulated implementation.

Source code for entity classes can be generated with the Hibernate Tools and the `hbm2java` exporter in your Ant build. The source artifact can be anything that can be read into a Hibernate metadata model—Hibernate XML mapping files are best if you want to customize the Java code generation.

Add the following target to your Ant build:

```
<target name="reveng.pojos"
        description="Produces Java classes from XML mappings">

    <hibernatetool destdir="${basedir}/src">

        <configuration>
```

```
    <fileset dir="${basedir}/src">
        <include name="**/*.hbm.xml"/>
    </fileset>
</configuration>

    <hbm2java/> <!-- Generate entity class source -->

</hibernatetool>

</target>
```

The `<configuration>` reads all Hibernate XML mapping files, and the `<hbm2-java>` exporter produces Java source code with the default strategy.

Customizing entity class generation

By default, hbm2java generates a simple entity class for each mapped entity. The class implements the `Serializable` marker interface, and it has accessor methods for all properties and the required constructor. All attributes of the class have private visibility for fields, although you can change that behavior with the `<meta>` element and attributes in the XML mapping files.

The first change to the default reverse engineering behavior you make is to restrict the visibility scope for the `Message`'s attributes. By default, all accessor methods are generated with public visibility. Let's say that `Message` objects are immutable; you wouldn't expose the setter methods on the public interface, but only the getter methods. Instead of enhancing the mapping of each property with a `<meta>` element, you can declare a meta-attribute at the class level, thus applying the setting to all properties in that class:

```
<class name="Message"
    table="MESSAGES">

        <meta attribute="scope-set">private</meta>
        ...

</class>
```

The `scope-set` attribute defines the visibility of property setter methods.

The hbm2java exporter also accepts meta-attributes on the next higher-level, in the root `<hibernate-mapping>` element, which are then applied to all classes mapped in the XML file. You can also add fine-grained meta-attributes to single property, collection, or component mappings.

One (albeit small) improvement of the generated entity class is the inclusion of the text of the `Message` in the output of the generated `toString()` method. The text is a good visual control element in the log output of the application. You can change the mapping of `Message` to include it in the generated code:

```
<property name="text" type="string">
    <meta attribute="use-in-tostring">true</meta>
    <column name="MESSAGE_TEXT" />
</property>
```

The generated code of the toString() method in Message.java looks like this:

```
public String toString() {
    StringBuffer buffer = new StringBuffer();
    buffer.append(getClass().getName())
        .append("@")
        .append( Integer.toHexString(hashCode()) )
        .append(" [");
        .append("text").append("='").append(getText()).append("' ");
        .append("]");

    return buffer.toString();
}
```

Meta-attributes can be inherited; that is, if you declare a use-in-tostring at the level of a <class> element, all properties of that class are included in the toString() method. This inheritance mechanism works for all hbm2java meta-attributes, but you can turn it off selectively:

```
<meta attribute="scope-class" inherit="false">public abstract</meta>
```

Setting inherit to false in the scope-class meta-attribute creates only the parent class of this <meta> element as public abstract, but not any of the (possibly) nested subclasses.

The hbm2java exporter supports, at the time of writing, 17 meta-attributes for fine-tuning code generation. Most are related to visibility, interface implementation, class extension, and predefined Javadoc comments. Refer to the Hibernate Tools documentation for a complete list.

If you use JDK 5.0, you can switch to automatically generated static imports and generics with the jdk5="true" setting on the <hbm2java> task. Or, you can produce EJB 3.0 entity classes with annotations.

Generating Java Persistence entity classes

Normally, you use either Hibernate XML mapping files or JPA annotations in your entity class source code to define your mapping metadata, so generating Java Persistence entity classes with annotations from XML mapping files doesn't seem reasonable. However, you can create entity class source code with annotations directly from JDBC metadata, and skip the XML mapping step. Look at the following Ant target:

```
<target name="reveng.entities"
        description="Produces Java entity classes in src directory">

    <hibernatetool destdir="${basedir}/src">

        <jdbcconfiguration
            propertyfile="${basedir}/helloworld.db.properties"
            revengfile="${basedir}/helloworld.reveng.xml"/>

        <hbm2java jdk5="true" ejb3="true"/>
        <hbm2cfgxml ejb3="true"/>

    </hibernatetool>

</target>
```

This target generates entity class source code with mapping annotations and a hibernate.cfg.xml file that lists these mapped classes. You can edit the Java source directly to customize the mapping, if the customization in helloworld.reveng.xml is too limited.

Also note that all exporters rely on templates written in the FreeMarker template language. You can customize the templates in whatever way you like, or even write your own. Even programmatic customization of code generation is possible. The Hibernate Tools reference documentation shows you how these options are used.

Other exporters and configurations are available with the Hibernate Tools:

- An <annotationconfiguration> replaces the regular <configuration> if you want to read mapping metadata from annotated Java classes, instead of XML mapping files. Its only argument is the location and name of a hibernate.cfg.xml file that contains a list of annotated classes. Use this approach to export a database schema from annotated classes.

- An <ejb3configuration> is equivalent to an <annotationconfiguration>, except that it can scan for annotated Java classes automatically on the classpath; it doesn't need a hibernate.cfg.xml file.

- The <hbm2dao> exporter can create additional Java source for a persistence layer, based on the *data access object* pattern. At the time of writing, the templates for this exporter are old and need updating. We expect that the finalized templates will be similar to the DAO code shown in chapter 16, section 16.2, "Creating a persistence layer."

- The <hbm2doc> exporter generates HTML files that document the tables and Java entities.

- The `<hbmtemplate>` exporter can be parameterized with a set of custom FreeMarker templates, and you can generate anything you want with this approach. Templates that produce a complete runable skeleton application with the JBoss Seam framework are bundled in the Hibernate Tools.

You can get creative with the import and export functionality of the tools. For example, you can read annotated Java classes with `<annotationconfiguration>` and export them with `<hbm2hbmxml>`. This allows you to develop with JDK 5.0 and the more convenient annotations but deploy Hibernate XML mapping files in production (on JDK 1.4).

Let's finish this chapter with some more advanced configuration options and integrate Hibernate with Java EE services.

2.4 Integration with Java EE services

We assume that you've already tried the "Hello World" example shown earlier in this chapter and that you're familiar with basic Hibernate configuration and how Hibernate can be integrated with a plain Java application. We'll now discuss more advanced native Hibernate configuration options and how a regular Hibernate application can utilize the Java EE services provided by a Java EE application server.

If you created your first JPA project with Hibernate Annotations and Hibernate EntityManager, the following configuration advice isn't really relevant for you—you're already deep inside Java EE land if you're using JPA, and no extra integration steps are required. Hence, you can skip this section if you use Hibernate EntityManager.

Java EE application servers such as JBoss AS, BEA WebLogic, and IBM WebSphere implement the standard (Java EE-specific) managed environment for Java. The three most interesting Java EE services Hibernate can be integrated with are JTA, JNDI, and JMX.

JTA allows Hibernate to participate in transactions on managed resources. Hibernate can look up managed resources (database connections) via JNDI and also bind itself as a service to JNDI. Finally, Hibernate can be deployed via JMX and then be managed as a service by the JMX container and monitored at runtime with standard JMX clients.

Let's look at each service and how you can integrate Hibernate with it.

2.4.1 Integration with JTA

The *Java Transaction API* (JTA) is the standardized service interface for transaction control in Java enterprise applications. It exposes several interfaces, such as the `UserTransaction` API for transaction demarcation and the `TransactionManager` API for participation in the transaction lifecycle. The transaction manager can coordinate a transaction that spans several resources—imagine working in two Hibernate `Sessions` on two databases in a single transaction.

A JTA transaction service is provided by all Java EE application servers. However, many Java EE services are usable stand-alone, and you can deploy a JTA provider along with your application, such as JBoss Transactions or ObjectWeb JOTM. We won't have much to say about this part of your configuration but focus on the integration of Hibernate with a JTA service, which is the same in full application servers or with stand-alone JTA providers.

Look at figure 2.6. You use the Hibernate `Session` interface to access your database(s), and it's Hibernate's responsibility to integrate with the Java EE services of the managed environment.

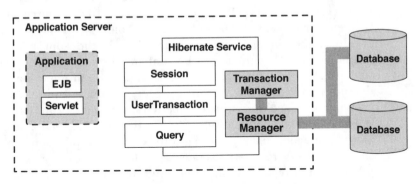

Figure 2.6 Hibernate in an environment with managed resources

In such a managed environment, Hibernate no longer creates and maintains a JDBC connection pool—Hibernate obtains database connections by looking up a `Datasource` object in the JNDI registry. Hence, your Hibernate configuration needs a reference to the JNDI name where managed connections can be obtained.

```
<hibernate-configuration>
<session-factory>

    <property name="hibernate.connection.datasource">
        java:/MyDatasource
```

```
    </property>

    <property name="hibernate.dialect">
        org.hibernate.dialect.HSQLDialect
    </property>
    ...

</session-factory>
</hibernate-configuration>
```

With this configuration file, Hibernate looks up database connections in JNDI using the name `java:/MyDatasource`. When you configure your application server and deploy your application, or when you configure your stand-alone JTA provider, this is the name to which you should bind the managed datasource. Note that a dialect setting is still required for Hibernate to produce the correct SQL.

> **NOTE** *Hibernate with Tomcat*—Tomcat isn't a Java EE application server; it's just a servlet container, albeit a servlet container with some features usually found only in application servers. One of these features may be used with Hibernate: the Tomcat connection pool. Tomcat uses the DBCP connection pool internally but exposes it as a JNDI datasource, just like a real application server. To configure the Tomcat datasource, you need to edit server.xml, according to instructions in the Tomcat JNDI/JDBC documentation. Hibernate can be configured to use this datasource by setting `hibernate.connection.datasource`. Keep in mind that Tomcat doesn't ship with a transaction manager, so you still have plain JDBC transaction semantics, which Hibernate can hide with its optional `Transaction` API. Alternatively, you can deploy a JTA-compatible stand-alone transaction manager along with your web application, which you should consider to get the standardized `UserTransaction` API. On the other hand, a regular application server (especially if it's modular like JBoss AS) may be easier to configure than Tomcat plus DBCP plus JTA, and it provides better services.

To fully integrate Hibernate with JTA, you need to tell Hibernate a bit more about your transaction manager. Hibernate has to hook into the transaction lifecycle, for example, to manage its caches. First, you need to tell Hibernate what transaction manager you're using:

```
<hibernate-configuration>
<session-factory>

    <property name="hibernate.connection.datasource">
        java:/MyDatasource
    </property>
```

```
<property name="hibernate.dialect">
    org.hibernate.dialect.HSQLDialect
</property>

<property name="hibernate.transaction.manager_lookup_class">
    org.hibernate.transaction.JBossTransactionManagerLookup
</property>

<property name="hibernate.transaction.factory_class">
    org.hibernate.transaction.JTATransactionFactory
</property>

...

</session-factory>
</hibernate-configuration>
```

You need to pick the appropriate lookup class for your application server, as you did in the preceding code—Hibernate comes bundled with classes for the most popular JTA providers and application servers. Finally, you tell Hibernate that you want to use the JTA transaction interfaces in the application to set transaction boundaries. The JTATransactionFactory does several things:

- It enables correct Session scoping and propagation for JTA if you decide to use the SessionFactory.getCurrentSession() method instead of opening and closing every Session manually. We discuss this feature in more detail in chapter 11, section 11.1, "Propagating the Hibernate session."

- It tells Hibernate that you're planning to call the JTA UserTransaction interface in your application to start, commit, or roll back system transactions.

- It also switches the Hibernate Transaction API to JTA, in case you don't want to work with the standardized UserTransaction. If you now begin a transaction with the Hibernate API, it checks whether an ongoing JTA transaction is in progress and, if possible, joins this transaction. If no JTA transaction is in progress, a new transaction is started. If you commit or roll back with the Hibernate API, it either ignores the call (if Hibernate joined an existing transaction) or sets the system transaction to commit or roll back. We don't recommend using the Hibernate Transaction API if you deploy in an environment that supports JTA. However, this setting keeps existing code portable between managed and nonmanaged environments, albeit with possibly different transactional behavior.

There are other built-in TransactionFactory options, and you can write your own by implementing this interface. The JDBCTransactionFactory is the default in a nonmanaged environment, and you have used it throughout this chapter in the simple "Hello World" example with no JTA. The CMTTransactionFactory should be enabled if you're working with JTA *and* EJBs, and if you plan to set transaction boundaries declaratively on your managed EJB components—in other words, if you deploy your EJB application on a Java EE application server but don't set transaction boundaries programmatically with the UserTransaction interface in application code.

Our recommended configuration options, ordered by preference, are as follows:

- If your application has to run in managed and nonmanaged environments, you should move the responsibility for transaction integration and resource management to the deployer. Call the JTA UserTransaction API in your application code, and let the deployer of the application configure the application server or a stand-alone JTA provider accordingly. Enable JTATransactionFactory in your Hibernate configuration to integrate with the JTA service, and set the right lookup class.

- Consider setting transaction boundaries declaratively, with EJB components. Your data access code then isn't bound to any transaction API, and the CMT-TransactionFactory integrates and handles the Hibernate Session for you behind the scenes. This is the easiest solution—of course, the deployer now has the responsibility to provide an environment that supports JTA *and* EJB components.

- Write your code with the Hibernate Transaction API and let Hibernate switch between the different deployment environments by setting either JDBCTransactionFactory or JTATransactionFactory. Be aware that transaction semantics may change, and the start or commit of a transaction may result in a no-op you may not expect. This is always the last choice when portability of transaction demarcation is needed.

FAQ   *How can I use several databases with Hibernate?*   If you want to work with several databases, you create several configuration files. Each database is assigned its own SessionFactory, and you build several SessionFactory instances from distinct Configuration objects. Each Session that is opened, from any SessionFactory, looks up a managed datasource in JNDI. It's now the responsibility of the transaction and resource manager to coordinate these resources—Hibernate only executes SQL statements on these database connections. Transaction boundaries are either set programmatically with JTA or handled by the container with EJBs and a declarative assembly.

Hibernate can not only look up managed resources in JNDI, it can also bind itself to JNDI. We'll look at that next.

2.4.2 *JNDI-bound SessionFactory*

We already touched on a question that every new Hibernate user has to deal with: How should a `SessionFactory` be stored, and how should it be accessed in application code? Earlier in this chapter, we addressed this problem by writing a `HibernateUtil` class that held a `SessionFactory` in a static field and provided the static `getSessionFactory()` method. However, if you deploy your application in an environment that supports JNDI, Hibernate can bind a `SessionFactory` to JNDI, and you can look it up there when needed.

> **NOTE** The *Java Naming and Directory Interface* API (JNDI) allows objects to be stored to and retrieved from a hierarchical structure (directory tree). JNDI implements the *Registry* pattern. Infrastructural objects (transaction contexts, datasources, and so on), configuration settings (environment settings, user registries, and so on) and even application objects (EJB references, object factories, and so on) can all be bound to JNDI.

The Hibernate `SessionFactory` automatically binds itself to JNDI if the `hibernate.session_factory_name` property is set to the name of the JNDI node. If your runtime environment doesn't provide a default JNDI context (or if the default JNDI implementation doesn't support instances of `Referenceable`), you need to specify a JNDI initial context using the `hibernate.jndi.url` and `hibernate.jndi.class` properties.

Here is an example Hibernate configuration that binds the `SessionFactory` to the name `java:/hibernate/MySessionFactory` using Sun's (free) file-system-based JNDI implementation, `fscontext.jar`:

```
hibernate.connection.datasource = java:/MyDatasource
    hibernate.transaction.factory_class = \
        org.hibernate.transaction.JTATransactionFactory
    hibernate.transaction.manager_lookup_class = \
        org.hibernate.transaction.JBossTransactionManagerLookup
    hibernate.dialect = org.hibernate.dialect.PostgreSQLDialect
    hibernate.session_factory_name = java:/hibernate/MySessionFactory
    hibernate.jndi.class = com.sun.jndi.fscontext.RefFSContextFactory
    hibernate.jndi.url = file:/auction/jndi
```

You can, of course, also use the XML-based configuration for this. This example isn't realistic, because most application servers that provide a connection pool through JNDI also have a JNDI implementation with a writable default context.

JBoss AS certainly has, so you can skip the last two properties and just specify a name for the SessionFactory.

> **NOTE** *JNDI with Tomcat*—Tomcat comes bundled with a read-only JNDI context, which isn't writable from application-level code after the startup of the servlet container. Hibernate can't bind to this context: You have to either use a full context implementation (like the Sun FS context) or disable JNDI binding of the SessionFactory by omitting the session_factory_name property in the configuration.

The SessionFactory is bound to JNDI when you build it, which means when Configuration.buildSessionFactory() is called. To keep your application code portable, you may want to implement this build and the lookup in HibernateUtil, and continue using that helper class in your data access code, as shown in listing 2.18.

Listing 2.18 HibernateUtil for JNDI lookup of SessionFactory

```
public class HibernateUtil {

    private static Context jndiContext;

    static {
        try {
            // Build it and bind it to JNDI
            new Configuration().buildSessionFactory();

            // Get a handle to the registry (reads jndi.properties)
            jndiContext = new InitialContext();

        } catch (Throwable ex) {
            throw new ExceptionInInitializerError(ex);
        }
    }

    public static SessionFactory getSessionFactory(String sfName) {
        SessionFactory sf;
        try {
            sf = (SessionFactory) jndiContext.lookup(sfName);
        } catch (NamingException ex) {
            throw new RuntimeException(ex);
        }
        return sf;
    }
}
```

Alternatively, you can look up the `SessionFactory` directly in application code with a JNDI call. However, you still need at least the `new Configuration().build-SessionFactory()` line of startup code somewhere in your application. One way to remove this last line of Hibernate startup code, and to completely eliminate the `HibernateUtil` class, is to deploy Hibernate as a JMX service (or by using JPA and Java EE).

2.4.3 JMX service deployment

The Java world is full of specifications, standards, and implementations of these. A relatively new, but important, standard is in its first version: the *Java Management Extensions* (JMX). JMX is about the management of systems components or, better, of system services.

Where does Hibernate fit into this new picture? Hibernate, when deployed in an application server, makes use of other services, like managed transactions and pooled datasources. Also, with Hibernate JMX integration, Hibernate can be a managed JMX service, depended on and used by others.

The JMX specification defines the following components:

- The *JMX MBean*—A reusable component (usually infrastructural) that exposes an interface for *management* (administration)
- The *JMX container*—Mediates generic access (local or remote) to the MBean
- The *JMX client*—May be used to administer any MBean via the JMX container

An application server with support for JMX (such as JBoss AS) acts as a JMX container and allows an MBean to be configured and initialized as part of the application server startup process. Your Hibernate service may be packaged and deployed as a JMX MBean; the bundled interface for this is `org.hibernate.jmx.HibernateService`. You can start, stop, and monitor the Hibernate core through this interface with any standard JMX client. A second MBean interface that can be deployed optionally is `org.hibernate.jmx.StatisticsService`, which lets you enable and monitor Hibernate's runtime behavior with a JMX client.

How JMX services and MBeans are deployed is vendor-specific. For example, on JBoss Application Server, you only have to add a jboss-service.xml file to your application's EAR to deploy Hibernate as a managed JMX service.

Instead of explaining every option here, see the reference documentation for JBoss Application Server. It contains a section that shows Hibernate integration and deployment step by step (http://docs.jboss.org/jbossas). Configuration and deployment on other application servers that support JMX should be similar, and you can adapt and port the JBoss configuration files.

2.5   Summary

In this chapter, you have completed a first Hibernate project. We looked at how Hibernate XML mapping files are written and what APIs you can call in Hibernate to interact with the database.

We then introduced Java Persistence and EJB 3.0 and explained how it can simplify even the most basic Hibernate application with automatic metadata scanning, standardized configuration and packaging, and dependency injection in managed EJB components.

If you have to get started with a legacy database, you can use the Hibernate toolset to reverse engineer XML mapping files from an existing schema. Or, if you work with JDK 5.0 and/or EJB 3.0, you can generate Java application code directly from an SQL database.

Finally, we looked at more advanced Hibernate integration and configuration options in a Java EE environment—integration that is already done for you if you rely on JPA or EJB 3.0.

A high-level overview and comparison between Hibernate functionality and Java Persistence is shown in table 2.1. (You can find a similar comparison table at the end of each chapter.)

Table 2.1   Hibernate and JPA comparison

Hibernate Core	Java Persistence and EJB 3.0
Integrates with everything, everywhere. Flexible, but sometimes configuration is complex.	Works in Java EE and Java SE. Simple and standardized configuration; no extra integration or special configuration is necessary in Java EE environments.
Configuration requires a list of XML mapping files or annotated classes.	JPA provider scans for XML mapping files and annotated classes automatically.
Proprietary but powerful. Continually improved native programming interfaces and query language.	Standardized and stable interfaces, with a sufficient subset of Hibernate functionality. Easy fallback to Hibernate APIs is possible.

In the next chapter, we introduce a more complex example application that we'll work with throughout the rest of the book. You'll see how to design and implement a domain model, and which mapping metadata options are the best choices in a larger project.

Domain models
and metadata

3

This chapter covers

- The CaveatEmptor example application
- POJO design for rich domain models
- Object/relational mapping metadata options

The "Hello World" example in the previous chapter introduced you to Hibernate; however, it isn't useful for understanding the requirements of real-world applications with complex data models. For the rest of the book, we use a much more sophisticated example application—CaveatEmptor, an online auction system—to demonstrate Hibernate and Java Persistence.

We start our discussion of the application by introducing a programming model for persistent classes. Designing and implementing the persistent classes is a multistep process that we'll examine in detail.

First, you'll learn how to identify the business entities of a problem domain. You create a conceptual model of these entities and their attributes, called a domain model, and you implement it in Java by creating persistent classes. We spend some time exploring exactly what these Java classes should look like, and we also look at the persistence capabilities of the classes, and how this aspect influences the design and implementation.

We then explore mapping metadata options—the ways you can tell Hibernate how your persistent classes and their properties relate to database tables and columns. This can involve writing XML documents that are eventually deployed along with the compiled Java classes and are read by Hibernate at runtime. Another option is to use JDK 5.0 metadata annotations, based on the EJB 3.0 standard, directly in the Java source code of the persistent classes. After reading this chapter, you'll know how to design the persistent parts of your domain model in complex real-world projects, and what mapping metadata option you'll primarily prefer and use.

Finally, in the last (probably optional) section of this chapter, we look at Hibernate's capability for representation independence. A relatively new feature in Hibernate allows you to create a domain model in Java that is fully dynamic, such as a model without any concrete classes but only `HashMaps`. Hibernate also supports a domain model representation with XML documents.

Let's start with the example application.

3.1 *The CaveatEmptor application*

The CaveatEmptor online auction application demonstrates ORM techniques and Hibernate functionality; you can download the source code for the application from http://caveatemptor.hibernate.org. We won't pay much attention to the user interface in this book (it could be web based or a rich client); we'll concentrate instead on the data access code. However, when a design decision about data access code that has consequences for the user interface has to be made, we'll naturally consider both.

In order to understand the design issues involved in ORM, let's pretend the CaveatEmptor application doesn't yet exist, and that you're building it from scratch. Our first task would be analysis.

3.1.1 *Analyzing the business domain*

A software development effort begins with analysis of the problem domain (assuming that no legacy code or legacy database already exists).

At this stage, you, with the help of problem domain experts, identify the main entities that are relevant to the software system. Entities are usually notions understood by users of the system: payment, customer, order, item, bid, and so forth. Some entities may be abstractions of less concrete things the user thinks about, such as a pricing algorithm, but even these would usually be understandable to the user. All these entities are found in the conceptual view of the business, which we sometimes call a business model. Developers and architects of object-oriented software analyze the business model and create an object-oriented model, still at the conceptual level (no Java code). This model may be as simple as a mental image existing only in the mind of the developer, or it may be as elaborate as a UML class diagram created by a computer-aided software engineering (CASE) tool like ArgoUML or TogetherJ. A simple model expressed in UML is shown in figure 3.1.

This model contains entities that you're bound to find in any typical auction system: category, item, and user. The entities and their relationships (and perhaps their attributes) are all represented by this model of the problem domain. We call this kind of object-oriented model of entities from the problem domain, encompassing only those entities that are of interest to the user, a domain model. It's an abstract view of the real world.

The motivating goal behind the analysis and design of a domain model is to capture the essence of the business information for the application's purpose. Developers and architects may, instead of an object-oriented model, also start the application design with a data model (possibly expressed with an Entity-Relationship diagram). We usually say that, with regard to persistence, there is little

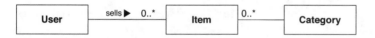

Figure 3.1 A class diagram of a typical online auction model

difference between the two; they're merely different starting points. In the end, we're most interested in the structure and relationships of the business entities, the rules that have to be applied to guarantee the integrity of data (for example, the multiplicity of relationships), and the logic used to manipulate the data.

In object modeling, there is a focus on polymorphic business logic. For our purpose and top-down development approach, it's helpful if we can implement our logical model in polymorphic Java; hence the first draft as an object-oriented model. We then derive the logical relational data model (usually without additional diagrams) and implement the actual physical database schema.

Let's see the outcome of our analysis of the problem domain of the Caveat-Emptor application.

3.1.2 *The CaveatEmptor domain model*

The CaveatEmptor site auctions many different kinds of items, from electronic equipment to airline tickets. Auctions proceed according to the English auction strategy: Users continue to place bids on an item until the bid period for that item expires, and the highest bidder wins.

In any store, goods are categorized by type and grouped with similar goods into sections and onto shelves. The auction catalog requires some kind of hierarchy of item categories so that a buyer can browse these categories or arbitrarily search by category and item attributes. Lists of items appear in the category browser and search result screens. Selecting an item from a list takes the buyer to an item-detail view.

An auction consists of a sequence of bids, and one is the winning bid. User details include name, login, address, email address, and billing information.

A web of trust is an essential feature of an online auction site. The web of trust allows users to build a reputation for trustworthiness (or untrustworthiness). Buyers can create comments about sellers (and vice versa), and the comments are visible to all other users.

A high-level overview of our domain model is shown in figure 3.2. Let's briefly discuss some interesting features of this model.

Each item can be auctioned only once, so you don't need to make Item distinct from any auction entities. Instead, you have a single auction item entity named Item. Thus, Bid is associated directly with Item. Users can write Comments about other users only in the context of an auction; hence the association between Item and Comment. The Address information of a User is modeled as a separate class, even though the User may have only one Address; they may alternatively have three, for home, billing, and shipping. You do allow the user to have

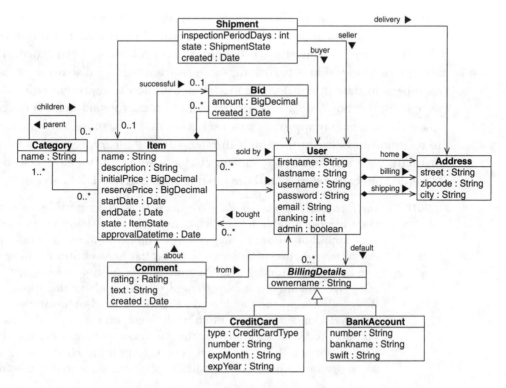

Figure 3.2   Persistent classes of the CaveatEmptor domain model and their relationships

many BillingDetails. The various billing strategies are represented as subclasses of an abstract class (allowing future extension).

A Category may be nested inside another Category. This is expressed by a recursive association, from the Category entity to itself. Note that a single Category may have multiple child categories but at most one parent. Each Item belongs to at least one Category.

The entities in a domain model should encapsulate state and behavior. For example, the User entity should define the name and address of a customer and the logic required to calculate the shipping costs for items (to this particular customer). The domain model is a rich object model, with complex associations, interactions, and inheritance relationships. An interesting and detailed discussion of object-oriented techniques for working with domain models can be found in *Patterns of Enterprise Application Architecture* (Fowler, 2003) or in *Domain-Driven Design* (Evans, 2003).

In this book, we won't have much to say about business rules or about the behavior of our domain model. This isn't because we consider it unimportant; rather, this concern is mostly orthogonal to the problem of persistence. It's the state of our entities that is persistent, so we concentrate our discussion on how to best represent state in our domain model, not on how to represent behavior. For example, in this book, we aren't interested in how tax for sold items is calculated or how the system may approve a new user account. We're more interested in how the relationship between users and the items they sell is represented and made persistent. We'll revisit this issue in later chapters, whenever we have a closer look at layered application design and the separation of logic and data access.

> **NOTE** *ORM without a domain model*—We stress that object persistence with full ORM is most suitable for applications based on a rich domain model. If your application doesn't implement complex business rules or complex interactions between entities (or if you have few entities), you may not need a domain model. Many simple and some not-so-simple problems are perfectly suited to table-oriented solutions, where the application is designed around the database data model instead of around an object-oriented domain model, often with logic executed in the database (stored procedures). However, the more complex and expressive your domain model, the more you'll benefit from using Hibernate; it shines when dealing with the full complexity of object/relational persistence.

Now that you have a (rudimentary) application design with a domain model, the next step is to implement it in Java. Let's look at some of the things you need to consider.

3.2 Implementing the domain model

Several issues typically must be addressed when you implement a domain model in Java. For instance, how do you separate the business concerns from the cross-cutting concerns (such as transactions and even persistence)? Do you need auto-mated or transparent persistence? Do you have to use a specific programming model to achieve this? In this section, we examine these types of issues and how to address them in a typical Hibernate application.

Let's start with an issue that any implementation must deal with: the separation of concerns. The domain model implementation is usually a central, organizing component; it's reused heavily whenever you implement new application functionality. For this reason, you should be prepared to go to some lengths to ensure that concerns other than business aspects don't leak into the domain model implementation.

3.2.1 Addressing leakage of concerns

The domain model implementation is such an important piece of code that it shouldn't depend on orthogonal Java APIs. For example, code in the domain model shouldn't perform JNDI lookups or call the database via the JDBC API. This allows you to reuse the domain model implementation virtually anywhere. Most importantly, it makes it easy to unit test the domain model without the need for a particular runtime environment or container (or the need for mocking any service dependencies). This separation emphasizes the distinction between logical unit testing and integration unit testing.

We say that the domain model should be concerned only with modeling the business domain. However, there are other concerns, such as persistence, transaction management, and authorization. You shouldn't put code that addresses these crosscutting concerns in the classes that implement the domain model. When these concerns start to appear in the domain model classes, this is an example of leakage of concerns.

The EJB standard solves the problem of leaky concerns. If you implement your domain classes using the entity programming model, the container takes care of some concerns for you (or at least lets you externalize those concerns into metadata, as annotations or XML descriptors). The EJB container prevents leakage of certain crosscutting concerns using interception. An EJB is a managed component, executed inside the EJB container; the container intercepts calls to your beans and executes its own functionality. This approach allows the container to implement the predefined crosscutting concerns—security, concurrency, persistence, transactions, and remoteness—in a generic way.

Unfortunately, the EJB 2.1 specification imposes many rules and restrictions on how you must implement a domain model. This, in itself, is a kind of leakage of concerns—in this case, the concerns of the container implementer have leaked! This was addressed in the EJB 3.0 specification, which is nonintrusive and much closer to the traditional JavaBean programming model.

Hibernate isn't an application server, and it doesn't try to implement all the crosscutting concerns of the full EJB specification. Hibernate is a solution for just one of these concerns: persistence. If you require declarative security and transaction management, you should access entity instances via a session bean, taking advantage of the EJB container's implementation of these concerns. Hibernate in an EJB container either replaces (EJB 2.1, entity beans with CMP) or implements (EJB 3.0, Java Persistence entities) the persistence aspect.

Hibernate persistent classes and the EJB 3.0 entity programming model offer transparent persistence. Hibernate and Java Persistence also provide automatic persistence.

Let's explore both terms in more detail and find an accurate definition.

3.2.2   *Transparent and automated persistence*

We use transparent to mean a complete separation of concerns between the persistent classes of the domain model and the persistence logic, where the persistent classes are unaware of—and have no dependency on—the persistence mechanism. We use automatic to refer to a persistence solution that relieves you of handling low-level mechanical details, such as writing most SQL statements and working with the JDBC API.

The `Item` class, for example, doesn't have any code-level dependency on any Hibernate API. Furthermore:

- Hibernate doesn't require that any special superclasses or interfaces be inherited or implemented by persistent classes. Nor are any special classes used to implement properties or associations. (Of course, the option to use both techniques is always there.) Transparent persistence improves code readability and maintenance, as you'll soon see.

- Persistent classes can be reused outside the context of persistence, in unit tests or in the user interface (UI) tier, for example. Testability is a basic requirement for applications with rich domain models.

- In a system with transparent persistence, objects aren't aware of the underlying data store; they need not even be aware that they are being persisted or retrieved. Persistence concerns are externalized to a generic persistence manager interface—in the case of Hibernate, the `Session` and `Query`. In JPA, the `EntityManager` and `Query` (which has the same name, but a different package and slightly different API) play the same roles.

Transparent persistence fosters a degree of portability; without special interfaces, the persistent classes are decoupled from any particular persistence solution. Our business logic is fully reusable in any other application context. You could easily change to another transparent persistence mechanism. Because JPA follows the same basic principles, there is no difference between Hibernate persistent classes and JPA entity classes.

By this definition of transparent persistence, certain nonautomated persistence layers are transparent (for example, the DAO pattern) because they decouple the persistence-related code with abstract programming interfaces. Only plain Java classes without dependencies are exposed to the business logic or contain the business logic. Conversely, some automated persistence layers (including EJB 2.1 entity instances and some ORM solutions) are nontransparent because they require special interfaces or intrusive programming models.

We regard transparency as required. Transparent persistence should be one of the primary goals of any ORM solution. However, no automated persistence solution is completely transparent: Every automated persistence layer, including Hibernate, imposes some requirements on the persistent classes. For example, Hibernate requires that collection-valued properties be typed to an interface such as `java.util.Set` or `java.util.List` and not to an actual implementation such as `java.util.HashSet` (this is a good practice anyway). Or, a JPA entity class has to have a special property, called the database identifier.

You now know why the persistence mechanism should have minimal impact on how you implement a domain model, and that transparent and automated persistence are required. What kind of programming model should you use? What are the exact requirements and contracts to observe? Do you need a special programming model at all? In theory, no; in practice, however, you should adopt a disciplined, consistent programming model that is well accepted by the Java community.

3.2.3 *Writing POJOs and persistent entity classes*

As a reaction against EJB 2.1 entity instances, many developers started talking about Plain Old Java Objects (POJOs),[1] a back-to-basics approach that essentially revives JavaBeans, a component model for UI development, and reapplies it to the business layer. (Most developers now use the terms POJO and JavaBean almost synonymously.) The overhaul of the EJB specification brought us new lightweight entities, and it would be appropriate to call them persistence-capable JavaBeans. Java developers will soon use all three terms as synonyms for the same basic design approach.

In this book, we use persistent class for any class implementation that is capable of persistent instances, we use POJO if some Java best practices are relevant,

---

[1] POJO is sometimes also written Plain *Ordinary* Java Objects. This term was coined in 2002 by Martin Fowler, Rebecca Parsons, and Josh Mackenzie.

and we use entity class when the Java implementation follows the EJB 3.0 and JPA specifications. Again, you shouldn't be too concerned about these differences, because the ultimate goal is to apply the persistence aspect as transparently as possible. Almost every Java class can be a persistent class, or a POJO, or an entity class if some good practices are followed.

Hibernate works best with a domain model implemented as POJOs. The few requirements that Hibernate imposes on your domain model implementation are also best practices for the POJO implementation, so most POJOs are Hibernate-compatible without any changes. Hibernate requirements are almost the same as the requirements for EJB 3.0 entity classes, so a POJO implementation can be easily marked up with annotations and made an EJB 3.0 compatible entity.

A POJO declares business methods, which define behavior, and properties, which represent state. Some properties represent associations to other user-defined POJOs.

A simple POJO class is shown in listing 3.1. This is an implementation of the User entity of your domain model.

Listing 3.1 POJO implementation of the User class

```
public class User
        implements Serializable {        ◁─┐  Declaration of
                                            │  Serializable
    private String username;
    private Address address;

    public User() {}    ◁─  No-argument class constructor

    public String getUsername() {          ◁─┐
        return username;
    }

    public void setUsername(String username) {  ◁─┤
        this.username = username;                   │  Property
    }                                               │  accessor
                                                    │  methods
    public Address getAddress() {          ◁─┤
        return address;
    }

    public void setAddress(Address address) {  ◁─┘
        this.address = address;
    }

    public MonetaryAmount calcShippingCosts(Address fromLocation) {
        ...
    }    ◁─  Business method
}
```

Hibernate doesn't require that persistent classes implement `Serializable`. However, when objects are stored in an `HttpSession` or passed by value using RMI, serialization is necessary. (This is likely to happen in a Hibernate application.) The class can be abstract and, if needed, extend a nonpersistent class.

Unlike the JavaBeans specification, which requires no specific constructor, Hibernate (and JPA) require a constructor with no arguments for every persistent class. Hibernate calls persistent classes using the Java Reflection API on this constructor to instantiate objects. The constructor may be nonpublic, but it has to be at least package-visible if runtime-generated proxies will be used for performance optimization. Proxy generation also requires that the class isn't declared final (nor has final methods)! (We'll come back to proxies in chapter 13, section 13.1, "Defining the global fetch plan.")

The properties of the POJO implement the attributes of the business entities—for example, the `username` of `User`. Properties are usually implemented as private or protected instance variables, together with public property accessor methods: a method for retrieving the value of the instance variable and a method for changing its value. These methods are known as the getter and setter, respectively. The example POJO in listing 3.1 declares getter and setter methods for the `username` and `address` properties.

The JavaBean specification defines the guidelines for naming these methods, and they allow generic tools like Hibernate to easily discover and manipulate the property value. A getter method name begins with `get`, followed by the name of the property (the first letter in uppercase); a setter method name begins with `set` and similarly is followed by the name of the property. Getter methods for Boolean properties may begin with `is` instead of `get`.

You can choose how the state of an instance of your persistent classes should be persisted by Hibernate, either through direct access to its fields or through accessor methods. Your class design isn't disturbed by these considerations. You can make some accessor methods nonpublic or completely remove them. Some getter and setter methods do something more sophisticated than access instance variables (validation, for example), but trivial accessor methods are common. Their primary advantage is providing an additional buffer between the internal representation and the public interface of the class, allowing independent refactoring of both.

The example in listing 3.1 also defines a business method that calculates the cost of shipping an item to a particular user (we left out the implementation of this method).

What are the requirements for JPA entity classes? The good news is that so far, all the conventions we've discussed for POJOs are also requirements for JPA entities. You have to apply some additional rules, but they're equally simple; we'll come back to them later.

Now that we've covered the basics of using POJO persistent classes as a programming model, let's see how to handle the associations between those classes.

3.2.4 *Implementing POJO associations*

You use properties to express associations between POJO classes, and you use accessor methods to navigate from object to object at runtime. Let's consider the associations defined by the Category class, as shown in figure 3.3.

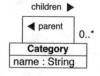

Figure 3.3 Diagram of the Category class with associations

As with all our diagrams, we left out the association-related attributes (let's call them parentCategory and childCategories) because they would clutter the illustration. These attributes and the methods that manipulate their values are called *scaffolding code*.

This is what the scaffolding code for the one-to-many self-association of Category looks like:

```
public class Category {
    private String name;
    private Category parentCategory;
    private Set childCategories = new HashSet();

    public Category() { }
    ...
}
```

To allow bidirectional navigation of the association, you require two attributes. The parentCategory field implements the single-valued end of the association and is declared to be of type Category. The many-valued end, implemented by the childCategories field, must be of collection type. You choose a Set, because duplicates are disallowed, and initialize the instance variable to a new instance of HashSet.

Hibernate requires interfaces for collection-typed attributes, so you must use java.util.Set or java.util.List rather than HashSet, for example. This is consistent with the requirements of the JPA specification for collections in entities. At runtime, Hibernate wraps the HashSet instance with an instance of one of Hibernate's own classes. (This special class isn't visible to the application code.) It's good practice to program to collection interfaces anyway, rather than concrete implementations, so this restriction shouldn't bother you.

You now have some private instance variables but no public interface to allow access from business code or property management by Hibernate (if it shouldn't access the fields directly). Let's add some accessor methods to the class:

```
public String getName() {
    return name;
}
public void setName(String name) {
    this.name = name;
}
public Set getChildCategories() {
    return childCategories;
}
public void setChildCategories(Set childCategories) {
    this.childCategories = childCategories;
}
public Category getParentCategory() {
    return parentCategory;
}
public void setParentCategory(Category parentCategory) {
    this.parentCategory = parentCategory;
}
```

Again, these accessor methods need to be declared public only if they're part of the external interface of the persistent class used by the application logic to create a relationship between two objects. However, managing the link between two Category instances is more difficult than setting a foreign key value in a database field. In our experience, developers are often unaware of this complication that arises from a network object model with bidirectional references. Let's walk through the issue step by step.

The basic procedure for adding a child Category to a parent Category looks like this:

```
Category aParent = new Category();
Category aChild = new Category();
aChild.setParentCategory(aParent);
aParent.getChildCategories().add(aChild);
```

Whenever a link is created between a parent Category and a child Category, two actions are required:

- The `parentCategory` of the child must be set, effectively breaking the association between the child and its old parent (there can only be one parent for any child).

- The child must be added to the `childCategories` collection of the new parent `Category`.

NOTE *Managed relationships in Hibernate*—Hibernate doesn't manage persistent associations. If you want to manipulate an association, you must write exactly the same code you would write without Hibernate. If an association is bidirectional, both sides of the relationship must be considered. Programming models like EJB 2.1 entity beans muddled this behavior by introducing container-managed relationships—the container automatically changes the other side of a relationship if one side is modified by the application. This is one of the reasons why code that uses EJB 2.1 entity beans couldn't be reused outside the container. EJB 3.0 entity associations are transparent, just like in Hibernate. If you ever have problems understanding the behavior of associations in Hibernate, just ask yourself, "What would I do without Hibernate?" Hibernate doesn't change the regular Java semantics.

It's a good idea to add a convenience method to the `Category` class that groups these operations, allowing reuse and helping ensure correctness, and in the end guarantee data integrity:

```
public void addChildCategory(Category childCategory) {
    if (childCategory == null)
      throw new IllegalArgumentException("Null child category!");
    if (childCategory.getParentCategory() != null)
      childCategory.getParentCategory().getChildCategories()
                                     .remove(childCategory);
    childCategory.setParentCategory(this);
    childCategories.add(childCategory);
}
```

The `addChildCategory()` method not only reduces the lines of code when dealing with `Category` objects, but also enforces the cardinality of the association. Errors that arise from leaving out one of the two required actions are avoided. This kind of grouping of operations should always be provided for associations, if possible. If you compare this with the relational model of foreign keys in a relational database, you can easily see how a network and pointer model complicates a simple operation: instead of a declarative constraint, you need procedural code to guarantee data integrity.

Because you want `addChildCategory()` to be the only externally visible muta-tor method for the child categories (possibly in addition to a `removeChildCate-gory()` method), you can make the `setChildCategories()` method private or drop it and use direct field access for persistence. The getter method still returns a modifiable collection, so clients can use it to make changes that aren't reflected on the inverse side. You should consider the static methods `Collections.unmod-ifiableCollection(c)` and `Collections.unmodifiableSet(s)`, if you prefer to wrap the internal collections before returning them in your getter method. The client then gets an exception if it tries to modify the collection; every modification is forced to go through the relationship-management method.

A different kind of relationship exists between the `Category` and `Item` classes: a bidirectional many-to-many association, as shown in figure 3.4.

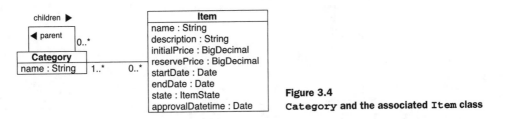

Figure 3.4
`Category` and the associated `Item` class

In the case of a many-to-many association, both sides are implemented with collec-tion-valued attributes. Let's add the new attributes and methods for accessing the `Item` relationship to the `Category` class, as shown in listing 3.2.

Listing 3.2 Category to Item scaffolding code

```
public class Category {
    ...
    private Set items = new HashSet();
    ...
    public Set getItems() {
        return items;
    }

    public void setItems(Set items) {
        this.items = items;
    }
}
```

The code for the Item class (the other end of the many-to-many association) is similar to the code for the Category class. You add the collection attribute, the standard accessor methods, and a method that simplifies relationship management, as in listing 3.3.

Listing 3.3   Item to Category scaffolding code

```
public class Item {

    private String name;
    private String description;
    ...
    private Set categories = new HashSet();
    ...

    public Set getCategories() {
        return categories;
    }

    private void setCategories(Set categories) {
        this.categories = categories;
    }

    public void addCategory(Category category) {
        if (category == null)
            throw new IllegalArgumentException("Null category");
        category.getItems().add(this);
        categories.add(category);
    }

}
```

The addCategory() method is similar to the addChildCategory() convenience method of the Category class. It's used by a client to manipulate the link between an Item and a Category. For the sake of readability, we won't show convenience methods in future code samples and assume you'll add them according to your own taste.

Using convenience methods for association handling isn't the only way to improve a domain model implementation. You can also add logic to your accessor methods.

3.2.5 Adding logic to accessor methods

One of the reasons we like to use JavaBeans-style accessor methods is that they provide encapsulation: The hidden internal implementation of a property can be changed without any changes to the public interface. This lets you abstract the internal data structure of a class—the instance variables—from the design of the database, if Hibernate accesses the properties at runtime through accessor methods. It also allows easier and independent refactoring of the public API and the internal representation of a class.

For example, if your database stores the name of a user as a single NAME column, but your User class has firstname and lastname properties, you can add the following persistent name property to the class:

```
public class User {
    private String firstname;
    private String lastname;
    ...

    public String getName() {
        return firstname + ' ' + lastname;
    }

    public void setName(String name) {
        StringTokenizer t = new StringTokenizer(name);
        firstname = t.nextToken();
        lastname = t.nextToken();
    }
    ....

}
```

Later, you'll see that a Hibernate custom type is a better way to handle many of these kinds of situations. However, it helps to have several options.

Accessor methods can also perform validation. For instance, in the following example, the setFirstName() method verifies that the name is capitalized:

```
public class User {
    private String firstname;
    ...

    public String getFirstname() {
        return firstname;
    }

    public void setFirstname(String firstname)
        throws InvalidNameException {

        if ( !StringUtil.isCapitalizedName(firstname) )
            throw new InvalidNameException(firstname);
        this.firstname = firstname;
    }
    ....

}
```

Hibernate may use the accessor methods to populate the state of an instance when loading an object from a database, and sometimes you'll prefer that this validation not occur when Hibernate is initializing a newly loaded object. In that case, it makes sense to tell Hibernate to directly access the instance variables.

Another issue to consider is dirty checking. Hibernate automatically detects object state changes in order to synchronize the updated state with the database. It's usually safe to return a different object from the getter method than the object passed by Hibernate to the setter. Hibernate compares the objects by value—not by object identity—to determine whether the property's persistent state needs to be updated. For example, the following getter method doesn't result in unnecessary SQL UPDATEs:

```
public String getFirstname() {
    return new String(firstname);
}
```

There is one important exception to this: Collections are compared by identity! For a property mapped as a persistent collection, you should return exactly the same collection instance from the getter method that Hibernate passed to the setter method. If you don't, Hibernate will update the database, even if no update is necessary, every time the state held in memory is synchronized with the database. This kind of code should almost always be avoided in accessor methods:

```
public void setNames(List namesList) {
    names = (String[]) namesList.toArray();
}

public List getNames() {
    return Arrays.asList(names);
}
```

Finally, you have to know how exceptions in accessor methods are handled if you configure Hibernate to use these methods when loading and storing instances. If a RuntimeException is thrown, the current transaction is rolled back, and the exception is yours to handle. If a checked application exception is thrown, Hibernate wraps the exception into a RuntimeException.

You can see that Hibernate doesn't unnecessarily restrict you with a POJO programming model. You're free to implement whatever logic you need in accessor methods (as long as you keep the same collection instance in both getter and setter). How Hibernate accesses the properties is completely configurable. This kind of transparency guarantees an independent and reusable domain model implementation. And everything we have explained and said so far is equally true for both Hibernate persistent classes and JPA entities.

Let's now define the object/relational mapping for the persistent classes.

3.3   *Object/relational mapping metadata*

ORM tools require metadata to specify the mapping between classes and tables, properties and columns, associations and foreign keys, Java types and SQL types, and so on. This information is called the object/relational mapping metadata. Metadata is data about data, and mapping metadata defines and governs the transformation between the different type systems and relationship representations in object-oriented and SQL systems.

It's your job as a developer to write and maintain this metadata. We discuss various approaches in this section, including metadata in XML files and JDK 5.0 source code annotations. Usually you decide to use one strategy in a particular project, and after reading these sections you'll have the background information to make an educated decision.

3.3.1   *Metadata in XML*

Any ORM solution should provide a human-readable, easily hand-editable mapping format, not just a GUI mapping tool. Currently, the most popular object/relational metadata format is XML. Mapping documents written in and with XML are lightweight, human readable, easily manipulated by version-control systems and text editors, and they can be customized at deployment time (or even at runtime, with programmatic XML generation).

But is XML-based metadata really the best approach? A certain backlash against the overuse of XML can be seen in the Java community. Every framework and application server seems to require its own XML descriptors.

In our view, there are three main reasons for this backlash:

- Metadata-based solutions have often been used inappropriately. Metadata is not, by nature, more flexible or maintainable than plain Java code.

- Many existing metadata formats weren't designed to be readable and easy to edit by hand. In particular, a major cause of pain is the lack of sensible defaults for attribute and element values, requiring significantly more typing than should be necessary. Even worse, some metadata schemas use only XML elements and text values, without any attributes. Another problem is schemas that are too generic, where every declaration is wrapped in a generic extension attribute of a meta element.

- Good XML editors, especially in IDEs, aren't as common as good Java coding environments. Worst, and most easily fixable, a document type declaration (DTD) often isn't provided, preventing autocompletion and validation.

There is no getting around the need for metadata in ORM. However, Hibernate was designed with full awareness of the typical metadata problems. The XML metadata format of Hibernate is extremely readable and defines useful default values. If attribute values are missing, reflection is used on the mapped class to determine defaults. Hibernate also comes with a documented and complete DTD. Finally, IDE support for XML has improved lately, and modern IDEs provide dynamic XML validation and even an autocomplete feature.

Let's look at the way you can use XML metadata in Hibernate. You created the Category class in the previous section; now you need to map it to the CATEGORY table in the database. To do that, you write the XML mapping document in listing 3.4.

Listing 3.4 Hibernate XML mapping of the Category class

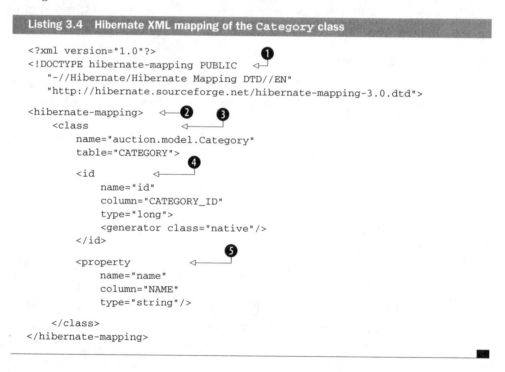

```
<?xml version="1.0"?>
<!DOCTYPE hibernate-mapping PUBLIC
    "-//Hibernate/Hibernate Mapping DTD//EN"
    "http://hibernate.sourceforge.net/hibernate-mapping-3.0.dtd">

<hibernate-mapping>
    <class
        name="auction.model.Category"
        table="CATEGORY">
        <id
            name="id"
            column="CATEGORY_ID"
            type="long">
            <generator class="native"/>
        </id>

        <property
            name="name"
            column="NAME"
            type="string"/>

    </class>
</hibernate-mapping>
```

1 The Hibernate mapping DTD should be declared in every mapping file—it's required for syntactic validation of the XML.

 Mappings are declared inside a <hibernate-mapping> element. You may include as many class mappings as you like, along with certain other special declarations that we'll mention later in the book.

❸ The class Category (in the auction.model package) is mapped to the CATEGORY table. Every row in this table represents one instance of type Category.

❹ We haven't discussed the concept of object identity, so you may be surprised by this mapping element. This complex topic is covered in the next chapter. To understand this mapping, it's sufficient to know that every row in the CATEGORY table has a primary key value that matches the object identity of the instance in memory. The <id> mapping element is used to define the details of object identity.

❺ The property name of type java.lang.String is mapped to a database NAME column. Note that the type declared in the mapping is a built-in Hibernate type (string), not the type of the Java property or the SQL column type. Think about this as the converter that represents a bridge between the other two type systems.

We've intentionally left the collection and association mappings out of this example. Association and especially collection mappings are more complex, so we'll return to them in the second part of the book.

Although it's possible to declare mappings for multiple classes in one mapping file by using multiple <class> elements, the recommended practice (and the practice expected by some Hibernate tools) is to use one mapping file per persistent class. The convention is to give the file the same name as the mapped class, appending a suffix (for example, Category.hbm.xml), and putting it in the same package as the Category class.

As already mentioned, XML mapping files aren't the only way to define mapping metadata in a Hibernate application. If you use JDK 5.0, your best choice is the Hibernate Annotations based on the EJB 3.0 and Java Persistence standard.

3.3.2   *Annotation-based metadata*

The basic idea is to put metadata next to the information it describes, instead of separating it physically into a different file. Java didn't have this functionality before JDK 5.0, so an alternative was developed. The XDoclet project introduced annotation of Java source code with meta-information, using special Javadoc tags with support for key/value pairs. Through nesting of tags, quite complex structures are supported, but only some IDEs allow customization of Javadoc templates for autocompletion and validation.

Java Specification Request (JSR) 175 introduced the annotation concept in the Java language, with type-safe and declared interfaces for the definition of annotations. Autocompletion and compile-time checking are no longer an issue. We found that annotation metadata is, compared to XDoclet, nonverbose and that it has better defaults. However, JDK 5.0 annotations are sometimes more difficult to read than XDoclet annotations, because they aren't inside regular comment blocks; you should use an IDE that supports configurable syntax highlighting of annotations. Other than that, we found no serious disadvantage in working with annotations in our daily work in the past years, and we consider annotation-meta-data support to be one of the most important features of JDK 5.0.

We'll now introduce mapping annotations and use JDK 5.0. If you have to work with JDK 1.4 but like to use annotation-based metadata, consider XDoclet, which we'll show afterwards.

Defining and using annotations

Before you annotate the first persistent class, let's see how annotations are created. Naturally, you'll usually use predefined annotations. However, knowing how to extend the existing metadata format or how to write your own annotations is a useful skill. The following code example shows the definition of an `Entity` annotation:

```
package javax.persistence;

@Target(TYPE)
@Retention(RUNTIME)
public @interface Entity {
    String name() default "";
}
```

The first line defines the package, as always. This annotation is in the package `javax.persistence`, the Java Persistence API as defined by EJB 3.0. It's one of the most important annotations of the specification—you can apply it on a POJO to make it a persistent entity class. The next line is an annotation that adds meta-information to the `@Entity` annotation (metadata about metadata). It specifies that the `@Entity` annotation can only be put on type declarations; in other words, you can only mark up classes with the `@Entity` annotation, not fields or methods. The retention policy chosen for this annotation is `RUNTIME`; other options (for other use cases) include removal of the annotation metadata during compilation, or only inclusion in byte-code without possible runtime reflectivity. You want to preserve all entity meta-information even at runtime, so Hibernate can read it on startup through Java Reflection. What follows in the example is the actual declaration of the annotation, including its interface name and its attributes (just one in this case, `name`, with an empty string default).

Let's use this annotation to make a POJO persistent class a Java Persistence entity:

```
package auction.model;

import javax.persistence.*;

@Entity
@Table(name = "ITEM")
public class Item {
    ...
}
```

This public class, `Item`, has been declared as a persistent entity. All of its properties are now automatically persistent with a default strategy. Also shown is a second annotation that declares the name of the table in the database schema this persistent class is mapped to. If you omit this information, the JPA provider defaults to the unqualified class name (just as Hibernate will if you omit the table name in an XML mapping file).

All of this is type-safe, and declared annotations are read with Java Reflection when Hibernate starts up. You don't need to write any XML mapping files, Hibernate doesn't need to parse any XML, and startup is faster. Your IDE can also easily validate and highlight annotations—they are regular Java types, after all.

One of the clear benefits of annotations is their flexibility for agile development. If you refactor your code, you rename, delete, or move classes and properties all the time. Most development tools and editors can't refactor XML element and attribute values, but annotations are part of the Java language and are included in all refactoring operations.

Which annotations should you apply? You have the choice among several standardized and vendor-specific packages.

Considering standards

Annotation-based metadata has a significant impact on how you write Java applications. Other programming environments, like C# and .NET, had this kind of support for quite a while, and developers adopted the metadata attributes quickly. In the Java world, the big rollout of annotations is happening with Java EE 5.0. All specifications that are considered part of Java EE, like EJB, JMS, JMX, and even the servlet specification, will be updated and use JDK 5.0 annotations for metadata needs. For example, web services in J2EE 1.4 usually require significant metadata in XML files, so we expect to see real productivity improvements with annotations. Or, you can let the web container inject an EJB handle into your servlet, by adding an annotation on a field. Sun initiated a specification effort (JSR 250) to take care of the annotations across specifications, defining common annotations for the whole Java platform. For you, however, working on a persistence layer, the most important specification is EJB 3.0 and JPA.

Annotations from the Java Persistence package are available in `javax.persistence` once you have included the JPA interfaces in your classpath. You can use these annotations to declare persistent entity classes, embeddable classes (we'll discuss these in the next chapter), properties, fields, keys, and so on. The JPA specification covers the basics and most relevant advanced mappings—everything you need to write a portable application, with a pluggable, standardized persistence layer that works inside and outside of any runtime container.

What annotations and mapping features aren't specified in Java Persistence? A particular JPA engine and product may naturally offer advantages—the so-called vendor extensions.

Utilizing vendor extensions

Even if you map most of your application's model with JPA-compatible annotations from the `javax.persistence` package, you'll have to use vendor extensions at some point. For example, almost all performance-tuning options you'd expect to be available in high-quality persistence software, such as fetching and caching settings, are only available as Hibernate-specific annotations.

Let's see what that looks like in an example. Annotate the `Item` entity source code again:

```
package auction.model;

import javax.persistence.*;

@Entity
@Table(name = "ITEM")
@org.hibernate.annotations.BatchSize(size = 10)
@org.hibernate.annotations.DiscriminatorFormula(
    "case when ITEM_IS_SPECIAL is not null then A else B end"
)
public class Item {
    ...
}
```

This example contains two Hibernate annotations. The first, `@BatchSize`, is a fetching option that can increase performance in situations we'll examine later in this book. The second, `@DiscriminatorFormula`, is a Hibernate mapping annotation that is especially useful for legacy schemas when class inheritance can't be determined with simple literal values (here it maps a legacy column `ITEM_IS_SPECIAL`—probably some kind of flag—to a literal value). Both annotations are prefixed with the `org.hibernate.annotations` package name.

Consider this a good practice, because you can now easily see what metadata of this entity class is from the JPA specification and which tags are vendor-specific. You can also easily search your source code for "org.hibernate.annotations" and get a complete overview of all nonstandard annotations in your application in a single search result.

If you switch your Java Persistence provider, you only have to replace the vendor-specific extensions, and you can expect a similar feature set to be available with most sophisticated solutions. Of course, we hope you'll never have to do this, and it doesn't happen often in practice—just be prepared.

Annotations on classes only cover metadata that is applicable for that particular class. However, you often need metadata at a higher level, for a whole package or even the whole application. Before we discuss these options, we'd like to introduce another mapping metadata format.

XML descriptors in JPA and EJB 3.0

The EJB 3.0 and Java Persistence standard embraces annotations aggressively. However, the expert group has been aware of the advantages of XML deployment descriptors in certain situations, especially for configuration metadata that changes with each deployment. As a consequence, every annotation in EJB 3.0 and JPA can be replaced with an XML descriptor element. In other words, you don't have to use annotations if you don't want to (although we strongly encourage you to reconsider and give annotations a try, if this is your first reaction to annotations).

Let's look at an example of a JPA XML descriptor for a particular persistence unit:

```xml
<?xml version="1.0" encoding="UTF-8"?>

<entity-mappings
  xmlns="http://java.sun.com/xml/ns/persistence/orm"
  xmlns:xsi="http://www.w3.org/2001/XMLSchema-instance"
  xsi:schemaLocation=
      "http://java.sun.com/xml/ns/persistence/orm orm_1_0.xsd"
  version="1.0">

    <persistence-unit-metadata>
        <xml-mapping-metadata-complete/>
        <persistence-unit-defaults>
            <schema>MY_SCHEMA</schema>
            <catalog>MY_CATALOG</catalog>
            <cascade-persist/>
        </persistence-unit-defaults>
    </persistence-unit-metadata>
```

```
<package>auction.model</package>

<entity class="Item" access="PROPERTY"
        metadata-complete="true">
    <attributes>
        <id name="id">
            <generated-value strategy="AUTO"/>
        </id>
    </attributes>
</entity>

</entity-mappings>
```

This XML is automatically picked up by the JPA provider if you place it in a file called orm.xml in your classpath, in the META-INF directory of the persistence unit. You can see that you only have to name an identifier property for a class; as in annotations, all other properties of the entity class are automatically considered persistent with a sensible default mapping.

You can also set default mappings for the whole persistence unit, such as the schema name and default cascading options. If you include the <xml-mapping-metadata-complete> element, the JPA provider completely ignores all annotations on your entity classes in this persistence unit and relies only on the mappings as defined in the orm.xml file. You can (redundantly in this case) enable this on an entity level, with metadata-complete="true". If enabled, the JPA provider assumes that all properties of the entity are mapped in XML, and that all annotations for this entity should be ignored.

If you don't want to ignore but instead want to override the annotation metadata, first remove the global <xml-mapping-metadata-complete> element from the orm.xml file. Also remove the metadata-complete="true" attribute from any entity mapping that should override, not replace, annotations:

```
<entity-mappings ...>

    <package>auction.model</package>

    <entity class="Item">
        <attributes>
            <basic name="initialPrice" optional="false">
                <column name="INIT_PRICE"/>
            </basic>
        </attributes>
    </entity>

</entity-mappings>
```

Here you map the initialPrice property to the INIT_PRICE column and specify it isn't nullable. Any annotation on the initialPrice property of the Item class is ignored, but all other annotations on the Item class are still applied. Also note that you didn't specify an access strategy in this mapping, so field or accessor method access is used depending on the position of the @Id annotation in Item. (We'll get back to this detail in the next chapter.)

An obvious problem with XML deployment descriptors in Java Persistence is their compatibility with native Hibernate XML mapping files. The two formats aren't compatible at all, and you should make a decision to use one or the other. The syntax of the JPA XML descriptor is much closer to the actual JPA annotations than to the native Hibernate XML mapping files.

You also need to consider vendor extensions when you make a decision for an XML metadata format. The Hibernate XML format supports all possible Hibernate mappings, so if something can't be mapped in JPA/Hibernate annotations, it can be mapped with native Hibernate XML files. The same isn't true with JPA XML descriptors—they only provide convenient externalized metadata that covers the specification. Sun does not allow vendor extensions with an additional namespace.

On the other hand, you can't override annotations with Hibernate XML mapping files; you have to define a complete entity class mapping in XML.

For these reasons, we don't show all possible mappings in all three formats; we focus on native Hibernate XML metadata and JPA/Hibernate annotations. However, you'll learn enough about the JPA XML descriptor to use it if you want to.

Consider JPA/Hibernate annotations the primary choice if you're using JDK 5.0. Fall back to native Hibernate XML mapping files if you want to externalize a particular class mapping or utilize a Hibernate extension that isn't available as an annotation. Consider JPA XML descriptors only if you aren't planning to use any vendor extension (which is, in practice, unlikely), or if you want to only override a few annotations, or if you require complete portability that even includes deployment descriptors.

But what if you're stuck with JDK 1.4 (or even 1.3) and still want to benefit from the better refactoring capabilities and reduced lines of code of inline metadata?

3.3.3 *Using XDoclet*

The XDoclet project has brought the notion of attribute-oriented programming to Java. XDoclet leverages the Javadoc tag format (@attribute) to specify class-, field-, or method-level metadata attributes. There is even a book about XDoclet from Manning Publications, *XDoclet in Action* (Walls and Richards, 2004).

XDoclet is implemented as an Ant task that generates Hibernate XML metadata (or something else, depending on the plug-in) as part of the build process.

Creating the Hibernate XML mapping document with XDoclet is straightforward; instead of writing it by hand, you mark up the Java source code of your persistent class with custom Javadoc tags, as shown in listing 3.5.

Listing 3.5   Using XDoclet tags to mark up Java classes with mapping metadata

```
/**
 * The Category class of the CaveatEmptor auction site domain model.
 *
 * @hibernate.class
 *  table="CATEGORY"
 */
public class Category {

    ...

    /**
     * @hibernate.id
     *  generator-class="native"
     *  column="CATEGORY_ID"
     */
    public Long getId() {
        return id;
    }

    ...

    /**
     * @hibernate.property
     */
    public String getName() {
        return name;
    }

    ...

}
```

With the annotated class in place and an Ant task ready, you can automatically generate the same XML document shown in the previous section (listing 3.4).

The downside to XDoclet is that it requires another build step. Most large Java projects are using Ant already, so this is usually a nonissue. Arguably, XDoclet mappings are less configurable at deployment time; but there is nothing stopping you from hand-editing the generated XML before deployment, so this is probably not a significant objection. Finally, support for XDoclet tag validation may not be available in your development environment. However, the latest IDEs support at least autocompletion of tag names. We won't cover XDoclet in this book, but you can find examples on the Hibernate website.

Whether you use XML files, JDK 5.0 annotations, or XDoclet, you'll often notice that you have to duplicate metadata in several places. In other words, you need to add global information that is applicable to more than one property, more than one persistent class, or even the whole application.

3.3.4 *Handling global metadata*

Consider the following situation: All of your domain model persistent classes are in the same package. However, you have to specify class names fully qualified, including the package, in every XML mapping file. It would be a lot easier to declare the package name once and then use only the short persistent class name. Or, instead of enabling direct field access for every single property through the `access="field"` mapping attribute, you'd rather use a single switch to enable field access for all properties. Class- or package-scoped metadata would be much more convenient.

Some metadata is valid for the whole application. For example, query strings can be externalized to metadata and called by a globally unique name in the application code. Similarly, a query usually isn't related to a particular class, and sometimes not even to a particular package. Other application-scoped metadata includes user-defined mapping types (converters) and data filter (dynamic view) definitions.

Let's walk through some examples of global metadata in Hibernate XML mappings and JDK 5.0 annotations.

Global XML mapping metadata

If you check the XML mapping DTD, you'll see that the `<hibernate-mapping>` root element has global options that are applied to the class mapping(s) inside it—some of these options are shown in the following example:

```
<hibernate-mapping
    schema="AUCTION"
    default-lazy="false"
    default-access="field"
    auto-import="false">

<class ...>
    ...
</class>

</hibernate-mapping>
```

The `schema` attribute enables a database schema prefix, `AUCTION`, used by Hibernate for all SQL statements generated for the mapped classes. By setting `default-lazy` to `false`, you enable default outer-join fetching for some class associations, a topic we'll discuss in chapter 13, section 13.1, "Defining the global fetch plan." (This `default-lazy="true"` switch has an interesting side effect: It switches to Hibernate 2.x default fetching behavior—useful if you migrate to Hibernate 3.x but don't want to update all fetching settings.) With `default-access`, you enable direct field access by Hibernate for all persistent properties of all classes mapped in this file. Finally, the `auto-import` setting is turned off for all classes in this file. We'll talk about importing and naming of entities in chapter 4, section 4.3, "Class mapping options."

> **TIP** *Mapping files with no class declarations*—Global metadata is required and present in any sophisticated application. For example, you may easily import a dozen interfaces, or externalize a hundred query strings. In large-scale applications, you often create mapping files without actual class mappings, and only imports, external queries, or global filter and type definitions. If you look at the DTD, you can see that `<class>` mappings are optional inside the `<hibernate-mapping>` root element. Split up and organize your global metadata into separate files, such as `AuctionTypes.hbm.xml`, `AuctionQueries.hbm.xml`, and so on, and load them in Hibernate's configuration just like regular mapping files. However, make sure that all custom types and filters are loaded before any other mapping metadata that applies these types and filters to class mappings.

Let's look at global metadata with JDK 5.0 annotations.

Global annotation metadata

Annotations are by nature woven into the Java source code for a particular class. Although it's possible to place global annotations in the source file of a class (at the top), we'd rather keep global metadata in a separate file. This is called package metadata, and it's enabled with a file named `package-info.java` in a particular package directory:

```
@org.hibernate.annotations.TypeDefs({
    @org.hibernate.annotations.TypeDef(
        name="monetary_amount_usd",
        typeClass = MonetaryAmountType.class,
        parameters = { @Parameter(name="convertTo", value="USD") }
    ),
    @org.hibernate.annotations.TypeDef(
        name="monetary_amount_eur",
        typeClass = MonetaryAmountType.class,
        parameters = { @Parameter(name="convertTo", value="EUR") }
    )
})
```

```
@org.hibernate.annotations.NamedQueries({
    @org.hibernate.annotations.NamedQuery(
        name = "findItemsOrderByPrice",
        query = "select i from Item i order by i.initialPrice)"
    )
})

package auction.persistence.types;
```

This example of a package metadata file, in the package `auction.persis-tence.types`, declares two Hibernate type converters. We'll discuss the Hibernate type system in chapter 5, section 5.2, "The Hibernate type system." You can now refer to the user-defined types in class mappings by their names. The same mechanism can be used to externalize queries and to define global identifier generators (not shown in the last example).

There is a reason the previous code example only includes annotations from the Hibernate package and no Java Persistence annotations. One of the (last-minute) changes made to the JPA specification was the removal of package visibility of JPA annotations. As a result, no Java Persistence annotations can be placed in a package-info.java file. If you need portable global Java Persistence metadata, put it in an orm.xml file.

Note that you have to name a package that contains a metadata file in your Hibernate or JPA persistence unit configuration if you aren't using automatic detection—see chapter 2, section 2.2.1, "Using Hibernate Annotations."

Global annotations (Hibernate and JPA) can also be placed in the source code of a particular class, right after the `import` section. The syntax for the annotations is the same as in the package-info.java file, so we won't repeat it here.

You now know how to write local and global mapping metadata. Another issue in large-scale applications is the portability of metadata.

Using placeholders

In any larger Hibernate application, you'll face the problem of native code in your mapping metadata—code that effectively binds your mapping to a particular database product. For example, SQL statements, such as in formula, constraint, or filter mappings, aren't parsed by Hibernate but are passed directly through to the database management system. The advantage is flexibility—you can call any native SQL function or keyword your database system supports. The disadvantage of putting native SQL in your mapping metadata is lost database portability, because your mappings, and hence your application, will work only for a particular DBMS (or even DBMS version).

Even simple things, such as primary key generation strategies, usually aren't portable across all database systems. In the next chapter, we discuss a special identifier generator called `native`, which is a built-in smart primary key generator. On Oracle, it uses a database sequence to generate primary key values for rows in a table; on IBM DB2, it uses a special identity primary key column by default. This is how you map it in XML:

```
<class name="Category" table="CATEGORY">

    <id name="id" column="CATEGORY_ID" type="long">
        <generator class="native"/>
    </id>

    ...
</class>
```

We'll discuss the details of this mapping later. The interesting part is the declaration `class="native"` as the identifier generator. Let's assume that the portability this generator provides isn't what you need, perhaps because you use a custom identifier generator, a class you wrote that implements the Hibernate `IdentifierGenerator` interface:

```
<id name="id" column="CATEGORY_ID" type="long">
    <generator class="auction.custom.MyOracleGenerator"/>
</id>
```

The XML mapping file is now bound to a particular database product, and you lose the database portability of the Hibernate application. One way to deal with this issue is to use a placeholder in your XML file that is replaced during build when the mapping files are copied to the target directory (Ant supports this). This mechanism is recommended only if you have experience with Ant or already need build-time substitution for other parts of your application.

A much more elegant variation is to use custom XML entities (not related to our application's business entities). Let's assume you need to externalize an element or attribute value in your XML files to keep it portable:

```
<id name="id" column="CATEGORY_ID" type="long">
    <generator class="&idgenerator;"/>
</id>
```

The `&idgenerator;` value is called an entity placeholder. You can define its value at the top of the XML file as an entity declaration, as part of the document type definition:

```
<?xml version="1.0"?>
<!DOCTYPE hibernate-mapping SYSTEM
```

```
    "http://hibernate.sourceforge.net/hibernate-mapping-3.0.dtd"
[
<!ENTITY idgenerator    "auction.custom.MyOracleGenerator">
]>
```

The XML parser will now substitute the placeholder on Hibernate startup, when mapping files are read.

You can take this one step further and externalize this addition to the DTD in a separate file and include the global options in all other mapping files:

```
<?xml version="1.0"?>
<!DOCTYPE hibernate-mapping SYSTEM
    "http://hibernate.sourceforge.net/hibernate-mapping-3.0.dtd"
[
<!ENTITY % globals SYSTEM "classpath://persistence/globals.dtd">
%globals;
]>
```

This example shows the inclusion of an external file as part of the DTD. The syntax, as often in XML, is rather crude, but the purpose of each line should be clear. All global settings are added to the globals.dtd file in the `persistence` package on the classpath:

```
<!ENTITY idgenerator    "auction.custom.MyOracleGenerator">
<!-- Add more options if needed... -->
```

To switch from Oracle to a different database system, just deploy a different globals.dtd file.

Often, you need not only substitute an XML element or attribute value but also to include whole blocks of mapping metadata in all files, such as when many of your classes share some common properties, and you can't use inheritance to capture them in a single location. With XML entity replacement, you can externalize an XML snippet to a separate file and include it in other XML files.

Let's assume all the persistent classes have a `dateModified` property. The first step is to put this mapping in its own file, say, DateModified.hbm.xml:

```
<property name="dateModified"
          column="DATE_MOD"
          type="timestamp"/>
```

This file needs no XML header or any other tags. Now you include it in the mapping file for a persistent class:

```
<?xml version="1.0"?>
<!DOCTYPE hibernate-mapping SYSTEM
    "http://hibernate.sourceforge.net/hibernate-mapping-3.0.dtd"
[
```

```
<!ENTITY datemodified  SYSTEM "classpath://model/DateModified.hbm.xml">
]>

<hibernate-mapping>

<class name="Item" table="ITEM"
    <id ...>

    &datemodified;

    ...
</class>
```

The content of DateModified.hbm.xml will be included and be substituted for the &datemodified; placeholder. This, of course, also works with larger XML snippets.

When Hibernate starts up and reads mapping files, XML DTDs have to be resolved by the XML parser. The built-in Hibernate entity resolver looks for the hibernate-mapping-3.0.dtd on the classpath; it should find the DTD in the hibernate3.jar file before it tries to look it up on the Internet, which happens automatically whenever an entity URL is prefixed with http://hibernate.source-forge.net/. The Hibernate entity resolver can also detect the classpath:// prefix, and the resource is then searched for in the classpath, where you can copy it on deployment. We have to repeat this FAQ: Hibernate never looks up the DTD on the Internet if you have a correct DTD reference in your mapping and the right JAR on the classpath.

The approaches we have described so far—XML, JDK 5.0 annotations, and XDoclet attributes—assume that all mapping information is known at development (or deployment) time. Suppose, however, that some information isn't known before the application starts. Can you programmatically manipulate the mapping metadata at runtime?

3.3.5 *Manipulating metadata at runtime*

It's sometimes useful for an application to browse, manipulate, or build new mappings at runtime. XML APIs like DOM, dom4j, and JDOM allow direct runtime manipulation of XML documents, so you could create or manipulate an XML document at runtime, before feeding it to the Configuration object.

On the other hand, Hibernate also exposes a configuration-time metamodel that contains all the information declared in your static mapping metadata. Direct programmatic manipulation of this metamodel is sometimes useful, especially for applications that allow for extension by user-written code. A more drastic approach would be complete programmatic and dynamic definition of the mapping metadata, without any static mapping. However, this is exotic and should be reserved for a particular class of fully dynamic applications, or application building kits.

The following code adds a new property, `motto`, to the `User` class:

```
// Get the existing mapping for User from Configuration
PersistentClass userMapping =
    cfg.getClassMapping(User.class.getName());

// Define a new column for the USER table
Column column = new Column();
column.setName("MOTTO");
column.setNullable(false);
column.setUnique(true);
userMapping.getTable().addColumn(column);

// Wrap the column in a Value
SimpleValue value = new SimpleValue();
value.setTable( userMapping.getTable() );
value.setTypeName("string");
value.addColumn(column);

// Define a new property of the User class
Property prop = new Property();
prop.setValue(value);
prop.setName("motto");
prop.setNodeName(prop.getName());
userMapping.addProperty(prop);

// Build a new session factory, using the new mapping
SessionFactory sf = cfg.buildSessionFactory();
```

A `PersistentClass` object represents the metamodel for a single persistent class, and you retrieve it from the `Configuration` object. `Column`, `SimpleValue`, and `Property` are all classes of the Hibernate metamodel and are available in the `org.hibernate.mapping` package.

> **TIP** Keep in mind that adding a property to an existing persistent class mapping, as shown here, is quite easy, but programmatically creating a new mapping for a previously unmapped class is more involved.

Once a `SessionFactory` is created, its mappings are immutable. The `Session-Factory` uses a different metamodel internally than the one used at configuration time. There is no way to get back to the original `Configuration` from the `SessionFactory` or `Session`. (Note that you can get the `SessionFactory` from a `Session` if you wish to access a global setting.) However, the application can read the `SessionFactory`'s metamodel by calling `getClassMetadata()` or `getCollection-Metadata()`. Here's an example:

```
Item item = ...;
ClassMetadata meta = sessionFactory.getClassMetadata(Item.class);
String[] metaPropertyNames =
            meta.getPropertyNames();
Object[] propertyValues =
            meta.getPropertyValues(item, EntityMode.POJO);
```

This code snippet retrieves the names of persistent properties of the Item class and the values of those properties for a particular instance. This helps you write generic code. For example, you may use this feature to label UI components or improve log output.

Although you've seen some mapping constructs in the previous sections, we haven't introduced any more sophisticated class and property mappings so far. You should now decide which mapping metadata option you'd like to use in your project and then read more about class and property mappings in the next chapter.

Or, if you're already an experienced Hibernate user, you can read on and find out how the latest Hibernate version allows you to represent a domain model without Java classes.

3.4 *Alternative entity representation*

In this book, so far, we've always talked about a domain model implementation based on Java classes—we called them POJOs, persistent classes, JavaBeans, or entities. An implementation of a domain model that is based on Java classes with regular properties, collections, and so on, is type-safe. If you access a property of a class, your IDE offers autocompletion based on the strong types of your model, and the compiler checks whether your source is correct. However, you pay for this safety with more time spent on the domain model implementation—and time is money.

In the following sections, we introduce Hibernate's ability to work with domain models that aren't implemented with Java classes. We're basically trading type-safety for other benefits and, because nothing is free, more errors at runtime whenever we make a mistake. In Hibernate, you can select an *entity mode* for your application, or even mix entity modes for a single model. You can even switch between entity modes in a single Session.

These are the three built-in entity modes in Hibernate:

- POJO—A domain model implementation based on POJOs, persistent classes. This is what you have seen so far, and it's the default entity mode.

- MAP—No Java classes are required; entities are represented in the Java application with HashMaps. This mode allows quick prototyping of fully dynamic applications.

- DOM4J—No Java classes are required; entities are represented as XML elements, based on the dom4j API. This mode is especially useful for exporting or importing data, or for rendering and transforming data through XSLT processing.

There are two reasons why you may want to skip the next section and come back later: First, a static domain model implementation with POJOs is the common case, and dynamic or XML representation are features you may not need right now. Second, we're going to present some mappings, queries, and other operations that you may not have seen so far, not even with the default POJO entity mode. However, if you feel confident enough with Hibernate, read on.

Let's start with the MAP mode and explore how a Hibernate application can be fully dynamically typed.

3.4.1 Creating dynamic applications

A dynamic domain model is a model that is dynamically typed. For example, instead of a Java class that represents an auction item, you work with a bunch of values in a Java Map. Each attribute of an auction item is represented by a key (the name of the attribute) and its value.

Mapping entity names

First, you need to enable this strategy by naming your business entities. In a Hibernate XML mapping file, you use the entity-name attribute:

```
<hibernate-mapping>

<class entity-name="ItemEntity" table="ITEM_ENTITY">
    <id name="id" type="long" column="ITEM_ID">
        <generator class="native"/>
    </id>

    <property name="initialPrice"
            type="big_decimal"
            column="INIT_PRICE"/>

    <property name="description"
            type="string"
            column="DESCRIPTION"/>

    <many-to-one name="seller"
            entity-name="UserEntity"
            column="USER_ID"/>
```

```
    </class>

    <class entity-name="UserEntity" table="USER_ENTITY">
        <id name="id" type="long" column="USER_ID">
            <generator class="native"/>
        </id>

        <property name="username"
                  type="string"
                  column="USERNAME"/>

        <bag name="itemsForSale" inverse="true" cascade="all">
            <key column="USER_ID"/>
            <one-to-many entity-name="ItemEntity"/>
        </bag>

    </class>

    </hibernate-mapping>
```

There are three interesting things to observe in this mapping file.

First, you mix several class mappings in one, something we didn't recommend earlier. This time you aren't really mapping Java classes, but logical names of entities. You don't have a Java source file and an XML mapping file with the same name next to each other, so you're free to organize your metadata in any way you like.

Second, the `<class name="...">` attribute has been replaced with `<class entity-name="...">`. You also append `...Entity` to these logical names for clarity and to distinguish them from other nondynamic mappings that you made earlier with regular POJOs.

Finally, all entity associations, such as `<many-to-one>` and `<one-to-many>`, now also refer to logical entity names. The `class` attribute in the association mappings is now `entity-name`. This isn't strictly necessary—Hibernate can recognize that you're referring to a logical entity name even if you use the `class` attribute. However, it avoids confusion when you later mix several representations.

Let's see what working with dynamic entities looks like.

Working with dynamic maps
To create an instance of one of your entities, you set all attribute values in a Java Map:

```
Map user = new HashMap();
user.put("username", "johndoe");

Map item1 = new HashMap();
item1.put("description", "An item for auction");
item1.put("initialPrice", new BigDecimal(99));
item1.put("seller", user);
```

```
Map item2 = new HashMap();
item2.put("description", "Another item for auction");
item2.put("initialPrice", new BigDecimal(123));
item2.put("seller", user);

Collection itemsForSale = new ArrayList();
itemsForSale.add(item1);
itemsForSale.add(item2);
user.put("itemsForSale", itemsForSale);

session.save("UserEntity", user);
```

The first map is a `UserEntity`, and you set the username attribute as a key/value pair. The next two maps are `ItemEntitys`, and here you set the link to the `seller` of each item by putting the `user` map into the `item1` and `item2` maps. You're effectively linking maps—that's why this representation strategy is sometimes also called "representation with maps of maps."

The collection on the inverse side of the one-to-many association is initialized with an `ArrayList`, because you mapped it with bag semantics (Java doesn't have a bag implementation, but the `Collection` interface has bag semantics). Finally, the `save()` method on the `Session` is given a logical entity name and the `user` map as an input parameter.

Hibernate knows that `UserEntity` refers to the dynamically mapped entity, and that it should treat the input as a map that has to be saved accordingly. Hibernate also cascades to all elements in the `itemsForSale` collection; hence, all item maps are also made persistent. One `UserEntity` and two `ItemEntitys` are inserted into their respective tables.

FAQ *Can I map a Set in dynamic mode?* Collections based on sets don't work with dynamic entity mode. In the previous code example, imagine that `itemsForSale` was a `Set`. A `Set` checks its elements for duplicates, so when you call `add(item1)` and `add(item2)`, the `equals()` method on these objects is called. However, `item1` and `item2` are Java `Map` instances, and the `equals()` implementation of a map is based on the key sets of the map. So, because both `item1` and `item2` are maps with the same keys, they aren't distinct when added to a `Set`. Use bags or lists only if you require collections in dynamic entity mode.

Hibernate handles maps just like POJO instances. For example, making a map persistent triggers identifier assignment; each map in persistent state has an identifier attribute set with the generated value. Furthermore, persistent maps are automatically checked for any modifications inside a unit of work. To set a new price on an item, for example, you can load it and then let Hibernate do all the work:

```
Long storedItemId = (Long) item1.get("id");

Session session = getSessionFactory().openSession();
session.beginTransaction();

Map loadedItemMap = (Map) session.load("ItemEntity", storedItemId);

loadedItemMap.put("initialPrice", new BigDecimal(100));

session.getTransaction().commit();
session.close();
```

All `Session` methods that have class parameters such as `load()` also come in an overloaded variation that accepts entity names. After loading an item map, you set a new price and make the modification persistent by committing the transaction, which, by default, triggers dirty checking and flushing of the `Session`.

You can also refer to entity names in HQL queries:

```
List queriedItemMaps =
    session.createQuery("from ItemEntity where initialPrice >= :p")
            .setParameter("p", new BigDecimal(100))
            .list();
```

This query returns a collection of `ItemEntity` maps. They are in persistent state.

Let's take this one step further and mix a POJO model with dynamic maps. There are two reasons why you would want to mix a static implementation of your domain model with a dynamic map representation:

- You want to work with a static model based on POJO classes by default, but sometimes you want to represent data easily as maps of maps. This can be particularly useful in reporting, or whenever you have to implement a generic user interface that can represent various entities dynamically.

- You want to map a single POJO class of your model to several tables and then select the table at runtime by specifying a logical entity name.

You may find other use cases for mixed entity modes, but they're so rare that we want to focus on the most obvious.

First, therefore, you'll mix a static POJO model and enable dynamic map representation for some of the entities, some of the time.

Mixing dynamic and static entity modes

To enable a mixed model representation, edit your XML mapping metadata and declare a POJO class name and a logical entity name:

```
<hibernate-mapping>

<class name="model.ItemPojo"
        entity-name="ItemEntity"
```

```
        table="ITEM_ENTITY">
    ...
    <many-to-one name="seller"
                 entity-name="UserEntity"
                 column="USER_ID"/>

</class>

<class name="model.UserPojo"
       entity-name="UserEntity"
       table="USER_ENTITY">
    ...
    <bag name="itemsForSale" inverse="true" cascade="all">
        <key column="USER_ID"/>
        <one-to-many entity-name="ItemEntity"/>
    </bag>

</class>

</hibernate-mapping>
```

Obviously, you also need the two classes, `model.ItemPojo` and `model.UserPojo`, that implement the properties of these entities. You still base the many-to-one and one-to-many associations between the two entities on logical names.

Hibernate will primarily use the logical names from now on. For example, the following code does not work:

```
UserPojo user = new UserPojo();
...
ItemPojo item1 = new ItemPojo();
...
ItemPojo item2 = new ItemPojo();
...
Collection itemsForSale = new ArrayList();
...

session.save(user);
```

The preceding example creates a few objects, sets their properties, and links them, and then tries to save the objects through cascading by passing the user instance to `save()`. Hibernate inspects the type of this object and tries to figure out what entity it is, and because Hibernate now exclusively relies on logical entity names, it can't find a mapping for `model.UserPojo`. You need to tell Hibernate the logical name when working with a mixed representation mapping:

```
...
session.save("UserEntity", user);
```

Once you change this line, the previous code example works. Next, consider loading, and what is returned by queries. By default, a particular `SessionFactory` is in POJO entity mode, so the following operations return instances of model.ItemPojo:

```
Long storedItemId = item1.getId();
ItemPojo loadedItemPojo =
    (ItemPojo) session.load("ItemEntity", storedItemId);

List queriedItemPojos =
    session.createQuery("from ItemEntity where initialPrice >= :p")
            .setParameter("p", new BigDecimal(100))
            .list();
```

You can switch to a dynamic map representation either globally or temporarily, but a global switch of the entity mode has serious consequences. To switch globally, add the following to your Hibernate configuration; e.g., in hibernate.cfg.xml:

```
<property name="default_entity_mode">dynamic-map</property>
```

All Session operations now either expect or return dynamically typed maps! The previous code examples that stored, loaded, and queried POJO instances no longer work; you need to store and load maps.

It's more likely that you want to switch to another entity mode temporarily, so let's assume that you leave the SessionFactory in the default POJO mode. To switch to dynamic maps in a particular Session, you can open up a new temporary Session on top of the existing one. The following code uses such a temporary Session to store a new auction item for an existing seller:

```
Session dynamicSession = session.getSession(EntityMode.MAP);

Map seller = (Map) dynamicSession.load("UserEntity", user.getId() );

Map newItemMap = new HashMap();
newItemMap.put("description", "An item for auction");
newItemMap.put("initialPrice", new BigDecimal(99));
newItemMap.put("seller", seller);

dynamicSession.save("ItemEntity", newItemMap);

Long storedItemId = (Long) newItemMap.get("id");

Map loadedItemMap =
    (Map) dynamicSession.load("ItemEntity", storedItemId);

List queriedItemMaps =
    dynamicSession
        .createQuery("from ItemEntity where initialPrice >= :p")
        .setParameter("p", new BigDecimal(100))
        .list();
```

The temporary dynamicSession that is opened with getSession() doesn't need to be flushed or closed; it inherits the context of the original Session. You use it

only to load, query, or save data in the chosen representation, which is the Entity-
Mode.MAP in the previous example. Note that you can't link a map with a POJO
instance; the seller reference has to be a HashMap, not an instance of UserPojo.

We mentioned that another good use case for logical entity names is the mapping of one POJO to several tables, so let's look at that.

Mapping a class several times

Imagine that you have several tables with some columns in common. For example, you could have ITEM_AUCTION and ITEM_SALE tables. Usually you map each
table to an entity persistent class, ItemAuction and ItemSale respectively. With
the help of entity names, you can save work and implement a single persistent
class.

To map both tables to a single persistent class, use different entity names (and
usually different property mappings):

```
<hibernate-mapping>

<class name="model.Item"
       entity-name="ItemAuction"
       table="ITEM_AUCTION">

    <id name="id" column="ITEM_AUCTION_ID">...</id>
    <property name="description" column="DESCRIPTION"/>
    <property name="initialPrice" column="INIT_PRICE"/>

</class>

<class name="model.Item"
       entity-name="ItemSale"
       table="ITEM_SALE">

    <id name="id" column="ITEM_SALE_ID">...</id>
    <property name="description" column="DESCRIPTION"/>
    <property name="salesPrice" column="SALES_PRICE"/>

</class>

</hibernate-mapping>
```

The model.Item persistent class has all the properties you mapped: id, description, initialPrice, and salesPrice. Depending on the entity name you use at
runtime, some properties are considered persistent and others transient:

```
Item itemForAuction = new Item();
itemForAuction.setDescription("An item for auction");
itemForAuction.setInitialPrice( new BigDecimal(99) );
session.save("ItemAuction", itemForAuction);

Item itemForSale = new Item();
itemForSale.setDescription("An item for sale");
```

```
itemForSale.setSalesPrice( new BigDecimal(123) );
session.save("ItemSale", itemForSale);
```

Thanks to the logical entity name, Hibernate knows into which table it should insert the data. Depending on the entity name you use for loading and querying entities, Hibernate selects from the appropriate table.

Scenarios in which you need this functionality are rare, and you'll probably agree with us that the previous use case isn't good or common.

In the next section, we introduce the third built-in Hibernate entity mode, the representation of domain entities as XML documents.

3.4.2 Representing data in XML

XML is nothing but a text file format; it has no inherent capabilities that qualify it as a medium for data storage or data management. The XML data model is weak, its type system is complex and underpowered, its data integrity is almost completely procedural, and it introduces hierarchical data structures that were outdated decades ago. However, data in XML format is attractive to work with in Java; we have nice tools. For example, we can transform XML data with XSLT, which we consider one of the best use cases.

Hibernate has no built-in functionality to store data in an XML format; it relies on a relational representation and SQL, and the benefits of this strategy should be clear. On the other hand, Hibernate can load and present data to the application developer in an XML format. This allows you to use a sophisticated set of tools without any additional transformation steps.

Let's assume that you work in default POJO mode and that you quickly want to obtain some data represented in XML. Open a temporary `Session` with the `EntityMode.DOM4J`:

```
Session dom4jSession = session.getSession(EntityMode.DOM4J);

Element userXML =
    (Element) dom4jSession.load(User.class, storedUserId);
```

What is returned here is a dom4j `Element`, and you can use the dom4j API to read and manipulate it. For example, you can pretty-print it to your console with the following snippet:

```
try {
    OutputFormat format = OutputFormat.createPrettyPrint();
    XMLWriter writer = new XMLWriter( System.out, format);
    writer.write( userXML );
} catch (IOException ex) {
    throw new RuntimeException(ex);
}
```

If we assume that you reuse the POJO classes and data from the previous examples, you see one `User` instance and two `Item` instances (for clarity, we no longer name them `UserPojo` and `ItemPojo`):

```
<User>
  <id>1</id>
  <username>johndoe</username>
  <itemsForSale>
    <Item>
      <id>2</id>
      <initialPrice>99</initialPrice>
      <description>An item for auction</description>
      <seller>1</seller>
    </Item>
    <Item>
      <id>3</id>
      <initialPrice>123</initialPrice>
      <description>Another item for auction</description>
      <seller>1</seller>
    </Item>
  </itemsForSale>
</User>
```

Hibernate assumes default XML element names—the entity and property names. You can also see that collection elements are embedded, and that circular references are resolved through identifiers (the `<seller>` element).

You can change this default XML representation by adding `node` attributes to your Hibernate mapping metadata:

```
<hibernate-mapping>

<class name="Item" table="ITEM_ENTITY" node="item">

    <id name="id" type="long" column="ITEM_ID" node="@id">
        <generator class="native"/>
    </id>

    <property name="initialPrice"
            type="big_decimal"
            column="INIT_PRICE"
            node="item-details/@initial-price"/>

    <property name="description"
            type="string"
            column="DESCRIPTION"
            node="item-details/@description"/>

    <many-to-one name="seller"
                class="User"
                column="USER_ID"
                embed-xml="false"
```

```
                        node="@seller-id"/>

    </class>

    <class name="User" table="USERS" node="user">

        <id name="id" type="long" column="USER_ID" node="@id">
            <generator class="native"/>
        </id>

        <property name="username"
                  type="string"
                  column="USERNAME"
                  node="@username"/>

        <bag name="itemsForSale" inverse="true" cascade="all"
            embed-xml="true" node="items-for-sale">
            <key column="USER_ID"/>
            <one-to-many class="Item"/>
        </bag>

    </class>

</hibernate-mapping>
```

Each node attribute defines the XML representation:

- A node="name" attribute on a <class> mapping defines the name of the XML element for that entity.

- A node="name" attribute on any property mapping specifies that the property content should be represented as the text of an XML element of the given name.

- A node="@name" attribute on any property mapping specifies that the property content should be represented as an XML attribute value of the given name.

- A node="name/@attname" attribute on any property mapping specifies that the property content should be represented as an XML attribute value of the given name, on a child element of the given name.

The embed-xml option is used to trigger embedding or referencing of associated entity data. The updated mapping results in the following XML representation of the same data you've seen before:

```
<user id="1" username="johndoe">
  <items-for-sale>
    <item id="2" seller-id="1">
      <item-details initial-price="99"
          description="An item for auction"/>
    </item>
```

```
    <item id="3" seller-id="1">
      <item-details initial-price="123"
          description="Another item for auction"/>
    </item>
  </items-for-sale>
</user>
```

Be careful with the `embed-xml` option—you can easily create circular references that result in an endless loop!

Finally, data in an XML representation is transactional and persistent, so you can modify queried XML elements and let Hibernate take care of updating the underlying tables:

```
Element itemXML =
    (Element) dom4jSession.get(Item.class, storedItemId);

itemXML.element("item-details")
        .attribute("initial-price")
        .setValue("100");

session.flush(); // Hibernate executes UPDATEs


Element userXML =
    (Element) dom4jSession.get(User.class, storedUserId);

Element newItem = DocumentHelper.createElement("item");
Element newItemDetails = newItem.addElement("item-details");
newItem.addAttribute("seller-id",
                    userXml.attribute("id").getValue() );
newItemDetails.addAttribute("initial-price", "123");
newItemDetails.addAttribute("description", "A third item");

dom4jSession.save(Item.class.getName(), newItem);

dom4jSession.flush(); // Hibernate executes INSERTs
```

There is no limit to what you can do with the XML that is returned by Hibernate. You can display, export, and transform it in any way you like. See the dom4j documentation for more information.

Finally, note that you can use all three built-in entity modes simultaneously, if you like. You can map a static POJO implementation of your domain model, switch to dynamic maps for your generic user interface, and export data into XML. Or, you can write an application that doesn't have any domain classes, only dynamic maps and XML. We have to warn you, though, that prototyping in the software industry often means that customers end up with the prototype that nobody wanted to throw away—would you buy a prototype car? We highly recommend that you rely on static domain models if you want to create a maintainable system.

We won't consider dynamic models or XML representation again in this book. Instead, we'll focus on static persistent classes and how they are mapped.

3.5 Summary

In this chapter, we focused on the design and implementation of a rich domain model in Java.

You now understand that persistent classes in a domain model should to be free of crosscutting concerns, such as transactions and security. Even persistence-related concerns should not leak into the domain model implementation. You also know how important transparent persistence is if you want to execute and test your business objects independently and easily.

You have learned the best practices and requirements for the POJO and JPA entity programming model, and what concepts they have in common with the old JavaBean specification. We had a closer look at the implementation of persistent classes, and how attributes and relationships are best represented.

To be prepared for the next part of the book, and to learn all the object/relational mapping options, you needed to make an educated decision to use either XML mapping files or JDK 5.0 annotations, or possibly a combination of both. You're now ready to write more complex mappings in both formats.

For convenience, table 3.1 summarizes the differences between Hibernate and Java Persistence related to concepts discussed in this chapter.

Table 3.1 Hibernate and JPA comparison chart for chapter 3

Hibernate Core	Java Persistence and EJB 3.0
Persistent classes require a no-argument constructor with public or protected visibility if proxy-based lazy loading is used.	The JPA specification mandates a no-argument constructor with public or protected visibility for all entity classes.
Persistent collections must be typed to interfaces. Hibernate supports all JDK interfaces.	Persistent collections must be typed to interfaces. Only a subset of all interfaces (no sorted collections, for example) is considered fully portable.
Persistent properties can be accessed through fields or accessor methods at runtime, or a completely customizable strategy can be applied.	Persistent properties of an entity class are accessed through fields or accessor methods, but not both if full portability is required.

Table 3.1   Hibernate and JPA comparison chart for chapter 3 *(continued)*

Hibernate Core	Java Persistence and EJB 3.0
The XML metadata format supports all possible Hibernate mapping options.	JPA annotations cover all basic and most advanced mapping options. Hibernate Annotations are required for exotic mappings and tuning.
XML mapping metadata can be defined globally, and XML placeholders are used to keep metadata free from dependencies.	Global metadata is only fully portable if declared in the standard orm.xml metadata file.

In the next part of the book, we show you all possible basic and some advanced mapping techniques, for classes, properties, inheritance, collections, and associations. You'll learn how to solve the structural object/relational mismatch.

Part 2

Mapping concepts and strategies

This part is all about actual object/relational mapping, from classes and properties to tables and columns. Chapter 4 starts with regular class and property mappings, and explains how you can map fine-grained Java domain models. Next, in chapter 5, you'll see how to map more complex class inheritance hierarchies and how to extend Hibernate's functionality with the powerful custom mapping type system. In chapters 6 and 7, we show you how to map Java collections and associations between classes, with many sophisticated examples. Finally, you'll find chapter 8 most interesting if you need to introduce Hibernate in an existing applications, or if you have to work with legacy database schemas and hand-written SQL. We also talk about customized SQL DDL for schema generation in this chapter.

After reading this part of the book, you'll be ready to create even the most complex mappings quickly and with the right strategy. You'll understand how the problem of inheritance mapping can be solved, and how collections and associations can be mapped. You'll also be able to tune and customize Hibernate for integration with any existing database schema or application.

Mapping
persistent classes

This chapter covers

- Understanding the entity and value-type concept
- Mapping classes with XML and annotations
- Fine-grained property and component mappings

157

This chapter presents the fundamental mapping options, explaining how classes and properties are mapped to tables and columns. We show and discuss how you can handle database identity and primary keys, and how various other metadata settings can be used to customize how Hibernate loads and stores objects. All mapping examples are done in Hibernate's native XML format, and with JPA annotations and XML descriptors, side by side. We also look closely at the mapping of fine-grained domain models, and at how properties and embedded components are mapped.

First, though, we define the essential distinction between entities and value types, and explain how you should approach the object/relational mapping of your domain model.

4.1 Understanding entities and value types

Entities are persistent types that represent first-class business objects (the term object is used here in its natural sense). In other words, some of the classes and types you have to deal with in an application are more important, which naturally makes others less important. You probably agree that in CaveatEmptor, Item is a more important class than String. User is probably more important than Address. What makes something important? Let's look at the issue from a different perspective.

4.1.1 Fine-grained domain models

A major objective of Hibernate is support for fine-grained domain models, which we isolated as the most important requirement for a rich domain model. It's one reason why we work with POJOs. In crude terms, fine-grained means more classes than tables.

For example, a user may have both a billing address and a home address. In the database, you may have a single USERS table with the columns BILLING_STREET, BILLING_CITY, and BILLING_ZIPCODE, along with HOME_STREET, HOME_CITY, and HOME_ZIPCODE. (Remember the problem of SQL types we discussed in chapter 1?)

In the domain model, you could use the same approach, representing the two addresses as six string-valued properties of the User class. But it's much better to model this using an Address class, where User has the billingAddress and homeAddress properties, thus using three classes for one table.

This domain model achieves improved cohesion and greater code reuse, and it's more understandable than SQL systems with inflexible type systems. In the past, many ORM solutions didn't provide especially good support for this kind of mapping.

Hibernate emphasizes the usefulness of fine-grained classes for implementing type safety and behavior. For example, many people model an email address as a string-valued property of User. A more sophisticated approach is to define an EmailAddress class, which adds higher-level semantics and behavior—it may provide a sendEmail() method.

This granularity problem leads us to a distinction of central importance in ORM. In Java, all classes are of equal standing—all objects have their own identity and lifecycle.

Let's walk through an example.

4.1.2 *Defining the concept*

Two people live in the same apartment, and they both register user accounts in CaveatEmptor. Naturally, each account is represented by one instance of User, so you have two entity instances. In the CaveatEmptor model, the User class has a homeAddress association with the Address class. Do both User instances have a runtime reference to the same Address instance or does each User instance have a reference to its own Address? If Address is supposed to support shared runtime references, it's an entity type. If not, it's likely a value type and hence is dependent on a single reference by an owning entity instance, which also provides identity.

We advocate a design with more classes than tables: One row represents multiple instances. Because database identity is implemented by primary key value, some persistent objects won't have their own identity. In effect, the persistence mechanism implements pass-by-value semantics for some classes! One of the objects represented in the row has its own identity, and others depend on that. In the previous example, the columns in the USERS table that contain address information are dependent on the identifier of the user, the primary key of the table. An instance of Address is dependent on an instance of User.

Hibernate makes the following essential distinction:

- An object of entity type has its own database identity (primary key value). An object reference to an entity instance is persisted as a reference in the database (a foreign key value). An entity has its own lifecycle; it may exist independently of any other entity. Examples in CaveatEmptor are User, Item, and Category.

- An object of value type has no database identity; it belongs to an entity instance and its persistent state is embedded in the table row of the owning entity. Value types don't have identifiers or identifier properties. The lifespan of a value type instance is bounded by the lifespan of the owning entity instance. A value type doesn't support shared references: If two users live in the same apartment, they each have a reference to their own homeAddress instance. The most obvious value types are classes like Strings and Integers, but all JDK classes are considered value types. User-defined classes can also be mapped as value types; for example, CaveatEmptor has Address and MonetaryAmount.

Identification of entities and value types in your domain model isn't an ad hoc task but follows a certain procedure.

4.1.3 *Identifying entities and value types*

You may find it helpful to add stereotype information to your UML class diagrams so you can immediately see and distinguish entities and value types. This practice also forces you to think about this distinction for all your classes, which is a first step to an optimal mapping and well-performing persistence layer. See figure 4.1 for an example.

The Item and User classes are obvious entities. They each have their own identity, their instances have references from many other instances (shared references), and they have independent lifecycles.

Identifying the Address as a value type is also easy: A particular Address instance is referenced by only a single User instance. You know this because the association has been created as a composition, where the User instance has been made fully responsible for the lifecycle of the referenced Address instance. Therefore, Address objects can't be referenced by anyone else and don't need their own identity.

The Bid class is a problem. In object-oriented modeling, you express a composition (the association between Item and Bid with the diamond), and an Item manages the lifecycles of all the Bid objects to which it has a reference (it's a collection of references). This seems reasonable, because the bids would be useless if

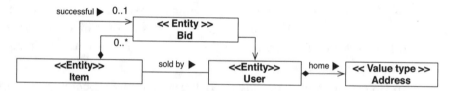

Figure 4.1 Stereotypes for entities and value types have been added to the diagram.

an Item no longer existed. But at the same time, there is another association to Bid: An Item may hold a reference to its successfulBid. The successful bid must also be one of the bids referenced by the collection, but this isn't expressed in the UML. In any case, you have to deal with possible shared references to Bid instances, so the Bid class needs to be an entity. It has a dependent lifecycle, but it must have its own identity to support shared references.

You'll often find this kind of mixed behavior; however, your first reaction should be to make everything a value-typed class and promote it to an entity only when absolutely necessary. Try to simplify your associations: Collections, for example, sometimes add complexity without offering any advantages. Instead of mapping a persistent collection of Bid references, you can write a query to obtain all the bids for an Item (we'll come back to this point again in chapter 7).

As the next step, take your domain model diagram and implement POJOs for all entities and value types. You have to take care of three things:

- *Shared references*—Write your POJO classes in a way that avoids shared references to value type instances. For example, make sure an Address object can be referenced by only one User. For example, make it immutable and enforce the relationship with the Address constructor.

- *Lifecycle dependencies*—As discussed, the lifecycle of a value-type instance is bound to that of its owning entity instance. If a User object is deleted, its Address dependent object(s) have to be deleted as well. There is no notion or keyword for this in Java, but your application workflow and user interface must be designed to respect and expect lifecycle dependencies. Persistence metadata includes the cascading rules for all dependencies.

- *Identity*—Entity classes need an identifier property in almost all cases. User-defined value-type classes (and JDK classes) don't have an identifier property, because instances are identified through the owning entity.

We'll come back to class associations and lifecycle rules when we discuss more advanced mappings later in the book. However, object identity is a subject you have to understand at this point.

4.2 Mapping entities with identity

It's vital to understand the difference between object identity and object equality before we discuss terms like database identity and the way Hibernate manages identity. Next, we explore how object identity and equality relate to database (primary key) identity.

4.2.1 *Understanding Java identity and equality*

Java developers understand the difference between Java object identity and equality. Object identity, ==, is a notion defined by the Java virtual machine. Two object references are identical if they point to the same memory location.

On the other hand, object equality is a notion defined by classes that implement the equals() method, sometimes also referred to as equivalence. Equivalence means that two different (nonidentical) objects have the same value. Two different instances of String are equal if they represent the same sequence of characters, even though they each have their own location in the memory space of the virtual machine. (If you're a Java guru, we acknowledge that String is a special case. Assume we used a different class to make the same point.)

Persistence complicates this picture. With object/relational persistence, a persistent object is an in-memory representation of a particular row of a database table. Along with Java identity (memory location) and object equality, you pick up database identity (which is the location in the persistent data store). You now have three methods for identifying objects:

- Objects are identical if they occupy the same memory location in the JVM. This can be checked by using the == operator. This concept is known as object identity.

- Objects are equal if they have the same value, as defined by the equals(Object o) method. Classes that don't explicitly override this method inherit the implementation defined by java.lang.Object, which compares object identity. This concept is known as equality.

- Objects stored in a relational database are identical if they represent the same row or, equivalently, if they share the same table and primary key value. This concept is known as database identity.

We now need to look at how database identity relates to object identity in Hibernate, and how database identity is expressed in the mapping metadata.

4.2.2 *Handling database identity*

Hibernate exposes database identity to the application in two ways:

- The value of the identifier property of a persistent instance
- The value returned by Session.getIdentifier(Object entity)

Adding an identifier property to entities

The identifier property is special—its value is the primary key value of the database row represented by the persistent instance. We don't usually show the identifier property in the domain model diagrams. In the examples, the identifier property is always named id. If myCategory is an instance of Category, calling myCategory.getId() returns the primary key value of the row represented by myCategory in the database.

Let's implement an identifier property for the Category class:

```
public class Category {
    private Long id;
    ...
    public Long getId() {
        return this.id;
    }

    private void setId(Long id) {
        this.id = id;
    }
    ...
}
```

Should you make the accessor methods for the identifier property private scope or public? Well, database identifiers are often used by the application as a convenient handle to a particular instance, even outside the persistence layer. For example, it's common for web applications to display the results of a search screen to the user as a list of summary information. When the user selects a particular element, the application may need to retrieve the selected object, and it's common to use a lookup by identifier for this purpose—you've probably already used identifiers this way, even in applications that rely on JDBC. It's usually appropriate to fully expose the database identity with a public identifier property accessor.

On the other hand, you usually declare the setId() method private and let Hibernate generate and set the identifier value. Or, you map it with direct field access and implement only a getter method. (The exception to this rule is classes with natural keys, where the value of the identifier is assigned by the application before the object is made persistent instead of being generated by Hibernate. We discuss natural keys in chapter 8.) Hibernate doesn't allow you to change the identifier value of a persistent instance after it's first assigned. A primary key value never changes—otherwise the attribute wouldn't be a suitable primary key candidate!

The Java type of the identifier property, java.lang.Long in the previous example, depends on the primary key type of the CATEGORY table and how it's mapped in Hibernate metadata.

Mapping the identifier property

A regular (noncomposite) identifier property is mapped in Hibernate XML files with the <id> element:

```
<class name="Category" table="CATEGORY">
<id name="id" column="CATEGORY_ID" type="long">
    <generator class="native"/>
</id>


...
</class>
```

The identifier property is mapped to the primary key column CATEGORY_ID of the table CATEGORY. The Hibernate type for this property is long, which maps to a BIGINT column type in most databases and which has also been chosen to match the type of the identity value produced by the native identifier generator. (We discuss identifier generation strategies in the next section.)

For a JPA entity class, you use annotations in the Java source code to map the identifier property:

```
@Entity
@Table(name="CATEGORY")
public class Category {
    private Long id;
    ...

    @Id
    @GeneratedValue(strategy = GenerationType.AUTO)
    @Column(name = "CATEGORY_ID")
    public Long getId() {
        return this.id;
    }

    private void setId(Long id) {
        this.id = id;
    }
    ...
}
```

The @Id annotation on the getter method marks it as the identifier property, and @GeneratedValue with the GenerationType.AUTO option translates into a native identifier generation strategy, like the native option in XML Hibernate mappings. Note that if you don't define a strategy, the default is also Generation-

Type.AUTO, so you could have omitted this attribute altogether. You also specify a database column—otherwise Hibernate would use the property name. The mapping type is implied by the Java property type, java.lang.Long.

Of course, you can also use direct field access for all properties, including the database identifier:

```
@Entity
@Table(name="CATEGORY")
public class Category {

    @Id @GeneratedValue
    @Column(name = "CATEGORY_ID")
    private Long id;
    ...

    public Long getId() {
        return this.id;
    }
    ...

}
```

Mapping annotations are placed on the field declaration when direct field access is enabled, as defined by the standard.

Whether field or property access is enabled for an entity depends on the position of the mandatory @Id annotation. In the preceding example, it's present on a field, so all attributes of the class are accessed by Hibernate through fields. The example before that, annotated on the getId() method, enables access to all attributes through getter and setter methods.

Alternatively, you can use JPA XML descriptors to create your identifier mapping:

```
<entity class="auction.model.Category" access="FIELD">
    <table name="CATEGORY"/>
    <attributes>
        <id name="id">
            <generated-value strategy="AUTO"/>
        </id>
        ...
    </attributes>
</entity>
```

In addition to operations for testing Java object identity, (a == b), and object equality, (a.equals(b)), you may now use a.getId().equals(b.getId()) to test database identity. What do these notions have in common? In what situations do they all return true? The time when all are true is called the scope of guaranteed object identity; and we'll come back to this subject in chapter 9, section 9.2, "Object identity and equality."

Using database identifiers in Hibernate is easy and straightforward. Choosing a good primary key (and key-generation strategy) may be more difficult. We discuss this issue next.

4.2.3 Database primary keys

Hibernate needs to know your preferred strategy for generating primary keys. First, though, let's define primary key.

Selecting a primary key

The candidate key is a column or set of columns that could be used to identify a particular row in a table. To become a primary key, a candidate key must satisfy the following properties:

- Its value (for any column of the candidate key) is never null.
- Each row has a unique value.
- The value of a particular row never changes.

If a table has only one identifying attribute, it's, by definition, the primary key. However, several columns or combinations of columns may satisfy these properties for a particular table; you choose between candidate keys to decide the best primary key for the table. Candidate keys not chosen as the primary key should be declared as unique keys in the database.

Many legacy SQL data models use natural primary keys. A natural key is a key with business meaning: an attribute or combination of attributes that is unique by virtue of its business semantics. Examples of natural keys are the U.S. Social Security Number and Australian Tax File Number. Distinguishing natural keys is simple: If a candidate key attribute has meaning outside the database context, it's a natural key, whether or not it's automatically generated. Think about the application users: If they refer to a key attribute when talking about and working with the application, it's a natural key.

Experience has shown that natural keys almost always cause problems in the long run. A good primary key must be unique, constant, and required (never null or unknown). Few entity attributes satisfy these requirements, and some that do can't be efficiently indexed by SQL databases (although this is an implementation detail and shouldn't be the primary motivation for or against a particular key). In addition, you should make certain that a candidate key definition can never change throughout the lifetime of the database before making it a primary key. Changing the value (or even definition) of a primary key, and all foreign keys that refer to it, is a frustrating task. Furthermore, natural candidate keys can often be found only by combining several columns in a composite natural key. These composite keys, although certainly appropriate for some relations (like a link table in a many-to-many relationship), usually make maintenance, ad-hoc queries, and schema evolution much more difficult.

For these reasons, we strongly recommend that you consider synthetic identifiers, also called surrogate keys. Surrogate keys have no business meaning—they're unique values generated by the database or application. Application users ideally don't see or refer to these key values; they're part of the system internals. Introducing a surrogate key column is also appropriate in a common situation: If there are no candidate keys, a table is by definition not a relation as defined by the relational model—it permits duplicate rows—and so you have to add a surrogate key column. There are a number of well-known approaches to generating surrogate key values.

Selecting a key generator

Hibernate has several built-in identifier-generation strategies. We list the most useful options in table 4.1.

Table 4.1 Hibernate's built-in identifier-generator modules

Generator name	JPA GenerationType	Options	Description
native	AUTO	–	The native identity generator picks other identity generators like identity, sequence, or hilo, depending on the capabilities of the underlying database. Use this generator to keep your mapping metadata portable to different database management systems.
identity	IDENTITY	–	This generator supports identity columns in DB2, MySQL, MS SQL Server, Sybase, and HypersonicSQL. The returned identifier is of type long, short, or int.

Table 4.1 Hibernate's built-in identifier-generator modules *(continued)*

Generator name	JPA GenerationType	Options	Description
`sequence`	SEQUENCE	`sequence, parameters`	This generator creates a sequence in DB2, PostgreSQL, Oracle, SAP DB, or Mckoi; or a generator in InterBase is used. The returned identifier is of type `long`, `short`, or `int`. Use the `sequence` option to define a catalog name for the sequence (`hibernate_ sequence` is the default) and `parameters` if you need additional settings creating a sequence to be added to the DDL.
`increment`	(Not available)	–	At Hibernate startup, this generator reads the maximum (numeric) primary key column value of the table and increments the value by one each time a new row is inserted. The generated identifier is of type `long`, `short`, or `int`. This generator is especially efficient if the single-server Hibernate application has exclusive access to the database but should not be used in any other scenario.
`hilo`	(Not available)	`table, column, max_lo`	A high/low algorithm is an efficient way to generate identifiers of type `long`, given a table and column (by default `hibernate_unique_key` and `next`, respectively) as a source of high values. The high/low algorithm generates identifiers that are unique only for a particular database. High values are retrieved from a global source and are made unique by adding a local low value. This algorithm avoids congestion when a single source for identifier values has to be accessed for many inserts. See "Data Modeling 101" (Ambler, 2002) for more information about the high/low approach to unique identifiers. This generator needs to use a separate database connection from time to time to retrieve high values, so it isn't supported with user-supplied database connections. In other words, don't use it with `sessionFactory.openSession(myConnection)`. The `max_lo` option defines how many low values are added until a new high value is fetched. Only settings greater than 1 are sensible; the default is 32767 (`Short.MAX_VALUE`).

Table 4.1 Hibernate's built-in identifier-generator modules *(continued)*

Generator name	JPA GenerationType	Options	Description
`seqhilo`	(Not available)	`sequence, parameters, max_lo`	This generator works like the regular `hilo` generator, except it uses a named database sequence to generate high values.
(JPA only)	TABLE	`table`, `catalog`, `schema`, `pkColumnName`, `valueColumnNam e`, `pkColumnValue`, `allocationSize`	Much like Hibernate's `hilo` strategy, TABLE relies on a database table that holds the last-generated integer primary key value, and each generator is mapped to one row in this table. Each row has two columns: `pkColumnName` and `valueColumnName`. The `pkColumn- Value` assigns each row to a particular generator, and the value column holds the last retrieved primary key. The persistence provider allocates up to `allocationSize` integers in each turn.
`uuid.hex`	(Not available)	`separator`	This generator is a 128-bit UUID (an algorithm that generates identifiers of type `string`, unique within a network). The IP address is used in combination with a unique timestamp. The UUID is encoded as a string of hexadecimal digits of length 32, with an optional `separator` string between each component of the UUID representation. Use this generator strategy only if you need globally unique identifiers, such as when you have to merge two databases regularly.
`guid`	(Not available)	-	This generator provides a database-generated globally unique identifier string on MySQL and SQL Server.
`select`	(Not available)	`key`	This generator retrieves a primary key assigned by a database trigger by selecting the row by some unique key and retrieving the primary key value. An additional unique candidate key column is required for this strategy, and the `key` option has to be set to the name of the unique key column.

Some of the built-in identifier generators can be configured with options. In a native Hibernate XML mapping, you define options as pairs of keys and values:

```
<id column="MY_ID">
    <generator class="sequence">
        <parameter name="sequence">MY_SEQUENCE</parameter>
        <parameter name="parameters">
            INCREMENT BY 1 START WITH 1
        </parameter>
    </generator>
</id>
```

You can use Hibernate identifier generators with annotations, even if no direct annotation is available:

```
@Entity
@org.hibernate.annotations.GenericGenerator(
    name = "hibernate-uuid",
    strategy = "uuid"
)
class name MyEntity {

    @Id
    @GeneratedValue(generator = "hibernate-uuid")
    @Column(name = "MY_ID")
    String id;
}
```

The @GenericGenerator Hibernate extension can be used to give a Hibernate identifier generator a name, in this case hibernate-uuid. This name is then referenced by the standardized generator attribute.

This declaration of a generator and its assignment by name also must be applied for sequence- or table-based identifier generation with annotations. Imagine that you want to use a customized sequence generator in all your entity classes. Because this identifier generator has to be global, it's declared in orm.xml:

```
<sequence-generator name="mySequenceGenerator"
    sequence-name="MY_SEQUENCE"
    initial-value="123"
    allocation-size="20"/>
```

This declares that a database sequence named MY_SEQUENCE with an initial value of 123 can be used as a source for database identifier generation, and that the persistence engine should obtain 20 values every time it needs identifiers. (Note, though, that Hibernate Annotations, at the time of writing, ignores the initial-Value setting.)

To apply this identifier generator for a particular entity, use its name:

```
@Entity
class name MyEntity {

    @Id @GeneratedValue(generator = "mySequenceGenerator")
    String id;
}
```

If you declared another generator with the same name at the entity level, before the `class` keyword, it would override the global identifier generator. The same approach can be used to declare and apply a `@TableGenerator`.

You aren't limited to the built-in strategies; you can create your own identifier generator by implementing Hibernate's `IdentifierGenerator` interface. As always, it's a good strategy to look at the Hibernate source code of the existing identifier generators for inspiration.

It's even possible to mix identifier generators for persistent classes in a single domain model, but for nonlegacy data we recommend using the same identifier generation strategy for all entities.

For legacy data and application-assigned identifiers, the picture is more complicated. In this case, we're often stuck with natural keys and especially composite keys. A composite key is a natural key that is composed of multiple table columns. Because composite identifiers can be a bit more difficult to work with and often only appear on legacy schemas, we only discuss them in the context of chapter 8, section 8.1, "Integrating legacy databases."

We assume from now on that you've added identifier properties to the entity classes of your domain model, and that after you completed the basic mapping of each entity and its identifier property, you continued to map value-typed properties of the entities. However, some special options can simplify or enhance your class mappings.

4.3 Class mapping options

If you check the `<hibernate-mapping>` and `<class>` elements in the DTD (or the reference documentation), you'll find a few options we haven't discussed so far:

- Dynamic generation of CRUD SQL statements
- Entity mutability control
- Naming of entities for querying
- Mapping package names
- Quoting keywords and reserved database identifiers
- Implementing database naming conventions

4.3.1 Dynamic SQL generation

By default, Hibernate creates SQL statements for each persistent class on startup. These statements are simple create, read, update, and delete operations for reading a single row, deleting a row, and so on.

How can Hibernate create an UPDATE statement on startup? After all, the columns to be updated aren't known at this time. The answer is that the generated SQL statement updates all columns, and if the value of a particular column isn't modified, the statement sets it to its old value.

In some situations, such as a legacy table with hundreds of columns where the SQL statements will be large for even the simplest operations (say, only one column needs updating), you have to turn off this startup SQL generation and switch to dynamic statements generated at runtime. An extremely large number of entities can also impact startup time, because Hibernate has to generate all SQL statements for CRUD upfront. Memory consumption for this query statement cache will also be high if a dozen statements must be cached for thousands of entities (this isn't an issue, usually).

Two attributes for disabling CRUD SQL generation on startup are available on the <class> mapping element:

```
<class name="Item"
    dynamic-insert="true"
    dynamic-update="true">
...
</class>
```

The dynamic-insert attribute tells Hibernate whether to include null property values in an SQL INSERT, and the dynamic-update attribute tells Hibernate whether to include unmodified properties in the SQL UPDATE.

If you're using JDK 5.0 annotation mappings, you need a native Hibernate annotation to enable dynamic SQL generation:

```
@Entity
@org.hibernate.annotations.Entity(
    dynamicInsert = true, dynamicUpdate = true
)
public class Item { ...
```

The second @Entity annotation from the Hibernate package extends the JPA annotation with additional options, including dynamicInsert and dynamicUpdate.

Sometimes you can avoid generating any UPDATE statement, if the persistent class is mapped immutable.

4.3.2 *Making an entity immutable*

Instances of a particular class may be immutable. For example, in CaveatEmptor, a Bid made for an item is immutable. Hence, no UPDATE statement ever needs to be executed on the BID table. Hibernate can also make a few other optimizations, such as avoiding dirty checking, if you map an immutable class with the mutable attribute set to false:

```
<hibernate-mapping default-access="field">
    <class name="Bid" mutable="false">
    ...
    </class>
</hibernate-mapping>
```

A POJO is immutable if no public setter methods for any properties of the class are exposed—all values are set in the constructor. Instead of private setter methods, you often prefer direct field access by Hibernate for immutable persistent classes, so you don't have to write useless accessor methods. You can map an immutable entity using annotations:

```
@Entity
@org.hibernate.annotations.Entity(mutable = false)
@org.hibernate.annotations.AccessType("field")
public class Bid { ...
```

Again, the native Hibernate @Entity annotation extends the JPA annotation with additional options. We have also shown the Hibernate extension annotation @AccessType here—this is an annotation you'll rarely use. As explained earlier, the default access strategy for a particular entity class is implicit from the position of the mandatory @Id property. However, you can use @AccessType to force a more fine-grained strategy; it can be placed on class declarations (as in the preceding example) or even on particular fields or accessor methods.

Let's have a quick look at another issue, the naming of entities for queries.

4.3.3 *Naming entities for querying*

By default, all class names are automatically "imported" into the namespace of the Hibernate query language, HQL. In other words, you can use the short class names without a package prefix in HQL, which is convenient. However, this auto-import can be turned off if two classes with the same name exist for a given SessionFactory, maybe in different packages of the domain model.

If such a conflict exists, and you don't change the default settings, Hibernate won't know which class you're referring to in HQL. You can turn off auto-import of names into the HQL namespace for particular mapping files with the `auto-import="false"` setting on the `<hibernate-mapping>` root element.

Entity names can also be imported explicitly into the HQL namespace. You can even import classes and interfaces that aren't explicitly mapped, so a short name can be used in polymorphic HQL queries:

```
<hibernate-mapping>
    <import class="auction.model.Auditable" rename="IAuditable"/>
</hibernate-mapping>
```

You can now use an HQL query such as `from IAuditable` to retrieve all persistent instances of classes that implement the `auction.model.Auditable` interface. (Don't worry if you don't know whether this feature is relevant to you at this point; we'll get back to queries later in the book.) Note that the `<import>` element, like all other immediate child elements of `<hibernate-mapping>`, is an application-wide declaration, so you don't have to (and can't) duplicate this in other mapping files.

With annotations, you can give an entity an explicit name, if the short name would result in a collision in the JPA QL or HQL namespace:

```
@Entity(name="AuctionItem")
public class Item { ... }
```

Now let's consider another aspect of naming: the declaration of packages.

4.3.4 Declaring a package name

All the persistent classes of the CaveatEmptor application are declared in the Java package `auction.model`. However, you don't want to repeat the full package name whenever this or any other class is named in an association, subclass, or component mapping. Instead, specify a `package` attribute:

```
<hibernate-mapping package="auction.model">
    <classname="Item" table="ITEM">
        ...
    </class>
</hibernate-mapping>
```

Now all unqualified class names that appear in this mapping document will be prefixed with the declared package name. We assume this setting in all mapping examples in this book and use unqualified names for CaveatEmptor model classes.

Names of classes and tables must be selected carefully. However, a name you've chosen may be reserved by the SQL database system, so the name has to be quoted.

4.3.5 *Quoting SQL identifiers*

By default, Hibernate doesn't quote table and column names in the generated SQL. This makes the SQL slightly more readable, and it also allows you to take advantage of the fact that most SQL databases are case insensitive when comparing unquoted identifiers. From time to time, especially in legacy databases, you encounter identifiers with strange characters or whitespace, or you wish to force case sensitivity. Or, if you rely on Hibernate's defaults, a class or property name in Java may be automatically translated to a table or column name that isn't allowed in your database management system. For example, the `User` class is mapped to a `USER` table, which is usually a reserved keyword in SQL databases. Hibernate doesn't know the SQL keywords of any DBMS product, so the database system throws an exception at startup or runtime.

If you quote a table or column name with backticks in the mapping document, Hibernate always quotes this identifier in the generated SQL. The following property declaration forces Hibernate to generate SQL with the quoted column name `"DESCRIPTION"`. Hibernate also knows that Microsoft SQL Server needs the variation `[DESCRIPTION]` and that MySQL requires `` `DESCRIPTION` ``.

```
<property name="description"
          column="`DESCRIPTION`"/>
```

There is no way, apart from quoting all table and column names in backticks, to force Hibernate to use quoted identifiers everywhere. You should consider renaming tables or columns with reserved keyword names whenever possible. Quoting with backticks works with annotation mappings, but it's an implementation detail of Hibernate and not part of the JPA specification.

4.3.6 *Implementing naming conventions*

We often encounter organizations with strict conventions for database table and column names. Hibernate provides a feature that allows you to enforce naming standards automatically.

Suppose that all table names in CaveatEmptor should follow the pattern `CE_<table name>`. One solution is to manually specify a `table` attribute on all `<class>` and collection elements in the mapping files. However, this approach is time-consuming and easily forgotten. Instead, you can implement Hibernate's `NamingStrategy` interface, as in listing 4.1.

Listing 4.1 NamingStrategy implementation

```java
public class CENamingStrategy extends ImprovedNamingStrategy {

    public String classToTableName(String className) {
        return StringHelper.unqualify(className);
    }

    public String propertyToColumnName(String propertyName) {
        return propertyName;
    }

    public String tableName(String tableName) {
        return "CE_" + tableName;
    }

    public String columnName(String columnName) {
        return columnName;
    }

    public String propertyToTableName(String className,
                                      String propertyName) {
        return "CE_"
                    + classToTableName(className)
                    + '_'
                    + propertyToColumnName(propertyName);
    }
}
```

You extend the `ImprovedNamingStrategy`, which provides default implementations for all methods of `NamingStrategy` you don't want to implement from scratch (look at the API documentation and source). The `classToTableName()` method is called only if a `<class>` mapping doesn't specify an explicit `table` name. The `propertyToColumnName()` method is called if a property has no explicit `column` name. The `tableName()` and `columnName()` methods are called when an explicit name is declared.

If you enable this `CENamingStrategy`, the class mapping declaration

```xml
<class name="BankAccount">
```

results in `CE_BANKACCOUNT` as the name of the table.

However, if a table name is specified, like this,

```xml
<class name="BankAccount" table="BANK_ACCOUNT">
```

then `CE_BANK_ACCOUNT` is the name of the table. In this case, `BANK_ACCOUNT` is passed to the `tableName()` method.

The best feature of the `NamingStrategy` interface is the potential for dynamic behavior. To activate a specific naming strategy, you can pass an instance to the Hibernate `Configuration` at startup:

```
Configuration cfg = new Configuration();
cfg.setNamingStrategy( new CENamingStrategy() );
SessionFactory sessionFactory sf =
                cfg.configure().buildSessionFactory();
```

This allows you to have multiple `SessionFactory` instances based on the same mapping documents, each using a different `NamingStrategy`. This is extremely useful in a multiclient installation, where unique table names (but the same data model) are required for each client. However, a better way to handle this kind of requirement is to use an SQL schema (a kind of namespace), as already discussed in chapter 3, section 3.3.4, "Handling global metadata."

You can set a naming strategy implementation in Java Persistence in your persistence.xml file with the `hibernate.ejb.naming_strategy` option.

Now that we have covered the concepts and most important mappings for entities, let's map value types.

4.4   Fine-grained models and mappings

After spending the first half of this chapter almost exclusively on entities and the respective basic persistent class-mapping options, we'll now focus on value types in their various forms. Two different kinds come to mind immediately: value-typed classes that came with the JDK, such as `String` or primitives, and value-typed classes defined by the application developer, such as `Address` and `MonetaryAmount`.

First, you map persistent class properties that use JDK types and learn the basic mapping elements and attributes. Then you attack custom value-typed classes and map them as embeddable components.

4.4.1   Mapping basic properties

If you map a persistent class, no matter whether it's an entity or a value type, all persistent properties have to be mapped explicitly in the XML mapping file. On the other hand, if a class is mapped with annotations, all of its properties are considered persistent by default. You can mark properties with the `@javax.persistence.Transient` annotation to exclude them, or use the `transient` Java keyword (which usually only excludes fields for Java serialization).

In a JPA XML descriptor, you can exclude a particular field or property:

```
<entity class="auction.model.User" access="FIELD">
    <attributes>
        ...
        <transient name="age"/>
    </attributes>
</entity>
```

A typical Hibernate property mapping defines a POJO's property name, a database column name, and the name of a Hibernate type, and it's often possible to omit the type. So, if `description` is a property of (Java) type `java.lang.String`, Hibernate uses the Hibernate type `string` by default (we come back to the Hibernate type system in the next chapter).

Hibernate uses reflection to determine the Java type of the property. Thus, the following mappings are equivalent:

```
<property name="description" column="DESCRIPTION" type="string"/>
<property name="description" column="DESCRIPTION"/>
```

It's even possible to omit the column name if it's the same as the property name, ignoring case. (This is one of the sensible defaults we mentioned earlier.)

For some more unusual cases, which you'll see more about later, you may need to use a `<column>` element instead of the `column` attribute in your XML mapping. The `<column>` element provides more flexibility: It has more optional attributes and may appear more than once. (A single property can map to more than one column, a technique we discuss in the next chapter.) The following two property mappings are equivalent:

```
<property name="description" column="DESCRIPTION" type="string"/>
<property name="description" type="string">
    <column name="DESCRIPTION"/>
</property>
```

The `<property>` element (and especially the `<column>` element) also defines certain attributes that apply mainly to automatic database schema generation. If you aren't using the `hbm2ddl` tool (see chapter 2, section 2.1.4, "Running and testing the application") to generate the database schema, you may safely omit these. However, it's preferable to include at least the `not-null` attribute, because Hibernate can then report illegal null property values without going to the database:

```
<property name="initialPrice" column="INITIAL_PRICE" not-null="true"/>
```

JPA is based on a configuration by exception model, so you could rely on defaults. If a property of a persistent class isn't annotated, the following rules apply:

- If the property is of a JDK type, it's automatically persistent. In other words, it's handled like `<property name="propertyName"/>` in a Hibernate XML mapping file.

- Otherwise, if the class of the property is annotated as `@Embeddable`, it's mapped as a component of the owning class. We'll discuss embedding of components later in this chapter.

- Otherwise, if the type of the property is `Serializable`, its value is stored in its serialized form. This usually isn't what you want, and you should always map Java classes instead of storing a heap of bytes in the database. Imagine maintaining a database with this binary information when the application is gone in a few years.

If you don't want to rely on these defaults, apply the `@Basic` annotation on a particular property. The `@Column` annotation is the equivalent of the XML `<column>` element. Here is an example of how you declare a property's value as required:

```
@Basic(optional = false)
@Column(nullable = false)
public BigDecimal getInitialPrice { return initialPrice; }
```

The `@Basic` annotation marks the property as not optional on the Java object level. The second setting, `nullable = false` on the column mapping, is only responsible for the generation of a `NOT NULL` database constraint. The Hibernate JPA implementation treats both options the same way in any case, so you may as well use only one of the annotations for this purpose.

In a JPA XML descriptor, this mapping looks the same:

```
<entity class="auction.model.Item" access="PROPERTY">
    <attributes>
        ...
        <basic name="initialPrice" optional="false">
            <column nullable="false"/>
        </basic>
    </attributes>
</entity>
```

Quite a few options in Hibernate metadata are available to declare schema constraints, such as `NOT NULL` on a column. Except for simple nullability, however, they're only used to produce DDL when Hibernate exports a database schema from mapping metadata. We'll discuss customization of SQL, including DDL, in chapter 8, section 8.3, "Improving schema DDL." On the other hand, the Hibernate Annotations package includes a more advanced and sophisticated data validation framework, which you can use not only to define database schema constraints in DDL, but also for data validation at runtime. We'll discuss it in chapter 17.

Are annotations for properties always on the accessor methods?

Customizing property access

Properties of a class are accessed by the persistence engine either directly (through fields) or indirectly (through getter and setter property accessor methods). In XML mapping files, you control the default access strategy for a class with the `default-access="field|property|noop|custom.Class"` attribute of the `hibernate-mapping root` element. An annotated entity inherits the default from the position of the mandatory `@Id` annotation. For example, if `@Id` has been declared on a field, not a getter method, all other property mapping annotations, like the name of the column for the item's `description` property, are also declared on fields:

```
@Column(name = "ITEM_DESCR")
private String description;

public String getDescription() { return description; }
```

This is the default behavior as defined by the JPA specification. However, Hibernate allows flexible customization of the access strategy with the `@org.hibernate.annotations.AccessType(<strategy>)` annotation:

- If `AccessType` is set on the class/entity level, all attributes of the class are accessed according to the selected strategy. Attribute-level annotations are expected on either fields or getter methods, depending on the strategy. This setting overrides any defaults from the position of the standard `@Id` annotations.

- If an entity defaults or is explicitly set for field access, the `AccessType("property")` annotation on a field switches this particular attribute to runtime access through property getter/setter methods. The position of the `AccessType` annotation is still the field.

- If an entity defaults or is explicitly set for property access, the `AccessType("field")` annotation on a getter method switches this particular attribute to runtime access through a field of the same name. The position of the `AccessType` annotation is still the getter method.

- Any `@Embedded` class inherits the default or explicitly declared access strategy of the owning root entity class.

- Any `@MappedSuperclass` properties are accessed with the default or explicitly declared access strategy of the mapped entity class.

You can also control access strategies on the property level in Hibernate XML mappings with the access attribute:

```
<property name="description"
          column="DESCR"
          access="field"/>
```

Or, you can set the access strategy for all class mappings inside a root <hibernate-mapping> element with the default-access attribute.

Another strategy besides field and property access that can be useful is noop. It maps a property that doesn't exist in the Java persistent class. This sounds strange, but it lets you refer to this "virtual" property in HQL queries (in other words, to use the database column in HQL queries only).

If none of the built-in access strategies are appropriate, you can define your own customized property-access strategy by implementing the interface org.hibernate.property.PropertyAccessor. Set the (fully qualified) class name on the access mapping attribute or @AccessType annotation. Have a look at the Hibernate source code for inspiration; it's a straightforward exercise.

Some properties don't map to a column at all. In particular, a derived property takes its value from an SQL expression.

Using derived properties

The value of a derived property is calculated at runtime by evaluating an expression that you define using the formula attribute. For example, you may map a totalIncludingTax property to an SQL expression:

```
<property name="totalIncludingTax"
          formula="TOTAL + TAX_RATE * TOTAL"
          type="big_decimal"/>
```

The given SQL formula is evaluated every time the entity is retrieved from the database (and not at any other time, so the result may be outdated if other properties are modified). The property doesn't have a column attribute (or sub-element) and never appears in an SQL INSERT or UPDATE, only in SELECTs. Formulas may refer to columns of the database table, they can call SQL functions, and they may even include SQL subselects. The SQL expression is passed to the underlying database as is; this is a good chance to bind your mapping file to a particular database product, if you aren't careful and rely on vendor-specific operators or keywords.

Formulas are also available with a Hibernate annotation:

```
@org.hibernate.annotations.Formula("TOTAL + TAX_RATE * TOTAL")
public BigDecimal getTotalIncludingTax() {
```

```
        return totalIncludingTax;
    }
```

The following example uses a correlated subselect to calculate the average amount of all bids for an item:

```
<property
    name="averageBidAmount"
    type="big_decimal"
    formula=
    "( select AVG(b.AMOUNT) from
        BID b where b.ITEM_ID = ITEM_ID )"/>
```

Notice that unqualified column names refer to columns of the table of the class to which the derived property belongs.

Another special kind of property relies on database-generated values.

Generated and default property values

Imagine a particular property of a class has its value generated by the database, usually when the entity row is inserted for the first time. Typical database-generated values are timestamp of creation, a default price for an item, and a trigger that runs for every modification.

Typically, Hibernate applications need to refresh objects that contain any properties for which the database generates values. Marking properties as generated, however, lets the application delegate this responsibility to Hibernate. Essentially, whenever Hibernate issues an SQL INSERT or UPDATE for an entity that has defined generated properties, it immediately does a SELECT afterwards to retrieve the generated values. Use the generated switch on a property mapping to enable this automatic refresh:

```
<property name="lastModified"
        column="LAST_MODIFIED"
        update="false"
        insert="false"
        generated="always"/>
```

Properties marked as database-generated must additionally be noninsertable and nonupdateable, which you control with the insert and update attributes. If both are set to false, the property's columns never appear in the INSERT or UPDATE statements—the property value is read-only. Also, you usually don't add a public setter method in your class for an immutable property (and switch to field access).

With annotations, declare immutability (and automatic refresh) with the @Generated Hibernate annotation:

```
@Column(updatable = false, insertable = false)
@org.hibernate.annotations.Generated(
    org.hibernate.annotations.GenerationTime.ALWAYS
)
private Date lastModified;
```

The settings available are `GenerationTime.ALWAYS` and `GenerationTime.INSERT`, and the equivalent options in XML mappings are `generated="always"` and `generated="insert"`.

A special case of database-generated property values are default values. For example, you may want to implement a rule that every auction item costs at least $1. First, you'd add this to your database catalog as the default value for the `INITIAL_PRICE` column:

```
create table ITEM (
    ...
    INITIAL_PRICE number(10,2) default '1',
    ...
);
```

If you use Hibernate's schema export tool, hbm2ddl, you can enable this output by adding a `default` attribute to the property mapping:

```
<class name="Item" table="ITEM"
       dynamic-insert="true" dynamic-update="true">
    ...
    <property name="initialPrice" type="big_decimal">
        <column name="INITIAL_PRICE"
                default="'1'"
                generated="insert"/>
    </property>
    ...
</class>
```

Note that you also have to enable dynamic insertion and update statement generation, so that the column with the default value isn't included in every statement if its value is `null` (otherwise a `NULL` would be inserted instead of the default value). Furthermore, an instance of `Item` that has been made persistent but not yet flushed to the database and not refreshed again won't have the default value set on the object property. In other words, you need to execute an explicit flush:

```
Item newItem = new Item(...);
session.save(newItem);

newItem.getInitialPrice();    // is null

session.flush();              // Trigger an INSERT
// Hibernate does a SELECT automatically

newItem.getInitialPrice();    // is $1
```

Because you set `generated="insert"`, Hibernate knows that an immediate additional `SELECT` is required to read the database-generated property value.

You can map default column values with annotations as part of the DDL definition for a column:

```
@Column(name = "INITIAL_PRICE",
        columnDefinition = "number(10,2) default '1'")
@org.hibernate.annotations.Generated(
    org.hibernate.annotations.GenerationTime.INSERT
)
private BigDecimal initalPrice;
```

The `columnDefinition` attribute includes the complete properties for the column DDL, with datatype and all constraints. Keep in mind that an actual nonportable SQL datatype may bind your annotation mapping to a particular database management system.

We'll come back to the topic of constraints and DDL customization in chapter 8, section 8.3, "Improving schema DDL."

Next, you'll map user-defined value-typed classes. You can easily spot them in your UML class diagrams if you search for a composition relationship between two classes. One of them is a dependent class, a component.

4.4.2 *Mapping components*

So far, the classes of the object model have all been entity classes, each with its own lifecycle and identity. The `User` class, however, has a special kind of association with the `Address` class, as shown in figure 4.2.

In object-modeling terms, this association is a kind of aggregation—a part-of relationship. Aggregation is a strong form of association; it has some additional semantics with regard to the lifecycle of objects. In this case, you have an even stronger form, composition, where the lifecycle of the part is fully dependent upon the lifecycle of the whole.

Object modeling experts and UML designers claim that there is no difference between this composition and other weaker styles of association when it comes to the actual Java implementation. But in the context of ORM, there is a big difference: A composed class is often a candidate value type.

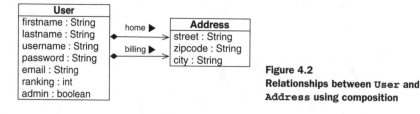

Figure 4.2
Relationships between `User` **and**
`Address` **using composition**

You map `Address` as a value type and `User` as an entity. Does this affect the implementation of the POJO classes?

Java has no concept of composition—a class or attribute can't be marked as a component or composition. The only difference is the object identifier: A component has no individual identity, hence the persistent component class requires no identifier property or identifier mapping. It's a simple POJO:

```java
public class Address {

    private String street;
    private String zipcode;
    private String city;

    public Address() {}

    public String getStreet() { return street; }
    public void setStreet(String street) { this.street = street; }

    public String getZipcode() { return zipcode; }
    public void setZipcode(String zipcode) {
        this.zipcode = zipcode; }

    public String getCity() { return city; }
    public void setCity(String city) { this.city = city; }

}
```

The composition between `User` and `Address` is a metadata-level notion; you only have to tell Hibernate that the `Address` is a value type in the mapping document or with annotations.

Component mapping in XML

Hibernate uses the term component for a user-defined class that is persisted to the same table as the owning entity, an example of which is shown in listing 4.2. (The use of the word component here has nothing to do with the architecture-level concept, as in software component.)

Listing 4.2 Mapping of the `User` class with a component `Address`

```xml
<class name="User" table="USER">

    <id name="id" column="USER_ID" type="long">
        <generator class="native"/>
    </id>

    <property name="loginName" column="LOGIN" type="string"/>

    <component name="homeAddress" class="Address">   ←❶
        <property name="street" type="string"
                column="HOME_STREET" not-null="true"/>
        <property name="city" type="string"
                column="HOME_CITY" not-null="true"/>
```

```
            <property name="zipcode" type="string"
                    column="HOME_ZIPCODE" not-null="true"/>
    </component>

    <component name="billingAddress" class="Address">
        <property name="street" type="string"
                column="BILLING_STREET" not-null="true"/>
        <property name="city" type="string"
                column="BILLING_CITY" not-null="true"/>
        <property name="zipcode" type="string"
                column="BILLING_ZIPCODE" not-null="true"/>
    </component>

    ...

</class>
```

1 You declare the persistent attributes of Address inside the <component> element. The property of the User class is named homeAddress.

2 You reuse the same component class to map another property of this type to the same table.

Figure 4.3 shows how the attributes of the Address class are persisted to the same table as the User entity.

Notice that, in this example, you model the composition association as unidirectional. You can't navigate from Address to User. Hibernate supports both unidirectional and bidirectional compositions, but unidirectional composition is far more common. An example of a bidirectional mapping is shown in listing 4.3.

<< Table >>
USERS
FIRSTNAME
LASTNAME
USERNAME
PASSWORD
EMAIL
...
HOME_STREET
HOME_ZIPCODE
HOME_CITY
BILLING_STREET
BILLING_ZIPCODE
BILLING_CITY

Component Columns

Component Columns

Figure 4.3   Table attributes of User with Address component

Listing 4.3   Adding a back-pointer to a composition

```
<component name="homeAddress" class="Address">
    <parent name="user"/>
    <property name="street" type="string"
            column="HOME_STREET" not-null="true"/>
    <property name="city" type="string"
            column="HOME_CITY" not-null="true"/>
    <property name="zipcode" type="stringshort"
            column="HOME_ZIPCODE" not-null="true"/>
</component>
```

In listing 4.3, the `<parent>` element maps a property of type `User` to the owning entity, which in this example is the property named `user`. You can then call `Address.getUser()` to navigate in the other direction. This is really a simple back-pointer.

A Hibernate component can own other components and even associations to other entities. This flexibility is the foundation of Hibernate's support for fine-grained object models. For example, you can create a `Location` class with detailed information about the home address of an `Address` owner:

```
<component name="homeAddress" class="Address">
    <parent name="user"/>

    <component name="location" class="Location">
        <property name="streetname" column="HOME_STREETNAME"/>
        <property name="streetside" column="HOME_STREETSIDE"/>
        <property name="housenumber" column="HOME_HOUSENR"/>
        <property name="floor" column="HOME_FLOOR"/>
    </component>

    <property name="city" type="string" column="HOME_CITY"/>
    <property name="zipcode" type="string" column="HOME_ZIPCODE"/>

</component>
```

The design of the `Location` class is equivalent to the `Address` class. You now have three classes, one entity, and two value types, all mapped to the same table.

Now let's map components with JPA annotations.

Annotating embedded classes

The Java Persistence specification calls components embedded classes. To map an embedded class with annotations, you can declare a particular property in the owning entity class as `@Embedded`, in this case the `homeAddress` of `User`:

```
@Entity
@Table(name = "USERS")
public class User {

    ...

    @Embedded
    private Address homeAddress;

    ...

}
```

If you don't declare a property as `@Embedded`, and it isn't of a JDK type, Hibernate looks into the associated class for the `@Embeddable` annotation. If it's present, the property is automatically mapped as a dependent component.

This is what the embeddable class looks like:

```
@Embeddable
public class Address {

    @Column(name = "ADDRESS_STREET", nullable = false)
    private String street;

    @Column(name = "ADDRESS_ZIPCODE", nullable = false)
    private String zipcode;

    @Column(name = "ADDRESS_CITY", nullable = false)
    private String city;

    ...
}
```

You can further customize the individual property mappings in the embeddable class, such as with the @Column annotation. The USERS table now contains, among others, the columns ADDRESS_STREET, ADDRESS_ZIPCODE, and ADDRESS_CITY. Any other entity table that contains component fields (say, an Order class that also has an Address) uses the same column options. You can also add a back-pointer property to the Address embeddable class and map it with @org.hibernate.annotations.Parent.

Sometimes you'll want to override the settings you made inside the embeddable class from outside for a particular entity. For example, here is how you can rename the columns:

```
@Entity
@Table(name = "USERS")
public class User {

    ...

    @Embedded
    @AttributeOverrides( {
        @AttributeOverride(name   = "street",
                           column = @Column(name="HOME_STREET") ),
        @AttributeOverride(name   = "zipcode",
                           column = @Column(name="HOME_ZIPCODE") ),
        @AttributeOverride(name   = "city",
                           column = @Column(name="HOME_CITY") )
    })
    private Address homeAddress;

    ...
}
```

The new @Column declarations in the User class override the settings of the embeddable class. Note that all attributes on the embedded @Column annotation are replaced, so they're no longer nullable = false.

In a JPA XML descriptor, a mapping of an embeddable class and a composition looks like the following:

```
<embeddable class="auction.model.Address access-type="FIELD"/>

<entity class="auction.model.User" access="FIELD">
    <attributes>
        ...
        <embedded name="homeAddress">
            <attribute-override name="street">
                <column name="HOME_STREET"/>
            </attribute-override>
            <attribute-override name="zipcode">
                <column name="HOME_ZIPCODE"/>
            </attribute-override>
            <attribute-override name="city">
                <column name="HOME_CITY"/>
            </attribute-override>
        </embedded>
    </attributes>
</entity>
```

There are two important limitations to classes mapped as components. First, shared references, as for all value types, aren't possible. The component homeAddress doesn't have its own database identity (primary key) and so can't be referred to by any object other than the containing instance of User.

Second, there is no elegant way to represent a null reference to an Address. In lieu of any elegant approach, Hibernate represents a null component as null values in all mapped columns of the component. This means that if you store a component object with all null property values, Hibernate returns a null component when the owning entity object is retrieved from the database.

You'll find many more component mappings (even collections of them) throughout the book.

4.5   *Summary*

In this chapter, you learned the essential distinction between entities and value types and how these concepts influence the implementation of your domain model as persistent Java classes.

Entities are the coarser-grained classes of your system. Their instances have an independent lifecycle and their own identity, and they can be referenced by many other instances. Value types, on the other hand, are dependent on a particular entity class. An instance of a value type has a lifecycle bound by its owning entity instance, and it can be referenced by only one entity—it has no individual identity.

We looked at Java identity, object equality, and database identity, and at what makes good primary keys. You learned which generators for primary key values are built into Hibernate, and how you can use and extend this identifier system.

You also learned various (mostly optional) class mapping options and, finally, how basic properties and value-type components are mapped in XML mappings and annotations.

For convenience, table 4.2 summarizes the differences between Hibernate and Java Persistence related to concepts discussed in this chapter.

Table 4.2 Hibernate and JPA comparison chart for chapter 4

Hibernate Core	Java Persistence and EJB 3.0
Entity- and value-typed classes are the essential concepts for the support of rich and fine-grained domain models.	The JPA specification makes the same distinction, but calls value types "embeddable classes." However, nested embeddable classes are considered a nonportable feature.
Hibernate supports 10 identifier generation strategies out-of-the-box.	JPA standardizes a subset of 4 identifier generators, but allows vendor extension.
Hibernate can access properties through fields, accessor methods, or with any custom `PropertyAccessor` implementation. Strategies can be mixed for a particular class.	JPA standardizes property access through fields or access methods, and strategies can't be mixed for a particular class without Hibernate extension annotations.
Hibernate supports formula properties and database-generated values.	JPA doesn't include these features, a Hibernate extension is needed.

In the next chapter, we'll attack inheritance and how hierarchies of entity classes can be mapped with various strategies. We'll also talk about the Hibernate mapping type system, the converters for value types we've shown in a few examples.

Inheritance and custom types

This chapter covers

- Inheritance mapping strategies
- The Hibernate mapping type system
- Customization of mapping types

We deliberately didn't talk much about inheritance mapping so far. Mapping a hierarchy of classes to tables can be a complex issue, and we'll present various strategies in this chapter. You'll learn which strategy to choose in a particular scenario.

The Hibernate type system, with all its built-in converters and transformers for Java value-typed properties to SQL datatypes, is the second big topic we discuss in this chapter.

Let's start with the mapping of entity inheritance.

5.1   Mapping class inheritance

A simple strategy for mapping classes to database tables might be "one table for every entity persistent class." This approach sounds simple enough and, indeed, works well until we encounter inheritance.

Inheritance is such a visible structural mismatch between the object-oriented and relational worlds because object-oriented systems model both is *a* and *has a* relationships. SQL-based models provide only *has a* relationships between entities; SQL database management systems don't support type inheritance—and even when it's available, it's usually proprietary or incomplete.

There are four different approaches to representing an inheritance hierarchy:

- Table per concrete class with implicit polymorphism—Use no explicit inheritance mapping, and default runtime polymorphic behavior.

- Table per concrete class—Discard polymorphism and inheritance relationships completely from the SQL schema.

- Table per class hierarchy—Enable polymorphism by denormalizing the SQL schema, and utilize a type discriminator column that holds type information.

- Table per subclass—Represent is *a* (inheritance) relationships as *has a* (foreign key) relationships.

This section takes a top-down approach; it assumes that you're starting with a domain model and trying to derive a new SQL schema. However, the mapping strategies described are just as relevant if you're working bottom up, starting with existing database tables. We'll show some tricks along the way that help you dealing with nonperfect table layouts.

5.1.1   Table per concrete class with implicit polymorphism

Suppose we stick with the simplest approach suggested. You can use exactly one table for each (nonabstract) class. All properties of a class, including inherited properties, can be mapped to columns of this table, as shown in figure 5.1.

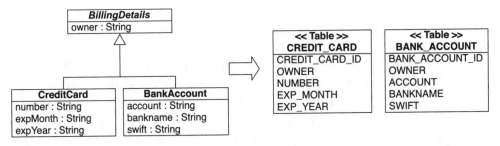

Figure 5.1 Mapping all concrete classes to an independent table

You don't have to do anything special in Hibernate to enable polymorphic behavior. The mapping for `CreditCard` and `BankAccount` is straightforward, each in its own entity `<class>` element, as we have done already for classes without a superclass (or persistent interfaces). Hibernate still knows about the superclass (or any interface) because it scans the persistent classes on startup.

The main problem with this approach is that it doesn't support polymorphic associations very well. In the database, associations are usually represented as foreign key relationships. In figure 5.1, if the subclasses are all mapped to different tables, a polymorphic association to their superclass (abstract `BillingDetails` in this example) can't be represented as a simple foreign key relationship. This would be problematic in our domain model, because `BillingDetails` is associated with `User`; both subclass tables would need a foreign key reference to the `USERS` table. Or, if `User` had a many-to-one relationship with `BillingDetails`, the `USERS` table would need a single foreign key column, which would have to refer both concrete subclass tables. This isn't possible with regular foreign key constraints.

Polymorphic queries (queries that return objects of all classes that match the interface of the queried class) are also problematic. A query against the superclass must be executed as several SQL SELECTs, one for each concrete subclass. For a query against the `BillingDetails` class Hibernate uses the following SQL:

```
select CREDIT_CARD_ID, OWNER, NUMBER, EXP_MONTH, EXP_YEAR ...
from CREDIT_CARD
```

```
select BANK_ACCOUNT_ID, OWNER, ACCOUNT, BANKNAME, ...
from BANK_ACCOUNT
```

Notice that a separate query is needed for each concrete subclass. On the other hand, queries against the concrete classes are trivial and perform well—only one of the statements is needed.

(Also note that here, and in other places in this book, we show SQL that is conceptually identical to the SQL executed by Hibernate. The actual SQL may look superficially different.)

A further conceptual problem with this mapping strategy is that several different columns, of different tables, share exactly the same semantics. This makes schema evolution more complex. For example, a change to a superclass property results in changes to multiple columns. It also makes it much more difficult to implement database integrity constraints that apply to all subclasses.

We recommend this approach (only) for the top level of your class hierarchy, where polymorphism isn't usually required, and when modification of the superclass in the future is unlikely.

Also, the Java Persistence interfaces don't support full polymorphic queries; only mapped entities (@Entity) can be officially part of a Java Persistence query (note that the Hibernate query interfaces are polymorphic, even if you map with annotations).

If you're relying on this implicit polymorphism, you map concrete classes with @Entity, as usual. However, you also have to duplicate the properties of the superclass to map them to all concrete class tables. By default, properties of the superclass are ignored and not persistent! You need to annotate the superclass to enable embedding of its properties in the concrete subclass tables:

```
@MappedSuperclass
public abstract class BillingDetails {

    @Column(name = "OWNER", nullable = false)
    private String owner;

        . . .

}
```

Now map the concrete subclasses:

```
@Entity
@AttributeOverride(name = "owner", column =
  @Column(name = "CC_OWNER", nullable = false)
)
public class CreditCard extends BillingDetails {

    @Id @GeneratedValue
    @Column(name = "CREDIT_CARD_ID")
    private Long id = null;

    @Column(name = "NUMBER", nullable = false)
    private String number;

    . . .

}
```

You can override column mappings from the superclass in a subclass with the `@AttributeOverride` annotation. You rename the `OWNER` column to `CC_OWNER` in the `CREDIT_CARD` table. The database identifier can also be declared in the superclass, with a shared column name and generator strategy for all subclasses.

Let's repeat the same mapping in a JPA XML descriptor:

```
<entity-mappings>

    <mapped-superclass class="auction.model.BillingDetails"
                       access="FIELD">
        <attributes>
            ...
        </attributes>
    </mapped-superclass>

    <entity class="auction.model.CreditCard" access="FIELD">
        <attribute-override name="owner">
            <column name="CC_OWNER" nullable="false"/>
        </attribute-override>
        <attributes>
            ...
        </attributes>
    </entity>
    ...
</entity-mappings>
```

> **NOTE** A component is a value type; hence, the normal entity inheritance rules presented in this chapter don't apply. However, you can map a subclass as a component by including all the properties of the superclass (or interface) in your component mapping. With annotations, you use the `@MappedSuperclass` annotation on the superclass of the embeddable component you're mapping just like you would for an entity. Note that this feature is available only in Hibernate Annotations and isn't standardized or portable.

With the help of the SQL `UNION` operation, you can eliminate most of the issues with polymorphic queries and associations, which are present with this mapping strategy.

5.1.2 *Table per concrete class with unions*

First, let's consider a union subclass mapping with `BillingDetails` as an abstract class (or interface), as in the previous section. In this situation, we again have two tables and duplicate superclass columns in both: `CREDIT_CARD` and `BANK_ACCOUNT`. What's new is a special Hibernate mapping that includes the superclass, as you can see in listing 5.1.

Listing 5.1 Using the `<union-subclass>` inheritance strategy

```
<hibernate-mapping>
    <class
        name="BillingDetails"         ❶
        abstract="true">              ⤶
                                  ❷
        <id                       ⤶
            name="id"
            column="BILLING_DETAILS_ID"
            type="long">
            <generator class="native"/>
        </id>
                          ❸
        <property         ⤶
            name="name"
            column="OWNER"
            type="string"/>

        ...
                     ❹
        <union-subclass     ⤶
            name="CreditCard" table="CREDIT_CARD">

            <property name="number" column="NUMBER"/>
            <property name="expMonth" column="EXP_MONTH"/>
            <property name="expYear" column="EXP_YEAR"/>

        </union-subclass>

        <union-subclass
            name="BankAccount" table="BANK_ACCOUNT">
            ...
    </class>
</hibernate-mapping>
```

❶ An abstract superclass or an interface has to be declared as `abstract="true"`; otherwise a separate table for instances of the superclass is needed.

❷ The database identifier mapping is shared for all concrete classes in the hierarchy. The CREDIT_CARD and the BANK_ACCOUNT tables both have a BILLING_DETAILS_ID primary key column. The database identifier property now has to be shared for all subclasses; hence you have to move it into BillingDetails and remove it from CreditCard and BankAccount.

❸ Properties of the superclass (or interface) are declared here and inherited by all concrete class mappings. This avoids duplication of the same mapping.

❹ A concrete subclass is mapped to a table; the table inherits the superclass (or interface) identifier and other property mappings.

The first advantage you may notice with this strategy is the shared declaration of superclass (or interface) properties. No longer do you have to duplicate these mappings for all concrete classes—Hibernate takes care of this. Keep in mind that the SQL schema still isn't aware of the inheritance; effectively, we've mapped two unrelated tables to a more expressive class structure. Except for the different primary key column name, the tables look exactly alike, as shown in figure 5.1.

In JPA annotations, this strategy is known as TABLE_PER_CLASS:

```
@Entity
@Inheritance(strategy = InheritanceType.TABLE_PER_CLASS)
public abstract class BillingDetails {

    @Id @GeneratedValue
    @Column(name = "BILLING_DETAILS_ID")
    private Long id = null;

    @Column(name = "OWNER", nullable = false)
    private String owner;

    ...
}
```

The database identifier and its mapping have to be present in the superclass, to be shared across all subclasses and their tables. An @Entity annotation on each subclass is all that is required:

```
@Entity
@Table(name = "CREDIT_CARD")
public class CreditCard extends BillingDetails {

    @Column(name = "NUMBER", nullable = false)
    private String number;

    ...
}
```

Note that TABLE_PER_CLASS is specified in the JPA standard as optional, so not all JPA implementations may support it. The actual implementation is also vendor dependent—in Hibernate, it's equivalent to a <union-subclass> mapping in XML files.

The same mapping looks like this in a JPA XML descriptor:

```
<entity-mappings>
    <entity class="auction.model.BillingDetails" access="FIELD">
        <inheritance strategy="TABLE_PER_CLASS"/>
        ...
    </entity>

    <entity class="auction.model.CreditCard" access="FIELD"/>
```

```
<entity class="auction.model.BankAccount" access="FIELD"/>

</entity-mappings>
```

If your superclass is concrete, then an additional table is needed to hold instances of that class. We have to emphasize again that there is still no relationship between the database tables, except for the fact that they share some similar columns. The advantages of this mapping strategy are clearer if we examine polymorphic queries. For example, a query for BillingDetails executes the following SQL statement:

```
select
    BILLING_DETAILS_ID, OWNER,
    NUMBER, EXP_MONTH, EXP_YEAR,
    ACCOUNT, BANKNAME, SWIFT
    CLAZZ_
from
  ( select
      BILLING_DETAILS_ID, OWNER,
      NUMBER, EXP_MONTH, EXP_YEAR,
      null as ACCOUNT, null as BANKNAME, null as SWIFT,
      1 as CLAZZ_
    from
      CREDIT_CARD

  union

  select
      BILLING_DETAILS_ID, OWNER,
      null as NUMBER, null as EXP_MONTH, null as EXP_YEAR, ...
      ACCOUNT, BANKNAME, SWIFT,
      2 as CLAZZ_
    from
      BANK_ACCOUNT
  )
```

This SELECT uses a FROM-clause subquery to retrieve all instances of BillingDetails from all concrete class tables. The tables are combined with a UNION operator, and a literal (in this case, 1 and 2) is inserted into the intermediate result; Hibernate reads this to instantiate the correct class given the data from a particular row. A union requires that the queries that are combined project over the same columns; hence, we have to pad and fill up nonexistent columns with NULL. You may ask whether this query will really perform better than two separate statements. Here we can let the database optimizer find the best execution plan to combine rows from several tables, instead of merging two result sets in memory as Hibernate's polymorphic loader engine would do.

Another much more important advantage is the ability to handle polymorphic associations; for example, an association mapping from User to BillingDetails would now be possible. Hibernate can use a UNION query to simulate a single table as the target of the association mapping. We cover this topic in detail in chapter 7, section 7.3, "Polymorphic associations."

So far, the inheritance mapping strategies we've discussed don't require extra consideration with regard to the SQL schema. No foreign keys are needed, and relations are properly normalized. This situation changes with the next strategy.

5.1.3 *Table per class hierarchy*

An entire class hierarchy can be mapped to a single table. This table includes columns for all properties of all classes in the hierarchy. The concrete subclass represented by a particular row is identified by the value of a type discriminator column. This approach is shown in figure 5.2.

This mapping strategy is a winner in terms of both performance and simplicity. It's the best-performing way to represent polymorphism—both polymorphic and nonpolymorphic queries perform well—and it's even easy to implement by hand. Ad-hoc reporting is possible without complex joins or unions. Schema evolution is straightforward.

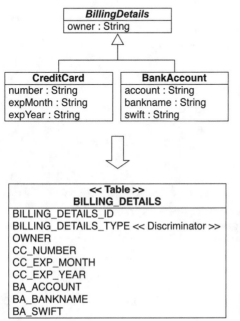

Figure 5.2
Mapping a whole class hierarchy to a single table

There is one major problem: Columns for properties declared by subclasses must be declared to be nullable. If your subclasses each define several nonnullable properties, the loss of NOT NULL constraints may be a serious problem from the point of view of data integrity. Another important issue is normalization. We've created functional dependencies between nonkey columns, violating the third normal form. As always, denormalization for performance can be misleading, because it sacrifices long-term stability, maintainability, and the integrity of data for immediate gains that may be also achieved by proper optimization of the SQL execution plans (in other words, ask your DBA).

In Hibernate, you use the <subclass> element to create a table per class hierarchy mapping, as in listing 5.2.

Listing 5.2   Hibernate <subclass> mapping

```
<hibernate-mapping>         ❶
    <class                       ←┘
        name="BillingDetails"
        table="BILLING_DETAILS">

        <id
            name="id"
            column="BILLING_DETAILS_ID"
            type="long">
            <generator class="native"/>
        </id>
                            ❷
        <discriminator       ←┘
            column="BILLING_DETAILS_TYPE"
            type="string"/>
                                ❸
        <property              ←┘
            name="owner"
            column="OWNER"
            type="string"/>

        . . .
                        ❹
        <subclass      ←┘
            name="CreditCard"
            discriminator-value="CC">

            <property name="number" column="CC_NUMBER"/>
            <property name="expMonth" column="CC_EXP_MONTH"/>
            <property name="expYear" column="CC_EXP_YEAR"/>

        </subclass>

        <subclass
            name="BankAccount"
            discriminator-value="BA">
```

```
    . . .
    </class>
</hibernate-mapping>
```

❶ The root class `BillingDetails` of the inheritance hierarchy is mapped to the table `BILLING_DETAILS`.

❷ You have to add a special column to distinguish between persistent classes: the discriminator. This isn't a property of the persistent class; it's used internally by Hibernate. The column name is `BILLING_DETAILS_TYPE`, and the values are strings—in this case, "CC" or "BA". Hibernate automatically sets and retrieves the discriminator values.

❸ Properties of the superclass are mapped as always, with a simple `<property>` element.

❹ Every subclass has its own `<subclass>` element. Properties of a subclass are mapped to columns in the `BILLING_DETAILS` table. Remember that `NOT NULL` constraints aren't allowed, because a `BankAccount` instance won't have an `expMonth` property, and the `CC_EXP_MONTH` field must be `NULL` for that row.

The `<subclass>` element can in turn contain other nested `<subclass>` elements, until the whole hierarchy is mapped to the table.

Hibernate generates the following SQL when querying the `BillingDetails` class:

```
select
    BILLING_DETAILS_ID, BILLING_DETAILS_TYPE, OWNER,
    CC_NUMBER, CC_EXP_MONTH, ..., BA_ACCOUNT, BA_BANKNAME, ...
from BILLING_DETAILS
```

To query the `CreditCard` subclass, Hibernate adds a restriction on the discriminator column:

```
select BILLING_DETAILS_ID, OWNER, CC_NUMBER, CC_EXP_MONTH, ...
from BILLING_DETAILS
where BILLING_DETAILS_TYPE='CC'
```

This mapping strategy is also available in JPA, as `SINGLE_TABLE`:

```
@Entity
@Inheritance(strategy = InheritanceType.SINGLE_TABLE)
@DiscriminatorColumn(
    name = "BILLING_DETAILS_TYPE",
    discriminatorType = DiscriminatorType.STRING
)
```

```
public abstract class BillingDetails {

    @Id @GeneratedValue
    @Column(name = "BILLING_DETAILS_ID")
    private Long id = null;

    @Column(name = "OWNER", nullable = false)
    private String owner;

    ...
}
```

If you don't specify a discriminator column in the superclass, its name defaults to DTYPE and its type to string. All concrete classes in the inheritance hierarchy can have a discriminator value; in this case, BillingDetails is abstract, and Credit-Card is a concrete class:

```
@Entity
@DiscriminatorValue("CC")
public class CreditCard extends BillingDetails {

    @Column(name = "CC_NUMBER")
    private String number;

    ...
}
```

Without an explicit discriminator value, Hibernate defaults to the fully qualified class name if you use Hibernate XML files and the entity name if you use annotations or JPA XML files. Note that no default is specified in Java Persistence for non-string discriminator types; each persistence provider can have different defaults.

This is the equivalent mapping in JPA XML descriptors:

```
<entity-mappings>
    <entity class="auction.model.BillingDetails" access="FIELD">
        <inheritance strategy="SINGLE_TABLE"/>
        <discriminator-column name="BILLING_DETAILS_TYPE"
            discriminator-type="STRING"/>
        ...
    </entity>

    <entity class="auction.model.CreditCard" access="FIELD">
        <discriminator-value>CC</discriminator-value>
        ...
    </entity>

</entity-mappings>
```

Sometimes, especially in legacy schemas, you don't have the freedom to include an extra discriminator column in your entity tables. In this case, you can apply a formula to calculate a discriminator value for each row:

```
<discriminator
  formula="case when CC_NUMBER is not null then 'CC' else 'BA' end"
  type="string"/>

    ...

<subclass
    name="CreditCard"
    discriminator-value="CC">
    ...
```

This mapping relies on an SQL CASE/WHEN expression to determine whether a particular row represents a credit card or a bank account (many developers never used this kind of SQL expression; check the ANSI standard if you aren't familiar with it). The result of the expression is a literal, CC or BA, which in turn is declared on the <subclass> mappings. Formulas for discrimination aren't part of the JPA specification. However, you can apply a Hibernate annotation:

```
@Entity
@Inheritance(strategy = InheritanceType.SINGLE_TABLE)
@org.hibernate.annotations.DiscriminatorFormula(
    "case when CC_NUMBER is not null then 'CC' else 'BA' end"
)
public abstract class BillingDetails {
    ...
}
```

The disadvantages of the table per class hierarchy strategy may be too serious for your design—after all, denormalized schemas can become a major burden in the long run. Your DBA may not like it at all. The next inheritance mapping strategy doesn't expose you to this problem.

5.1.4 *Table per subclass*

The fourth option is to represent inheritance relationships as relational foreign key associations. Every class/subclass that declares persistent properties—including abstract classes and even interfaces—has its own table.

Unlike the table per concrete class strategy we mapped first, the table here contains columns only for each noninherited property (each property declared by the subclass itself) along with a primary key that is also a foreign key of the superclass table. This approach is shown in figure 5.3.

If an instance of the CreditCard subclass is made persistent, the values of properties declared by the BillingDetails superclass are persisted to a new row of the BILLING_DETAILS table. Only the values of properties declared by the subclass are persisted to a new row of the CREDIT_CARD table. The two rows are linked together

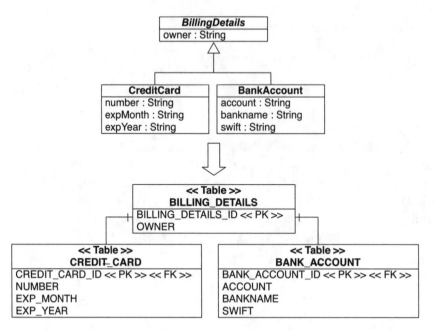

Figure 5.3 Mapping all classes of the hierarchy to their own table

by their shared primary key value. Later, the subclass instance may be retrieved from the database by joining the subclass table with the superclass table.

The primary advantage of this strategy is that the SQL schema is normalized. Schema evolution and integrity constraint definition are straightforward. A polymorphic association to a particular subclass may be represented as a foreign key referencing the table of that particular subclass.

In Hibernate, you use the `<joined-subclass>` element to create a table per subclass mapping. See listing 5.3.

Listing 5.3 Hibernate `<joined-subclass>` mapping

```
<hibernate-mapping>      ❶
    <class              ↵
        name="BillingDetails"
        table="BILLING_DETAILS">

        <id
            name="id"
            column="BILLING_DETAILS_ID"
            type="long">
            <generator class="native"/>
```

```
        </id>

        <property
            name="owner"
            column="OWNER"
            type="string"/>

            ...
        <joined-subclass   <┘
            name="CreditCard"
            table="CREDIT_CARD">

            <key column="CREDIT_CARD_ID"/>   <┘

            <property name="number" column="NUMBER"/>
            <property name="expMonth" column="EXP_MONTH"/>
            <property name="expYear" column="EXP_YEAR"/>

        </joined-subclass>

        <joined-subclass
            name="BankAccount"
            table="BANK_ACCOUNT">
        ...

    </class>
</hibernate-mapping>
```

❶ The root class `BillingDetails` is mapped to the table `BILLING_DETAILS`. Note that no discriminator is required with this strategy.

❷ The new `<joined-subclass>` element maps a subclass to a new table—in this example, `CREDIT_CARD`. All properties declared in the joined subclass are mapped to this table.

❸ A primary key is required for the `CREDIT_CARD` table. This column also has a foreign key constraint to the primary key of the `BILLING_DETAILS` table. A Credit-Card object lookup requires a join of both tables. A `<joined-subclass>` element may contain other nested `<joined-subclass>` elements, until the whole hierarchy has been mapped.

Hibernate relies on an outer join when querying the `BillingDetails` class:

```
select BD.BILLING_DETAILS_ID, BD.OWNER,
       CC.NUMBER, CC.EXP_MONTH, ..., BA.ACCOUNT, BA.BANKNAME, ...
    case
        when CC.CREDIT_CARD_ID is not null then 1
        when BA.BANK_ACCOUNT_ID is not null then 2
        when BD.BILLING_DETAILS_ID is not null then 0
    end as CLAZZ_
```

```
from BILLING_DETAILS BD
    left join CREDIT_CARD CC
      on BD.BILLING_DETAILS_ID = CC.CREDIT_CARD_ID
    left join BANK_ACCOUNT BA
      on BD.BILLING_DETAILS_ID = BA.BANK_ACCOUNT_ID
```

The SQL CASE statement detects the existence (or absence) of rows in the subclass tables CREDIT_CARD and BANK_ACCOUNT, so Hibernate can determine the concrete subclass for a particular row of the BILLING_DETAILS table.

To narrow the query to the subclass, Hibernate uses an inner join:

```
select BD.BILLING_DETAILS_ID, BD.OWNER, CC.NUMBER, ...
from CREDIT_CARD CC
    inner join BILLING_DETAILS BD
      on BD.BILLING_DETAILS_ID = CC.CREDIT_CARD_ID
```

As you can see, this mapping strategy is more difficult to implement by hand—even ad-hoc reporting is more complex. This is an important consideration if you plan to mix Hibernate code with handwritten SQL.

Furthermore, even though this mapping strategy is deceptively simple, our experience is that performance can be unacceptable for complex class hierarchies. Queries always require either a join across many tables or many sequential reads.

Let's map the hierarchy with the same strategy and annotations, here called the JOINED strategy:

```
@Entity
@Inheritance(strategy = InheritanceType.JOINED)
public abstract class BillingDetails {

    @Id @GeneratedValue
    @Column(name = "BILLING_DETAILS_ID")
    private Long id = null;

    ...
}
```

In subclasses, you don't need to specify the join column if the primary key column of the subclass table has (or is supposed to have) the same name as the primary key column of the superclass table:

```
@Entity
public class BankAccount {
    ...
}
```

This entity has no identifier property; it automatically inherits the BILLING_ DETAILS_ID property and column from the superclass, and Hibernate knows how to join the tables together if you want to retrieve instances of BankAccount. Of course, you can specify the column name explicitly:

```
@Entity
@PrimaryKeyJoinColumn(name = "CREDIT_CARD_ID")
public class CreditCard {
    ...
}
```

Finally, this is the equivalent mapping in JPA XML descriptors:

```
<entity-mappings>

    <entity class="auction.model.BillingDetails" access="FIELD">
        <inheritance strategy="JOINED"/>
        ...
    </entity>

    <entity class="auction.model.BankAccount" access="FIELD"/>
    <entity class="auction.model.CreditCard" access="FIELD">
        <primary-key-join-column name="CREDIT_CARD_ID"/>
    </entity>

</entity-mappings>
```

Before we show you when to choose which strategy, let's consider mixing inheritance mapping strategies in a single class hierarchy.

5.1.5 *Mixing inheritance strategies*

You can map whole inheritance hierarchies by nesting <union-subclass>, <subclass>, and <joined-subclass> mapping elements. You can't mix them—for example, to switch from a table-per-class hierarchy with a discriminator to a normalized table-per-subclass strategy. Once you've made a decision for an inheritance strategy, you have to stick to it.

This isn't completely true, however. With some Hibernate tricks, you can switch the mapping strategy for a particular subclass. For example, you can map a class hierarchy to a single table, but for a particular subclass, switch to a separate table with a foreign key mapping strategy, just as with table per subclass. This is possible with the <join> mapping element:

```
<hibernate-mapping>
<class name="BillingDetails"
    table="BILLING_DETAILS">

    <id>...</id>

    <discriminator
        column="BILLING_DETAILS_TYPE"
        type="string"/>
```

```
    . . .

<subclass
    name="CreditCard"
    discriminator-value="CC">

    <join table="CREDIT_CARD">
        <key column="CREDIT_CARD_ID"/>

        <property name="number" column="CC_NUMBER"/>
        <property name="expMonth" column="CC_EXP_MONTH"/>
        <property name="expYear" column="CC_EXP_YEAR"/>
        . . .
    </join>

</subclass>

<subclass
    name="BankAccount"
    discriminator-value="BA">

    <property name=account" column="BA_ACCOUNT"/>
    . . .
</subclass>

. . .

</class>
</hibernate-mapping>
```

The <join> element groups some properties and tells Hibernate to get them from a secondary table. This mapping element has many uses, and you'll see it again later in the book. In this example, it separates the CreditCard properties from the table per hierarchy into the CREDIT_CARD table. The CREDIT_CARD_ID column of this table is at the same time the primary key, and it has a foreign key constraint referencing the BILLING_DETAILS_ID of the hierarchy table. The BankAccount subclass is mapped to the hierarchy table. Look at the schema in figure 5.4.

At runtime, Hibernate executes an outer join to fetch BillingDetails and all subclass instances polymorphically:

```
select
    BILLING_DETAILS_ID, BILLING_DETAILS_TYPE, OWNER,
    CC.CC_NUMBER, CC.CC_EXP_MONTH, CC.CC_EXP_YEAR,
    BA_ACCOUNT, BA_BANKNAME, BA_SWIFT
from
    BILLING_DETAILS
left outer join
    CREDIT_CARD CC
        on BILLING_DETAILS_ID = CC.CREDIT_CARD_ID
```

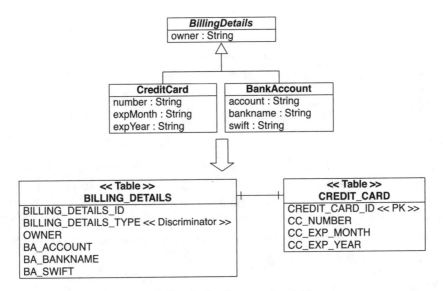

Figure 5.4 Breaking out a subclass to its own secondary table

You can also use the `<join>` trick for other subclasses in your class hierarchy. However, if you have an exceptionally wide class hierarchy, the outer join can become a problem. Some database systems (Oracle, for example) limit the number of tables in an outer join operation. For a wide hierarchy, you may want to switch to a different fetching strategy that executes an immediate second select instead of an outer join:

```
<subclass
    name="CreditCard"
    discriminator-value="CC">

    <join table="CREDIT_CARD" fetch="select">
        <key column="CREDIT_CARD_ID"/>
        ...
    </join>

</subclass>
```

Java Persistence also supports this mixed inheritance mapping strategy with annotations. Map the superclass `BillingDetails` with `InheritanceType.SINGLE_TABLE`, as you did before. Now map the subclass you want to break out of the single table to a secondary table.

```
@Entity
@DiscriminatorValue("CC")
@SecondaryTable(
```

```
    name = "CREDIT_CARD",
    pkJoinColumns = @PrimaryKeyJoinColumn(name = "CREDIT_CARD_ID")
)
public class CreditCard extends BillingDetails {

    @Column(table = "CREDIT_CARD",
            name = "CC_NUMBER",
            nullable = false)
    private String number;
    ...
}
```

If you don't specify a primary key join column for the secondary table, the name of the primary key of the single inheritance table is used—in this case, BILLING_DETAILS_ID. Also note that you need to map all properties that are moved into the secondary table with the name of that secondary table.

You also want more tips about how to choose an appropriate combination of mapping strategies for your application's class hierarchies.

5.1.6 *Choosing a strategy*

You can apply all mapping strategies to abstract classes and interfaces. Interfaces may have no state but may contain accessor method declarations, so they can be treated like abstract classes. You can map an interface with <class>, <union-sub-class>, <subclass>, or <joined-subclass>, and you can map any declared or inherited property with <property>. Hibernate won't try to instantiate an abstract class, even if you query or load it.

> **NOTE** Note that the JPA specification doesn't support any mapping annotation on an interface! This will be resolved in a future version of the specification; when you read this book, it will probably be possible with Hibernate Annotations.

Here are some rules of thumb:

- If you don't require polymorphic associations or queries, lean toward table-per-concrete-class—in other words, if you never or rarely query for BillingDetails and you have no class that has an association to BillingDetails (our model has). An explicit UNION-based mapping should be preferred, because (optimized) polymorphic queries and associations will then be possible later. Implicit polymorphism is mostly useful for queries utilizing non-persistence-related interfaces.

- If you do require polymorphic associations (an association to a superclass, hence to all classes in the hierarchy with dynamic resolution of the concrete class at runtime) or queries, and subclasses declare relatively few properties (particularly if the main difference between subclasses is in their behavior), lean toward table-per-class-hierarchy. Your goal is to minimize the number of nullable columns and to convince yourself (and your DBA) that a denormalized schema won't create problems in the long run.

- If you do require polymorphic associations or queries, and subclasses declare many properties (subclasses differ mainly by the data they hold), lean toward table-per-subclass. Or, depending on the width and depth of your inheritance hierarchy and the possible cost of joins versus unions, use table-per-concrete-class.

By default, choose table-per-class-hierarchy only for simple problems. For more complex cases (or when you're overruled by a data modeler insisting on the importance of nullability constraints and normalization), you should consider the table-per-subclass strategy. But at that point, ask yourself whether it may not be better to remodel inheritance as delegation in the object model. Complex inheritance is often best avoided for all sorts of reasons unrelated to persistence or ORM. Hibernate acts as a buffer between the domain and relational models, but that doesn't mean you can ignore persistence concerns when designing your classes.

When you start thinking about mixing inheritance strategies, remember that implicit polymorphism in Hibernate is smart enough to handle more exotic cases. For example, consider an additional interface in our application, Electronic-PaymentOption. This is a business interface that doesn't have a persistence aspect—except that in our application, a persistent class such as CreditCard will likely implement this interface. No matter how you map the BillingDetails hierarchy, Hibernate can answer a query from ElectronicPaymentOption correctly. This even works if other classes, which aren't part of the BillingDetails hierarchy, are mapped persistent and implement this interface. Hibernate always know what tables to query, which instances to construct, and how to return a polymorphic result.

Finally, you can also use <union-subclass>, <subclass>, and <joined-subclass> mapping elements in a separate mapping file (as a top-level element instead of <class>). You then have to declare the class that is extended, such as <subclass name="CreditCard" extends="BillingDetails">, and the superclass mapping must be loaded programmatically before the subclass mapping file (you don't have to worry about this order when you list mapping resources in the XML configuration file). This technique allows you to extend a class hierarchy without modifying the mapping file of the superclass.

You now know everything you need to know about the mapping of entities, properties, and inheritance hierarchies. You can already map complex domain models. In the second half of this chapter, we discuss another important feature that you should know by heart as a Hibernate user: the Hibernate mapping type system.

5.2 The Hibernate type system

In chapter 4, we first distinguished between entity and value types—a central concept of ORM in Java. We must elaborate on that distinction in order for you to fully understand the Hibernate type system of entities, value types, and mapping types.

5.2.1 Recapitulating entity and value types

Entities are the coarse-grained classes in your system. You usually define the features of a system in terms of the entities involved. *The user places a bid for an item* is a typical feature definition; it mentions three entities. Classes of value types often don't even appear in the business requirements—they're usually the fine-grained classes representing strings, numbers, and monetary amounts. Occasionally, value types do appear in feature definitions: *the user changes billing address* is one example, assuming that `Address` is a value type.

More formally, an entity is any class whose instances have their own persistent identity. A value type is a class that doesn't define some kind of persistent identity. In practice, this means that entity types are classes with identifier properties, and value type classes depend on an entity.

At runtime, you have a network of entity instances interleaved with value type instances. The entity instances may be in any of the three persistent lifecycle states: transient, detached, or persistent. We don't consider these lifecycle states to apply to the value type instances. (We'll come back to this discussion of object states in chapter 9.)

Therefore, entities have their own lifecycle. The `save()` and `delete()` methods of the Hibernate `Session` interface apply to instances of entity classes, never to value type instances. The persistence lifecycle of a value type instance is completely tied to the lifecycle of the owning entity instance. For example, the username becomes persistent when the user is saved; it never becomes persistent independently of the user.

In Hibernate, a value type may define associations; it's possible to navigate from a value type instance to some other entity. However, it's never possible to navigate from the other entity back to the value type instance. Associations always point to entities. This means that a value type instance is owned by exactly one entity when it's retrieved from the database; it's never shared.

At the level of the database, any table is considered an entity. However, Hibernate provides certain constructs to hide the existence of a database-level entity from the Java code. For example, a many-to-many association mapping hides the intermediate association table from the application. A collection of strings (more accurately, a collection of value-typed instances) behaves like a value type from the point of view of the application; however, it's mapped to its own table. Although these features seem nice at first (they simplify the Java code), we have over time become suspicious of them. Inevitably, these hidden entities end up needing to be exposed to the application as business requirements evolve. The many-to-many association table, for example, often has additional columns added as the application matures. We're almost prepared to recommend that every database-level entity be exposed to the application as an entity class. For example, we would be inclined to model the many-to-many association as two one-to-many associations to an intervening entity class. We'll leave the final decision to you, however, and come back to the topic of many-to-many entity associations in the future chapters.

Entity classes are always mapped to the database using `<class>`, `<union-subclass>`, `<subclass>`, and `<joined-subclass>` mapping elements. How are value types mapped?

You've already met two different kinds of value type mappings: `<property>` and `<component>`. The value type of a component is obvious: It's the class that is mapped as embeddable. However, the type of a property is a more generic notion. Consider this mapping of the CaveatEmptor `User` and email address:

```
<property name="email"
          column="EMAIL"
          type="string"/>
```

Let's focus on that `type="string"` attribute. You know that in ORM you have to deal with Java types and SQL datatypes. The two different type systems must be bridged. This is the job of the Hibernate mapping types, and `string` is the name of a built-in Hibernate mapping type.

The `string` mapping type isn't the only one built into Hibernate. Hibernate comes with various mapping types that define default persistence strategies for primitive Java types and certain JDK classes.

5.2.2 Built-in mapping types

Hibernate's built-in mapping types usually share the name of the Java type they map. However, there may be more than one Hibernate mapping type for a particular Java type.

The built-in types may not be used to perform arbitrary conversions, such as mapping a VARCHAR database value to a Java `Integer` property value. You may define your own custom value types for this kind of conversation, as shown later in this chapter.

We now discuss the basic, date and time, locator object, and various other built-in mapping types and show you what Java and SQL datatype they handle.

Java primitive mapping types

The basic mapping types in table 5.1 map Java primitive types (or their wrapper types) to appropriate built-in SQL standard types.

Table 5.1 Primitive types

Mapping type	Java type	Standard SQL built-in type
`integer`	`int` or `java.lang.Integer`	`INTEGER`
`long`	`long` or `java.lang.Long`	`BIGINT`
`short`	`short` or `java.lang.Short`	`SMALLINT`
`float`	`float` or `java.lang.Float`	`FLOAT`
`double`	`double` or `java.lang.Double`	`DOUBLE`
`big_decimal`	`java.math.BigDecimal`	`NUMERIC`
`character`	`java.lang.String`	`CHAR(1)`
`string`	`java.lang.String`	`VARCHAR`
`byte`	`byte` or `java.lang.Byte`	`TINYINT`
`boolean`	`boolean` or `java.lang.Boolean`	`BIT`
`yes_no`	`boolean` or `java.lang.Boolean`	`CHAR(1)` (`'Y'` or `'N'`)
`true_false`	`boolean` or `java.lang.Boolean`	`CHAR(1)` (`'T'` or `'F'`)

You've probably noticed that your database doesn't support some of the SQL types mentioned in table 5.1. The listed type names are names of ANSI-standard datatypes. Most database vendors ignore this part of the SQL standard (because their legacy type systems often predate the standard). However, the JDBC driver provides a partial abstraction of vendor-specific SQL datatypes, allowing Hibernate to work with ANSI-standard types when executing DML. For database-specific DDL generation, Hibernate translates from the ANSI-standard type to an appropriate vendor-specific type, using the built-in support for specific SQL dialects. (This means you usually don't have to worry about SQL datatypes if you're using Hibernate for data access and SQL schema definition.)

Furthermore, the Hibernate type system is smart and can switch SQL datatypes depending on the defined length of a value. The most obvious case is string: If you declare a string property mapping with a length attribute, Hibernate picks the correct SQL datatype depending on the selected dialect. For MySQL, for example, a length of up to 65535 results in a regular VARCHAR(length) column when Hibernate exports the schema. For a length of up to 16777215, a MEDIUMTEXT datatype is used. Larger string mappings result in a LONGTEXT. Check your SQL dialect (the source code comes with Hibernate) if you want to know the ranges for this and other mapping types. You can customize this behavior by subclassing your dialect and overriding these settings.

Most dialects also support setting the scale and precision of decimal SQL datatypes. For example, a precision or scale setting in your mapping of a BigDecimal creates a NUMERIC(precision, scale) datatype for MySQL.

Finally, the yes_no and true_false mapping types are converters that are mostly useful for legacy schemas and Oracle users; Oracle DBMS products don't have a built-in boolean or truth-valued type (the only built-in datatype actually required by the relational data model).

Date and time mapping types

Table 5.2 lists Hibernate types associated with dates, times, and timestamps. In your domain model, you may choose to represent date and time data using java.util.Date, java.util.Calendar, or the subclasses of java.util.Date defined in the java.sql package. This is a matter of taste, and we leave the decision to you—make sure you're consistent, however. (In practice, binding your domain model to types from the JDBC package isn't the best idea.)

A caveat: If you map a java.util.Date property with timestamp (the most common case), Hibernate returns a java.sql.Timestamp when loading the property from the database. Hibernate has to use the JDBC subclass because it includes

Table 5.2   Date and time types

Mapping type	Java type	Standard SQL built-in type
date	`java.util.Date` or `java.sql.Date`	DATE
time	`java.util.Date` or `java.sql.Time`	TIME
timestamp	`java.util.Date` or `java.sql.Timestamp`	TIMESTAMP
calendar	`java.util.Calendar`	TIMESTAMP
calendar_date	`java.util.Calendar`	DATE

nanosecond information that may be present in the database. Hibernate can't just cut off this information. This can lead to problems if you try to compare your `java.util.Date` properties with the `equals()` method, because it isn't symmetric with the `java.sql.Timestamp` subclass `equals()` method. First, the right way (in any case) to compare two `java.util.Date` objects, which also works for any subclass, is `aDate.getTime() > bDate.getTime()` (for a greater-than comparison). Second, you can write a custom mapping type that cuts off the database nanosecond information and returns a `java.util.Date` in all cases. Currently (although this may change in the future), no such mapping type is built into Hibernate.

Binary and large value mapping types

Table 5.3 lists Hibernate types for handling binary data and large values. Note that only `binary` is supported as the type of an identifier property.

If a property in your persistent Java class is of type `byte[]`, Hibernate can map it to a `VARBINARY` column with the `binary` mapping type. (Note that the real SQL

Table 5.3   Binary and large value types

Mapping type	Java type	Standard SQL built-in type
binary	`byte[]`	VARBINARY
text	`java.lang.String`	CLOB
clob	`java.sql.Clob`	CLOB
blob	`java.sql.Blob`	BLOB
serializable	Any Java class that implements `java.io.Serializable`	VARBINARY

type depends on the dialect; for example, in PostgreSQL, the SQL type is BYTEA, and in Oracle it's RAW.) If a property in your persistent Java class is of type java.lang.String, Hibernate can map it to an SQL CLOB column, with the text mapping type.

Note that in both cases, Hibernate initializes the property value right away, when the entity instance that holds the property variable is loaded. This is inconvenient when you have to deal with potentially large values.

One solution is lazy loading through interception of field access, on demand. However, this approach requires bytecode instrumentation of your persistent classes for the injection of extra code. We'll discuss lazy loading through bytecode instrumentation and interception in chapter 13, section 13.1.6, "Lazy loading with interception."

A second solution is a different kind of property in your Java class. JDBC supports locator objects (LOBs) directly.[1] If your Java property is of type java.sql.Clob or java.sql.Blob, you can map it with the clob or blob mapping type to get lazy loading of large values without bytecode instrumentation. When the owner of the property is loaded, the property value is a locator object—effectively, a pointer to the real value that isn't yet materialized. Once you access the property, the value is materialized. This on-demand loading works only as long as the database transaction is open, so you need to access any property of such a type when the owning entity instance is in a persistent and transactional state, not in detached state. Your domain model is now also bound to JDBC, because the import of the java.sql package is required. Although domain model classes are executable in isolated unit tests, you can't access LOB properties without a database connection.

Mapping properties with potentially large values is slightly different if you rely on Java Persistence annotations. By default, a property of type java.lang.String is mapped to an SQL VARCHAR column (or equivalent, depending on the SQL dialect). If you want to map a java.lang.String, char[], Character[], or even a java.sql.Clob typed property to a CLOB column, you need to map it with the @Lob annotation:

```
@Lob
@Column(name = "ITEM_DESCRIPTION")
private String description;
```

---

[1] Jim Starkey, who came up with the idea of LOBs, says that the terms BLOB and CLOB don't mean anything but were created by the marketing department. You can interpret them any way you like. We prefer *locator objects*, as a hint that they work like pointers.

```
@Lob
@Column(name = "ITEM_IMAGE")
private byte[] image;
```

The same is true for any property that is of type byte[], Byte[], or java.sql.Blob. Note that for all cases, except properties that are of java.sql.Clob or java.sql.Blob type, the values are again loaded immediately by Hibernate, and not lazily on demand. Instrumenting bytecode with interception code is again an option to enable lazy loading of individual properties transparently.

To create and set a java.sql.Blob or java.sql.Clob value, if you have these property types in your domain model, use the static Hibernate.createBlob() and Hibernate.createClob() methods and provide a byte array, an input stream, or a string.

Finally, note that both Hibernate and JPA provide a serialization fallback for any property type that is Serializable. This mapping type converts the value of a property to a byte stream that is then stored in a VARBINARY (or equivalent) column. When the owner of the property is loaded, the property value is deserialized. Naturally, you should use this strategy with extreme caution (data lives longer than an application), and it may be useful only for temporary data (user preferences, login session data, and so on).

JDK mapping types

Table 5.4 lists Hibernate types for various other Java types of the JDK that may be represented as a VARCHAR in the database.

You may have noticed that <property> isn't the only Hibernate mapping element that has a type attribute.

Table 5.4 Other JDK-related types

Mapping type	Java type	Standard SQL built-in type
class	java.lang.Class	VARCHAR
locale	java.util.Locale	VARCHAR
timezone	java.util.TimeZone	VARCHAR
currency	java.util.Currency	VARCHAR

5.2.3 *Using mapping types*

All of the basic mapping types may appear almost anywhere in the Hibernate mapping document, on normal property, identifier property, and other mapping elements. The <id>, <property>, <version>, <discriminator>, <index> and <element> elements all define an attribute named type.

You can see how useful the built-in mapping types are in this mapping for the BillingDetails class:

```
<class name="BillingDetails" table="BILLING_DETAILS">
    <id name="id" type="long" column="BILLING_DETAILS_ID">
        <generator class="native"/>
    </id>
    <discriminator type="character" column="BILLING_DETAILS_TYPE"/>
    <property name="number" type="string"/>
    ....
</class>
```

The BillingDetails class is mapped as an entity. Its discriminator, identifier, and name properties are value typed, and we use the built-in Hibernate mapping types to specify the conversion strategy.

It isn't often necessary to explicitly specify a built-in mapping type in the XML mapping document. For instance, if you have a property of Java type java.lang.String, Hibernate discovers this using reflection and selects string by default. We can easily simplify the previous mapping example:

```
<class name="BillingDetails" table="BILLING_DETAILS">
    <id name="id" column="BILLING_DETAILS_ID">
        <generator class="native"/>
    </id>
    <discriminator type="character" column="BILLING_DETAILS_TYPE"/>
    <property name="number"/>
    ....
</class>
```

Hibernate also understands type="java.lang.String"; it doesn't have to use reflection then. The most important case where this approach doesn't work well is a java.util.Date property. By default, Hibernate interprets a java.util.Date as a timestamp mapping. You need to explicitly specify type="time" or type="date" if you don't wish to persist both date and time information.

With JPA annotations, the mapping type of a property is automatically detected, just like in Hibernate. For a java.util.Date or java.util.Calendar property, the Java Persistence standard requires that you select the precision with a @Temporal annotation:

```
@Temporal(TemporalType.TIMESTAMP)
@Column(nullable = false, updatable = false)
private Date startDate;
```

On the other hand, Hibernate Annotations, relaxing the rules of the standard, defaults to `TemporalType.TIMESTAMP`—options are `TemporalType.TIME` and `TemporalType.DATE`.

In other rare cases, you may want to add the `@org.hibernate.annotations.Type` annotation to a property and declare the name of a built-in or custom Hibernate mapping type explicitly. This is a much more common extension as soon as you start writing your own custom mapping types, which you'll do later in this chapter.

The equivalent JPA XML descriptor is as follows:

```
<entity class="auction.model.Item" access="FIELD">
    <attributes>
        ...
        <basic name="startDate">
            <column nullable="false" updatable="false"/>
            <temporal>TIMESTAMP</temporal>
        </basic>
    </attributes>
</entity>
```

For each of the built-in mapping types, a constant is defined by the class `org.hibernate.Hibernate`. For example, `Hibernate.STRING` represents the `string` mapping type. These constants are useful for query parameter binding, as discussed in more detail in chapters 14 and 15:

```
session.createQuery("from Item i where i.description like :desc")
    .setParameter("desc", d, Hibernate.STRING)
    .list();
```

Note that you may as well use the `setString()` argument binding method in this case. Type constants are also useful for programmatic manipulation of the Hibernate mapping metamodel, as discussed in chapter 3.

Hibernate isn't limited to the built-in mapping types. We consider the extensible mapping-type system one of the core features and an important aspect that makes Hibernate so flexible.

5.3 Creating custom mapping types

Object-oriented languages like Java make it easy to define new types by writing new classes. This is a fundamental part of the definition of object-orientation. If we were then limited to the predefined built-in Hibernate mapping types when declaring properties of our persistent classes, we would lose much of Java's expressiveness. Furthermore, our domain model implementation would be tightly coupled to the physical data model, because new type conversions would be impossible.

Most ORM solutions that we have seen provide support for user-defined strategies for performing type conversions. These are often called converters. For example, the user can create a new strategy for persisting a property of JDK type `Integer` to a `VARCHAR` column. Hibernate provides a similar, much more powerful, feature called custom mapping types.

First you need to understand when it's appropriate to write your own custom mapping type, and which Hibernate extension point is relevant for you. We'll then write some custom mapping types and explore the options.

5.3.1 *Considering custom mapping types*

As an example, take the mapping of the `Address` class from previous chapters, as a component:

```
<component name="homeAddress" class="Address">

    <property name="street" type="string" column="HOME_STREET"/>
    <property name="city" type="string"   column="HOME_CITY"/>
    <property name="zipcode" type="string" column="HOME_ZIPCODE"/>

</component>
```

This value type mapping is straightforward; all properties of the new user-defined Java type are mapped to individual columns of a built-in SQL datatype. However, you can alternatively map it as a simple property, with a custom mapping type:

```
<property name="homeAddress"
          type="auction.persistence.CustomAddressType">

    <column name="HOME_STREET"/>
    <column name="HOME_CITY"/>
    <column name="HOME_ZIPCODE"/>

</property>
```

This is also probably the first time you've seen a single `<property>` element with several `<column>` elements nested inside. We're moving the responsibility for translating and converting between an `Address` value type (it isn't even named anywhere) and the named three columns to a separate class: `auction.persistence.CustomAddressType`. This class is now responsible for loading and saving this property. Note that no Java code changes in the domain model implementation—the homeAddress property is of type `Address`.

Granted, the benefit of replacing a component mapping with a custom mapping type is dubious in this case. As long as you require no special conversion when loading and saving this object, the CustomAddressType you now have to write is just additional work. However, you can already see that custom mapping types provide an additional buffer—something that may come in handy in the long run when extra conversion is required. Of course, there are better use cases for custom mapping types, as you'll soon see. (Many examples of useful Hibernate mapping types can be found on the Hibernate community website.)

Let's look at the Hibernate extension points for the creation of custom mapping types.

5.3.2 *The extension points*

Hibernate provides several interfaces that applications may use when defining custom mapping types. These interfaces reduce the work involved in creating new mapping types and insulate the custom type from changes to the Hibernate core. This allows you to easily upgrade Hibernate and keep your existing custom mapping types.

The extension points are as follows:

- org.hibernate.usertype.UserType—The basic extension point, which is useful in many situations. It provides the basic methods for custom loading and storing of value type instances.

- org.hibernate.usertype.CompositeUserType—An interface with more methods than the basic UserType, used to expose internals about your value type class to Hibernate, such as the individual properties. You can then refer to these properties in Hibernate queries.

- org.hibernate.usertype.UserCollectionType—A rarely needed interface that's used to implement custom collections. A custom mapping type implementing this interface isn't declared on a property mapping but is useful only for custom collection mappings. You have to implement this type if you want to persist a non-JDK collection and preserve additional semantics persistently. We discuss collection mappings and this extension point in the next chapter.

- org.hibernate.usertype.EnhancedUserType—An interface that extends UserType and provides additional methods for marshalling value types to and from XML representations, or enables a custom mapping type for use in identifier and discriminator mappings.

- `org.hibernate.usertype.UserVersionType`—An interface that extends `UserType` and provides additional methods enabling the custom mapping type for usage in entity version mappings.

- `org.hibernate.usertype.ParameterizedType`—A useful interface that can be combined with all others to provide configuration settings—that is, parameters defined in metadata. For example, you can write a single `Money-Converter` that knows how to translate values into Euro or US dollars, depending on a parameter in the mapping.

We'll now create some custom mapping types. You shouldn't consider this an unnecessary exercise, even if you're happy with the built-in Hibernate mapping types. In our experience, every sophisticated application has many good use cases for custom mapping types.

5.3.3 *The case for custom mapping types*

The `Bid` class defines an `amount` property, and the `Item` class defines an initialPrice property; both are monetary values. So far, we've used only a simple `BigDecimal` to represent the value, mapped with `big_decimal` to a single `NUMERIC` column.

Suppose you want to support multiple currencies in the auction application and that you have to refactor the existing domain model for this (customer-driven) change. One way to implement this change would be to add new properties to `Bid` and `Item`: `amountCurrency` and `initialPriceCurrency`. You could then map these new properties to additional `VARCHAR` columns with the built-in currency mapping type. We hope you never use this approach!

Instead, you should create a new `MonetaryAmount` class that encapsulates both currency and amount. Note that this is a class of your domain model; it doesn't have any dependency on Hibernate interfaces:

```
public class MonetaryAmount implements Serializable {

    private final BigDecimal amount;
    private final Currency currency;

    public MonetaryAmount(BigDecimal amount, Currency currency) {
        this.amount = amount;
        this.currency = currency;
    }

    public BigDecimal getAmount() { return amount; }

    public Currency getCurrency() { return currency; }
```

```
public boolean equals(Object o) { ... }
public int hashCode() { ...}

}
```

We have made `MonetaryAmount` an immutable class. This is a good practice in Java because it simplifies coding. Note that you have to implement `equals()` and `hashCode()` to finish the class (there is nothing special to consider here). You use this new `MonetaryAmount` to replace the `BigDecimal` of the `initialPrice` property in `Item`. You can and should use it for all other `BigDecimal` prices in any persistent classes, such as the `Bid.amount`, and in business logic—for example, in the billing system.

Let's map the refactored `initialPrice` property of `Item`, with its new `MonetaryAmount` type to the database.

5.3.4 Creating a UserType

Imagine that you're working with a legacy database that represents all monetary amounts in USD. The application is no longer restricted to a single currency (that was the point of the refactoring), but it takes some time for the database team to make the changes. You need to convert the amount to USD when persisting `MonetaryAmount` objects. When you load from the database, you convert it back to the currency the user selected in his or her preferences.

Create a new `MonetaryAmountUserType` class that implements the Hibernate interface `UserType`. This is your custom mapping type, shown in listing 5.4.

Listing 5.4 Custom mapping type for monetary amounts in USD

```
public class MonetaryAmountUserType
        implements UserType {
    public int[] sqlTypes() {             ❶
        return new int[]{ Hibernate.BIG_DECIMAL.sqlType() };
    }

    public Class returnedClass() { return MonetaryAmount.class; }   ❷

    public boolean isMutable() { return false; }    ❸

    public Object deepCopy(Object value) {  return value; }    ❹

    public Serializable disassemble(Object value)     ❺
        { return (Serializable) value; }

    public Object assemble(Serializable cached, Object owner)    ❻
        { return cached; }

    public Object replace(Object original,     ❼
                          Object target,
```

```
                              Object owner)
      { return original; }
    public boolean equals(Object x, Object y) {     ←─ ❽
        if (x == y) return true;
        if (x == null || y == null) return false;
        return x.equals(y);
    }

    public int hashCode(Object x) {
        return x.hashCode();
    }
                                                     ❾
    public Object nullSafeGet(ResultSet resultSet,  ←─
                              String[] names,
                              Object owner)
          throws SQLException {

        BigDecimal valueInUSD = resultSet.getBigDecimal(names[0]);
        // Deferred check after first read
        if (resultSet.wasNull()) return null;
        Currency userCurrency = User.getPreferences().getCurrency();
        MonetaryAmount amount = new MonetaryAmount(valueInUSD, "USD");
        return amount.convertTo(userCurrency);
    }
                                                          ❿
    public void nullSafeSet(PreparedStatement statement,  ←─
                            Object value,
                            int index)
          throws HibernateException, SQLException {

        if (value == null) {
          statement.setNull(index, Hibernate.BIG_DECIMAL.sqlType());
        } else {
          MonetaryAmount anyCurrency = (MonetaryAmount)value;
          MonetaryAmount amountInUSD =
            MonetaryAmount.convert( anyCurrency,
                                    Currency.getInstance("USD") );
          statement.setBigDecimal(index, amountInUSD.getAmount ());
        }
    }
  }
```

❶ The `sqlTypes()` method tells Hibernate what SQL column types to use for DDL schema generation. Notice that this method returns an array of type codes. A UserType may map a single property to multiple columns, but this legacy data model has only a single numeric column. By using the Hibernate.BIG_DECIMAL.sqlType() method, you let Hibernate decide the exact SQL datatype for the given database dialect. Alternatively, return a constant from `java.sql.Types`.

2 The `returnedClass()` method tells Hibernate what Java value type class is mapped by this `UserType`.

3 Hibernate can make some minor performance optimizations for immutable types like this one, for example, when comparing snapshots during dirty checking. The `isMutable()` method tells Hibernate that this type is immutable.

4 The `UserType` is also partially responsible for creating a snapshot of a value in the first place. Because `MonetaryAmount` is an immutable class, the `deepCopy()` method returns its argument. In the case of a mutable type, it would need to return a copy of the argument to be used as the snapshot value.

5 The `disassemble()` method is called when Hibernate puts a `MonetaryAmount` into the second-level cache. As you'll learn later, this is a cache of data that stores information in a serialized form.

6 The `assemble()` method does the opposite of disassembly: It can transform cached data into an instance of `MonetaryAmount`. As you can see, implementation of both routines is easy for immutable types.

7 Implement `replace()` to handle merging of detached object state. As you'll see later in the book, the process of merging involves an original and a target object, whose state must be combined. Again, for immutable value types, return the first argument. For mutable types, at least return a deep copy of the first argument. For mutable types that have component fields, you probably want to apply a recursive merging routine.

8 The `UserType` is responsible for dirty checking property values. The `equals()` method compares the current property value to a previous snapshot and determines whether the property is dirty and must by saved to the database. The `hashCode()` of two equal value typed instances has to be the same. We usually delegate this method to the actual value type class—in this case, the `hashCode()` method of the given `MonetaryAmount` object.

9 The `nullSafeGet()` method retrieves the property value from the JDBC `ResultSet`. You can also access the owner of the component if you need it for the conversion. All database values are in USD, so you convert it to the currency the user has currently set in his preferences. (Note that it's up to you to implement this conversion and preference handling.)

⑩ The `nullSafeSet()` method writes the property value to the JDBC `Prepared-Statement`. This method takes whatever currency is set and converts it to a simple `BigDecimal` USD amount before saving.

You now map the `initialPrice` property of `Item` as follows:

```
<property name="initialPrice"
         column="INITIAL_PRICE"
         type="persistence.MonetaryAmountUserType"/>
```

Note that you place the custom user type into the `persistence` package; it's part of the persistence layer of the application, not the domain model or business layer.

To use a custom type in annotations, you have to add a Hibernate extension:

```
@org.hibernate.annotations.Type(
    type = " persistence.MonetaryAmountUserType"
)
@Column(name = "INITIAL_PRICE")
private MonetaryAmount initialPrice;
```

This is the simplest kind of transformation that a `UserType` can perform. Much more sophisticated things are possible. A custom mapping type can perform validation; it can read and write data to and from an LDAP directory; it can even retrieve persistent objects from a different database. You're limited mainly by your imagination.

In reality, we'd prefer to represent both the amount and currency of monetary amounts in the database, especially if the schema isn't legacy but can be defined (or updated quickly). Let's assume you now have two columns available and can store the `MonetaryAmount` without much conversion. A first option may again be a simple `<component>` mapping. However, let's try to solve it with a custom mapping type.

(Instead of writing a new custom type, try to adapt the previous example for two columns. You can do this without changing the Java domain model classes—only the converter needs to be updated for this new requirement and the additional column named in the mapping.)

The disadvantage of a simple `UserType` implementation is that Hibernate doesn't know anything about the individual properties inside a `MonetaryAmount`. All it knows is the custom type class and the column names. The Hibernate query engine (discussed in more detail later) doesn't know how to query for `amount` or a particular `currency`.

You write a `CompositeUserType` if you need the full power of Hibernate queries. This (slightly more complex) interface exposes the properties of the `MonetaryAmount` to Hibernate queries. We'll now map it again with this more flexible customization interface to two columns, effectively producing an equivalent to a component mapping.

5.3.5 Creating a CompositeUserType

To demonstrate the flexibility of custom mappings types, you don't change the `MonetaryAmount` class (and other persistent classes) at all—you change only the custom mapping type, as shown in listing 5.5.

Listing 5.5 Custom mapping type for monetary amounts in new database schemas

```
public class MonetaryAmountCompositeUserType
        implements CompositeUserType {
    // public int[] sqlTypes()...              ←❶
    public Class returnedClass...
    public boolean isMutable...
    public Object deepCopy...
    public Serializable disassemble...
    public Object assemble...
    public Object replace...
    public boolean equals...
    public int hashCode...

    public Object nullSafeGet(ResultSet resultSet,    ←❷
                              String[] names,
                              SessionImplementor session,
                              Object owner)
            throws SQLException {

        BigDecimal value = resultSet.getBigDecimal( names[0] );
        if (resultSet.wasNull()) return null;
        Currency currency =
            Currency.getInstance(resultSet.getString( names[1] ) );
        return new MonetaryAmount(value, currency);
    }

    public void nullSafeSet(PreparedStatement statement,   ←❸
                            Object value,
                            int index,
                            SessionImplementor session)
            throws SQLException {

        if (value==null) {
            statement.setNull(index, Hibernate.BIG_DECIMAL.sqlType());
            statement.setNull(index+1, Hibernate.CURRENCY.sqlType());
        } else {
```

```
                MonetaryAmount amount = (MonetaryAmount) value;
                String currencyCode =
                            amount.getCurrency().getCurrencyCode();
                statement.setBigDecimal( index, amount.getAmount() );
                statement.setString( index+1, currencyCode );
            }
        }
        public String[] getPropertyNames() {
            return new String[] { "amount", "currency" };
        }
        public Type[] getPropertyTypes() {
            return new Type[] { Hibernate.BIG_DECIMAL,
                                Hibernate.CURRENCY };
        }
        public Object getPropertyValue(Object component, int property) {
            MonetaryAmount monetaryAmount = (MonetaryAmount) component;
            if (property == 0)
                return monetaryAmount.getAmount();
            else
                return monetaryAmount.getCurrency();
        }
        public void setPropertyValue(Object component,
                                     int property,
                                     Object value) {
          throw new
            UnsupportedOperationException("Immutable MonetaryAmount!");
        }
    }
```

④ at `public String[] getPropertyNames() {`
⑤ at `public Type[] getPropertyTypes() {`
⑥ at `public Object getPropertyValue(Object component, int property) {`
⑦ at `public void setPropertyValue(Object component,`

❶ The `CompositeUserType` interface requires the same housekeeping methods as the `UserType` you created earlier. However, the `sqlTypes()` method is no longer needed.

❷ Loading a value now is straightforward: You transform two column values in the result set to two property values in a new `MonetaryAmount` instance.

❸ Saving a value involves setting two parameters on the prepared statement.

❹ A `CompositeUserType` exposes the properties of the value type through `getPropertyNames()`.

❺ The properties each have their own type, as defined by `getPropertyTypes()`. The types of the SQL columns are now implicit from this method.

❻ The `getPropertyValue()` method returns the value of an individual property of the `MonetaryAmount`.

❼ The `setPropertyValue()` method sets the value of an individual property of the `MonetaryAmount`.

The `initialPrice` property now maps to two columns, so you need to declare both in the mapping file. The first column stores the value; the second stores the currency of the `MonetaryAmount`:

```
<property name="initialPrice"
          type="persistence.MonetaryAmountCompositeUserType">
    <column name="INITIAL_PRICE"/>
    <column name="INITIAL_PRICE_CURRENCY"/>
</property>
```

If `Item` is mapped with annotations, you have to declare several columns for this property. You can't use the `javax.persistence.Column` annotation several times, so a new, Hibernate-specific annotation is needed:

```
@org.hibernate.annotations.Type(
    type = "persistence.MonetaryAmountUserType"
)
@org.hibernate.annotations.Columns(columns = {
    @Column(name="INITIAL_PRICE"),
    @Column(name="INITIAL_PRICE_CURRENCY", length = 2)
})
private MonetaryAmount initialPrice;
```

In a Hibernate query, you can now refer to the `amount` and `currency` properties of the custom type, even though they don't appear anywhere in the mapping document as individual properties:

```
from Item i
where i.initialPrice.amount > 100.0
  and i.initialPrice.currency = 'AUD'
```

You have extended the buffer between the Java object model and the SQL database schema with the new custom composite type. Both representations are now more robust to changes. Note that the number of columns isn't relevant for your choice of `UserType` versus `CompositeUserType`—only your desire to expose value type properties for Hibernate queries.

Parameterization is a helpful feature for all custom mapping types.

5.3.6 *Parameterizing custom types*

Let's assume that you face the initial problem again: conversion of money to a different currency when storing it to the database. Often, problems are more subtle than a generic conversion; for example, you may store US dollars in some tables and Euros in others. You still want to write a single custom mapping type for this, which can do arbitrary conversions. This is possible if you add the `ParameterizedType` interface to your `UserType` or `CompositeUserType` classes:

```
public class MonetaryAmountConversionType
    implements UserType, ParameterizedType {

    // Configuration parameter
    private Currency convertTo;

    public void setParameterValues(Properties parameters) {
       this.convertTo = Currency.getInstance(
                             parameters.getProperty("convertTo")
                      );
    }

    // ... Housekeeping methods

    public Object nullSafeGet(ResultSet resultSet,
                              String[] names,
                              SessionImplementor session,
                              Object owner)
          throws SQLException {

       BigDecimal value = resultSet.getBigDecimal( names[0] );
       if (resultSet.wasNull()) return null;
       // When loading, take the currency from the database
       Currency currency = Currency.getInstance(
                             resultSet.getString( names[1] )
                             );
       return new MonetaryAmount(value, currency);
    }

    public void nullSafeSet(PreparedStatement statement,
                            Object value,
                            int index,
                            SessionImplementor session)
          throws SQLException {

       if (value==null) {
           statement.setNull(index, Types.NUMERIC);
       } else {
           MonetaryAmount amount = (MonetaryAmount) value;
           // When storing, convert the amount to the
           // currency this converter was parameterized with
           MonetaryAmount dbAmount =
               MonetaryAmount.convert(amount, convertTo);
           statement.setBigDecimal( index, dbAmount.getAmount() );
           statement.setString( index+1,
                               dbAmount.getCurrencyCode() );
       }
    }
}
```

We left out the usual mandatory housekeeping methods in this example. The important additional method is setParameterValues() of the Parameterized-Type interface. Hibernate calls this method on startup to initialize this class with a convertTo parameter. The nullSafeSet() methods uses this setting to convert to the target currency when saving a MonetaryAmount. The nullSafeGet() method takes the currency that is present in the database and leaves it to the client to deal with the currency of a loaded MonetaryAmount (this asymmetric implementation isn't the best idea, naturally).

You now have to set the configuration parameters in your mapping file when you apply the custom mapping type. A simple solution is the nested <type> mapping on a property:

```
<property name="initialPrice">
    <column name="INITIAL_PRICE"/>
    <column name="INITIAL_PRICE_CUR"/>
    <type name="persistence.MonetaryAmountConversionType">
        <param name="convertTo">USD</param>
    </type>
</property>
```

However, this is inconvenient and requires duplication if you have many monetary amounts in your domain model. A better strategy uses a separate definition of the type, including all parameters, under a unique name that you can then reuse across all your mappings. You do this with a separate <typedef>, an element (you can also use it without parameters):

```
<typedef class="persistence.MonetaryAmountConversionType"
        name="monetary_amount_usd">
    <param name="convertTo">USD</param>
</typedef>

<typedef class="persistence.MonetaryAmountConversionType"
        name="monetary_amount_eur">
    <param name="convertTo">EUR</param>
</typedef>
```

What we show here is a binding of a custom mapping type with some arguments to the names monetary_amount_usd and monetary_amount_eur. This definition can be placed anywhere in your mapping files; it's a child element of <hibernate-mapping> (as mentioned earlier in the book, larger applications have often one or several MyCustomTypes.hbm.xml files with no class mappings). With Hibernate extensions, you can define named custom types with parameters in annotations:

```
@org.hibernate.annotations.TypeDefs({
    @org.hibernate.annotations.TypeDef(
        name="monetary_amount_usd",
        typeClass = persistence.MonetaryAmountConversionType.class,
        parameters = { @Parameter(name="convertTo", value="USD") }
    ),
    @org.hibernate.annotations.TypeDef(
        name="monetary_amount_eur",
        typeClass = persistence.MonetaryAmountConversionType.class,
        parameters = { @Parameter(name="convertTo", value="EUR") }
    )
})
```

This annotation metadata is global as well, so it can be placed outside any Java class declaration (right after the `import` statements) or in a separate file, `package-info.java`, as discussed in chapter 2, section 2.2.1, "Using Hibernate Annotations." A good location in this system is in a `package-info.java` file in the `persistence` package.

In XML mapping files and annotation mappings, you now refer to the defined type name instead of the fully qualified class name of your custom type:

```
<property name="initialPrice"
          type="monetary_amount_usd">
    <column name="INITIAL_PRICE"/>
    <column name="INITIAL_PRICE_CUR"/>
</property>
```

```
@org.hibernate.annotations.Type(type = "monetary_amount_eur")
@org.hibernate.annotations.Columns({
  @Column(name = "BID_AMOUNT"),
  @Column(name = "BID_AMOUNT_CUR")
})
private MonetaryAmount bidAmount;
```

Let's look at a different, extremely important, application of custom mapping types. The type-safe enumeration design pattern can be found in almost all applications.

5.3.7 *Mapping enumerations*

An enumeration type is a common Java idiom where a class has a constant (small) number of immutable instances. In CaveatEmptor, this can be applied to credit cards: for example, to express the possible types a user can enter and the application offers (Mastercard, Visa, and so on). Or, you can enumerate the possible ratings a user can submit in a `Comment`, about a particular auction.

In older JDKs, you had to implement such classes (let's call them CreditCard-Type and Rating) yourself, following the type-safe enumeration pattern. This is still the right way to do it if you don't have JDK 5.0; the pattern and compatible custom mapping types can be found on the Hibernate community website.

Using enumerations in JDK 5.0

If you use JDK 5.0, you can use the built-in language support for type-safe enumerations. For example, a Rating class looks as follows:

```
package auction.model;

public enum Rating {
    EXCELLENT, OK, BAD
}
```

The Comment class has a property of this type:

```
public class Comment {
    ...
    private Rating rating;
    private Item auction;
    ...
}
```

This is how you use the enumeration in the application code:

```
Comment goodComment =
    new Comment(Rating.EXCELLENT, thisAuction);
```

You now have to persist this Comment instance and its Rating. One approach is to use the actual name of the enumeration and save it to a VARCHAR column in the COMMENTS table. This RATING column will then contain EXCELLENT, OK, or BAD, depending on the Rating given.

Let's write a Hibernate UserType that can load and store VARCHAR-backed enumerations, such as the Rating.

Writing a custom enumeration handler

Instead of the most basic UserType interface, we now want to show you the EnhancedUserType interface. This interface allows you to work with the Comment entity in XML representation mode, not only as a POJO (see the discussion of data representations in chapter 3, section 3.4, "Alternative entity representation"). Furthermore, the implementation you'll write can support any VARCHAR-backed enumeration, not only Rating, thanks to the additional Parameterized-Type interface.

Look at the code in listing 5.6.

Listing 5.6 Custom mapping type for string-backed enumerations

```java
public class StringEnumUserType
        implements EnhancedUserType, ParameterizedType {

    private Class<Enum> enumClass;

    public void setParameterValues(Properties parameters) {     ①
        String enumClassName =
            parameters.getProperty("enumClassname");
        try {
            enumClass = ReflectHelper.classForName(enumClassName);
        } catch (ClassNotFoundException cnfe) {
            throw new
                HibernateException("Enum class not found", cnfe);
        }
    }

    public Class returnedClass() {     ②
        return enumClass;
    }

    public int[] sqlTypes() {     ③
        return new int[] { Hibernate.STRING.sqlType() };
    }

    public boolean isMutable...     ④
    public Object deepCopy...
    public Serializable disassemble...
    public Object replace...
    public Object assemble...
    public boolean equals...
    public int hashCode...

    public Object fromXMLString(String xmlValue) {     ⑤
        return Enum.valueOf(enumClass, xmlValue);
    }

    public String objectToSQLString(Object value) {
        return '\'' + ( (Enum) value ).name() + '\'';
    }

    public String toXMLString(Object value) {
        return ( (Enum) value ).name();
    }

    public Object nullSafeGet(ResultSet rs,     ⑥
                              String[] names,
                              Object owner)
            throws SQLException {
        String name = rs.getString( names[0] );
        return rs.wasNull() ? null : Enum.valueOf(enumClass, name);     ⑦
    }

    public void nullSafeSet(PreparedStatement st,
```

```
                                Object value,
                                int index)
              throws SQLException {
        if (value == null) {
            st.setNull(index, Hibernate.STRING.sqlType());
        } else {
            st.setString( index, ( (Enum) value ).name() );
        }
    }

}
```

❶ The configuration parameter for this custom mapping type is the name of the enumeration class it's used for, such as `Rating`.

❷ It's also the class that is returned from this method.

❸ A single `VARCHAR` column is needed in the database table. You keep it portable by letting Hibernate decide the SQL datatype.

❹ These are the usual housekeeping methods for an immutable type.

❺ The following three methods are part of the `EnhancedUserType` and are used for XML marshalling.

❻ When you're loading an enumeration, you get its name from the database and create an instance.

❼ When you're saving an enumeration, you store its name.

Next, you'll map the `rating` property with this new custom type.

Mapping enumerations with XML and annotations

In the XML mapping, first create a custom type definition:

```
<typedef class="persistence.StringEnumUserType"
        name="rating">
    <param name="enumClassname">auction.model.Rating</param>
</typedef>
```

You can now use the type named `rating` in the `Comment` class mapping:

```
<property  name="rating"
           column="RATING"
           type="rating"
           not-null="true"
           update="false"
           access="field"/>
```

Because ratings are immutable, you map it as `update="false"` and enable direct field access (no setter method for immutable properties). If other classes besides `Comment` have a `Rating` property, use the defined custom mapping type again.

The definition and declaration of this custom mapping type in annotations looks the same as the one you did in the previous section.

On the other hand, you can rely on the Java Persistence provider to persist enumerations. If you have a property in one of your annotated entity classes of type `java.lang.Enum` (such as the `rating` in your `Comment`), and it isn't marked as `@Transient` or `transient` (the Java keyword), the Hibernate JPA implementation must persist this property out of the box without complaining; it has a built-in type that handles this. This built-in mapping type has to default to a representation of an enumeration in the database. The two common choices are string representation, as you implemented for native Hibernate with a custom type, or ordinal representation. An ordinal representation saves the position of the selected enumeration option: for example, 1 for EXCELLENT, 2 for OK, and 3 for BAD. The database column also defaults to a numeric column. You can change this default enumeration mapping with the `Enumerated` annotation on your property:

```
public class Comment {
    ...

    @Enumerated(EnumType.STRING)
    @Column(name = "RATING", nullable = false, updatable = false)
    private Rating rating;
    ...
}
```

You've now switched to a string-based representation, effectively the same representation your custom type can read and write. You can also use a JPA XML descriptor:

```
<entity class="auction.model.Item" access="PROPERTY">
  <attributes>
    ...
    <basic name="rating">
        <column name="RATING" nullable="false" updatable="false"/>
        <enumerated>STRING</enumerated>
    </basic>
  </attributes>
</entity>
```

You may (rightfully) ask why you have to write your own custom mapping type for enumerations when obviously Hibernate, as a Java Persistence provider, can persist and load enumerations out of the box. The secret is that Hibernate Annotations includes several custom mapping types that implement the behavior defined by Java Persistence. You could use these custom types in XML mappings; however, they aren't user friendly (they need many parameters) and weren't written for that purpose. You can check the source (such as `org.hibernate.type.EnumType` in Hibernate Annotations) to learn their parameters and decide if you want to use them directly in XML.

Querying with custom mapping types

One further problem you may run into is using enumerated types in Hibernate queries. For example, consider the following query in HQL that retrieves all comments that are rated "bad":

```
Query q =
    session.createQuery(
      "from Comment c where c.rating = auction.model.Rating.BAD"
    );
```

Although this query works if you persist your enumeration as a string (the query parser uses the enumeration value as a constant), it doesn't work if you selected ordinal representation. You have to use a bind parameter and set the rating value for the comparison programmatically:

```
Query q =
    session.createQuery("from Comment c where c.rating = :rating");

Properties params = new Properties();
params.put("enumClassname",
            "auction.model.Rating");

q.setParameter("rating", Rating.BAD,
                Hibernate.custom(StringEnumUserType.class, params)
                );
```

The last line in this example uses the static helper method `Hibernate.custom()` to convert the custom mapping type to a Hibernate `Type`; this is a simple way to tell Hibernate about your enumeration mapping and how to deal with the `Rating.BAD` value. Note that you also have to tell Hibernate about any initialization properties the parameterized type may need.

Unfortunately, there is no API in Java Persistence for arbitrary and custom query parameters, so you have to fall back to the Hibernate `Session` API and create a Hibernate `Query` object.

We recommend that you become intimately familiar with the Hibernate type system and that you consider the creation of custom mapping types an essential skill—it will be useful in every application you develop with Hibernate or JPA.

5.4 *Summary*

In this chapter, you learned how inheritance hierarchies of entities can be mapped to the database with the four basic inheritance mapping strategies: table per concrete class with implicit polymorphism, table per concrete class with unions, table per class hierarchy, and the normalized table per subclass strategy. You've seen how these strategies can be mixed for a particular hierarchy and when each strategy is most appropriate.

We also elaborated on the Hibernate entity and value type distinction, and how the Hibernate mapping type system works. You used various built-in types and wrote your own custom types by utilizing the Hibernate extension points such as `UserType` and `ParameterizedType`.

Table 5.5 shows a summary you can use to compare native Hibernate features and Java Persistence.

Table 5.5 Hibernate and JPA comparison chart for chapter 5

Hibernate Core	Java Persistence and EJB 3.0
Supports four inheritance mapping strategies. Mixing of inheritance strategies is possible.	Four inheritance mapping strategies are standardized; mixing strategies in one hierarchy isn't considered portable. Only table per class hierarchy and table per subclass are required for JPA-compliant providers.
A persistent supertype can be an abstract class or an interface (with property accessor methods only).	A persistent supertype can be an abstract class; mapped interfaces aren't considered portable.
Provides flexible built-in mapping types and converters for value typed properties.	There is automatic detection of mapping types, with standardized override for temporal and enum mapping types. Hibernate extension annotation is used for any custom mapping type declaration.
Powerful extendable type system.	The standard requires built-in types for enumerations, LOBs, and many other value types for which you'd have to write or apply a custom mapping type in native Hibernate.

The next chapter introduces collection mappings and discusses how you can handle collections of value typed objects (for example, a collection of `Strings`) and collections that contain references to entity instances.

Mapping collections
and entity associations

This chapter covers

- Basic collection mapping strategies
- Mapping collections of value types
- Mapping a parent/children entity relationship

Two important (and sometimes difficult to understand) topics didn't appear in the previous chapters: the mapping of collections, and the mapping of associations between entity classes.

Most developers new to Hibernate are dealing with collections and entity associations for the first time when they try to map a typical *parent/child relationship*. But instead of jumping right into the middle, we start this chapter with basic collection mapping concepts and simple examples. After that, you'll be prepared for the first collection in an entity association—although we'll come back to more complicated entity association mappings in the next chapter. To get the full picture, we recommend you read both chapters.

6.1 Sets, bags, lists, and maps of value types

An object of *value type* has no database identity; it belongs to an entity instance, and its persistent state is embedded in the table row of the owning entity—at least, if an entity has a reference to a single instance of a valuetype. If an entity class has a collection of value types (or a collection of references to value-typed instances), you need an additional table, the so-called collection table.

Before you map collections of value types to collection tables, remember that value-typed classes don't have identifiers or identifier properties. The lifespan of a value-type instance is bounded by the lifespan of the owning entity instance. A value type doesn't support shared references.

Java has a rich collection API, so you can choose the collection interface and implementation that best fits your domain model design. Let's walk through the most common collection mappings.

Suppose that sellers in CaveatEmptor are able to attach images to Items. An image is accessible only via the containing item; it doesn't need to support associations from any other entity in your system. The application manages the collection of images through the Item class, adding and removing elements. An image object has no life outside of the collection; it's dependent on an Item entity.

In this case, it isn't unreasonable to model the image class as a value type. Next. you need to decide what collection to use.

6.1.1 Selecting a collection interface

The idiom for a collection property in the Java domain model is always the same:

```
private <<Interface>> images = new <<Implementation>>();

...
// Getter and setter methods
```

Use an interface to declare the type of the property, not an implementation. Pick a matching implementation, and initialize the collection right away; doing so avoids uninitialized collections (we don't recommend initializing collections late, in constructors or setter methods).

If you work with JDK 5.0, you'll likely code with the generic versions of the JDK collections. Note that this isn't a requirement; you can also specify the contents of the collection explicitly in mapping metadata. Here's a typical generic Set with a type parameter:

```
private Set<String> images = new HashSet<String>();
...
// Getter and setter methods
```

Out of the box, Hibernate supports the most important JDK collection interfaces. In other words, it knows how to preserve the semantics of JDK collections, maps, and arrays in a persistent fashion. Each interface has a matching implementation supported by Hibernate, and it's important that you use the right combination. Hibernate only *wraps* the collection object you've already initialized on declaration of the field (or sometimes replaces it, if it's not the right one).

Without extending Hibernate, you can choose from the following collections:

- A java.util.Set is mapped with a <set> element. Initialize the collection with a java.util.HashSet. The order of its elements isn't preserved, and duplicate elements aren't allowed. This is the most common persistent collection in a typical Hibernate application.

- A java.util.SortedSet can be mapped with <set>, and the sort attribute can be set to either a comparator or natural ordering for in-memory sorting. Initialize the collection with a java.util.TreeSet instance.

- A java.util.List can be mapped with <list>, preserving the position of each element with an additional index column in the collection table. Initialize with a java.util.ArrayList.

- A java.util.Collection can be mapped with <bag> or <idbag>. Java doesn't have a Bag interface or an implementation; however, java.util.Collection allows bag semantics (possible duplicates, no element order is preserved). Hibernate supports persistent bags (it uses lists internally but ignores the index of the elements). Use a java.util.ArrayList to initialize a bag collection.

- A java.util.Map can be mapped with <map>, preserving key and value pairs. Use a java.util.HashMap to initialize a property.

- A `java.util.SortedMap` can be mapped with `<map>` element, and the `sort` attribute can be set to either a comparator or natural ordering for in-memory sorting. Initialize the collection with a `java.util.TreeMap` instance.

- Arrays are supported by Hibernate with `<primitive-array>` (for Java primitive value types) and `<array>` (for everything else). However, they're rarely used in domain models, because Hibernate can't wrap array properties. You lose lazy loading without bytecode instrumentation, and optimized dirty checking, essential convenience and performance features for persistent collections.

The JPA standard doesn't name all these options. The possible standard collection property types are `Set`, `List`, `Collection`, and `Map`. Arrays aren't considered.

Furthermore, the JPA specification only specifies that collection properties hold references to entity objects. Collections of value types, such as simple `String` instances, aren't standardized. However, the specification document already mentions that future versions of JPA will support collection elements of embeddable classes (in other words, value types). You'll need vendor-specific support if you want to map collections of value types with annotations. Hibernate Annotations include that support, and we'd expect many other JPA vendors support the same.

If you want to map collection interfaces and implementations not directly supported by Hibernate, you need to tell Hibernate about the semantics of your custom collections. The extension point in Hibernate is called `Persistent-Collection`; usually you extend one of the existing `PersistentSet`, `Persistent-Bag`, or `PersistentList` classes. Custom persistent collections are not very easy to write and we don't recommend doing this if you aren't an experienced Hibernate user. An example can be found in the Hibernate test suite source code, as part of your Hibernate download package.

We now go through several scenarios, always implementing the collection of item images. You map it first in XML and then with Hibernate's support for collection annotations. For now, assume that the image is stored somewhere on the filesystem and that you keep just the filename in the database. How images are stored and loaded with this approach isn't discussed; we focus on the mapping.

6.1.2 *Mapping a set*

The simplest implementation is a `Set` of `String` image filenames. First, add a collection property to the `Item` class:

```
private Set images = new HashSet();
...
public Set getImages() {
    return this.images;
}
public void setImages(Set images) {
    this.images = images;
}
```

Now, create the following mapping in the Item's XML metadata:

```
<set name="images" table="ITEM_IMAGE">

    <key column="ITEM_ID"/>

    <element type="string" column="FILENAME" not-null="true"/>
</set>
```

The image filenames are stored in a table named ITEM_IMAGE, the collection table. From the point of view of the database, this table is a separate entity, a separate table, but Hibernate hides this for you. The <key> element declares the foreign key column in the collection table that references the primary key ITEM_ID of the owning entity. The <element> tag declares this collection as a collection of value type instances—in this case, of strings.

A set can't contain duplicate elements, so the primary key of the ITEM_IMAGE collection table is a composite of both columns in the <set> declaration: ITEM_ID and FILENAME. You can see the schema in figure 6.1.

ITEM

ITEM_ID	NAME
1	Foo
2	Bar
3	Baz

ITEM_IMAGE

ITEM_ID	FILENAME
1	fooimage1.jpg
1	fooimage2.jpg
2	barimage1.jpg

Figure 6.1
Table structure and example data for a collection of strings

It doesn't seem likely that you would allow the user to attach the same image more than once, but let's suppose you did. What kind of mapping would be appropriate in that case?

6.1.3 *Mapping an identifier bag*

An unordered collection that permits duplicate elements is called a *bag*. Curiously, the Java Collections framework doesn't include a bag implementation. However, the java.util.Collection interface has bag semantics, so you only need a matching implementation. You have two choices:

- Write the collection property with the `java.util.Collection` interface, and, on declaration, initialize it with an `ArrayList` of the JDK. Map the collection in Hibernate with a standard `<bag>` or `<idbag>` element. Hibernate has a built-in `PersistentBag` that can deal with lists; however, consistent with the contract of a bag, it ignores the position of elements in the `ArrayList`. In other words, you get a persistent `Collection`.

- Write the collection property with the `java.util.List` interface, and, on declaration, initialize it with an `ArrayList` of the JDK. Map it like the previous option, but expose a different collection interface in the domain model class. This approach works but isn't recommended, because clients using this collection property may think the order of elements is always preserved, which isn't the case if it's mapped as a `<bag>` or `<idbag>`.

We recommend the first option. Change the type of `images` in the `Item` class from `Set` to `Collection`, and initialize it with an `ArrayList`:

```
private Collection images = new ArrayList();
...
public Collection getImages() {
    return this.images;
}

public void setImages(Collection images) {
    this.images = images;
}
```

Note that the setter method accepts a `Collection`, which can be anything in the JDK collection interface hierarchy. However, Hibernate is smart enough to replace this when persisting the collection. (It also relies on an `ArrayList` internally, like you did in the declaration of the field.)

You also have to modify the collection table to permit duplicate FILENAMEs; the table needs a different primary key. An `<idbag>` mapping adds a surrogate key column to the collection table, much like the synthetic identifiers you use for entity classes:

```
<idbag name="images" table="ITEM_IMAGE">

    <collection-id type="long" column="ITEM_IMAGE_ID">
        <generator class="sequence"/>
    </collection-id>

    <key column="ITEM_ID"/>

    <element type="string" column="FILENAME" not-null="true"/>
</idbag>
```

ITEM	
ITEM_ID	NAME
1	Foo
2	Bar
3	Baz

ITEM_IMAGE		
ITEM_IMAGE_ID	ITEM_ID	FILENAME
1	1	fooimage1.jpg
2	1	fooimage1.jpg
3	3	barimage1.jpg

Figure 6.2   A surrogate primary key allows duplicate bag elements.

In this case, the primary key is the generated ITEM_IMAGE_ID, as you can see in figure 6.2. Note that the `native` generator for primary keys isn't supported for `<idbag>` mappings; you have to name a concrete strategy. This usually isn't a problem, because real-world applications often use a customized identifier generator anyway. You can also isolate your identifier generation strategy with placeholders; see chapter 3, section 3.3.4.3, "Using placeholders."

Also note that the ITEM_IMAGE_ID column isn't exposed to the application in any way. Hibernate manages it internally.

A more likely scenario is one in which you wish to preserve the order in which images are attached to the Item. There are a number of good ways to do this; one way is to use a real list, instead of a bag.

6.1.4   Mapping a list

First, let's update the Item class:

```
private List images = new ArrayList();
...
public List getImages() {
    return this.images;
}

public void setImages(List images) {
    this.images = images;
}
```

A `<list>` mapping requires the addition of an *index column* to the collection table. The index column defines the position of the element in the collection. Thus, Hibernate is able to preserve the ordering of the collection elements. Map the collection as a `<list>`:

```
<list name="images" table="ITEM_IMAGE">

    <key column="ITEM_ID"/>

    <list-index column="POSITION"/>
```

```
    <element type="string" column="FILENAME" not-null="true"/>
</list>
```

(There is also an index element in the XML DTD, for compatibility with Hibernate 2.x. The new list-index is recommended; it's less confusing and does the same thing.)

The primary key of the collection table is a composite of ITEM_ID and POSITION. Notice that duplicate elements (FILENAME) are now allowed, which is consistent with the semantics of a list, see figure 6.3.

ITEM

ITEM_ID	NAME
1	Foo
2	Bar
3	Baz

ITEM_IMAGE

ITEM_ID	POSITION	FILENAME
1	0	fooimage1.jpg
1	1	fooimage2.jpg
1	2	foomage3.jpg

Figure 6.3   The collection table preserves the position of each element.

The index of the persistent list starts at zero. You could change this, for example, with <list-index base="1".../> in your mapping. Note that Hibernate adds null elements to your Java list if the index numbers in the database aren't continuous.

Alternatively, you could map a Java array instead of a list. Hibernate supports this; an array mapping is virtually identical to the previous example, except with different element and attribute names (<array> and <array-index>). However, for reasons explained earlier, Hibernate applications rarely use arrays.

Now, suppose that the images for an item have user-supplied names in addition to the filename. One way to model this in Java is a map, with names as keys and filenames as values of the map.

6.1.5   *Mapping a map*

Again, make a small change to the Java class:

```
private Map images = new HashMap();
...
public Map getImages() {
    return this.images;
}
public void setImages(Map images) {
    this.images = images;
}
```

Mapping a <map> (pardon us) is similar to mapping a list.

ITEM

ITEM_ID	NAME
1	Foo
2	Bar
3	Baz

ITEM_IMAGE

ITEM_ID	IMAGENAME	FILENAME
1	Image One	fooimage1.jpg
1	Image Two	fooimage2.jpg
1	Image Three	foomage3.jpg

Figure 6.4   Tables for a map, using strings as indexes and elements

```
<map name="images" table="ITEM_IMAGE">

    <key column="ITEM_ID"/>

    <map-key column="IMAGENAME" type="string"/>

    <element type="string" column="FILENAME" not-null="true"/>
</map>
```

The primary key of the collection table is a composite of ITEM_ID and IMAGENAME. The IMAGENAME column holds the keys of the map. Again, duplicate elements are allowed; see figure 6.4 for a graphical view of the tables.

This map is unordered. What if you want to always sort your map by the name of the image?

6.1.6 Sorted and ordered collections

In a startling abuse of the English language, the words *sorted* and *ordered* mean different things when it comes to Hibernate persistent collections. A *sorted collection* is sorted in memory using a Java comparator. An *ordered collection* is ordered at the database level using an SQL query with an order by clause.

Let's make the map of images a sorted map. First, you need to change the initialization of the Java property to a java.util.TreeMap and switch to the java.util.SortedMap interface:

```
private SortedMap images = new TreeMap();
...
public SortedMap getImages() {
    return this.images;
}

public void setImages(SortedMap images) {
    this.images = images;
}
```

Hibernate handles this collection accordingly, if you map it as sorted:

```
<map name="images"
        table="ITEM_IMAGE"
        sort="natural">

    <key column="ITEM_ID"/>

    <map-key column="IMAGENAME" type="string"/>

    <element type="string" column="FILENAME" not-null="true"/>
</map>
```

By specifying `sort="natural"`, you tell Hibernate to use a `SortedMap` and to sort the image names according to the `compareTo()` method of `java.lang.String`. If you need some other sort algorithm (for example, reverse alphabetical order), you may specify the name of a class that implements `java.util.Comparator` in the `sort` attribute. For example:

```
<map name="images"
        table="ITEM_IMAGE"
        sort="auction.util.comparator.ReverseStringComparator">

    <key column="ITEM_ID"/>

    <map-key column="IMAGENAME" type="string"/>

    <element type="string" column="FILENAME" not-null="true"/>
</map>
```

A `java.util.SortedSet` (with a `java.util.TreeSet` implementation) is mapped like this:

```
<set name="images"
        table="ITEM_IMAGE"
        sort="natural">

    <key column="ITEM_ID"/>

    <element type="string" column="FILENAME" not-null="true"/>
</set>
```

Bags may not be sorted (there is no `TreeBag`, unfortunately), nor may lists; the order of list elements is defined by the list index.

Alternatively, instead of switching to the `Sorted*` interfaces and the (`Tree*` implementations), you may want to work with a linked map and to sort elements on the database side, not in memory. Keep the `Map`/`HashMap` declaration in the Java class, and create the following mapping:

```
<map name="images"
        table="ITEM_IMAGE"
        order-by="IMAGENAME asc">
```

```
    <key column="ITEM_ID"/>

    <map-key column="IMAGENAME" type="string"/>

    <element type="string" column="FILENAME" not-null="true"/>
</map>
```

The expression in the `order-by` attribute is a fragment of an SQL order by clause. In this case, Hibernate orders the collection elements by the IMAGENAME column in ascending order during loading of the collection. You can even include an SQL function call in the `order-by` attribute:

```
<map name="images"
     table="ITEM_IMAGE"
     order-by="lower(FILENAME) asc">

    <key column="ITEM_ID"/>

    <map-key column="IMAGENAME" type="string"/>

    <element type="string" column="FILENAME" not-null="true"/>
</map>
```

You can order by any column of the collection table. Internally, Hibernate uses a `LinkedHashMap`, a variation of a map that preserves the insertion order of key elements. In other words, the order that Hibernate uses to add the elements to the collection, during loading of the collection, is the iteration order you see in your application. The same can be done with a set: Hibernate internally uses a `LinkedHashSet`. In your Java class, the property is a regular `Set/HashSet`, but Hibernate's internal wrapping with a `LinkedHashSet` is again enabled with the `order-by` attribute:

```
<set name="images"
     table="ITEM_IMAGE"
     order-by="FILENAME asc">

    <key column="ITEM_ID"/>

    <element type="string" column="FILENAME" not-null="true"/>
</set>
```

You can also let Hibernate order the elements of a bag for you during collection loading. Your Java collection property is either `Collection/ArrayList` or `List/ArrayList`. Internally, Hibernate uses an `ArrayList` to implement a bag that preserves insertion-iteration order:

```
<idbag name="images"
       table="ITEM_IMAGE"
       order-by="ITEM_IMAGE_ID desc">
```

```
        <collection-id type="long" column="ITEM_IMAGE_ID">
            <generator class="sequence"/>
        </collection-id>

        <key column="ITEM_ID"/>

        <element type="string" column="FILENAME" not-null="true"/>
    </idbag>
```

The linked collections Hibernate uses internally for sets and maps are available only in JDK 1.4 or later; older JDKs don't come with a LinkedHashMap and LinkedHashSet. Ordered bags are available in all JDK versions; internally, an ArrayList is used.

In a real system, it's likely that you'll need to keep more than just the image name and filename. You'll probably need to create an Image class for this extra information. This is the perfect use case for a collection of components.

6.2 Collections of components

You could map Image as an entity class and create a one-to-many relationship from Item to Image. However, this isn't necessary, because Image can be modeled as a value type: Instances of this class have a dependent lifecycle, don't need their own identity, and don't have to support shared references.

As a value type, the Image class defines the properties name, filename, sizeX, and sizeY. It has a single association with its owner, the Item entity class, as shown in figure 6.5.

As you can see from the composition association style (the black diamond), Image is a component of Item, and Item is the entity that is responsible for the lifecycle of Image instances. The multiplicity of the association further declares this association as many-valued—that is, many (or zero) Image instances for the same Item instance.

Let's walk through the implementation of this in Java and through a mapping in XML.

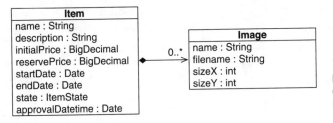

Figure 6.5
Collection of Image components in Item

6.2.1 *Writing the component class*

First, implement the `Image` class as a regular POJO. As you know from chapter 4, component classes don't have an identifier property. You must implement `equals()` (and `hashCode()`) and compare the `name`, `filename`, `sizeX`, and `sizeY` properties. Hibernate relies on this equality routine to check instances for modifications. A custom implementation of `equals()` and `hashCode()` isn't required for all component classes (we would have mentioned this earlier). However, we recommend it for any component class because the implementation is straightforward, and "better safe than sorry" is a good motto.

The `Item` class may have a `Set` of images, with no duplicates allowed. Let's map this to the database.

6.2.2 *Mapping the collection*

Collections of components are mapped similarly to collections of JDK value type. The only difference is the use of `<composite-element>` instead of an `<element>` tag. An ordered set of images (internally, a `LinkedHashSet`) can be mapped like this:

```
<set name="images"
    table="ITEM_IMAGE"
    order-by="IMAGENAME asc">

    <key column="ITEM_ID"/>

    <composite-element class="Image">
      <property name="name" column="IMAGENAME" not-null="true"/>
      <property name="filename" column="FILENAME" not-null="true"/>
      <property name="sizeX" column="SIZEX" not-null="true"/>
      <property name="sizeY" column="SIZEY" not-null="true"/>
    </composite-element>
</set>
```

The tables with example data are shown in figure 6.6.

This is a set, so the primary key of the collection table is a composite of the key column and all element columns: `ITEM_ID`, `IMAGENAME`, `FILENAME`, `SIZEX`, and `SIZEY`. Because these columns all appear in the primary key, you needed to declare them with `not-null="true"` (or make sure they're `NOT NULL` in any existing schema). No column in a composite primary key can be nullable—you can't identify what you don't know. This is probably a disadvantage of this particular mapping. Before you improve this (as you may guess, with an identifier bag), let's enable bidirectional navigation.

ITEM

ITEM_ID	ITEM_NAME
1	Foo
2	Bar
3	Baz

ITEM_IMAGE

ITEM_ID	IMAGENAME	FILENAME	SIZEX	SIZEY
1	Foo	Foo.jpg	123	123
1	Bar	Bar.jpg	420	80
2	Baz	Baz.jpg	50	60

Figure 6.6
Example data tables for a collection of components mapping

6.2.3 *Enabling bidirectional navigation*

The association from Item to Image is unidirectional. You can navigate to the images by accessing the collection through an Item instance and iterating: anItem.getImages().iterator(). This is the only way you can get these image objects; no other entity holds a reference to them (value type again).

On the other hand, navigating from an image back to an item doesn't make much sense. However, it may be convenient to access a back pointer like anImage.getItem() in some cases. Hibernate can fill in this property for you if you add a <parent> element to the mapping:

```
<set name="images"
     table="ITEM_IMAGE"
     order-by="IMAGE_NAME asc">

    <key column="ITEM_ID"/>

    <composite-element class="Image">
        <parent name="item"/>
        <property name="name" column="IMAGENAME" not-null="true"/>
        <property name="filename" column="FILENAME" not-null="true"/>
        <property name="sizeX" column="SIZEX" not-null="true"/>
        <property name="sizeY" column="SIZEY" not-null="true"/>
    </composite-element>
</set>
```

True bidirectional navigation is impossible, however. You can't retrieve an Image independently and then navigate back to its parent Item. This is an important issue: You can load Image instances by querying for them. But these Image objects won't have a reference to their owner (the property is null) when you query in HQL or with a Criteria. They're retrieved as scalar values.

Finally, declaring all properties as not-null is something you may not want. You need a different primary key for the IMAGE collection table, if any of the property columns are nullable.

6.2.4 *Avoiding not-null columns*

Analogous to the additional surrogate identifier property an <idbag> offers, a surrogate key column would come in handy now. As a side effect, an <idset> would also allow duplicates—a clear conflict with the notion of a set. For this and other reasons (including the fact that nobody ever asked for this feature), Hibernate doesn't offer an <idset> or any surrogate identifier collection other than an <idbag>. Hence, you need to change the Java property to a Collection with bag semantics:

```
private Collection images = new ArrayList();
...
public Collection getImages() {
    return this.images;
}

public void setImages(Collection images) {
    this.images = images;
}
```

This collection now also allows duplicate Image elements—it's the responsibility of your user interface, or any other application code, to avoid these duplicate elements if you require set semantics. The mapping adds the surrogate identifier column to the collection table:

```
<idbag name="images"
       table="ITEM_IMAGE"
       order-by="IMAGE_NAME asc">

    <collection-id type="long" column="ITEM_IMAGE_ID">
        <generator class="sequence"/>
    </collection-id>
    <key column="ITEM_ID"/>

    <composite-element class="Image">
        <property name="name" column="IMAGENAME"/>
        <property name="filename" column="FILENAME" not-null="true"/>
        <property name="sizeX" column="SIZEX"/>
        <property name="sizeY" column="SIZEY"/>
    </composite-element>
</idbag>
```

The primary key of the collection table is now the ITEM_IMAGE_ID column, and it isn't important that you implement equals() and hashCode() on the Image class

ITEM_IMAGE

ITEM_IMAGE_ID	ITEM_ID	IMAGENAME	FILENAME	SIZEX	SIZEY
1	1	Foo	Foo.jpg	123	123
2	1	Bar	Bar.jpg	420	80
3	2	Baz	Baz.jpg	NULL	NULL

Figure 6.7 Collection of `Image` components using a bag with surrogate key

(at least, Hibernate doesn't require it). Nor do you have to declare the properties with `not-null="true"`. They may be nullable, as can be seen in figure 6.7.

We should point out that there isn't a great deal of difference between this bag mapping and a standard parent/child entity relationship like the one you map later in this chapter. The tables are identical. The choice is mainly a matter of taste. A parent/child relationship supports shared references to the child entity and true bidirectional navigation. The price you'd pay is more complex lifecycles of objects. Value-typed instances can be created and associated with the persistent `Item` by adding a new element to the collection. They can be disassociated and permanently deleted by removing an element from the collection. If `Image` would be an entity class that supports shared references, you'd need more code in your application for the same operations, as you'll see later.

Another way to switch to a different primary key is a map. You can remove the name property from the `Image` class and use the image name as the key of a map:

```
<map name="images"
    table="ITEM_IMAGE"
    order-by="IMAGENAME asc">

    <key column="ITEM_ID"/>

    <map-key type="string" column="IMAGENAME"/>

    <composite-element class="Image">
        <property name="filename" column="FILENAME" not-null="true"/>
        <property name="sizeX" column="SIZEX"/>
        <property name="sizeY" column="SIZEY"/>
    </composite-element>
</map>
```

The primary key of the collection table is now a composite of `ITEM_ID` and `IMAGE-NAME`.

A composite element class like `Image` isn't limited to simple properties of basic type like `filename`. It may contain other components, mapped with `<nested-composite-element>`, and even `<many-to-one>` associations to entities. It can't own collections, however. A composite element with a many-to-one association is useful, and we come back to this kind of mapping in the next chapter.

This wraps up our discussion of basic collection mappings in XML. As we mentioned at the beginning of this section, mapping collections of value types with annotations is different compared with mappings in XML; at the time of writing, it isn't part of the Java Persistence standard but is available in Hibernate.

6.3   *Mapping collections with annotations*

The Hibernate Annotations package supports nonstandard annotations for the mapping of collections that contain value-typed elements, mainly `org.hibernate.annotations.CollectionOfElements`. Let's walk through some of the most common scenarios again.

6.3.1   *Basic collection mapping*

The following maps a simple collection of `String` elements:

```
@org.hibernate.annotations.CollectionOfElements(
    targetElement = java.lang.String.class
)
@JoinTable(
    name = "ITEM_IMAGE",
    joinColumns = @JoinColumn(name = "ITEM_ID")
)
@Column(name = "FILENAME", nullable = false)
private Set<String> images = new HashSet<String>();
```

The collection table `ITEM_IMAGE` has two columns; together, they form the composite primary key. Hibernate can automatically detect the type of the element if you use generic collections. If you don't code with generic collections, you need to specify the element type with the `targetElement` attribute—in the previous example it's therefore optional.

To map a persistent `List`, add `@org.hibernate.annotations.IndexColumn` with an optional base for the index (default is zero):

```
@org.hibernate.annotations.CollectionOfElements
@JoinTable(
    name = "ITEM_IMAGE",
    joinColumns = @JoinColumn(name = "ITEM_ID")
)
@org.hibernate.annotations.IndexColumn(
    name="POSITION", base = 1
```

```
)
@Column(name = "FILENAME")
private List<String> images = new ArrayList<String>();
```

If you forget the index column, this list would be treated as a bag collection, equivalent to a <bag> in XML.

For collections of value types, you'd usually use <idbag> to get a surrogate primary key on the collection table. A <bag> of value typed elements doesn't really work; duplicates would be allowed at the Java level, but not in the database. On the other hand, pure bags are great for one-to-many entity associations, as you'll see in chapter 7.

To map a persistent map, use @org.hibernate.annotations.MapKey:

```
@org.hibernate.annotations.CollectionOfElements
@JoinTable(
    name = "ITEM_IMAGE",
    joinColumns = @JoinColumn(name = "ITEM_ID")
)
@org.hibernate.annotations.MapKey(
    columns = @Column(name="IMAGENAME")
)
@Column(name = "FILENAME")
private Map<String, String> images = new HashMap<String, String>();
```

If you forget the map key, the keys of this map would be automatically mapped to the column MAPKEY.

If the keys of the map are not simple strings but of an embeddable class, you can specify multiple map key columns that hold the individual properties of the embeddable component. Note that @org.hibernate.annotations.MapKey is a more powerful replacement for @javax.persistence.MapKey, which isn't very useful (see chapter 7, section 7.2.4 "Mapping maps").

6.3.2 *Sorted and ordered collections*

A collection can also be sorted or ordered with Hibernate annotations:

```
@org.hibernate.annotations.CollectionOfElements
@JoinTable(
    name = "ITEM_IMAGE",
    joinColumns = @JoinColumn(name = "ITEM_ID")
)
@Column(name = "FILENAME", nullable = false)
@org.hibernate.annotations.Sort(
    type = org.hibernate.annotations.SortType.NATURAL
)
private SortedSet<String> images = new TreeSet<String>();
```

(Note that without the @JoinColumn and/or @Column, Hibernate applies the usual naming conventions and defaults for the schema.) The @Sort annotation supports various SortType attributes, with the same semantics as the XML mapping options. The shown mapping uses a java.util.SortedSet (with a java.util.TreeSet implementation) and natural sort order. If you enable SortType.COMPARATOR, you also need to set the comparator attribute to a class that implements your comparison routine. Maps can also be sorted; however, as in XML mappings, there is no sorted Java bag or a sorted list (which has a persistent ordering of elements, by definition).

Maps, sets, and even bags, can be ordered on load, by the database, through an SQL fragment in the ORDER BY clause:

```
@org.hibernate.annotations.CollectionOfElements
@JoinTable(
    name = "ITEM_IMAGE",
    joinColumns = @JoinColumn(name = "ITEM_ID")
)
@Column(name = "FILENAME", nullable = false)
@org.hibernate.annotations.OrderBy(
    clause = "FILENAME asc"
)
private Set<String> images = new HashSet<String>();
```

The clause attribute of the Hibernate-specific @OrderBy annotation is an SQL fragment that is passed on directly to the database; it can even contain function calls or any other native SQL keyword. See our explanation earlier for details about the internal implementation of sorting and ordering; the annotations are equivalent to the XML mappings.

6.3.3 *Mapping a collection of embedded objects*

Finally, you can map a collection of components, of user-defined value-typed elements. Let's assume that you want to map the same Image component class you've seen earlier in this chapter, with image names, sizes, and so on.

You need to add the @Embeddable component annotation on that class to enable embedding:

```
@Embeddable
public class Image {

    @org.hibernate.annotations.Parent
    Item item;

    @Column(length = 255, nullable = false)
    private String name;
```

```
@Column(length = 255, nullable = false)
private String filename;

@Column(nullable = false)
private int sizeX;

@Column(nullable = false)
private int sizeY;

... // Constructor, accessor methods, equals()/hashCode()
}
```

Note that you again map a back pointer with a Hibernate annotation; anImage.getItem() can be useful. You can leave out this property if you don't need this reference. Because the collection table needs all the component columns as the composite primary key, it's important that you map these columns as NOT NULL. You can now embed this component in a collection mapping and even override column definitions (in the following example you override the name of a single column of the component collection table; all others are named with the default strategy):

```
@org.hibernate.annotations.CollectionOfElements
@JoinTable(
    name = "ITEM_IMAGE",
    joinColumns = @JoinColumn(name = "ITEM_ID")
)
@AttributeOverride(
    name = "element.name",
    column = @Column(name = "IMAGENAME",
                     length = 255,
                     nullable = false)
)
private Set<Image> images = new HashSet<Image>();
```

To avoid the non-nullable component columns you need a surrogate primary key on the collection table, like <idbag> provides in XML mappings. With annotations, use the @CollectionId Hibernate extension:

```
@org.hibernate.annotations.CollectionOfElements
@JoinTable(
    name = "ITEM_IMAGE",
    joinColumns = @JoinColumn(name = "ITEM_ID")
)
@CollectionId(
    columns = @Column(name = "ITEM_IMAGE_ID"),
    type = @org.hibernate.annotations.Type(type = "long"),
    generator = "sequence"
)
private Collection<Image> images = new ArrayList<Image>();
```

You've now mapped all the basic and some more complex collections with XML mapping metadata, and annotations. Switching focus, we now consider collections with elements that aren't value types, but references to other entity instances. Many Hibernate users try to map a typical parent/children entity relationship, which involves a collection of entity references.

6.4   *Mapping a parent/children relationship*

From our experience with the Hibernate user community, we know that the first thing many developers try to do when they begin using Hibernate is a mapping of a parent/children relationship. This is usually the first time you encounter collections. It's also the first time you have to think about the differences between entities and value types, or get lost in the complexity of ORM.

Managing the associations between classes and the relationships between tables is at the heart of ORM. Most of the difficult problems involved in implementing an ORM solution relate to association management.

You mapped relationships between classes of value type in the previous section and earlier in the book, with varying multiplicity of the relationship ends. You map a *one* multiplicity with a simple <property> or as a <component>. The *many* association multiplicity requires a collection of value types, with <element> or <composite-element> mappings.

Now you want to map one- and many-valued relationships between entity classes. Clearly, entity aspects such as *shared references* and *independent lifecycle* complicate this relationship mapping. We'll approach these issues step by step; and, in case you aren't familiar with the term *multiplicity*, we'll also discuss that.

The relationship we show in the following sections is always the same, between the Item and Bid entity classes, as can be seen in figure 6.8.

Memorize this class diagram. But first, there's something we need to explain up front.

If you've used EJB CMP 2.0, you're familiar with the concept of a managed association (or managed relationship). CMP associations are called container managed relationships (CMRs) for a reason. Associations in CMP are inherently bidirectional. A change made to one side of an association is instantly reflected at the other side. For example, if you call aBid.setItem(anItem), the container automatically calls anItem.getBids().add(aBid).

Figure 6.8
Relationship between Item and Bid

POJO-oriented persistence engines such as Hibernate don't implement managed associations, and POJO standards such as EJB 3.0 and Java Persistence don't require managed associations. Contrary to EJB 2.0 CMR, Hibernate and JPA associations are all inherently *unidirectional*. As far as Hibernate is concerned, the association from Bid to Item is a *different association* than the association from Item to Bid! This is a good thing—otherwise your entity classes wouldn't be usable outside of a runtime container (CMR was a major reason why EJB 2.1 entities were considered problematic).

Because associations are so important, you need a precise language for classifying them.

6.4.1 *Multiplicity*

In describing and classifying associations, we'll almost always use the term *multiplicity*. In our example, the multiplicity is just two bits of information:

- Can there be more than one Bid for a particular Item?
- Can there be more than one Item for a particular Bid?

After glancing at the domain model (see figure 6.8), you can conclude that the association from Bid to Item is a *many-to-one* association. Recalling that associations are directional, you classify the inverse association from Item to Bid as a *one-to-many* association.

There are only two more possibilities: *many-to-many* and *one-to-one*. We'll get back to these in the next chapter.

In the context of object persistence, we aren't interested in whether *many* means two or a maximum of five or unrestricted. And we're only barely interested in optionality of most associations; we don't especially care whether an associated instance is required or if the other end in an association can be NULL (meaning zero-to-many and to-zero association) However, these are important aspects in your relational data schema that influence your choice of integrity rules and the constraints you define in SQL DDL (see chapter 8, section 8.3, "Improving schema DDL").

6.4.2 *The simplest possible association*

The association from Bid to Item (and vice versa) is an example of the simplest possible kind of entity association. You have two properties in two classes. One is a collection of references, and the other a single reference.

First, here's the Java class implementation of Bid:

```
public class Bid {
    ...

    private Item item;

    public void setItem(Item item) {
        this.item = item;
    }

    public Item getItem() {
        return item;
    }

    ...

}
```

Next, this is the Hibernate mapping for this association:

```
<class
    name="Bid"
    table="BID">
    ...
    <many-to-one
        name="item"
        column="ITEM_ID"
        class="Item"
        not-null="true"/>

</class>
```

This mapping is called a *unidirectional many-to-one association*. (Actually, because it's unidirectional, you don't know what is on the other side, and you could just as well call this mapping a unidirectional to-one association mapping.) The column ITEM_ID in the BID table is a foreign key to the primary key of the ITEM table.

You name the class Item, which is the target of this association, explicitly. This is usually optional, because Hibernate can determine the target type with reflection on the Java property.

You added the not-null attribute because you can't have a bid without an item—a constraint is generated in the SQL DDL to reflect this. The foreign key column ITEM_ID in the BID can never be NULL, the association is not to-zero-or-one. The table structure for this association mapping is shown in figure 6.9.

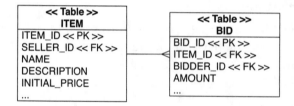

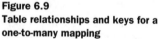

Figure 6.9
Table relationships and keys for a one-to-many mapping

In JPA, you map this association with the @ManyToOne annotation, either on the field or getter method, depending on the access strategy for the entity (determined by the position of the @Id annotation):

```
public class Bid {
    ...
    @ManyToOne( targetEntity = auction.model.Item.class )
    @JoinColumn(name = "ITEM_ID", nullable = false)
    private Item item;

    ...
}
```

There are two optional elements in this mapping. First, you don't have to include the targetEntity of the association; it's implicit from the type of the field. An explicit targetEntity attribute is useful in more complex domain models—for example, when you map a @ManyToOne on a getter method that returns a *delegate class*, which mimics a particular target entity interface.

The second optional element is the @JoinColumn. If you don't declare the name of the foreign key column, Hibernate automatically uses a combination of the target entity name and the database identifier property name of the target entity. In other words, if you don't add a @JoinColumn annotation, the default name for the foreign key column is item plus id, separated with an underscore. However, because you want to make the foreign key column NOT NULL, you need the annotation anyway to set nullable = false. If you generate the schema with the Hibernate Tools, the optional="false" attribute on the @ManyToOne would also result in a NOT NULL constraint on the generated column.

This was easy. It's critically important to realize that you can write a complete application without using anything else. (Well, maybe a shared primary key one-to-one mapping from time to time, as shown in the next chapter.) You don't need to map the other side of this class association, and you've already mapped everything present in the SQL schema (the foreign key column). If you need the Item instance for which a particular Bid was made, call aBid.getItem(), utilizing the entity association you created. On the other hand, if you need all bids that have been made for an item, you can write a query (in whatever language Hibernate supports).

One of the reasons you use a full object/relational mapping tool like Hibernate is, of course, that you don't want to write that query.

6.4.3 *Making the association bidirectional*

You want to be able to easily fetch all the bids for a particular item without an explicit query, by navigating and iterating through the network of persistent objects. The most convenient way to do this is with a collection property on `Item`: `anItem.getBids().iterator()`. (Note that there are other good reasons to map a collection of entity references, but not many. Always try to think of these kinds of collection mappings as a feature, not a requirement. If it gets too difficult, don't do it.)

You now map a collection of entity references by making the relationship between `Item` and `Bid` bidirectional.

First add the property and scaffolding code to the `Item` class:

```
public class Item {
    ...

    private Set bids = new HashSet();

    public void setBids(Set bids) {
        this.bids = bids;
    }

    public Set getBids() {
        return bids;
    }

    public void addBid(Bid bid) {
        bid.setItem(this);
        bids.add(bid);
    }

    ...

}
```

You can think of the code in `addBid()` (a convenience method) as implementing a managed association in the object model! (We had more to say about these methods in chapter 3, section 3.2, "Implementing the domain model." You may want to review the code examples there.)

A basic mapping for this one-to-many association looks like this:

```
<class
    name="Item"
    table="ITEM">
    ...

    <set name="bids">
        <key column="ITEM_ID"/>
```

```
        <one-to-many class="Bid"/>
    </set>

</class>
```

If you compare this with the collection mappings earlier in this chapter, you see that you map the content of the collection with a different element, <one-to-many>. This indicates that the collection contains not value type instances, but references to entity instances. Hibernate now knows how to treat shared references and the lifecycle of the associated objects (it disables all the implicit dependent lifecycle of value type instances). Hibernate also knows that the table used for the collection is the same table the target entity class is mapped to—the <set> mapping needs no table attribute.

The column mapping defined by the <key> element is the foreign key column ITEM_ID of the BID table, the same column you already mapped on the other side of the relationship.

Note that the table schema didn't change; it's the same as it was before you mapped the many side of the association. There is, however, one difference: The not null="true" attribute is missing. The problem is that you now have two different unidirectional associations mapped to the same foreign key column. What side controls that column?

At runtime, there are two different in-memory representations of the same foreign key value: the item property of Bid and an element of the bids collection held by an Item. Suppose the application modifies the association, by, for example, adding a bid to an item in this fragment of the addBid() method:

```
bid.setItem(item);
bids.add(bid);
```

This code is fine, but in this situation, Hibernate detects two changes to the in-memory persistent instances. From the point of view of the database, only one value has to be updated to reflect these changes: the ITEM_ID column of the BID table.

Hibernate doesn't transparently detect the fact that the two changes refer to the same database column, because at this point you've done nothing to indicate that this is a bidirectional association. In other words, you've mapped the same column twice (it doesn't matter that you did this in two mapping files), and Hibernate always needs to know about this because it can't detect this duplicate automatically (there is no reasonable default way it could be handled).

You need one more thing in the association mapping to make this a real bidirectional association mapping. The `inverse` attribute tells Hibernate that the collection is a mirror image of the `<many-to-one>` association on the other side:

```
<class
    name="Item"
    table="ITEM">
    ...

    <set name="bids"
        inverse="true">

        <key column="ITEM_ID"/>
        <one-to-many class="Bid"/>

    </set>

</class>
```

Without the `inverse` attribute, Hibernate tries to execute two different SQL statements, both updating the same foreign key column, when you manipulate the link between two instances. By specifying `inverse="true"`, you explicitly tell Hibernate which end of the link it should not synchronize with the database. In this example, you tell Hibernate that it should propagate changes made at the `Bid` end of the association to the database, ignoring changes made only to the `bids` collection.

If you only call `anItem.getBids().add(bid)`, no changes are made persistent! You get what you want only if the other side, `aBid.setItem(anItem)`, is set correctly. This is consistent with the behavior in Java without Hibernate: If an association is bidirectional, you have to create the link with pointers on two sides, not just one. It's the primary reason why we recommend convenience methods such as `addBid()`—they take care of the bidirectional references in a system without container-managed relationships.

Note that an `inverse` side of an association mapping is always ignored for the generation of SQL DDL by the Hibernate schema export tools. In this case, the `ITEM_ID` foreign key column in the `BID` table gets a `NOT NULL` constraint, because you've declared it as such in the noninverse `<many-to-one>` mapping.

(Can you switch the inverse side? The `<many-to-one>` element doesn't have an `inverse` attribute, but you can map it with `update="false"` and `insert="false"` to effectively ignore it for any `UPDATE` or `INSERT` statements. The collection side is then noninverse and considered for insertion or updating of the foreign key column. We'll do this in the next chapter.)

Let's map this inverse collection side again, with JPA annotations:

```
public class Item {

    ...

    @OneToMany(mappedBy = "item")
    private Set<Bid> bids = new HashSet<Bid>();

    ...

}
```

The `mappedBy` attribute is the equivalent of the `inverse` attribute in XML mappings; however, it has to name the inverse property of the target entity. Note that you don't specify the foreign key column again here (it's mapped by the other side), so this isn't as verbose as the XML.

You now have a working *bidirectional* many-to-one association (which could also be called a bidirectional one-to-many association). One final option is missing if you want to make it a true parent/children relationship.

6.4.4 *Cascading object state*

The notion of a parent and a child implies that one takes care of the other. In practice, this means you need fewer lines of code to manage a relationship between a parent and a child, because some things can be taken care of automatically. Let's explore the options.

The following code creates a new `Item` (which we consider the parent) and a new `Bid` instance (the child):

```
Item newItem = new Item();
Bid newBid = new Bid();

newItem.addBid(newBid); // Set both sides of the association

session.save(newItem);
session.save(newBid);
```

The second call to `session.save()` seems redundant, if we're talking about a true parent/children relationship. Hold that thought, and think about entities and value types again: If both classes are entities, their instances have a completely independent lifecycle. New objects are transient and have to be made persistent if you want to store them in the database. Their relationship doesn't influence their lifecycle, if they're entities. If `Bid` would be a value type, the state of a `Bid` instance is the same as the state of its owning entity. In this case, however, `Bid` is a separate entity with its own completely independent state. You have three choices:

- Take care of the independent instances yourself, and execute additional save() and delete() calls on the Bid objects when needed—in addition to the Java code needed to manage the relationship (adding and removing references from collections, and so on).

- Make the Bid class a value type (a component). You can map the collection with a `<composite-element>` and get the implicit lifecycle. However, you lose other aspects of an entity, such as possible shared references to an instance.

- Do you need shared references to Bid objects? Currently, a particular Bid instance isn't referenced by more than one Item. However, imagine that a User entity also has a collection of bids, made by the user. To support shared references, you have to map Bid as an entity. Another reason you need shared references is the successfulBid association from Item in the full CaveatEmptor model. In this case, Hibernate offers *transitive persistence*, a feature you can enable to save lines of code and to let Hibernate manage the lifecycle of associated entity instances automatically.

You don't want to execute more persistence operations than absolutely necessary, and you don't want to change your domain model—you need shared references to Bid instances. The third option is what you'll use to simplify this parent/children example.

Transitive persistence

When you instantiate a new Bid and add it to an Item, the bid should become persistent automatically. You'd like to avoid making the Bid persistent explicitly with an extra save() operation.

To enable this transitive state across the association, add a cascade option to the XML mapping:

```
<class
    name="Item"
    table="ITEM">
    ...

    <set name="bids"
        inverse="true"
        cascade="save-update">

        <key column="ITEM_ID"/>
        <one-to-many class="Bid"/>

    </set>

</class>
```

The `cascade="save-update"` attribute enables transitive persistence for `Bid` instances, if a particular `Bid` is referenced by a persistent `Item`, in the collection.

The `cascade` attribute is directional: It applies to only one end of the association. You could also add `cascade="save-update"` to the `<many-to-one>` association in the mapping of `Bid`, but because bids are created after items, doing so doesn't make sense.

JPA also supports cascading entity instance state on associations:

```
public class Item {

    ...

    @OneToMany(cascade = { CascadeType.PERSIST, CascadeType.MERGE },
               mappedBy = "item")
    private Set<Bid> bids = new HashSet<Bid>();

    ...

}
```

Cascading options are *per operation* you'd like to be transitive. For native Hibernate, you cascade the `save` and `update` operations to associated entities with `cascade="save-update"`. Hibernate's object state management always bundles these two things together, as you'll learn in future chapters. In JPA, the (almost) equivalent operations are `persist` and `merge`.

You can now simplify the code that links and saves an `Item` and a `Bid`, in native Hibernate:

```
Item newItem = new Item();
Bid newBid = new Bid();

newItem.addBid(newBid); // Set both sides of the association

session.save(newItem);
```

All entities in the bids collection are now persistent as well, just as they would be if you called `save()` on each `Bid` manually. With the JPA `EntityManager` API, the equivalent to a `Session`, the code is as follows:

```
Item newItem = new Item();
Bid newBid = new Bid();

newItem.addBid(newBid); // Set both sides of the association

entityManager.persist(newItem);
```

Don't worry about the `update` and `merge` operations for now; we'll come back to them later in the book.

FAQ   *What is the effect of* cascade *on* inverse? Many new Hibernate users ask
this question. The answer is simple: The cascade attribute has nothing to
do with the inverse attribute. They often appear on the same collection
mapping. If you map a collection of entities as inverse="true", you're
controlling the generation of SQL for a bidirectional association mapping. It's a hint that tells Hibernate you mapped the same foreign key
column twice. On the other hand, cascading is used as a convenience feature. If you decide to cascade operations from one side of an entity relationship to associated entities, you save the lines of code needed to
manage the state of the other side manually. We say that object state
becomes *transitive*. You can cascade state not only on collections of entities, but on all entity association mappings. cascade and inverse have in
common the fact that they don't appear on collections of value types or
on any other value-type mappings. The rules for these are implied by the
nature of value types.

Are you finished now? Well, perhaps not quite.

Cascading deletion

With the previous mapping, the association between Bid and Item is fairly loose.
So far, we have only considered making things persistent as a transitive state. What
about deletion?

It seems reasonable that deletion of an item implies deletion of all bids for the
item. In fact, this is what the composition (the filled out diamond) in the UML
diagram means. With the current cascading operations, you have to write the following code to make that happen:

```
Item anItem = // Load an item

// Delete all the referenced bids
for ( Iterator<Bid> it = anItem.getBids().iterator();
    it.hasNext(); ) {

  Bid bid = it.next();

  it.remove();                 // Remove reference from collection
  session.delete(bid);         // Delete it from the database
}

session.delete(anItem);        // Finally, delete the item
```

First you remove the references to the bids by iterating the collection. You delete
each Bid instance in the database. Finally, the Item is deleted. Iterating and
removing the references in the collection seems unnecessary; after all, you'll
delete the Item at the end anyway. If you can guarantee that no other object (or

row in any other table) holds a reference to these bids, you can make the deletion transitive.

Hibernate (and JPA) offer a cascading option for this purpose. You can enable cascading for the `delete` operation:

```
<set name="bids"
     inverse="true"
     cascade="save-update, delete">
...
```

The operation you cascade in JPA is called `remove`:

```
public class Item {
    ...

    @OneToMany(cascade = { CascadeType.PERSIST,
                           CascadeType.MERGE,
                           CascadeType.REMOVE },
             mappedBy = "item")
    private Set<Bid> bids = new HashSet<Bid>();

    ...

}
```

The same code to delete an item and all its bids is reduced to the following, in Hibernate or with JPA:

```
Item anItem = // Load an item
session.delete(anItem);
entityManager.remove(anItem);
```

The `delete` operation is now cascaded to all entities referenced in the collection. You no longer have to worry about removal from the collection and manually deleting those entities one by one.

Let's consider one further complication. You may have shared references to the `Bid` objects. As suggested earlier, a `User` may have a collection of references to the `Bid` instances they made. You can't delete an item and all its bids without removing these references first. You may get an exception if you try to commit this transaction, because a foreign key constraint may be violated.

You have to *chase the pointers*. This process can get ugly, as you can see in the following code, which removes all references from all users who have references before deleting the bids and finally the item:

```
Item anItem = // Load an item

// Delete all the referenced bids
for ( Iterator<Bid> it = anItem.getBids().iterator();
      it.hasNext(); ) {
```

```
Bid bid = it.next();

// Remove references from users who have made this bid
Query q = session.createQuery(
  "from User u where :bid in elements(u.bids)"
);
q.setParameter("bid", bid);
Collection usersWithThisBid = q.list();

for (Iterator itUsers = usersWithThisBid.iterator();
     itUsers.hasNext();) {
     User user = (User) itUsers.next();
     user.getBids().remove(bid);
    }
  }
}

session.delete(anItem);
// Finally, delete the item and the associated bids
```

Obviously, the additional query (in fact, many queries) isn't what you want. However, in a network object model, you don't have any choice other than executing code like this if you want to correctly set pointers and references—there is no persistent garbage collector or other automatic mechanism. No Hibernate cascading option helps you; you have to chase all references to an entity before you finally delete it.

(This isn't the whole truth: Because the BIDDER_ID foreign key column that represents the association from User to Bid is in the BID table, these references are automatically removed at the database level if a row in the BID table is deleted. This doesn't affect any objects that are already present in memory in the current unit of work, and it also doesn't work if BIDDER_ID is mapped to a different (intermediate) table. To make sure all references and foreign key columns are nulled out, you need to chase pointers in Java.)

On the other hand, if you don't have shared references to an entity, you should rethink your mapping and map the bids as a collection components (with the Bid as a <composite-element>). With an <idbag> mapping, even the tables look the same:

```
<class
    name="Item"
    table="ITEM">
    ...

    <idbag name="bids" table="BID">

        <collection-id type="long" column="BID_ID">
            <generator class="sequence"/>
        </collection-id>
```

```
        <key column="ITEM_ID" not-null="true"/>

        <composite-element class="Bid">
            <parent name="item"/>
            <property .../>
            ...
        </composite-element>

    </idbag>

</class>
```

The separate mapping for Bid is no longer needed.

If you really want to make this a one-to-many entity association, Hibernate offers another convenience option you may be interested in.

Enabling orphan deletion

The cascading option we explain now is somewhat difficult to understand. If you followed the discussion in the previous section, you should be prepared.

Imagine you want to delete a Bid from the database. Note that you aren't deleting the parent (the Item) in this case. The goal is to remove a row in the BID table. Look at this code:

```
anItem.getBids().remove(aBid);
```

If the collection has the Bid mapped as a collection of components, as in the previous section, this code triggers several operations:

- The aBid instance is removed from the collection Item.bids.

- Because Bid is mapped as a value type, and no other object can hold a reference to the aBid instance, the row representing this bid is deleted from the BID table by Hibernate.

In other words, Hibernate assumes that aBid is an orphan if it's removed from its owning entity's collection. No other in-memory persistent object is holding a reference to it. No foreign key value that references this row can be present in the database. Obviously, you designed your object model and mapping this way by making the Bid class an embeddable component.

However, what if Bid is mapped as an entity and the collection is a <one-to-many>? The code changes to

```
anItem.getBids().remove(aBid);
session.delete(aBid);
```

The aBid instance has its own lifecycle, so it can exist outside of the collection. By deleting it manually, you guarantee that nobody else will hold a reference to it, and the row can be removed safely. You may have removed all other references manually. Or, if you didn't, the database constraints prevent any inconsistency, and you see a foreign key constraint exception.

Hibernate offers you a way to declare this guarantee for collections of entity references. You can tell Hibernate, "If I remove an element from this collection, it will be an entity reference, and it's going to be the only reference to that entity instance. You can safely delete it." The code that worked for deletion with a collection of components works with collections of entity references.

This option is called *cascade orphan delete.* You can enable it on a collection mapping in XML as follows:

```
<set name="bids"
    inverse="true"
    cascade="save-update, delete, delete-orphan">
...
```

With annotations, this feature is available only as a Hibernate extension:

```
public class Item {
    ...

    @OneToMany(cascade = { CascadeType.PERSIST,
                           CascadeType.MERGE,
                           CascadeType.REMOVE },
            mappedBy = "item")
    @org.hibernate.annotations.Cascade(
        value = org.hibernate.annotations.CascadeType.DELETE_ORPHAN
    )
    private Set<Bid> bids = new HashSet<Bid>();

    ...

}
```

Also note that this trick works only for collections of entity references in a one-to-many association; conceptually, no other entity association mapping supports it. You should ask yourself at this point, with so many cascading options set on your collection, whether a simple collection of components may be easier to handle. After all, you've enabled a dependent lifecycle for objects referenced in this collection, so you may as well switch to the implicit and fully dependent lifecycle of components.

Finally, let's look at the mapping in a JPA XML descriptor:

```
<entity-mappings>

    <entity class="auction.model.Item" access="FIELD">
        ...
        <one-to-many name="bids" mapped-by="item">
```

```
        <cascade>
            <cascade-persist/>
            <cascade-merge/>
            <cascade-remove/>
        </cascade>
      </one-to-many>
  </entity>
  <entity class="auction.model.Bid" access="FIELD">
      ...
      <many-to-one name="item">
          <join-column name="ITEM_ID"/>
      </many-to-one>
  </entity>

</entity-mappings>
```

Note that the Hibernate extension for cascade orphan deletion isn't available in this case.

6.5 Summary

You're probably a little overwhelmed by all the new concepts we introduced in this chapter. You may have to read it a few times, and we encourage you to try the code (and watch the SQL log). Many of the strategies and techniques we've shown in this chapter are key concepts of object/relational mapping. If you master collection mappings, and once you've mapped your first parent/children entity association, you'll have the worst behind you. You'll already be able to build entire applications!

Table 6.1 summarizes the differences between Hibernate and Java Persistence related to concepts discussed in this chapter.

Table 6.1 Hibernate and JPA comparison chart for chapter 6

Hibernate Core	Java Persistence and EJB 3.0
Hibernate provides mapping support for sets, lists, maps, bags, identifier bags, and arrays. All JDK collection interfaces are supported, and extension points for custom persistent collections are available.	Standardized persistent sets, lists, maps, and bags are supported.
Collections of value types and components are supported.	Hibernate Annotations is required for collections of value types and embeddable objects.
Parent/children entity relationships are supported, with transitive state cascading on associations per operation.	You can map entity associations and enable transitive state cascading on associations per operation.

Table 6.1 Hibernate and JPA comparison chart for chapter 6 *(continued)*

Hibernate Core	Java Persistence and EJB 3.0
Automatic deletion of orphaned entity instances is built in.	Hibernate Annotations is required for automatic deletion of orphaned entity instances.

We've covered only a tiny subset of the entity association options in this chapter. The remaining options we explore in detail in the next chapter are either rare or variations of the techniques we've just described.

Advanced entity association mappings

This chapter covers
- Mapping one-to-one and many-to-one entity associations
- Mapping one-to-many and many-to-many entity associations
- Polymorphic entity associations

When we use the word *associations*, we always refer to relationships between entities. In the previous chapter, we demonstrated a unidirectional many-to-one association, made it bidirectional, and finally turned it into a parent/children relationship (one-to-many and many-to-one with cascading options).

One reason we discuss more advanced entity mappings in a separate chapter is that quite a few of them are considered rare, or at least optional.

It's absolutely possible to only use component mappings and many-to-one (occasionally one-to-one) entity associations. You can write a sophisticated application without ever mapping a collection! Of course, efficient and easy access to persistent data, by iterating a collection for example, is one of the reasons why you use full object/relational mapping and not a simple JDBC query service. However, some exotic mapping features should be used with care and even *avoided* most of the time.

We'll point out recommended and optional mapping techniques in this chapter, as we show you how to map entity associations with all kinds of multiplicity, with and without collections.

7.1 Single-valued entity associations

Let's start with one-to-one entity associations.

We argued in chapter 4 that the relationships between `User` and `Address` (the user has a `billingAddress`, `homeAddress`, and `shippingAddress`) are best represented with a `<component>` mapping. This is usually the simplest way to represent one-to-one relationships, because the lifecycle is almost always dependent in such a case, it's either an aggregation or a composition in UML.

But what if you want a dedicated table for `Address`, and you map both `User` and `Address` as entities? One benefit of this model is the possibility for shared references—another entity class (let's say `Shipment`) can also have a reference to a particular `Address` instance. If a `User` has a reference to this instance, as their `shippingAddress`, the `Address` instance has to support shared references and needs its own identity.

In this case, `User` and `Address` classes have a true *one-to-one association*. Look at the revised class diagram in figure 7.1.

The first change is a mapping of the `Address` class as a stand-alone entity:

```
<class name="Address" table="ADDRESS">
    <id name="id" column="ADDRESS_ID">
        <generator .../>
    </id>
    <property name="street" column="STREET"/>
```

```
        <property name="city" column="CITY"/>
        <property name="zipcode" column="ZIPCODE"/>
    </class>
```

We assume you won't have any difficulty creating the same mapping with annotations or changing the Java class to an entity, with an identifier property—this is the only change you have to make.

Now let's create the association mappings from other entities to that class. There are several choices, the first being a *primary key one-to-one* association.

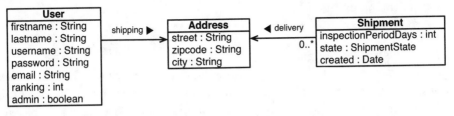

Figure 7.1 `Address` as an entity with two associations referencing the same instance

7.1.1 *Shared primary key associations*

Rows in two tables related by a primary key association share the same primary key values. The main difficulty with this approach is ensuring that associated instances are assigned the same primary key value when the objects are saved. Before we try to solve this problem, let's see how you map the primary key association.

Mapping a primary key association with XML

The XML mapping element that maps an entity association to a shared primary key entity is `<one-to-one>`. First you need a new property in the `User` class:

```
public class User {
    ...
    private Address shippingAddress;
    // Getters and setters
}
```

Next, map the association in `User.hbm.xml`:

```
<one-to-one name="shippingAddress"
            class="Address"
            cascade="save-update"/>
```

You add a cascading option that is natural for this model: If a `User` instance is made persistent, you usually also want its `shippingAddress` to become persistent. Hence, the following code is all that is needed to save both objects:

```
User newUser = new User();
Address shippingAddress = new Address();

newUser.setShippingAddress(shippingAddress);

session.save(newUser);
```

Hibernate inserts a row into the USERS table and a row into the ADDRESS table. But wait, this doesn't work! How can Hibernate possibly know that the record in the ADDRESS table needs to get the same primary key value as the USERS row? At the beginning of this section, we intentionally didn't show you any primary-key generator in the mapping of Address.

You need to enable a special identifier generator.

The foreign identifier generator

If an Address instance is saved, it needs to get the primary key value of a User object. You can't enable a regular identifier generator, let's say a database sequence. The special `foreign` identifier generator for Address has to know where to get the right primary key value.

The first step to create this identifier binding between Address and User is a bidirectional association. Add a new user property to the Address entity:

```
public class Address {
    ...
     private User user;
    // Getters and setters
}
```

Map the new user property of an Address in Address.hbm.xml:

```
<one-to-one name="user"
            class="User"
            constrained="true"/>
```

This mapping not only makes the association bidirectional, but also, with `constrained="true"`, adds a foreign key constraint linking the primary key of the ADDRESS table to the primary key of the USERS table. In other words, the database guarantees that an ADDRESS row's primary key references a valid USERS primary key. (As a side effect, Hibernate can now also enable lazy loading of users when a shipping address is loaded. The foreign key constraint means that a user has to exist for a particular shipping address, so a proxy can be enabled without hitting the database. Without this constraint, Hibernate has to hit the database to find out if there is a user for the address; the proxy would then be redundant. We'll come back to this in later chapters.)

You can now use the special `foreign` identifier generator for Address objects:

```
<class name="Address" table="ADDRESS">

    <id name="id" column="ADDRESS_ID">
        <generator class="foreign">
            <param name="property">user</param>
        </generator>
    </id>
    ...
    <one-to-one name="user"
                class="User"
                constrained="true"/>

</class>
```

This mapping seems strange at first. Read it as follows: When an Address is saved, the primary key value is taken from the user property. The user property is a reference to a User object; hence, the primary key value that is inserted is the same as the primary key value of that instance. Look at the table structure in figure 7.2.

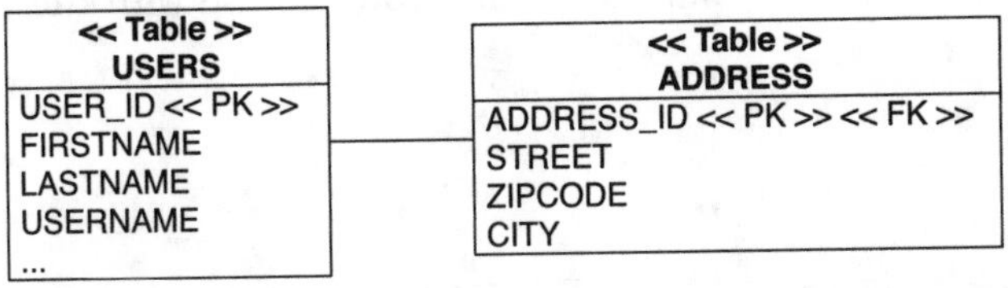

Figure 7.2
The USERS and ADDRESS tables have the same primary keys.

The code to save both objects now has to consider the bidirectional relationship, and it finally works:

```
User newUser = new User();
Address shippingAddress = new Address();

newUser.setShippingAddress(shippingAddress);
shippingAddress.setUser(newUser);              // Bidirectional

session.save(newUser);
```

Let's do the same with annotations.

Shared primary key with annotations

JPA supports one-to-one entity associations with the @OneToOne annotation. To map the association of shippingAddress in the User class as a shared primary key association, you also need the @PrimaryKeyJoinColumn annotation:

```
@OneToOne
@PrimaryKeyJoinColumn
private Address shippingAddress;
```

This is all that is needed to create a unidirectional one-to-one association on a shared primary key. Note that you need @PrimaryKeyJoinColumns (plural) instead if you map with composite primary keys. In a JPA XML descriptor, a one-to-one mapping looks like this:

```
<entity-mappings>

    <entity class="auction.model.User" access="FIELD">
        ...
        <one-to-one name="shippingAddress">
            <primary-key-join-column/>
        </one-to-one>
    </entity>

</entity-mappings>
```

The JPA specification doesn't include a standardized method to deal with the problem of shared primary key generation, which means you're responsible for setting the identifier value of an Address instance correctly before you save it (to the identifier value of the linked User instance). Hibernate has an extension annotation for custom identifier generators which you can use with the Address entity (just like in XML):

```
@Entity
@Table(name = "ADDRESS")
public class Address {

    @Id @GeneratedValue(generator = "myForeignGenerator")
    @org.hibernate.annotations.GenericGenerator(
        name = "myForeignGenerator",
        strategy = "foreign",
        parameters = @Parameter(name = "property", value = "user")
    )
    @Column(name = "ADDRESS_ID")
    private Long id;

    ...
    private User user;
}
```

Shared primary key one-to-one associations aren't uncommon but are relatively rare. In many schemas, a *to-one* association is represented with a foreign key field and a unique constraint.

7.1.2 *One-to-one foreign key associations*

Instead of sharing a primary key, two rows can have a foreign key relationship. One table has a foreign key column that references the primary key of the associated table. (The source and target of this foreign key constraint can even be the same table: This is called a *self-referencing* relationship.)

Let's change the mapping from a `User` to an `Address`. Instead of the shared primary key, you now add a `SHIPPING_ADDRESS_ID` column in the `USERS` table:

```
<class name="User" table="USERS">

    <many-to-one name="shippingAddress"
                 class="Address"
                 column="SHIPPING_ADDRESS_ID"
                 cascade="save-update"
                 unique="true"/>

</class>
```

The mapping element in XML for this association is `<many-to-one>`—not `<one-to-one>`, as you might have expected. The reason is simple: You don't care what's on the target side of the association, so you can treat it like a *to-one* association without the *many* part. All you want is to express "This entity has a property that is a reference to an instance of another entity" and use a foreign key field to represent that relationship. The database schema for this mapping is shown in figure 7.3.

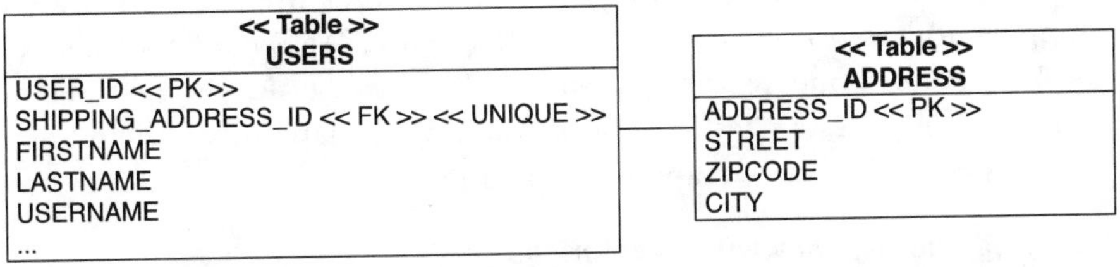

Figure 7.3 A one-to-one foreign key association between USERS and ADDRESS

An additional constraint enforces this relationship as a real *one* to one. By making the `SHIPPING_ADDRESS_ID` column `unique`, you declare that a particular address can be referenced by at most one user, as a shipping address. This isn't as strong as the guarantee from a shared primary key association, which allows a particular address to be referenced by at most one user, period. With several foreign key columns (let's say you also have unique `HOME_ADDRESS_ID` and `BILLING_ADDRESS_ID`), you can reference the same address target row several times. But in any case, two users can't share the same address for the same purpose.

Let's make the association from `User` to `Address` bidirectional.

Inverse property reference
The last foreign key association was mapped from `User` to `Address` with `<many-to-one>` and a `unique` constraint to guarantee the desired multiplicity. What mapping

element can you add on the `Address` side to make this association bidirectional, so that access from `Address` to `User` is possible in the Java domain model?

In XML, you create a `<one-to-one>` mapping with a property reference attribute:

```
<one-to-one name="user"
            class="User"
            property-ref="shippingAddress"/>
```

You tell Hibernate that the `user` property of the `Address` class is the inverse of a property on the other side of the association. You can now call `anAddress.getUser()` to access the user who's shipping address you've given. There is no additional column or foreign key constraint; Hibernate manages this pointer for you.

Should you make this association bidirectional? As always, the decision is up to you and depends on whether you need to navigate through your objects in that direction in your application code. In this case, we'd probably conclude that the bidirectional association doesn't make much sense. If you call `anAddress.getUser()`, you are saying "give me the user who has this address has its shipping address," not a very reasonable request. We recommend that a foreign key-based one-to-one association, with a unique constraint on the foreign key column—is almost always best represented without a mapping on the other side.

Let's repeat the same mapping with annotations.

Mapping a foreign key with annotations

The JPA mapping annotations also support a one-to-one relationship between entities based on a foreign key column. The main difference compared to the mappings earlier in this chapter is the use of `@JoinColumn` instead of `@PrimaryKeyJoinColumn`.

First, here's the to-one mapping from `User` to `Address` with the unique constraint on the `SHIPPING_ADDRESS_ID` foreign key column. However, instead of a `@ManyToOne` annotation, this requires a `@OneToOne` annotation:

```
public class User {
    ...

    @OneToOne
    @JoinColumn(name="SHIPPING_ADDRESS_ID")
    private Address shippingAddress;

    ...
}
```

Hibernate will now enforce the multiplicity with the unique constraint. If you want to make this association bidirectional, you need another @OneToOne mapping in the Address class:

```
public class Address {
    ...

    @OneToOne(mappedBy = "shippingAddress")
    private User user;

    ...
}
```

The effect of the mappedBy attribute is the same as the property-ref in XML mapping: a simple inverse declaration of an association, naming a property on the target entity side.

The equivalent mapping in JPA XML descriptors is as follows:

```
<entity-mappings>

    <entity class="auction.model.User" access="FIELD">
        ...
        <one-to-one name="shippingAddress">
            <join-column name="SHIPPING_ADDRESS_ID"/>
        </one-to-one>
    </entity>

    <entity class="auction.model.Address" access="FIELD">
        ...
        <one-to-one name="user" mapped-by="shippingAddress"/>
    </entity>

</entity-mappings>
```

You've now completed two basic single-ended association mappings: the first with a shared primary key, the second with a foreign key reference. The last option we want to discuss is a bit more exotic: mapping a one-to-one association with the help of an additional table.

7.1.3 *Mapping with a join table*

Let's take a break from the complex CaveatEmptor model and consider a different scenario. Imagine you have to model a data schema that represents an office allocation plan in a company. Common entities include people working at desks. It seems reasonable that a desk may be vacant and have no person assigned to it. On the other hand, an employee may work at home, with the same result. You're dealing with an *optional* one-to-one association between Person and Desk.

If you apply the mapping techniques we discussed in the previous sections, you may come to the following conclusions: Person and Desk are mapped to two tables, with one of them (let's say the PERSON table) having a foreign key column that references the other table (such as ASSIGNED_DESK_ID) with an additional unique constraint (so two people can't be assigned the same desk). The relationship is optional if the foreign key column is nullable.

On second thought, you realize that the assignment between persons and desks calls for another table that represents ASSIGNMENT. In the current design, this table has only two columns: PERSON_ID and DESK_ID. The multiplicity of these foreign key columns is enforced with a unique constraint on both—a particular person and desk can only be assigned once, and only one such an assignment can exist.

It also seems likely that one day you'll need to extend this schema and add columns to the ASSIGNMENT table, such as the date when a person was assigned to a desk. As long as this isn't the case, however, you can use object/relational mapping to hide the intermediate table and create a one-to-one Java entity association between only two classes. (This situation changes completely once additional columns are introduced to ASSIGNMENT.)

Where does such an optional one-to-one relationship exist in CaveatEmptor?

The CaveatEmptor use case

Let's consider the Shipment entity in CaveatEmptor again and discuss its purpose. Sellers and buyers interact in CaveatEmptor by starting and bidding on auctions. The shipment of the goods seems to be outside the scope of the application; the seller and the buyer agree on a method of shipment and payment after the auction ends. They can do this offline, outside of CaveatEmptor. On the other hand, you could offer an extra *escrow service* in CaveatEmptor. Sellers would use this service to create a trackable shipment once the auction completed. The buyer would pay the price of the auction item to a trustee (you), and you'd inform the seller that the money was available. Once the shipment arrived and the buyer accepted it, you'd transfer the money to the seller.

If you've ever participated in an online auction of significant value, you've probably used such an escrow service. But you want more service in CaveatEmptor. Not only will you provide trust services for completed auctions, but you'll also allow users to create a trackable and trusted shipment for any deal they make outside an auction, outside CaveatEmptor.

This scenario calls for a Shipment entity with an optional one-to-one association to an Item. Look at the class diagram for this domain model in figure 7.4.

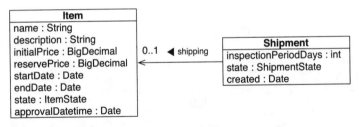

Figure 7.4   A shipment has an optional link with a single auction item.

In the database schema, you add an intermediate link table called `ITEM_SHIPMENT`. A row in this table represents a `Shipment` made in the context of an auction. The tables are shown in figure 7.5.

You now map two classes to three tables: first in XML, and then with annotations.

Mapping a join table in XML

The property that represents the association from `Shipment` to `Item` is called `auction`:

```
public class Shipment {

    ...
    private Item auction;
    ...
    // Getter/setter methods
}
```

Because you have to map this association with a foreign key column, you need the `<many-to-one>` mapping element in XML. However, the foreign key column isn't in the `SHIPMENT` table, it's in the `ITEM_SHIPMENT` join table. With the help of the `<join>` mapping element, you move it there.

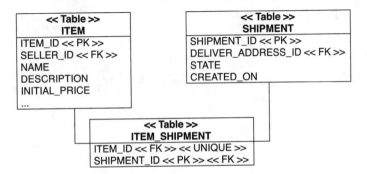

Figure 7.5   An optional one-to-many relationship mapped to a join table

```
<class name="Shipment" table="SHIPMENT">

    <id name="id" column="SHIPMENT_ID">...</id>

    ...

    <join table="ITEM_SHIPMENT" optional="true">
        <key column="SHIPMENT_ID"/>
        <many-to-one name="auction"
                    column="ITEM_ID"
                    not-null="true"
                    unique="true"/>
    </join>

</class>
```

The join table has two foreign key columns: SHIPMENT_ID, referencing the primary key of the SHIPMENT table; and ITEM_ID, referencing the ITEM table. The ITEM_ID column is unique; a particular item can be assigned to exactly one shipment. Because the primary key of the join table is SHIPMENT_ID, which makes this column also unique, you have a guaranteed one-to-one multiplicity between Shipment and Item.

By setting optional="true" on the <join> mapping, you tell Hibernate that it should insert a row into the join table only if the properties grouped by this mapping are non-null. But if a row needs to be inserted (because you called aShipment.setAuction(anItem)), the NOT NULL constraint on the ITEM_ID column applies.

You could map this association bidirectional, with the same technique on the other side. However, optional one-to-one associations are unidirectional most of the time.

JPA also supports association join tables as *secondary tables* for an entity.

Mapping secondary join tables with annotations

You can map an optional one-to-one association to an intermediate join table with annotations:

```
public class Shipment {

    @OneToOne
    @JoinTable(
        name="ITEM_SHIPMENT",
        joinColumns = @JoinColumn(name = "SHIPMENT_ID"),
        inverseJoinColumns = @JoinColumn(name = "ITEM_ID")
    )
    private Item auction;
    ...
    // Getter/setter methods
}
```

You don't have to specify the SHIPMENT_ID column because it's automatically considered to be the join column; it's the primary key column of the SHIPMENT table.

Alternatively, you can map properties of a JPA entity to more than one table, as demonstrated in "Moving properties into a secondary table" in chapter 8, section 8.1.3. First, you need to declare the secondary table for the entity:

```
@Entity
@Table(name = "SHIPMENT")
@SecondaryTable(name = "ITEM_SHIPMENT")
public class Shipment {

    @Id @GeneratedValue
    @Column(name = "SHIPMENT_ID")
    private Long id;

    ...
}
```

Note that the @SecondaryTable annotation also supports attributes to declare the foreign-key column name—the equivalent of the <key column="..."/> you saw earlier in XML and the joinColumn(s) in a @JoinTable. If you don't specify it, the primary-key column name of the entity is used—in this case, again SHIPMENT_ID.

The auction property mapping is a @OneToOne; and as before, the foreign key column referencing the ITEM table is moved to the intermediate secondary table:

```
...
public class Shipment {
    ...
    @OneToOne
    @JoinColumn(table = "ITEM_SHIPMENT", name = "ITEM_ID")
    private Item auction;
}
```

The table for the target @JoinColumn is named explicitly. Why would you use this approach instead of the (simpler) @JoinTable strategy? Declaring a secondary table for an entity is useful if not only one property (the many-to-one in this case) but several properties must be moved into the secondary table. We don't have a great example with Shipment and Item, but if your ITEM_SHIPMENT table would have additional columns, mapping these columns to properties of the Shipment entity might be useful.

This completes our discussion of one-to-one association mappings. To summarize, use a shared primary key association if one of the two entities seems more important and can act as the primary key source. Use a foreign key association in all other cases, and a hidden intermediate join table when your one-to-one association is optional.

We now focus on many-valued entity associations, including more options for one-to-many, and finally, many-to-many mappings.

7.2   Many-valued entity associations

A *many-valued* entity association is by definition a collection of entity references. You mapped one of these in the previous chapter, section 6.4, "Mapping a parent/children relationship." A parent entity instance has a collection of references to many child objects—hence, *one-to-many*.

One-to-many associations are the most important kind of entity association that involves a collection. We go so far as to discourage the use of more exotic association styles when a simple bidirectional many-to-one/one-to-many will do the job. A many-to-many association may always be represented as two many-to-one associations to an intervening class. This model is usually more easily extensible, so we tend not to use many-to-many associations in applications. Also remember that you don't have to map *any* collection of entities, if you don't want to; you can always write an explicit query instead of direct access through iteration.

If you decide to map collections of entity references, there are a few options and more complex situations that we discuss now, including a many-to-many relationship.

7.2.1   One-to-many associations

The parent/children relationship you mapped earlier was a bidirectional association, with a `<one-to-many>` and a `<many-to-one>` mapping. The *many* end of this association was implemented in Java with a `Set`; you had a collection of `bids` in the `Item` class.

Let's reconsider this mapping and focus on some special cases.

Considering bags

It's *possible* to use a `<bag>` mapping instead of a set for a bidirectional one-to-many association. Why would you do this?

Bags have the most efficient performance characteristics of all the collections you can use for a bidirectional one-to-many entity association (in other words, if the collection side is `inverse="true"`). By default, collections in Hibernate are loaded only when they're accessed for the first time in the application. Because a bag doesn't have to maintain the index of its elements (like a list) or check for duplicate elements (like a set), you can add new elements to the bag without triggering the loading. This is an important feature if you're going to map a possibly large collection of entity references. On the other hand, you can't eager-fetch two collections of bag type simultaneously (for example, if bids and images of an Item were one-to-many bags). We'll come back to fetching strategies in chapter 13, section 13.1, "Defining the global fetch plan." In general we would say that a bag is the best inverse collection for a one-to-many association.

To map a bidirectional one-to-many association as a bag, you have to replace the type of the bids collection in the Item persistent class with a Collection and an ArrayList implementation. The mapping for the association between Item and Bid is left essentially unchanged:

```
<class name="Bid"
       table="BID">
    ...
    <many-to-one name="item"
                 column="ITEM_ID"
                 class="Item"
                 not-null="true"/>

</class>
<class name="Item"
       table="ITEM">
    ...
    <bag name="bids"
         inverse="true">
        <key column="ITEM_ID"/>
        <one-to-many class="Bid"/>
    </bag>

</class>
```

You rename the <set> element to <bag>, making no other changes. Even the tables are the same: The BID table has the ITEM_ID foreign key column. In JPA, all Collection and List properties are considered to have bag semantics, so the following is equivalent to the XML mapping:

```
public class Item {
    ...

    @OneToMany(mappedBy = "item")
    private Collection<Bid> bids = new ArrayList<Bid>();

    ...

}
```

A bag also allows duplicate elements, which the set you mapped earlier didn't. It turns out that this isn't relevant in this case, because *duplicate* means you've added a particular reference to the same Bid instance several times. You wouldn't do this in your application code. But even if you add the same reference several times to this collection, Hibernate ignores it—it's mapped inverse.

Unidirectional and bidirectional lists

If you need a real list to hold the position of the elements in a collection, you have to store that position in an additional column. For the one-to-many mapping, this also means you should change the `bids` property in the `Item` class to `List` and initialize the variable with an `ArrayList` (or keep the `Collection` interface from the previous section, if you don't want to expose this behavior to a client of the class).

The additional column that holds the position of a reference to a `Bid` instance is the `BID_POSITION`, in the mapping of `Item`:

```
<class name="Item"
       table="ITEM">
    ...
    <list name="bids">
        <key column="ITEM_ID"/>
        <list-index column="BID_POSITION"/>
        <one-to-many class="Bid"/>
    </list>

</class>
```

So far this seems straightforward; you've changed the collection mapping to `<list>` and added the `<list-index>` column `BID_POSITION` to the collection table (which in this case is the `BID` table). Verify this with the table shown in figure 7.6.

This mapping isn't really complete. Consider the `ITEM_ID` foreign key column: It's NOT NULL (a bid has to reference an item). The first problem is that you don't specify this constraint in the mapping. Also, because this mapping is unidirectional (the collection is noninverse), you have to assume that there is no opposite side mapped to the same foreign key column (where this constraint could be declared). You need to add a `not-null="true"` attribute to the `<key>` element of the collection mapping:

BID

BID_ID	ITEM_ID	BID_POSITION	AMOUNT	CREATED_ON
1	1	0	99.00	19.04.08 23:11
2	1	1	123.00	19.04.08 23:12
3	2	0	433.00	20.04.08 09:30

Figure 7.6
Storing the position of each bid in the list collection

```
<class name="Item"
       table="ITEM">
    ...
    <list name="bids">
        <key column="ITEM_ID" not-null="true"/>
        <list-index column="BID_POSITION"/>
        <one-to-many class="Bid"/>
    </list>

</class>
```

Note that the attribute has to be on the `<key>` mapping, not on a possible nested `<column>` element. Whenever you have a noninverse collection of entity references (most of the time a one-to-many with a list, map, or array) and the foreign key join column in the target table is not nullable, you need to tell Hibernate about this. Hibernate needs the hint to order INSERT and UPDATE statements correctly, to avoid a constraint violation.

Let's make this bidirectional with an `item` property of the `Bid`. If you follow the examples from earlier chapters, you might want to add a `<many-to-one>` on the `ITEM_ID` foreign key column to make this association bidirectional, and enable `inverse="true"` on the collection. Remember that Hibernate ignores the state of an inverse collection! This time, however, the collection contains information that is needed to update the database correctly: the position of its elements. If only the state of each `Bid` instance is considered for synchronization, and the collection is inverse and ignored, Hibernate has no value for the `BID_POSITION` column.

If you map a bidirectional one-to-many entity association with an indexed collection (this is also true for maps and arrays), you have to switch the inverse sides. You can't make an indexed collection `inverse="true"`. The collection becomes responsible for state synchronization, and the *one* side, the `Bid`, has to be made inverse. However, there is no `inverse="true"` for a many-to-one mapping so you need to simulate this attribute on a `<many-to-one>`:

```
<class name="Bid"
       table="BID">
    ...
    <many-to-one name="item"
                 column="ITEM_ID"
                 class="Item"
                 not-null="true"
                 insert="false"
                 update="false"/>

</class>
```

Setting `insert` and `update` to `false` has the desired effect. As we discussed earlier, these two attributes used together make a property effectively *read-only*. This side of the association is therefore ignored for any write operations, and the state of the collection (including the index of the elements) is the relevant state when the in-memory state is synchronized with the database. You've switched the inverse/noninverse sides of the association, a requirement if you switch from a set or bag to a list (or any other indexed collection).

The equivalent in JPA, an indexed collection in a bidirectional one-to-many mapping, is as follows:

```
public class Item {
    ...

    @OneToMany
    @JoinColumn(name = "ITEM_ID", nullable = false)
    @org.hibernate.annotations.IndexColumn(name = "BID_POSITION")
    private List<Bid> bids = new ArrayList<Bid>();

    ...

}
```

This mapping is noninverse because no `mappedBy` attribute is present. Because JPA doesn't support persistent indexed lists (only *ordered* with an `@OrderBy` at load time), you need to add a Hibernate extension annotation for index support. Here's the other side of the association in `Bid`:

```
public class Bid {
    ...

    @ManyToOne
    @JoinColumn(name = "ITEM_ID", nullable = false,
                updatable = false, insertable = false)
    private Item item;

    ...

}
```

We now discuss one more scenario with a one-to-many relationship: an association mapped to an intermediate join table.

Optional one-to-many association with a join table

A useful addition to the `Item` class is a `buyer` property. You can then call `anItem.getBuyer()` to access the `User` who made the winning bid. (Of course, `anItem.getSuccessfulBid().getBidder()` can provide the same access with a

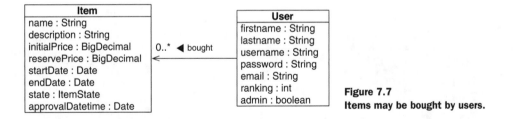

Figure 7.7
Items may be bought by users.

different path.) If made bidirectional, this association will also help to render a screen that shows all auctions a particular user has won: You call aUser.get-BoughtItems() instead of writing a query.

From the point of view of the User class, the association is one-to-many. The classes and their relationship are shown in figure 7.7.

Why is this association different than the one between Item and Bid? The multiplicity 0..* in UML indicates that the reference is *optional.* This doesn't influence the Java domain model much, but it has consequences for the underlying tables. You expect a BUYER_ID foreign key column in the ITEM table. The column has to be nullable—a particular Item may not have been bought (as long as the auction is still running).

You can accept that the foreign key column can be NULL and apply additional constraints ("allowed to be NULL only if the auction end time hasn't been reached or if no bid has been made"). We always try to avoid nullable columns in a relational database schema. Information that is unknown degrades the quality of the data you store. Tuples represent propositions that are *true,* you can't assert something you don't know. And, in practice, many developers and DBAs don't create the right constraint and rely on (often buggy) application code to provide data integrity.

An optional entity association, be it one-to-one or one-to-many, is best represented in an SQL database with a join table. See figure 7.8 for an example schema.

You added a join table earlier in this chapter, for a one-to-one association. To guarantee the multiplicity of one-to-one, you applied *unique* constraints on both foreign key columns of the join table. In the current case, you have a one-to-many multiplicity, so only the ITEM_ID column of the ITEM_BUYER table is unique. A particular item can be bought only once.

Let's map this in XML. First, here's the boughtItems collection of the User class.

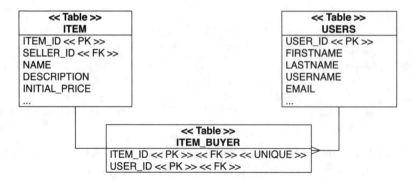

Figure 7.8   An optional relationship with a join table avoids nullable foreign key columns.

```
<set name="boughtItems" table="ITEM_BUYER">
    <key column="USER_ID"/>
    <many-to-many class="Item"
                  column="ITEM_ID"
                  unique="true"/>
</set>
```

You use a Set as the collection type. The collection table is the join table, ITEM_BUYER; its primary key is a composite of USER_ID and ITEM_ID. The new mapping element you haven't seen before is <many-to-many>; it's required because the regular <one-to-many> doesn't know anything about join tables. By forcing a unique constraint on the foreign key column that references the target entity table, you effectively force a one-to-many multiplicity.

You can map this association bidirectional with the buyer property of Item. Without the join table, you'd add a <many-to-one> with a BUYER_ID foreign key column in the ITEM table. With the join table, you have to move this foreign key column into the join table. This is possible with a <join> mapping:

```
<join table="ITEM_BUYER"
      optional="true"
      inverse="true">
    <key column="ITEM_ID" unique="true" not-null="true"/>
    <many-to-one name="buyer" column="USER_ID"/>
</join>
```

Two important details: First, the association is optional, and you tell Hibernate not to insert a row into the join table if the grouped properties (only one here, buyer) are null. Second, this is a bidirectional entity association. As always, one side has to be the inverse end. You've chosen the <join> to be inverse; Hibernate now uses the collection state to synchronize the database and ignores the state of the Item.buyer property. As long as your collection is not an indexed variation (a list, map, or array), you can reverse this by declaring the collection inverse="true". The Java code to create a link between a bought item and a user object is the same in both cases:

```
aUser.getBoughtItems().add(anItem);
anItem.setBuyer(aUser);
```

You can map secondary tables in JPA to create a one-to-many association with a join table. First, map a @ManyToOne to a join table:

```
@Entity
public class Item {
    @ManyToOne
    @JoinTable(
        name = "ITEM_BUYER",
        joinColumns = {@JoinColumn(name = "ITEM_ID")},
        inverseJoinColumns = {@JoinColumn(name = "USER_ID")}
    )
    private User buyer;
    ...
}
```

At the time of writing, this mapping has the limitation that you can't set it to optional="true"; hence, the USER_ID column is nullable. If you try to add a nullable="false" attribute on the @JoinColumn, Hibernate Annotations thinks that you want the whole buyer property to never be null. Furthermore, the primary key of the join table is now the ITEM_ID column only. This is fine, because you don't want duplicate items in this table—they can be bought only once.

To make this mapping bidirectional, add a collection on the User class and make it inverse with mappedBy:

```
@OneToMany(mappedBy = "buyer")
private Set<Item> boughtItems = new HashSet<Item>();
```

We showed a <many-to-many> XML mapping element in the previous section for a one-to-many association on a join table. The @JoinTable annotation is the equivalent in annotations. Let's map a real many-to-many association.

7.2.2 Many-to-many associations

The association between Category and Item is a many-to-many association, as can be seen in figure 7.9.

In a real system, you may not have a many-to-many association. Our experience is that there is almost always other information that must be attached to each link between associated instances (such as the date and time when an item was added

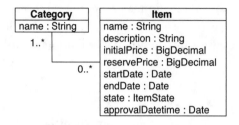

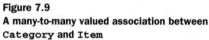

Figure 7.9
A many-to-many valued association between
`Category` **and** `Item`

to a category) and that the best way to represent this information is via an intermediate *association class*. In Hibernate, you can map the association class as an entity and map two one-to-many associations for either side. Perhaps more conveniently, you can also map a composite element class, a technique we show later.

It's the purpose of this section to implement a real many-to-many entity association. Let's start with a unidirectional example.

A simple unidirectional many-to-many association

If you require only unidirectional navigation, the mapping is straightforward. Unidirectional many-to-many associations are essentially no more difficult than the collections of value-type instances we discussed earlier. For example, if the `Category` has a set of `Items`, you can create this mapping:

```
<set name="items"
     table="CATEGORY_ITEM"
     cascade="save-update">
   <key column="CATEGORY_ID"/>
   <many-to-many class="Item" column="ITEM_ID"/>
</set>
```

The join table (or *link table*, as some developers call it) has two columns: the foreign keys of the `CATEGORY` and `ITEM` tables. The primary key is a composite of both columns. The full table structure is shown in figure 7.10.

In JPA annotations, many-to-many associations are mapped with the `@ManyToMany` attribute:

```
@ManyToMany
@JoinTable(
    name = "CATEGORY_ITEM",
    joinColumns = {@JoinColumn(name = "CATEGORY_ID")},
    inverseJoinColumns = {@JoinColumn(name = "ITEM_ID")}
)
private Set<Item> items = new HashSet<Item>();
```

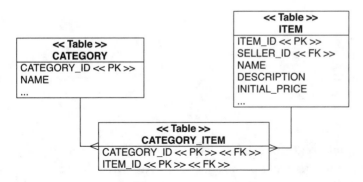

Figure 7.10   Many-to-many entity association mapped to an association table

In Hibernate XML you can also switch to an `<idbag>` with a separate primary key column on the join table:

```
<idbag name="items"
       table="CATEGORY_ITEM"
       cascade="save-update">
    <collection-id type="long" column="CATEGORY_ITEM_ID">
        <generator class="sequence"/>
    </collection-id>
    <key column="CATEGORY_ID"/>
    <many-to-many class="Item" column="ITEM_ID"/>
</idbag>
```

As usual with an `<idbag>` mapping, the primary key is a surrogate key column, `CATEGORY_ITEM_ID`. Duplicate links are therefore allowed; the same `Item` can be added twice to a `Category`. (This doesn't seem to be a useful feature.) With annotations, you can switch to an identifier bag with the Hibernate `@CollectionId`:

```
@ManyToMany
@CollectionId(
    columns = @Column(name = "CATEGORY_ITEM_ID"),
    type = @org.hibernate.annotations.Type(type = "long"),
    generator = "sequence"
)
@JoinTable(
    name = "CATEGORY_ITEM",
    joinColumns = {@JoinColumn(name = "CATEGORY_ID")},
    inverseJoinColumns = {@JoinColumn(name = "ITEM_ID")}
)
private Collection<Item> items = new ArrayList<Item>();
```

A JPA XML descriptor for a regular many-to-many mapping with a set (you can't use a Hibernate extension for identifier bags) looks like this:

```
<entity class="auction.model.Category" access="FIELD">
    ...
    <many-to-many name="items">
        <join-table name="CATEGORY_ITEM">
            <join-column name="CATEGORY_ID"/>
            <inverse-join-column name="ITEM_ID"/>
        </join-table>
    </many-to-many>

</entity>
```

You may even switch to an indexed collection (a map or list) in a many-to-many association. The following example maps a list in Hibernate XML:

```
<list name="items"
      table="CATEGORY_ITEM"
      cascade="save-update">
    <key column="CATEGORY_ID"/>
    <list-index column="DISPLAY_POSITION"/>
    <many-to-many class="Item" column="ITEM_ID"/>
</list>
```

The primary key of the link table is a composite of the CATEGORY_ID and DISPLAY_POSITION columns; this mapping guarantees that the position of each Item in a Category is persistent. Or, with annotations:

```
@ManyToMany
@JoinTable(
    name = "CATEGORY_ITEM",
    joinColumns = {@JoinColumn(name = "CATEGORY_ID")},
    inverseJoinColumns = {@JoinColumn(name = "ITEM_ID")}
)
@org.hibernate.annotations.IndexColumn(name = "DISPLAY_POSITION")
private List<Item> items = new ArrayList<Item>();
```

As discussed earlier, JPA only supports ordered collections (with an optional @OrderBy annotation or ordered by primary key), so you again have to use a Hibernate extension for indexed collection support. If you don't add an @Index-Column, the List is stored with bag semantics (no guaranteed persistent order of elements).

Creating a link between a Category and an Item is easy:

```
aCategory.getItems().add(anItem);
```

Bidirectional many-to-many associations are slightly more difficult.

A bidirectional many-to-many association

You know that one side in a bidirectional association has to be mapped as inverse because you have named the foreign key column(s) twice. The same principle applies to bidirectional many-to-many associations: Each row of the link table is represented by two collection elements, one element at each end of the association. An association between an `Item` and a `Category` is represented in memory by the `Item` instance in the `items` collection of the `Category`, but also by the `Category` instance in the `categories` collection of the `Item`.

Before we discuss the mapping of this bidirectional case, you have to be aware that the code to create the object association also changes:

```
aCategory.getItems().add(anItem);
anItem.getCategories().add(aCategory);
```

As always, a bidirectional association (no matter of what multiplicity) requires that you set both ends of the association.

When you map a bidirectional many-to-many association, you must declare one end of the association using `inverse="true"` to define which side's state is used to update the join table. You can choose which side should be inverse.

Recall this mapping of the `items` collection from the previous section:

```
<class name="Category" table="CATEGORY">
    ...
    <set name="items"
        table="CATEGORY_ITEM"
        cascade="save-update">
        <key column="CATEGORY_ID"/>
        <many-to-many class="Item" column="ITEM_ID"/>
    </set>
```

You may reuse this mapping for the `Category` end of the bidirectional association and map the other side as follows:

```
<class name="Item" table="ITEM">
    ...
    <set name="categories"
        table="CATEGORY_ITEM"
        inverse="true"
        cascade="save-update">
        <key column="ITEM_ID"/>
        <many-to-many class="Category" column="CATEGORY_ID"/>
    </set>
</class>
```

Note the `inverse="true"`. Again, this setting tells Hibernate to ignore changes made to the `categories` collection and that the other end of the association, the `items` collection, is the representation that should be synchronized with the database if you link instances in Java code.

You have enabled `cascade="save-update"` for both ends of the collection. This isn't unreasonable, we suppose. On the other hand, the cascading options `all`, `delete`, and `delete-orphans` aren't meaningful for many-to-many associations. (This is good point to test if you understand entities and value types—try to come up with reasonable answers why these cascading options don't make sense for a many-to-many association.)

In JPA and with annotations, making a many-to-many association bidirectional is easy. First, the noninverse side:

```
@ManyToMany
@JoinTable(
    name = "CATEGORY_ITEM",
    joinColumns = {@JoinColumn(name = "CATEGORY_ID")},
    inverseJoinColumns = {@JoinColumn(name = "ITEM_ID")}
)
private Set<Item> items = new HashSet<Item>();
```

Now the opposite inverse side:

```
@ManyToMany(mappedBy = "items")
private Set<Category> categories = new HashSet<Category>();
```

As you can see, you don't have to repeat the join-table declaration on the inverse side.

What types of collections may be used for bidirectional many-to-many associations? Do you need the same type of collection at each end? It's reasonable to map, for example, a <list> for the noninverse side of the association and a <bag> on the inverse side.

For the inverse end, <set> is acceptable, as is the following bag mapping:

```
<class name="Item" table="ITEM">
    ...
    <bag name="categories"
        table="CATEGORY_ITEM"
        inverse="true"
        cascade="save-update">
      <key column="ITEM_ID"/>
      <many-to-many class="Category" column="CATEGORY_ID"/>
    </bag>
</class>
```

In JPA, a bag is a collection without a persistent index:

```
@ManyToMany(mappedBy = "items")
private Collection<Category> categories = new ArrayList<Category>();
```

No other mappings can be used for the inverse end of a many-to-many association. Indexed collections (lists and maps) don't work, because Hibernate won't initialize or maintain the index column if the collection is inverse. In other words, a many-to-many association can't be mapped with indexed collections on both sides.

We already frowned at the use of many-to-many associations, because additional columns on the join table are almost always inevitable.

7.2.3 Adding columns to join tables

In this section, we discuss a question that is asked frequently by Hibernate users: What do I do if my join table has additional columns, not only two foreign key columns?

Imagine that you need to record some information each time you add an Item to a Category. For example, you may need to store the date and the name of the user who added the item to this category. This requires additional columns on the join table, as you can see in figure 7.11.

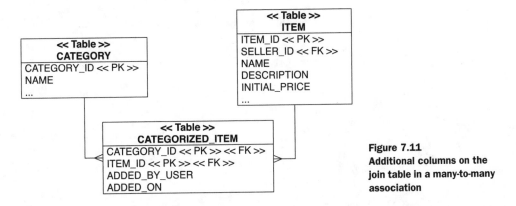

Figure 7.11
Additional columns on the join table in a many-to-many association

You can use two common strategies to map such a structure to Java classes. The first strategy requires an intermediate entity class for the join table and is mapped with one-to-many associations. The second strategy utilizes a collection of components, with a value-type class for the join table.

Mapping the join table to an intermediate entity

The first option we discuss now resolves the many-to-many relationship between Category and Item with an intermediate entity class, CategorizedItem. Listing 7.1 shows this entity class, which represents the join table in Java, including JPA annotations:

Listing 7.1 An entity class that represents a link table with additional columns

```java
@Entity
@Table(name = "CATEGORIZED_ITEM")
public class CategorizedItem {

    @Embeddable
    public static class Id implements Serializable {

        @Column(name = "CATEGORY_ID")
        private Long categoryId;

        @Column(name = "ITEM_ID")
        private Long itemId;

        public Id() {}

        public Id(Long categoryId, Long itemId) {
            this.categoryId = categoryId;
            this.itemId = itemId;
        }
        public boolean equals(Object o) {
            if (o != null && o instanceof Id) {
                Id that = (Id)o;
                return this.categoryId.equals(that.categoryId) &&
                       this.itemId.equals(that.itemId);
            } else {
                return false;
            }
        }

        public int hashCode() {
            return categoryId.hashCode() + itemId.hashCode();
        }
    }

    @EmbeddedId
    private Id id = new Id();

    @Column(name = "ADDED_BY_USER")
    private String username;

    @Column(name = "ADDED_ON")
    private Date dateAdded = new Date();

    @ManyToOne
    @JoinColumn(name="ITEM_ID",
                insertable = false,
                updatable = false)
    private Item item;

    @ManyToOne
    @JoinColumn(name="CATEGORY_ID",
                insertable = false,
                updatable = false)
    private Category category;
```

```
    public CategorizedItem() {}

    public CategorizedItem(String username,
                           Category category,
                           Item item) {
        // Set fields
        this.username = username;

        this.category = category;
        this.item = item;

        // Set identifier values
        this.id.categoryId = category.getId();
        this.id.itemId = item.getId();

        // Guarantee referential integrity
        category.getCategorizedItems().add(this);
        item.getCategorizedItems().add(this);
    }

    // Getter and setter methods
    ...
}
```

An entity class needs an identifier property. The primary key of the join table is CATEGORY_ID and ITEM_ID, a composite. Hence, the entity class also has a composite key, which you encapsulate in a static nested class for convenience. You can also see that constructing a CategorizedItem involves setting the values of the identifier—composite key values are assigned by the application. Pay extra attention to the constructor and how it sets the field values and guarantees referential integrity by managing collections on either side of the association.

Let's map this class to the join table in XML:

```
<class name="CategorizedItem"
       table="CATEGORY_ITEM"
       mutable="false">

    <composite-id name="id" class="CategorizedItem$Id">
        <key-property name="categoryId"
                      access="field"
                      column="CATEGORY_ID"/>

        <key-property name="itemId"
                      access="field"
                      column="ITEM_ID"/>
    </composite-id>

    <property name="dateAdded"
              column="ADDED_ON"
              type="timestamp"
```

```
                              not-null="true"/>
          <property name="username"
                    column="ADDED_BY_USER"
                    type="string"
                    not-null="true"/>

          <many-to-one name="category"
                       column="CATEGORY_ID"
                       not-null="true"
                       insert="false"
                       update="false"/>

          <many-to-one name="item"
                       column="ITEM_ID"
                       not-null="true"
                       insert="false"
                       update="false"/>

    </class>
```

The entity class is mapped as immutable—you'll never update any properties after creation. Hibernate accesses <composite-id> fields directly—you don't need getters and setters in this nested class. The two <many-to-one> mappings are effectively read-only; insert and update are set to false. This is necessary because the columns are mapped twice, once in the composite key (which is responsible for insertion of the values) and again for the many-to-one associations.

The Category and Item entities (can) have a one-to-many association to the CategorizedItem entity, a collection. For example, in Category:

```
<set name="categorizedItems"
     inverse="true">
    <key column="CATEGORY_ID"/>
    <one-to-many class="CategorizedItem"/>
</set>
```

And here's the annotation equivalent:

```
@OneToMany(mappedBy = "category")
private Set<CategorizedItem> categorizedItems =
                            new HashSet<CategorizedItem>();
```

There is nothing special to consider here; it's a regular bidirectional one-to-many association with an inverse collection. Add the same collection and mapping to Item to complete the association. This code creates and stores a link between a category and an item:

```
CategorizedItem newLink =
    new CategorizedItem(aUser.getUsername(), aCategory, anItem);

session.save(newLink);
```

The referential integrity of the Java objects is guaranteed by the constructor of `CategorizedItem`, which manages the collection in `aCategory` and in `anItem`. Remove and delete the link between a category and an item:

```
aCategory.getCategorizedItems().remove( theLink );
anItem.getCategorizedItems().remove( theLink );

session.delete(theLink);
```

The primary advantage of this strategy is the possibility for bidirectional navigation: You can get all items in a category by calling `aCategory.getCategorizedItems()` and the also navigate from the opposite direction with `anItem.getCategorizedItems()`. A disadvantage is the more complex code needed to manage the `CategorizedItem` entity instances to create and remove associations—they have to be saved and deleted independently, and you need some infrastructure in the `CategorizedItem` class, such as the composite identifier. However, you can enable transitive persistence with cascading options on the collections from `Category` and `Item` to `CategorizedItem`, as explained in chapter 12, section 12.1, "Transitive persistence."

The second strategy for dealing with additional columns on the join table doesn't need an intermediate entity class; it's simpler.

Mapping the join table to a collection of components

First, simplify the `CategorizedItem` class, and make it a value type, without an identifier or any complex constructor:

```java
public class CategorizedItem {
    private String username;
    private Date dateAdded = new Date();
    private Item item;
    private Category category;

    public CategorizedItem(String username,
                           Category category,
                           Item item) {
        this.username = username;
        this.category = category;
        this.item = item;
    }
    ...

    // Getter and setter methods
    // Don't forget the equals/hashCode methods
}
```

As for all value types, this class has to be owned by an entity. The owner is the `Category`, and it has a collection of these components:

```
<class name="Category" table="CATEGORY">

    ...

    <set name="categorizedItems" table="CATEGORY_ITEM">
        <key column="CATEGORY_ID"/>
        <composite-element class="CategorizedItem">
            <parent name="category"/>

            <many-to-one name="item"
                        column="ITEM_ID"
                        not-null="true"
                        class="Item"/>

            <property name="username" column="ADDED_BY_USER"/>
            <property name="dateAdded" column="ADDED_ON"/>

        </composite-element>
    </set>

</class>
```

This is the complete mapping for a many-to-many association with extra columns on the join table. The `<many-to-one>` element represents the association to `Item`; the `<property>` mappings cover the extra columns on the join table. There is only one change to the database tables: The `CATEGORY_ITEM` table now has a primary key that is a composite of all columns, not only `CATEGORY_ID` and `ITEM_ID`, as in the previous section. Hence, all properties should never be `nullable`—otherwise you can't identify a row in the join table. Except for this change, the tables still look as shown in figure 7.11.

You can enhance this mapping with a reference to the `User` instead of just the user's name. This requires an additional `USER_ID` column on the join table, with a foreign key to `USERS`. This is a *ternary association* mapping:

```
<set name="categorizedItems" table="CATEGORY_ITEM">
    <key column="CATEGORY_ID"/>
    <composite-element class="CategorizedItem">
        <parent name="category"/>

        <many-to-one name="item"
                    column="ITEM_ID"
                    not-null="true"
                    class="Item"/>

        <many-to-one name="user"
                    column="USER_ID"
                    not-null="true"
                    class="User"/>

        <property name="dateAdded" column="ADDED_ON"/>

    </composite-element>
</set>
```

This is a fairly exotic beast!

The advantage of a collection of components is clearly the implicit lifecycle of the link objects. To create an association between a `Category` and an `Item`, add a new `CategorizedItem` instance to the collection. To break the link, remove the element from the collection. No extra cascading settings are required, and the Java code is simplified:

```
CategorizedItem aLink =
    new CategorizedItem(aUser.getUserName(), aCategory, anItem);

aCategory.getCategorizedItems().add( aLink );

aCategory.getCategorizedItems().remove( aLink );
```

The downside of this approach is that there is no way to enable bidirectional navigation: A component (such as `CategorizedItem`) can't, by definition, have shared references. You can't navigate from `Item` to `CategorizedItem`. However, you can write a query to retrieve the objects you need.

Let's do the same mapping with annotations. First, make the component class `@Embeddable`, and add the component column and association mappings:

```
@Embeddable
public class CategorizedItem {

    @org.hibernate.annotations.Parent // Optional back-pointer
    private Category category;

    @ManyToOne
    @JoinColumn(name = "ITEM_ID",
                nullable = false,
                updatable = false)
    private Item item;

    @ManyToOne
    @JoinColumn(name = "USER_ID",
                nullable = false,
                updatable = false)
    private User user;

    @Temporal(TemporalType.TIMESTAMP)
    @Column(name = "ADDED_ON", nullable = false, updatable = false)
    private Date dateAdded;

    ...
    // Constructor
    // Getter and setter methods
    // Don't forget the equals/hashCode methods
}
```

Now map this as a collection of components in the `Category` class:

```
@org.hibernate.annotations.CollectionOfElements
@JoinTable(
    name = "CATEGORY_ITEM",
    joinColumns = @JoinColumn(name = "CATEGORY_ID")
)
private Set<CategorizedItem> categorizedItems =
                            new HashSet<CategorizedItem>();
```

That's it: You've mapped a ternary association with annotations. What looked incredibly complex at the beginning has been reduced to a few lines of annotation metadata, most of it optional.

The last collection mapping we'll explore are `Maps` of entity references.

7.2.4 Mapping maps

You mapped a Java `Map` in the last chapter—the keys and values of the `Map` were value types, simple strings. You can create more complex maps; not only can the keys be references to entities, but so can the values. The result can therefore be a ternary association.

Values as references to entities

First, let's assume that only the value of each map entry is a reference to another entity. The key is a value type, a `long`. Imagine that the `Item` entity has a map of `Bid` instances and that each map entry is a pair of `Bid` identifier and reference to a `Bid` instance. If you iterate through `anItem.getBidsByIdentifier()`, you iterate through map entries that look like (1, <reference to Bid with PK 1>), (2, <reference to Bid with PK 2>), and so on.

The underlying tables for this mapping are nothing special; you again have an `ITEM` and a `BID` table, with an `ITEM_ID` foreign key column in the `BID` table. Your motivation here is a slightly different representation of the data in the application, with a `Map`.

In the `Item` class, include a `Map`:

```
@MapKey(name="id")
@OneToMany
private Map<Long,Bid> bidsByIdentifier = new HashMap<Long,Bid>();
```

New here is the `@MapKey` element of JPA—it maps a property of the target entity as key of the map. The default if you omit the `name` attribute is the identifier property of the target entity (so the name here is redundant). Because the keys of a map form a set, values are expected to be unique for a particular map—this is the case for `Bid` primary keys but likely not for any other property of `Bid`.

In Hibernate XML, this mapping is as follows:

```
<map name="bidsByIdentifier">
    <key column="ITEM_ID"/>
    <map-key type="long" formula="BID_ID"/>
    <one-to-many class="Bid"/>
</map>
```

The `formula` key for a map makes this column read-only, so it's never updated when you modify the map. A more common situation is a map in the middle of a ternary association.

Ternary associations

You may be a little bored by now, but we promise this is the last time we'll show another way to map the association between `Category` and `Item`. Let's summarize what you already know about this many-to-many association:

- It can be mapped with two collections on either side and a join table that has only two foreign key columns. This is a regular many-to-many association mapping.

- It can be mapped with an intermediate entity class that represents the join table, and any additional columns therein. A one-to-many association is mapped on either side (`Category` and `Item`), and a bidirectional many-to-one equivalent is mapped in the intermediate entity class.

- It can be mapped unidirectional, with a join table represented as a value type component. The `Category` entity has a collection of components. Each component has a reference to its owning `Category` and a many-to-one entity association to an `Item`. (You can also switch the words `Category` and `Item` in this explanation.)

You previously turned the last scenario into a ternary association by adding another many-to-one entity association to a `User`. Let's do the same with a `Map`.

A `Category` has a `Map` of `Item` instances—the key of each map entry is a reference to an `Item`. The value of each map entry is the `User` who added the `Item` to the `Category`. This strategy is appropriate if there are no additional columns on the join table; see the schema in figure 7.12.

The advantage of this strategy is that you don't need any intermediate class, no entity or value type, to represent the `ADDED_BY_USER_ID` column of the join table in your Java application.

First, here's the `Map` property in `Category` with a Hibernate extension annotation.

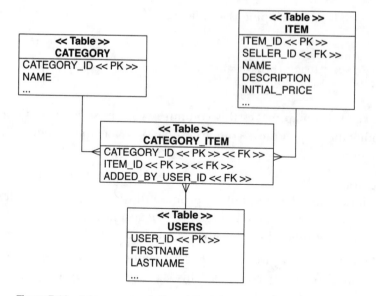

Figure 7.12 A ternary association with a join table between three entities

```
@ManyToMany
@org.hibernate.annotations.MapKeyManyToMany(
    joinColumns = @JoinColumn(name = "ITEM_ID")
)
@JoinTable(
    name = "CATEGORY_ITEM",
    joinColumns = @JoinColumn(name = "CATEGORY_ID"),
    inverseJoinColumns = @JoinColumn(name = "USER_ID")
)
private Map<Item,User> itemsAndUser = new HashMap<Item,User>();
```

The Hibernate XML mapping includes a new element, `<map-key-many-to-many>`:

```
<map name="itemsAndUser" table="CATEGORY_ITEM">
    <key column="CATEGORY_ID"/>
    <map-key-many-to-many column="ITEM_ID" class="Item"/>
    <many-to-many column="ADDED_BY_USER_ID" class="User"/>
</map>
```

To create a link between all three entities, if all your instances are already in persistent state, add a new entry to the map:

```
aCategory.getItemsAndUser().add( anItem, aUser );
```

To remove the link, remove the entry from the map. As an exercise, you can try to make this mapping bidirectional, with a collection of `categories` in `Item`.

Remember that this has to be an inverse collection mapping, so it doesn't support indexed collections.

Now that you know all the association mapping techniques for normal entities, we still have to consider inheritance and associations to the various levels of an inheritance hierarchy. What we really want is *polymorphic* behavior. Let's see how Hibernate deals with polymorphic entity associations.

7.3 *Polymorphic associations*

Polymorphism is a defining feature of object-oriented languages like Java. Support for polymorphic associations and polymorphic queries is an absolutely basic feature of an ORM solution like Hibernate. Surprisingly, we've managed to get this far without needing to talk much about polymorphism. Even more surprisingly, there is not much to say on the topic—polymorphism is so easy to use in Hibernate that we don't need to spend a lot of effort explaining it.

To get an overview, we first consider a many-to-one association to a class that may have subclasses. In this case, Hibernate guarantees that you can create links to any subclass instance just like you would to instances of the superclass.

7.3.1 *Polymorphic many-to-one associations*

A *polymorphic association* is an association that may refer instances of a subclass of the class that was explicitly specified in the mapping metadata. For this example, consider the `defaultBillingDetails` property of `User`. It references one particular `BillingDetails` object, which at runtime can be any concrete instance of that class. The classes are shown in figure 7.13.

You map this association to the abstract class `BillingDetails` as follows in User.hbm.xml.

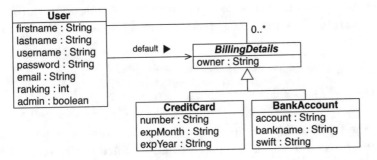

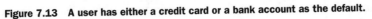
Figure 7.13 A user has either a credit card or a bank account as the default.

```
<many-to-one name="defaultBillingDetails"
             class="BillingDetails"
             column="DEFAULT_BILLING_DETAILS_ID"/>
```

But because `BillingDetails` is abstract, the association must refer to an instance of one of its subclasses—`CreditCard` or `CheckingAccount`—at runtime.

You don't have to do anything special to enable polymorphic associations in Hibernate; specify the name of any mapped persistent class in your association mapping (or let Hibernate discover it using reflection), and then, if that class declares any `<union-subclass>`, `<subclass>`, or `<joined-subclass>` elements, the association is naturally polymorphic.

The following code demonstrates the creation of an association to an instance of the `CreditCard` subclass:

```
CreditCard cc = new CreditCard();
cc.setNumber(ccNumber);
cc.setType(ccType);
cc.setExpiryDate(ccExpiryDate);

User user = (User) session.get(User.class, userId);
user.addBillingDetails(cc); // Add it to the one-to-many association

user.setDefaultBillingDetails(cc);

// Complete unit of work
```

Now, when you navigate the association in a second unit of work, Hibernate automatically retrieves the `CreditCard` instance:

```
User user = (User) secondSession.get(User.class, userId);

// Invoke the pay() method on the actual subclass instance
user.getDefaultBillingDetails().pay(amount);
```

There is just one thing to watch out for: If `BillingDetails` was mapped with `lazy="true"` (which is the default), Hibernate would proxy the `defaultBilling-Details` association target. In this case, you wouldn't be able to perform a type-cast to the concrete class `CreditCard` at runtime, and even the `instanceof` operator would behave strangely:

```
User user = (User) session.get(User.class, userid);
BillingDetails bd = user.getDefaultBillingDetails();
System.out.println( bd instanceof CreditCard ); // Prints "false"
CreditCard cc = (CreditCard) bd; // ClassCastException!
```

In this code, the typecast fails because `bd` is a proxy instance. When a method is invoked on the proxy, the call is delegated to an instance of `CreditCard` that is fetched lazily (it's an instance of a runtime-generated subclass, so `instanceof` also fails). Until this initialization occurs, Hibernate doesn't know what the subtype of the given instance is—this would require a database hit, which you try to avoid with lazy loading in the first place. To perform a proxy-safe typecast, use `load()`:

```
User user = (User) session.get(User.class, userId);
BillingDetails bd = user.getDefaultBillingDetails();

// Narrow the proxy to the subclass, doesn't hit the database
CreditCard cc =
    (CreditCard) session.load( CreditCard.class, bd.getId() );
expiryDate = cc.getExpiryDate();
```

After the call to `load()`, `bd` and `cc` refer to two different proxy instances, which both delegate to the same underlying `CreditCard` instance. However, the second proxy has a different interface, and you can call methods (like `getExpiryDate()`) that apply only to this interface.

Note that you can avoid these issues by avoiding lazy fetching, as in the following code, using an eager fetch query:

```
User user = (User)session.createCriteria(User.class)
    .add(Restrictions.eq("id", uid) )
    .setFetchMode("defaultBillingDetails", FetchMode.JOIN)
    .uniqueResult();

// The users defaultBillingDetails have been fetched eagerly
CreditCard cc = (CreditCard) user.getDefaultBillingDetails();
expiryDate = cc.getExpiryDate();
```

Truly object-oriented code shouldn't use `instanceof` or numerous typecasts. If you find yourself running into problems with proxies, you should question your design, asking whether there is a more polymorphic approach. Hibernate also offers bytecode instrumentation as an alternative to lazy loading through proxies; we'll get back to fetching strategies in chapter 13, section 13.1, "Defining the global fetch plan."

One-to-one associations are handled the same way. What about many-valued associations—for example, the collection of `billingDetails` for each `User`?

7.3.2 Polymorphic collections

A `User` may have references to many `BillingDetails`, not only a single default (one of the many *is* the default). You map this with a bidirectional one-to-many association.

In `BillingDetails`, you have the following:

```
<many-to-one name="user"
             class="User"
             column="USER_ID"/>
```

In the Users mapping you have:

```
<set name="billingDetails"
    inverse="true">
    <key column="USER_ID"/>
    <one-to-many class="BillingDetails"/>
</set>
```

Adding a CreditCard is easy:

```
CreditCard cc = new CreditCard();
cc.setNumber(ccNumber);
cc.setType(ccType);
cc.setExpMonth(...);
cc.setExpYear(...);

User user = (User) session.get(User.class, userId);

// Call convenience method that sets both sides of the association
user.addBillingDetails(cc);

// Complete unit of work
```

As usual, addBillingDetails() calls getBillingDetails().add(cc) and cc.set-User(this) to guarantee the integrity of the relationship by setting both pointers.

You may iterate over the collection and handle instances of CreditCard and CheckingAccount polymorphically (you probably don't want to bill users several times in the final system, though):

```
User user = (User) session.get(User.class, userId);

for( BillingDetails bd : user.getBillingDetails() ) {
    // Invoke CreditCard.pay() or BankAccount.pay()
    bd.pay(paymentAmount);
}
```

In the examples so far, we assumed that BillingDetails is a class mapped explicitly and that the inheritance mapping strategy is *table per class hierarchy*, or normalized with *table per subclass*.

However, if the hierarchy is mapped with *table per concrete class* (implicit polymorphism) or explicitly with *table per concrete class with union*, this scenario requires a more sophisticated solution.

7.3.3   *Polymorphic associations to unions*

Hibernate supports the polymorphic many-to-one and one-to-many associations shown in the previous sections even if a class hierarchy is mapped with the *table per concrete class* strategy. You may wonder how this works, because you may not have a table for the superclass with this strategy; if so, you can't reference or add a foreign key column to BILLING_DETAILS.

Review our discussion of *table per concrete class with union* in chapter 5, section 5.1.2, "Table per concrete class with unions." Pay extra attention to the polymorphic query Hibernate executes when retrieving instances of `BillingDetails`. Now, consider the following collection of `BillingDetails` mapped for `User`:

```
<set name="billingDetails"
     inverse="true">
    <key column="USER_ID"/>
    <one-to-many class="BillingDetails"/>
</set>
```

If you want to enable the polymorphic union feature, a requirement for this polymorphic association is that it's inverse; there must be a mapping on the opposite side. In the mapping of `BillingDetails`, with `<union-subclass>`, you have to include a `<many-to-one>` association:

```
<class name="BillingDetails" abstract="true">

    <id name="id" column="BILLING_DETAILS_ID" .../>

    <property .../>

    <many-to-one name="user"
                 column="USER_ID"
                 class="User"/>

    <union-subclass name="CreditCard" table="CREDIT_CARD">
        <property .../>
    </union-subclass>

    <union-subclass name="BankAccount" table="BANK_ACCOUNT">
        <property .../>
    </union-subclass>

</class>
```

You have two tables for both concrete classes of the hierarchy. Each table has a foreign key column, `USER_ID`, referencing the `USERS` table. The schema is shown in figure 7.14.

Now, consider the following data-access code:

```
aUser.getBillingDetails().iterator().next();
```

<< Table >> **CREDIT_CARD**
BILLING_DETAILS_ID << PK >>
USER_ID << FK >>
OWNER
NUMBER
EXP_MONTH
EXP_YEAR

<< Table >> **BANK_ACCOUNT**
BILLING_DETAILS_ID << PK >>
USER_ID << FK >>
OWNER
ACCOUNT
BANKNAME
SWIFT

Figure 7.14 Two concrete classes mapped to two separate tables

Hibernate executes a UNION query to retrieve all instances that are referenced in this collection:

```
select
    BD.*
from
  ( select
      BILLING_DETAILS_ID, USER_ID, OWNER,
      NUMBER, EXP_MONTH, EXP_YEAR,
      null as ACCOUNT, null as BANKNAME, null as SWIFT,
      1 as CLAZZ
    from
      CREDIT_CARD

    union

    select
      BILLING_DETAILS_ID, USER_ID, OWNER,
      null as NUMBER, null as EXP_MONTH, null as EXP_YEAR
      ACCOUNT, BANKNAME, SWIFT,
      2 as CLAZZ
    from
      BANK_ACCOUNT
  ) BD
where
    BD.USER_ID = ?
```

The FROM-clause subselect is a union of all concrete class tables, and it includes the USER_ID foreign key values for all instances. The outer select now includes a restriction in the WHERE clause to all rows referencing a particular user.

This magic works great for retrieval of data. If you manipulate the collection and association, the noninverse side is used to update the USER_ID column(s) in the concrete table. In other words, the modification of the inverse collection has no effect: The value of the user property of a CreditCard or BankAccount instance is taken.

Now consider the many-to-one association defaultBillingDetails again, mapped with the DEFAULT_BILLING_DETAILS_ID column in the USERS table. Hibernate executes a UNION query that looks similar to the previous query to retrieve this instance, if you access the property. However, instead of a restriction in the WHERE clause to a particular user, the restriction is made on a particular BILLING_DETAILS_ID.

Important: Hibernate cannot and will not create a foreign key constraint for DEFAULT_BILLING_DETAILS_ID with this strategy. The target table of this reference can be any of the concrete tables, which can't be constrained easily. You should consider writing a custom integrity rule for this column with a database trigger.

One problematic inheritance strategy remains: *table per concrete class* with implicit polymorphism.

7.3.4 *Polymorphic table per concrete class*

In chapter 5, section 5.1.1, "Table per concrete class with implicit polymorphism," we defined the *table per concrete class* mapping strategy and observed that this mapping strategy makes it difficult to represent a polymorphic association, because you can't map a foreign key relationship to a table of the abstract superclass. There is no table for the superclass with this strategy; you have tables only for concrete classes. You also can't create a UNION, because Hibernate doesn't know what unifies the concrete classes; the superclass (or interface) isn't mapped anywhere.

Hibernate doesn't support a polymorphic billingDetails one-to-many collection in User, if this inheritance mapping strategy is applied on the BillingDetails hierarchy. If you need polymorphic many-to-one associations with this strategy, you'll have to resort to a hack. The technique we'll show you in this section should be your last choice. Try to switch to a <union-subclass> mapping first.

Suppose that you want to represent a polymorphic many-to-one association from User to BillingDetails, where the BillingDetails class hierarchy is mapped with a *table per concrete class* strategy and implicit polymorphic behavior in Hibernate. You have a CREDIT_CARD table and a BANK_ACCOUNT table, but no BILLING_DETAILS table. Hibernate needs two pieces of information in the USERS table to uniquely identify the associated default CreditCard or BankAccount:

- The name of the table in which the associated instance resides
- The identifier of the associated instance

The USERS table requires a DEFAULT_BILLING_DETAILS_TYPE column in addition to the DEFAULT_BILLING_DETAILS_ID. This extra column works as an additional discriminator and requires a Hibernate <any> mapping in User.hbm.xml:

```
<any name="defaultBillingDetails"
    id-type="long"
    meta-type="string">
    <meta-value value="CREDIT_CARD" class="CreditCard"/>
    <meta-value value="BANK_ACCOUNT" class="BankAccount"/>
    <column name="DEFAULT_BILLING_DETAILS_TYPE"/>
    <column name="DEFAULT_BILLING_DETAILS_ID"/>
</any>
```

The meta-type attribute specifies the Hibernate type of the DEFAULT_BILLING_DETAILS_TYPE column; the id-type attribute specifies the type of the DEFAULT_

BILLING_DETAILS_ID column (it's necessary for CreditCard and BankAccount to have the same identifier type).

The <meta-value> elements tell Hibernate how to interpret the value of the DEFAULT_BILLING_DETAILS_TYPE column. You don't need to use the full table name here—you can use any value you like as a type discriminator. For example, you can encode the information in two characters:

```
<any name="defaultBillingDetails"
    id-type="long"
    meta-type="string">
    <meta-value value="CC" class="CreditCard"/>
    <meta-value value="CA" class="BankAccount"/>
    <column name="DEFAULT_BILLING_DETAILS_TYPE"/>
    <column name="DEFAULT_BILLING_DETAILS_ID"/>
</any>
```

An example of this table structure is shown in figure 7.15.

Here is the first major problem with this kind of association: You can't add a foreign key constraint to the DEFAULT_BILLING_DETAILS_ID column, because some values refer to the BANK_ACCOUNT table and others to the CREDIT_CARD table. Thus, you need to come up with some other way to ensure integrity (a trigger, for example). This is the same issue you'd face with a <union-subclass> strategy.

Furthermore, it's difficult to write SQL table joins for this association. In particular, the Hibernate query facilities don't support this kind of association mapping, nor may this association be fetched using an outer join. We discourage the use of <any> associations for all but the *most* special cases. Also note that this mapping

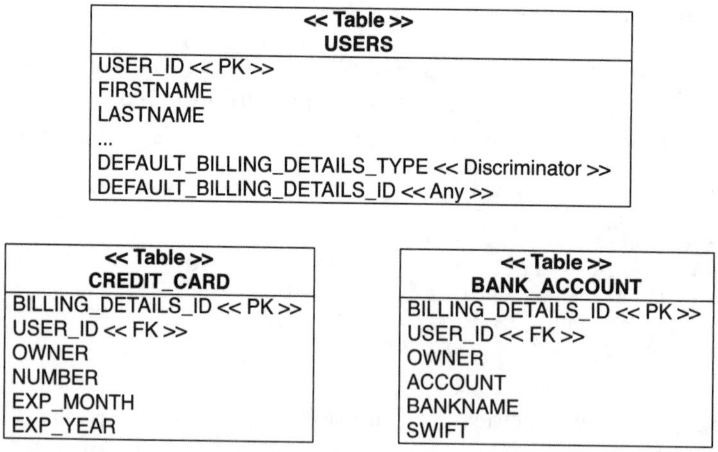

Figure 7.15   Using a discriminator column with an *any* association

technique isn't available with annotations or in Java Persistence (this mapping is so rare that nobody asked for annotation support so far).

As you can see, as long as you don't plan to create an association to a class hierarchy mapped with implicit polymorphism, associations are straightforward; you don't usually need to think about it. You may be surprised that we didn't show any JPA or annotation example in the previous sections—the runtime behavior is the same, and you don't need any extra mapping to get it.

7.4 Summary

In this chapter, you learned how to map more complex entity associations. Many of the techniques we've shown are rarely needed and may be unnecessary if you can simplify the relationships between your classes. In particular, many-to-many entity associations are often best represented as two one-to-many associations to an intermediate entity class, or with a collection of components.

Table 7.1 shows a summary you can use to compare native Hibernate features and Java Persistence.

Table 7.1 Hibernate and JPA comparison chart for chapter 7

Hibernate Core	Java Persistence and EJB 3.0
Hibernate supports key generation for shared primary key one-to-one association mappings.	Standardized one-to-one mapping is supported. Automatic shared primary key generation is possible through a Hibernate extension.
Hibernate supports all entity association mappings across join tables.	Standardized association mappings are available across secondary tables.
Hibernate supports mapping of lists with persistent indexes.	Persistent indexes require a Hibernate extension annotation.
Hibernate supports fully polymorphic behavior. It provides extra support for *any* association mappings to an inheritance hierarchy mapped with implicit polymorphism.	Fully polymorphic behavior is available, but there is no annotation support for *any* mappings.

In the next chapter, we'll focus on legacy database integration and how you can customize the SQL that Hibernate generates automatically for you. This chapter is interesting not only if you have to work with legacy schemas, but also if you want to improve your new schema with custom DDL, for example.

Legacy databases
and custom SQL

This chapter covers

- Legacy database integration and tricky mappings
- Customization of SQL statements
- Improving the SQL schema with custom DDL

Many examples presented in this chapter are about "difficult" mappings. The first time you'll likely have problems creating a mapping is with a legacy database schema that can't be modified. We discuss typical issues you encounter in such a scenario and how you can bend and twist your mapping metadata instead of changing your application or database schema.

We also show you how you can override the SQL Hibernate generates automatically. This includes SQL queries, DML (create, update, delete) operations, as well as Hibernate's automatic DDL-generation feature. You'll see how to map stored procedures and user-defined SQL functions, and how to apply the right integrity rules in your database schema. This section will be especially useful if your DBA needs full control (or if you're a DBA and want to optimize Hibernate at the SQL level).

As you can see, the topics in this chapter are diverse; you don't have to read them all at once. You can consider a large part of this chapter to be reference material and come back when you face a particular issue.

8.1 Integrating legacy databases

In this section, we hope to cover all the things you may encounter when you have to deal with an existing legacy database or (and this is often synonymous) a weird or broken schema. If your development process is top-down, however, you may want to skip this section. Furthermore, we recommend that you first read all chapters about class, collection, and association mappings before you attempt to reverse-engineer a complex legacy schema.

We have to warn you: When your application inherits an existing legacy database schema, you should usually make as few changes to the existing schema as possible. Every change that you make to the schema could break other existing applications that access the database. Possibly expensive migration of existing data is also something you need to evaluate. In general, it isn't possible to build a new application and make no changes to the existing data model—a new application usually means additional business requirements that naturally require evolution of the database schema.

We'll therefore consider two types of problems: problems that relate to the changing business requirements (which generally can't be solved without schema changes) and problems that relate only to how you wish to represent the same business problem in your new application (these can usually, but not always, be solved without database schema changes). It should be clear that the first kind of problem is usually visible by looking at just the logical data model. The second more often relates to the implementation of the logical data model as a physical database schema.

If you accept this observation, you'll see that the kinds of problems that require schema changes are those that necessitate addition of new entities, refactoring of existing entities, addition of new attributes to existing entities, and modification to the associations between entities. The problems that can be solved without schema changes usually involve inconvenient table or column definitions for a particular entity. In this section, we'll concentrate on these kinds of problems.

We assume that you've tried to reverse-engineer your existing schema with the Hibernate toolset, as described in chapter 2, section 2.3, "Reverse engineering a legacy database." The concepts and solutions discussed in the following sections assume that you have basic object/relational mapping in place and that you need to make additional changes to get it working. Alternatively, you can try to write the mapping completely by hand without the reverse-engineering tools.

Let's start with the most obvious problem: legacy primary keys.

8.1.1 Handling primary keys

We've already mentioned that we think natural primary keys can be a bad idea. Natural keys often make it difficult to refactor the data model when business requirements change. They may even, in extreme cases, impact performance. Unfortunately, many legacy schemas use (natural) composite keys heavily and, for the reason we discourage the use of composite keys, it may be difficult to change the legacy schema to use noncomposite natural or surrogate keys.

Therefore, Hibernate supports the use of natural keys. If the natural key is a composite key, support is via the <composite-id> mapping. Let's map both a composite and a noncomposite natural primary key.

Mapping a natural key

If you encountered a USERS table in a legacy schema, it's likely that USERNAME is the actual primary key. In this case, you have no surrogate identifier that is automatically generated. Instead, you enable the assigned identifier generator strategy to indicate to Hibernate that the identifier is a natural key assigned by the application before the object is saved:

```
<class name="User" table="USERS">
    <id name="username" column="USERNAME" length="16">
        <generator class="assigned"/>
    </id>

    ...
</class>
```

The code to save a new User is as follows:

```
User user = new User();
user.setUsername("johndoe"); // Assign a primary key value
user.setFirstname("John");
user.setLastname("Doe");
session.saveOrUpdate(user); // Will result in an INSERT
// System.out.println( session.getIdentifier(user) );
session.flush();
```

How does Hibernate know that saveOrUpdate() requires an INSERT and not an UPDATE? It doesn't, so a trick is needed: Hibernate queries the USERS table for the given username, and if it's found, Hibernate updates the row. If it isn't found, insertion of a new row is required and done. This is certainly not the best solution, because it triggers an additional hit on the database.

Several strategies avoid the SELECT:

- Add a <version> or a <timestamp> mapping, and a property, to your entity. Hibernate manages both values internally for optimistic concurrency control (discussed later in the book). As a side effect, an empty timestamp or a 0 or NULL version indicates that an instance is new and has to be inserted, not updated.

- Implement a Hibernate Interceptor, and hook it into your Session. This extension interface allows you to implement the method isTransient() with any custom procedure you may need to distinguish old and new objects.

On the other hand, if you're happy to use save() and update() explicitly instead of saveOrUpdate(), Hibernate doesn't have to distinguish between transient and detached instances—you do this by selecting the right method to call. (This issue is, in practice, the only reason to not use saveOrUpdate() all the time, by the way.)

Mapping natural primary keys with JPA annotations is straightforward:

```
@Id
private String username;
```

If no identifier generator is declared, Hibernate assumes that it has to apply the regular select-to-determine-state-unless-versioned strategy and expects the application to take care of the primary key value assignment. You can again avoid the SELECT by extending your application with an interceptor or by adding a version-control property (version number or timestamp).

Composite natural keys extend on the same ideas.

Mapping a composite natural key

Suppose that the primary key of the USERS table consists of a USERNAME and DEPARTMENT_NR. You can add a property named departmentNr to the User class and create the following mapping:

```
<class name="User" table="USERS">

    <composite-id>
        <key-property name="username"
                      column="USERNAME"/>

        <key-property name="departmentNr"
                      column="DEPARTMENT_NR"/>
    </composite-id>

    ...
</class>
```

The code to save a new User looks like this:

```
User user = new User();

// Assign a primary key value
user.setUsername("johndoe");
user.setDepartmentNr(42);

// Set property values
user.setFirstname("John");
user.setLastname("Doe");

session.saveOrUpdate(user);
session.flush();
```

Again, keep in mind that Hibernate executes a SELECT to determine what save-OrUpdate() should do—unless you enable versioning control or a custom Interceptor. But what object can/should you use as the identifier when you call load() or get()? Well, it's possible to use an instance of the User class, for example:

```
User user = new User();

// Assign a primary key value
user.setUsername("johndoe");
user.setDepartmentNr(42);

// Load the persistent state into user
session.load(User.class, user);
```

In this code snippet, User acts as its own identifier class. It's more elegant to define a separate composite identifier class that declares just the key properties. Call this class UserId:

```
public class UserId implements Serializable {
    private String username;
```

```
        private Integer departmentNr;

        public UserId(String username, Integer departmentNr) {
            this.username = username;
            this.departmentNr = departmentNr;
        }

        // Getters...

        public int hashCode() {
            int result;
                result = username.hashCode();
                result = 29 * result + departmentNr.hashCode();
                return result;
        }

        public boolean equals(Object other) {
            if (other==null) return false;
            if ( !(other instanceof UserId) ) return false;
            UserId that = (UserId) other;
            return this.username.equals(that.username) &&
                this.departmentNr.equals(that.departmentNr);
        }
    }
}
```

It's critical that you implement equals() and hashCode() correctly, because Hibernate relies on these methods for cache lookups. Identifier classes are also expected to implement Serializable.

You now remove the username and departmentNr properties from User and add a userId property. Create the following mapping:

```
<class name="User" table="USERS">

    <composite-id name="userId" class="UserId">
        <key-property name="username"
                    column="USERNAME"/>

        <key-property name="departmentNr"
                    column="DEPARTMENT_NR"/>
    </composite-id>

    ...
</class>
```

Save a new instance of User with this code:

```
UserId id = new UserId("johndoe", 42);

User user = new User();

// Assign a primary key value
user.setUserId(id);

// Set property values
```

```
user.setFirstname("John");
user.setLastname("Doe");

session.saveOrUpdate(user);
session.flush();
```

Again, a SELECT is needed for saveOrUpdate() to work. The following code shows
how to load an instance:

```
UserId id = new UserId("johndoe", 42);

User user = (User) session.load(User.class, id);
```

Now, suppose that the DEPARTMENT_NR is a foreign key referencing the DEPART-
MENT table, and that you wish to represent this association in the Java domain
model as a many-to-one association.

Foreign keys in composite primary keys

We recommend that you map a foreign key column that is also part of a composite primary key with a regular <many-to-one> element, and disable any Hibernate inserts or updates of this column with insert="false" update="false", as
follows:

```
<class name="User" table="USER">

    <composite-id name="userId" class="UserId">
        <key-property name="username"
                      column="USERNAME"/>

        <key-property name="departmentId"
                      column="DEPARTMENT_ID"/>
    </composite-id>

    <many-to-one name="department"
                 class="Department"
                 column="DEPARTMENT_ID"
                 insert="false" update="false"/>
    ...
</class>
```

Hibernate now ignores the department property when updating or inserting a
User, but you can of course read it with johndoe.getDepartment(). The relationship between a User and Department is now managed through the departmentId
property of the UserId composite key class:

```
UserId id = new UserId("johndoe", department.getId() );

User user = new User();

// Assign a primary key value
user.setUserId(id);
```

```
// Set property values
user.setFirstname("John");
user.setLastname("Doe");
user.setDepartment(department);

session.saveOrUpdate(user);
session.flush();
```

Only the identifier value of the department has any effect on the persistent state; the setDepartment(department) call is done for consistency: Otherwise, you'd have to refresh the object from the database to get the department set after the flush. (In practice you can move all these details into the constructor of your composite identifier class.)

An alternative approach is a <key-many-to-one>:

```
<class name="User" table="USER">

    <composite-id name="userId" class="UserId">
        <key-property name="username"
                      column="USERNAME"/>

        <key-many-to-one name="department"
                         class="Department"
                         column="DEPARTMENT_ID"/>
    </composite-id>

    ...
</class>
```

However, it's usually inconvenient to have an association in a composite identifier class, so this approach isn't recommended except in special circumstances. The <key-many-to-one> construct also has limitations in queries: You can't restrict a query result in HQL or Criteria across a <key-many-to-one> join (although it's possible these features will be implemented in a later Hibernate version).

Foreign keys to composite primary keys

Because USERS has a composite primary key, any referencing foreign key is also composite. For example, the association from Item to User (the seller) is now mapped with a composite foreign key.

Hibernate can hide this detail from the Java code with the following association mapping from Item to User:

```
<many-to-one name="seller" class="User">
    <column name="USERNAME"/>
    <column name="DEPARTMENT_ID"/>
</many-to-one>
```

Any collection owned by the User class also has a composite foreign key—for example, the inverse association, items, sold by this user:

```
<set name="itemsForAuction" inverse="true">
    <key>
        <column name="USERNAME"/>
        <column name="DEPARTMENT_ID"/>
    </key>
    <one-to-many class="Item"/>
</set>
```

Note that the order in which columns are listed is important and should match the order in which they appear in the <composite-id> element of the primary key mapping of User.

This completes our discussion of the basic composite key mapping technique in Hibernate. Mapping composite keys with annotations is almost the same, but as always, small differences are important.

Composite keys with annotations

The JPA specification covers strategies for handling composite keys. You have three options:

- Encapsulate the identifier properties in a separate class and mark it @Embeddable, like a regular component. Include a property of this component type in your entity class, and map it with @Id for an application-assigned strategy.

- Encapsulate the identifier properties in a separate class without any annotations on it. Include a property of this type in your entity class, and map it with @EmbeddedId.

- Encapsulate the identifier properties in a separate class. Now—and this is different that what you usually do in native Hibernate—duplicate all the identifier properties in the entity class. Then, annotate the entity class with @IdClass and specify the name of your encapsulated identifier class.

The first option is straightforward. You need to make the UserId class from the previous section embeddable:

```
@Embeddable
public class UserId implements Serializable {
    private String username;
    private String departmentNr;

    ...
}
```

As for all component mappings, you can define extra mapping attributes on the fields (or getter methods) of this class. To map the composite key of User, set the generation strategy to application assigned by omitting the @GeneratedValue annotation:

```
@Id
@AttributeOverrides({
    @AttributeOverride(name    = "username",
                       column = @Column(name="USERNAME") ),
    @AttributeOverride(name    = "departmentNr",
                       column = @Column(name="DEP_NR") )
})
private UserId userId;
```

Just as you did with regular component mappings earlier in the book, you can override particular attribute mappings of the component class, if you like.

The second composite-key mapping strategy doesn't require that you mark up the UserId primary key class. Hence, no @Embeddable and no other annotation on that class is needed. In the owning entity, you map the composite identifier property with @EmbeddedId, again, with optional overrides:

```
@EmbeddedId
@AttributeOverrides({
    @AttributeOverride(name    = "username",
                       column = @Column(name="USERNAME") ),
    @AttributeOverride(name    = "departmentNr",
                       column = @Column(name="DEP_NR") )
})
private UserId userId;
```

In a JPA XML descriptor, this mapping looks as follows:

```
<embeddable class="auction.model.UserId" access ="PROPERTY">
    <attributes>
        <basic name="username">
            <column name="UNAME"/>
        </basic>
        <basic name="departmentNr">
            <column name="DEPARTMENT_NR"/>
        </basic>
    </attributes>
</embeddable>

<entity class="auction.model.User" access="FIELD">
    <attributes>
        <embedded-id name="userId">
            <attribute-override name="username">
                <column name="USERNAME"/>
            </attribute-override>
```

```
                    <attribute-override name="departmentNr">
                        <column name="DEP_NR"/>
                    </attribute-override>
                </embedded-id>
                ...
            </attributes>
        </entity>
```

The third composite-key mapping strategy is a bit more difficult to understand, especially for experienced Hibernate users. First, you encapsulate all identifier attributes in a separate class—as in the previous strategy, no extra annotations on that class are needed. Now you duplicate all the identifier properties in the entity class:

```
@Entity
@Table(name = "USERS")
@IdClass(UserId.class)
public class User {

    @Id
    private String username;

    @Id
    private String departmentNr;

    // Accessor methods, etc.
    ...
}
```

Hibernate inspects the @IdClass and singles out all the duplicate properties (by comparing name and type) as identifier properties and as part of the primary key. All primary key properties are annotated with @Id, and depending on the position of these elements (field or getter method), the entity defaults to field or property access.

Note that this last strategy is also available in Hibernate XML mappings; however, it's somewhat obscure:

```
<composite-id class="UserId" mapped="true">
    <key-property name="username"
                  column="USERNAME"/>

    <key-property name="departmentNr"
                  column="DEP_NR"/>
</composite-id>
```

You omit the identifier property name of the entity (because there is none), so Hibernate handles the identifier internally. With mapped="true", you enable the last JPA mapping strategy, so all key properties are now expected to be present in both the User and the UserId classes.

This composite identifier mapping strategy looks as follows if you use JPA XML descriptors:

```
<entity class="auction.model.User" access="FIELD">
    <id-class class="auction.model.UserId"/>
    <attributes>
        <id name="username"/>
        <id name="departmentNr"/>
    </attributes>
</entity>
```

Because we didn't find a compelling case for this last strategy defined in Java Persistence, we have to assume that it was added to the specification to support some legacy behavior (EJB 2.x entity beans).

Composite foreign keys are also possible with annotations. Let's first map the association from `Item` to `User`:

```
@ManyToOne
@JoinColumns({
    @JoinColumn(name="USERNAME", referencedColumnName = "USERNAME"),
    @JoinColumn(name="DEP_NR", referencedColumnName = "DEP_NR")
})
private User seller;
```

The primary difference between a regular `@ManyToOne` and this mapping is the number of columns involved—again, the order is important and should be the same as the order of the primary key columns. However, if you declare the `referencedColumnName` for each column, order isn't important, and both the source and target tables of the foreign key constraint can have different column names.

The inverse mapping from `User` to `Item` with a collection is even more straightforward:

```
@OneToMany(mappedBy = "seller")
private Set<Item> itemsForAuction = new HashSet<Item>();
```

This inverse side needs the `mappedBy` attribute, as usual for bidirectional associations. Because this is the inverse side, it doesn't need any column declarations.

In legacy schemas, a foreign key often doesn't reference a primary key.

Foreign key referencing nonprimary keys

Usually, a foreign key constraint references a primary key. A foreign key constraint is an integrity rule that guarantees that the referenced table has one row with a key value that matches the key value in the referencing table and given row. Note that a foreign key constraint can be self-referencing; in other words, a column with a foreign key constraint can reference the primary key column of the same table. (The `PARENT_CATEGORY_ID` in the CaveatEmptor `CATEGORY` table is one example.)

Legacy schemas sometimes have foreign key constraints that don't follow the simple "FK references PK" rule. Sometimes a foreign key references a nonprimary key: a simple unique column, a natural nonprimary key. Let's assume that in Cave-atEmptor, you need to handle a legacy natural key column called CUSTOMER_NR on the USERS table:

```
<class name="User" table="USERS">

    <id name="id" column="USER_ID">...</id>

    <property name="customerNr"
              column="CUSTOMER_NR"
              not-null="true"
              unique="true"/>

</class>
```

The only thing that is probably new to you in this mapping is the unique attribute. This is one of the SQL customization options in Hibernate; it's not used at runtime (Hibernate doesn't do any uniqueness validation) but to export the database schema with hbm2ddl. If you have an existing schema with a natural key, you assume that it's unique. For completeness, you can and should repeat such important constraints in your mapping metadata—maybe you'll use it one day to export a fresh schema.

Equivalent to the XML mapping, you can declare a column as unique in JPA annotations:

```
@Column(name = "CUSTOMER_NR", nullable = false, unique=true)
private int customerNr;
```

The next issue you may discover in the legacy schema is that the ITEM table has a foreign key column, SELLER_NR. In an ideal world, you would expect this foreign key to reference the primary key, USER_ID, of the USERS table. However, in a legacy schema, it may reference the natural unique key, CUSTOMER_NR. You need to map it with a property reference:

```
<class name="Item" table="ITEM">

    <id name="id" column="ITEM_ID">...</id>

    <many-to-one name="seller" column="SELLER_NR"
                 property-ref="customerNr"/>

</class>
```

You'll encounter the property-ref attribute in more exotic Hibernate mappings. It's used to tell Hibernate that "this is a mirror of the named property." In the previous example, Hibernate now knows the target of the foreign key reference. One further thing to note is that `property-ref` requires the target property to be unique, so `unique="true"`, as shown earlier, is needed for this mapping.

If you try to map this association with JPA annotations, you may look for an equivalent to the `property-ref` attribute. You map the association with an explicit reference to the natural key column, CUSTOMER_NR:

```
@ManyToOne
@JoinColumn(name="SELLER_NR", referencedColumnName = "CUSTOMER_NR")
private User seller;
```

Hibernate now knows that the referenced target column is a natural key and manages the foreign key relationship accordingly.

To complete this example, you make this association mapping between the two classes bidirectional, with a mapping of an `itemsForAuction` collection on the User class. First, here it is in XML:

```
<class name="User" table="USERS">

    <id name="id" column="USER_ID">...</id>

    <property name="customerNr" column="CUSTOMER_NR" unique="true"/>

    <set name="itemsForAuction" inverse="true">
        <key column="SELLER_NR" property-ref="customerNr"/>
        <one-to-many class="Item"/>
    </set>

</class>
```

Again the foreign key column in ITEM is mapped with a property reference to customerNr. In annotations, this is a lot easier to map as an inverse side:

```
@OneToMany(mappedBy = "seller")
private Set<Item> itemsForAuction = new HashSet<Item>();
```

Composite foreign key referencing nonprimary keys

Some legacy schemas are even more complicated than the one discussed before: A foreign key might be a composite key and, by design, reference a composite natural nonprimary key!

Let's assume that USERS has a natural composite key that includes the FIRST-NAME, LASTNAME, and BIRTHDAY columns. A foreign key may reference this natural key, as shown in figure 8.1.

To map this, you need to group several properties under the same name—otherwise you can't name the composite in a `property-ref`. Apply the `<properties>` element to group the mappings:

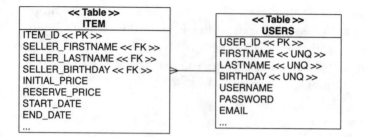

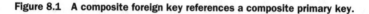

Figure 8.1   A composite foreign key references a composite primary key.

```
<class name="User" table="USERS">

    <id name="id" column="USER_ID">...</id>

    <properties name="nameAndBirthday" unique="true" update="false">
        <property name="firstname" column="FIRSTNAME"/>
        <property name="lastname" column="LASTNAME"/>
        <property name="birthday" column="BIRTHDAY" type="date"/>
    </properties>

    <set name="itemsForAuction" inverse="true">
        <key property-ref="nameAndBirthday">
            <column name="SELLER_FIRSTNAME"/>
            <column name="SELLER_LASTNAME"/>
            <column name="SELLER_BIRTHDAY"/>
        </key>
        <one-to-many class="Item"/>
    </set>

</class>
```

As you can see, the <properties> element is useful not only to give several properties a name, but also to define a multicolumn unique constraint or to make several properties immutable. For the association mappings, the order of columns is again important:

```
<class name="Item" table="ITEM">

    <id name="id" column="ITEM_ID">...</id>

    <many-to-one name="seller" property-ref="nameAndBirthday">
        <column name="SELLER_FIRSTNAME"/>
        <column name="SELLER_LASTNAME"/>
        <column name="SELLER_BIRTHDAY"/>
    </many-to-one>

</class>
```

Fortunately, it's often straightforward to clean up such a schema by refactoring foreign keys to reference primary keys—if you can make changes to the database that don't disturb other applications sharing the data.

This completes our exploration of natural, composite, and foreign key-related problems you may have to deal with when you try to map a legacy schema. Let's move on to other interesting special mapping strategies.

Sometimes you can't make any changes to a legacy database—not even creating tables or views. Hibernate can map classes, properties, and even parts of associations to a simple SQL statement or expression. We call these kinds of mappings formula mappings.

8.1.2 Arbitrary join conditions with formulas

Mapping a Java artifact to an SQL expression is useful for more than integrating a legacy schema. You created two formula mappings already: The first, "Using derived properties," in chapter 4, section 4.4.1, was a simple derived read-only property mapping. The second formula calculated the discriminator in an inheritance mapping; see chapter 5, section 5.1.3, "Table per class hierarchy."

You'll now apply formulas for a more exotic purposes. Keep in mind that some of the mappings you'll see now are complex, and you may be better prepared to understand them after reading all the chapters in part 2 of this book.

Understanding the use case

You now map a literal join condition between two entities. This sounds more complex than it is in practice. Look at the two classes shown in figure 8.2.

A particular `Item` may have several `Bid`s—this is a one-to-many association. But it isn't the only association between the two classes; the other, a unidirectional

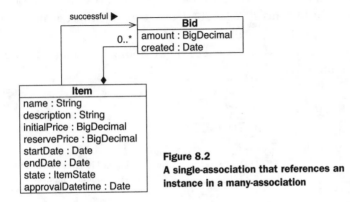

Figure 8.2
A single-association that references an instance in a many-association

one-to-one, is needed to single out one particular `Bid` instance as the winning bid. You map the first association because you'd like to be able to get all the bids for an auctioned item by calling `anItem.getBids()`. The second association allows you to call `anItem.getSuccessfulBid()`. Logically, one of the elements in the collection is also the successful bid object referenced by `getSuccessfulBid()`.

The first association is clearly a bidirectional one-to-many/many-to-one association, with a foreign key `ITEM_ID` in the `BID` table. (If you haven't mapped this before, look at chapter 6, section 6.4, "Mapping a parent/children relationship.")

The one-to-one association is more difficult; you can map it several ways. The most natural is a uniquely constrained foreign key in the `ITEM` table referencing a row in the `BID` table—the winning row, for example a `SUCCESSFUL_BID_ID` column.

Legacy schemas often need a mapping that isn't a simple foreign key relationship.

Mapping a formula join condition

Imagine that each row in the `BID` table has a flag column to mark the winning bid, as shown in figure 8.3. One `BID` row has the flag set to `true`, and all other rows for this auction item are naturally `false`. Chances are good that you won't find a constraint or an integrity rule for this relationship in a legacy schema, but we ignore this for now and focus on the mapping to Java classes.

To make this mapping even more interesting, assume that the legacy schema didn't use the SQL `BOOLEAN` datatype but a `CHAR(1)` field and the values `T` (for true) and `F` (for false) to simulate the boolean switch. Your goal is to map this flag column to a `successfulBid` property of the `Item` class. To map this as an object reference, you need a literal join condition, because there is no foreign key Hibernate can use for a join. In other words, for each `ITEM` row, you need to join a row from the `BID` table that has the `SUCCESSFUL` flag set to `T`. If there is no such row, the `anItem.getSuccessfulBid()` call returns `null`.

Let's first map the `Bid` class and a `successful` boolean property to the `SUCCESSFUL` database column:

<< Table >> ITEM	<< Table >> BID
ITEM_ID << PK >>	BID_ID << PK >>
SELLER_ID << FK >>	ITEM_ID << FK >>
INITIAL_PRICE	AMOUNT
RESERVE_PRICE	CREATED_ON
...	SUCCESSFUL

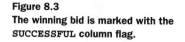

Figure 8.3
The winning bid is marked with the
`SUCCESSFUL` **column flag.**

```
<class name="Bid" table="BID">

    <id name="id" column="BID_ID"...

    <property name="amount"
                    ...

    <properties name="successfulReference">

        <property name="successful"
                    column="SUCCESSFUL"
                    type="true_false"/>
                    ...

        <many-to-one name="item"
                    class="Item"
                    column="ITEM_ID"/>
                    ...

    </properties>

    <many-to-one name="bidder"
                    class="User"
                    column="BIDDER_ID"/>
                    ...

</class>
```

The `type="true_false"` attribute creates a mapping between a Java `boolean` primitive (or its wrapper) property and a simple `CHAR(1)` column with `T/F` literal values—it's a built-in Hibernate mapping type. You again group several properties with `<properties>` under a name that you can reference in other mappings. What is new here is that you can group a `<many-to-one>`, not only basic properties.

The real trick is happening on the other side, for the mapping of the `successfulBid` property of the `Item` class:

```
<class name="Item" table="ITEM">

    <id name="id" column="ITEM_ID"...

    <property name="initialPrice"
        ...

    <one-to-one name="successfulBid"
                    property-ref="successfulReference">
        <formula>'T'</formula>
        <formula>ITEM_ID</formula>
    </one-to-one>

    <set name="bids" inverse="true">
        <key column="ITEM_ID"/>
        <one-to-many class="Bid"/>
    </set>

</class>
```

Ignore the <set> association mapping in this example; this is the regular one-to-many association between Item and Bid, bidirectional, on the ITEM_ID foreign key column in BID.

> **NOTE** *Isn't <one-to-one> used for primary key associations?* Usually, a <one-to-one> mapping is a primary key relationship between two entities, when rows in both entity tables share the same primary key value. However, by using a formula with a property-ref, you can apply it to a foreign key relationship. In the example shown in this section, you could replace the <one-to-one> element with <many-to-one>, and it would still work.

The interesting part is the <one-to-one> mapping and how it relies on a property-ref and literal formula values as a join condition when you work with the association.

Working with the association

The full SQL query for retrieval of an auction item and its successful bid looks like this:

```
select
    i.ITEM_ID,
    i.INITIAL_PRICE,
    ...
    b.BID_ID,
    b.AMOUNT,
    b.SUCCESSFUL,
    b.BIDDER_ID,
    ...
from
    ITEM i
left outer join
    BID b
        on 'T' = b.SUCCESSFUL
        and i.ITEM_ID = b.ITEM_ID
where
    i.ITEM_ID = ?
```

When you load an Item, Hibernate now joins a row from the BID table by applying a join condition that involves the columns of the successfulReference property. Because this is a grouped property, you can declare individual expressions for each of the columns involved, in the right order. The first one, 'T', is a literal, as you can see from the quotes. Hibernate now includes 'T' = SUCCESSFUL in the join condition when it tries to find out whether there is a successful row in the BID table. The second expression isn't a literal but a column name (no quotes).

Hence, another join condition is appended: `i.ITEM_ID = b.ITEM_ID`. You can expand this and add more join conditions if you need additional restrictions.

Note that an outer join is generated because the item in question may not have a successful bid, so `NULL` is returned for each `b.*` column. You can now call `anItem.getSuccessfulBid()` to get a reference to the successful bid (or `null` if none exists).

Finally, with or without database constraints, you can't just implement an `item.setSuccessfulBid()` method that only sets the value on a private field in the `Item` instance. You have to implement a small procedure in this setter method that takes care of this special relationship and the flag property on the bids:

```
public class Item {
    ...

    private Bid successfulBid;
    private Set<Bid> bids = new HashSet<Bid>();

    public Bid getSuccessfulBid() {
        return successfulBid;
    }

    public void setSuccessfulBid(Bid successfulBid) {
        if (successfulBid != null) {

            for (Bid bid : bids)
                bid.setSuccessful(false);

            successfulBid.setSuccessful(true);
            this.successfulBid = successfulBid;
        }
    }

}
```

When `setSuccessfulBid()` is called, you set all bids to not successful. Doing so may trigger the loading of the collection—a price you have to pay with this strategy. Then, the new successful bid is marked and set as an instance variable. Setting the flag updates the `SUCCESSFUL` column in the `BID` table when you save the objects. To complete this (and to fix the legacy schema), your database-level constraints need to do the same as this method. (We'll come back to constraints later in this chapter.)

One of the things to remember about this literal join condition mapping is that it can be applied in many other situations, not only for successful or default relationships. Whenever you need some arbitrary join condition appended to your queries, a formula is the right choice. For example, you could use it in a

<many-to-many> mapping to create a literal join condition from the association table to the entity table(s).

Unfortunately, at the time of writing, Hibernate Annotations doesn't support arbitrary join conditions expressed with formulas. The grouping of properties under a reference name also wasn't possible. We expect that these features will closely resemble the XML mapping, once they're available.

Another issue you may encounter in a legacy schema is that it doesn't integrate nicely with your class granularity. Our usual recommendation to have more classes than tables may not work, and you may have to do the opposite and join arbitrary tables into one class.

8.1.3 *Joining arbitrary tables*

We've already shown the <join> mapping element in an inheritance mapping in chapter 5; see section 5.1.5, "Mixing inheritance strategies." It helped to break out properties of a particular subclass into a separate table, out of the primary inheritance hierarchy table. This generic functionality has more uses—however, we have to warn you that <join> can also be a bad idea. Any properly designed system should have more classes than tables. Splitting a single class into separate tables is something you should do only when you need to merge several tables in a legacy schema into a single class.

Moving properties into a secondary table

Suppose that in CaveatEmptor, you aren't keeping a user's address information with the user's main information in the USERS table, mapped as a component, but in a separate table. This is shown in figure 8.4. Note that each BILLING_ADDRESS has a foreign key USER_ID, which is in turn the primary key of the BILLING_ ADDRESS table.

To map this in XML, you need to group the properties of the Address in a <join> element:

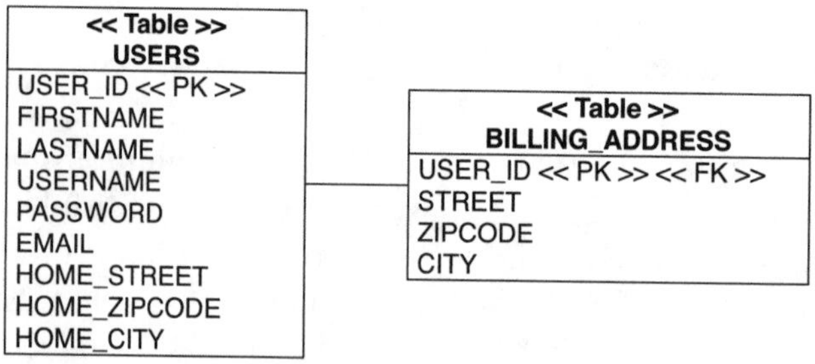

Figure 8.4
Breaking out the billing address data into a secondary table

```
<class name="User" table="USERS">
    <id>...

    <join table="BILLING_ADDRESS" optional="true">
        <key column="USER_ID"/>
        <component name="billingAddress" class="Address">
            <property    name="street"
                         type="string"
                         column="STREET"
                         length="255"/>
                <property    name="zipcode"
                             type="string"
                             column="ZIPCODE"
                             length="16"/>
                <property    name="city"
                             type="string"
                             column="CITY"
                             length="255"/>
        </component>
    </join>

</class>
```

You don't have to join a component; you can as well join individual properties or even a <many-to-one> (we did this in the previous chapter for optional entity associations). By setting optional="true", you indicate that the component property may also be null for a User with no billingAddress, and that no row should then be inserted into the secondary table. Hibernate also executes an outer join instead of an inner join to retrieve the row from the secondary table. If you declared fetch="select" on the <join> mapping, a secondary select would be used for that purpose.

The notion of a secondary table is also included in the Java Persistence specification. First, you have to declare a secondary table (or several) for a particular entity:

```
@Entity
@Table(name = "USERS")
@SecondaryTable(
    name = "BILLING_ADDRESS",
    pkJoinColumns = {
        @PrimaryKeyJoinColumn(name="USER_ID")
    }
)
public class User {
    ...
}
```

Each secondary table needs a name and a join condition. In this example, a foreign key column references the primary key column of the USERS table, just like earlier in the XML mapping. (This is the default join condition, so you can only declare the secondary table name, and nothing else). You can probably see that the syntax of annotations is starting to become an issue and code is more difficult to read. The good news is that you won't have to use secondary tables often.

The actual component property, billingAddress, is mapped as a regular @Embedded class, just like a regular component. However, you need to override each component property column and assign it to the secondary table, in the User class:

```java
@Embedded
@AttributeOverrides( {
    @AttributeOverride(
        name   = "street",
        column = @Column(name="STREET",
                         table = "BILLING_ADDRESS")
    ),
    @AttributeOverride(
        name   = "zipcode",
        column = @Column(name="ZIPCODE",
                         table = "BILLING_ADDRESS")
    ),
    @AttributeOverride(
        name   = "city",
        column = @Column(name="CITY",
                         table = "BILLING_ADDRESS")
    )
})
private Address billingAddress;
```

This is no longer easily readable, but it's the price you pay for mapping flexibility with declarative metadata in annotations. Or, you can use a JPA XML descriptor:

```xml
<entity class="auction.model.User" access="FIELD">
    <table name="USERS"/>
    <secondary-table name="BILLING_ADDRESS">
        <primary-key-join-column
            referenced-column-name="USER_ID"/>
    </secondary-table>
    <attributes>
        ...
        <embedded name="billingAddress">
            <attribute-override name="street">
                <column name="STREET" table="BILLING_ADDRESS"/>
            </attribute-override>
            <attribute-override name="zipcode">
```

```
                <column name="ZIPCODE" table="BILLING_ADDRESS"/>
            </attribute-override>
            <attribute-override name="city">
                <column name="CITY" table="BILLING_ADDRESS"/>
            </attribute-override>
        </embedded>
    </attributes>
</entity>
```

Another, even more exotic use case for the `<join>` element is inverse joined properties or components.

Inverse joined properties

Let's assume that in CaveatEmptor you have a legacy table called `DAILY_BILLING`. This table contains all the open payments, executed in a nightly batch, for any auctions. The table has a foreign key column to `ITEM`, as you can see in figure 8.5.

Each payment includes a `TOTAL` column with the amount of money that will be billed. In CaveatEmptor, it would be convenient if you could access the price of a particular auction by calling `anItem.getBillingTotal()`.

You can map the column from the `DAILY_BILLING` table into the `Item` class. However, you never insert or update it from this side; it's read-only. For that reason, you map it inverse—a simple mirror of the (supposed, you don't map it here) other side that takes care of maintaining the column value:

```
<class name="Item" table="ITEM">
    <id>...

    <join table="DAILY_BILLING" optional="true" inverse="true">
        <key column="ITEM_ID"/>
        <property    name="billingTotal"
                     type="big_decimal"
                     column="TOTAL"/>
    </join>

</class>
```

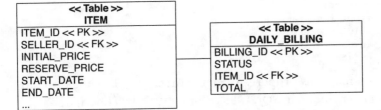

Figure 8.5 The daily billing summary references an item and contains the total sum.

Note that an alternative solution for this problem is a derived property using a formula expression and a correlated subquery:

```
<property name="billingTotal"
          type="big_decimal"
          formula="( select db.TOTAL from DAILY_BILLING db
                     where db.ITEM_ID = ITEM_ID )"/>
```

The main difference is the SQL SELECT used to load an ITEM: The first solution defaults to an outer join, with an optional second SELECT if you enable `<join fetch="select">`. The derived property results in an embedded subselect in the select clause of the original query. At the time of writing, inverse join mappings aren't supported with annotations, but you can use a Hibernate annotation for formulas.

As you can probably guess from the examples, `<join>` mappings come in handy in many situations. They're even more powerful if combined with formulas, but we hope you won't have to use this combination often.

One further problem that often arises in the context of working with legacy data are database triggers.

8.1.4 Working with triggers

There are some reasons for using triggers even in a brand-new database, so legacy data isn't the only scenerio in which they can cause problems. Triggers and object state management with an ORM software are almost always an issue, because triggers may run at inconvenient times or may modify data that isn't synchronized with the in-memory state.

Triggers that run on INSERT

Suppose the ITEM table has a CREATED column, mapped to a created property of type Date, that is initialized by a trigger that executes automatically on insertion. The following mapping is appropriate:

```
<property name="created"
          type="timestamp"
          column="CREATED"
          insert="false"
          update="false"/>
```

Notice that you map this property insert="false" update="false" to indicate that it isn't to be included in SQL INSERTs or UPDATEs by Hibernate.

After saving a new Item, Hibernate isn't aware of the value assigned to this column by the trigger, because it occurred after the INSERT of the item row. If you need the generated value in the application, you must explicitly tell Hibernate to reload the object with an SQL SELECT. For example:

```
Item item = new Item();
...
Session session = getSessionFactory().openSession();
Transaction tx = session.beginTransaction();

session.save(item);
session.flush(); // Force the INSERT to occur
session.refresh(item); // Reload the object with a SELECT

System.out.println( item.getCreated() );

tx.commit();
session.close();
```

Most problems involving triggers may be solved in this way, using an explicit flush() to force immediate execution of the trigger, perhaps followed by a call to refresh() to retrieve the result of the trigger.

Before you add refresh() calls to your application, we have to tell you that the primary goal of the previous section was to show you when to use refresh(). Many Hibernate beginners don't understand its real purpose and often use it incorrectly. A more formal definition of refresh() is "refresh an in-memory instance in persistent state with the current values present in the database."

For the example shown, a database trigger filling a column value after insertion, a much simpler technique can be used:

```
<property name="created"
          type="timestamp"
          column="CREATED"
          generated="insert"
          insert="false"
          update="false"/>
```

With annotations, use a Hibernate extension:

```
@Temporal(TemporalType.TIMESTAMP)
@org.hibernate.annotations.Generated(
    org.hibernate.annotations.GenerationTime.INSERT
)
@Column(name = "CREATED", insertable = false, updatable = false)
private Date created;
```

We have already discussed the generated attribute in detail in chapter 4, section 4.4.1.3, "Generated and default property values." With generated="insert", Hibernate automatically executes a SELECT after insertion, to retrieve the updated state.

There is one further problem to be aware of when your database executes triggers: reassociation of a detached object graph and triggers that run on each UPDATE.

Triggers that run on UPDATE

Before we discuss the problem of ON UPDATE triggers in combination with reattachment of objects, we need to point out an additional setting for the generated attribute:

```
<version name="version"
        column="OBJ_VERSION"
        generated="always"/>
...
<timestamp name="lastModified"
        column="LAST_MODIFIED"
        generated="always"/>
...
<property name="lastModified"
        type="timestamp"
        column="LAST_MODIFIED"
        generated="always"
        insert="false"
        update="false"/>
```

With annotations, the equivalent mappings are as follows:

```
@Version
@org.hibernate.annotations.Generated(
    org.hibernate.annotations.GenerationTime.ALWAYS
)
@Column(name = "OBJ_VERSION")
private int version;

@Version
@org.hibernate.annotations.Generated(
    org.hibernate.annotations.GenerationTime.ALWAYS
)
@Column(name = "LAST_MODIFIED")
private Date lastModified;

@Temporal(TemporalType.TIMESTAMP)
@org.hibernate.annotations.Generated(
    org.hibernate.annotations.GenerationTime.ALWAYS
)
@Column(name = "LAST_MODIFIED", insertable = false, updatable = false)
private Date lastModified;
```

With always, you enable Hibernate's automatic refreshing not only for insertion but also for updating of a row. In other words, whenever a version, timestamp, or any property value is generated by a trigger that runs on UPDATE SQL statements, you need to enable this option. Again, refer to our earlier discussion of generated properties in section 4.4.1.

Let's look at the second issue you may run into if you have triggers running on updates. Because no snapshot is available when a detached object is reattached to a new `Session` (with `update()` or `saveOrUpdate()`), Hibernate may execute unnecessary SQL UPDATE statements to ensure that the database state is synchronized with the persistence context state. This may cause an UPDATE trigger to fire inconveniently. You avoid this behavior by enabling `select-before-update` in the mapping for the class that is persisted to the table with the trigger. If the ITEM table has an update trigger, add the following attribute to your mapping:

```
<class name="Item"
       table="ITEM"
       select-before-update="true">
   ...
</class>
```

This setting forces Hibernate to retrieve a snapshot of the current database state using an SQL SELECT, enabling the subsequent UPDATE to be avoided if the state of the in-memory `Item` is the same. You trade the inconvenient UPDATE for an additional SELECT.

A Hibernate annotation enables the same behavior:

```
@Entity
@org.hibernate.annotations.Entity(selectBeforeUpdate = true)
public class Item { ... }
```

Before you try to map a legacy scheme, note that the SELECT before an update only retrieves the state of the entity instance in question. No collections or associated instances are eagerly fetched, and no prefetching optimization is active. If you start enabling `selectBeforeUpdate` for many entities in your system, you'll probably find that the performance issues introduced by the nonoptimized selects are problematic. A better strategy uses merging instead of reattachment. Hibernate can then apply some optimizations (outer joins) when retrieving database snapshots. We'll talk about the differences between reattachment and merging later in the book in more detail.

Let's summarize our discussion of legacy data models: Hibernate offers several strategies to deal with (natural) composite keys and inconvenient columns easily. Before you try to map a legacy schema, our recommendation is to carefully examine whether a schema change is possible. In our experience, many developers immediately dismiss database schema changes as too complex and time-consuming and look for a Hibernate solution. This sometimes isn't justified, and you should consider schema evolution a natural part of your schema's lifecycle. If tables change, then a data export, some transformation, and an import may solve the problem. One day of work may save many days in the long run.

Legacy schemas often also require customization of the SQL generated by Hibernate, be it for data manipulation (DML) or schema definition (DDL).

8.2   *Customizing SQL*

SQL started its life in the 1970s but wasn't (ANSI) standardized until 1986. Although each update of the SQL standard has seen new (and many controversial) features, every DBMS product that supports SQL does so in its own unique way. The burden of portability is again on the database application developers. This is where Hibernate helps: Its built-in query mechanisms, HQL and the `Criteria` API, produce SQL that depends on the configured database dialect. All other automatically generated SQL (for example, when a collection has to be retrieved on demand) is also produced with the help of dialects. With a simple switch of the dialect, you can run your application on a different DBMS.

To support this portability, Hibernate has to handle three kinds of operations:

- Every data-retrieval operation results in `SELECT` statements being executed. Many variations are possible; for example, database products may use a different syntax for the join operation or how a result can be limited to a particular number of rows.

- Every data modification requires the execution of Data Manipulation Language (DML) statements, such as `UPDATE`, `INSERT`, and `DELETE`. DML often isn't as complex as data retrieval, but it still has product-specific variations.

- A database schema must be created or altered before DML and data retrieval can be executed. You use Data Definition Language (DDL) to work on the database catalog; it includes statements such as `CREATE`, `ALTER`, and `DROP`. DDL is almost completely vendor specific, but most products have at least a similar syntax structure.

Another term we use often is CRUD, for create, read, update, and delete. Hibernate generates all this SQL for you, for all CRUD operations and schema definition. The translation is based on an `org.hibernate.dialect.Dialect` implementation—Hibernate comes bundled with dialects for all popular SQL database management systems. We encourage you to look at the source code of the dialect you're using; it's not difficult to read. Once you're more experienced with

Hibernate, you may even want to extend a dialect or write your own. For example, to register a custom SQL function for use in HQL selects, you'd extend an existing dialect with a new subclass and add the registration code—again, check the existing source code to find out more about the flexibility of the dialect system.

On the other hand, you sometimes need more control than Hibernate APIs (or HQL) provide, when you need to work on a lower level of abstraction. With Hibernate you can override or completely replace all CRUD SQL statements that will be executed. You can customize and extend all DDL SQL statements that define your schema, if you rely on Hibernate's automatic schema-export tool (you don't have to).

Furthermore Hibernate allows you to get a plain JDBC `Connection` object at all times through `session.connection()`. You should use this feature as a last resort, when nothing else works or anything else would be more difficult than plain JDBC. With the newest Hibernate versions, this is fortunately exceedingly rare, because more and more features for typical stateless JDBC operations (bulk updates and deletes, for example) are built-in, and many extension points for custom SQL already exist.

This custom SQL, both DML and DDL, is the topic of this section. We start with custom DML for create, read, update, and delete operations. Later, we integrate stored database procedures to do the same work. Finally, we look at DDL customization for the automatic generation of a database schema and how you can create a schema that represents a good starting point for the optimization work of a DBA.

Note that at the time of writing this detailed customization of automatically generated SQL isn't available in annotations; hence, we use XML metadata exclusively in the following examples. We expect that a future version of Hibernate Annotations will include better support for SQL customization.

8.2.1 *Writing custom CRUD statements*

The first custom SQL you'll write is used to load entities and collections. (Most of the following code examples show almost the same SQL Hibernate executes by default, without much customization—this helps you to understand the mapping technique more quickly.)

Loading entities and collections with custom SQL

For each entity class that requires a custom SQL operation to load an instance, you define a `<loader>` reference to a named query:

```
<class name="User" table="USERS">
    <id name="id" column="USER_ID"...
```

```
<loader query-ref="loadUser"/>
...

</class>
```

The `loadUser` query can now be defined anywhere in your mapping metadata, separate and encapsulated from its use. This is an example of a simple query that retrieves the data for a `User` entity instance:

```
<sql-query name="loadUser">
    <return alias="u" class="User"/>
    select
        us.USER_ID      as {u.id},
        us.FIRSTNAME    as {u.firstname},
        us.LASTNAME     as {u.lastname},
        us.USERNAME     as {u.username},
        us."PASSWORD"   as {u.password},
        us.EMAIL        as {u.email},
        us.RANKING      as {u.ranking},
        us.IS_ADMIN     as {u.admin},
        us.CREATED      as {u.created},
        us.HOME_STREET  as {u.homeAddress.street},
        us.HOME_ZIPCODE as {u.homeAddress.zipcode},
        us.HOME_CITY    as {u.homeAddress.city},
        us.DEFAULT_BILLING_DETAILS_ID as {u.defaultBillingDetails}
    from
        USERS us
    where
        us.USER_ID = ?
</sql-query>
```

As you can see, the mapping from column names to entity properties uses a simple aliasing. In a named loader query for an entity, you have to SELECT the following columns and properties:

- The primary key columns and primary key property or properties, if a composite primary key is used.

- All scalar properties, which must be initialized from their respective column(s).

- All composite properties which must be initialized. You can address the individual scalar elements with the following aliasing syntax: `{entity-alias.componentProperty.scalarProperty}`.

- All foreign key columns, which must be retrieved and mapped to the respective `many-to-one` property. See the `DEFAULT_BILLING_DETAILS_ID` example in the previous snippet.

- All scalar properties, composite properties, and many-to-one entity references that are inside a `<join>` element. You use an inner join to the secondary table if all the joined properties are never NULL; otherwise, an outer join is appropriate. (Note that this isn't shown in the example.)

- If you enable lazy loading for scalar properties, through bytecode instrumentation, you don't need to load the lazy properties. See chapter 13, section 13.1.6, "Lazy loading with interception."

The `{propertyName}` aliases as shown in the previous example are not absolutely necessary. If the name of a column in the result is the same as the name of a mapped column, Hibernate can automatically bind them together.

You can even call a mapped query by name in your application with `session.getNamedQuery("loadUser")`. Many more things are possible with custom SQL queries, but we'll focus on basic SQL customization for CRUD in this section. We come back to other relevant APIs in chapter 15, section 15.2, "Using native SQL queries."

Let's assume that you also want to customize the SQL that is used to load a collection—for example, the `items` sold by a `User`. First, declare a loader reference in the collection mapping:

```
<set name="items" inverse="true">
    <key column="SELLER_ID" not-null="true"/>
    <one-to-many class="Item"/>
    <loader query-ref="loadItemsForUser"/>
</set>
```

The named query `loadItemsForUser` looks almost the same as the entity loader:

```
<sql-query name="loadItemsForUser">
    <load-collection alias="i" role="User.items"/>
    select
        {i.*}
    from
        ITEM i
    where
        i.SELLER_ID = :id
</sql-query>
```

There are two major differences: One is the `<load-collection>` mapping from an alias to a collection role; it should be self-explanatory. What is new in this query is an automatic mapping from the SQL table alias ITEM i to the properties of all items with `{i.*}`. You created a connection between the two by using the same alias: the symbol `i`. Furthermore, you're now using a named parameter, `:id`, instead of a simple positional parameter with a question mark. You can use whatever syntax you prefer.

Sometimes, loading an entity instance and a collection is better done in a single query, with an outer join (the entity may have an empty collection, so you can't use an inner join). If you want to apply this eager fetch, don't declare a loader references for the collection. The entity loader takes care of the collection retrieval:

```
<sql-query name="loadUser">
    <return alias="u" class="User"/>
    <return-join alias="i" property="u.items"/>
    select
        {u.*}, {i.*}
    from
        USERS u
    left outer join ITEM i
        on u.USER_ID = i.SELLER_ID
    where
        u.USER_ID = ?
</sql-query>
```

Note how you use the `<return-join>` element to bind an alias to a collection property of the entity, effectively linking both aliases together. Further note that this technique also works if you'd like to eager-fetch one-to-one and many-to-one associated entities in the original query. In this case, you may want an inner join if the associated entity is mandatory (the foreign key can't be NULL) or an outer join if the target is optional. You can retrieve many single-ended associations eagerly in one query; however, if you (outer-) join more than one collection, you create a Cartesian product, effectively multiplying all collection rows. This can generate huge results that may be slower than two queries. You'll meet this limitation again when we discuss fetching strategies in chapter 13.

As mentioned earlier, you'll see more SQL options for object loading later in the book. We now discuss customization of insert, update, and delete operations, to complete the CRUD basics.

Custom insert, update, and delete

Hibernate produces all trivial CRUD SQL at startup. It caches the SQL statements internally for future use, thus avoiding any runtime cost of SQL generation for the most common operations. You've seen how you can override the R of CRUD, so let's do the same for CUD.

For each entity or collection, you can define custom CUD SQL statements inside the `<sql-insert>`, `<sql-delete>`, and `<sql-update>` element, respectively:

```
<class name="User" table="USERS">

    <id name="id" column="USER_ID"...

    ...

    <join table="BILLING_ADDRESS" optional="true">
        <key column="USER_ID"/>
        <component name="billingAddress" class="Address">
            <property ...
        </component>

        <sql-insert>
            insert into BILLING_ADDRESS
                            (STREET, ZIPCODE, CITY, USER_ID)
            values (?, ?, ?, ?)
        </sql-insert>

        <sql-update>...</sql-update>

        <sql-delete>...</sql-delete>

    </join>

    <sql-insert>
        insert into USERS (FIRSTNAME, LASTNAME, USERNAME,
                            "PASSWORD", EMAIL, RANKING, IS_ADMIN,
                            CREATED, DEFAULT_BILLING_DETAILS_ID,
                            HOME_STREET, HOME_ZIPCODE, HOME_CITY,
                            USER_ID)
        values (?, ?, ?, ?, ?, ?, ?, ?, ?, ?, ?, ?, ?)
    </sql-insert>

    <sql-update>...</sql-update>

    <sql-delete>...</sql-delete>

</class>
```

This mapping example may look complicated, but it's really simple. You have two tables in a single mapping: the primary table for the entity, USERS, and the secondary table BILLING_ADDRESS from your legacy mapping earlier in this chapter. Whenever you have secondary tables for an entity, you have to include them in any custom SQL—hence the <sql-insert>, <sql-delete>, and <sql-update> elements in both the <class> and the <join> sections of the mapping.

The next issue is the binding of arguments for the statements. For CUD SQL customization, only positional parameters are supported at the time of writing. But what is the right order for the parameters? There is an internal order to how Hibernate binds arguments to SQL parameters. The easiest way to figure out the right SQL statement and parameter order is to let Hibernate generate one for you. Remove your custom SQL from the mapping file, enable DEBUG logging for the `org.hibernate.persister.entity` package, and watch (or search) the Hibernate startup log for lines similar to these:

```
AbstractEntityPersister - Insert 0: insert into USERS (FIRSTNAME,
  LASTNAME, USERNAME, "PASSWORD", EMAIL, RANKING, IS_ADMIN,
  CREATED, DEFAULT_BILLING_DETAILS_ID, HOME_STREET, HOME_ZIPCODE,
  HOME_CITY, USER_ID) values (?, ?, ?, ?, ?, ?, ?, ?, ?, ?, ?, ?, ?)
AbstractEntityPersister - Update 0: update USERS set
  FIRSTNAME=?, LASTNAME=?, "PASSWORD"=?, EMAIL=?, RANKING=?,
  IS_ADMIN=?, DEFAULT_BILLING_DETAILS_ID=?, HOME_STREET=?,
  HOME_ZIPCODE=?, HOME_CITY=? where USER_ID=?
...
```

You can now copy the statements you want to customize into your mapping file and make the necessary changes. For more information on logging in Hibernate, refer to "Enabling logging statistics" in chapter 2, in section 2.1.3.

You've now mapped CRUD operations to custom SQL statements. On the other hand, dynamic SQL isn't the only way how you can retrieve and manipulate data. Predefined and compiled procedures stored in the database can also be mapped to CRUD operations for entities and collections.

8.2.2 *Integrating stored procedures and functions*

Stored procedures are common in database application development. Moving code closer to the data and executing it inside the database has distinct advantages.

First, you don't have to duplicate functionality and logic in each program that accesses the data. A different point of view is that a lot of business logic shouldn't be duplicated, so it can be applied all the time. This includes procedures that guarantee the integrity of the data: for example, constraints that are too complex to be implemented declaratively. You'll usually also find triggers in a database that has procedural integrity rules.

Stored procedures have advantages for all processing on large amounts of data, such as reporting and statistical analysis. You should always try to avoid moving large data sets on your network and between your database and application servers, so a stored procedure is a natural choice for mass data operations. Or, you can implement a complex data-retrieval operation that assembles data with several queries before it passes the final result to the application client.

On the other hand, you'll often see (legacy) systems that implement even the most basic CRUD operations with a stored procedure. As a variation of this, systems that don't allow any direct SQL DML, but only stored procedure calls, also had (and sometimes still have) their place.

You may start integrating existing stored procedures for CRUD or for mass data operations, or you may begin writing your own stored procedure first.

Writing a procedure

Programming languages for stored procedures are usually proprietary. Oracle PL/SQL, a procedural dialect of SQL, is very popular (and available with variations in other database products). Some databases even support stored procedures written in Java. Standardizing Java stored procedures was part of the SQLJ effort, which, unfortunately, hasn't been successful.

You'll use the most common stored procedure systems in this section: Oracle databases and PL/SQL. It turns out that stored procedures in Oracle, like so many other things, are always different than you expect; we'll tell you whenever something requires extra attention.

A stored procedure in PL/SQL has to be created in the database catalog as source code and then compiled. Let's first write a stored procedure that can load all User entities that match a particular criterion:

```
<database-object>
    <create>
        create or replace procedure SELECT_USERS_BY_RANK
        (
         OUT_RESULT out SYS_REFCURSOR,
         IN_RANK    in  int
        ) as
        begin
         open OUT_RESULT for
         select
             us.USER_ID         as USER_ID,
             us.FIRSTNAME       as FIRSTNAME,
             us.LASTNAME        as LASTNAME,
             us.USERNAME        as USERNAME,
             us."PASSWORD"      as PASSWD,
             us.EMAIL           as EMAIL,
             us.RANKING         as RANKING,
             us.IS_ADMIN        as IS_ADMIN,
             us.CREATED         as CREATED,
             us.HOME_STREET     as HOME_STREET,
             us.HOME_ZIPCODE    as HOME_ZIPCODE,
             us.HOME_CITY       as HOME_CITY,
             ba.STREET          as BILLING_STREET,
             ba.ZIPCODE         as BILLING_ZIPCODE,
             ba.CITY            as BILLING_CITY,
             us.DEFAULT_BILLING_DETAILS_ID
                                as DEFAULT_BILLING_DETAILS_ID
        from
             USERS us
```

```
            left outer join
                BILLING_ADDRESS ba
                    on us.USER_ID = ba.USER_ID
            where
                    us.RANKING >= IN_RANK;
        end;
    </create>
    <drop>
        drop procedure SELECT_USERS_BY_RANK
    </drop>
</database-object>
```

You embed the DDL for the stored procedure in a `<database-object>` element for creation and removal. That way, Hibernate automatically creates and drops the procedure when the database schema is created and updated with the `hbm2ddl` tool. You could also execute the DDL by hand on your database catalog. Keeping it in your mapping files (in whatever location seems appropriate, such as in `MyStoredProcedures.hbm.xml`) is a good choice if you're working on a nonlegacy system with no existing stored procedures. We'll come back to other options for the `<database-object>` mapping later in this chapter.

As before, the stored procedure code in the example is straightforward: a join query against the base tables (primary and secondary tables for the `User` class) and a restriction by `RANKING`, an input argument to the procedure.

You must observe a few rules for stored procedures mapped in Hibernate. Stored procedures support `IN` and `OUT` parameters. If you use stored procedures with Oracle's own JDBC drivers, Hibernate requires that the first parameter of the stored procedure is an `OUT`; and for stored procedures that are supposed to be used for queries, the query result is supposed to be returned in this parameter. In Oracle 9 or newer, the type of the `OUT` parameter has to be a `SYS_REFCURSOR`. In older versions of Oracle, you must define your own reference cursor type first, called `REF CURSOR`—examples can be found in Oracle product documentation. All other major database management systems (and drivers for the Oracle DBMS not from Oracle) are JDBC-compliant, and you can return a result directly in the stored procedure without using an `OUT` parameter. For example, a similar procedure in Microsoft SQL Server would look as follows:

```
create procedure SELECT_USERS_BY_RANK
    @IN_RANK int
    as
    select
        us.USER_ID          as USER_ID,
        us.FIRSTNAME        as FIRSTNAME,
        us.LASTNAME         as LASTNAME,
```

```
    ...
from
    USERS us
where us.RANKING >= @IN_RANK
```

Let's map this stored procedure to a named query in Hibernate.

Querying with a procedure

A stored procedure for querying is mapped as a regular named query, with some minor differences:

```
<sql-query name="loadUsersByRank" callable="true">
    <return alias="u" class="User">
        <return-property name="id"          column="USER_ID"/>
        <return-property name="firstname"   column="FIRSTNAME"/>
        <return-property name="lastname"    column="LASTNAME"/>
        <return-property name="username"    column="USERNAME"/>
        <return-property name="password"    column="PASSWD"/>
        <return-property name="email"       column="EMAIL"/>
        <return-property name="ranking"     column="RANKING"/>
        <return-property name="admin"       column="IS_ADMIN"/>
        <return-property name="created"     column="CREATED"/>
        <return-property name="homeAddress">
            <return-column name="HOME_STREET"/>
            <return-column name="HOME_ZIPCODE"/>
            <return-column name="HOME_CITY"/>
        </return-property>
        <return-property name="billingAddress">
            <return-column name="BILLING_STREET"/>
            <return-column name="BILLING_ZIPCODE"/>
            <return-column name="BILLING_CITY"/>
        </return-property>
        <return-property name="defaultBillingDetails"
                         column="DEFAULT_BILLING_DETAILS_ID"/>
    </return>
    { call SELECT_USERS_BY_RANK(?, :rank) }
</sql-query>
```

The first difference, compared to a regular SQL query mapping, is the `callable="true"` attribute. This enables support for callable statements in Hibernate and correct handling of the output of the stored procedure. The following mappings bind the column names returned in the procedures result to the properties of a `User` object. One special case needs extra consideration: If multicolumn properties, including components (`homeAddress`), are present in the class, you need to map their columns in the right order. For example, the `homeAddress` property is mapped as a `<component>` with three properties, each to its own column. Hence, the stored procedure mapping includes three columns bound to the `homeAddress` property.

The `call` of the stored procedure prepares one `OUT` (the question mark) and a named input parameter. If you aren't using the Oracle JDBC drivers (other drivers or a different DBMS), you don't need to reserve the first `OUT` parameter; the result can be returned directly from the stored procedure.

Look at the regular class mapping of the `User` class. Notice that the column names returned by the procedure in this example are the same as the column names you already mapped. You can omit the binding of each property and let Hibernate take care of the mapping automatically:

```
<sql-query name="loadUsersByRank" callable="true">
    <return class="User"/>
    { call SELECT_USERS_BY_RANK(?, :rank) }
</sql-query>
```

The responsibility for returning the correct columns, for all properties and foreign key associations of the class with the same names as in the regular mappings, is now moved into the stored procedure code. Because you have aliases in the stored procedure already (`select ... us.FIRSTNAME as FIRSTNAME...`), this is straightforward. Or, if only some of the columns returned in the result of the procedure have different names than the ones you mapped already as your properties, you only need to declare these:

```
<sql-query name="loadUsersByRank" callable="true">
    <return class="User">
        <return-property name="firstname"    column="FNAME"/>
        <return-property name="lastname"     column="LNAME"/>
    </return>
    { call SELECT_USERS_BY_RANK(?, :rank) }
</sql-query>
```

Finally, let's look at the `call` of the stored procedure. The syntax you're using here, `{ call PROCEDURE() }`, is defined in the SQL standard and portable. A non-portable syntax that works for Oracle is `begin PROCEDURE(); end;`. It's recommended that you always use the portable syntax. The procedure has two parameters. As explained, the first is reserved as an output parameter, so you use a positional parameter symbol (`?`). Hibernate takes care of this parameter if you configured a dialect for an Oracle JDBC driver. The second is an input parameter you have to supply when executing the call. You can either use only positional parameters or mix named and positional parameters. We prefer named parameters for readability.

Querying with this stored procedure in the application looks like any other named query execution:

```
Query q = session.getNamedQuery("loadUsersByRank");
q.setParameter("rank", 12);
List result = q.list();
```

At the time of writing, mapped stored procedures can be enabled as named queries, as you did in this section, or as loaders for an entity, similar to the `loadUser` example you mapped earlier.

Stored procedures can not only query and load data, but also manipulate data. The first use case for this is mass data operations, executed in the database tier. You shouldn't map this in Hibernate but should execute it with plain JDBC: `session.connection().prepareCallableStatement();` and so on. The data-manipulation operations you can map in Hibernate are the creation, deletion, and update of an entity object.

Mapping CUD to a procedure

Earlier, you mapped `<sql-insert>`, `<sql-delete>`, and `<sql-update>` elements for a class to custom SQL statements. If you'd like to use stored procedures for these operations, change the mapping to callable statements:

```
<class name="User">
    ...

    <sql-update callable="true" check="none">
        { call UPDATE_USER(?, ?, ?, ?, ?, ?, ?, ?, ?, ?, ?, ?, ?) }
    </sql-update>

</class>
```

With the current version of Hibernate, you have the same problem as before: the binding of values to the positional parameters. First, the stored procedure must have the same number of input parameters as expected by Hibernate (enable the SQL log as shown earlier to get a generated statement you can copy and paste). The parameters again must be in the same order as expected by Hibernate.

Consider the `check="none"` attribute. For correct (and, if you enabled it) optimistic locking, Hibernate needs to know whether this custom update operation was successful. Usually, for dynamically generated SQL, Hibernate looks at the number of updated rows returned from an operation. If the operation didn't or couldn't update any rows, an optimistic locking failure occurs. If you write your own custom SQL operation, you can customize this behavior as well.

With `check="none"`, Hibernate expects your custom procedure to deal internally with failed updates (for example, by doing a version check of the row that needs to be updated) and expects your procedure to throw an exception if something goes wrong. In Oracle, such a procedure is as follows:

```
<database-object>
    <create>
        create or replace procedure UPDATE_USER
         (IN_FIRSTNAME  in varchar,
          IN_LASTNAME   in varchar,
          IN_PASSWORD   in varchar,
          ...
         )
        as
          rowcount INTEGER;
        begin

          update USERS set
            FIRSTNAME   = IN_FIRSTNAME,
            LASTNAME    = IN_LASTNAME,
            "PASSWORD"  = IN_PASSWORD,
          where
            OBJ_VERSION = ...;

          rowcount := SQL%ROWCOUNT;
          if rowcount != 1 then
              RAISE_APPLICATION_ERROR( -20001, 'Version check failed');
          end if;

        end;

    </create>
    <drop>
        drop procedure UPDATE_USER
    </drop>
</database-object>
```

The SQL error is caught by Hibernate and converted into an optimistic locking exception you can then handle in application code. Other options for the check attribute are as follows:

- If you enable check="count", Hibernate checks the number of modified rows using the plain JDBC API. This is the default and used when you write dynamic SQL without stored procedures.

- If you enable check="param", Hibernate reserves an OUT parameter to get the return value of the stored procedure call. You need to add an additional question mark to your call and, in your stored procedure, return the row count of your DML operation on this (first) OUT parameter. Hibernate then validates the number of modified rows for you.

Mappings for insertion and deletion are similar; all of these must declare how optimistic lock checking is performed. You can copy a template from the Hibernate startup log to get the correct order and number of parameters.

Finally, you can also map stored functions in Hibernate. They have slightly different semantics and use cases.

Mapping stored functions

A stored function only has input parameters—no output parameters. However, it can return a value. For example, a stored function can return the rank of a user:

```
<database-object>
    <create>
        create or replace function GET_USER_RANK
         (IN_USER_ID int)
        return int is
         RANK int;
        begin
            select
                RANKING
            into
                RANK
            from
                USERS
            where
                USER_ID = IN_USER_ID;

            return RANK;
        end;
    </create>
    <drop>
        drop function GET_USER_RANK
    </drop>
</database-object>
```

This function returns a scalar number. The primary use case for stored functions that return scalars is embedding a call in regular SQL or HQL queries. For example, you can retrieve all users who have a higher rank than a given user:

```
String q = "from User u where u.ranking > get_user_rank(:userId)";
List result = session.createQuery(q)
                .setParameter("userId", 123)
                .list();
```

This query is in HQL; thanks to the pass-through functionality for function calls in the WHERE clause (not in any other clause though), you can call any stored function in your database directly. The return type of the function should match the operation: in this case, the greater-than comparison with the `ranking` property, which is also numeric.

If your function returns a resultset cursor, as in previous sections, you can even map it as a named query and let Hibernate marshal the resultset into an object graph.

Finally, remember that stored procedures and functions, especially in legacy databases, sometimes can't be mapped in Hibernate; in such cases you have to fall back to plain JDBC. Sometimes you can wrap a legacy stored procedure with another stored procedure that has the parameter interface expected by Hibernate. There are too many varieties and special cases to be covered in a generic mapping tool. However, future versions of Hibernate will improve mapping capabilities—we expect better handling of parameters (no more counting of question marks) and support for arbitrary input and output arguments to be available in the near future.

You've now completed customization of runtime SQL queries and DML. Let's switch perspective and customize the SQL used for the creation and modification of the database schema, the DDL.

8.3   *Improving schema DDL*

Customizing the DDL in your Hibernate application is something you'll usually consider only when you generate the database schema with Hibernate's toolset. If a schema already exists, such customizations won't affect the runtime behavior of Hibernate.

You can export DDL to a text file or execute it directly on your database whenever you run your integration tests. Because DDL is mostly vendor-specific, every option you put in your mapping metadata has the potential to bind the metadata to a particular database product—keep this in mind when applying the following features.

We separate DDL customization into two categories:

- Naming automatically generated database objects, such as tables, columns, and constraints explicitly in mapping metadata, instead of relying on the automatic naming derived from the Java class and property names by Hibernate. We already discussed the built-in mechanism and options for quoting and extending names in chapter 4, section 4.3.5, "Quoting SQL identifiers." We next look at other options you can enable to beautify your generated DDL scripts.

- Handling additional database objects, such as indexes, constraints, and stored procedures in your mapping metadata. Earlier in this chapter, you added arbitrary CREATE and DROP statements to XML mapping files with the <database-object> element. You can also enable the creation of indexes and constraints with additional mapping elements inside the regular class and property mappings.

8.3.1 *Custom SQL names and datatypes*

In listing 8.1, you add attributes and elements to the mapping of the Item class.

Listing 8.1 Additional elements in the Item mapping for hbm2ddl

```
<class name="Item" table="ITEMS">

    <id name="id" type="string">
        <column name="ITEM_ID" sql-type="char(32)"/>      ❶
        <generator class="uuid"/>
    </id>

    <property name="initialPrice" type="big_decimal">
        <column name="INIT_PRICE"
                not-null="true"                            ❷
                precision="10"
                scale="2"/>
    </property>

    <property name="description" type="string"             ❸
            column="ITM_DESCRIPTION" length="4000"/>

    <set name="categories" table="CATEGORY_ITEM" cascade="none">
        <key>
            <column name="ITEM_ID" sql-type="char(32)"/>   ❹
        </key>
        <many-to-many class="Category">
            <column name="CATEGORY_ID" sql-type="char(32)"/>
        </many-to-many>
    </set>

    ...

</class>
```

❶ The hbm2ddl exporter generates a VARCHAR typed column if a property (even the identifier property) is of mapping type string. You know that the identifier generator uuid always generates 32-character strings; therefore you switch to a CHAR SQL type and also set its size fixed at 32 characters. The <column> element is required for this declaration, because no attribute supports the SQL datatype on the <id> element.

❷ For decimal types, you can declare the precision and scale. This example creates the column as INIT_PRICE number(10,2) on an Oracle dialect; however, for databases that don't support types with decimal precision, a simple INIT_PRICE numeric (this is in HSQL) is produced.

❸ For the description field, you add DDL attributes on the <property> element instead of a nested <column> element. The DESCRIPTION column is generated as VARCHAR(4000)—a limitation of a variable character field in an Oracle database (in Oracle, it would be VARCHAR2(4000) in the DDL, but the dialect takes care of this).

❹ A <column> element can also be used to declare the foreign key fields in an association mapping. Otherwise, the columns of your association table CATEGORY_ITEM would be VARCHAR(32) instead of the more appropriate CHAR(32) type.

The same customization is possible in annotations, see listing 8.2.

Listing 8.2 Additional annotations for customization of DDL export

```
@Entity
@Table(name = "ITEMS")
public class Item {

    @Id
    @Column(name = "ITEM_ID", columnDefinition = "char(32)")
    @GeneratedValue(generator = "hibernate-uuid.hex")
    @org.hibernate.annotations.GenericGenerator(
            name = "hibernate-uuid.hex",
            strategy = "uuid.hex"
    )
    Private String id;

    @Column(name = "INIT_PRICE", nullable = false,
            precision = 10, scale = 2)
    BigDecimal initialPrice;

    @Column(name = "ITM_DESCRIPTION", length = 4000)
    Private String description;

    @ManyToMany
    @JoinTable(
        name = "CATEGORY_ITEM",
        joinColumns =
            { @JoinColumn(name = "ITEM_ID",
                        columnDefinition = "char(32)")
            },
        inverseJoinColumns =
```

```
            { @JoinColumn(name = "CATEGORY_ID",
                          columnDefinition = "char(32)")
            }
        )
    Private Set<Category> categories = new HashSet<Category>();

    ...
}
```

You have to use one Hibernate extension to name the nonstandard identifier generator. All other customizations of the generated SQL DDL are done with annotations of the JPA specification. One attribute deserves special attention: The `columnDefinition` isn't the same as `sql-type` in a Hibernate mapping file. It's more flexible: The JPA persistence provider appends the whole string after the column name in the `CREATE TABLE` statement, as in `ITEM_ID char(32)`.

Customization of names and data types is the absolute minimum you should consider. We recommend that you always improve the quality of your database schema (and ultimately, the quality of the data that is stored) with the appropriate integrity rules.

8.3.2 *Ensuring data consistency*

Integrity rules are an important part of your database schema. The most important responsibility of your database is to protect your information and to guarantee that it's never in an inconsistent state. This is called consistency, and it's part of the ACID criteria commonly applied to transactional database management systems.

Rules are part of your business logic, so you usually have a mix of business-related rules implemented in your application code and in your database. Your application is written so as to avoid any violation of the database rules. However, it's the job of the database management system to never allow any false (in the business logic sense) information to be stored permanently—for example, if one of the applications accessing the database has bugs. Systems that ensure integrity only in application code are prone to data corruption and often degrade the quality of the database over time. Keep in mind that the primary purpose of most business applications is to produce valuable business data in the long run.

In contrast to ensuring data consistency in procedural (or object-oriented) application code, database-management systems allow you to implement integrity rules declaratively as part of your data schema. The advantages of declarative rules include fewer possible errors in code and a chance for the database-management system to optimize data access.

We identify four levels of rules:

- *Domain constraint*—A domain is (loosely speaking, and in the database world) a datatype in a database. Hence, a domain constraint defines the range of possible values a particular datatype can handle. For example, an int datatype is usable for integer values. A char datatype can hold character strings: for example, all characters defined in ASCII. Because we mostly use datatypes that are built in to the database management system, we rely on the domain constraints as defined by the vendor. If you create user-defined datatypes (UDT), you'll have to define their constraints. If they're supported by your SQL database, you can use the (limited) support for custom domains to add additional constraints for particular datatypes.

- *Column constraint*—Restricting a column to hold values of a particular domain is equivalent to adding a column constraint. For example, you declare in DDL that the INITIAL_PRICE column holds values of the domain MONEY, which internally uses the datatype number(10,2). You use the datatype directly most of the time, without defining a domain first. A special column constraint in an SQL database is NOT NULL.

- *Table constraint*—An integrity rule that applies to a single row or several rows is a table constraint. A typical declarative table constraints is UNIQUE (all rows are checked for duplicate values). A sample rule affecting only a single row is "end date of an auction must be later than the start date."

- *Database constraint*—If a rule applies to more than one table, it has database scope. You should already be familiar with the most common database constraint, the foreign key. This rule guarantees the integrity of references between rows, usually in separate tables, but not always (self-referencing foreign key constraints aren't uncommon).

Most (if not all) SQL database-management systems support the mentioned levels of constraints and the most important options in each. In addition to simple keywords, such as NOT NULL and UNIQUE, you can usually also declare more complex rules with the CHECK constraint that applies an arbitrary SQL expression. Still, integrity constraints are one of the weak areas in the SQL standard, and solutions from vendors can differ significantly.

Furthermore, nondeclarative and procedural constraints are possible with database triggers that intercept data-modification operations. A trigger can then implement the constraint procedure directly or call an existing stored procedure.

Like DDL for stored procedures, you can add trigger declarations to your Hibernate mapping metadata with the `<database-object>` element for inclusion in the generated DDL.

Finally, integrity constraints can be checked immediately when a data-modification statement is executed, or the check can be deferred until the end of a transaction. The violation response in SQL databases is usually rejection, without any possibility of customization.

We now have a closer look at the implementation of integrity constraints.

8.3.3 Adding domains and column constraints

The SQL standard includes domains, which, unfortunately, not only are rather limited but also are often not supported by the DBMS. If your system supports SQL domains, you can use them to add constraints to datatypes:

```
create domain EMAILADDRESS as varchar
    constraint DOMAIN_EMAILADDRESS
    check ( IS_EMAILADDRESS(value) );
```

You can now use this domain identifier as a column type when creating a table:

```
create table USERS (
    ...
    USER_EMAIL EMAILADDRESS(255) not null,
    ...
);
```

The (relatively minor) advantage of domains in SQL is the abstraction of common constraints into a single location. Domain constraints are always checked immediately when data is inserted and modified. To complete the previous example, you also have to write the stored function `IS_EMAILADDRESS` (you can find many regular expressions to do this on the Web). Adding the new domain in a Hibernate mapping is simple as an `sql-type`:

```
<property name="email" type="string">
    <column name="USER_EMAIL"
            length="255"
            not-null="true"
            sql-type="EMAILADDRESS"/>
</property>
```

With annotations, declare your own `columnDefinition`:

```
@Column(name = "USER_EMAIL", length = 255,
        columnDefinition = "EMAILADDRESS(255) not null")
String email;
```

If you want to create and drop the domain declaration automatically with the rest of your schema, put it into a <database-object> mapping.

SQL supports additional column constraints. For example, the business rules allow only alphanumeric characters in user login names:

```
create table USERS (
    ...
    USERNAME varchar(16) not null
        check(regexp_like(USERNAME,'^[[:alpha:]]+$')),
    ...
);
```

You may not be able to use this expression in your DBMS unless it supports regular expressions. Single-column check constraints are declared in Hibernate mappings on the <column> mapping element:

```
<property name="username" type="string">
    <column name="USERNAME"
            length="16"
            not-null="true"
            check="regexp_like(USERNAME,'^[[:alpha:]]+$')"/>
</property>
```

Check constraints in annotations are available only as a Hibernate extension:

```
@Column(name = "USERNAME", length = 16,
        nullable = false, unique = true)
@org.hibernate.annotations.Check(
    constraints = "regexp_like(USERNAME,'^[[:alpha:]]+$')"
)
private String username;
```

Note that you have a choice: Creating and using a domain or adding a single-column constraint has the same effect. In the long run, domains are usually easier to maintain and more likely to avoid duplication.

Let's look at the next level of rules: single and multirow table constraints.

8.3.4 *Table-level constraints*

Imagine that you want to guarantee that a CaveatEmptor auction can't end before it started. You write the application code to prevent users from setting the start-Date and endDate properties on an Item to wrong values. You can do this in the user interface or in the setter methods of the properties. In the database schema, you add a single-row table constraint:

```
create table ITEM (
    ...
    START_DATE timestamp not null,
```

```
        END_DATE timestamp not null,
        ...
        check (START_DATE < END_DATE)
);
```

Table constraints are appended in the CREATE TABLE DDL and can contain arbitrary SQL expressions. You include the constraint expression in your Hibernate mapping file on the <class> mapping element:

```
<class name="Item"
       table="ITEM"
       check="START_DATE &lt; END_DATE">
```

Note that the < character must be escaped as < in XML. With annotations, you need to add a Hibernate extension annotation to declare check constraints:

```
@Entity
@org.hibernate.annotations.Check(
    constraints = "START_DATE < END_DATE"
)
public class Item { ... }
```

Multirow table constraints can be implemented with more complex expressions. You may need a subselect in the expression to do this, which may not be supported in your DBMS—check your product documentation first. However, there are common multirow table constraints you can add directly as attributes in Hibernate mappings. For example, you identify the login name of a User as unique in the system:

```
<property name="username" type="string">
    <column name="USERNAME"
            length="16"
            not-null="true"
            check="regexp_like(USERNAME,'^[[:alpha:]]+$')"
            unique="true"/>
</property>
```

Unique constraint declaration is also possible in annotation metadata:

```
@Column(name = "USERNAME", length = 16, nullable = false,
        unique = true)
@org.hibernate.annotations.Check(
    constraints = "regexp_like(USERNAME,'^[[:alpha:]]+$')"
)
private String username;
```

And, of course, you can do this in JPA XML descriptors (there is no check constraint, however):

```
<entity class="auction.model.User" access="FIELD">
    <attributes>
        ...
        <basic name="username">
            <column name="USERNAME"
                    length="16"
                    nullable="false"
                    unique="true"/>
        </basic>
    </attributes>
</entity>
```

The exported DDL includes the unique constraint:

```
create table USERS (
    ...
    USERNAME varchar(16) not null unique
        check(regexp_like(USERNAME,'^[[:alpha:]]+$')),
    ...
);
```

A unique constraint can also span several columns. For example, CaveatEmptor
supports a tree of nested Category objects. One of the business rules says that a
particular category can't have the same name as any of its siblings. Hence, you
need a multicolumn multirow constraint that guarantees this uniqueness:

```
<class name="Category" table="CATEGORY">
    ...
    <property name="name">
      <column name="CAT_NAME"
              unique-key="unique_siblings"/>
    </property>

    <many-to-one name="parent" class="Category">
      <column name="PARENT_CATEGORY_ID"
              unique-key="unique_siblings"/>
    </many-to-one>
    ...
</class>
```

You assign an identifier to the constraint with the unique-key attribute so you can
refer to it several times in one class mapping and group columns for the same
constraint. However, the identifier isn't used in the DDL to name the constraint:

```
create table CATEGORY (
    ...
    CAT_NAME varchar(255) not null,
    PARENT_CATEGORY_ID integer,
    ...
    unique (CAT_NAME, PARENT_CATEGORY_ID)
);
```

If you want to create a unique constraint with annotations that spans several columns, you need to declare it on the entity, not on a single column:

```
@Entity
@Table(name = "CATEGORY",
   uniqueConstraints = {
       @UniqueConstraint(columnNames =
           {"CAT_NAME", "PARENT_CATEGORY_ID"} )
   }
)
public class Category { ... }
```

With JPA XML descriptors, multicolumn constraints are as follows:

```
<entity class="Category" access="FIELD">
    <table name="CATEGORY">
        <unique-constraint>
            <column-name>CAT_NAME</column-name>
            <column-name>PARENT_CATEGORY_ID</column-name>
        </unique-constraint>
    </table>
...
```

Completely custom constraints, including an identifier for the database catalog, can be added to your DDL with the `<database-object>` element:

```
<database-object>
    <create>
        alter table CATEGORY add constraint UNIQUE_SIBLINGS
            unique (CAT_NAME, PARENT_CATEGORY_ID);
    </create>
    <drop>
        drop constraint UNIQUE_SIBLINGS
    </drop>
</database-object;
```

This functionality isn't available in annotations. Note that you can add a Hibernate XML metadata file with all your custom database DDL objects in your annotation-based application.

Finally, the last category of constraints includes database-wide rules that span several tables.

8.3.5 Database constraints

You can create a rule that spans several tables with a join in a subselect in any check expression. Instead of referring only to the table on which the constraint is declared, you may query (usually for the existence or nonexistence of a particular piece of information) a different table.

Another technique to create a database-wide constraint uses custom triggers that run on insertion or update of rows in particular tables. This is a procedural approach that has the already-mentioned disadvantages but is inherently flexible.

By far the most common rules that span several tables are referential integrity rules. They're widely known as foreign keys, which are a combination of two things: a key value copy from a related row and a constraint that guarantees that the referenced value exists. Hibernate creates foreign key constraints automatically for all foreign key columns in association mappings. If you check the DDL produced by Hibernate, you may notice that these constraints also have automatically generated database identifiers—names that aren't easy to read and that make debugging more difficult:

```
alter table ITEM add constraint FK1FF7F1F09FA3CB90
    foreign key (SELLER_ID) references USERS;
```

This DDL declares the foreign key constraint for the `SELLER_ID` column in the `ITEM` table. It references the primary key column of the `USERS` table. You can customize the name of the constraint in the `<many-to-one>` mapping of the `Item` class with the `foreign-key` attribute:

```
<many-to-one name="seller"
        class="User"
        column="SELLER_ID"
        foreign-key="FK_SELLER_ID"/>
```

With annotations, use a Hibernate extension:

```
@ManyToOne
@JoinColumn(name = "SELLER_ID")
@org.hibernate.annotations.ForeignKey(name = "FK_SELLER_ID")
private User seller;
```

And a special syntax is required for foreign keys created for a many-to-many association:

```
@ManyToMany
@JoinTable(...)
@org.hibernate.annotations.ForeignKey(
    name = "FK_CATEGORY_ID",
    inverseName = "FK_ITEM_ID"
)
private Set<Category> categories...
```

If you want to automatically generate DDL that isn't distinguishable from what a human DBA would write, customize all your foreign key constraints in all your mapping metadata. Not only is this good practice, but it also helps significantly

If you want to create a unique constraint with annotations that spans several columns, you need to declare it on the entity, not on a single column:

```
@Entity
@Table(name = "CATEGORY",
    uniqueConstraints = {
        @UniqueConstraint(columnNames =
            {"CAT_NAME", "PARENT_CATEGORY_ID"} )
    }
)
public class Category { ... }
```

With JPA XML descriptors, multicolumn constraints are as follows:

```
<entity class="Category" access="FIELD">
    <table name="CATEGORY">
        <unique-constraint>
            <column-name>CAT_NAME</column-name>
            <column-name>PARENT_CATEGORY_ID</column-name>
        </unique-constraint>
    </table>
    ...
```

Completely custom constraints, including an identifier for the database catalog, can be added to your DDL with the `<database-object>` element:

```
<database-object>
    <create>
        alter table CATEGORY add constraint UNIQUE_SIBLINGS
            unique (CAT_NAME, PARENT_CATEGORY_ID);
    </create>
    <drop>
        drop constraint UNIQUE_SIBLINGS
    </drop>
</database-object>
```

This functionality isn't available in annotations. Note that you can add a Hibernate XML metadata file with all your custom database DDL objects in your annotation-based application.

Finally, the last category of constraints includes database-wide rules that span several tables.

8.3.5 *Database constraints*

You can create a rule that spans several tables with a join in a subselect in any check expression. Instead of referring only to the table on which the constraint is declared, you may query (usually for the existence or nonexistence of a particular piece of information) a different table.

```
                    type="timestamp"
                    index="IDX_END_DATE"/>
```

The automatically produced DDL now includes an additional statement:

```
create index IDX_END_DATE on ITEM (END_DATE);
```

The same functionality is available with annotations, as a Hibernate extension:

```
@Column(name = "END_DATE", nullable = false, updatable = false)
@org.hibernate.annotations.Index(name = "IDX_END_DATE")
private Date endDate;
```

You can create a multicolumn index by setting the same identifier on several property (or column) mappings. Any other index option, such as UNIQUE INDEX (which creates an additional multirow table-level constraint), the indexing method (common are btree, hash, and binary), and any storage clause (for example, to create the index in a separate tablespace) can be set only in completely custom DDL with <database-object>.

A multicolumn index with annotations is defined at the entity level, with a custom Hibernate annotation that applies additional attributes to table mapping:

```
@Entity
@Table(name="ITEMS")
@org.hibernate.annotations.Table(
  appliesTo = "ITEMS",  indexes =
    @org.hibernate.annotations.Index(
      name = "IDX_INITIAL_PRICE",
      columnNames = { "INITIAL_PRICE", "INITIAL_PRICE_CURRENCY" }
    )
)
public class Item { ... }
```

Note that @org.hibernate.annotations.Table isn't a replacement for @javax.perisistence.Table, so if you need to override the default table name, you still need the regular @Table.

We recommend that you get the excellent book *SQL Tuning* by Dan Tow (Tow, 2003) if you want to learn efficient database-optimization techniques and especially how indexes can get you closer to the best-performing execution plan for your queries.

One mapping we have shown a few times in this chapter is <database-object>. It has some other options that we haven't discussed yet.

8.3.7 *Adding auxiliary DDL*

Hibernate creates the basic DDL for your tables and constraints automatically; it even creates sequences if you have a particular identifier generator. However, there is some DDL that Hibernate can't create automatically. This includes all kinds of highly vendor-specific performance options and any other DDL that is relevant only for the physical storage of data (tablespaces, for example).

One reason this kind of DDL has no mapping elements or annotations is that there are too many variations and possibilities—nobody can or wants to maintain more than 25 database dialects with all the possible combinations of DDL. A second, much more important reason, is that you should always ask your DBA to finalize your database schema. For example, did you know that indexes on foreign key columns can hurt performance in some situations and therefore aren't automatically generated by Hibernate? We recommend that DBAs get involved early and verify the automatically generated DDL from Hibernate.

A common process, if you're starting with a new application and new database, is to generate DDL with Hibernate automatically during development; database performance concerns shouldn't and usually don't play an important role at that stage. At the same time (or later, during testing), a professional DBA verifies and optimizes the SQL DDL and creates the final database schema. You can export the DDL into a text file and hand it to your DBA.

Or—and this is the option you've seen a few times already—you can add customized DDL statements to your mapping metadata:

```
<database-object>
    <create>
        [CREATE statement]
    </create>
    <drop>
        [DROP statement]
    </drop>

    <dialect-scope name="org.hibernate.dialect.Oracle9Dialect"/>
    <dialect-scope name="org.hibernate.dialect.OracleDialect"/>

</database-object>
```

The `<dialect-scope>` elements restrict the custom `CREATE` or `DROP` statements to a particular set of configured database dialects, which is useful if you're deploying on several systems and need different customizations.

If you need more programmatic control over the generated DDL, implement the `AuxiliaryDatabaseObject` interface. Hibernate comes bundled with a convenience implementation that you can subclass; you can then override methods selectively:

```
package auction.persistence;

import org.hibernate.mapping.*;
```

```
import org.hibernate.dialect.Dialect;
import org.hibernate.engine.Mapping;

public class CustomDDLExtension
    extends AbstractAuxiliaryDatabaseObject {

    public CustomDDLExtension() {
        addDialectScope("org.hibernate.dialect.Oracle9Dialect");
    }

    public String sqlCreateString(Dialect dialect,
                                  Mapping mapping,
                                  String defaultCatalog,
                                  String defaultSchema) {

        return "[CREATE statement]";
    }

    public String sqlDropString(Dialect dialect,
                                String defaultCatalog,
                                String defaultSchema) {

        return "[DROP statement]";
    }
}
```

You can add dialect scopes programmatically and even access some mapping information in the `sqlCreateString()` and `sqlDropString()` methods. This gives you a lot of flexibility regarding how you create and write your DDL statements. You have to enable this custom class in your mapping metadata:

```
<database-object>
    <definition class="auction.persistence.CustomDDLExtension"/>
    <dialect-scope name="org.hibernate.dialect.OracleDialect"/>
</database-object>
```

Additional dialect scopes are cumulative; the previous examples all apply to two dialects.

8.4 Summary

In this chapter, we looked at issues that you may run into when you have to deal with a legacy database schema. Natural keys, composite keys, and foreign keys are often inconvenient and need to be mapped with extra care. Hibernate also offers formulas, little SQL expressions in your mapping file, that can help you to deal with a legacy schema you can't change.

Usually, you also rely on Hibernate's automatically generated SQL for all create, read, update, and delete operations in your application. In this chapter, you've learned how to customize this SQL with your own statements and how to integrate Hibernate with stored procedures and stored functions.

In the last section, we explored the generation of database schemas and how you can customize and extend your mappings to include all kinds of constraints, indexes, and arbitrary DDL that your DBA may recommend.

Table 8.1 shows a summary you can use to compare native Hibernate features and Java Persistence.

Table 8.1 Hibernate and JPA comparison chart for chapter 8

Hibernate Core	Java Persistence and EJB 3.0
Hibernate supports any kind of natural and composite primary key, including foreign keys to natural keys, composite primary keys, and foreign keys in composite primary keys.	Standardized support is provided for natural and composite keys, equivalent to Hibernate.
Hibernate supports arbitrary association join conditions with formula mappings and property references.	No standard or annotation support is provided for grouped property references at the time of writing.
Hibernate supports basic joins of secondary tables for a particular entity class.	Standardized support is provided for secondary tables and basic joins.
Hibernate supports trigger integration and generated property settings.	Hibernate Annotations supports generated properties and trigger integration.
Hibernate lets you customize all SQL DML statements with options in XML mapping metadata.	At the time of writing, no support is provided for SQL DML customization with annotations.
Hibernate lets you customize SQL DDL for automatic schema generation. Arbitrary SQL DDL statements can be included in XML mapping metadata.	JPA standardizes basic DDL declarations, but not all features of the XML mapping metadata are supported with annotations.

You now know everything (well, as much as we can show in a single book) there is to know about mapping classes to schemas. In the next part of the book, we'll discuss how to use the persistence manager APIs to load and store objects, how transactions and conversations are implemented, and how to write queries.

Part 3

Conversational object processing

In this part of the book, we explain how to work with persistent objects. Chapter 9 shows you how to load and store objects with the Hibernate and Java Persistence programming interfaces. Transactions and concurrency control are another important topic, discussed in detail in chapter 10. We then implement conversations in chapter 11 and show you how this concept can improve the design of your system. Chapters 12 and 13 focus on efficiency and how Hibernate features can make your life easier when you have to load and modify large and complex datasets. Querying, query languages, and APIs are examined in detail in chapters 14 and 15. In chapter 16, we bring it all together by designing and testing a layered application with ORM persistence.

After reading this part, you'll know how to work with Hibernate and Java Persistence programming interfaces and how to load, modify, and store objects efficiently. You'll understand how transactions work and why conversational processing can open up new ways for application design. You'll be ready to optimize any object modification scenario, write complex queries, and apply the best fetching and caching strategy to increase performance and scalability.

Working with objects

9

This chapter covers

- The lifecycle and states of objects
- Working with the Hibernate API
- Working with the Java Persistence API

You now have an understanding of how Hibernate and ORM solve the static aspects of the object/relational mismatch. With what you know so far, it's possible to solve the structural mismatch problem, but an *efficient* solution to the problem requires something more. You must investigate strategies for runtime data access, because they're crucial to the performance of your applications. You basically have learn how to control the state of objects.

This and the following chapters cover the *behavioral* aspect of the object/relational mismatch. We consider these problems to be at least as important as the structural problems discussed in previous chapters. In our experience, many developers are only really aware of the structural mismatch and rarely pay attention to the more dynamic behavioral aspects of the mismatch.

In this chapter, we discuss the lifecycle of objects—how an object becomes persistent, and how it stops being considered persistent—and the method calls and other actions that trigger these transitions. The Hibernate persistence manager, the `Session`, is responsible for managing object state, so we discuss how to use this important API. The main Java Persistence interface in EJB 3.0 is called `EntityManager`, and thanks to its close resemblance with Hibernate APIs, it will be easy to learn alongside. Of course, you can skip quickly through this material if you aren't working with Java Persistence or EJB 3.0—we encourage you to read about both options and then decide what is better for your application.

Let's start with persistent objects, their lifecycle, and the events which trigger a change of persistent state. Although some of the material may be formal, a solid understanding of the *persistence lifecycle* is essential.

9.1   *The persistence lifecycle*

Because Hibernate is a transparent persistence mechanism—classes are unaware of their own persistence capability—it's possible to write application logic that is unaware whether the objects it operates on represent persistent state or temporary state that exists only in memory. The application shouldn't necessarily need to care that an object is persistent when invoking its methods. You can, for example, invoke the `calculateTotalPrice()` business method on an instance of the `Item` class without having to consider persistence at all; e.g., in a unit test.

Any application with persistent state must interact with the persistence service whenever it needs to propagate state held in memory to the database (or vice versa). In other words, you have to call Hibernate (or the Java Persistence) interfaces to store and load objects.

When interacting with the persistence mechanism in that way, it's necessary for the application to concern itself with the state and lifecycle of an object with respect to persistence. We refer to this as the *persistence lifecycle*: the states an object goes through during its life. We also use the term *unit of work*: a set of operations you consider one (usually atomic) group. Another piece of the puzzle is the *persistence context* provided by the persistence service. Think of the persistence context as a cache that remembers all the modifications and state changes you made to objects in a particular unit of work (this is somewhat simplified, but it's a good starting point).

We now dissect all these terms: object and entity states, persistence contexts, and managed scope. You're probably more accustomed to thinking about what *statements* you have to manage to get stuff in and out of the database (via JDBC and SQL). However, one of the key factors of your success with Hibernate (and Java Persistence) is your understanding of state management, so stick with us through this section.

9.1.1 *Object states*

Different ORM solutions use different terminology and define different states and state transitions for the persistence lifecycle. Moreover, the object states used internally may be different from those exposed to the client application. Hibernate defines only four states, hiding the complexity of its internal implementation from the client code.

The object states defined by Hibernate and their transitions in a state chart are shown in figure 9.1. You can also see the method calls to the persistence manager API that trigger transitions. This API in Hibernate is the `Session`. We discuss this chart in this chapter; refer to it whenever you need an overview.

We've also included the states of Java Persistence entity instances in figure 9.1. As you can see, they're almost equivalent to Hibernate's, and most methods of the `Session` have a counterpart on the `EntityManager` API (shown in italics). We say that Hibernate is a *superset* of the functionality provided by the *subset* standardized in Java Persistence.

Some methods are available on both APIs; for example, the `Session` has a `persist()` operation with the same semantics as the `EntityManager`'s counterpart. Others, like `load()` and `getReference()`, also share semantics, with a different method name.

During its life, an object can transition from a transient object to a persistent object to a detached object. Let's explore the states and transitions in more detail.

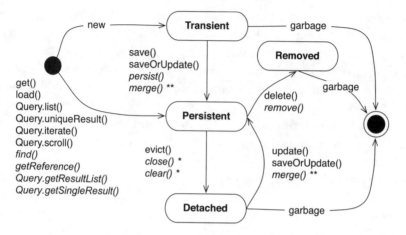

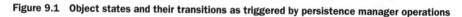

* Hibernate & JPA, affects all instances in the persistence context
** Merging returns a persistent instance, original doesn't change state

Figure 9.1   Object states and their transitions as triggered by persistence manager operations

Transient objects

Objects instantiated using the new operator aren't immediately persistent. Their state is *transient*, which means they aren't associated with any database table row and so their state is lost as soon as they're no longer referenced by any other object. These objects have a lifespan that effectively ends at that time, and they become inaccessible and available for garbage collection. Java Persistence doesn't include a term for this state; entity objects you just instantiated are *new*. We'll continue to refer to them as *transient* to emphasize the potential for these instances to become managed by a persistence service.

Hibernate and Java Persistence consider all transient instances to be nontransactional; any modification of a transient instance isn't known to a persistence context. This means that Hibernate doesn't provide any roll-back functionality for transient objects.

Objects that are referenced only by other transient instances are, by default, also transient. For an instance to transition from transient to persistent state, to become managed, requires either a call to the persistence manager or the creation of a reference from an already persistent instance.

Persistent objects

A *persistent* instance is an entity instance with a *database identity*, as defined in chapter 4, section 4.2, "Mapping entities with identity." That means a persistent and managed instance has a primary key value set as its database identifier. (There are some variations to *when* this identifier is assigned to a persistent instance.)

Persistent instances may be objects instantiated by the application and then made persistent by calling one of the methods on the persistence manager. They may even be objects that became persistent when a reference was created from another persistent object that is already managed. Alternatively, a persistent instance may be an instance retrieved from the database by execution of a query, by an identifier lookup, or by navigating the object graph starting from another persistent instance.

Persistent instances are always associated with a *persistence context.* Hibernate caches them and can detect whether they have been modified by the application.

There is much more to be said about this state and how an instance is managed in a persistence context. We'll get back to this later in this chapter.

Removed objects

You can delete an entity instance in several ways: For example, you can remove it with an explicit operation of the persistence manager. It may also become available for deletion if you remove all references to it, a feature available only in Hibernate or in Java Persistence with a Hibernate extension setting (orphan deletion for entities).

An object is in the *removed* state if it has been scheduled for deletion at the end of a unit of work, but it's still managed by the persistence context until the unit of work completes. In other words, a removed object shouldn't be reused because it will be deleted from the database as soon as the unit of work completes. You should also discard any references you may hold to it in the application (of course, after you finish working with it—for example, after you've rendered the removal-confirmation screen your users see).

Detached objects

To understand *detached* objects, you need to consider a typical transition of an instance: First it's transient, because it just has been created in the application. Now you make it persistent by calling an operation on the persistence manager. All of this happens in a single unit of work, and the persistence context for this unit of work is synchronized with the database at some point (when an SQL INSERT occurs).

The unit of work is now completed, and the persistence context is closed. But the application still has a *handle:* a reference to the instance that was saved. As long as the persistence context is active, the state of this instance is *persistent.* At the end of a unit of work, the persistence context closes. What is the state of the object you're holding a reference to now, and what can you do with it?

We refer to these objects as *detached*, indicating that their state is no longer guaranteed to be synchronized with database state; they're no longer attached to a persistence context. They still contain persistent data (which may soon be stale). You can continue working with a detached object and modify it. However, at some point you probably want to make those changes persistent—in other words, bring the detached instance back into persistent state.

Hibernate offers two operations, *reattachment* and *merging*, to deal with this situation. Java Persistence only standardizes merging. These features have a deep impact on how multitiered applications may be designed. The ability to return objects from one persistence context to the presentation layer and later reuse them in a new persistence context is a main selling point of Hibernate and Java Persistence. It enables you to create *long* units of work that span user think-time. We call this kind of long-running unit of work a *conversation*. We'll get back to detached objects and conversations soon.

You should now have a basic understanding of object states and how transitions occur. Our next topic is the persistence context and the management of objects it provides.

9.1.2 *The persistence context*

You may consider the persistence context to be a cache of managed entity instances. The persistence context isn't something you see in your application; it isn't an API you can call. In a Hibernate application, we say that one `Session` has one internal persistence context. In a Java Persistence application, an `EntityManager` has a persistence context. All entities in persistent state and managed in a unit of work are cached in this context. We walk through the `Session` and `EntityManager` APIs later in this chapter. Now you need to know what this (internal) persistence context is buying you.

The persistence context is useful for several reasons:

- Hibernate can do automatic dirty checking and transactional write-behind.
- Hibernate can use the persistence context as a first-level cache.
- Hibernate can guarantee a scope of Java object identity.
- Hibernate can extend the persistence context to span a whole conversation.

All these points are also valid for Java Persistence providers. Let's look at each feature.

Automatic dirty checking

Persistent instances are managed in a persistence context—their state is synchronized with the database at the end of the unit of work. When a unit of work completes, state held in memory is propagated to the database by the execution of SQL INSERT, UPDATE, and DELETE statements (DML). This procedure may also occur at other times. For example, Hibernate may synchronize with the database before execution of a query. This ensures that queries are aware of changes made earlier during the unit of work.

Hibernate doesn't update the database row of every single persistent object in memory at the end of the unit of work. ORM software must have a strategy for detecting which persistent objects have been modified by the application. We call this *automatic dirty checking*. An object with modifications that have not yet been propagated to the database is considered *dirty*. Again, this state isn't visible to the application. With *transparent transaction-level write-behind*, Hibernate propagates state changes to the database as late as possible but hides this detail from the application. By executing DML as late as possible (toward the end of the database transaction), Hibernate tries to keep lock-times in the database as short as possible. (DML usually creates locks in the database that are held until the transaction completes.)

Hibernate is able to detect exactly which *properties* have been modified so that it's possible to include only the columns that need updating in the SQL UPDATE statement. This may bring some performance gains. However, it's usually not a significant difference and, in theory, could harm performance in some environments. By default, Hibernate includes all columns of a mapped table in the SQL UPDATE statement (hence, Hibernate can generate this basic SQL at startup, not at runtime). If you want to update only modified columns, you can enable dynamic SQL generation by setting dynamic-update="true" in a class mapping. The same mechanism is implemented for insertion of new records, and you can enable runtime generation of INSERT statements with dynamic-insert="true". We recommend you consider this setting when you have an extraordinarily large number of columns in a table (say, more than 50); at some point, the overhead network traffic for unchanged fields will be noticeable.

In rare cases, you may also want to supply your own dirty checking algorithm to Hibernate. By default, Hibernate compares an old snapshot of an object with the snapshot at synchronization time, and it detects any modifications that require an update of the database state. You can implement your own routine by supplying a custom findDirty() method with an org.hibernate.Interceptor for a Session. We'll show you an implementation of an interceptor later in the book.

We'll also get back to the synchronization process (known as *flushing*) and when it occurs later in this chapter.

The persistence context cache

A persistence context is a cache of persistent entity instances. This means it remembers all persistent entity instances you've handled in a particular unit of work. Automatic dirty checking is one of the benefits of this caching. Another benefit is *repeatable read* for entities and the performance advantage of a unit of work-scoped cache.

For example, if Hibernate is told to load an object by primary key (a lookup by identifier), it can first check the persistence context for the current unit of work. If the entity is found there, no database hit occurs—this is a repeatable read for an application. The same is true if a query is executed through one of the Hibernate (or Java Persistence) interfaces. Hibernate reads the result set of the query and marshals entity objects that are then returned to the application. During this process, Hibernate interacts with the current persistence context. It tries to resolve every entity instance in this cache (by identifier); only if the instance can't be found in the current persistence context does Hibernate read the rest of the data from the result set.

The persistence context cache offers significant performance benefits and improves the isolation guarantees in a unit of work (you get repeatable read of entity instances for free). Because this cache only has the scope of a unit of work, it has no real disadvantages, such as lock management for concurrent access—a unit of work is processed in a single thread at a time.

The persistence context cache sometimes helps avoid unnecessary database traffic; but, more important, it ensures that:

- The persistence layer isn't vulnerable to stack overflows in the case of circular references in a graph of objects.

- There can never be conflicting representations of the same database row at the end of a unit of work. In the persistence context, at most a single object represents any database row. All changes made to that object may be safely written to the database.

- Likewise, changes made in a particular persistence context are always immediately visible to all other code executed inside that persistence context and its unit of work (the repeatable read for entities guarantee).

You don't have to do anything special to enable the persistence context cache. It's always on and, for the reasons shown, can't be turned off.

Later in this chapter, we'll show you how objects are added to this cache (basically, whenever they become persistent) and how you can manage this cache (by detaching objects manually from the persistence context, or by clearing the persistence context).

The last two items on our list of benefits of a persistence context, the guaranteed scope of identity and the possibility to extend the persistence context to span a conversation, are closely related concepts. To understand them, you need to take a step back and consider objects in detached state from a different perspective.

9.2 Object identity and equality

A basic Hibernate client/server application may be designed with server-side units of work that span a single client request. When a request from the application user requires data access, a new unit of work is started. The unit of work ends when processing is complete and the response for the user is ready. This is also called the *session-per-request* strategy (you can replace the word *session* with *persistence context* whenever you read something like this, but it doesn't roll off the tongue as well).

We already mentioned that Hibernate can support an implementation of a possibly long-running unit of work, called a conversation. We introduce the concept of conversations in the following sections as well as the fundamentals of object identity and when objects are considered equal—which can impact how you think about and design conversations.

Why is the concept of a conversation useful?

9.2.1 Introducing conversations

For example, in web applications, you don't usually maintain a database transaction across a user interaction. Users take a long time to think about modifications, but, for scalability reasons, you must keep database transactions short and release database resources as soon as possible. You'll likely face this issue whenever you need to guide the user through several screens to complete a unit of work (from the user's perspective)—for example, to fill an online form. In this common scenario, it's extremely useful to have the support of the persistence service, so you can implement such a conversation with a minimum of coding and best scalability.

Two strategies are available to implement a conversation in a Hibernate or Java Persistence application: with detached objects or by extending a persistence context. Both have strength and weaknesses.

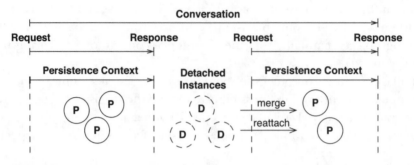

Figure 9.2   Conversation implementation with detached object state

The *detached* object state and the already mentioned features of reattachment or merging are ways to implement a conversation. Objects are held in detached state during user think-time, and any modification of these objects is made persistent manually through reattachment or merging. This strategy is also called *session-per-request-with-detached-objects.* You can see a graphical illustration of this conversation pattern in figure 9.2.

A persistence context only spans the processing of a particular request, and the application manually reattaches and merges (and sometimes detaches) entity instances during the conversation.

The alternative approach doesn't require manual reattachment or merging: With the *session-per-conversation* pattern, you *extend* a persistence context to span the whole unit of work (see figure 9.3).

First we have a closer look at detached objects and the problem of *identity* you'll face when you implement a conversation with this strategy.

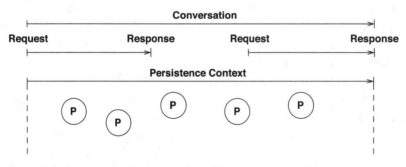

Figure 9.3   Conversation implementation with an extended persistence context

9.2.2 *The scope of object identity*

As application developers, we identify an object using Java object identity (a==b). If an object changes state, is the Java identity guaranteed to be the same in the new state? In a layered application, that may not be the case.

In order to explore this, it's extremely important to understand the relationship between Java identity, a==b, and database identity, x.getId().equals(y.getId()). Sometimes they're equivalent; sometimes they aren't. We refer to the conditions under which Java identity is equivalent to database identity as the *scope of object identity.*

For this scope, there are three common choices:

- A primitive persistence layer with *no identity scope* makes no guarantees that if a row is accessed twice the same Java object instance will be returned to the application. This becomes problematic if the application modifies two different instances that both represent the same row in a single unit of work. (How should we decide which state should be propagated to the database?)

- A persistence layer using *persistence context-scoped identity* guarantees that, in the scope of a single persistence context, only one object instance represents a particular database row. This avoids the previous problem and also allows for some caching at the context level.

- *Process-scoped identity* goes one step further and guarantees that only one object instance represents the row in the whole process (JVM).

For a typical web or enterprise application, persistence context-scoped identity is preferred. Process-scoped identity does offer some potential advantages in terms of cache utilization and the programming model for reuse of instances across multiple units of work. However, in a pervasively multithreaded application, the cost of always synchronizing shared access to persistent objects in the global identity map is too high a price to pay. It's simpler, and more scalable, to have each thread work with a distinct set of persistent instances in each persistence context.

We would say that Hibernate implements persistence context-scoped identity. So, by nature, Hibernate is best suited for highly concurrent data access in multiuser applications. However, we already mentioned some issues you'll face when objects aren't associated with a persistence context. Let's discuss this with an example.

The Hibernate identity scope is the scope of a persistence context. Let's see how this works in code with Hibernate APIs—the Java Persistence code is the equivalent with `EntityManager` instead of `Session`. Even though we haven't shown you much about these interfaces, the following examples are simple, and you should have no problems understanding the methods we call on the `Session`.

If you request two objects using the same database identifier value in the same `Session`, the result is two references to the same in-memory instance. Listing 9.1 demonstrates this with several `get()` operations in two `Sessions`.

Listing 9.1   The guaranteed scope of object identity in Hibernate

```
Session session1 = sessionFactory.openSession();
Transaction tx1 = session1.beginTransaction();

// Load Item with identifier value "1234"
Object a = session1.get(Item.class, new Long(1234) );
Object b = session1.get(Item.class, new Long(1234) );

( a==b ) // True, persistent a and b are identical

tx1.commit();
session1.close();

// References a and b are now to an object in detached state

Session session2 = sessionFactory.openSession();
Transaction tx2 = session2.beginTransaction();

Object c = session2.get(Item.class, new Long(1234) );

( a==c ) // False, detached a and persistent c are not identical

tx2.commit();
session2.close();
```

Object references a and b have not only the same database identity, but also the same Java identity, because they're obtained in the same `Session`. They reference the same persistent instance known to the persistence context for that unit of work. Once you're outside this boundary, however, Hibernate doesn't guarantee Java identity, so a and c aren't identical. Of course, a test for database identity, `a.getId().equals( c.getId() )`, will still return `true`.

If you work with objects in detached state, you're dealing with objects that are living outside of a guaranteed scope of object identity.

9.2.3   The identity of detached objects

If an object reference leaves the scope of guaranteed identity, we call it a *reference to a detached object*. In listing 9.1, all three object references, a, b, and c, are equal if we only consider database identity—their primary key value. However, they aren't identical in-memory object instances. This can lead to problems if you treat them as equal in detached state. For example, consider the following extension of the code, after `session2` has ended:

```
...
session2.close();

Set allObjects = new HashSet();
allObjects.add(a);
allObjects.add(b);
allObjects.add(c);
```

All three references have been added to a `Set`. All are references to detached objects. Now, if you check the size of the collection, the number of elements, what result do you expect?

First you have to realize the contract of a Java `Set`: No duplicate elements are allowed in such a collection. Duplicates are detected by the `Set`; whenever you add an object, its `equals()` method is called automatically. The added object is checked against all other elements already in the collection. If `equals()` returns `true` for any object already in the collection, the addition doesn't occur.

If you know the implementation of `equals()` for the objects, you can find out the number of elements you can expect in the `Set`. By default, all Java classes inherit the `equals()` method of `java.lang.Object`. This implementation uses a double-equals (`==`) comparison; it checks whether two references refer to the same in-memory instance on the Java heap.

You may guess that the number of elements in the collection is *two*. After all, a and b are references to the same in-memory instance; they have been loaded in the same persistence context. Reference c is obtained in a second `Session`; it refers to a different instance on the heap. You have three references to two instances. However, you know this only because you've seen the code that loaded the objects. In a real application, you may not know that a and b are loaded in the same `Session` and c in another.

Furthermore, you obviously expect that the collection has exactly one element, because a, b, and c represent the same database row.

Whenever you work with objects in detached state, and especially if you test them for equality (usually in hash-based collections), you need to supply your own implementation of the `equals()` and `hashCode()` methods for your persistent classes.

Understanding equals() and hashCode()

Before we show you how to implement your own equality routine. we have to bring two important points to your attention. First, in our experience, many Java developers never had to override the equals() and hashCode() methods before using Hibernate (or Java Persistence). Traditionally, Java developers seem to be unaware of the intricate details of such an implementation. The longest discussion threads on the public Hibernate forum are about this equality problem, and the "blame" is often put on Hibernate. You should be aware of the fundamental issue: Every object-oriented programming language with hash-based collections requires a custom equality routine if the default contract doesn't offer the desired semantics. The detached object state in a Hibernate application exposes you to this problem, maybe for the first time.

On the other hand, you may not have to override equals() and hashCode(). The identity scope guarantee provided by Hibernate is sufficient if you never compare detached instances—that is, if you never put detached instances into the same Set. You may decide to design an application that doesn't use detached objects. You can apply an extended persistence context strategy for your conversation implementation and eliminate the detached state from your application completely. This strategy also extends the scope of guaranteed object identity to span the whole conversation. (Note that you still need the discipline to not compare detached instances obtained in two conversations!)

Let's assume that you want to use detached objects and that you have to test them for equality with your own routine. You can implement equals() and hashCode() several ways. Keep in mind that when you override equals(), you always need to also override hashCode() so the two methods are *consistent*. If two objects are equal, they must have the same hashcode.

A clever approach is to implement equals() to compare just the database identifier property (often a surrogate primary key) value:

```
public class User {
    ...

    public boolean equals(Object other) {
        if (this==other) return true;
        if (id==null) return false;
        if ( !(other instanceof User) ) return false;
        final User that = (User) other;
        return this.id.equals( that.getId() );
    }

    public int hashCode() {
        return id==null ?
```

```
            System.identityHashCode(this) :
            id.hashCode();
    }

}
```

Notice how this `equals()` method falls back to Java identity for transient instances (if `id==null`) that don't have a database identifier value assigned yet. This is reasonable, because they can't possibly be equal to a detached instance, which has an identifier value.

Unfortunately, this solution has one huge problem: Identifier values aren't assigned by Hibernate until an object becomes persistent. If a transient object is added to a `Set` before being saved, its hash value may change while it's contained by the `Set`, contrary to the contract of `java.util.Set`. In particular, this problem makes cascade save (discussed later in the book) useless for sets. We strongly discourage this solution (*database identifier equality*).

A better way is to include all persistent properties of the persistent class, *apart* from any database identifier property, in the `equals()` comparison. This is how most people perceive the meaning of `equals()`; we call it *by value* equality.

When we say *all properties,* we don't mean to include collections. Collection state is associated with a different table, so it seems wrong to include it. More important, you don't want to force the entire object graph to be retrieved just to perform `equals()`. In the case of `User`, this means you shouldn't include the `boughtItems` collection in the comparison. This is the implementation you can write:

```
public class User {
    ...

    public boolean equals(Object other) {
        if (this==other) return true;
        if ( !(other instanceof User) ) return false;
        final User that = (User) other;
        if ( !this.getUsername().equals( that.getUsername() ) )
            return false;
        if ( !this.getPassword().equals( that.getPassword() ) )
            return false;
        return true;
    }

    public int hashCode() {
        int result = 14;
        result = 29 * result + getUsername().hashCode();
        result = 29 * result + getPassword().hashCode();
        return result;
    }

}
```

However, there are again two problems with this approach. First, instances from different `Sessions` are no longer equal if one is modified (for example, if the user changes the password). Second, instances with different database identity (instances that represent different rows of the database table) can be considered equal unless some combination of properties is guaranteed to be unique (the database columns have a unique constraint). In the case of user, there is a unique property: `username`.

This leads us to the preferred (and semantically correct) implementation of an equality check. You need a *business key*.

Implementing equality with a business key

To get to the solution that we recommend, you need to understand the notion of a *business key*. A business key is a property, or some combination of properties, that is unique for each instance with the same database identity. Essentially, it's the natural key that you would use if you weren't using a surrogate primary key instead. Unlike a natural primary key, it isn't an absolute requirement that the business key never changes—as long as it changes rarely, that's enough.

We argue that essentially every entity class should have *some* business key, even if it includes all properties of the class (this would be appropriate for some immutable classes). The business key is what the user thinks of as uniquely identifying a particular record, whereas the surrogate key is what the application and database use.

Business key equality means that the `equals()` method compares only the properties that form the business key. This is a perfect solution that avoids all the problems described earlier. The only downside is that it requires extra thought to identify the correct business key in the first place. This effort is required anyway; it's important to identify any unique keys if your database must ensure data integrity via constraint checking.

For the `User` class, `username` is a great candidate business key. It's never null, it's unique with a database constraint, and it changes rarely, if ever:

```
public class User {
    ...

    public boolean equals(Object other) {
        if (this==other) return true;
        if ( !(other instanceof User) ) return false;
        final User that = (User) other;
        return this.username.equals( that.getUsername() );
    }

    public int hashCode() {
```

```
            return username.hashCode();
        }

    }
```

For some other classes, the business key may be more complex, consisting of a combination of properties. Here are some hints that should help you identify a business key in your classes:

- Consider what attributes users of your application will refer to when they have to identify an object (in the real world). How do users tell the difference between one object and another if they're displayed on the screen? This is probably the business key you're looking for.

- Every attribute that is immutable is probably a good candidate for the business key. Mutable attributes may be good candidates, if they're updated rarely or if you can control the situation when they're updated.

- Every attribute that has a UNIQUE database constraint is a good candidate for the business key. Remember that the precision of the business key has to be good enough to avoid overlaps.

- Any date or time-based attribute, such as the creation time of the record, is usually a good component of a business key. However, the accuracy of System.currentTimeMillis() depends on the virtual machine and operating system. Our recommended safety buffer is 50 milliseconds, which may not be accurate enough if the time-based property is the single attribute of a business key.

- You can use database identifiers as part of the business key. This seems to contradict our previous statements, but we aren't talking about the database identifier of the given class. You may be able to use the database identifier of an associated object. For example, a candidate business key for the Bid class is the identifier of the Item it was made for together with the bid amount. You may even have a unique constraint that represents this composite business key in the database schema. You can use the identifier value of the associated Item because it never changes during the lifecycle of a Bid—setting an already persistent Item is required by the Bid constructor.

If you follow our advice, you shouldn't have much difficulty finding a good business key for all your business classes. If you have a difficult case, try to solve it without considering Hibernate—after all, it's purely an object-oriented problem. Notice that it's almost *never* correct to override equals() on a subclass and include another property in the comparison. It's a little tricky to satisfy the requirements that equality be both symmetric and transitive in this case; and, more important, the business key may not correspond to any well-defined candidate natural key in the database (subclass properties may be mapped to a different table).

You may have also noticed that the `equals()` and `hashCode()` methods always access the properties of the "other" object via the getter methods. This is extremely important, because the object instance passed as `other` may be a proxy object, not the actual instance that holds the persistent state. To initialize this proxy to get the property value, you need to access it with a getter method. This is one point where Hibernate isn't *completely* transparent. However, it's a good practice to use getter methods instead of direct instance variable access anyway.

Let's switch perspective now and consider an implementation strategy for conversations that doesn't require detached objects and doesn't expose you to any of the problems of detached object equality. If the identity scope issues you'll possibly be exposed to when you work with detached objects seem too much of a burden, the second conversation-implementation strategy may be what you're looking for. Hibernate and Java Persistence support the implementation of conversations with an *extended* persistence context: the *session-per-conversation* strategy.

9.2.4 *Extending a persistence context*

A particular conversation reuses the same persistence context for all interactions. All request processing during a conversation is managed by the same persistence context. The persistence context isn't closed after a request from the user has been processed. It's disconnected from the database and held in this state during user think-time. When the user continues in the conversation, the persistence context is reconnected to the database, and the next request can be processed. At the end of the conversation, the persistence context is synchronized with the database and closed. The next conversation starts with a fresh persistence context and doesn't reuse any entity instances from the previous conversation; the pattern is repeated.

Note that this eliminates the *detached* object state! All instances are either transient (not known to a persistence context) or persistent (attached to a particular persistence context). This also eliminates the need for manual reattachment or merging of object state between contexts, which is one of the advantages of this strategy. (You still may have detached objects *between* conversations, but we consider this a special case that you should try to avoid.)

In Hibernate terms, this strategy uses a single `Session` for the duration of the conversation. Java Persistence has built-in support for extended persistence contexts and can even automatically store the disconnected context for you (in a stateful EJB session bean) between requests.

We'll get back to conversations later in the book and show you all the details about the two implementation strategies. You don't have to choose one right now, but you should be aware of the consequences these strategies have on object state and object identity, and you should understand the necessary transitions in each case.

We now explore the persistence manager APIs and how you make the theory behind object states work in practice.

9.3 The Hibernate interfaces

Any transparent persistence tool includes a *persistence manager* API. This persistence manager usually provides services for the following:

- Basic CRUD (create, retrieve, update, delete) operations
- Query execution
- Control of transactions
- Management of the persistence context

The persistence manager may be exposed by several different interfaces. In the case of Hibernate, these are `Session`, `Query`, `Criteria`, and `Transaction`. Under the covers, the implementations of these interfaces are coupled tightly together.

In Java Persistence, the main interface you interact with is the `EntityManager`; it has the same role as the Hibernate `Session`. Other Java Persistence interfaces are `Query` and `EntityTransaction` (you can probably guess what their counterpart in native Hibernate is).

We'll now show you how to load and store objects with Hibernate and Java Persistence. Sometimes both have exactly the same semantics and API, and even the method names are the same. It's therefore much more important to keep your eyes open for little differences. To make this part of the book easier to understand, we decided to use a different strategy than usual and explain Hibernate first and then Java Persistence.

Let's start with Hibernate, assuming that you write an application that relies on the native API.

9.3.1 Storing and loading objects

In a Hibernate application, you store and load objects by essentially changing their state. You do this in units of work. A single unit of work is a set of operations considered an atomic group. If you're guessing now that this is closely related to transactions, you're right. But, it isn't necessarily the same thing. We have to approach this step by step; for now, consider a unit of work a particular sequence of state changes to your objects that you'd group together.

First you have to begin a unit of work.

Beginning a unit of work

At the beginning of a unit of work, an application obtains an instance of Session from the application's SessionFactory:

```
Session session = sessionFactory.openSession();
Transaction tx = session.beginTransaction();
```

At this point, a new persistence context is also initialized for you, and it will manage all the objects you work with in that Session. The application may have multiple SessionFactorys if it accesses several databases. How the SessionFactory is created and how you get access to it in your application code depends on your deployment environment and configuration—you should have the simple HibernateUtil startup helper class ready if you followed the setup in "Handling the SessionFactory" in chapter 2, section 2.1.3.

You should never create a new SessionFactory just to service a particular request. Creation of a SessionFactory is extremely expensive. On the other hand, Session creation is extremely *inexpensive*. The Session doesn't even obtain a JDBC Connection until a connection is required.

The second line in the previous code begins a Transaction on another Hibernate interface. All operations you execute inside a unit of work occur inside a transaction, no matter if you read or write data. However, the Hibernate API is optional, and you may begin a transaction in any way you like—we'll explore these options in the next chapter. If you use the Hibernate Transaction API, your code works in all environments, so you'll do this for all examples in the following sections.

After opening a new Session and persistence context, you use it to load and save objects.

Making an object persistent

The first thing you want to do with a Session is make a new transient object persistent with the save() method (listing 9.2).

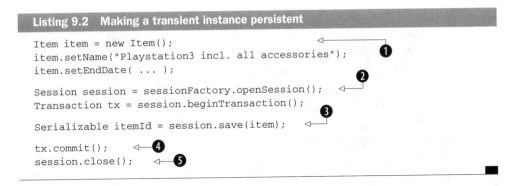

Listing 9.2 Making a transient instance persistent

```
Item item = new Item();                                         ❶
item.setName("Playstation3 incl. all accessories");
item.setEndDate( ... );
                                                                ❷
Session session = sessionFactory.openSession();
Transaction tx = session.beginTransaction();
                                                                ❸
Serializable itemId = session.save(item);

tx.commit();        ❹
session.close();    ❺
```

A new transient object `item` is instantiated as usual ❶. Of course, you may also instantiate it after opening a `Session`; they aren't related yet. A new `Session` is opened using the `SessionFactory` ❷. You start a new transaction.

A call to `save()` ❸ makes the transient instance of `Item` persistent. It's now associated with the current `Session` and its persistence context.

The changes made to persistent objects have to be synchronized with the database at some point. This happens when you `commit()` the Hibernate `Transaction` ❹. We say a *flush* occurs (you can also call `flush()` manually; more about this later). To synchronize the persistence context, Hibernate obtains a JDBC connection and issues a single SQL `INSERT` statement. Note that this isn't always true for insertion: Hibernate guarantees that the `item` object has an assigned database identifier after it has been saved, so an earlier `INSERT` may be necessary, depending on the identifier generator you have enabled in your mapping. The `save()` operation also returns the database identifier of the persistent instance.

The `Session` can finally be closed ❺, and the persistence context ends. The reference `item` is now a reference to an object in detached state.

You can see the same unit of work and how the object changes state in figure 9.4.

It's better (but not required) to fully initialize the `Item` instance before managing it with a `Session`. The SQL `INSERT` statement contains the values that were

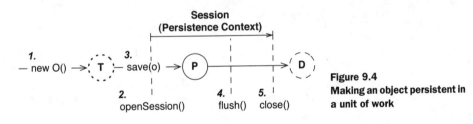

Figure 9.4
Making an object persistent in a unit of work

held by the object at the point when save() was called. You can modify the object after calling save(), and your changes will be propagated to the database as an (additional) SQL UPDATE.

Everything between session.beginTransaction() and tx.commit() occurs in one transaction. For now, keep in mind that all database operations in transaction scope either completely succeed or completely fail. If one of the UPDATE or INSERT statements made during flushing on tx.commit() fails, all changes made to persistent objects in this transaction are rolled back at the database level. However, Hibernate doesn't roll back in-memory changes to persistent objects. This is reasonable because a failure of a transaction is normally nonrecoverable, and you have to discard the failed Session immediately. We'll discuss exception handling later in the next chapter.

Retrieving a persistent object

The Session is also used to query the database and retrieve existing persistent objects. Hibernate is especially powerful in this area, as you'll see later in the book. Two special methods are provided for the simplest kind of query: retrieval by identifier. The get() and load() methods are demonstrated in listing 9.3.

Listing 9.3   Retrieval of a Item by identifier

```
Session session = sessionFactory.openSession();
Transaction tx = session.beginTransaction();

Item item = (Item) session.load(Item.class, new Long(1234));
// Item item = (Item) session.get(Item.class, new Long(1234));

tx.commit();
session.close();
```

You can see the same unit of work in figure 9.5.

The retrieved object item is in persistent state and as soon as the persistence context is closed, in detached state.

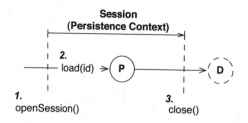

Figure 9.5
Retrieving a persistent object by identifier

The one difference between get() and load() is how they indicate that the instance could not be found. If no row with the given identifier value exists in the database, get() returns null. The load() method throws an ObjectNotFound-Exception. It's your choice what error-handling you prefer.

More important, the load() method may return a *proxy*, a placeholder, without hitting the database. A consequence of this is that you may get an ObjectNotFoundException later, as soon as you try to access the returned placeholder and force its initialization (this is also called *lazy loading*; we discuss load optimization in later chapters.) The load() method always tries to return a proxy, and only returns an initialized object instance if it's already managed by the current persistence context. In the example shown earlier, no database hit occurs at all! The get() method on the other hand never returns a proxy, it always hits the database.

You may ask why this option is useful—after all, you retrieve an object to access it. It's common to obtain a persistent instance to assign it as a reference to another instance. For example, imagine that you need the item only for a single purpose: to set an association with a Comment: aComment.setForAuction(item). If this is all you plan to do with the item, a proxy will do fine; there is no need to hit the database. In other words, when the Comment is saved, you need the foreign key value of an item inserted into the COMMENT table. The proxy of an Item provides just that: an identifier value wrapped in a placeholder that looks like the real thing.

Modifying a persistent object

Any persistent object returned by get(), load(), or any entity queried is already associated with the current Session and persistence context. It can be modified, and its state is synchronized with the database (see listing 9.4).

Figure 9.6 shows this unit of work and the object transitions.

Listing 9.4   Modifying a persistent instance

```
Session session = sessionFactory.openSession();
Transaction tx = session.beginTransaction();

Item item = (Item) session.get(Item.class, new Long(1234));

item.setDescription("This Playstation is as good as new!");

tx.commit();
session.close();
```

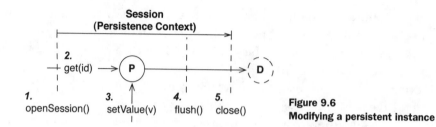

Figure 9.6
Modifying a persistent instance

First, you retrieve the object from the database with the given identifier. You modify the object, and these modifications are propagated to the database during flush when `tx.commit()` is called. This mechanism is called *automatic dirty checking*—that means Hibernate tracks and saves the changes you make to an object in persistent state. As soon as you close the `Session`, the instance is considered detached.

Making a persistent object transient

You can easily make a persistent object transient, removing its persistent state from the database, with the `delete()` method (see listing 9.5).

Listing 9.5   Making a persistent object transient using delete()

```
Session session = sessionFactory.openSession();
Transaction tx = session.beginTransaction();

Item item = (Item) session.load(Item.class, new Long(1234));

session.delete(item);

tx.commit();
session.close();
```

Look at figure 9.7.

The `item` object is in *removed* state after you call `delete()`; you shouldn't continue working with it, and, in most cases, you should make sure any reference to it

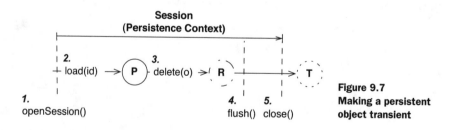

Figure 9.7
Making a persistent object transient

in your application is removed. The SQL DELETE is executed only when the Session's persistence context is synchronized with the database at the end of the unit of work. After the Session is closed, the item object is considered an ordinary transient instance. The transient instance is destroyed by the garbage collector if it's no longer referenced by any other object. Both the in-memory object instance and the persistent database row will have been removed.

FAQ   *Do I have to load an object to delete it?*   Yes, an object has to be loaded into the persistence context; an instance has to be in persistent state to be removed (note that a proxy is good enough). The reason is simple: You may have Hibernate interceptors enabled, and the object must be passed through these interceptors to complete its lifecycle. If you delete rows in the database directly, the interceptor won't run. Having said that, Hibernate (and Java Persistence) offer bulk operations that translate into direct SQL DELETE statements; we'll discuss these operations in chapter 12, section 12.2, "Bulk and batch operations."

Hibernate can also roll back the identifier of any entity that has been deleted, if you enable the hibernate.use_identifier_rollback configuration option. In the previous example, Hibernate sets the database identifier property of the deleted item to null after deletion and flushing, if the option is enabled. It's then a clean transient instance that you can reuse in a future unit of work.

Replicating objects

The operations on the Session we have shown you so far are all common; you need them in every Hibernate application. But Hibernate can help you with some special use cases—for example, when you need to retrieve objects from one database and store them in another. This is called *replication* of objects.

Replication takes detached objects loaded in one Session and makes them persistent in another Session. These Sessions are usually opened from two different SessionFactorys that have been configured with a mapping for the same persistent class. Here is an example:

```
Session session = sessionFactory1.openSession();
Transaction tx = session.beginTransaction();
Item item = (Item) session.get(Item.class, new Long(1234));
tx.commit();
session.close();

Session session2 = sessionFactory2.openSession();
Transaction tx2 = session2.beginTransaction();
session2.replicate(item, ReplicationMode.LATEST_VERSION);
tx2.commit();
session2.close();
```

The ReplicationMode controls the details of the replication procedure:

- ReplicationMode.IGNORE—Ignores the object when there is an existing database row with the same identifier in the target database.

- ReplicationMode.OVERWRITE—Overwrites any existing database row with the same identifier in the target database.

- ReplicationMode.EXCEPTION—Throws an exception if there is an existing database row with the same identifier in the target database.

- ReplicationMode.LATEST_VERSION—Overwrites the row in the target database if its version is earlier than the version of the object, or ignores the object otherwise. Requires enabled Hibernate optimistic concurrency control.

You may need replication when you reconcile data entered into different databases, when you're upgrading system configuration information during product upgrades (which often involves a migration to a new database instance), or when you need to roll back changes made during non-ACID transactions.

You now know the persistence lifecycle and the basic operations of the persistence manager. Using these together with the persistent class mappings we discussed in earlier chapters, you may now create your own small Hibernate application. Map some simple entity classes and components, and then store and load objects in a stand-alone application. You don't need a web container or application server: Write a main() method, and call the Session as we discussed in the previous section.

In the next sections, we cover the *detached* object state and the methods to reattach and merge detached objects between persistence contexts. This is the foundation knowledge you need to implement long units of work—conversations. We assume that you're familiar with the scope of object identity as explained earlier in this chapter.

9.3.2 *Working with detached objects*

Modifying the item after the Session is closed has no effect on its persistent representation in the database. As soon as the persistence context is closed, item becomes a *detached* instance.

If you want to save modifications you made to a detached object, you have to either *reattach* or *merge* it.

Reattaching a modified detached instance

A detached instance may be reattached to a new `Session` (and managed by this new persistence context) by calling `update()` on the detached object. In our experience, it may be easier for you to understand the following code if you rename the `update()` method in your mind to `reattach()`—however, there is a good reason it's called updating.

The `update()` method forces an update to the persistent state of the object in the database, always scheduling an SQL UPDATE. See listing 9.6 for an example of detached object handling.

Listing 9.6 Updating a detached instance

```
item.setDescription(...); // Loaded in previous Session

Session sessionTwo = sessionFactory.openSession();
Transaction tx = sessionTwo.beginTransaction();

sessionTwo.update(item);

item.setEndDate(...);

tx.commit();
sessionTwo.close();
```

It doesn't matter if the `item` object is modified before or after it's passed to `update()`. The important thing here is that the call to `update()` is reattaching the detached instance to the new `Session` (and persistence context). Hibernate always treats the object as dirty and schedules an SQL UPDATE., which will be executed during flush. You can see the same unit of work in figure 9.8.

You may be surprised and probably hoped that Hibernate could know that you modified the detached `item`'s description (or that Hibernate should know you did *not* modify anything). However, the new `Session` and its fresh persistence context don't have this information. Neither does the detached object contain some internal list of all the modifications you've made. Hibernate has to assume that an

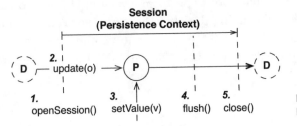

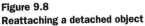

Figure 9.8
Reattaching a detached object

UDPATE in the database is needed. One way to avoid this UDPATE statement is to configure the class mapping of Item with the select-before-update="true" attribute. Hibernate then determines whether the object is dirty by executing a SELECT statement and comparing the object's current state to the current database state.

If you're sure you haven't modified the detached instance, you may prefer another method of reattachment that doesn't always schedule an update of the database.

Reattaching an unmodified detached instance

A call to lock() associates the object with the Session and its persistence context without forcing an update, as shown in listing 9.7.

Listing 9.7   Reattaching a detached instance with lock()

```
Session sessionTwo = sessionFactory.openSession();
Transaction tx = sessionTwo.beginTransaction();

sessionTwo.lock(item, LockMode.NONE);

item.setDescription(...);
item.setEndDate(...);

tx.commit();
sessionTwo.close();
```

In this case, it *does* matter whether changes are made before or after the object has been reattached. Changes made before the call to lock() aren't propagated to the database, you use it only if you're sure the detached instance hasn't been modified. This method only guarantees that the object's state changes from detached to persistent and that Hibernate will manage the persistent object again. Of course, any modifications you make to the object once it's in managed persistent state require updating of the database.

We discuss Hibernate lock modes in the next chapter. By specifying Lock-Mode.NONE here, you tell Hibernate not to perform a version check or obtain any database-level locks when reassociating the object with the Session. If you specified LockMode.READ, or LockMode.UPGRADE, Hibernate would execute a SELECT statement in order to perform a version check (and to lock the row(s) in the database for updating).

Making a detached object transient

Finally, you can make a detached instance transient, deleting its persistent state from the database, as in listing 9.8.

Listing 9.8 Making a detached object transient using `delete()`

```
Session session = sessionFactory.openSession();
Transaction tx = session.beginTransaction();

session.delete(item);

tx.commit();
session.close();
```

This means you don't have to reattach (with `update()` or `lock()`) a detached instance to delete it from the database. In this case, the call to `delete()` does two things: It reattaches the object to the `Session` and then schedules the object for deletion, executed on `tx.commit()`. The state of the object after the `delete()` call is *removed*.

Reattachment of detached objects is only one possible way to transport data between several `Session`s. You can use another option to synchronize modifications to a detached instance with the database, through *merging* of its state.

Merging the state of a detached object

Merging of a detached object is an alternative approach. It can be complementary to or can replace reattachment. Merging was first introduced in Hibernate to deal with a particular case where reattachment was no longer sufficient (the old name for the `merge()` method in Hibernate 2.x was `saveOrUpdateCopy()`). Look at the following code, which tries to reattach a detached object:

```
item.getId(); // The database identity is "1234"
item.setDescription(...);

Session session = sessionFactory.openSession();
Transaction tx = session.beginTransaction();

Item item2 = (Item) session.get(Item.class, new Long(1234));

session.update(item); // Throws exception!

tx.commit();
session.close();
```

Given is a detached `item` object with the database identity 1234. After modifying it, you try to reattach it to a new `Session`. However, before reattachment, another instance that represents the same database row has already been loaded into the persistence context of that Session. Obviously, the reattachment through update() clashes with this already persistent instance, and a NonUniqueObjectException is thrown. The error message of the exception is *A persistent instance with the same database identifier is already associated with the Session!* Hibernate can't decide which object represents the current state.

You can resolve this situation by reattaching the item first; then, because the object is in persistent state, the retrieval of item2 is unnecessary. This is straightforward in a simple piece of code such as the example, but it may be impossible to refactor in a more sophisticated application. After all, a client sent the detached object to the persistence layer to have it managed, and the client may not (and shouldn't) be aware of the managed instances already in the persistence context.

You can let Hibernate merge item and item2 automatically:

```
item.getId() // The database identity is "1234"
item.setDescription(...);

Session session= sessionFactory.openSession();
Transaction tx = session.beginTransaction();

Item item2 = (Item) session.get(Item.class, new Long(1234));    ❷

Item item3 = (Item) session.merge(item);    ❸

(item == item2) // False
(item == item3) // False
(item2 == item3) // True

return item3;

tx.commit();
session.close();
```

Look at this unit of work in figure 9.9.

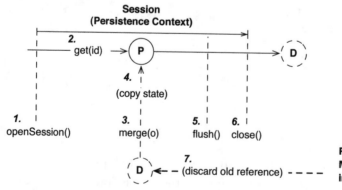

Figure 9.9
Merging a detached instance into a persistent instance

The merge(item) call ❸ results in several actions. First, Hibernate checks whether a persistent instance in the persistence context has the same database identifier as the detached instance you're merging. In this case, this is true: item and item2, which were loaded with get() ❷, have the same primary key value.

If there is an equal persistent instance in the persistence context, Hibernate *copies* the state of the detached instance onto the persistent instance ❹. In other words, the new description that has been set on the detached item is also set on the persistent item2.

If there is no equal persistent instance in the persistence context, Hibernate loads it from the database (effectively executing the same retrieval by identifier as you did with get()) and then merges the detached state with the retrieved object's state. This is shown in figure 9.10.

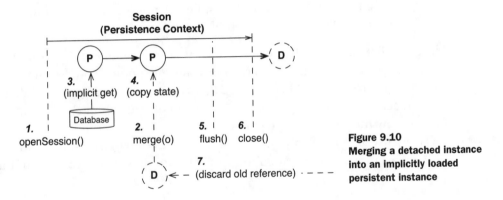

Figure 9.10
Merging a detached instance into an implicitly loaded persistent instance

If there is no equal persistent instance in the persistence context, and a lookup in the database yields no result, a new persistent instance is created, and the state of the merged instance is copied onto the new instance. This new object is then scheduled for insertion into the database and returned by the merge() operation.

An insertion also occurs if the instance you passed into merge() was a transient instance, not a detached object.

The following questions are likely on your mind:

- What exactly is copied from item to item2? Merging includes all value-typed properties and all additions and removals of elements to any collection.

- What state is item in? Any detached object you merge with a persistent instance stays detached. It doesn't change state; it's unaffected by the merge operation. Therefore, item and the other two references aren't the same in Hibernate's identity scope. (The first two identity checks in the last example.) However, item2 and item3 *are* identical references to the same persistent in-memory instance.

- Why is item3 returned from the merge() operation? The merge() operation always returns a handle to the persistent instance it has merged the state into. This is convenient for the client that called merge(), because it can now either continue working with the detached item object and merge it again when needed, or discard this reference and continue working with item3. The difference is significant: If, before the Session completes, subsequent modifications are made to item2 or item3 after merging, the client is completely unaware of these modifications. The client has a handle only to the detached item object, which is now getting stale. However, if the client decides to throw away item after merging and continue with the returned item3, it has a new handle on up-to-date state. Both item and item2 should be considered obsolete after merging.

Merging of state is slightly more complex than reattachment. We consider it an essential operation you'll likely have to use at some point if you design your application logic around detached objects. You can use this strategy as an alternative for reattachment and merge every time instead of reattaching. You can also use it to make any transient instance persistent. As you'll see later in this chapter, this is the standardized model of Java Persistence; reattachment isn't supported.

We haven't paid much attention so far to the persistence context and how it manages persistent objects.

9.3.3 *Managing the persistence context*

The persistence context does many things for you: automatic dirty checking, guaranteed scope of object identity, and so on. It's equally important that you know some of the details of its management, and that you sometimes influence what goes on behind the scenes.

Controlling the persistence context cache

The persistence context is a cache of persistent objects. Every object in persistent state is known to the persistence context, and a duplicate, a *snapshot* of each persistent instance, is held in the cache. This snapshot is used internally for dirty checking, to detect any modifications you made to your persistent objects.

Many Hibernate users who ignore this simple fact run into an OutOfMemory-Exception. This is typically the case when you load thousands of objects in a Session but never intend to modify them. Hibernate still has to create a snapshot of each object in the persistence context cache and keep a reference to the managed object, which can lead to memory exhaustion. (Obviously, you should execute a *bulk data operation* if you modify thousands of objects—we'll get back to this kind of unit of work in chapter 12, section 12.2, "Bulk and batch operations.")

The persistence context cache never shrinks automatically. To reduce or regain the memory consumed by the persistence context in a particular unit of work, you have to do the following:

- Keep the size of your persistence context to the necessary minimum. Often, many persistent instances in your `Session` are there by accident—for example, because you needed only a few but queried for many. Make objects persistent only if you absolutely need them in this state; extremely large graphs can have a serious performance impact and require significant memory for state snapshots. Check that your queries return only objects you need. As you'll see later in the book, you can also execute a query in Hibernate that returns objects in read-only state, without creating a persistence context snapshot.

- You can call `session.evict(object)` to detach a persistent instance manually from the persistence context cache. You can call `session.clear()` to detach *all* persistent instances from the persistence context. Detached objects aren't checked for dirty state; they aren't managed.

- With `session.setReadOnly(object, true)`, you can disable dirty checking for a particular instance. The persistence context will no longer maintain the snapshot if it's read-only. With `session.setReadOnly(object, false)`, you can re-enable dirty checking for an instance and force the recreation of a snapshot. Note that these operations don't change the object's state.

At the end of a unit of work, all the modifications you made have to be synchronized with the database through SQL DML statements. This process is called *flushing* of the persistence context.

Flushing the persistence context

The Hibernate `Session` implements *write-behind*. Changes to persistent objects made in the scope of a persistence context aren't immediately propagated to the database. This allows Hibernate to coalesce many changes into a minimal number of database requests, helping minimize the impact of network latency. Another excellent side-effect of executing DML as late as possible, toward the end of the transaction, is shorter lock durations inside the database.

For example, if a single property of an object is changed twice in the same persistence context, Hibernate needs to execute only one SQL UPDATE. Another example of the usefulness of write-behind is that Hibernate is able to take advantage of the JDBC batch API when executing multiple UPDATE, INSERT, or DELETE statements.

The synchronization of a persistence context with the database is called *flushing*. Hibernate flushes occur at the following times:

- When a Transaction on the Hibernate API is committed
- Before a query is executed
- When the application calls session.flush() explicitly

Flushing the Session state to the database at the end of a unit of work is required in order to make the changes durable and is the common case. Note that automatic flushing when a transaction is committed is a feature of the Hibernate API! Committing a transaction with the JDBC API doesn't trigger a flush. Hibernate doesn't flush before every query. If changes are held in memory that would affect the results of the query, Hibernate synchronizes first by default.

You can control this behavior by explicitly setting the Hibernate FlushMode via a call to session.setFlushMode(). The default flush mode is FlushMode.AUTO and enables the behavior described previously. If you chose FlushMode.COMMIT, the persistence context isn't flushed before query execution (it's flushed only when you call Transaction.commit() or Session.flush() manually). This setting may expose you to stale data: Modifications you make to managed objects only in memory may conflict with the results of the query. By selecting Flush-Mode.MANUAL, you may specify that only explicit calls to flush() result in synchronization of managed state with the database.

Controlling the FlushMode of a persistence context will be necessary later in the book, when we extend the context to span a conversation.

Repeated flushing of the persistence context is often a source for performance issues, because all dirty objects in the persistence context have to be detected at flush-time. A common cause is a particular unit-of-work pattern that repeats a query-modify-query-modify sequence many times. Every modification leads to a flush and a dirty check of all persistent objects, before each query. A Flush-Mode.COMMIT may be appropriate in this situation.

Always remember that the performance of the flush process depends in part on the size of the persistence context—the number of persistent objects it manages. Hence, the advice we gave for managing the persistence context, in the previous section, also applies here.

You've now seen the most important strategies and some optional ones for interacting with objects in a Hibernate application and what methods and operations are available on a Hibernate `Session`. If you plan to work only with Hibernate APIs, you can skip the next section and go directly to the next chapter and read about transactions. If you want to work on your objects with Java Persistence and/or EJB 3.0 components, read on.

9.4 The Java Persistence API

We now store and load objects with the Java Persistence API. This is the API you use either in a Java SE application or with EJB 3.0 components, as a vendor-independent alternative to the Hibernate native interfaces.

You've read the first sections of this chapter and know the object states defined by JPA and how they're related to Hibernate's. Because the two are similar, the first part of this chapter applies no matter what API you'll choose. It follows that the way you interact with your objects, and how you manipulate the database, are also similar. So, we also assume that you have learned the Hibernate interfaces in the previous section (you also miss all the illustrations if you skip the previous section; we won't repeat them here). This is important for another reason: JPA provides a *subset* of functionality of the *superset* of Hibernate native APIs. In other words, there are good reasons to fall back to native Hibernate interfaces whenever you need to. You can expect that the majority of the functionality you'll need in an application is covered by the standard, and that this is rarely necessary.

As in Hibernate, you store and load objects with JPA by manipulating the current state of an object. And, just as in Hibernate, you do this in a unit of work, a set of operations considered to be atomic. (We still haven't covered enough ground to explain all about transactions, but we will soon.)

To begin a unit of work in a Java Persistence application, you need to get an `EntityManager` (the equivalent to the Hibernate `Session`). However, where you open a `Session` from a `SessionFactory` in a Hibernate application, a Java Persistence application can be written with *managed* and *unmanaged* units of work. Let's keep this simple, and assume that you first want to write a JPA application that doesn't benefit from EJB 3.0 components in a managed environment.

9.4.1 Storing and loading objects

The term *unmanaged* refers to the possibility to create a persistence layer with Java Persistence that runs and works without any special runtime environment. You can use JPA without an application server, outside of any runtime container, in a plain Java SE application. This can be a servlet application (the web container doesn't provide anything you'd need for persistence) or a simple `main()` method. Another common case is local persistence for desktop applications, or persistence for two-tiered systems, where a desktop application accesses a remote database tier (although there is no good reason why you can't use a lightweight modular application server with EJB 3.0 support in such a scenario).

Beginning a unit of work in Java SE

In any case, because you don't have a container that could provide an `EntityManager` for you, you need to create one manually. The equivalent of the Hibernate `SessionFactory` is the JPA `EntityManagerFactory`:

```
EntityManagerFactory emf =
    Persistence.createEntityManagerFactory("caveatemptorDatabase");
EntityManager em = emf.createEntityManager();
EntityTransaction tx = em.getTransaction();
tx.begin();
```

The first line of code is part of your system configuration. You should create one `EntityManagerFactory` for each persistence unit you deploy in a Java Persistence application. We covered this already in chapter 2, section 2.2.2, "Using Hibernate EntityManager," so we won't repeat it here. The next three lines are equivalent to how you'd begin a unit of work in a stand-alone Hibernate application: First, an `EntityManager` is created, and then a transaction is started. To familiarize yourself with EJB 3.0 jargon, you can call this `EntityManager` *application-managed*. The transaction you started here also has a special description: It's a *resource-local* transaction. You're controlling the resources involved (the database in this case) directly in your application code; no runtime container takes care of this for you.

The `EntityManager` has a fresh persistence context assigned when it's created. In this context, you store and load objects.

Making an entity instance persistent

An entity class is the same as one of your Hibernate persistent classes. Of course, you'd usually prefer annotations to map your entity classes, as a replacement of Hibernate XML mapping files. After all, the (primary) reason you're using Java Persistence is the benefit of standardized interfaces and mappings.

Let's create a new instance of an entity and bring it from transient into persistent state:

```
Item item = new Item();
item.setName("Playstation3 incl. all accessories");
item.setEndDate( ... );
```

```
EntityManager em = emf.createEntityManager();
EntityTransaction tx = em.getTransaction();
tx.begin();

em.persist(item);

tx.commit();
em.close();
```

This code should look familiar if you've followed the earlier sections of this chapter. The transient item entity instance becomes persistent as soon as you call persist() on it; it's now managed in the persistence context. Note that persist() doesn't return the database identifier value of the entity instance (this little difference, compared to Hibernate's save() method, will be important again when you implement conversations in "Delaying insertion until flush-time" in chapter 11, section 11.2.3.

FAQ　*Should I use persist() on the Session?*　The Hibernate Session interface also features a persist() method. It has the same semantics as the persist() operation of JPA. However, there's an important difference between the two operations with regard to flushing. During synchronization, a Hibernate Session doesn't *cascade* the persist() operation to associated entities and collections, even if you mapped an association with this option. It's only cascaded to entities that are reachable when you call persist()! Only save() (and update()) are cascaded at flush-time if you use the Session API. In a JPA application, however, it's the other way round: Only persist() is cascaded at flush-time.

Managed entity instances are monitored. Every modification you make to an instance in persistent state is at some point synchronized with the database (unless you abort the unit of work). Because the EntityTransaction is managed by the application, you need to do the commit() manually. The same rule applies to the application-controlled EntityManager: You need to release all resources by closing it.

Retrieving an entity instance

The EntityManager is also used to query the database and retrieve persistent entity instances. Java Persistence supports sophisticated query features (which we'll cover later in the book). The most basic is as always the *retrieval by identifier.*

```
EntityManager em = emf.createEntityManager();
EntityTransaction tx = em.getTransaction();
tx.begin();

Item item = em.find(Item.class, new Long(1234));
```

```
tx.commit();
em.close();
```

You don't need to cast the returned value of the `find()` operation; it's a generic method. and its return type is set as a side effect of the first parameter. This is a minor but convenient benefit of the Java Persistence API—Hibernate native methods have to work with older JDKs that don't support generics.

The retrieved entity instance is in a persistent state and can now be modified inside the unit of work or be detached for use outside of the persistence context. If no persistent instance with the given identifier can be found, `find()` returns `null`. The `find()` operation always hits the database (or a vendor-specific transparent cache), so the entity instance is always initialized during loading. You can expect to have all of its values available later in detached state.

If you don't want to hit the database, because you aren't sure you'll need a fully initialized instance, you can tell the `EntityManager` to attempt the retrieval of a placeholder:

```
EntityManager em = emf.createEntityManager();
EntityTransaction tx = em.getTransaction();
tx.begin();

Item item = em.getReference(Item.class, new Long(1234));

tx.commit();
em.close();
```

This operation returns either the fully initialized `item` (for example, if the instance was already available in the current persistence context) or a *proxy* (a hollow placeholder).

As soon as you try to access any property of the item that isn't the database identifier property, an additional `SELECT` is executed to fully initialize the placeholder. This also means you should expect an `EntityNotFoundException` at this point (or even earlier, when `getReference()` is executed). A logical conclusion is that if you decide to detach the `item` reference, no guarantees are made that it will be fully initialized (unless, of course, you access one of its nonidentifier properties before detachment).

Modifying a persistent entity instance

An entity instance in persistent state is managed by the current persistence context. You can modify it and expect that the persistence context flushes the necessary SQL DML at synchronization time. This is the same automatic dirty checking feature provided by the Hibernate `Session`:

```
EntityManager em = emf.createEntityManager();
EntityTransaction tx = em.getTransaction();
tx.begin();

Item item = em.find(Item.class, new Long(1234));
item.setDescription(...);

tx.commit();
em.close();
```

A persistent entity instance is retrieved by its identifier value. Then, you modify one of its mapped properties (a property that hasn't been annotated with @Transient or the transient Java keyword). In this code example, the next synchronization with the database occurs when the resource-local transaction is committed. The Java Persistence engine executes the necessary DML, in this case an UDPATE.

Making a persistent entity instance transient

If you want to remove the state of an entity instance from the database, you have to make it transient. Use the remove() method on your EntityManager:

```
EntityManager em = emf.createEntityManager();
EntityTransaction tx = em.getTransaction();
tx.begin();

Item item = em.find(Item.class, new Long(1234));

em.remove(item);

tx.commit();
em.close();
```

The semantics of the remove() Java Persistence method are the same as the delete() method's on the Hibernate Session. The previously persistent object is now in *removed* state, and you should discard any reference you're holding to it in the application. An SQL DELETE is executed during the next synchronization of the persistence context. The JVM garbage collector detects that the item is no longer referenced by anyone and finally deletes the last trace of the object. However, note that you can't call remove() on an entity instance in detached state, or an exception will be thrown. You have to merge the detached instance first and then remove the merged object (or, alternatively, get a reference with the same identifier, and remove that).

Flushing the persistence context

All modifications made to persistent entity instances are synchronized with the database at some point, a process called *flushing*. This write-behind behavior is the same as Hibernate's and guarantees the best scalability by executing SQL DML as late as possible.

The persistence context of an `EntityManager` is flushed whenever `commit()` on an `EntityTransaction` is called. All the previous code examples in this section of the chapter have been using that strategy. However, JPA implementations are allowed to synchronize the persistence context at other times, if they wish.

Hibernate, as a JPA implementation, synchronizes at the following times:

- When an `EntityTransaction` is committed
- Before a query is executed
- When the application calls `em.flush()` explicitly

These are the same rules we explained for native Hibernate in the previous section. And as in native Hibernate, you can control this behavior with a JPA interface, the `FlushModeType`:

```
EntityManager em = emf.createEntityManager();
em.setFlushMode(FlushModeType.COMMIT);
EntityTransaction tx = em.getTransaction();
tx.begin();

Item item = em.find(Item.class, new Long(1234));
item.setDescription(...);

List result = em.createQuery(...).getResultList();

tx.commit();
em.close();
```

Switching the `FlushModeType` to `COMMIT` for an `EntityManager` disables automatic synchronization before queries; it occurs only when the transaction is committed or when you flush manually. The default `FlushModeType` is `AUTO`.

Just as with native Hibernate, controlling the synchronization behavior of a persistence context will be important functionality for the implementation of conversations, which we'll attack later.

You now know the basic operations of Java Persistence, and you can go ahead and store and load some entity instances in your own application. Set up your system as described in chapter 2, section 2.2, "Starting a Java Persistence project," and map some classes to your database schema with annotations. Write a `main()` method that uses an `EntityManager` and an `EntityTransaction`; we think you'll soon see how easy it is to use Java Persistence even without EJB 3.0 managed components or an application server.

Let's discuss how you work with detached entity instances.

9.4.2   *Working with detached entity instances*

We assume you already know how a detached object is defined (if you don't, read the first section of this chapter again). You don't necessarily have to know how you'd work with detached objects in Hibernate, but we'll refer you to earlier sections if a strategy with Java Persistence is the same as in native Hibernate.

First, let's see again how entity instances become detached in a Java Persistence application.

JPA persistence context scope

You've used Java Persistence in a Java SE environment, with application-managed persistence contexts and transactions. Every persistent and managed entity instance becomes detached when the persistence context is closed. But wait—we didn't tell you when the persistence context is closed.

If you're familiar with native Hibernate, you already know the answer: The persistence context ends when the `Session` is closed. The `EntityManager` is the equivalent in JPA; and by default, if you created the `EntityManager` yourself, the persistence context is scoped to the lifecycle of that `EntityManager` instance.

Look at the following code:

```
EntityManager em = emf.createEntityManager();
EntityTransaction tx = em.getTransaction();

tx.begin();
Item item = em.find(Item.class, new Long(1234));
tx.commit();

Item.setDescription(...);

tx.begin();
User user = em.find(User.class, new Long(3456));
user.setPassword("secret");
tx.commit();

em.close();
```

In the first transaction, you retrieve an `Item` object. The transaction then completes, but the `item` is still in persistent state. Hence, in the second transaction, you not only load a `User` object, but also update the modified persistent `item` when the second transaction is committed (in addition to an update for the dirty `user` instance).

Just like in native Hibernate code with a `Session`, the persistence context begins with `createEntityManager()` and ends with `close()`.

Closing the persistence context isn't the only way to detach an entity instance.

Manual detachment of entity instances

An entity instance becomes detached when it leaves the persistence context. A method on the `EntityManager` allows you to clear the persistence context and detach all persistent instances:

```
EntityManager em = emf.createEntityManager();
EntityTransaction tx = em.getTransaction();

tx.begin();
Item item = em.find(Item.class, new Long(1234));

em.clear();

item.setDescription(...); // Detached entity instance!

tx.commit();
em.close();
```

After the `item` is retrieved, you clear the persistence context of the `EntityMan-ager`. All entity instances that have been managed by that persistence context are now detached. The modification of the detached instance isn't synchronized with the database during commit.

> **FAQ** *Where is eviction of individual instances?* The Hibernate `Session` API features the `evict(object)` method. Java Persistence doesn't have this capability. The reason is probably only known by some expert group members—we can't explain it. (Note that this is a nice way of saying that experts couldn't agree on the semantics of the operation.) You can only clear the persistence context completely and detach all persistent objects. You have to fall back to the `Session` API as described in chapter 2, section 2.2.4, "Switching to Hibernate interfaces," if you want to evict individual instances from the persistence context.

Obviously you also want to save any modifications you made to a detached entity instance at some point.

Merging detached entity instances

Whereas Hibernate offers two strategies, *reattachment* and *merging*, to synchronize any changes of detached objects with the database, Java Persistence only offers the latter. Let's assume you've retrieved an `item` entity instance in a previous persistence context, and now you want to modify it and save these modifications.

```
EntityManager em = emf.createEntityManager();
EntityTransaction tx = em.getTransaction();
tx.begin();

Item item = em.find(Item.class, new Long(1234));
```

```
tx.commit();
em.close();

item.setDescription(...); // Detached entity instance!

EntityManager em2 = emf.createEntityManager();
EntityTransaction tx2 = em2.getTransaction();
tx2.begin();

Item mergedItem = (Item) em2.merge(item);

tx2.commit();
em2.close();
```

The item is retrieved in a first persistence context and merged, after modification in detached state, into a new persistence context. The merge() operation does several things:

First, the Java Persistence engine checks whether a persistent instance in the persistence context has the same database identifier as the detached instance you're merging. Because, in our code examples, there is no equal persistent instance in the second persistence context, one is retrieved from the database through lookup by identifier. Then, the detached entity instance is *copied* onto the persistent instance. In other words, the new description that has been set on the detached item is also set on the persistent mergedItem, which is returned from the merge() operation.

If there is no equal persistent instance in the persistence context, and a lookup by identifier in the database is negative, the merged instance is copied onto a fresh persistent instance, which is then inserted into the database when the second persistence context is synchronized with the database.

Merging of state is an alternative to reattachment (as provided by native Hibernate). Refer to our earlier discussion of merging with Hibernate in section 9.3.2, "Merging the state of a detached object"; both APIs offer the same semantics, and the notes there apply for JPA mutatis mutandis.

You're now ready to expand your Java SE application and experiment with the persistence context and detached objects in Java Persistence. Instead of only storing and loading entity instances in a single unit of work, try to use several and try to merge modifications of detached objects. Don't forget to watch your SQL log to see what's going on behind the scenes.

Once you've mastered basic Java Persistence operations with Java SE, you'll probably want to do the same in a managed environment. The benefits you get from JPA in a full EJB 3.0 container are substantial. No longer do you have to manage EntityManager and EntityTransaction yourself. You can focus on what you're supposed to do: load and store objects.

9.5   *Using Java Persistence in EJB components*

A managed runtime environment implies some sort of container. Your application components live inside this container. Most containers these days are implemented using an interception technique, method calls on objects are intercepted and any code that needs to be executed before (or after) the method is applied. This is perfect for any *cross-cutting concerns*: Opening and closing an `EntityManager`, because you need it *inside* the method that is called, is certainly one. Your business logic doesn't need to be concerned with this aspect. Transaction demarcation is another concern a container can take care of for you. (You'll likely find other aspects in any application.)

Unlike older application servers from the EJB 2.x era, containers that support EJB 3.0 and other Java EE 5.0 services are easy to install and use—refer to our discussion in chapter 2, section 2.2.3, "Introducing EJB components," to prepare your system for the following section. Furthermore, the EJB 3.0 programming model is based on plain Java classes. You shouldn't be surprised if you see us writing many EJBs in this book; most of the time, the only difference from a plain JavaBean is a simple annotation, a declaration that you wish to use a service provided by the environment the component will run in. If you can't modify the source code and add an annotation, you can turn a class into an EJB with an XML deployment descriptor. Hence, (almost) every class can be a managed component in EJB 3.0, which makes it much easier for you to benefit from Java EE 5.0 services.

The entity classes you've created so far aren't enough to write an application. You also want stateless or stateful session beans, components that you can use to encapsulate your application logic. Inside these components, you need the services of the container: for example, you usually want the container to *inject* an `EntityManager`, so that you can load and store entity instances.

9.5.1   *Injecting an EntityManager*

Remember how you create an instance of an `EntityManager` in Java SE? You have to open it from an `EntityManagerFactory` and close it manually. You also have to begin and end a resource-local transaction with the `EntityTransaction` interface.

In an EJB 3.0 server, a container-managed `EntityManager` is available through *dependency injection.* Consider the following EJB session bean that implements a particular action in the CaveatEmptor application:

```
@Stateless
public class ManageAuctionBean implements ManageAuction {

    // Use field injection:
```

```
@PersistenceContext
private EntityManager em;

// or setter injection:
//
// @PersistenceContext
// public void setEntityManager(EntityManager em) {
//    this.em = em;
// }

@TransactionAttribute(TransactionAttributeType.REQUIRED)
public Item findAuctionByName(String name) {
    return (Item) em.createQuery()...
    ...
}
}
```

It's a stateless action, and it implements the ManageAuction interface. These details of stateless EJBs aren't our concern at this time, what is interesting is that you can access the EntityManager in the findAuctionByName() method of the action. The container automatically *injects* an instance of an EntityManager into the em field of the bean, before the action method executes. The visibility of the field isn't important for the container, but you need to apply the @Persistence-Context annotation to indicate that you want the container's service. You could also create a public setter method for this field and apply the annotation on this method. This is the recommended approach if you also plan to set the Entity-Manager manually—for example, during integration or functional testing.

The injected EntityManager is maintained by the container. You don't have to flush or close it, nor do you have to start and end a transaction—in the previous example you tell the container that the findAuctionByName() method of the session bean *requires* a transaction. (This is the default for all EJB session bean methods.) A transaction must be active when the method is called by a client (or a new transaction is started automatically). When the method returns, the transaction either continues or is committed, depending on whether it was started for this method.

The persistence context of the injected container-managed EntityManager is bound to the scope of the transaction, Hence, it's flushed automatically and closed when the transaction ends. This is an important difference, if you compare it with earlier examples that showed JPA in Java SE! The persistence context there wasn't scoped to the transaction but to the EntityManager instance you closed explicitly. The transaction-scoped persistence context is the natural default for a stateless bean, as you'll see when you focus on conversation implementation and transactions later, in the following chapters.

A nice trick that obviously works only with JBoss EJB 3.0 is the automatic injection of a `Session` object, instead of an `EntityManager`:

```
@Stateless
public class ManageAuctionBean implements ManageAuction {

    @PersistenceContext
    private Session session;
    ...

}
```

This is mostly useful if you have a managed component that would rely on the Hibernate API.

Here is a variation that works with two databases—that is, two persistence units:

```
@Stateless
public class ManageAuctionBean implements ManageAuction {

    @PersistenceContext(unitName = "auctionDB")
    private EntityManager auctionEM;

    @PersistenceContext(unitName = "auditDB")
    private EntityManager auditEM;

    @TransactionAttribute(TransactionAttributeType.REQUIRED)
    public void createAuction(String name, BigDecimal price) {
        Item newItem = new Item(name, price);
        auctionEM.persist(newItem);
        auditEM.persist( new CreateAuctionEvent(newItem) );
        ...
    }

}
```

The `unitName` refers to the configured and deployed persistence unit. If you work with one database (one `EntityManagerFactory` or one `SessionFactory`), you don't need to declare the name of the persistence unit for injection. Note that `EntityManager` instances from two different persistence units aren't sharing the same persistence context. Naturally, both are independent caches of managed entity objects, but that doesn't mean they can't participate in the same system transaction.

If you write EJBs with Java Persistence, the choice is clear: You want the `EntityManager` with the right persistence context injected into your managed components by the container. An alternative you'll rarely use is the *lookup* of a container-managed `EntityManager`.

9.5.2   Looking up an EntityManager

Instead of letting the container inject an `EntityManager` on your field or setter method, you can look it up from JNDI when you need it:

```
@Stateless
@PersistenceContext(name = "em/auction", unitName = "auctionDB")
public class ManageAuctionBean implements ManageAuction {

    @Resource
    SessionContext ctx;

    @TransactionAttribute(TransactionAttributeType.REQUIRED)
    public Item findAuctionByName(String name) {
        EntityManager em = (EntityManager) ctx.lookup("em/auction");

        return (Item) em.createQuery()...
    }

}
```

Several things are happening in this code snippet: First, you declare that you want the component environment of the bean populated with an `EntityManager` and that the name of the bound reference is supposed to be `em/auction`. The full name in JNDI is `java:comp/env/em/auction`—the `java:comp/env/` part is the so called *bean-naming context*. Everything in that subcontext of JNDI is bean-dependent. In other words, the EJB container reads this annotation and knows that it has to bind an `EntityManager` for this bean only, at runtime when the bean executes, under the namespace in JNDI that is reserved for this bean.

You look up the `EntityManager` in your bean implementation with the help of the `SessionContext`. The benefit of this context is that it automatically prefixes the name you're looking for with `java:comp/env/`; hence, it tries to find the reference in the bean's naming context, and not the global JNDI namespace. The `@Resource` annotation instructs the EJB container to inject the `SessionContext` for you.

A persistence context is created by the container when the first method on the `EntityManager` is called, and it's flushed and closed when the transaction ends—when the method returns.

Injection and lookup are also available if you need an `EntityManagerFactory`.

9.5.3   Accessing an EntityManagerFactory

An EJB container also allows you to access an `EntityManagerFactory` for a persistence unit directly. Without a managed environment, you have to create the `EntityManagerFactory` with the help of the `Persistence` bootstrap class. In a container, you can again utilize automatic dependency injection to get an EntityManagerFactory:

```
@Stateless
public class ManageAuctionBean implements ManageAuction {

    @PersistenceUnit(unitName = "auctionDB")
    EntityManagerFactory auctionDB;

    @TransactionAttribute(TransactionAttributeType.REQUIRED)
    public Item findAuctionByName(String name) {
        EntityManager em = auctionDB.createEntityManager();
        ...
        Item item = (Item) em.createQuery()...
        ...
        em.flush();
        em.close();
        return item;
    }

}
```

The unitName attribute is optional and only required if you have more than one configured persistence unit (several databases). The EntityManager you created from the injected factory is again application-managed—the container won't flush this persistence context, nor close it. It's rare that you mix container-managed factories with application-managed EntityManager instances, but doing so is useful if you need more control over the lifecycle of an EntityManager in an EJB component.

You may create an EntityManager *outside* of any JTA transaction boundaries; for example, in an EJB method that doesn't require a transaction context. It's then your responsibility to notify the EntityManager that a JTA transaction is active, when needed, with the joinTransaction() method. Note that this operation doesn't bind or scope the persistence context to the JTA transaction; it's only a hint that switches the EntityManager to transactional behavior internally.

The previous statements aren't complete: If you close() the EntityManager, it doesn't immediately close its persistence context, if this persistence context has been associated with a transaction. The persistence context is closed when the transaction completes. However, any call of the closed EntityManager throws an exception (except for the getTransaction() method in Java SE and the isOpen() method). You can switch this behavior with the hibernate. ejb.discard_ pc_on_close configuration setting. You don't have to worry about this if you never call the EntityManager outside of transaction boundaries.

Another reason for accessing your `EntityManagerFactory` may be that you want to access a particular vendor extension on this interface, like we discussed in chapter 2, section 2.2.4, "Switching to Hibernate interfaces."

You can also look up an `EntityManagerFactory` if you bind it to the EJB's naming context first:

```
@Stateless
@PersistenceUnit(name= "emf/auction", unitName = "auctionDB")
public class ManageAuctionBean implements ManageAuction {

    @Resource
    SessionContext ctx;

    @TransactionAttribute(TransactionAttributeType.REQUIRED)
    public Item findAuctionByName(String name) {
        EntityManagerFactory auctionDB =
            (EntityManagerFactory) ctx.lookup("emf/auction");

        EntityManager em = auctionDB.createEntityManager();
        ...
        Item item = (Item) em.createQuery()...
        ...

        em.flush();
        em.close();
        return item;
    }
}
```

Again, there is no particular advantage if you compare the lookup technique with automatic injection.

9.6 Summary

We've covered a lot of ground in this chapter. You now know that the basic interfaces in Java Persistence aren't much different from those provided by Hibernate. Loading and storing objects is almost the same. The scope of the persistence context is slightly different, though; in Hibernate, it's by default the same as the `Session` scope. In Java Persistence, the scope of the persistence context varies, depending on whether you create an `EntityManager` yourself, or you let the container manage and bind it to the current transaction scope in an EJB component.

Table 9.1 shows a summary you can use to compare native Hibernate features and Java Persistence.

We've already talked about conversations in an application and how you can design them with detached objects or with an extended persistence context. Although we haven't had time to discuss every detail, you can probably already see

Table 9.1 Hibernate and JPA comparison chart for chapter 9

Hibernate Core	Java Persistence and EJB 3.0
Hibernate defines and relies on four object states: transient, persistent, removed, and detached.	Equivalent object states are standardized and defined in EJB 3.0.
Detached objects can be reattached to a new persistence context or merged onto persistent instances.	Only merging is supported with the Java Persistence management interfaces.
At flush-time, the `save()` and `update()` operations can be cascaded to all associated and reachable instances. The `persist()` operation can only be cascaded to reachable instances at call-time.	At flush-time, the `persist()` operation can be cascaded to all associated and reachable instances. If you fall back to the `Session` API, `save()` and `update()` are only cascaded to reachable instances at call-time.
A `get()` hits the database; a `load()` may return a proxy.	A `find()` hits the database; a `getReference()` may return a proxy.
Dependency injection of a `Session` in an EJB works only in JBoss Application Server.	Dependency injection of an `EntityManager` works in all EJB 3.0 components.

that working with detached objects requires discipline (outside of the guaranteed scope of object identity) and manual reattachment or merging. In practice, and from our experience over the years, we recommend that you consider detached objects a secondary option and that you first look at an implementation of conversations with an extended persistence context.

Unfortunately, we still don't have all the pieces to write a really sophisticated application with conversations. You may especially miss more information about transactions. The next chapter covers transaction concepts and interfaces.

10
Transactions and concurrency

This chapter covers

- Database transactions
- Transactions with Hibernate and Java Persistence
- Nontransactional data access

In this chapter, we finally talk about *transactions* and how you create and control units of work in a application. We'll show you how transactions work at the lowest level (the database) and how you work with transactions in an application that is based on native Hibernate, on Java Persistence, and with or without Enterprise JavaBeans.

Transactions allow you to set the boundaries of a unit of work: an atomic group of operations. They also help you isolate one unit of work from another unit of work in a multiuser application. We talk about concurrency and how you can control concurrent data access in your application with pessimistic and optimistic strategies.

Finally, we look at nontransactional data access and when you should work with your database in autocommit mode.

10.1 *Transaction essentials*

Let's start with some background information. Application functionality requires that several things be done at the same time. For example, when an auction finishes, three different tasks have to be performed by the CaveatEmptor application:

1 Mark the winning (highest amount) bid.

2 Charge the seller the cost of the auction.

3 Notify the seller and successful bidder.

What happens if you can't bill the auction costs because of a failure in the external credit-card system? The business requirements may state that either all listed actions must succeed or none must succeed. If so, you call these steps collectively a *transaction* or *unit of work*. If only one step fails, the whole unit of work must fail. This is known as *atomicity*, the notion that all operations are executed as an atomic unit.

Furthermore, transactions allow multiple users to work concurrently with the same data without compromising the integrity and correctness of the data; a particular transaction should not be visible to other concurrently running transactions. Several strategies are important to fully understand this *isolation* behavior, and we'll explore them in this chapter.

Transactions have other important attributes, such as *consistency* and *durability*. Consistency means that a transaction works on a consistent set of data: a set of data that is hidden from other concurrently running transactions and that is left in a clean and consistent state after the transactions completes. Your database integrity rules guarantee consistency. You also want *correctness* of a transaction. For example, the business rules dictate that the seller is charged once, not twice. This is a reasonable assumption, but you may not be able to express it with database constraints. Hence, the correctness of a transaction is the responsibility of the application, whereas consistency is the responsibility of the database. *Durability* means that once a transaction completes, all changes made during that transaction become persistent and aren't lost even if the system subsequently fails.

Together, these transaction attributes are known as the *ACID* criteria.

Database transactions have to be short. A single transaction usually involves only a single batch of database operations. In practice, you also need a concept that allows you to have long-running *conversations*, where an atomic group of database operations occur in not one but several batches. Conversations allow the user of your application to have think-time, while still guaranteeing atomic, isolated, and consistent behavior.

Now that we've defined our terms, we can talk about transaction *demarcation* and how you can define the boundaries of a unit of work.

10.1.1 *Database and system transactions*

Databases implement the notion of a unit of work as a *database transaction*. A database transaction groups data-access operations—that is, SQL operations. All SQL statements execute inside a transaction; there is no way to send an SQL statement to a database outside of a database transaction. A transaction is guaranteed to end in one of two ways: It's either completely *committed* or completely *rolled back*. Hence, we say database transactions are *atomic*. In figure 10.1, you can see this graphically.

To execute all your database operations inside a transaction, you have to mark the boundaries of that unit of work. You must start the transaction and at some point, commit the changes. If an error occurs (either while executing operations or when committing the transaction), you have to roll back the transaction to leave the data in a consistent state. This is known as *transaction demarcation* and, depending on the technique you use, involves more or less manual intervention.

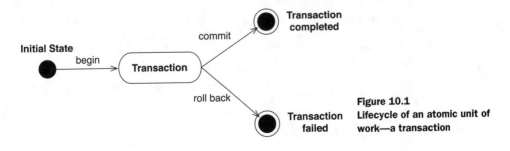

Figure 10.1
Lifecycle of an atomic unit of work—a transaction

In general, transaction boundaries that begin and end a transaction can be set either programmatically in application code or declaratively.

Programmatic transaction demarcation

In a nonmanaged environment, the JDBC API is used to mark transaction boundaries. You begin a transaction by calling `setAutoCommit(false)` on a JDBC Connection and end it by calling `commit()`. You may, at any time, force an immediate rollback by calling `rollback()`.

In a system that manipulates data in several databases, a particular unit of work involves access to more than one resource. In this case, you can't achieve atomicity with JDBC alone. You need a *transaction manager* that can handle several resources in one *system transaction*. Such transaction-processing systems expose the *Java Transaction API* (JTA) for interaction with the developer. The main API in JTA is the `UserTransaction` interface with methods to `begin()` and `commit()` a system transaction.

Furthermore, programmatic transaction management in a Hibernate application is exposed to the application developer via the Hibernate `Transaction` interface. You aren't forced to use this API—Hibernate also lets you begin and end JDBC transactions directly, but this usage is discouraged because it binds your code to direct JDBC. In a Java EE environment (or if you installed it along with your Java SE application), a JTA-compatible transaction manager is available, so you should call the JTA `UserTransaction` interface to begin and end a transaction programmatically. However, the Hibernate `Transaction` interface, as you may have guessed, also works on top of JTA. We'll show you all these options and discuss portability concerns in more detail.

Programmatic transaction demarcation with Java Persistence also has to work inside and outside of a Java EE application server. Outside of an application server, with plain Java SE, you're dealing with resource-local transactions; this is what the `EntityTransaction` interface is good for—you've seen it in previous chapters. Inside an application server, you call the JTA `UserTransaction` interface to begin and end a transaction.

Let's summarize these interfaces and when they're used:

- `java.sql.Connection`—Plain JDBC transaction demarcation with `setAutoCommit(false)`, `commit()`, and `rollback()`. It can but shouldn't be used in a Hibernate application, because it binds your application to a plain JDBC environment.

- `org.hibernate.Transaction`—Unified transaction demarcation in Hibernate applications. It works in a nonmanaged plain JDBC environment and also in an application server with JTA as the underlying system transaction service. The main benefit, however, is tight integration with persistence context management—for example, a `Session` is flushed automatically when you commit. A persistence context can also have the scope of this transaction (useful for conversations; see the next chapter). Use this API in Java SE if you can't have a JTA-compatible transaction service.

- `javax.transaction.UserTransaction`—Standardized interface for programmatic transaction control in Java; part of JTA. This should be your primary choice whenever you have a JTA-compatible transaction service and want to control transactions programmatically.

- `javax.persistence.EntityTransaction`—Standardized interface for programmatic transaction control in Java SE applications that use Java Persistence.

Declarative transaction demarcation, on the other hand, doesn't require extra coding; and by definition, it solves the problem of portability.

Declarative transaction demarcation

In your application, you declare (for example, with annotations on methods) when you wish to work inside a transaction. It's then the responsibility of the application deployer and the runtime environment to handle this concern. The standard container that provides declarative transaction services in Java is an EJB container, and the service is also called *container-managed transactions* (CMT). We'll again write EJB session beans to show how both Hibernate and Java Persistence can benefit from this service.

Before you decide on a particular API, or for declarative transaction demarcation, let's explore these options step by step. First, we assume you're going to use native Hibernate in a plain Java SE application (a client/server web application, desktop application, or any two-tier system). After that, you'll refactor the code to run in a managed Java EE environment (and see how to avoid that refactoring in the first place). We also discuss Java Persistence along the way.

10.1.2 Transactions in a Hibernate application

Imagine that you're writing a Hibernate application that has to run in plain Java; no container and no managed database resources are available.

Programmatic transactions in Java SE

You configure Hibernate to create a JDBC connection pool for you, as you did in "The database connection pool" in chapter 2, section 2.1.3. In addition to the connection pool, no additional configuration settings are necessary if you're writing a Java SE Hibernate application with the `Transaction` API:

- The `hibernate.transaction.factory_class` option defaults to `org.hibernate.transaction.JDBCTransactionFactory`, which is the correct factory for the `Transaction` API in Java SE and for direct JDBC.

- You can extend and customize the `Transaction` interface with your own implementation of a `TransactionFactory`. This is rarely necessary but has some interesting use cases. For example, if you have to write an audit log whenever a transaction is started, you can add this logging to a custom `Transaction` implementation.

Hibernate obtains a JDBC connection for each `Session` you're going to work with:

```
Session session = null;
Transaction tx = null;

try {
    session = sessionFactory.openSession();
    tx = session.beginTransaction();

    concludeAuction(session);

    tx.commit();
} catch (RuntimeException ex) {
    tx.rollback();
} finally {
    session.close();
}
```

A Hibernate `Session` is lazy. This is a good thing—it means it doesn't consume any resources unless they're absolutely needed. A JDBC `Connection` from the connection pool is obtained only when the database transaction begins. The call to `beginTransaction()` translates into `setAutoCommit(false)` on the fresh JDBC `Connection`. The `Session` is now bound to this database connection, and all SQL statements (in this case, all SQL required to conclude the auction) are sent on this connection. All database statements execute inside the same database transaction. (We assume that the `concludeAuction()` method calls the given `Session` to access the database.)

We already talked about *write-behind* behavior, so you know that the bulk of SQL statements are executed as late as possible, when the persistence context of the

Session is flushed. This happens when you call commit() on the Transaction, by default. After you commit the transaction (or roll it back), the database connection is released and unbound from the Session. Beginning a new transaction with the same Session obtains another connection from the pool.

Closing the Session releases all other resources (for example, the persistence context); all managed persistent instances are now considered detached.

FAQ *Is it faster to roll back read-only transactions?* If code in a transaction reads data but doesn't modify it, should you roll back the transaction instead of committing it? Would this be faster? Apparently, some developers found this to be faster in some special circumstances, and this belief has spread through the community. We tested this with the more popular database systems and found no difference. We also failed to discover any source of real numbers showing a performance difference. There is also no reason why a database system should have a suboptimal implementation—why it should not use the fastest transaction cleanup algorithm internally. Always commit your transaction and roll back if the commit fails. Having said that, the SQL standard includes a SET TRANSACTION READ ONLY statement. Hibernate doesn't support an API that enables this setting, although you could implement your own custom Transaction and TransactionFactory to add this operation. We recommend you first investigate if this is supported by your database and what the possible performance benefits, if any, will be.

We need to discuss exception handling at this point.

Handling exceptions

If concludeAuction() as shown in the last example (or flushing of the persistence context during commit) throws an exception, you must force the transaction to roll back by calling tx.rollback(). This rolls back the transaction immediately, so no SQL operation you sent to the database has any permanent effect.

This seems straightforward, although you can probably already see that catching RuntimeException whenever you want to access the database won't result in nice code.

NOTE *A history of exceptions*—Exceptions and how they should be handled always end in heated debates between Java developers. It isn't surprising that Hibernate has some noteworthy history as well. Until Hibernate 3.x, all exceptions thrown by Hibernate were *checked* exceptions, so every Hibernate API forced the developer to catch and handle exceptions. This strategy was influenced by JDBC, which also throws only checked exceptions. However, it soon became clear that this doesn't make sense, because all exceptions thrown by Hibernate are fatal. In many cases, the best a developer can do in this situation is to clean up, display an error message, and exit the application. Therefore, starting with Hibernate 3.x, all exceptions thrown by Hibernate are subtypes of the unchecked `Runtime-Exception`, which is usually handled in a single location in an application. This also makes any Hibernate template or wrapper API obsolete.

First, even though we admit that you wouldn't write your application code with dozens (or hundreds) of `try`/`catch` blocks, the example we showed isn't complete. This is an example of the standard idiom for a Hibernate unit of work with a database transaction that contains real exception handling:

```
Session session = null;
Transaction tx = null;

try {
    session = sessionFactory.openSession();
    tx = session.beginTransaction();

    tx.setTimeout(5);

    concludeAuction(session);

    tx.commit();
} catch (RuntimeException ex) {
    try {
        tx.rollback();
    } catch (RuntimeException rbEx) {
        log.error("Couldn't roll back transaction", rbEx);
    }
    throw ex;
} finally {
    session.close();
}
```

Any Hibernate operation, including flushing the persistence context, can throw a `RuntimeException`. Even rolling back a transaction can throw an exception! You want to catch this exception and log it; otherwise, the original exception that led to the rollback is swallowed.

An optional method call in the example is `setTimeout()`, which takes the number of seconds a transaction is allowed to run. However, *real* monitored transactions aren't available in a Java SE environment. The best Hibernate can do if you run this code outside of an application server (that is, without a transaction manager) is to set the number of seconds the driver will wait for a `Prepared-Statement` to execute (Hibernate exclusively uses prepared statements). If the limit is exceeded, an `SQLException` is thrown.

You don't want to use this example as a template in your own application, because you should hide the exception handling with generic infrastructure code. You can, for example, write a single error handler for `RuntimeException` that knows when and how to roll back a transaction. The same can be said about opening and closing a `Session`. We discuss this with more realistic examples later in the next chapter and again in chapter 16, section 16.1.3, "The Open Session in View pattern."

Hibernate throws *typed* exceptions, all subtypes of `RuntimeException` that help you identify errors:

- The most common `HibernateException` is a generic error. You have to either check the exception message or find out more about the cause by calling `getCause()` on the exception.

- A `JDBCException` is any exception thrown by Hibernate's internal JDBC layer. This kind of exception is always caused by a particular SQL statement, and you can get the offending statement with `getSQL()`. The internal exception thrown by the JDBC connection (the JDBC driver, actually) is available with `getSQLException()` or `getCause()`, and the database- and vendor-specific error code is available with `getErrorCode()`.

- Hibernate includes subtypes of `JDBCException` and an internal converter that tries to translate the vendor-specific error code thrown by the database driver into something more meaningful. The built-in converter can produce `JDBCConnectionException`, `SQLGrammarException`, `LockAquisition-Exception`, `DataException`, and `ConstraintViolationException` for the most important database dialects supported by Hibernate. You can either manipulate or enhance the dialect for your database, or plug in a `SQLExceptionConverterFactory` to customize this conversion.

- Other `RuntimeExceptions` thrown by Hibernate should also abort a transaction. You should always make sure you catch `RuntimeException`, no matter what you plan to do with any fine-grained exception-handling strategy.

You now know what exceptions you should catch and when to expect them. However, one question is probably on your mind: What should you do *after* you've caught an exception?

All exceptions thrown by Hibernate are fatal. This means you have to roll back the database transaction and close the current `Session`. You aren't allowed to continue working with a `Session` that threw an exception.

Usually, you also have to exit the application after you close the `Session` following an exception, although there are some exceptions (for example, `StaleObjectStateException`) that naturally lead to a new attempt (possibly after interacting with the application user again) in a new `Session`. Because these are closely related to conversations and concurrency control, we'll cover them later.

> **FAQ**   *Can I use exceptions for validation?*   Some developers get excited once they see how many fine-grained exception types Hibernate can throw. This can lead you down the wrong path. For example, you may be tempted to catch the `ConstraintViolationException` for validation purposes. If a particular operation throws this exception, why not display a (customized depending on the error code and text) failure message to application users and let them correct the mistake? This strategy has two significant disadvantages. First, throwing unchecked values against the database to see what sticks isn't the right strategy for a scalable application. You want to implement at least some data-integrity validation in the application layer. Second, all exceptions are fatal for your current unit of work. However, this isn't how application users will interpret a validation error—they expect to still be inside a unit of work. Coding around this mismatch is awkward and difficult. Our recommendation is that you use the fine-grained exception types to display better looking (fatal) error messages. Doing so helps you during development (no fatal exceptions should occur in production, ideally) and also helps any customer-support engineer who has to decide quickly if it's an application error (constraint violated, wrong SQL executed) or if the database system is under load (locks couldn't be acquired).

Programmatic transaction demarcation in Java SE with the Hibernate `Transaction` interface keeps your code portable. It can also run inside a managed environment, when a transaction manager handles the database resources.

Programmatic transactions with JTA

A managed runtime environment compatible with Java EE can manage resources for you. In most cases, the resources that are managed are database connections, but any resource that has an adaptor can integrate with a Java EE system (messaging or legacy systems, for example). Programmatic transaction demarcation on those resources, if they're transactional, is unified and exposed to the developer with JTA; `javax.transaction.UserTransaction` is the primary interface to begin and end transactions.

The common managed runtime environment is a Java EE application server. Of course, application servers provide many more services, not only management of resources. Many Java EE services are modular—installing an application server isn't the only way to get them. You can obtain a *stand-alone* JTA provider if managed resources are all you need. Open source stand-alone JTA providers include *JBoss Transactions* (http://www.jboss.com/products/transactions), *ObjectWeb JOTM* (http://jotm.objectweb.org), and others. You can install such a JTA service along with your Hibernate application (in Tomcat, for example). It will manage a pool of database connections for you, provide JTA interfaces for transaction demarcation, and provide managed database connections through a JNDI registry.

The following are benefits of managed resources with JTA and reasons to use this Java EE service:

- A transaction-management service can unify all resources, no matter of what type, and expose transaction control to you with a single standardized API. This means that you can *replace* the Hibernate `Transaction` API and use JTA directly everywhere. It's then the responsibility of the application deployer to install the application on (or with) a JTA-compatible runtime environment. This strategy moves portability concerns where they belong; the application relies on standardized Java EE interfaces, and the runtime environment has to provide an implementation.

- A Java EE transaction manager can enlist multiple resources in a single transaction. If you work with several databases (or more than one resource), you probably want a *two-phase commit* protocol to guarantee atomicity of a transaction across resource boundaries. In such a scenario, Hibernate is configured with several `SessionFactory`s, one for each database, and their `Session`s obtain managed database connections that all participate in the same system transaction.

- The quality of JTA implementations is usually higher compared to simple JDBC connection pools. Application servers and stand-alone JTA providers that are modules of application servers usually have had more testing in high-end systems with a large transaction volume.

- JTA providers don't add unnecessary overhead at runtime (a common misconception). The simple case (a single JDBC database) is handled as efficiently as with plain JDBC transactions. The connection pool managed behind a JTA service is probably much better software than a random connection pooling library you'd use with plain JDBC.

Let's assume that you aren't sold on JTA and that you want to continue using the Hibernate `Transaction` API to keep your code runnable in Java SE *and* with managed Java EE services, without any code changes. To deploy the previous code examples, which all call the Hibernate `Transaction` API, on a Java EE application server, you need to switch the Hibernate configuration to JTA:

- The `hibernate.transaction.factory_class` option must be set to `org.hibernate.transaction.JTATransactionFactory`.

- Hibernate needs to know the JTA implementation on which you're deploying, for two reasons: First, different implementations may expose the JTA `UserTransaction`, which Hibernate has to call internally now, under different names. Second, Hibernate has to hook into the synchronization process of the JTA transaction manager to handle its caches. You have to set the `hibernate.transaction.manager_lookup_class` option to configure both: for example, to `org.hibernate.transaction.JBossTransaction-ManagerLookup`. Lookup classes for the most common JTA implementations and application servers are packaged with Hibernate (and can be customized if needed). Check the Javadoc for the package.

- Hibernate is no longer responsible for managing a JDBC connection pool; it obtains managed database connections from the runtime container. These connections are exposed by the JTA provider through JNDI, a global registry. You must configure Hibernate with the right name for your database resources on JNDI, as you did in chapter 2, section 2.4.1, "Integration with JTA."

Now the same piece of code you wrote earlier for Java SE directly on top of JDBC will work in a JTA environment with managed datasources:

```
Session session = null;
Transaction tx = null;

try {
    session = sessionFactory.openSession();
    tx = session.beginTransaction();

    tx.setTimeout(5);

    concludeAuction(session);

    tx.commit();
} catch (RuntimeException ex) {
    try {
        tx.rollback();
    } catch (RuntimeException rbEx) {
        log.error("Couldn't roll back transaction", rbEx);
    }
    throw ex;
```

```
    } finally {
        session.close();
    }
```

However, the database connection-handling is slightly different. Hibernate obtains a managed database connection for each `Session` you're using and, again, tries to be as lazy as possible. Without JTA, Hibernate would hold on to a particular database connection from the beginning until the end of the transaction. With a JTA configuration, Hibernate is even more aggressive: A connection is obtained and used for only a single SQL statement and then is immediately returned to the managed connection pool. The application server guarantees that it will hand out the same connection during the same transaction, when it's needed again for another SQL statement. This aggressive connection-release mode is Hibernate's internal behavior, and it doesn't make any difference for your application and how you write code. (Hence, the code example is line-by-line the same as the last one.)

A JTA system supports global transaction timeouts; it can monitor transactions. So, `setTimeout()` now controls the global JTA timeout setting—equivalent to calling `UserTransaction.setTransactionTimeout()`.

The Hibernate `Transaction` API guarantees portability with a simple change of Hibernate configuration. If you want to move this responsibility to the application deployer, you should write your code against the standardized JTA interface, instead. To make the following example a little more interesting, you'll also work with two databases (two `SessionFactorys`) inside the same system transaction:

```
UserTransaction utx = (UserTransaction) new InitialContext()
                        .lookup("java:comp/UserTransaction");

Session session1 = null;
Session session2 = null;

try {
    utx.begin();

    session1 = auctionDatabase.openSession();
    session2 = billingDatabase.openSession();

    concludeAuction(session1);
    billAuction(session2);

    session1.flush();
    session2.flush();

    utx.commit();
} catch (RuntimeException ex) {
    try {
```

```
        utx.rollback();
    } catch (RuntimeException rbEx) {
        log.error("Couldn't roll back transaction", rbEx);
    }
    throw ex;
} finally {
    session1.close();
    session2.close();
}
```

(Note that this code snippet can throw some other, checked exceptions, like a `NamingException` from the JNDI lookup. You need to handle these accordingly.)

First, a handle on a JTA `UserTransaction` must be obtained from the JNDI registry. Then, you begin and end a transaction, and the (container-provided) database connections used by all Hibernate `Sessions` are enlisted in that transaction automatically. Even if you aren't using the `Transaction` API, you should still configure `hibernate.transaction.factory_class` and `hibernate.transaction.manager_lookup_class` for JTA and your environment, so that Hibernate can interact with the transaction system internally.

With default settings, it's also your responsibility to `flush()` each `Session` manually to synchronize it with the database (to execute all SQL DML). The Hibernate `Transaction` API did this automatically for you. You also have to close all `Sessions` manually. On the other hand, you can enable the `hibernate.transaction.flush_before_completion` and/or the `hibernate.transaction.auto_close_session` configuration options and let Hibernate take care of this for you again—flushing and closing is then part of the internal synchronization procedure of the transaction manager and occurs before (and after, respectively) the JTA transaction ends. With these two settings enabled the code can be simplified to the following:

```
UserTransaction utx = (UserTransaction) new InitialContext()
                    .lookup("java:comp/UserTransaction");

Session session1 = null;
Session session2 = null;

try {
    utx.begin();

    session1 = auctionDatabase.openSession();
    session2 = billingDatabase.openSession();

    concludeAuction(session1);
    billAuction(session2);

    utx.commit();
} catch (RuntimeException ex) {
```

```
    try {
        utx.rollback();
    } catch (RuntimeException rbEx) {
        log.error("Couldn't roll back transaction", rbEx);
    }
    throw ex;
}
```

The `session1` and `session2` persistence context is now flushed automatically during commit of the `UserTransaction`, and both are closed after the transaction completes.

Our advice is to use JTA directly whenever possible. You should always try to move the responsibility for portability outside of the application and, if you can, require deployment in an environment that provides JTA.

Programmatic transaction demarcation requires application code written against a transaction demarcation interface. A much nicer approach that avoids any nonportable code spread throughout your application is *declarative* transaction demarcation.

Container-managed transactions

Declarative transaction demarcation implies that a container takes care of this concern for you. You *declare* if and how you want your code to participate in a transaction. The responsibility to provide a container that supports declarative transaction demarcation is again where it belongs, with the application deployer.

CMT is a standard feature of Java EE and, in particular, EJB. The code we'll show you next is based on EJB 3.0 session beans (Java EE only); you define transaction boundaries with annotations. Note that the actual data-access code doesn't change if you have to use the older EJB 2.1 session beans; however, you have to write an EJB deployment descriptor in XML to create your transaction assembly—this is optional in EJB 3.0.

(A stand-alone JTA implementation doesn't provide container-managed and declarative transactions. However, JBoss Application Server is available as a modular server with a minimal footprint, and it can provide only JTA and an EJB 3.0 container, if needed.)

Suppose that an EJB 3.0 session bean implements an action that ends an auction. The code you previously wrote with programmatic JTA transaction demarcation is moved into a stateless session bean:

```
@Stateless
public class ManageAuctionBean implements ManageAuction {

    @TransactionAttribute(TransactionAttributeType.REQUIRED)
```

```
public void endAuction(Item item) {
    Session session1 = auctionDatabase.openSession();
    Session session2 = billingDatabase.openSession();

    concludeAuction(session1, item);
    billAuction(session2, item);
}
...
}
```

The container notices your declaration of a `TransactionAttribute` and applies it to the `endAuction()` method. If no system transaction is running when the method is called, a new transaction is started (it's `REQUIRED`). Once the method returns, and if the transaction was started when the method was called (and not by anyone else), the transaction commits. The system transaction is automatically rolled back if the code inside the method throws a `RuntimeException`.

We again show two `SessionFactorys` for two databases, for the sake of the example. They could be assigned with a JNDI lookup (Hibernate can bind them there at startup) or from an enhanced version of `HibernateUtil`. Both obtain database connections that are enlisted with the same container-managed transaction. And, if the container's transaction system and the resources support it, you again get a two-phase commit protocol that ensures atomicity of the transaction across databases.

You have to set some configuration options to enable CMT with Hibernate:

- The `hibernate.transaction.factory_class` option must be set to `org.hibernate.transaction.CMTTransactionFactory`.

- You need to set `hibernate.transaction.manager_lookup_class` to the right lookup class for your application server.

Also note that all EJB session beans default to CMT, so if you want to disable CMT and call the JTA `UserTransaction` directly in any session bean method, annotate the EJB class with `@TransactionManagement(TransactionManagementType.BEAN)`. You're then working with *bean-managed transactions* (BMT). Even if it may work in most application servers, mixing CMT and BMT in a single bean isn't allowed by the Java EE specification.

The CMT code already looks much nicer than the programmatic transaction demarcation. If you configure Hibernate to use CMT, it knows that it should flush and close a `Session` that participates in a system transaction automatically. Furthermore, you'll soon improve this code and even remove the two lines that open a Hibernate `Session`.

Let's look at transaction handling in a Java Persistence application.

10.1.3 *Transactions with Java Persistence*

With Java Persistence, you also have the design choice to make between programmatic transaction demarcation in application code or declarative transaction demarcation handled automatically by the runtime container. Let's investigate the first option with plain Java SE and then repeat the examples with JTA and EJB components.

The description *resource-local* transaction applies to all transactions that are controlled by the application (programmatic) and that aren't participating in a global system transaction. They translate directly into the native transaction system of the resource you're dealing with. Because you're working with JDBC databases, this means a resource-local transaction translates into a JDBC database transaction.

Resource-local transactions in JPA are controlled with the EntityTransaction API. This interface exists not for portability reasons, but to enable particular features of Java Persistence—for instance, flushing of the underlying persistence context when you commit a transaction.

You've seen the standard idiom of Java Persistence in Java SE many times. Here it is again with exception handling:

```
EntityManager em = null;
EntityTransaction tx = null;

try {
    em = emf.createEntityManager();
    tx = em.getTransaction();
    tx.begin();

    concludeAuction(em);

    tx.commit();
} catch (RuntimeException ex) {
    try {
        tx.rollback();
    } catch (RuntimeException rbEx) {
        log.error("Couldn't roll back transaction", rbEx);
    }
    throw ex;
} finally {
    em.close();
}
```

This pattern is close to its Hibernate equivalent, with the same implications: You have to manually begin and end a database transaction, and you must guarantee that the application-managed EntityManager is closed in a finally block. (Although we often show code examples that don't handle exceptions or are wrapped in a try/catch block, this isn't optional.)

Exceptions thrown by JPA are subtypes of `RuntimeException`. Any exception invalidates the current persistence context, and you aren't allowed to continue working with the `EntityManager` once an exception has been thrown. Therefore, all the strategies we discussed for Hibernate exception handling also apply to Java Persistence exception handling. In addition, the following rules apply:

- Any exception thrown by any method of the `EntityManager` interfaces triggers an automatic rollback of the current transaction.

- Any exception thrown by any method of the `javax.persistence.Query` interface triggers an automatic rollback of the current transaction, except for `NoResultException` and `NonUniqueResultException`. So, the previous code example that catches all exceptions also executes a rollback for these exceptions.

Note that JPA doesn't offer fine-grained SQL exception types. The most common exception is `javax.persistence.PersistenceException`. All other exceptions thrown are subtypes of `PersistenceException`, and you should consider them all fatal except `NoResultException` and `NonUniqueResultException`. However, you may call `getCause()` on any exception thrown by JPA and find a wrapped native Hibernate exception, including the fine-grained SQL exception types.

If you use Java Persistence inside an application server or in an environment that at least provides JTA (see our earlier discussions for Hibernate), you call the JTA interfaces for programmatic transaction demarcation. The `EntityTransaction` interface is available only for resource-local transactions.

JTA transactions with Java Persistence

If your Java Persistence code is deployed in an environment where JTA is available, and you want to use JTA system transactions, you need to call the JTA `UserTransaction` interface to control transaction boundaries programmatically:

```
UserTransaction utx = (UserTransaction) new InitialContext()
                        .lookup("java:comp/UserTransaction");
EntityManager em = null;

try {
    utx.begin();

    em = emf.createEntityManager();

    concludeAuction(em);

    utx.commit();
} catch (RuntimeException ex) {
    try {
```

```
        utx.rollback();
    } catch (RuntimeException rbEx) {
        log.error("Couldn't roll back transaction", rbEx);
    }
    throw ex;
} finally {
    em.close();
}
```

The persistence context of the `EntityManager` is scoped to the JTA transaction. All SQL statements flushed by this `EntityManager` are executed inside the JTA transaction on a database connection that is enlisted with the transaction. The persistence context is flushed and closed automatically when the JTA transaction commits. You could use several `EntityManagers` to access several databases in the same system transaction, just as you'd use several `Sessions` in a native Hibernate application.

Note that the scope of the persistence context changed! It's now scoped to the JTA transaction, and any object that was in persistent state during the transaction is considered detached once the transaction is committed.

The rules for exception handling are equivalent to those for resource-local transactions. If you use JTA in EJBs, don't forget to set `@TransactionManagement(TransactionManagementType.BEAN)` on the class to enable BMT.

You won't often use Java Persistence with JTA and not also have an EJB container available. If you don't deploy a stand-alone JTA implementation, a Java EE 5.0 application server will provide both. Instead of programmatic transaction demarcation, you'll probably utilize the declarative features of EJBs.

Java Persistence and CMT

Let's refactor the `ManageAuction` EJB session bean from the earlier Hibernate-only examples to Java Persistence interfaces. You also let the container inject an `EntityManager`:

```
@Stateless
public class ManageAuctionBean implements ManageAuction {

    @PersistenceContext(unitName = "auctionDB")
    private EntityManager auctionEM;

    @PersistenceContext(unitName = "billingDB")
    private EntityManager billingEM;

    @TransactionAttribute(TransactionAttributeType.REQUIRED)
    public void endAuction(Item item)
                    throws AuctionNotValidException {

        concludeAuction(auctionEM, item);
```

```
        billAuction(billingEM, item);
    }
    ...
}
```

Again, what happens inside the `concludeAuction()` and `billAuction()` methods isn't relevant for this example; assume that they need the `EntityManagers` to access the database. The `TransactionAttribute` for the `endAuction()` method requires that all database access occurs inside a transaction. If no system transaction is active when `endAuction()` is called, a new transaction is started for this method. If the method returns, and if the transaction was started for this method, it's committed. Each `EntityManager` has a persistence context that spans the scope of the transaction and is flushed automatically when the transaction commits. The persistence context has the same scope as the `endAuction()` method, if no transaction is active when the method is called.

Both persistence units are configured to deploy on JTA, so two managed database connections, one for each database, are enlisted inside the same transaction, and atomicity is guaranteed by the transaction manager of the application server.

You declare that the `endAuction()` method may throw an `AuctionNotValidEx-ception`. This is a custom exception you write; before ending the auction, you check if everything is correct (the end time of the auction has been reached, there is a bid, and so on). This is a checked exception that is a subtype of `java.lang.Exception`. An EJB container treats this as an *application exception* and doesn't trigger any action if the EJB method throws this exception. However, the container recognizes *system exceptions*, which by default are all unchecked `RuntimeExceptions` that may be thrown by an EJB method. A system exception thrown by an EJB method enforces an automatic rollback of the system transaction.

In other words, you don't need to catch and rethrow any system exception from your Java Persistence operations—let the container handle them. You have two choices how you can roll back a transaction if an application exception is thrown: First, you can catch it and call the JTA `UserTransaction` manually, and set it to roll back. Or you can add an `@ApplicationException(rollback = true)` annotation to the class of `AuctionNotValidException`—the container will then recognize that you wish an automatic rollback whenever an EJB method throws this application exception.

You're now ready to use Java Persistence and Hibernate inside and outside of an application server, with or without JTA, and in combination with EJBs and container-managed transactions. We've discussed (almost) all aspects of transaction atomicity. Naturally, you probably still have questions about the *isolation* between concurrently running transactions.

10.2 Controlling concurrent access

Databases (and other transactional systems) attempt to ensure *transaction isolation*, meaning that, from the point of view of each concurrent transaction, it appears that no other transactions are in progress. Traditionally, this has been implemented with *locking*. A transaction may place a lock on a particular item of data in the database, temporarily preventing access to that item by other transactions. Some modern databases such as Oracle and PostgreSQL implement transaction isolation with *multiversion concurrency control* (MVCC) which is generally considered more scalable. We'll discuss isolation assuming a locking model; most of our observations are also applicable to multiversion concurrency, however.

How databases implement concurrency control is of the utmost importance in your Hibernate or Java Persistence application. Applications *inherit* the isolation guarantees provided by the database management system. For example, Hibernate never locks anything in memory. If you consider the many years of experience that database vendors have with implementing concurrency control, you'll see the advantage of this approach. On the other hand, some features in Hibernate and Java Persistence (either because you use them or by design) can improve the isolation guarantee beyond what is provided by the database.

We discuss concurrency control in several steps. We explore the lowest layer and investigate the transaction isolation guarantees provided by the database. Then, we look at Hibernate and Java Persistence features for pessimistic and optimistic concurrency control at the application level, and what other isolation guarantees Hibernate can provide.

10.2.1 Understanding database-level concurrency

Your job as a Hibernate application developer is to understand the capabilities of your database and how to change the database isolation behavior if needed in your particular scenario (and by your data integrity requirements). Let's take a step back. If we're talking about isolation, you may assume that two things are either isolated or not isolated; there is no grey area in the real world. When we talk about database transactions, complete isolation comes at a high price. Several *isolation levels* are available, which, naturally, weaken full isolation but increase performance and scalability of the system.

Transaction isolation issues

First, let's look at several phenomena that may occur when you weaken full transaction isolation. The ANSI SQL standard defines the standard transaction isolation levels in terms of which of these phenomena are permissible in a database management system:

A *lost update* occurs if two transactions both update a row and then the second transaction aborts, causing both changes to be lost. This occurs in systems that don't implement locking. The concurrent transactions aren't isolated. This is shown in figure 10.2.

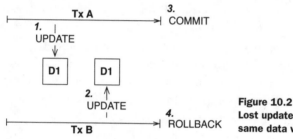

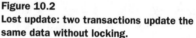

Figure 10.2
Lost update: two transactions update the same data without locking.

A *dirty read* occurs if a one transaction reads changes made by another transaction that has not yet been committed. This is dangerous, because the changes made by the other transaction may later be rolled back, and invalid data may be written by the first transaction, see figure 10.3.

An *unrepeatable read* occurs if a transaction reads a row twice and reads different state each time. For example, another transaction may have written to the row and committed between the two reads, as shown in figure 10.4.

A special case of unrepeatable read is the *second lost updates problem*. Imagine that two concurrent transactions both read a row: One writes to it and commits, and then the second writes to it and commits. The changes made by the first writer are lost. This issue is especially relevant if you think about application

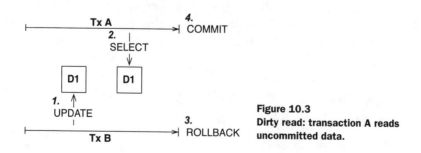

Figure 10.3
Dirty read: transaction A reads uncommitted data.

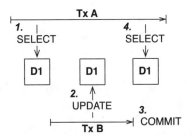

Figure 10.4
Unrepeatable read: transaction A executes two
nonrepeatable reads

conversations that need several database transactions to complete. We'll explore
this case later in more detail.

A *phantom read* is said to occur when a transaction executes a query twice, and
the second result set includes rows that weren't visible in the first result set or rows
that have been deleted. (It need not necessarily be *exactly* the same query.) This
situation is caused by another transaction inserting or deleting rows between the
execution of the two queries, as shown in figure 10.5.

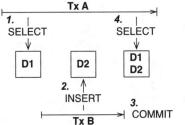

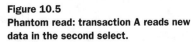

Figure 10.5
Phantom read: transaction A reads new
data in the second select.

Now that you understand all the bad things that can occur, we can define the
transaction isolation levels and see what problems they prevent.

ANSI transaction isolation levels

The standard isolation levels are defined by the ANSI SQL standard, but they
aren't peculiar to SQL databases. JTA defines exactly the same isolation levels, and
you'll use these levels to declare your desired transaction isolation later. With
increased levels of isolation comes higher cost and serious degradation of performance and scalability:

- A system that permits dirty reads but not lost updates is said to operate in
  read uncommitted isolation. One transaction may not write to a row if another
  uncommitted transaction has already written to it. Any transaction may read
  any row, however. This isolation level may be implemented in the database-management system with exclusive write locks.

- A system that permits unrepeatable reads but not dirty reads is said to implement *read committed* transaction isolation. This may be achieved by using shared read locks and exclusive write locks. Reading transactions don't block other transactions from accessing a row. However, an uncommitted writing transaction blocks all other transactions from accessing the row.

- A system operating in *repeatable read* isolation mode permits neither unrepeatable reads nor dirty reads. Phantom reads may occur. Reading transactions block writing transactions (but not other reading transactions), and writing transactions block all other transactions.

- *Serializable* provides the strictest transaction isolation. This isolation level emulates serial transaction execution, as if transactions were executed one after another, serially, rather than concurrently. Serializability may not be implemented using only row-level locks. There must instead be some other mechanism that prevents a newly inserted row from becoming visible to a transaction that has already executed a query that would return the row.

How exactly the locking system is implemented in a DBMS varies significantly; each vendor has a different strategy. You should study the documentation of your DBMS to find out more about the locking system, how locks are escalated (from row-level, to pages, to whole tables, for example), and what impact each isolation level has on the performance and scalability of your system.

It's nice to know how all these technical terms are defined, but how does that help you choose an isolation level for your application?

Choosing an isolation level

Developers (ourselves included) are often unsure what transaction isolation level to use in a production application. Too great a degree of isolation harms scalability of a highly concurrent application. Insufficient isolation may cause subtle, unreproduceable bugs in an application that you'll never discover until the system is working under heavy load.

Note that we refer to *optimistic locking* (with versioning) in the following explanation, a concept explained later in this chapter. You may want to skip this section and come back when it's time to make the decision for an isolation level in your application. Picking the correct isolation level is, after all, highly dependent on your particular scenario. Read the following discussion as recommendations, not carved in stone.

Hibernate tries hard to be as transparent as possible regarding transactional semantics of the database. Nevertheless, caching and optimistic locking affect these semantics. What is a sensible database isolation level to choose in a Hibernate application?

First, eliminate the *read uncommitted* isolation level. It's extremely dangerous to use one transaction's uncommitted changes in a different transaction. The rollback or failure of one transaction will affect other concurrent transactions. Rollback of the first transaction could bring other transactions down with it, or perhaps even cause them to leave the database in an incorrect state. It's even possible that changes made by a transaction that ends up being rolled back could be committed anyway, because they could be read and then propagated by another transaction that *is* successful!

Secondly, most applications don't need *serializable* isolation (phantom reads aren't usually problematic), and this isolation level tends to scale poorly. Few existing applications use serializable isolation in production, but rather rely on pessimistic locks (see next sections) that effectively force a serialized execution of operations in certain situations.

This leaves you a choice between *read committed* and *repeatable read*. Let's first consider repeatable read. This isolation level eliminates the possibility that one transaction can overwrite changes made by another concurrent transaction (the second lost updates problem) if all data access is performed in a single atomic database transaction. A read lock held by a transaction prevents any write lock a concurrent transaction may wish to obtain. This is an important issue, but enabling repeatable read isn't the only way to resolve it.

Let's assume you're using versioned data, something that Hibernate can do for you automatically. The combination of the (mandatory) persistence context cache and versioning already gives you most of the nice features of repeatable read isolation. In particular, versioning prevents the second lost updates problem, and the persistence context cache also ensures that the state of the persistent instances loaded by one transaction is isolated from changes made by other transactions. So, read-committed isolation for all database transactions is acceptable if you use versioned data.

Repeatable read provides more reproducibility for query result sets (only for the duration of the database transaction); but because phantom reads are still possible, that doesn't appear to have much value. You can obtain a repeatable-read guarantee explicitly in Hibernate for a particular transaction and piece of data (with a pessimistic lock).

Setting the transaction isolation level allows you to choose a good default locking strategy for all your database transactions. How do you set the isolation level?

Setting an isolation level

Every JDBC connection to a database is in the default isolation level of the DBMS—usually read committed or repeatable read. You can change this default in the DBMS configuration. You may also set the transaction isolation for JDBC connections on the application side, with a Hibernate configuration option:

```
hibernate.connection.isolation = 4
```

Hibernate sets this isolation level on every JDBC connection obtained from a connection pool before starting a transaction. The sensible values for this option are as follows (you may also find them as constants in `java.sql.Connection`):

- 1—Read uncommitted isolation
- 2—Read committed isolation
- 4—Repeatable read isolation
- 8—Serializable isolation

Note that Hibernate never changes the isolation level of connections obtained from an application server-provided database connection in a managed environment! You can change the default isolation using the configuration of your application server. (The same is true if you use a stand-alone JTA implementation.)

As you can see, setting the isolation level is a global option that affects all connections and transactions. From time to time, it's useful to specify a more restrictive lock for a particular transaction. Hibernate and Java Persistence rely on optimistic concurrency control, and both allow you to obtain additional locking guarantees with version checking and pessimistic locking.

10.2.2 Optimistic concurrency control

An optimistic approach always assumes that everything will be OK and that conflicting data modifications are rare. Optimistic concurrency control raises an error only at the end of a unit of work, when data is written. Multiuser applications usually default to optimistic concurrency control and database connections with a read-committed isolation level. Additional isolation guarantees are obtained only when appropriate; for example, when a repeatable read is required. This approach guarantees the best performance and scalability.

Understanding the optimistic strategy

To understand optimistic concurrency control, imagine that two transactions read a particular object from the database, and both modify it. Thanks to the read-committed isolation level of the database connection, neither transaction will run into

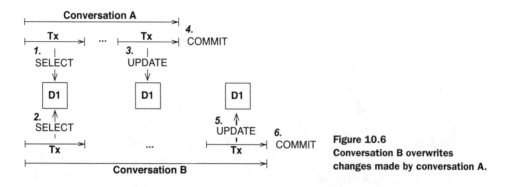

Figure 10.6
Conversation B overwrites
changes made by conversation A.

any dirty reads. However, reads are still nonrepeatable, and updates may also be lost. This is a problem you'll face when you think about conversations, which are atomic transactions from the point of view of your users. Look at figure 10.6.

Let's assume that two users select the same piece of data at the same time. The user in conversation A submits changes first, and the conversation ends with a successful commit of the second transaction. Some time later (maybe only a second), the user in conversation B submits changes. This second transaction also commits successfully. The changes made in conversation A have been lost, and (potentially worse) modifications of data committed in conversation B may have been based on stale information.

You have three choices for how to deal with lost updates in these second transactions in the conversations:

- *Last commit wins*—Both transactions commit successfully, and the second commit overwrites the changes of the first. No error message is shown.

- *First commit wins*—The transaction of conversation A is committed, and the user committing the transaction in conversation B gets an error message. The user must restart the conversation by retrieving fresh data and go through all steps of the conversation again with nonstale data.

- *Merge conflicting updates*—The first modification is committed, and the transaction in conversation B aborts with an error message when it's committed. The user of the failed conversation B may however apply changes selectively, instead of going through all the work in the conversation again.

If you don't enable optimistic concurrency control, and by default it isn't enabled, your application runs with a *last commit wins* strategy. In practice, this issue of lost updates is frustrating for application users, because they may see all their work lost without an error message.

Obviously, *first commit wins* is much more attractive. If the application user of conversation B commits, he gets an error message that reads, *Somebody already committed modifications to the data you're about to commit. You've been working with stale data. Please restart the conversation with fresh data.* It's your responsibility to design and write the application to produce this error message and to direct the user to the beginning of the conversation. Hibernate and Java Persistence help you with automatic optimistic locking, so that you get an exception whenever a transaction tries to commit an object that has a conflicting updated state in the database.

Merge conflicting changes, is a variation of *first commit wins*. Instead of displaying an error message that forces the user to go back all the way, you offer a dialog that allows the user to merge conflicting changes manually. This is the best strategy because no work is lost and application users are less frustrated by optimistic concurrency failures. However, providing a dialog to merge changes is much more time-consuming for you as a developer than showing an error message and forcing the user to repeat all the work. We'll leave it up to you whether you want to use this strategy.

Optimistic concurrency control can be implemented many ways. Hibernate works with automatic versioning.

Enabling versioning in Hibernate

Hibernate provides automatic versioning. Each entity instance has a version, which can be a number or a timestamp. Hibernate increments an object's version when it's modified, compares versions automatically, and throws an exception if a conflict is detected. Consequently, you add this version property to all your persistent entity classes to enable optimistic locking:

```
public class Item {
    ...
    private int version;
    ...
}
```

You can also add a getter method; however, version numbers must not be modified by the application. The <version> property mapping in XML must be placed immediately after the identifier property mapping:

```
<class name="Item" table="ITEM">
    <id .../>

    <version name="version" access="field" column="OBJ_VERSION"/>

    ...
</class>
```

The version number is just a counter value—it doesn't have any useful semantic value. The additional column on the entity table is used by your Hibernate application. Keep in mind that all other applications that access the same database can (and probably should) also implement optimistic versioning and utilize the same version column. Sometimes a timestamp is preferred (or exists):

```
public class Item {
    ...
    private Date lastUpdated;
    ...
}

<class name="Item" table="ITEM">
    <id .../>

    <timestamp name="lastUpdated"
               access="field"
               column="LAST_UPDATED"/>
    ...
</class>
```

In theory, a timestamp is slightly less safe, because two concurrent transactions may both load and update the same item in the same millisecond; in practice, this won't occur because a JVM usually doesn't have millisecond accuracy (you should check your JVM and operating system documentation for the guaranteed precision).

Furthermore, retrieving the current time from the JVM isn't necessarily safe in a clustered environment, where nodes may not be time synchronized. You can switch to retrieval of the current time from the database machine with the `source="db"` attribute on the `<timestamp>` mapping. Not all Hibernate SQL dialects support this (check the source of your configured dialect), and there is always the overhead of hitting the database for every increment.

We recommend that new projects rely on versioning with version numbers, not timestamps.

Optimistic locking with versioning is enabled as soon as you add a `<version>` or a `<timestamp>` property to a persistent class mapping. There is no other switch.

How does Hibernate use the version to detect a conflict?

Automatic management of versions
Every DML operation that involves the now versioned `Item` objects includes a version check. For example, assume that in a unit of work you load an `Item` from the database with version 1. You then modify one of its value-typed properties, such as the price of the `Item`. When the persistence context is flushed, Hibernate detects

that modification and increments the version of the Item to 2. It then executes the SQL UPDATE to make this modification permanent in the database:

```
update ITEM set INITIAL_PRICE='12.99', OBJ_VERSION=2
    where ITEM_ID=123 and OBJ_VERSION=1
```

If another concurrent unit of work updated and committed the same row, the OBJ_VERSION column no longer contains the value 1, and the row isn't updated. Hibernate checks the row count for this statement as returned by the JDBC driver—which in this case is the number of rows updated, zero—and throws a StaleObjectStateException. The state that was present when you loaded the Item is no longer present in the database at flush-time; hence, you're working with stale data and have to notify the application user. You can catch this exception and display an error message or a dialog that helps the user restart a conversation with the application.

What modifications trigger the increment of an entity's version? Hibernate increments the version number (or the timestamp) whenever an entity instance is dirty. This includes all dirty value-typed properties of the entity, no matter if they're single-valued, components, or collections. Think about the relationship between User and BillingDetails, a one-to-many entity association: If a Credit-Card is modified, the version of the related User isn't incremented. If you add or remove a CreditCard (or BankAccount) from the collection of billing details, the version of the User is incremented.

If you want to disable automatic increment for a particular value-typed property or collection, map it with the optimistic-lock="false" attribute. The inverse attribute makes no difference here. Even the version of an owner of an inverse collection is updated if an element is added or removed from the inverse collection.

As you can see, Hibernate makes it incredibly easy to manage versions for optimistic concurrency control. If you're working with a legacy database schema or existing Java classes, it may be impossible to introduce a version or timestamp property and column. Hibernate has an alternative strategy for you.

Versioning without version numbers or timestamps

If you don't have version or timestamp columns, Hibernate can still perform automatic versioning, but only for objects that are retrieved and modified in the same persistence context (that is, the same Session). If you need optimistic locking for conversations implemented with detached objects, you *must* use a version number or timestamp that is transported with the detached object.

This alternative implementation of versioning checks the current database state against the unmodified values of persistent properties at the time the object was retrieved (or the last time the persistence context was flushed). You may enable this functionality by setting the `optimistic-lock` attribute on the class mapping:

```
<class name="Item" table="ITEM" optimistic-lock="all">
    <id .../>
    ...
</class>
```

The following SQL is now executed to flush a modification of an `Item` instance:

```
update ITEM set ITEM_PRICE='12.99'
where ITEM_ID=123
  and ITEM_PRICE='9.99'
  and ITEM_DESCRIPTION="An Item"
  and ...
  and SELLER_ID=45
```

Hibernate lists all columns and their last known nonstale values in the WHERE clause of the SQL statement. If any concurrent transaction has modified any of these values, or even deleted the row, this statement again returns with zero updated rows. Hibernate then throws a `StaleObjectStateException`.

Alternatively, Hibernate includes only the modified properties in the restriction (only ITEM_PRICE, in this example) if you set `optimistic-lock="dirty"`. This means two units of work may modify the same object concurrently, and a conflict is detected only if they both modify the same value-typed property (or a foreign key value). In most cases, this isn't a good strategy for business entities. Imagine that two people modify an auction item concurrently: One changes the price, the other the description. Even if these modifications don't conflict at the lowest level (the database row), they may conflict from a business logic perspective. Is it OK to change the price of an item if the description changed completely? You also need to enable `dynamic-update="true"` on the class mapping of the entity if you want to use this strategy, Hibernate can't generate the SQL for these dynamic UPDATE statements at startup.

We don't recommend versioning without a version or timestamp column in a new application; it's a little slower, it's more complex, and it doesn't work if you're using detached objects.

Optimistic concurrency control in a Java Persistence application is pretty much the same as in Hibernate.

Versioning with Java Persistence

The Java Persistence specification assumes that concurrent data access is handled optimistically, with versioning. To enable automatic versioning for a particular entity, you need to add a version property or field:

```
@Entity
public class Item {
    ...
    @Version
    @Column(name = "OBJ_VERSION")
    private int version;
    ...
}
```

Again, you can expose a getter method but can't allow modification of a version value by the application. In Hibernate, a version property of an entity can be of any numeric type, including primitives, or a `Date` or `Calendar` type. The JPA specification considers only `int`, `Integer`, `short`, `Short`, `long`, `Long`, and `java.sql.Timestamp` as portable version types.

Because the JPA standard doesn't cover optimistic versioning without a version attribute, a Hibernate extension is needed to enable versioning by comparing the old and new state:

```
@Entity
@org.hibernate.annotations.Entity(
    optimisticLock = org.hibernate.annotations.OptimisticLockType.ALL
)
public class Item {
    ...
}
```

You can also switch to `OptimisticLockType.DIRTY` if you only wish to compare modified properties during version checking. You then also need to set the `dynamicUpdate` attribute to `true`.

Java Persistence doesn't standardize which entity instance modifications should trigger an increment of the version. If you use Hibernate as a JPA provider, the defaults are the same—every value-typed property modification, including additions and removals of collection elements, triggers a version increment. At the time of writing, no Hibernate annotation for disabling of version increments on particular properties and collections is available, but a feature request for `@OptimisticLock(excluded=true)` exists. Your version of Hibernate Annotations probably includes this option.

Hibernate EntityManager, like any other Java Persistence provider, throws a `javax.persistence.OptimisticLockException` when a conflicting version is detected. This is the equivalent of the native `StaleObjectStateException` in Hibernate and should be treated accordingly.

We've now covered the basic isolation levels of a database connection, with the conclusion that you should almost always rely on read-committed guarantees from your database. Automatic versioning in Hibernate and Java Persistence prevents lost updates when two concurrent transactions try to commit modifications on the same piece of data. To deal with nonrepeatable reads, you need additional isolation guarantees.

10.2.3 *Obtaining additional isolation guarantees*

There are several ways to prevent nonrepeatable reads and upgrade to a higher isolation level.

Explicit pessimistic locking

We already discussed switching all database connections to a higher isolation level than read committed, but our conclusion was that this is a bad default when scalability of the application is a concern. You need better isolation guarantees only for a particular unit of work. Also remember that the persistence context cache provides repeatable reads for entity instances in persistent state. However, this isn't always sufficient.

For example, you may need repeatable read for scalar queries:

```
Session session = sessionFactory.openSession();
Transaction tx = session.beginTransaction();

Item i = (Item) session.get(Item.class, 123);

String description = (String)
        session.createQuery("select i.description from Item i" +
                            " where i.id = :itemid")
                .setParameter("itemid", i.getId() )
                .uniqueResult();

tx.commit();
session.close();
```

This unit of work executes two reads. The first retrieves an entity instance by identifier. The second read is a scalar query, loading the description of the already loaded `Item` instance again. There is a small window in this unit of work in which a concurrently running transaction may commit an updated item description between the two reads. The second read then returns this committed data, and the variable `description` has a different value than the property `i.getDescription()`.

This example is simplified, but it's enough to illustrate how a unit of work that mixes entity and scalar reads is vulnerable to nonrepeatable reads, if the database transaction isolation level is read committed.

Instead of switching all database transactions into a higher and nonscalable isolation level, you obtain stronger isolation guarantees when necessary with the `lock()` method on the Hibernate `Session`:

```
Session session = sessionFactory.openSession();
Transaction tx = session.beginTransaction();

Item i = (Item) session.get(Item.class, 123);

session.lock(i, LockMode.UPGRADE);

String description = (String)
        session.createQuery("select i.description from Item i" +
                            " where i.id = :itemid")
            .setParameter("itemid", i.getId() )
            .uniqueResult();

tx.commit();
session.close();
```

Using `LockMode.UPGRADE` results in a pessimistic lock held on the database for the row(s) that represent the `Item` instance. Now no concurrent transaction can obtain a lock on the same data—that is, no concurrent transaction can modify the data between your two reads. This can be shortened as follows:

```
Session session = sessionFactory.openSession();
Transaction tx = session.beginTransaction();

Item i = (Item) session.get(Item.class, 123, LockMode.UPGRADE);
...
```

A `LockMode.UPGRADE` results in an SQL `SELECT ... FOR UPDATE` or similar, depending on the database dialect. A variation, `LockMode.UPGRADE_NOWAIT`, adds a clause that allows an immediate failure of the query. Without this clause, the database usually waits when the lock can't be obtained (perhaps because a concurrent transaction already holds a lock). The duration of the wait is database-dependent, as is the actual SQL clause.

FAQ   *Can I use long pessimistic locks?* The duration of a pessimistic lock in Hibernate is a single database transaction. This means you can't use an exclusive lock to block concurrent access for longer than a single database transaction. We consider this a good thing, because the only solution would be an extremely expensive lock held in memory (or a so-called *lock table* in the database) for the duration of, for example, a whole conversation. These kinds of locks are sometimes called *offline* locks. This is almost always a performance bottleneck; every data access involves additional lock checks to a synchronized lock manager. Optimistic locking, however, is the perfect concurrency control strategy and performs well in long-running conversations. Depending on your conflict-resolution options (that is, if you had enough time to implement *merge changes*), your application users are as happy with it as with blocked concurrent access. They may also appreciate not being locked out of particular screens while others look at the same data.

Java Persistence defines `LockModeType.READ` for the same purpose, and the `EntityManager` also has a `lock()` method. The specification doesn't require that this lock mode is supported on nonversioned entities; however, Hibernate supports it on all entities, because it defaults to a pessimistic lock in the database.

The Hibernate lock modes

Hibernate supports the following additional `LockModes`:

- `LockMode.NONE`—Don't go to the database unless the object isn't in any cache.

- `LockMode.READ`—Bypass all caches, and perform a version check to verify that the object in memory is the same version that currently exists in the database.

- `LockMode.UPDGRADE`—Bypass all caches, do a version check (if applicable), and obtain a database-level pessimistic upgrade lock, if that is supported. Equivalent to `LockModeType.READ` in Java Persistence. This mode transparently falls back to `LockMode.READ` if the database SQL dialect doesn't support a `SELECT ... FOR UPDATE` option.

- `LockMode.UPDGRADE_NOWAIT`—The same as `UPGRADE`, but use a `SELECT ... FOR UPDATE NOWAIT`, if supported. This disables waiting for concurrent lock releases, thus throwing a locking exception immediately if the lock can't be obtained. This mode transparently falls back to `LockMode.UPGRADE` if the database SQL dialect doesn't support the `NOWAIT` option.

- `LockMode.FORCE`—Force an increment of the objects version in the database, to indicate that it has been modified by the current transaction. Equivalent to `LockModeType.WRITE` in Java Persistence.

- `LockMode.WRITE`—Obtained automatically when Hibernate has written to a row in the current transaction. (This is an internal mode; you may not specify it in your application.)

By default, load() and get() use LockMode.NONE. A LockMode.READ is most useful with session.lock() and a detached object. Here's an example:

```
Item item = ... ;
Bid bid = new Bid();
item.addBid(bid);
...
Transaction tx = session.beginTransaction();
session.lock(item, LockMode.READ);
tx.commit();
```

This code performs a version check on the detached Item instance to verify that the database row wasn't updated by another transaction since it was retrieved, before saving the new Bid by cascade (assuming the association from Item to Bid has cascading enabled).

(Note that EntityManager.lock() doesn't reattach the given entity instance—it only works on instances that are already in managed persistent state.)

Hibernate LockMode.FORCE and LockModeType.WRITE in Java Persistence have a different purpose. You use them to force a version update if by default no version would be incremented.

Forcing a version increment

If optimistic locking is enabled through versioning, Hibernate increments the version of a modified entity instance automatically. However, sometimes you want to increment the version of an entity instance manually, because Hibernate doesn't consider your changes to be a modification that should trigger a version increment.

Imagine that you modify the owner name of a CreditCard:

```
Session session = getSessionFactory().openSession();
Transaction tx = session.beginTransaction();

User u = (User) session.get(User.class, 123);

u.getDefaultBillingDetails().setOwner("John Doe");

tx.commit();
session.close();
```

When this Session is flushed, the version of the BillingDetail's instance (let's assume it's a credit card) that was modified is incremented automatically by Hibernate. This may not be what you want—you may want to increment the version of the owner, too (the User instance).

Call lock() with LockMode.FORCE to increment the version of an entity instance:

```
Session session = getSessionFactory().openSession();
Transaction tx = session.beginTransaction();

User u = (User) session.get(User.class, 123);

session.lock(u, LockMode.FORCE);

u.getDefaultBillingDetails().setOwner("John Doe");

tx.commit();
session.close();
```

Any concurrent unit of work that works with the same `User` row now knows that this data was modified, even if only one of the values that you'd consider part of the whole aggregate was modified. This technique is useful in many situations where you modify an object and want the version of a root object of an aggregate to be incremented. Another example is a modification of a bid amount for an auction item (if these amounts aren't immutable): With an explicit version increment, you can indicate that the item has been modified, even if none of its value-typed properties or collections have changed. The equivalent call with Java Persistence is `em.lock(o, LockModeType.WRITE)`.

You now have all the pieces to write more sophisticated units of work and create conversations. We need to mention one final aspect of transactions, however, because it becomes essential in more complex conversations with JPA. You must understand how autocommit works and what nontransactional data access means in practice.

10.3   *Nontransactional data access*

Many DBMSs enable the so called *autocommit mode* on every new database connection by default. The autocommit mode is useful for ad hoc execution of SQL.

Imagine that you connect to your database with an SQL console and that you run a few queries, and maybe even update and delete rows. This interactive data access is ad hoc; most of the time you don't have a plan or a sequence of statements that you consider a unit of work. The default autocommit mode on the database connection is perfect for this kind of data access—after all, you don't want to type `begin a transaction` and `end a transaction` for every SQL statement you write and execute. In autocommit mode, a (short) database transaction begins and ends for each SQL statement you send to the database. You're working effectively *nontransactionally*, because there are no atomicity or isolation guarantees for your session with the SQL console. (The only guarantee is that a single SQL statement is atomic.)

An application, by definition, always executes a planned sequence of statements. It seems reasonable that you therefore always create transaction boundaries to group your statements into units that are atomic. Therefore, the autocommit mode has no place in an application.

10.3.1 *Debunking autocommit myths*

Many developers still like to work with an autocommit mode, often for reasons that are vague and not well defined. Let's first debunk a few of these reasons before we show you how to access data nontransactionally if you want (or have) to:

- Many application developers think they can talk to a database outside of a transaction. This obviously isn't possible; no SQL statement can be send to a database outside of a database transaction. The term *nontransactional* data access means there are no explicit transaction boundaries, no system transaction, and that the behavior of data access is that of the autocommit mode. It doesn't mean no physical database transactions are involved.

- If your goal is to improve performance of your application by using the autocommit mode, you should think again about the implications of many small transactions. Significant overhead is involved in starting and ending a database transaction for every SQL statement, and it may decrease the performance of your application.

- If your goal is to improve the scalability of your application with the autocommit mode, think again: A longer-running database transaction, instead of many small transactions for every SQL statement, may hold database locks for a longer time and probably won't scale as well. However, thanks to the Hibernate persistence context and write-behind of DML, all write locks in the database are already held for a short time. Depending on the isolation level you enable, the cost of read locks is likely negligible. Or, you may use a DBMS with multiversion concurrency that doesn't require read locks (Oracle, PostgreSQL, Informix, Firebird), because readers are never blocked by default.

- Because you're working nontransactionally, not only do you give up any transactional atomicity of a group of SQL statements, but you also have weaker isolation guarantees if data is modified concurrently. Repeatable reads based on read locks are impossible with autocommit mode. (The persistence context cache helps here, naturally.)

Many more issues must be considered when you introduce nontransactional data access in your application. We've already noted that introducing a new type of transaction, namely *read-only transactions*, can significantly complicate any future modification of your application. The same is true if you introduce nontransactional operations.

You would then have three different kinds of data access in your application: in regular transactions, in read-only transactions, and now also nontransactional, with no guarantees. Imagine that you have to introduce an operation that writes data into a unit of work that was supposed to only read data. Imagine that you have to reorganize operations that were nontransactional to be transactional.

Our recommendation is to not use the autocommit mode in an application, and to apply read-only transactions only when there is an obvious performance benefit or when future code changes are highly unlikely. Always prefer regular ACID transactions to group your data-access operations, regardless of whether you read or write data.

Having said that, Hibernate and Java Persistence allow nontransactional data access. In fact, the EJB 3.0 specification forces you to access data nontransactionally if you want to implement atomic long-running conversations. We'll approach this subject in the next chapter. Now we want to dig a little deeper into the consequences of the autocommit mode in a plain Hibernate application. (Note that, despite our negative remarks, there are some good use cases for the autocommit mode. In our experience autocommit is often enabled for the wrong reasons and we wanted to wipe the slate clean first.)

10.3.2 *Working nontransactionally with Hibernate*

Look at the following code, which accesses the database without transaction boundaries:

```
Session session = sessionFactory.openSession();

session.get(Item.class, 1231);

session.close();
```

By default, in a Java SE environment with a JDBC configuration, this is what happens if you execute this snippet:

1 A new `Session` is opened. It doesn't obtain a database connection at this point.

2 The call to `get()` triggers an SQL SELECT. The `Session` now obtains a JDBC `Connection` from the connection pool. Hibernate, by default, immediately

turns off the autocommit mode on this connection with `setAutoCom-mit(false)`. This effectively starts a JDBC transaction!

3 The `SELECT` is executed inside this JDBC transaction. The `Session` is closed, and the connection is returned to the pool and released by Hibernate—Hibernate calls `close()` on the JDBC `Connection`. What happens to the uncommitted transaction?

The answer to that question is, "It depends!" The JDBC specification doesn't say anything about pending transactions when `close()` is called on a connection. What happens depends on how the vendors implement the specification. With Oracle JDBC drivers, for example, the call to `close()` commits the transaction! Most other JDBC vendors take the sane route and roll back any pending transaction when the JDBC `Connection` object is closed and the resource is returned to the pool.

Obviously, this won't be a problem for the `SELECT` you've executed, but look at this variation:

```
Session session = getSessionFactory().openSession();

Long generatedId = session.save(item);

session.close();
```

This code results in an `INSERT` statement, executed inside a transaction that is never committed or rolled back. On Oracle, this piece of code inserts data permanently; in other databases, it may not. (This situation is slightly more complicated: The `INSERT` is executed only if the identifier generator requires it. For example, an identifier value can be obtained from a `sequence` without an `INSERT`. The persistent entity is then queued until flush-time insertion—which never happens in this code. An `identity` strategy requires an immediate `INSERT` for the value to be generated.)

We haven't even touched on autocommit mode yet but have only highlighted a problem that can appear if you try to work without setting explicit transaction boundaries. Let's assume that you still think working without transaction demarcation is a good idea and that you want the regular autocommit behavior. First, you have to tell Hibernate to allow autocommitted JDBC connections in the Hibernate configuration:

```
<property name="connection.autocommit">true</property>
```

With this setting, Hibernate no longer turns off autocommit when a JDBC connection is obtained from the connection pool—it *enables* autocommit if the connection isn't already in that mode. The previous code examples now work predictably, and the JDBC driver wraps a short transaction around every SQL statement that is send to the database—with the implications we listed earlier.

In which scenarios would you enable the autocommit mode in Hibernate, so that you can use a `Session` without beginning and ending a transaction manually? Systems that benefit from autocommit mode are systems that require on-demand (lazy) loading of data, in a particular `Session` and persistence context, but in which it is difficult to wrap transaction boundaries around all code that might trigger on-demand data retrieval. This is usually not the case in web applications that follow the design patterns we discuss in chapter 16. On the other hand, desktop applications that access the database tier through Hibernate often require on-demand loading without explicit transaction boundaries. For example, if you double-click on a node in a Java Swing tree view, all children of that node have to be loaded from the database. You'd have to wrap a transaction around this event manually; the autocommit mode is a more convenient solution. (Note that we are not proposing to open and close `Sessions` on demand!)

10.3.3 *Optional transactions with JTA*

The previous discussion focused on autocommit mode and nontransactional data access in an application that utilizes unmanaged JDBC connections, where Hibernate manages the connection pool. Now imagine that you want to use Hibernate in a Java EE environment, with JTA and probably also CMT. The `connection.autocommit` configuration option has no effect in this environment. Whether autocommit is used depends on your transaction assembly.

Imagine that you have an EJB session bean that marks a particular method as nontransactional:

```
@Stateless
public class ItemFinder {

    @TransactionAttribute(TransactionAttributeType.NOT_SUPPORTED)
    public Item findItemById(Long id) {
        Session s = getSessionFactory().openSession();
        Item item = (Item) s.get(Item.class, id);
        s.close();
        return item;
    }
}
```

The `findItemById()` method produces an immediate SQL `SELECT` that returns the `Item` instance. Because the method is marked as not supporting a transaction context, no transaction is started for this operation, and any existing transaction context is suspended for the duration of this method. The `SELECT` is effectively executed in autocommit mode. (Internally, an autocommitted JDBC connection is assigned to serve this `Session`.)

Finally, you need to know that the default `FlushMode` of a `Session` changes when no transaction is in progress. The default behavior, `FlushMode.AUTO`, results in a synchronization before every HQL, SQL, or `Criteria` query. This is bad, of course, because DML `UPDATE`, `INSERT`, and `DELETE` operations execute in addition to a `SELECT` for the query. Because you're working in autocommit mode, these modifications are permanent. Hibernate prevents this by disabling automatic flushing when you use a `Session` outside of transaction boundaries. You then have to expect that queries may return stale data or data that is conflicting with the state of data in your current `Session`—effectively the same issue you have to deal with when `FlushMode.MANUAL` is selected.

We'll get back to nontransactional data access in the next chapter, in our discussion of conversations. You should consider autocommit behavior a feature that you'd possibly use in conversations with Java Persistence or EJBs, and when wrapping programmatic transaction boundaries around all data access events would be difficult (in a desktop application, for example). In most other cases, autocommit results in systems that are difficult to maintain, with now performance or scalability benefit. (In our opinion, RDBMS vendors should not enable autocommit by default. SQL query consoles and tools should enable autocommit mode on a connection, when necessary.)

10.4 Summary

In this chapter, you learned about transactions, concurrency, isolation, and locking. You now know that Hibernate relies on the database concurrency control mechanism but provides better isolation guarantees in a transaction, thanks to automatic versioning and the persistence context cache. You learned how to set transaction boundaries programmatically with the Hibernate API, JTA `UserTransaction`, and the JPA `EntityTransaction` interface. We also looked at transaction assembly with EJB 3.0 components and how you can work nontransactionally with autocommit mode.

Table 10.1 shows a summary you can use to compare native Hibernate features and Java Persistence.

Table 10.1   Hibernate and JPA comparison chart for chapter 10

Hibernate Core	Java Persistence and EJB 3.0
The `Transaction` API can be configured for JDBC and JTA.	The `EntityTransaction` API is only useful with resource-local transactions.
Hibernate can be configured to integrate with JTA and container-managed transactions in EJBs.	With Java Persistence, no extra configuration besides the database connection name changes between Java SE and Java EE.
Hibernate defaults to optimistic concurrency control for best scalability, with automatic versioning.	Java Persistence standardizes optimistic concurrency control with automatic versioning.

We've now finished our discussion and exploration of the fundamentals involved in storing and loading objects in a transactional fashion. Next, we'll bring all the pieces together by creating more realistic conversations between the user and the application.

11

Implementing conversations

You've tried the examples in previous chapters and stored and loaded objects inside transactions. Very likely you've noticed that code examples of five lines are excellent to help you understand a particular issue and learn an API and how objects change their state. If you take the next step and try to apply what you've learned in your own application, you'll probably soon realize that you're missing two important concepts.

The first concept we'll show you in this chapter—*persistence context propagation*—is useful when you have to call several classes to complete a particular action in your application and they all need database access. So far, we had only a single method that opened and closed a persistence context (a `Session` or an `Entity-Manager`) internally. Instead of passing the persistence context between classes and methods manually, we'll show you the mechanisms in Hibernate and Java Persistence that can take care of propagation automatically. Hibernate can help you to create more complex units of work.

The next design problem you'll run into is that of application flow when your application user has to be guided through several screens to complete a unit of work. You must create code that controls the navigation from screen to screen—however, this is outside of the scope of persistence, and we won't have much to say about it in this chapter. What is partly the responsibility of the persistence mechanism is the atomicity and isolation of data access for a unit of work that spans possible user think-time. We call a unit of work that completes in several client/server request and response cycles a *conversation*. Hibernate and Java Persistence offer several strategies for the implementation of conversations, and in this chapter we show you how the pieces fit together with realistic examples.

We start with Hibernate and then, in the second half of the chapter, discuss JPA conversations. Let's create more complex data access examples first, to see how several classes can reuse the same persistence context through automatic propagation.

11.1 Propagating the Hibernate Session

Recall the use case we introduced in the previous chapter: An event that triggers the end of an auction has to be processed (chapter 10, section 10.1, "Transaction essentials"). For the following examples, it doesn't matter who triggered this event; probably an automatic timer ends auctions when their end date and time is reached. It could also be a human operator who triggers the event.

To process the event, you need to execute a sequence of operations: check the winning bid for the auction, charge the cost of the auction, notify the seller and winner, and so on. You could write a single class that has one big procedure. A better design is to move the responsibility for each of these steps into reusable smaller components and to separate them by concern. We'll have much more to say about this in chapter 16. For now, assume that you followed our advice and that several classes need to be called inside the same unit of work to process the closing of an auction.

11.1.1 *The use case for Session propagation*

Look at the code example in Listing 11.1, which controls the processing of the event.

Listing 11.1 Controller code that closes and ends an auction

```
public class ManageAuction {

    ItemDAO       itemDAO = new ItemDAO();
    PaymentDAO  paymentDAO = new PaymentDAO();

    public void endAuction(Item item) {

        // Reattach item
        itemDAO.makePersistent(item);

        // Set winning bid
        Bid winningBid = itemDAO.getMaxBid( item.getId() );
        item.setSuccessfulBid(winningBid);
        item.setBuyer( winningBid.getBidder() );

        // Charge seller
        Payment payment = new Payment(item);
        paymentDAO.makePersistent(payment);

        // Notify seller and winner
        ...
    }
    ...
}
```

The `ManageAuction` class is called a *controller*. Its responsibility is to coordinate all the steps necessary to process a particular event. The method `endAuction()` is called by the timer (or user interface) when the event is triggered. The controller doesn't contain all the code necessary to complete and close the auction; it delegates as much as possible to other classes. First, it needs two stateless service objects called *data access objects* (DAOs) to complete its work—they're instantiated directly for each instance of the controller. The endAuction() method uses the DAOs when it needs to access the database. For example, the ItemDAO is used to reattach the detached item and to query the database for the highest bid. The PaymentDAO is used to make a transient new payment persistent. You don't even need to see how the seller and winner of the auction are notified—you have enough code to demonstrate that context propagation is required.

The code in listing 11.1 doesn't work. First, there is no transaction demarcation. All the code in endAuction() is to be considered an atomic unit of work: It either all fails or all completes successfully. So, you need to wrap a transaction around all these operations. You'll do that with different APIs next.

A more difficult problem is the persistence context. Imagine that ItemDAO and PaymentDAO use a different persistence context in every method (they're stateless). In other words, itemDAO.getMaxBid() and paymentDAO.makePersistent() both open, flush, and close their own persistence context (a Session or an EntityManager). This is an anti-pattern that should be avoided at all times! In the Hibernate world, it's known as *session-per-operation,* and it's the first thing a good Hibernate developer should take care of when examining an application design for performance bottlenecks. A single persistence context shouldn't be used to process a particular operation, but the whole event (which, naturally, may require several operations). The scope of the persistence context is often the same scope as the database transaction. This is also known as *session-per-request;* see figure 11.1.

Let's add transaction demarcation to the ManageAuction controller and propagate the persistence context between data access classes.

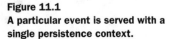

Figure 11.1
**A particular event is served with a
single persistence context.**

11.1.2 *Propagation through thread-local*

Hibernate offers automatic persistence-context propagation for stand-alone Java applications with plain Java SE and for any application that uses JTA with or without EJBs. We strongly encourage you to consider this feature in your own application, because all the alternatives are less sophisticated.

In Hibernate, you can access the current `Session` to access the database. For example, consider the `ItemDAO` implementation with Hibernate:

```
public class ItemDAO {

    public Bid getMaxBid(Long itemId) {
        Session s = getSessionFactory().getCurrentSession();
        return (Bid) s.createQuery("...").uniqueResult();
    }
    ...

}
```

The method `getSessionFactory()` returns the global `SessionFactory`. How it does that is entirely up to you and how you configure and deploy your application—it could come from a static variable (`HibernateUtil`), be looked up from the JNDI registry, or be injected manually when the `ItemDAO` is instantiated. This kind of dependency management is trivial; the `SessionFactory` is a thread-safe object.

The `getCurrentSession()` method on the `SessionFactory` is what we want to discuss. (The `PaymentDAO` implementation also uses the current `Session` in all methods.) What is the current `Session`, what does *current* refer to? Let's add transaction demarcation to the controller that calls `ItemDAO` and `PaymentDAO`, see listing 11.2.

Listing 11.2 Adding transaction demarcation to the controller

```
public class ManageAuction {

    ItemDAO     itemDAO = new ItemDAO();
    PaymentDAO  paymentDAO = new PaymentDAO();

    public void endAuction(Item item) {
        try {
            // Begin unit of work
            sf.getCurrentSession().beginTransaction();

            // Reattach item
            itemDAO.makePersistent(item);

            // Set winning bid
            Bid winningBid = itemDAO.getMaxBid( item.getId() );
```

```
        item.setWinningBid(winningBid);
        item.setBuyer( winningBid.getBidder() );

        // Charge seller
        Payment payment = new Payment(item);
        paymentDAO.makePersistent(payment);

        // Notify seller and winner
        ...

        // End unit of work
        sf.getCurrentSession().getTransaction().commit();
    } catch (RuntimeException ex) {
        try {
            sf.getCurrentSession().getTransaction().rollback();
        } catch (RuntimeException rbEx) {
            log.error("Couldn't roll back transaction," rbEx);
        }
        throw ex;
    }
}
...
}
```

The unit of work starts when the endAuction() method is called. If sessionFactory.getCurrentSession() is called for the first time in the current Java thread, a new Session is opened and returned—you get a fresh persistence context. You immediately begin a database transaction on this new Session, with the Hibernate Transaction interface (which translates to JDBC transactions in a Java SE application).

All the data-access code that calls getCurrentSession() on the global shared SessionFactory gets access to the same current Session—if it's called in the same thread. The unit of work completes when the Transaction is committed (or rolled back). Hibernate also flushes and closes the current Session and its persistence context if you commit or roll back the transaction. The implication here is that a call to getCurrentSession() after commit or rollback produces a new Session and a fresh persistence context.

You effectively apply the same scope to the database transaction and the persistence context. Usually, you'll want to improve this code by moving the transaction and exception handling outside of the method implementation. A straightforward solution is a *transaction interceptor*; you'll write one in chapter 16.

Internally, Hibernate binds the current Session to the currently running Java thread. (In the Hibernate community, this is also known as the *ThreadLocal Session* pattern.) You have to enable this binding in your Hibernate configuration by setting the `hibernate.current_session_context_class` property to `thread`.

If you deploy your application with JTA, you can enable a slightly different strategy that scopes *and* binds the persistence context directly to the system transaction.

11.1.3 *Propagation with JTA*

In previous sections, we always recommended the JTA service to handle transactions, and we now repeat this recommendation. JTA offers, among many other things, a standardized transaction demarcation interface that avoids the pollution of code with Hibernate interfaces. Listing 11.3 shows the `ManageAuction` controller refactored with JTA.

Listing 11.3 Transaction demarcation with JTA in the controller

```
public class ManageAuction {

    UserTransaction utx = null;
    ItemDAO      itemDAO = new ItemDAO();
    PaymentDAO  paymentDAO = new PaymentDAO();

    public ManageAuction() throws NamingException {
        utx = (UserTransaction) new InitialContext()
                .lookup("UserTransaction");
    }

    public void endAuction(Item item) throws Exception {
        try {
            // Begin unit of work
            utx.begin();

            // Reattach item
            itemDAO.makePersistent(item);

            // Set winning bid
            Bid winningBid = itemDAO.getMaxBid( item.getId() );
            item.setWinningBid(winningBid);
            item.setBuyer( winningBid.getBidder() );

            // Charge seller
            Payment payment = new Payment(item);
            paymentDAO.makePersistent(payment);

            // Notify seller and winner
            ...

            // End unit of work
            utx.commit();

        } catch (Exception ex) {
            try {
```

```
                    utx.rollback();
                } catch (Exception rbEx) {
                    log.error("Couldn't roll back transaction", rbEx);
                }
                throw ex;
            }
        }
        ...
    }
```

This code is free from any Hibernate imports. And, more important, the `ItemDAO` and `PaymentDAO` classes, which internally use `getCurrentSession()`, are unchanged. A new persistence context begins when `getCurrentSession()` is called for the first time in one of the DAO classes. The current `Session` is bound automatically to the current JTA system transaction. When the transaction completes, either through commit or rollback, the persistence context is flushed and the internally bound current `Session` is closed.

The exception handling in this code is slightly different compared to the previous example without JTA, because the `UserTransaction` API may throw checked exceptions (and the JNDI lookup in the constructor may also fail).

You don't have to enable this JTA-bound persistence context if you configure your Hibernate application for JTA; `getCurrentSession()` always returns a `Session` scoped and bound to the current JTA system transaction.

(Note that you can't use the Hibernate `Transaction` interface together with the `getCurrentSession()` feature and JTA. You need a `Session` to call `beginTransaction()`, but a `Session` must be bound to the current JTA transaction—a chicken and egg problem. This again emphasizes that you should always use JTA when possible and Hibernate `Transaction` only if you can't use JTA.)

11.1.4 *Propagation with EJBs*

If you write your controller as an EJB and apply container-managed transactions, the code (in listing 11.4) is even cleaner.

Listing 11.4 Transaction demarcation with CMT in the controller

```
@Stateless
public class ManageAuctionBean implements ManageAuction {

    ItemDAO      itemDAO = new ItemDAO();
    PaymentDAO   paymentDAO = new PaymentDAO();

    @TransactionAttribute(TransactionAttributeType.REQUIRED)
```

```
public void endAuction(Item item) {

    // Reattach item
    itemDAO.makePersistent(item);

    // Set winning bid
    Bid winningBid = itemDAO.getMaxBid( item.getId() );
    item.setWinningBid(winningBid);
    item.setBuyer( winningBid.getBidder() );

    // Charge seller
    Payment payment = new Payment(item);
    paymentDAO.makePersistent(payment);

    // Notify seller and winner
    ...
}
...
}
```

The current `Session` is bound to the transaction that is started for the `endAuc-tion()` method, and it's flushed and closed when this method returns. All code that runs inside this method and calls `sessionFactory.getCurrentSession()` gets the same persistence context.

If you compare this example with the first nonworking example, listing 11.1, you'll see that you had to add only some annotations to make it work. The `@TransactionAttribute` is even optional—it defaults to `REQUIRED`. This is why EJB 3.0 offers a *simplified programming model.* Note that you haven't used a JPA interface so far; the data access classes still rely on the current Hibernate `Session`. You can refactor this easily later—concerns are cleanly separated.

You now know how the persistence context is scoped to transactions to serve a particular event and how you can create more complex data-access operations that require propagation and sharing of a persistence context between several objects. Hibernate internally uses the current thread or the current JTA system transaction to bind the current `Session` and persistence context. The scope of the `Session` and persistence context is the same as the scope of the Hibernate `Trans-action` or JTA system transaction.

We now focus on the second design concept that can significantly improve how you design and create database applications. We'll implement long-running conversations, a sequence of interactions with the application user that spans user think-time.

11.2 Conversations with Hibernate

You've been introduced to the concept of conversations several times throughout the previous chapters. The first time, we said that conversations are units of work that span user think-time. We then explored the basic building blocks you have to put together to create conversational applications: detached objects, reattachment, merging, and the alternative strategy with an extended persistence context.

It's now time to see all these options in action. We build on the previous example, the closing and completion of an auction, and turn it into a conversation.

11.2.1 Providing conversational guarantees

You already implemented a conversation—it just wasn't long. You implemented the shortest possible conversation: a conversation that spanned a single request from the application user: The user (let's assume we're talking about a human operator) clicks the Complete Auction button in the CaveatEmptor administration interface. This requested event is then processed, and a response showing that the action was successful is presented to the operator.

In practice, short conversations are common. Almost all applications have more complex conversations—more sophisticated sequences of actions that have to be grouped together as one unit. For example, the human operator who clicks the Complete Auction button does so because they're convinced this auction should be completed. They make this decision by looking at the data presented on the screen—how did the information get there? An earlier request was sent to the application and triggered the loading of an auction for display. From the application user's point of view, this loading of data is part of the same unit of work. It seems reasonable that the application also should know that both events—the loading of an auction item for display and the completion of an auction—are supposed to be in the same unit of work. We're expanding our concept of a unit of work and adopting the point of view of the application user. You group both events into the same conversation.

The application user expects some guarantees while going through this conversation with the application:

- The auction the user is about to close and end isn't modified while they look at it. Completion of the auction requires that the data on which this decision is based is still unchanged when the completion occurs. Otherwise, the operator is working with stale data and probably will make a wrong decision.

- The conversation is atomic: At any time the user can abort the conversation, and all changes they made are rolled back. This isn't a big issue in our current scenario, because only the last event would make any permanent changes; the first request only loads data for display. However, more complex conversations are possible and common.

You as the application developer wish to implement these guarantees with as little work as possible.

We now show you how to implement long conversations with Hibernate, with and without EJBs. The first decision you'll have to make, in any environment, is between a strategy that utilizes *detached objects* and a strategy that *extends the persistence context*.

11.2.2 Conversations with detached objects

Let's create the conversation with native Hibernate interfaces and a detached object strategy. The conversation has two steps: The first step loads an object, and the second step makes changes to the loaded object persistent. The two steps are shown in figure 11.2.

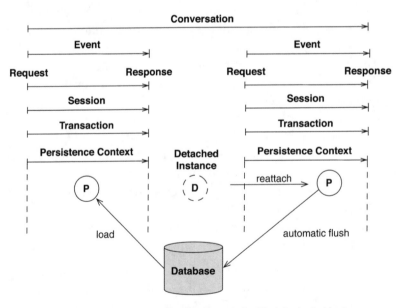

Figure 11.2   A two-step conversation implemented with detached objects

The first step requires a Hibernate `Session` to retrieve an instance by its identifier (assume this is a given parameter). You'll write another `ManageAuction` controller that can handle this event:

```
public class ManageAuction {

    public Item getAuction(Long itemId) {
        Session s = sf.getCurrentSession();

        s.beginTransaction();

        Item item = (Item) s.get(Item.class, itemId);

        s.getTransaction().commit();

        return item;
    }
    ...
}
```

We simplified the code a little to avoid cluttering the example—you know exception handling isn't really optional. Note that this is a much simpler version than the one we showed previously; we want to show you the minimum code needed to understand conversations. You can also write this controller with DAOs, if you like.

A new `Session`, persistence context, and database transaction begin when the `getAuction()` method is called. An object is loaded from the databases, the transaction commits, and the persistence context is closed. The `item` object is now in a detached state and is returned to the client that called this method. The client works with the detached object, displays it, and possibly even allows the user to modify it.

The second step in the conversation is the completion of the auction. That is the purpose of another method on the `ManageAuction` controller. Compared to previous examples, you again simplify the `endAuction()` method to avoid any unnecessary complication:

```
public class ManageAuction {

    public Item getAuction(Long itemId) ...
    ...

    public void endAuction(Item item) {
        Session s = sf.getCurrentSession();

        s.beginTransaction();

        // Reattach item
        s.update(item);

        // Set winning bid
        // Charge seller
```

```
        // Notify seller and winner
        ...

        s.getTransaction().commit();
    }

}
```

The client calls the endAuction() method and passes back the detached item instance—this is the same instance returned in the first step. The update() operation on the Session reattaches the detached object to the persistence context and schedules an SQL UDPATE. Hibernate must assume that the client modified the object while it was detached. (Otherwise, if you're certain that it hasn't been modified, a lock() would be sufficient.) The persistence context is flushed automatically when the second transaction in the conversation commits, and any modifications to the once detached and now persistent object are synchronized with the database.

The saveOrUpdate() method is in practice more useful than upate(), save(), or lock(): In complex conversations, you don't know if the item is in detached state or if it's new and transient and must be saved. The automatic state-detection provided by saveOrUpdate() becomes even more useful when you not only work with single instances, but also want to reattach or persist a network of connected objects and apply cascading options. Also reread the definition of the merge() operation and when to use merging instead of reattachment: "Merging the state of a detached object" in chapter 9, section 9.3.2.

So far, you've solved only one of the conversation implementation problems: little code was required to implement the conversation. However, the application user still expects that the unit of work is not only isolated from concurrent modifications, but also atomic.

You isolate concurrent conversations with optimistic locking. As a rule, you shouldn't apply a pessimistic concurrency-control strategy that spans a long-running conversation—this implies expensive and nonscalable locking. In other words, you don't prevent two operators from seeing the same auction item. You hope that this happens rarely: You're optimistic. But if it happens, you have a conflict resolution strategy in place. You need to enable Hibernate's automatic versioning for the Item persistent class, as you did in "Enabling versioning in Hibernate" in chapter 10, section 10.2.2. Then, every SQL UPDATE or DELETE at any time during the conversation will include a version check against the state present in the database. You get a StaleObjectStateException if this check fails and then have to take appropriate action. In this case, you present an error message to the user ("Sorry, somebody modified the same auction!") and force a restart of the conversation from step one.

How can you make the conversation atomic? The conversation spans several persistence contexts and several database transactions. But this isn't the scope of a unit of work from the point of view of the application user; she considers the conversation to be an atomic group of operations that either all fail or all succeed. In the current conversation this isn't a problem, because you modify and persist data only in the last (second) step. Any conversation that only reads data and delays all reattachment of modified objects until the last step is automatically atomic and can be aborted at any time. If a conversation reattaches and commits modifications to the database in an intermediate step, it's no longer atomic.

One solution is to not flush the persistence contexts on commit—that is, to set a `FlushMode.MANUAL` on a `Session` that isn't supposed to persist modifications (of course, not for the last step of the conversation). Another option is to use *compensation* actions that *undo* any step that made permanent changes, and to call the appropriate compensation actions when the user aborts the conversation. We won't have much to say about writing compensation actions; they depend on the conversation you're implementing.

Next, you implement the same conversation with a different strategy, eliminating the detached object state. You extend the persistence context to span the whole conversation.

11.2.3 Extending a Session for a conversation

The Hibernate `Session` has an internal persistence context. You can implement a conversation that doesn't involve detached objects by *extending* the persistence context to span the whole conversation. This is known as the *session-per-conversation* strategy, as shown in figure 11.3.

A new `Session` and persistence context are opened at the beginning of a conversation. The first step, loading of the `Item` object, is implemented in a first database transaction. The `Session` is automatically disconnected from the underlying JDBC `Connection` as soon as you commit the database transaction. You can now hold on to this disconnected `Session` and its internal persistence context during user think-time. As soon as the user continues in the conversation and executes the next step, you reconnect the `Session` to a fresh JDBC `Connection` by beginning a second database transaction. Any object that has been loaded in this conversation is in persistent state: It's never detached. Hence, all modifications you made to any persistent object are flushed to the database as soon as you call `flush()` on the `Session`. You have to disable automatic flushing of the `Session` by

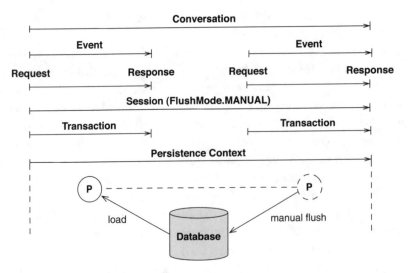

Figure 11.3   A disconnected persistence context extended to span a conversation

setting a FlushMode.MANUAL—you should do this when the conversation begins and the Session is opened.

Modifications made in concurrent conversations are isolated, thanks to optimistic locking and Hibernate's automatic version-checking during flushing. Atomicity of the conversation is guaranteed if you don't flush the Session until the last step, the end of the conversation—if you close the unflushed Session, you effectively abort the conversation.

We need to elaborate on one exception to this behavior: the time of insertion of new entity instances. Note that this isn't a problem in this example, but it's something you'll have to deal with in more complex conversations.

Delaying insertion until flush-time

To understand the problem, think about the way objects are saved and how their identifier value is assigned. Because you don't save any new objects in the Complete Auction conversation, you haven't seen this issue. But any conversation in which you save objects in an intermediate step may not be atomic.

The save() method on the Session requires that the new database identifier of the saved instance must be returned. So, the identifier value has to be generated when the save() method is called. This is no problem with most identifier generator strategies; for example, Hibernate can call a sequence, do the in-memory increment, or ask the hilo generator for a new value. Hibernate doesn't have to execute an SQL INSERT to return the identifier value on save() and assign it to the now-persistent instance.

The exceptions are identifier-generation strategies that are triggered after the INSERT occurs. One of them is identity, the other is select; both require that a row is inserted first. If you map a persistent class with these identifier generators, an immediate INSERT is executed when you call save()! Because you're committing database transactions during the conversation, this insertion may have permanent effects.

Look at the following slightly different conversation code that demonstrates this effect:

```
Session session = getSessionFactory().openSession();
session.setFlushMode(FlushMode.MANUAL);

// First step in the conversation
session.beginTransaction();
Item item = (Item) session.get(Item.class, new Long(123) );
session.getTransaction().commit();

// Second step in the conversation
session.beginTransaction();
Item newItem = new Item();
Long newId = (Long) session.save(newItem); // Triggers INSERT!
session.getTransaction().commit();

// Roll back the conversation!
session.close();
```

You may expect that the whole conversation, the two steps, can be rolled back by closing the unflushed persistence context. The insertion of the newItem is supposed to be delayed until you call flush() on the Session, which never happens in this code. This is the case only if you don't pick identity or select as your identifier generator. With these generators, an INSERT must be executed in the second step of the conversation, and the INSERT is committed to the database.

One solution uses compensation actions that you execute to undo any possible insertions made during a conversation that is aborted, in addition to closing the unflushed persistence context. You'd have to manually delete the row that was inserted. Another solution is a different identifier generator, such as a sequence, that supports generation of new identifier values without insertion.

The persist() operation exposes you to the same problem. However, it also provides an alternative (and better) solution. It can delay insertions, even with post-insert identifier generation, if you call it outside of a transaction:

```
Session session = getSessionFactory().openSession();
session.setFlushMode(FlushMode.MANUAL);

// First step in the conversation
session.beginTransaction();
Item item = (Item) session.get(Item.class, new Long(1));
session.getTransaction().commit();

// Second step in the conversation
Item newItem = new Item();
session.persist(newItem);

// Roll back the conversation!
session.close();
```

The persist() method can delay inserts because it doesn't have to return an identifier value. Note that the newItem entity is in persistent state after you call persist(), but it has no identifier value assigned if you map the persistent class with an identity or select generator strategy. The identifier value is assigned to the instance when the INSERT occurs, at flush-time. No SQL statement is executed when you call persist() outside of a transaction. The newItem object has only been queued for insertion.

Keep in mind that the problem we've discussed depends on the selected identifier generator strategy—you may not run into it, or you may be able to avoid it. The nontransactional behavior of persist() will be important again later in this chapter, when you write conversations with JPA and not Hibernate interfaces.

Let's first complete the implementation of a conversation with an extended Session. With a session-per-conversation strategy, you no longer have to detach and reattach (or merge) objects manually in your code. You must implement infrastructure code that can reuse the same Session for a whole conversation.

Managing the current Session

The current Session support we discussed earlier is a switchable mechanism. You've already seen two possible internal strategies: One was thread-bound, and the other bound the current Session to the JTA transaction. Both, however, closed the Session at the end of the transaction. You need a different scope of the Session for the session-per-conversation pattern, but you still want to be able to access the current Session in your application code.

A third built-in option does exactly what you want for the session-per-conversation strategy. You have to enable it by setting the hibernate.current_session_context_class configuration option to managed. The other built-in options we've discussed are thread and jta, the latter being enabled implicitly if you configure Hibernate for JTA deployment. Note that all these built-in options are implementations of the org.hibernate.context.CurrentSessionContext interface; you could write your own implementation and name the class in the configuration. This usually isn't necessary, because the built-in options cover most cases.

The Hibernate built-in implementation you just enabled is called *managed* because it delegates the responsibility for managing the scope, the start and end of the current `Session`, to you. You manage the scope of the `Session` with three static methods:

```
public class ManagedSessionContext implements CurrentSessionContext {
    public static Session bind(Session session) { ... }
    public static Session unbind(SessionFactory factory) { ... }
    public static boolean hasBind(SessionFactory factory) { ... }
}
```

You can probably already guess what the implementation of a session-per-conversation strategy has to do:

- When a conversation starts, a new `Session` must be opened and bound with `ManagedSessionContext.bind()` to serve the first request in the conversation. You also have to set `FlushMode.MANUAL` on that new `Session`, because you don't want any persistence context synchronization to occur behind your back.

- All data-access code that now calls `sessionFactory.getCurrentSession()` receives the `Session` you bound.

- When a request in the conversation completes, you need to call `ManagedSessionContext.unbind()` and store the now disconnected `Session` somewhere until the next request in the conversation is made. Or, if this was the last request in the conversation, you need to flush and close the `Session`.

All these steps can be implemented in an *interceptor.*

Creating a conversation interceptor

You need an interceptor that is triggered automatically for each request event in a conversation. If you use EJBs, as you'll do soon, you get much of this infrastructure code for free. If you write a non-Java EE application, you have to write your own interceptor. There are many ways how to do this; we show you an abstract interceptor that only demonstrates the concept. You can find working and tested interceptor implementations for web applications in the CaveatEmptor download in the `org.hibernate.ce.auction.web.filter` package.

Let's assume that the interceptor runs whenever an event in a conversation has to be processed. We also assume that each event must go through a front door controller and its `execute()` action method—the easiest scenario. You can now wrap an interceptor around this method; that is, you write an interceptor that is

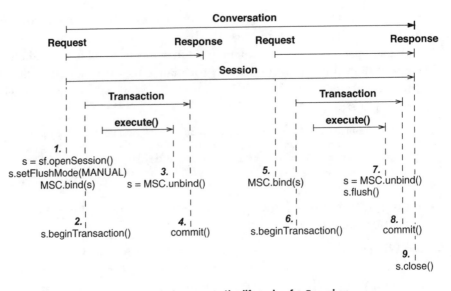

Figure 11.4 Interception of events to manage the lifecycle of a Session

called before and after this method executes. This is shown in figure 11.4; read the numbered items from left to right.

When the first request in a conversation hits the server, the interceptor runs and opens a new Session ❶; automatic flushing of this Session is immediately disabled. This Session is then bound into Hibernate's ManagedSessionContext. A transaction is started ❷ before the interceptor lets the controller handle the event. All code that runs inside this controller (or any DAO called by the controller) can now call sessionFactory.getCurrentSession() and work with the Session. When the controller finishes its work, the interceptor runs again and unbinds the current Session ❸. After the transaction is committed ❹, the Session is disconnected automatically and can be stored during user think-time.

Now the server waits for the second request in the conversation.

As soon as the second request hits the server, the interceptor runs, detects that there is a disconnected stored Session, and binds it into the ManagedSession-Context ❺. The controller handles the event after a transaction was started by the interceptor ❻. When the controller finishes its work, the interceptor runs again and unbinds the current Session from Hibernate. However, instead of disconnecting and storing it, the interceptor now detects that this is the end of the conversation and that the Session needs to be flushed ❼, before the transaction is committed ❽. Finally, the conversation is complete and the interceptor closes the Session ❾.

This sounds more complex than it is in code. Listing 11.5 is a pseudoimplementation of such an interceptor:

Listing 11.5 An interceptor implements the session-per-conversation strategy

```java
public class ConversationInterceptor {

    public Object invoke(Method method) {

        // Which Session to use?
        Session currentSession = null;

        if (disconnectedSession == null) {
            // Start of a new conversation
            currentSession = sessionFactory.openSession();
            currentSession.setFlushMode(FlushMode.MANUAL);
        } else {
            // In the middle of a conversation
            currentSession = disconnectedSession;
        }

        // Bind before processing event
        ManagedSessionContext.bind(currentSession);

        // Begin a database transaction, reconnects Session
        currentSession.beginTransaction();

        // Process the event by invoking the wrapped execute()
        Object returnValue = method.invoke();

        // Unbind after processing the event
        currentSession =
            ManagedSessionContext.unbind(sessionFactory);

        // Decide if this was the last event in the conversation
        if ( returnValue.containsEndOfConversationToken() ) {

            // The event was the last event: flush, commit, close
            currentSession.flush();
            currentSession.getTransaction().commit();
            currentSession.close();

            disconnectedSession = null; // Clean up

        } else {

            // Event was not the last event, continue conversation
            currentSession.getTransaction().commit(); // Disconnects
            disconnectedSession = currentSession;
        }

        return returnValue;
    }
}
```

The `invoke(Method)` interceptor wraps around the `execute()` operation of the controller. This interception code runs every time a request from the application user has to be processed. When it returns, you check whether the return value contains a special token or marker. This token signals that this was the last event that has to be processed in a particular conversation. You now flush the `Session`, commit all changes, and close the `Session`. If this wasn't the last event of the conversation, you commit the database transaction, store the disconnected `Session`, and continue to wait for the next event in the conversation.

This interceptor is transparent for any client code that calls `execute()`. It's also transparent to any code that runs inside `execute ()`: Any data access operation uses the current `Session`; concerns are separated properly. We don't even have to show you the data-access code, because it's free from any database transaction demarcation or `Session` handling. Just load and store objects with `getCurrentSession()`.

The following questions are probably on your mind:

- *Where is the* `disconnectedSession` *stored while the application waits for the user to send the next request in a conversation?* It can be stored in the `HttpSession` or even in a stateful EJB. If you don't use EJBs, this responsibility is delegated to your application code. If you use EJB 3.0 and JPA, you can bind the scope of the persistence context, the equivalent of a `Session`, to a stateful EJB— another advantage of the simplified programming model.

- *Where does the special token that marks the end of the conversation come from?* In our abstract example, this token is present in the return value of the `execute()` method. There are many ways to implement such a special signal to the interceptor, as long as you find a way to transport it there. Putting it in the result of the event processing is a pragmatic solution.

This completes our discussion of persistence-context propagation and conversation implementation with Hibernate. We shortened and simplified quite a few examples in the past sections to make it easier for you to understand the concepts. If you want to go ahead and implement more sophisticated units of work with Hibernate, we suggest that you first also read chapter 16.

On the other hand, if you aren't using Hibernate APIs but want to work with Java Persistence and EJB 3.0 components, read on.

11.3 Conversations with JPA

We now look at persistence context propagation and conversation implementation with JPA and EJB 3.0. Just as with native Hibernate, you must consider three points when you want to implement conversations with Java Persistence:

- You want to propagate the persistence context so that one persistence context is used for all data access in a particular request. In Hibernate, this functionality is built in with the `getCurrentSession()` feature. JPA doesn't have this feature if it's deployed stand-alone in Java SE. On the other hand, thanks to the EJB 3.0 programming model and the well-defined scope and lifecycle of transactions and managed components, JPA in combination with EJBs is much more powerful than native Hibernate.

- If you decide to use a detached objects approach as your conversation implementation strategy, you need to make changes to detached objects persistent. Hibernate offers reattachment and merging; JPA only supports merging. We discussed the differences in the previous chapter in detail, but we want to revisit it briefly with more realistic conversation examples.

- If you decide to use the session-per-conversation approach as your conversation implementation strategy, you need to extend the persistence context to span a whole conversation. We look at the JPA persistence context scopes and explore how you can implement extended persistence contexts with JPA in Java SE and with EJB components.

Note that we again have to deal with JPA in two different environments: in plain Java SE and with EJBs in a Java EE environment. You may be more interested in one or the other when you read this section. We previously approached the subject of conversations with Hibernate by first talking about context propagation and then discussing long conversations. With JPA and EJB 3.0, we'll explore both at the same time, but in separate sections for Java SE and Java EE.

We first implement conversations with JPA in a Java SE application without any managed components or container. We're often going to refer to the differences between native Hibernate conversations, so make sure you understood the previous sections of this chapter. Let's discuss the three issues we identified earlier: persistence context propagation, merging of detached instances, and extended persistence contexts.

11.3.1 *Persistence context propagation in Java SE*

Consider again the controller from listing 11.1. This code relies on DAOs that execute the persistence operations. Here is again the implementation of such a data access object with Hibernate APIs:

```
public class ItemDAO {

    public Bid getMaxBid(Long itemId) {
        Session s = getSessionFactory().getCurrentSession();
        return (Bid) s.createQuery("...").uniqueResult();
    }
    ...

}
```

If you try to refactor this with JPA, your only choice seems to be this:

```
public class ItemDAO {

    public Bid getMaxBid(Long itemId) {
        Bid maxBid;
        EntityManager em = null;
        EntityTransaction tx = null;
        try {
            em  = getEntityManagerFactory().createEntityManager();
            tx = em.getTransaction();
            tx.begin();

            maxBid = (Bid) em.createQuery("...")
                            .getSingleResult();
            tx.commit();
        } finally {
            em.close();
        }
        return maxBid;
    }
    ...

}
```

No persistence-context propagation is defined in JPA, if the application handles the `EntityManager` on its own in Java SE. There is no equivalent to the `getCurrentSession()` method on the Hibernate `SessionFactory`.

The only way to get an `EntityManager` in Java SE is through instantiation with the `createEntityManager()` method on the factory. In other words, all your data access methods use their own `EntityManager` instance—this is the *session-per-operation* antipattern we identified earlier! Worse, there is no sensible location for transaction demarcation that spans several data access operations.

There are three possible solutions for this issue:

- You can instantiate an `EntityManager` for the whole DAO when the DAO is created. This doesn't get you the *persistence-context-per-request* scope, but it's slightly better than one persistence context per operation. However, transaction demarcation is still an issue with this strategy; all DAO operations on all DAOs still can't be grouped as one atomic and isolated unit of work.

- You can instantiate a single `EntityManager` in your controller and pass it into all DAOs when you create the DAOs (constructor injection). This solves the problem. The code that handles an `EntityManager` can be paired with transaction demarcation code in a single location, the controller.

- You can instantiate a single `EntityManager` in an interceptor and bind it to a `ThreadLocal` variable in a helper class. The DAOs retrieve the current `EntityManager` from the `ThreadLocal`. This strategy simulates the `getCurrentSession()` functionality in Hibernate. The interceptor can also include transaction demarcation, and you can wrap the interceptor around your controller methods. Instead of writing this infrastructure yourself, consider EJBs first.

We leave it to you which strategy you prefer for persistence-context propagation in Java SE. Our recommendation is to consider Java EE components, EJBs, and the powerful context propagation that is then available to you. You can easily deploy a lightweight EJB container with your application, as you did in chapter 2, section 2.2.3, "Introducing EJB components."

Let's move on to the second item on the list: the modification of detached instances in long conversations.

11.3.2 *Merging detached objects in conversations*

We already elaborated on the detached object concept and how you can reattach modified instances to a new persistence context or, alternatively, merge them into the new persistence context. Because JPA offers persistence operations only for merging, review the examples and notes about merging with native Hibernate code (in "Merging the state of a detached object" in chapter 9, section 9.3.2.) and the discussion of detached objects in JPA, chapter 9, section 9.4.2, "Working with detached entity instances."

Here we want to focus on a question we brought up earlier and look at it from a slightly different perspective. The question is, "Why is a persistent instance returned from the `merge()` operation?"

The long conversation you previously implemented with Hibernate has two steps, two events. In the first event, an auction item is retrieved for display. In the second event, the (probably modified) item is reattached to a new persistence context and the auction is closed.

Listing 11.6 shows the same controller, which can serve both events, with JPA and merging:

Listing 11.6   A controller that uses JPA to merge a detached object

```
public class ManageAuction {

    public Item getAuction(Long itemId) {
        EntityManager em = emf.createEntityManager();
        EntityTransaction tx = em.getTransaction();

        tx.begin();

        Item item = em.find(Item.class, itemId);

        tx.commit();
        em.close();

        return item;
    }

    public Item endAuction(Item item) {
        EntityManager em = emf.createEntityManager();
        EntityTransaction tx = em.getTransaction();

        tx.begin();

        // Merge item
        Item mergedItem = em.merge(item);

        // Set winning bid
        // Charge seller
        // Notify seller and winner
        // ... this code uses mergedItem!

        tx.commit();
        em.close();

        return mergedItem;
    }

}
```

There should be no code here that surprises you—you've seen all these operations many times. Consider the client that calls this controller, which is usually some kind of presentation code. First, the getAuction() method is called to retrieve an Item instance for display. Some time later, the second event is triggered, and the endAuction() method is called. The detached Item instance is passed into this method; however, the method also returns an Item instance. The returned Item, mergedItem, is a different instance! The client now has two Item objects: the old one and the new one.

As we pointed out in "Merging the state of a detached object" in section 9.3.2, the reference to the old instance should be considered obsolete by the client: It doesn't represent the latest state. Only the mergedItem is a reference to the up-to-date state. With merging instead of reattachment, it becomes the client's responsibility to discard obsolete references to stale objects. This usually isn't an issue, if you consider the following client code:

```
ManageAuction controller = new ManageAuction();

// First event
Item item = controller.getAuction( 12341 );

// Item is displayed on screen and modified...
item.setDescription("[SOLD] An item for sale");

// Second event
item = controller.endAuction(item);
```

The last line of code sets the merged result as the item variable value, so you effectively update this variable with a new reference. Keep in mind that this line updates only this variable. Any other code in the presentation layer that still has a reference to the old instance must also refresh variables—be careful. This effectively means that your presentation code has to be aware of the differences between reattachment and merge strategies.

We've observed that applications that have been constructed with an *extended persistence context* strategy are often easier to understand than applications that rely heavily on detached objects.

11.3.3 *Extending the persistence context in Java SE*

We already discussed the scope of a persistence context with JPA in Java SE in chapter 10, section 10.1.3, "Transactions with Java Persistence." Now we elaborate on these basics and focus on examples that show an extended persistence context with a conversation implementation.

The default persistence context scope

In JPA without EJBs, the persistence context is bound to the lifecycle and scope of an EntityManager instance. To reuse the same persistence context for all events in a conversation, you only have to reuse the same EntityManager to process all events.

An unsophisticated approach delegates this responsibility to the client of the conversation controller:

```
public static class ManageAuctionExtended {

    EntityManager em;

    public ManageAuctionExtended(EntityManager em) {
        this.em = em;
    }

    public Item getAuction(Long itemId) {
        EntityTransaction tx = em.getTransaction();

        tx.begin();

        Item item = em.find(Item.class, itemId);

        tx.commit();

        return item;
    }

    public Item endAuction(Item item) {
        EntityTransaction tx = em.getTransaction();

        tx.begin();

        // Merge item
        Item mergedItem = em.merge(item);

        // Set winning bid
        // Charge seller
        // Notify seller and winner
        // ... this code uses mergedItem!

        tx.commit();

        return mergedItem;
    }
}
```

The controller expects that the persistence context for the whole conversation is set in its constructor. The client now creates and closes the `EntityManager`:

```
// Begin persistence context and conversation
EntityManager em = emf.createEntityManager();

ManageAuctionExtended controller = new ManageAuctionExtended(em);

// First event
Item item = controller.getAuction( 12341 );

// Item is displayed on screen and modified...
item.setDescription("[SOLD] An item for sale");

// Second event
controller.endAuction(item);

// End persistence context and conversation
em.close();
```

Naturally, an interceptor that wraps the `getAuction()` and `endAuction()` methods and supplies the correct `EntityManager` instance can be more convenient. It also avoids the concern leaking upward to the presentation layer. You'd get this interceptor for free if you wrote your controller as a stateful EJB session bean.

When you try to apply this strategy with an extended persistence context that spans the whole conversation, you'll probably run into an issue that can break atomicity of the conversation—automatic flushing.

Preventing automatic flushing

Consider the following conversation, which adds an event as an intermediate step:

```
// Begin persistence context and conversation
EntityManager em = emf.createEntityManager();

ManageAuctionExtended controller = new ManageAuctionExtended(em);

// First event
Item item = controller.getAuction( 12341 );

// Item is displayed on screen and modified...
item.setDescription("[SOLD] An item for sale");

// Second event
if ( !controller.sellerHasEnoughMoney(seller) )
    throw new RuntimeException("Seller can't afford it!");

// Third event
controller.endAuction(item);

// End persistence context and conversation
em.close();
```

From looking at this new conversation client code, when do you think the updated item description is saved in the database? It depends on the flushing of the persistence context. You know that the default `FlushMode` in JPA is `AUTO`, which enables synchronization before a query is executed, and when a transaction is committed. The atomicity of the conversation depends on the implementation of the `sellerHasEnoughMoney()` method and whether it executes a query or commits a transaction.

Let's assume you wrap the operations that execute inside that method with a regular transaction block:

```
public class ManageAuctionExtended {
    ...

    public boolean sellerHasEnoughMoney(User seller) {
        EntityTransaction tx = em.getTransaction();
        tx.begin();
```

```
        boolean sellerCanAffordIt = (Boolean)
            em.createQuery("select...").getSingleResult();

        tx.commit();

        return sellerCanAffordIt;
    }

    ...

}
```

The code snippet even includes two calls that trigger the flushing of the Entity-
Manager's persistence context. First, FlushMode.AUTO means that the execution of
the query triggers a flush. Second, the transaction commit triggers another flush.
This obviously isn't what you want—you want to make the whole conversation
atomic and prevent any flushing before the last event is completed.

Hibernate offers org.hibernate.FlushMode.MANUAL, which decouples transaction demarcation from the synchronization. Unfortunately, due to disagree-
ments among the members of the JSR-220 expert group, javax.persis-
tence.FlushMode only offers AUTO and COMMIT. Before we show you the "official"
solution, here is how you can get FlushMode.MANUAL by falling back to a Hibernate API:

```
// Prepare Hibernate-specific EntityManager parameters
Map params = new HashMap();
params.put("org.hibernate.flushMode," "MANUAL");

// Begin persistence context with custom parameters
EntityManager em = emf.createEntityManager(params);

// Alternative: Fall back and disable automatic flushing
((org.hibernate.Session)em.getDelegate())
    .setFlushMode(org.hibernate.FlushMode.MANUAL);

// Begin conversation
ManageAuction controller = new ManageAuction(em);

// First event
Item item = controller.getAuction( 12341 );

// Item is displayed on screen and modified...
item.setDescription("[SOLD] An item for sale");

// Second event
if ( !controller.sellerHasEnoughMoney(seller) )
    throw new RuntimeException("Seller can't afford it!");

// Third event
controller.endAuction(item);

// End persistence context and conversation
em.close();
```

Don't forget that em.flush() must be called manually, in the last transaction in the third event—otherwise no modifications are made persistent:

```
public static class ManageAuctionExtended {
    ...
    public Item endAuction(Item item) {
        EntityTransaction tx = em.getTransaction();

        tx.begin();

        // Merge item
        ...
        // Set winning bid
        ...

        em.flush(); // Commit the conversation

        tx.commit();

        return mergedItem;
    }
}
```

The official architectural solution relies on nontransactional behavior. Instead of a simple FlushMode setting, you need to code your data-access operations without transaction boundaries. One of the reasons given by expert group members about the missing FlushMode is that "a transaction commit should make all modifications permanent." So, you can only disable flushing for the second step in the conversation by removing transaction demarcation:

```
public class ManageAuction {
    ...

    public boolean sellerHasEnoughMoney(User seller) {
        boolean sellerCanAffordIt = (Boolean)
            em.createQuery("select ...").getSingleResult();
        return sellerCanAffordIt;
    }

    ...
}
```

This code doesn't trigger a flush of the persistence context, because the Entity-Manager is used outside of any transaction boundaries. The EntityManager that executes this query is now working in autocommit mode, with all the interesting consequences we covered earlier in section 10.3, "Nontransactional data access." Even worse, you lose the ability to have repeatable reads: If the same query is executed twice, the two queries each execute on their own database connection in autocommit mode. They can return different results, so the database transaction isolation levels *repeatable read* and *serializable* have no effect. In other words, with the official solution, you can't get repeatable-read database transaction isolation and at the same time disable automatic flushing. The persistence-context cache can provide repeatable read only for entity queries, not for scalar queries.

We highly recommend that you consider Hibernate's `FlushMode.MANUAL` setting if you implement conversations with JPA. We also expect that this problem will be fixed in a future release of the specification; (almost) all JPA vendors already include a proprietary flush mode setting with the same effect as `org.hibernate.FlushMode.MANUAL`.

You now know how to write JPA conversations with detached entity instances and extended persistence contexts. We laid the foundation in the previous sections for the next step: the implementation of conversations with JPA *and* EJBs. If you now have the impression that JPA is more cumbersome than Hibernate, we think you may be surprised at how easy conversations are to implement once you introduce EJBs.

11.4 Conversations with EJB 3.0

We have to go through our list again: persistence context propagation, handling of detached objects, and extended persistence contexts that span the whole conversation. This time, you'll add EJBs to the mix.

We don't have much more to say about detached entity instances and how you can merge modifications between persistence contexts in a conversation—the concept and the API to use are exactly the same in Java SE and with EJBs.

On the other hand, persistence-context propagation and extended persistence-context management with JPA become much easier when you introduce EJBs and then rely on the standardized context propagation rules and the integration of JPA with the EJB 3.0 programming model.

Let's first focus on the persistence-context propagation in EJB invocations.

11.4.1 Context propagation with EJBs

JPA and EJB 3.0 define how the persistence context is handled in an application and the rules that apply if several classes (or EJB components) use an `EntityManager`. The most common case in an application with EJBs is a container-managed and injected `EntityManager`. You turn the `ItemDAO` class into a managed stateless EJB component with an annotation, and rewrite the code to use `EntityManager`:

```
@Stateless
public class ItemDAOBean implements ItemDAO {

    @PersistenceContext
```

```
    private EntityManager em;

    @TransactionAttribute(TransactionAttributeType.REQUIRED)
    public Bid getMaxBid(Long itemId) {
        return (Bid) em.createQuery("...").getSingleResult();
    }
    ...

}
```

The EJB container injects an `EntityManager` when a client of this bean calls `get-MaxBid()`. The persistence context for that `EntityManager` is the current persistence context (more about this soon). If no transaction is in progress when `getMaxBid()` is called, a new transaction is started and committed when `getMax-Bid()` returns.

NOTE Many developers didn't use EJB session beans for DAO classes with EJB 2.1. In EJB 3.0, all components are plain Java objects and there is no reason you shouldn't get the container's services with a few simple annotations (or an XML deployment descriptor, if you don't like annotations).

Wiring EJB components

Now that `ItemDAO` is an EJB component (don't forget to also refactor `PaymentDAO` if you follow the examples from earlier conversation implementations with Hibernate), you can wire it into the also refactored `ManageAuction` component through dependency injection and wrap the whole operation in a single transaction:

```
@Stateless
public class ManageAuctionBean implements ManageAuction {

    @EJB
    ItemDAO itemDAO;

    @EJB
    PaymentDAO paymentDAO;

    @TransactionAttribute(TransactionAttributeType.REQUIRED)
    public Item endAuction(Item item) {

        // Merge item
        itemDAO.makePersistent(item);

        // Set winning bid
        Bid winningBid = itemDAO.getMaxBid( item.getId() );
        item.setWinningBid(winningBid);
        item.setBuyer( winningBid.getBidder() );

        // Charge seller
        Payment payment = new Payment(item);
        paymentDAO.makePersistent(payment);
```

```
        // Notify seller and winner
        ...
        return item;
    }
    ...
}
```

The EJB container injects the desired components based on your declaration of fields with @EJB—the interface names ItemDAO and PaymentDAO are enough information for the container to find the required components.

Let's focus on the transaction and persistence-context propagation rules that apply to this component assembly.

Propagation rules

First, a system transaction is required and is started if a client calls ManageAuction.endAuction(). The transaction is therefore committed by the container when this method returns. This is the scope of the system transaction. Any other stateless component methods that are called and that either require or support transactions (like the DAO methods) inherit the same transaction context. If you use an EntityManager in any of these stateless components, the persistence context you're working with is automatically the same, scoped to the system transaction. Note that this isn't the case if you use JPA in a Java SE application: The EntityManager instance defines the scope of the persistence context (we elaborated on this earlier).

When ItemDAO and PaymentDAO, both stateless components, are invoked inside the system transaction, both inherit the persistence context scoped to the transaction. The container injects an EntityManager instance into itemDAO and paymentDAO with the current persistence context behind the scenes.

(Internally, if a client obtains a ManageAuction controller, the container grabs an idle ManageAuctionBean instance from its pool of stateless beans, injects an idle stateless ItemDAOBean and PaymentDAOBean, sets the persistence context on all the components that need it, and returns the ManageAuction bean handle to the client for invocation. This is of course somewhat simplified.)

These are the formalized rules for persistence-context scoping and propagation:

- If a container-provided (through injection or obtained through lookup) EntityManager is invoked for the first time, a persistence context begins. By default, it's transaction-scoped and closes when the system transaction is committed or rolled back. It's automatically flushed when the transaction is committed.

- If a container-provided (through injection or obtained through lookup) `EntityManager` is invoked for the first time, a persistence context begins. If no system transaction is active at that time, the persistence context is short and serves only the single method call. Any SQL triggered by any such method call executes on a database connection in autocommit mode. All entity instances that are (possibly) retrieved in that `EntityManager` call become detached immediately.

- If a stateless component (such as `ItemDAO`) is invoked, and the caller has an active transaction *and* the transaction is propagated into the called component (because `ItemDAO` methods require or support transactions), any persistence context bound to the JTA transaction is propagated with the transaction.

- If a stateless component (such as `ItemDAO`) is invoked, and the caller doesn't have an active transaction (for example, `ManageAuction.endAuction()` doesn't start a transaction), or the transaction isn't propagated into the called component (because `ItemDAO` methods don't require or support a transaction), a new persistence context is created when the `EntityManager` is called inside the stateless component. In other words, no propagation of a persistence context occurs if no transaction is propagated.

These rules look complex if you read only the formal definition; however, in practice they translate into a natural behavior. The persistence context is automatically scoped and bound to the JTA system transaction, if there is one—you only have to learn the rules for transaction propagation to know how the persistence context is propagated. If there is no JTA system transaction, the persistence context serves a single `EntityManager` call.

You used `TransactionAttributeType.REQUIRED` in almost all the examples so far. This is the most common attribute applied in transaction assemblies; after all, EJB is a programming model for transactional processing. Only once did we show `TransactionAttributeType.NOT_SUPPORTED`, when we discussed nontransactional data access with a Hibernate `Session` in chapter 10 section 10.3.3, "Optional transactions with JTA".

Also remember that you need nontransactional data access in JPA, to disable automatic flushing of the persistence context in a long conversation—the problem of the missing `FlushMode.MANUAL` again.

We now take a closer look at the transaction attribute types and how you can implement a conversation with EJBs and manual flushing of an extended persistence context.

11.4.2 Extended persistence contexts with EJBs

In the previous section, you only worked with persistence contexts that were scoped to the JTA system transaction. The container injected an `EntityManager` automatically, and it transparently handled the persistence context flushing and closing.

If you want to implement a conversation with EJBs and an *extended* persistence context, you have two choices:

- You can write a stateful session bean as a conversation controller. The persistence context can be automatically scoped to the lifecycle of the stateful bean, which is a convenient approach. The persistence context is closed automatically when the stateful EJB is removed.

- You can create an `EntityManager` yourself with the `EntityManagerFactory`. The persistence context of this `EntityManager` is application-managed—you must flush and close it manually. You also have to use the `joinTransaction()` operation to notify the `EntityManager` if you call it inside JTA transaction boundaries. You'll almost always prefer the first strategy with stateful session beans.

You implement the same conversation as before in Java SE: three steps that must be completed as one atomic unit of work: Retrieval of an auction item for display and modification, a liquidity check of the seller account, and finally the closing of the auction.

You again have to decide how you want to disable automatic flushing of the extended persistence context during the conversation, to preserve atomicity. You can choose between the Hibernate vendor extension with `FlushMode.MANUAL` and the official approach with nontransactional operations.

Disabling flushing with a Hibernate extension

Let's first write a stateful EJB, the conversation controller, with the easier Hibernate extension:

```
@Stateful
@TransactionAttribute(TransactionAttributeType.REQUIRED)
public class ManageAuctionBean implements ManageAuction {

    @PersistenceContext(
        type = PersistenceContextType.EXTENDED,
        properties = @PersistenceProperty(
                        name="org.hibernate.flushMode",
                        value="MANUAL")
    )
```

```
EntityManager em;

public Item getAuction(Long itemId) {
    return em.find(Item.class, itemId);
}

public boolean sellerHasEnoughMoney(User seller) {
    boolean sellerCanAffordIt = (Boolean)
        em.createQuery("select...").getSingleResult();
    return sellerCanAffordIt;
}

@Remove
public void endAuction(Item item, User buyer) {
    // Set winning bid
    // Charge seller
    // Notify seller and winner
    item.setBuyer(...);

    em.flush();
}

}
```

This bean implements the three methods of the `ManageAuction` interface (we don't have to show you this interface). First, it's a stateful EJB; the container creates and reserves an instance for a particular client. When a client obtains a handle to this EJB for the first time, a new instance is created and a new extended persistence context is injected by the container. The persistence context is now bound to the lifecycle of the EJB instance and is closed when the method marked as `@Remove` returns. Notice how you can read the methods of the EJB like a story of your conversation, one step after another. You can annotate several methods with `@Remove`; for example, you can add a `cancel()` method to undo all conversation steps. This is a strong and convenient programming model for conversations, all built-in for free with EJB 3.0.

Next is the problem of automatic flushing. All methods of the `ManageAuction-Bean` require a transaction; you declare this on the class level. The `sellerHasEnoughMoney()` method, step two in the conversation, flushes the persistence context before executing the query and again when the transaction of that method returns. To prevent that, you declare that the injected persistence context should be in `FlushMode.MANUAL`, a Hibernate extension. It's now your responsibility to flush the persistence context whenever you want to write the queued SQL DML to the database—you do this only once at the end of the conversation.

Your transaction assembly is now decoupled from the flush behavior of the persistence engine.

Disabling flushing by disabling transactions

The official solution, according to the EJB 3.0 specification, mixes these two concerns. You prevent automatic flushing by making all steps of the conversation (except the last one) nontransactional:

```
@Stateful
@TransactionAttribute(TransactionAttributeType.NOT_SUPPORTED)
public class ManageAuctionBean implements ManageAuction {

    @PersistenceContext(type = PersistenceContextType.EXTENDED)
    EntityManager em;

    public Item getAuction(Long itemId) {
        return em.find(Item.class, itemId);
    }

    public boolean sellerHasEnoughMoney(User seller) {
        boolean sellerCanAffordIt = (Boolean)
            em.createQuery("select...").getSingleResult();
        return sellerCanAffordIt;
    }

    @Remove
    @TransactionAttribute(TransactionAttributeType.REQUIRED)
    public void endAuction(Item item, User buyer) {
        // Set winning bid
        // Charge seller
        // Notify seller and winner
        item.setBuyer(...);
    }

}
```

In this implementation, you switch to a different default for all methods, `TransactionAttributeType.NOT_SUPPORTED`, and require a transaction only for the `endAuction()` method. This last transaction also flushes the persistence context at commit time.

All methods that now call the `EntityManager` without transactions are effectively running in autocommit mode, which we discussed in the previous chapter.

Complex transaction assemblies

You've now used a few different `TransactionAttributeType` annotations; see the complete list of available options in Table 11.1.

The most commonly used transaction attribute type is `REQUIRED`, which is the default for all stateless and stateful EJB methods. To disable automatic flushing of the extended persistence context for a method in a stateful session bean, switch to `NOT_SUPPORTED` or even `NEVER`.

Table 11.1 EJB 3.0 declarative transaction attribute types

Attribute name	Description
REQUIRED	A method must be invoked with a transaction context. If the client doesn't have a transaction context, the container starts a transaction and enlists all resources (datasources, and so on) used with that transaction. If this method calls other transactional components, the transaction is propagated. The container commits the transaction when the method returns, before the result is send to the client.
NOT_SUPPORTED	If a method is invoked within the transaction context propagated from the client, the caller's transaction is suspended and reactivated when the method returns. If the caller has no transaction context, no transaction is started for the method. All used resources aren't enlisted with a transaction (autocommit occurs).
SUPPORTS	If a method is invoked within the transaction context propagated from the client, it joins that transaction context with the same result as REQUIRED. If the caller has no transaction context, no transaction is started, with the same result as NOT_SUPPORTED. This transaction attribute type should be used only for methods that can handle both cases correctly.
REQUIRES_NEW	A method is always executed inside a new transaction context, with the same consequences and behavior as with REQUIRED. Any propagated client transaction is suspended and resumes when the method returns and the new transaction is completed.
MANDATORY	A method must be called with an active transaction context. It then joins this transaction context and propagates it further, if needed. If no transaction context is present at call time, an exception is thrown.
NEVER	This is the opposite of MANDATORY. An exception is thrown if a method is called with an active transaction context.

You have to be aware of the transaction- and persistence-context propagation rules when you design your conversations with stateful EJBs, or if you want to mix stateless and stateful components:

- If a stateful session bean that has an extended persistence context calls (effectively instantiates) another stateful session bean that also has a persistence context, the second stateful session bean inherits the persistence context from the caller. The lifecycle of the persistence context is bound to the first stateful session bean; it's closed when both session beans have been removed. This behavior is recursive if more stateful session beans are involved. This behavior is also independent of any transaction rules and transaction propagation.

- If an `EntityManager` is used in a method of stateful session bean that has a bound extended persistence context, and this method requires/supports the client's JTA transaction, then an exception is raised if the caller of the method also propagates a *different* persistence context with its transaction. (This is a rare design issue.)

One gotcha is hidden in these rules: Imagine that the stateful `ManageAuction` controller doesn't call the `EntityManager` directly, but that it delegates to other components (data access objects, for example). It still has and is responsible for the extended persistence context, although the `EntityManager` is never used directly. This persistence context has to be propagated to all other components that are called: i.e., into `ItemDAO` and `PaymentDAO`.

If you implement your DAOs as stateless session beans, as you did before, they won't inherit the extended persistence context if they are called from a nontransactional method in a stateful controller. This is the stateful controller again, calling a DAO:

```
@Stateful
@TransactionAttribute(TransactionAttributeType.NOT_SUPPORTED)
public class ManageAuctionBean implements ManageAuction {

    @PersistenceContext(type = PersistenceContextType.EXTENDED)
    EntityManager em;

    @EJB
    PaymentDAO paymentDAO;

    public boolean sellerHasEnoughMoney(User seller) {
        return paymentDAO.checkLiquidity(seller);
    }

    ...
}
```

The `sellerHashEnoughMoney()` method doesn't start a transaction, to avoid automatic flushing of the persistence context on commit in the middle of the conversation. The problem is the call to the DAO, which is a stateless EJB. To get the persistence context propagated into the stateless EJB call, you need to propagate a transaction context. If `paymentDAO.checkLiquidity()` uses an `EntityManager`, it gets new persistence context!

The second problem lies in the `PaymentDAO` stateless session bean:

```
@Stateless
public class PaymentDAO {

    @PersistenceContext
    EntityManager em;
```

```
public boolean checkLiquidity(User u) {
    boolean hasMoney = (Boolean)
        em.createQuery("select...").getSingleResult();
    return hasMoney;
}
...
}
```

Because no persistence context is propagated into the checkLiquidity() method when it's called, a new persistence context is created to server this single operation. This is the session-per-operation antipattern! Worse, you now have two (or more) persistence contexts in one request and in the conversation, and you'll run into data aliasing problems (no identity scope guarantee).

If you implement your DAOs as stateful session beans, they inherit the persistence context from the calling stateful session bean controller. In this case, the persistence context is propagated through instantiation, not through transaction propagation.

Write your DAOs as stateful EJBs if you write your controller as a stateful session bean. This issue is another nasty side effect of the missing FlushMode.MANUAL that can seriously impact how you design and layer applications. We recommend you rely on the Hibernate extension until the EJB 3.0 (or 3.1?) specification is fixed. With FlushMode.MANUAL, your controllers don't have to use TransactionAttributeType.NOT_SUPPORTED, and the persistence context is always propagated along with your transaction (and you can mix stateless and stateful EJB calls easily).

We'll get back to this issue in chapter 16, when we write more complex application code and DAOs.

11.5 Summary

In this chapter, you implemented conversations with Hibernate, JPA, and EJB 3.0 components. You learned how to propagate the current Hibernate Session and the persistence context to create more complex layered applications without leaking concerns. You've also seen that persistence-context propagation is a deeply integrated feature of EJB 3.0 and that a persistence context can be easily bound to the JTA (or CMT) transaction scope. You've seen how FlushMode.MANUAL, a Hibernate feature, can disable flushing of your persistence context independently from your transaction assembly.

Table 11.2 shows a summary you can use to compare native Hibernate features and Java Persistence.

Table 11.2   Hibernate and JPA comparison chart for chapter 11

Hibernate Core	Java Persistence and EJB 3.0
Persistence context propagation is available with thread or JTA transaction binding in Java SE and Java EE. Persistence contexts are either scoped to the transaction, or managed by the application.	Java Persistence standardizes a persistence context propagation model for Java EE only, deeply integrated with EJB 3.0 components. Persistence context scoping, to transactions or to stateful session beans, is well defined.
Hibernate supports a conversation implementation with detached objects, these objects can be reattached or merged during a conversation.	Java Persistence standardizes merging of detached objects, but has no support for reattachment.
Hibernate supports disabling automatic flushing of persistence contexts for long conversations with the `FlushMode.MANUAL` option.	Disabling automatic flushing of an extended persistence context requires nontransactional event processing (with serious restrictions on application design and layering) or a Hibernate fallback to `FlushMode.MANUAL`.

In the next chapter, we'll look at various options you should rely on whenever you need to work with more complex and larger datasets. You'll see how transitive persistence works with Hibernate's cascading model, how to execute batch and bulk operations efficiently, and how to hook into and manipulate the Hibernate default behavior when objects are loaded and stored.

12

Modifying objects
efficiently

This chapter shows you how to make data manipulations more efficient. We optimize and reduce the amount of code that is necessary to store objects and discuss the most efficient processing options. You should be familiar with the basic object states and the persistence interfaces; the previous chapters are required reading to understand this chapter.

First we'll show you how transitive persistence can make your work with complex object networks easier. The cascading options you can enable in Hibernate and Java Persistence applications significantly reduce the amount of code that's otherwise needed to insert, update, or delete several objects at the same time.

We then discuss how large datasets are best handled, with batch operations in your application or with bulk operations that execute directly in the database.

Finally, we show you data filtering and interception, both of which offer transparent hooks into the loading and storing process inside Hibernate's engine. These features let you influence or participate in the lifecycle of your objects without writing complex application code and without binding your domain model to the persistence mechanism.

Let's start with transitive persistence and store more than one object at a time.

12.1 *Transitive persistence*

Real, nontrivial applications work not only with single objects, but rather with networks of objects. When the application manipulates a network of persistent objects, the result may be an object graph consisting of persistent, detached, and transient instances. *Transitive persistence* is a technique that allows you to propagate persistence to transient and detached subgraphs automatically.

For example, if you add a newly instantiated `Category` to the already persistent hierarchy of categories, it should become automatically persistent without a call to `save()` or `persist()`. We gave a slightly different example in chapter 6, section 6. 4, "Mapping a parent/children relationship," when you mapped a parent/child relationship between `Bid` and `Item`. In this case, bids were not only automatically made persistent when they were added to an item, but they were also automatically deleted when the owning item was deleted. You effectively made `Bid` an entity that was completely dependent on another entity, `Item` (the `Bid` entity isn't a value type, it still supports shared reference).

There is more than one model for transitive persistence. The best known is *persistence by reachability*; we discuss it first. Although some basic principles are the same, Hibernate uses its own, more powerful model, as you'll see later. The same is true for Java Persistence, which also has the concept of transitive persistence and almost all the options Hibernate natively provides.

12.1.1 *Persistence by reachability*

An object persistence layer is said to implement *persistence by reachability* if any instance becomes persistent whenever the application creates an object reference to the instance from another instance that is already persistent. This behavior is illustrated by the object diagram (note that this isn't a class diagram) in figure 12.1.

In this example, Computer is a persistent object. The objects Desktop PCs and Monitors are also persistent: They're reachable from the Computer Category instance. Electronics and Cellphones are transient. Note that we assume navigation is possible only to child categories, but not to the parent—for example, you can call computer.getChildCategories(). Persistence by reachability is a recursive algorithm. All objects reachable from a persistent instance become persistent either when the original instance is made persistent or just before in-memory state is synchronized with the datastore.

Persistence by reachability guarantees referential integrity; any object graph can be completely re-created by loading the persistent root object. An application may walk the object network from association to association without ever having to worry about the persistent state of the instances. (SQL databases have a different approach to referential integrity, relying on declarative and procedural constraints to detect a misbehaving application.)

In the purest form of persistence by reachability, the database has some top-level or root object, from which all persistent objects are reachable. Ideally, an instance should become transient and be deleted from the database if it isn't reachable via references from the root persistent object.

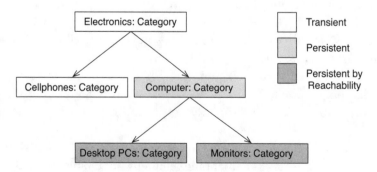

Figure 12.1 Persistence by reachability with a root persistent object

Neither Hibernate nor other ORM solutions implement this—in fact, there is no analog of the root persistent object in an SQL database and no persistent garbage collector that can detect unreferenced instances. Object-oriented data stores may implement a garbage-collection algorithm, similar to the one implemented for in-memory objects by the JVM. But this option is not available in the ORM world; scanning all tables for unreferenced rows won't perform acceptably.

So, persistence by reachability is at best a halfway solution. It helps you make transient objects persistent and propagate their state to the database without many calls to the persistence manager. However, at least in the context of SQL databases and ORM, it isn't a full solution to the problem of making persistent objects transient (removing their state from the database). This turns out to be a much more difficult problem. You can't remove all reachable instances when you remove an object—other persistent instances may still hold references to them (remember that entities can be shared). You can't even safely remove instances that aren't referenced by any persistent object in memory; the instances in memory are only a small subset of all objects represented in the database.

Let's look at Hibernate's more flexible transitive persistence model.

12.1.2 *Applying cascading to associations*

Hibernate's transitive persistence model uses the same basic concept as persistence by reachability: Object associations are examined to determine transitive state. Furthermore, Hibernate allows you to specify a *cascade style* for each association mapping, which offers much more flexibility and fine-grained control for all state transitions. Hibernate reads the declared style and cascades operations to associated objects automatically.

By default, Hibernate doesn't navigate an association when searching for transient or detached objects, so saving, deleting, reattaching, merging, and so on, a `Category` has no effect on any child category referenced by the `childCategories` collection of the parent. This is the opposite of the persistence by reachability default behavior. If, for a particular association, you wish to enable transitive persistence, you must override this default in the mapping metadata.

These settings are called *cascading* options. They're available for every entity association mapping (one-to-one, one-to-many, many-to-many), in XML and annotation syntax. See table 12.1 for a list of all settings and a description of each option.

In XML mapping metadata, you put the `cascade="..."` attribute on `<one-to-one>` or `<many-to-one>` mapping element to enable transitive state changes. All collections mappings (`<set>`, `<bag>`, `<list>`, and `<map>`) support the

Table 12.1   Hibernate and Java Persistence entity association cascading options

XML attribute	Annotation Description
None	(Default) Hibernate ignores the association.
save-update	`org.hibernate.annotations.CascadeType.SAVE_UPDATE` Hibernate navigates the association when the `Session` is flushed and when an object is passed to `save()` or `update()`, and saves newly instantiated transient instances and persist changes to detached instances.
persist	`javax.persistence.CascadeType.PERSIST` Hibernate makes any associated transient instance persistent when an object is passed to `persist()`. If you use native Hibernate, cascading occurs only at call-time. If you use the `EntityManager` module, this operation is cascaded when the persistence context is flushed.
merge	`Javax.persistence.CascadeType.MERGE` Hibernate navigates the association and merges the associated detached instances with equivalent persistent instances when an object is passed to `merge()`. Reachable transient instances are made persistent.
delete	`org.hibernate.annotations.CascadeType.DELETE` Hibernate navigates the association and deletes associated persistent instances when an object is passed to `delete()` or `remove()`.
remove	`javax.persistence.CascadeType.REMOVE` This option enables cascading deletion to associated persistent instances when an object is passed to `remove()` or `delete()`.
lock	`org.hibernate.annotations.CascadeType.LOCK` This option cascades the `lock()` operation to associated instances, reattaching them to the persistence context if the objects are detached. Note that the `LockMode` isn't cascaded; Hibernate assumes that you don't want pessimistic locks on associated objects—for example, because a pessimistic lock on the root object is good enough to avoid concurrent modification.
replicate	`org.hibernate.annotations.CascadeType.REPLICATE` Hibernate navigates the association and cascades the `replicate()` operation to associated objects.
evict	`org.hibernate.annotations.CascadeType.EVICT` Hibernate evicts associated objects from the persistence context when an object is passed to `evict()` on the Hibernate `Session`.
refresh	`javax.persistence.CascadeType.REFRESH` Hibernate rereads the state of associated objects from the database when an object is passed to `refresh()`.

Table 12.1 Hibernate and Java Persistence entity association cascading options *(continued)*

XML attribute	Annotation Description
all	`javax.persistence.CascadeType.ALL` This setting includes and enables all cascading options listed previously.
delete- orphan	`org.hibernate.annotations.CascadeType.DELETE_ORPHAN` This extra and special setting enables deletion of associated objects when they're removed from the association, that is, from a collection. If you enable this setting on an entity collection, you're telling Hibernate that the associated objects don't have shared references and can be safely deleted when a reference is removed from the collection.

cascade attribute. The `delete-orphan` setting, however, is applicable only to collections. Obviously, you never have to enable transitive persistence for a collection that references value-typed classes—here the lifecycle of the associated objects is dependent and implicit. Fine-grained control of dependent lifecycle is relevant and available only for associations between entities.

FAQ *What is the relationship between* cascade *and* inverse? There is no relationship; both are different notions. The noninverse end of an association is used to generate the SQL statements that manage the association in the database (insertion and update of the foreign key column(s)). Cascading enables transitive object state changes across entity class associations.

Here are a few examples of cascading options in XML mapping files. Note that this code isn't from a single entity mapping or a single class, but only illustrative:

```
<many-to-one name="parent"
             column="PARENT_CATEGORY_ID"
             class="Category"
             cascade="save-update, persist, merge"/>

...

<one-to-one name="shippingAddress"
            class="Address"
            cascade="save-update, lock"/>

...

<set name="bids" cascade="all, delete-orphan"
     inverse="true">
   <key column ="ITEM_ID"/>
   <one-to-many class="Bid"/>
</set>
```

As you can see, several cascading options can be combined and applied to a particular association as a comma-separated list. Further note that delete-orphan isn't included in all.

Cascading options are declared with annotations in two possible ways. First, all the association mapping annotations, @ManyToOne, @OneToOne, @OneToMany, and @ManyToMany, support a cascade attribute. The value of this attribute is a single or a list of javax.persistence.CascadeType values. For example, the XML illustrative mapping done with annotations looks like this:

```
@ManyToOne(cascade = { CascadeType.PERSIST, CascadeType.MERGE })
@JoinColumn(name = "PARENT_CATEGORY_ID", nullable = true)
private Category parent;

...

@OneToMany(cascade = CascadeType.ALL)
private Set<Bid> bids = new HashSet<Bid>();
```

Obviously, not all cascading types are available in the standard javax.persistence package. Only cascading options relevant for EntityManager operations, such as persist() and merge(), are standardized. You have to use a Hibernate extension annotation to apply any Hibernate-only cascading option:

```
@ManyToOne(cascade = { CascadeType.PERSIST, CascadeType.MERGE })
@org.hibernate.annotations.Cascade(
    org.hibernate.annotations.CascadeType.SAVE_UPDATE
)
@JoinColumn(name = "PARENT_CATEGORY_ID", nullable = true)
private Category parent;

...

@OneToOne
@org.hibernate.annotations.Cascade({
    org.hibernate.annotations.CascadeType.SAVE_UPDATE,
    org.hibernate.annotations.CascadeType.LOCK
})
@PrimaryKeyJoinColumn
private Address shippingAddress;

...

@OneToMany(cascade = CascadeType.ALL)
@org.hibernate.annotations.Cascade(
    org.hibernate.annotations.CascadeType.DELETE_ORPHAN
)
private Set<Bid> bids = new HashSet<Bid>();
```

A Hibernate extension cascading option can be used either as an addition to the options already set on the association annotation (first and last example) or as a stand-alone setting if no standardized option applies (second example).

Hibernate's association-level cascade style model is both richer and less safe than persistence by reachability. Hibernate doesn't make the same strong guarantees of referential integrity that persistence by reachability provides. Instead, Hibernate partially delegates referential integrity concerns to the foreign key constraints of the underlying SQL database.

There is a good reason for this design decision: It allows Hibernate applications to use *detached* objects efficiently, because you can control reattachment and merging of a detached object graph at the association level. But cascading options aren't available only to avoid unnecessary reattachment or merging: They're useful whenever you need to handle more than one object at a time.

Let's elaborate on the transitive state concept with some example association mappings. We recommend that you read the next section in one turn, because each example builds on the previous one.

12.1.3 *Working with transitive state*

CaveatEmptor administrators are able to create new categories, rename categories, and move subcategories around in the category hierarchy. This structure can be seen in figure 12.2.

Now, you map this class and the association, using XML:

Figure 12.2
Category class with associations to itself

```
<class name="Category" table="CATEGORY">
    ...
    <property name="name" column="CATEGORY_NAME"/>

    <many-to-one name="parentCategory"
                 class="Category"
                 column="PARENT_CATEGORY_ID"
                 cascade="none"/>

    <set name="childCategories"
         table="CATEGORY"
         cascade="save-update"
         inverse="true">
        <key column="PARENT_CATGORY_ID"/>
        <one-to-many class="Category"/>
    </set>
    ...
</class>
```

This is a recursive bidirectional one-to-many association. The one-valued end is mapped with the <many-to-one> element and the Set typed property with the

<set>. Both refer to the same foreign key column PARENT_CATEGORY_ID. All columns are in the same table, CATEGORY.

Creating a new category

Suppose you create a new Category, as a child category of Computer; see figure 12.3.

You have several ways to create this new Laptops object and save it in the database. You can go back to the database and retrieve the Computer category to which the new Laptops category will belong, add the new category, and commit the transaction:

```
Session session = sessionFactory.openSession();
Transaction tx = session.beginTransaction();

Category computer =
          (Category) session.load(Category.class, computerId);

Category laptops = new Category("Laptops");

computer.getChildCategories().add(laptops);
laptops.setParentCategory(computer);

tx.commit();
session.close();
```

The computer instance is persistent (note how you use load() to work with a proxy and avoid the database hit), and the childCategories association has cascade-save enabled. Hence, this code results in the new laptops category becoming persistent when tx.commit() is called, as Hibernate cascades the persistent state to the childCategories collection elements of computer. Hibernate examines the state of the objects and their relationships when the persistence context is flushed and queues an INSERT statement.

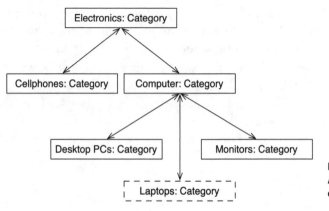

Figure 12.3
Adding a new Category to the object graph

Creating a new category in a detached fashion

Let's do the same thing again, but this time create the link between Computer and Laptops outside of the persistence context scope:

```
Category computer =
            (Category) session.get() // Loaded in previous Session

Category laptops = new Category("Laptops");

computer.getChildCategories().add(laptops);
laptops.setParentCategory(computer);
```

You now have the detached fully initialized (no proxy) `computer` object, loaded in a previous `Session`, associated with the new transient `laptops` object (and vice versa). You make this change to the objects persistent by saving the new object in a second Hibernate `Session`, a new persistence context:

```
Session session = sessionFactory.openSession();
Transaction tx = session.beginTransaction();

// Persist one new category and the link to its parent category
session.save(laptops);

tx.commit();
session.close();
```

Hibernate inspects the database identifier property of the `laptops.parentCategory` object and correctly creates the reference to the Computer category in the database. Hibernate inserts the identifier value of the parent into the foreign key field of the new Laptops row in `CATEGORY`.

You can't obtain a detached proxy for `computer` in this example, because `computer.getChildCategories()` would trigger initialization of the proxy and you'd see a `LazyInitializationException`: The `Session` is already closed. You can't walk the object graph across uninitialized boundaries in detached state.

Because you have `cascade="none"` defined for the `parentCategory` association, Hibernate ignores changes to any of the other categories in the hierarchy (Computer, Electronics)! It doesn't cascade the call to `save()` to entities referred by this association. If you enabled `cascade="save-update"` on the `<many-to-one>` mapping of `parentCategory`, Hibernate would navigate the whole graph of objects in memory, synchronizing all instances with the database. This is an obvious overhead you'd prefer to avoid.

In this case, you neither need nor want transitive persistence for the `parentCategory` association.

Saving several new instances with transitive persistence

Why do we have cascading operations? You could save the `laptop` object, as shown in the previous example, without using any cascade mapping. Well, consider the following case:

```
Category computer = ... // Loaded in a previous Session

Category laptops = new Category("Laptops");
Category laptopUltraPortable = new Category("Ultra-Portable");
Category laptopTabletPCs = new Category("Tablet PCs");

laptops.addChildCategory(laptopUltraPortable);
laptops.addChildCategory(laptopTabletPCs);

computer.addChildCategory(laptops);
```

(Notice that the convenience method `addChildCategory()` sets both ends of the association link in one call, as described earlier in the book.)

It would be undesirable to have to save each of the three new categories individually in a new `Session`. Fortunately, because you mapped the `childCategories` association (the collection) with `cascade="save-update"`, you don't need to. The same code shown earlier, which saved the single Laptops category, will save all three new categories in a new `Session`:

```
Session session = sessionFactory.openSession();
Transaction tx = session.beginTransaction();

// Persist all three new Category instances
session.save(laptops);

tx.commit();
session.close();
```

You're probably wondering why the cascade style is called `cascade="save-update"` rather then merely `cascade="save"`. Having just made all three categories persistent previously, suppose you make the following changes to the category hierarchy in a subsequent event, outside of a `Session` (you're working on detached objects again):

```
laptops.setName("Laptop Computers");                      // Modify
laptopUltraPortable.setName("Ultra-Portable Notebooks");  // Modify
laptopTabletPCs.setName("Tablet Computers");              // Modify

Category laptopBags = new Category("Laptop Bags");
laptops.addChildCategory(laptopBags);                     // Add
```

You add a new category (`laptopBags`) as a child of the Laptops category, and modify all three existing categories. The following code propagates all these changes to the database:

```
Session session = sessionFactory.openSession();
Transaction tx = session.beginTransaction();

// Update three old Category instances and insert the new one
session.saveOrUpdate(laptops);

tx.commit();
session.close();
```

Because you specify cascade="save-update" on the childCategories collection, Hibernate determines what is needed to persist the objects to the database. In this case, it queues three SQL UPDATE statements (for laptops, laptop-UltraPortable, laptopTablePCs) and one INSERT (for laptopBags). The saveOrUpdate() method tells Hibernate to propagate the state of an instance to the database by creating a new database row if the instance is a new transient instance or updating the existing row if the instance is a detached instance.

More experienced Hibernate users use saveOrUpdate() exclusively; it's much easier to let Hibernate decide what is new and what is old, especially in a more complex network of objects with mixed state. The only (not really serious) disadvantage of exclusive saveOrUpdate() is that it sometimes can't guess whether an instance is old or new without firing a SELECT at the database—for example, when a class is mapped with a natural composite key and no version or timestamp property.

How does Hibernate detect which instances are old and which are new? A range of options is available. Hibernate assumes that an instance is an unsaved transient instance if:

- The identifier property is null.
- The version or timestamp property (if it exists) is null.
- A new instance of the same persistent class, created by Hibernate internally, has the same database identifier value as the given instance.
- You supply an unsaved-value in the mapping document for the class, and the value of the identifier property matches. The unsaved-value attribute is also available for version and timestamp mapping elements.
- Entity data with the same identifier value isn't in the second-level cache.
- You supply an implementation of org.hibernate.Interceptor and return Boolean.TRUE from Interceptor.isUnsaved() after checking the instance in your own code.

In the CaveatEmptor domain model, you use the nullable type java.lang.Long as your identifier property type everywhere. Because you're using generated, synthetic identifiers, this solves the problem. New instances have a `null` identifier property value, so Hibernate treats them as transient. Detached instances have a nonnull identifier value, so Hibernate treats them accordingly.

It's rarely necessary to customize the automatic detection routines built into Hibernate. The `saveOrUpdate()` method always knows what to do with the given object (or any reachable objects, if cascading of `save-update` is enabled for an association). However, if you use a natural composite key and there is no version or timestamp property on your entity, Hibernate has to hit the database with a `SELECT` to find out if a row with the same composite identifier already exists. In other words, we recommend that you almost always use `saveOrUpdate()` instead of the individual `save()` or `update()` methods, Hibernate is smart enough to do the right thing and it makes transitive "all of this should be in persistent state, no matter if new or old" much easier to handle.

We've now discussed the basic transitive persistence options in Hibernate, for saving new instances and reattaching detached instances with as few lines of code as possible. Most of the other cascading options are equally easy to understand: `persist`, `lock`, `replicate`, and `evict` do what you would expect—they make a particular `Session` operation transitive. The `merge` cascading option has effectively the same consequences as `save-update`.

It turns out that object deletion is a more difficult thing to grasp; the `delete-orphan` setting in particular causes confusion for new Hibernate users. This isn't because it's complex, but because many Java developers tend to forget that they're working with a network of pointers.

Considering transitive deletion

Imagine that you want to delete a `Category` object. You have to pass this object to the `delete()` method on a `Session`; it's now in *removed* state and will be gone from the database when the persistence context is flushed and committed. However, you'll get a *foreign key constraint violation* if any other `Category` holds a reference to the deleted row at that time (maybe because it was still referenced as the parent of others).

It's your responsibility to delete all links to a `Category` before you delete the instance. This is the normal behavior of entities that support shared references. Any value-typed property (or component) value of an entity instance is deleted automatically when the owning entity instance is deleted. Value-typed collection elements (for example, the collection of `Image` objects for an `Item`) are deleted if you remove the references from the owning collection.

In certain situations, you want to delete an entity instance by removing a reference from a collection. In other words, you can guarantee that once you remove the reference to this entity from the collection, no other reference will exist. Therefore, Hibernate can delete the entity safely after you've removed that single last reference. Hibernate assumes that an orphaned entity with no references should be deleted. In the example domain model, you enable this special cascading style for the collection (it's only available for collections) of bids, in the mapping of Item:

```
<set name="bids"
     cascade="all, delete-orphan"
     inverse="true">
    <key column="ITEM_ID"/>
    <one-to-many class="Bid"/>
</set>
```

You can now delete Bid objects by removing them from this collection—for example, in detached state:

```
Item anItem = ... // Loaded in previous Session

anItem.getBids().remove(aBid);
anItem.getBids().remove(anotherBid);

Session session = sessionFactory.openSession();
Transaction tx = session.beginTransaction();

session.saveOrUpdate(anItem);

tx.commit();
session.close();
```

If you don't enable the delete-orphan option, you have to explicitly delete the Bid instances after removing the last reference to them from the collection:

```
Item anItem = ... // Loaded in previous Session

anItem.getBids().remove(aBid);
anItem.getBids().remove(anotherBid);

Session session = sessionFactory.openSession();
Transaction tx = session.beginTransaction();

session.delete(aBid);
session.delete(anotherBid);

session.saveOrUpdate(anItem);

tx.commit();
session.close();
```

Automatic deletion of orphans saves you two lines of code—two lines of code that are inconvenient. Without orphan deletion, you'd have to remember all the Bid objects you wish to delete—the code that removes an element from the collection is often in a different layer than the code that executes the delete() operation. With orphan deletion enabled, you can remove orphans from the collection, and Hibernate will assume that they're no longer referenced by any other entity. Note again that orphan deletion is implicit if you map a collection of components; the extra option is relevant only for a collection of entity references (almost always a <one-to-many>).

Java Persistence and EJB 3.0 also support transitive state changes across entity associations. The standardized cascading options are similar to Hibernate's, so you can learn them easily.

12.1.4 *Transitive associations with JPA*

The Java Persistence specification supports annotations for entity associations that enable cascading object manipulation. Just as in native Hibernate, each Entity-Manager operation has an equivalent cascading style. For example, consider the Category tree (parent and children associations) mapped with annotations:

```
@Entity
public class Category {

    private String name;

    @ManyToOne
    public Category parentCategory;

    @OneToMany(mappedBy = "parentCategory",
               cascade = { CascadeType.PERSIST,
                           CascadeType.MERGE }
              )
    public Set<Category> childCategories = new HashSet<Category>();
    ...
}
```

You enable standard cascading options for the persist() and merge() operations. You can now create and modify Category instances in persistent or detached state, just as you did earlier with native Hibernate:

```
Category computer = ... // Loaded in a previous persistence context

Category laptops = new Category("Laptops");
Category laptopUltraPortable = new Category("Ultra-Portable");
Category laptopTabletPCs = new Category("Tablet PCs");

laptops.addChildCategory(laptopUltraPortable);
laptops.addChildCategory(laptopTabletPCs);

computer.setName("Desktops and Laptops");
computer.addChildCategory(laptops);
```

```
EntityManager em = emf.createEntityManager();
EntityTransaction tx = em.getTransaction();
tx.begin();

computer = em.merge(computer);

tx.commit();
em.close();
```

A single call to merge() makes any modification and addition persistent. Remember that merge() isn't the same as reattachment: It returns a new value that you should bind to the current variable as a handle to current state after merging.

Some cascading options aren't standardized, but Hibernate specific. You map these annotations (they're all in the org.hibernate.annotations package) if you're working with the Session API or if you want an extra setting for Entity-Manager (for example, org.hibernate.annotations.CascadeType.DELETE_ORPHAN). Be careful, though—custom cascading options in an otherwise pure JPA application introduce implicit object state changes that may be difficult to communicate to someone who doesn't expect them.

In the previous sections, we've explored the entity association cascading options with Hibernate XML mapping files and Java Persistence annotations. With transitive state changes, you save lines of code by letting Hibernate navigate and cascade modifications to associated objects. We recommend that you consider which associations in your domain model are candidates for transitive state changes and then implement this with cascading options. In practice, it's extremely helpful if you also write down the cascading option in the UML diagram of your domain model (with stereotypes) or any other similar documentation that is shared between developers. Doing so improves communication in your development team, because everybody knows which operations and associations imply cascading state changes.

Transitive persistence isn't the only way you can manipulate many objects with a single operation. Many applications have to modify large object sets: For example, imagine that you have to set a flag on 50,000 Item objects. This is a bulk operation that is best executed directly in the database.

12.2 Bulk and batch operations

You use object/relational mapping to move data into the application tier so that you can use an object-oriented programming language to process that data. This is a good strategy if you're implementing a multiuser online transaction processing application, with small to medium size data sets involved in each unit of work.

On the other hand, operations that require massive amounts of data are best *not* executed in the application tier. You should move the operation closer to the location of the data, rather than the other way round. In an SQL system, the DML statements UPDATE and DELETE execute directly in the database and are often sufficient if you have to implement an operation that involves thousands of rows. More complex operations may require more complex procedures to run inside the database; hence, you should consider *stored procedures* as one possible strategy.

You can fall back to JDBC and SQL at all times in Hibernate or Java Persistence applications. In this section, we'll show you how to avoid this and how to execute bulk and batch operations with Hibernate and JPA.

12.2.1 *Bulk statements with HQL and JPA QL*

The Hibernate Query Language (HQL) is similar to SQL. The main difference between the two is that HQL uses class names instead of table names, and property names instead of column names. It also understands inheritance—that is, whether you're querying with a superclass or an interface.

The JPA query language, as defined by JPA and EJB 3.0, is a *subset* of HQL. Hence, all queries and statements that are valid JPA QL are also valid HQL. The statements we'll show you now, for bulk operations that execute directly in the database, are available in JPA QL and HQL. (Hibernate adopted the standardized bulk operations from JPA.)

The available statements support updating and deleting objects directly in the database without the need to retrieve the objects into memory. A statement that can select data and insert it as new entity objects is also provided.

Updating objects directly in the database

In the previous chapters, we've repeated that you should think about *state management* of objects, not how SQL statements are managed. This strategy assumes that the objects you're referring to are available in memory. If you execute an SQL statement that operates directly on the rows in the database, any change you make doesn't affect the in-memory objects (in whatever state they may be). In other words, any direct DML statement bypasses the Hibernate persistence context (and all caches).

A pragmatic solution that avoids this issue is a simple convention: Execute any direct DML operations first in a fresh persistence context. Then, use the Hibernate Session or EntityManager to load and store objects. This convention guarantees that the persistence context is unaffected by any statements executed earlier. Alternatively, you can selectively use the refresh() operation to reload the state of a persistent object from the database, if you know it's been modified behind the back of the persistence context.

Hibernate and JPA offer DML operations that are a little more powerful than plain SQL. Let's look at the first operation in HQL and JPA QL, an UPDATE:

```
Query q =
    session.createQuery("update Item i set i.isActive = :isActive");
q.setBoolean("isActive", true);
int updatedItems = q.executeUpdate();
```

This HQL statement (or JPA QL statement, if executed with the EntityManager) looks like an SQL statement. However, it uses an entity name (class name) and a property name. It's also integrated into Hibernate's parameter binding API. The number of updated entity objects is returned—not the number of updated rows. Another benefit is that the HQL (JPA QL) UPDATE statement works for inheritance hierarchies:

```
Query q = session.createQuery(
    "update CreditCard set stolenOn <= :now where type = 'Visa'"
);
q.setTimestamp("now", new Date() );
int updatedCreditCards = q.executeUpdate();
```

The persistence engine knows how to execute this update, even if several SQL statements have to be generated; it updates several base tables (because Credit-Card is mapped to several superclass and subclass tables). This example also doesn't contain an alias for the entity class—it's optional. However, if you use an alias, all properties must be prefixed with an alias. Also note that HQL (and JPA QL) UPDATE statements can reference only a single entity class; you can't write a single statement to update Item and CreditCard objects simultaneously, for example. Subqueries are allowed in the WHERE clause; any joins are allowed only in these subqueries.

Direct DML operations, by default, don't affect any version or timestamp values of the affected entities (this is standardized in Java Persistence). With HQL, however, you can increment the version number of directly modified entity instances:

```
Query q =
    session.createQuery(
        "update versioned Item i set i.isActive = :isActive"
    );
q.setBoolean("isActive", true);
int updatedItems = q.executeUpdate();
```

(The versioned keyword is not allowed if your version or timestamp property relies on a custom org.hibernate.usertype.UserVersionType.)

The second HQL (JPA QL) bulk operation we introduce is the DELETE:

```
Query q = session.createQuery(
    "delete CreditCard c where c.stolenOn is not null"
);
int updatedCreditCards = q.executeUpdate();
```

The same rules as for UPDATE statements apply: no joins, single entity class only, optional aliases, subqueries allowed in the WHERE clause.

Just like SQL bulk operations, HQL (and JPA QL) bulk operations don't affect the persistence context, they bypass any cache. Credit cards or items in memory aren't updated if you execute one of these examples.

The last HQL bulk operation can create objects directly in the database.

Creating new objects directly in the database

Let's assume that all your customers' Visa cards have been stolen. You write two bulk operations to mark the day they were stolen (well, the day you discovered the theft) and to remove the compromised credit-card data from your records. Because you work for a responsible company, you have to report the stolen credit cards to the authorities and affected customers. So, before you delete the records, you extract everything that was stolen and create a few hundred (or thousand) StolenCreditCard objects. This is a new class you write just for that purpose:

```
public class StolenCreditCard {

    private Long id;

    private String type;
    private String number;
    private String expMonth;
    private String expYear;
    private String ownerFirstname;
    private String ownerLastname;
    private String ownerLogin;
    private String ownerEmailAddress;
    private Address ownerHomeAddress;

    ... // Constructors, getter and setter methods
}
```

You now map this class to its own STOLEN_CREDIT_CARD table, either with an XML file or JPA annotations (you shouldn't have any problem doing this on your own). Next, you need a statement that executes directly in the database, retrieves all compromised credit cards, and creates new StolenCreditCard objects:

```
Query q = session.createQuery(
    "insert into StolenCreditCard
        (type, number, expMonth, expYear,
```

```
            ownerFirstname, onwerLastname, ownerLogin,
            ownerEmailAddress, ownerHomeAddress)
    select
            c.type, c.number, c.expMonth, c.expYear,
            u.firstname, u.lastname, u.username,
            u.email, u.homeAddress
        from CreditCard c join c.user u
        where c.stolenOn is not null"
);

int createdObjects = q.executeUpdate();
```

This operation does two things: First, the details of `CreditCard` records and the respective owner (a `User`) are selected. The result is then directly inserted into the table to which the `StolenCreditCard` class is mapped.

Note the following:

- The properties that are the target of an `INSERT ... SELECT` (in this case, the `StolenCreditCard` properties you list) have to be for a particular sub-class, not an (abstract) superclass. Because `StolenCreditCard` isn't part of an inheritance hierarchy, this isn't an issue.

- The types returned by the `SELECT` must match the types required for the `INSERT`—in this case, lots of `string` types and a component (the same type of component for selection and insertion).

- The database identifier for each `StolenCreditCard` object will be generated automatically by the identifier generator you map it with. Alternatively, you can add the identifier property to the list of inserted properties and supply a value through selection. Note that automatic generation of identifier values works only for identifier generators that operate directly inside the database, such as sequences or identity fields.

- If the generated objects are of a versioned class (with a `version` or `timestamp` property), a fresh version (zero, or timestamp of today) will also be generated. Alternatively, you can select a version (or timestamp) value and add the version (or timestamp) property to the list of inserted properties.

Finally, note that `INSERT ... SELECT` is available only with HQL; JPA QL doesn't standardize this kind of statement—hence, your statement may not be portable.

HQL and JPA QL bulk operations cover many situations in which you'd usually resort to plain SQL. On the other hand, sometimes you can't exclude the application tier in a mass data operation.

12.2.2 *Processing with batches*

Imagine that you have to manipulate all Item objects, and that the changes you have to make aren't as trivial as setting a flag (which you've done with a single statement previously). Let's also assume that you can't create an SQL stored procedure, for whatever reason (maybe because your application has to work on database-management systems that don't support stored procedures). Your only choice is to write the procedure in Java and to retrieve a massive amount of data into memory to run it through the procedure.

You should execute this procedure by *batching* the work. That means you create many smaller datasets instead of a single dataset that wouldn't even fit into memory.

Writing a procedure with batch updates

The following code loads 100 Item objects at a time for processing:

```
Session session = sessionFactory.openSession();
Transaction tx = session.beginTransaction();

ScrollableResults itemCursor =
    session.createQuery("from Item").scroll();

int count=0;
while ( itemCursor.next() ) {
    Item item = (Item) itemCursor.get(0);
    modifyItem(item);
    if ( ++count % 100 == 0 ) {
        session.flush();
        session.clear();
    }
}

tx.commit();
session.close();
```

You use an HQL query (a simple one) to load all Item objects from the database. But instead of retrieving the result of the query completely into memory, you open an online *cursor*. A cursor is a pointer to a result set that stays in the database. You can control the cursor with the ScrollableResults object and move it along the result. The get(int i) call retrieves a single object into memory, the object the cursor is currently pointing to. Each call to next() forwards the cursor to the next object. To avoid memory exhaustion, you flush() and clear() the persistence context before loading the next 100 objects into it.

A flush of the persistence context writes the changes you made to the last 100 Item objects to the database. For best performance, you should set the size of the Hibernate (and JDBC) configuration property hibernate.jdbc.batch_size to the same size as your procedure batch: 100. All UDPATE statements that are executed during flushing are then also batched at the JDBC level.

(Note that you should disable the second-level cache for any batch operations; otherwise, each modification of an object during the batch procedure must be propagated to the second-level cache for that persistent class. This is an unnecessary overhead. You'll learn how to control the second-level cache in the next chapter.)

The Java Persistence API unfortunately doesn't support cursor-based query results. You have to call org.hibernate.Session and org.hibernate.Query to access this feature.

The same technique can be used to create and persist a large number of objects.

Inserting many objects in batches

If you have to create a few hundred or thousand objects in a unit of work, you may run into memory exhaustion. Every object that is passed to insert() or persist() is added to the persistence context cache.

A straightforward solution is to flush and clear the persistence context after a certain number of objects. You effectively batch the inserts:

```
Session session = sessionFactory.openSession();
Transaction tx = session.beginTransaction();

for ( int i=0; i<100000; i++ ) {
    Item item = new Item(...);
    session.save(item);
    if ( i % 100 == 0 ) {
        session.flush();
        session.clear();
    }
}

tx.commit();
session.close();
```

Here you create and persist 100,000 objects, 100 at a time. Again, remember to set the hibernate.jdbc.batch_size configuration property to an equivalent value and disable the second-level cache for the persistent class. Caveat: Hibernate silently disables JDBC batch inserts if your entity is mapped with an identity identifier generator; many JDBC drivers don't support batching in that case.

Another option that completely avoids memory consumption of the persistence context (by effectively disabling it) is the StatelessSession interface.

12.2.3 *Using a stateless Session*

The persistence context is an essential feature of the Hibernate and Java Persistence engine. Without a persistence context, you wouldn't be able to manipulate object state and have Hibernate detect your changes automatically. Many other things also wouldn't be possible.

However, Hibernate offers you an alternative interface, if you prefer to work with your database by executing statements. This statement-oriented interface, org.hibernate.StatelessSession, feels and works like plain JDBC, except that you get the benefit from mapped persistent classes and Hibernate's database portability.

Imagine that you want to execute the same "update all item objects" procedure you wrote in an earlier example with this interface:

```
Session session = sessionFactory.openStatelessSession();
Transaction tx = session.beginTransaction();

ScrollableResults itemCursor =
    session.createQuery("from Item").scroll();

while ( itemCursor.next() ) {
    Item item = (Item) itemCursor.get(0);
    modifyItem(item);
    session.update(item);
}

tx.commit();
session.close();
```

The batching is gone in this example—you open a StatelessSession. You no longer work with objects in persistent state; everything that is returned from the database is in detached state. Hence, after modifying an Item object, you need to call update() to make your changes permanent. Note that this call no longer reattaches the detached and modified item. It executes an immediate SQL UPDATE; the item is again in detached state after the command.

Disabling the persistence context and working with the StatelessSession interface has some other serious consequences and conceptual limitations (at least, if you compare it to a regular Session):

- A StatelessSession doesn't have a persistence context cache and doesn't interact with any other second-level or query cache. Everything you do results in immediate SQL operations.

- Modifications to objects aren't automatically detected (no dirty checking), and SQL operations aren't executed as late as possible (no write-behind).

- No modification of an object and no operation you call are cascaded to any associated instance. You're working with instances of a single entity class.

- Any modifications to a collection that is mapped as an entity association (one-to-many, many-to-many) are ignored. Only collections of value types are considered. You therefore shouldn't map entity associations with collections, but only the noninverse side with foreign keys to many-to-one; handle the relationship through one side only. Write a query to obtain data you'd otherwise retrieve by iterating through a mapped collection.

- The `StatelessSession` bypasses any enabled `org.hibernate.Interceptor` and can't be intercepted through the event system (both features are discussed later in this chapter).

- You have no guaranteed scope of object identity. The same query produces two different in-memory detached instances. This can lead to data-aliasing effects if you don't carefully implement the `equals()` method of your persistent classes.

Good use cases for a `StatelessSession` are rare; you may prefer it if manual batching with a regular `Session` becomes cumbersome. Remember that the `insert()`, `update()`, and `delete()` operations have naturally different semantics than the equivalent `save()`, `update()`, and `delete()` operations on a regular `Session`. (They probably should have different names, too; the `StatelessSession` API was added to Hibernate ad hoc, without much planning. The Hibernate developer team discussed renaming this interface in a future version of Hibernate; you may find it under a different name in the Hibernate version you're using.)

So far in this chapter, we've shown how you can store and manipulate many objects with the most efficient strategy through cascading, bulk, and batch operations. We'll now consider interception and data filtering, and how you can hook into Hibernate's processing in a transparent fashion.

12.3 Data filtering and interception

Imagine that you don't want to see all the data in your database. For example, the currently logged-in application user may not have the rights to see everything. Usually, you add a condition to your queries and restrict the result dynamically. This becomes difficult if you have to handle a concern such as security or temporal data ("Show me only data from last week," for example). Even more difficult is a restriction on collections; if you iterate through the Item objects in a Category, you'll see all of them.

One possible solution for this problem uses database views. SQL doesn't standardize dynamic views—views that can be restricted and moved at runtime with some parameter (the currently logged-in user, a time period, and so on). Few databases offer more flexible view options, and if they're available, they're pricey and/or complex (Oracle offers a Virtual Private Database addition, for example).

Hibernate provides an alternative to dynamic database views: *data filters* with dynamic parameterization at runtime. We'll look at the use cases and application of data filters in the following sections.

Another common issue in database applications is crosscutting concerns that require knowledge of the data that is stored or loaded. For example, imagine that you have to write an audit log of every data modification in your application. Hibernate offers an org.hibernate.Interceptor interface that allows you to hook into the internal processing of Hibernate and execute side effects such as audit logging. You can do much more with interception, and we'll show you a few tricks after we've completed our discussion of data filters.

The Hibernate core is based on an event/listener model, a result of the last refactoring of the internals. If an object must be loaded, for example, a LoadEvent is fired. The Hibernate core is implemented as default listeners for such events, and this system has public interfaces that let you plug in your own listeners if you like. The event system offers complete customization of any imaginable operation that happens inside Hibernate, and should be considered a more powerful alternative to interception—we'll show you how to write a custom listener and handle events yourself.

Let's first apply dynamic data filtering in a unit of work.

12.3.1 *Dynamic data filters*

The first use case for dynamic data filtering is related to data security. A User in CaveatEmptor has a ranking property. Now assume that users can only bid on items that are offered by other users with an equal or lower rank. In business terms, you have several groups of users that are defined by an arbitrary rank (a number), and users can trade only within their group.

You can implement this with complex queries. For example, let's say you want to show all the Item objects in a Category, but only those items that are sold by users in the same group (with an equal or lower rank than the logged-in user). You'd write an HQL or Criteria query to retrieve these items. However, if you use aCategory.getItems() and navigate to these objects, all Item instances would be visible.

You solve this problem with a dynamic filter.

Defining a data filter

A dynamic data filter is defined with a global unique name, in mapping metadata. You can add this global filter definition in any XML mapping file you like, as long as it's inside a <hibernate-mapping> element:

```
<filter-def name="limitItemsByUserRank">
    <filter-param name="currentUserRank" type="int"/>
</filter-def>
```

This filter is named limitItemsByUserRank and accepts one runtime argument of type int. You can put the equivalent @org.hibernate.annotations.FilterDef annotation on any class you like (or into package metadata); it has no effect on the behavior of that class:

```
@org.hibernate.annotations.FilterDef(
    name="limitItemsByUserRank",
    parameters = {
        @org.hibernate.annotations.ParamDef(
            name = "currentUserRank", type = "int"
        )
    }
)
```

The filter is inactive now; nothing (except maybe the name) indicates that it's supposed to apply to Item objects. You have to apply and implement the filter on the classes or collections you want to filter.

Applying and implementing the filter

You want to apply the defined filter on the Item class so that no items are visible if the logged-in user doesn't have the necessary rank:

```
<class name="Item" table="ITEM">
    ...

    <filter name="limitItemsByUserRank"
            condition=":currentUserRank >=
                        (select u.RANK from USER u
                        where u.USER_ID = SELLER_ID)"/>

</class>
```

The <filter> element can be set for a class mapping. It applies a named filter to instances of that class. The condition is an SQL expression that's passed through directly to the database system, so you can use any SQL operator or function. It must evaluate to *true* if a record should pass the filter. In this example, you use a subquery to obtain the rank of the seller of the item. Unqualified columns, such as SELLER_ID, refer to the table to which the entity class is mapped. If the currently logged-in user's rank isn't greater than or equal than the rank returned by the subquery, the Item instance is filtered out.

Here is the same in annotations on the Item entity:

```
@Entity
@Table(name = "ITEM")
@org.hibernate.annotations.Filter(
    name = "limitItemsByUserRank",
    condition=":currentUserRank >= " +
                "(select u.RANK from USER u" +
                " where u.USER_ID = SELLER_ID)"
)
public class Item implements { ... }
```

You can apply several filters by grouping them within a @org.hibernate.annotations.Filters annotation. A defined and applied filter, if enabled for a particular unit of work, filters out any Item instance that doesn't pass the condition. Let's enable it.

Enabling the filter

You've defined a data filter and applied it to a persistent class. It's still not filtering anything; it must be enabled and parameterized in the application for a particular Session (the EntityManager doesn't support this API—you have to fall back to Hibernate interfaces for this functionality):

```
Filter filter = session.enableFilter("limitItemsByUserRank");
filter.setParameter("currentUserRank", loggedInUser.getRanking());
```

You enable the filter by name; this method returns a Filter instance. This object accepts the runtime arguments. You must set the parameters you have defined. Other useful methods of the Filter are getFilterDefinition() (which allows you to iterate through the parameter names and types) and validate() (which throws a HibernateException if you forgot to set a parameter). You can also set a list of arguments with setParameterList(), this is mostly useful if your SQL condition contains an expression with a quantifier operator (the IN operator, for example).

Now every HQL or Criteria query that is executed on the filtered Session restricts the returned Item instances:

```
List<Item> filteredItems =
                session.createQuery("from Item").list();
List<Item> filteredItems =
                session.createCriteria(Item.class).list();
```

Two object-retrieval methods are *not* filtered: retrieval by identifier and navigational access to Item instances (such as from a Category with aCategory.get-
Items()).

Retrieval by identifier can't be restricted with a dynamic data filter. It's also
conceptually wrong: If you know the identifier of an Item, why shouldn't you be
allowed to see it? The solution is to filter the identifiers—that is, not expose identifiers that are restricted in the first place. Similar reasoning applies to filtering of
many-to-one or one-to-one associations. If a many-to-one association was filtered
(for example, by returning null if you call anItem.getSeller()), the multiplicity
of the association would change! This is also conceptually wrong and not the
intent of filters.

You can solve the second issue, navigational access, by applying the same filter
on a collection.

Filtering collections

So far, calling aCategory.getItems() returns all Item instances that are referenced by that Category. This can be restricted with a filter applied to a collection:

```
<class name="Category" table="CATEGORY">

    ...

    <set name="items" table="CATEGORY_ITEM">
        <key column="CATEGORY_ID"/>
        <many-to-many class="Item" column="ITEM_ID">

            <filter name="limitItemsByUserRank"
                    condition=":currentUserRank >=
                                (select u.RANK from USERS u where
    u.USER_ID = SELLER_ID)"/>
        </many-to-many>
    </set>

</class>
```

In this example, you don't apply the filter to the collection element but to the
<many-to-many>. Now the unqualified SELLER_ID column in the subquery refer-
ences the target of the association, the ITEM table, not the CATEGORY_ITEM join
table of the association. With annotations, you can apply a filter on a
many-to-many association with @org.hibernate.annotations.FilterJoin-
Table(s) on the @ManyToMany field or getter method.

If the association between `Category` and `Item` was one-to-many, you'd created the following mapping:

```
<class name="Category" table="CATEGORY">

    ...

    <set name="items">
        <key column="CATEGORY_ID"/>
        <one-to-many class="Item"/>

        <filter name="limitItemsByUserRank"
                condition=":currentUserRank >=
                            (select u.RANK from USERS u
    where u.USER_ID = SELLER_ID)"/>
    </set>

</class>
```

With annotations, you just place the `@org.hibernate.annotations.Filter(s)` on the right field or getter method, next to the `@OneToMany` or `@ManyToMany` annotation.

If you now enable the filter in a `Session`, all iteration through a collection of `items` of a `Category` is filtered.

If you have a default filter condition that applies to many entities, declare it with your filter definition:

```
<filter-def name="limitByRegion"
            condition="REGION >= :showRegion">
    <filter-param name="showRegion" type="int"/>
</filter-def>
```

If applied to an entity or collection with or without an additional condition and enabled in a `Session`, this filter always compares the `REGION` column of the entity table with the runtime `showRegion` argument.

There are many other excellent use cases for dynamic data filters.

Use cases for dynamic data filters

Hibernate's dynamic filters are useful in many situations. The only limitation is your imagination and your skill with SQL expressions. Typical use cases are as follows:

- *Security limits*—A common problem is the restriction of data access given some arbitrary security-related condition. This can be the rank of a user, a particular group the user must belong to, or a role the user has been assigned.

- *Regional data*—Often, data is stored with a regional code (for example, all business contacts of a sales team). Each salesperson works only on a dataset that covers their region.

- *Temporal data*—Many enterprise applications need to apply time-based views on data (for example, to see a dataset as it was last week). Hibernate's data filters can provide basic temporal restrictions that help you implement this kind of functionality.

Another useful concept is the interception of Hibernate internals, to implement orthogonal concerns.

12.3.2 Intercepting Hibernate events

Let's assume that you want to write an audit log of all object modifications. This audit log is kept in a database table that contains information about changes made to other data—specifically, about the *event* that results in the change. For example, you may record information about creation and update events for auction `Items`. The information that is recorded usually includes the user, the date and time of the event, what type of event occurred, and the item that was changed.

Audit logs are often handled using database triggers. On the other hand, it's sometimes better for the application to take responsibility, especially if portability between different databases is required.

You need several elements to implement audit logging. First, you have to mark the persistent classes for which you want to enable audit logging. Next, you define *what* information should be logged, such as the user, date, time, and type of modification. Finally, you tie it all together with an `org.hibernate.Interceptor` that automatically creates the audit trail.

Creating the marker interface

First, create a marker interface, `Auditable`. You use this interface to mark all persistent classes that should be automatically audited:

```
package auction.model;

public interface Auditable {
    public Long getId();
}
```

This interface requires that a persistent entity class exposes its identifier with a getter method; you need this property to log the audit trail. Enabling audit logging for a particular persistent class is then trivial. You add it to the class declaration—for example, for `Item`:

```
public class Item implements Auditable { ... }
```

Of course, if the `Item` class didn't expose a public `getId()` method, you'd need to add it.

Creating and mapping the log record

Now create a new persistent class, `AuditLogRecord`. This class represents the information you want to log in your audit database table:

```
public class AuditLogRecord {

    public String message;
    public Long entityId;
    public Class entityClass;
    public Long userId;
    public Date created;

    AuditLogRecord() {}

    public AuditLogRecord(String message,
                          Long entityId,
                          Class entityClass,
                          Long userId) {
        this.message = message;
        this.entityId = entityId;
        this.entityClass = entityClass;
        this.userId = userId;
        this.created = new Date();
    }
}
```

You shouldn't consider this class part of your domain model! Hence you expose all attributes as public; it's unlikely you'll have to refactor that part of the application. The `AuditLogRecord` is part of your persistence layer and possibly shares the same package with other persistence related classes, such as `HibernateUtil` or your custom `UserType` extensions.

Next, map this class to the `AUDIT_LOG` database table:

```
<hibernate-mapping default-access="field">

<class name="persistence.audit.AuditLogRecord"
       table="AUDIT_LOG" mutable="false">

    <id type="long" column="AUDIT_LOG_ID">
        <generator class="native"/>
    </id>

    <property    name="message"
                 type="string"
                 column="MESSAGE"
                 length="255"
```

```
                        not-null="true"/>
        <property    name="entityId"
                     type="long"
                     column="ENTITY_ID"
                     not-null="true"/>

        <property    name="entityClass"
                     type="class"
                     column="ENTITY_CLASS"
                     not-null="true"/>

        <property    name="userId"
                     type="long"
                     column="USER_ID"
                     not-null="true"/>

        <property    name="created"
                     column="CREATED"
                     type="java.util.Date"
                     update="false"
                     not-null="true"/>

    </class>

</hibernate-mapping>
```

You map the default access to a `field` strategy (no getter methods in the class) and, because `AuditLogRecord` objects are never updated, map the class as `mutable="false"`. Note that you don't declare an identifier property name (the class has no such property); Hibernate therefore manages the surrogate key of an `AuditLogRecord` internally. You aren't planning to use the `AuditLogRecord` in a detached fashion, so it doesn't need to contain an identifier property. However, if you mapped this class with annotation as a Java Persistence entity, an identifier property would be required. We think that you won't have any problems creating this entity mapping on your own.

Audit logging is a somewhat orthogonal concern to the business logic that causes the loggable event. It's possible to mix logic for audit logging with the business logic, but in many applications it's preferable that audit logging be handled in a central piece of code, transparently to the business logic (and especially when you rely on cascading options). Creating a new `AuditLogRecord` and saving it whenever an `Item` is modified is certainly something you wouldn't do manually. Hibernate offers an `Interceptor` extension interface.

Writing an interceptor

A `logEvent()` method should be called automatically when you call `save()`. The best way to do this with Hibernate is to implement the `Interceptor` interface. Listing 12.1 shows an interceptor for audit logging.

Listing 12.1 Implementation of an interceptor for audit logging

```
public class AuditLogInterceptor extends EmptyInterceptor {

    private Session session;
    private Long userId;

    private Set inserts = new HashSet();
    private Set updates = new HashSet();

    public void setSession(Session session) {
        this.session=session;
    }

    public void setUserId(Long userId) {
        this.userId=userId;
    }

    public boolean onSave(Object entity,
                          Serializable id,
                          Object[] state,
                          String[] propertyNames,
                          Type[] types)
            throws CallbackException {

        if (entity instanceof Auditable)
            inserts.add(entity);

        return false;
    }

    public boolean onFlushDirty(Object entity,
                                Serializable id,
                                Object[] currentState,
                                Object[] previousState,
                                String[] propertyNames,
                                Type[] types)
            throws CallbackException {
        if (entity instanceof Auditable)
            updates.add(entity);

        return false;
    }

    public void postFlush(Iterator iterator)
                throws CallbackException {
        try {
            for (Iterator it = inserts.iterator(); it.hasNext();) {
```

```
            Auditable entity = (Auditable) it.next();
            AuditLog.logEvent("create",
                              entity,
                              userId,
                              session.connection());
        }
        for (Iterator it = updates.iterator(); it.hasNext();) {
            Auditable entity = (Auditable) it.next();
            AuditLog.logEvent("update",
                              entity,
                              userId,
                              session.connection());
        }
    } finally {
        inserts.clear();
        updates.clear();
    }
}
}
```

The Hibernate `Interceptor` API has many more methods than shown in this example. Because you're extending the `EmptyInterceptor`, instead of implementing the interface directly, you can rely on default semantics of all methods you don't override. The interceptor has two interesting aspects.

This interceptor needs the `session` and `userId` attributes to do its work; a client using this interceptor must set both properties. The other interesting aspect is the audit-log routine in `onSave()` and `onFlushDirty()`: You add new and updated entities to the `inserts` and `updates` collections. The `onSave()` interceptor method is called whenever an entity is saved by Hibernate; the `onFlush-Dirty()` method is called whenever Hibernate detects a dirty object.

The actual logging of the audit trail is done in the `postFlush()` method, which Hibernate calls after executing the SQL that synchronizes the persistence context with the database. You use the static call `AuditLog.logEvent()` (a class and method we discuss next) to log the event. Note that you can't log events in `onSave()`, because the identifier value of a transient entity may not be known at this point. Hibernate guarantees to set entity identifiers during flush, so `post-Flush()` is the correct place to log this information.

Also note how you use the `session`: You pass the JDBC connection of a given `Session` to the static call to `AuditLog.logEvent()`. There is a good reason for this, as we'll discuss in more detail.

Let's first tie it all together and see how you enable the new interceptor.

Enabling the interceptor

You need to assign the `Interceptor` to a Hibernate `Session` when you first open the session:

```
AuditLogInterceptor interceptor = new AuditLogInterceptor();
Session session = getSessionFactory().openSession(interceptor);
Transaction tx = session.beginTransaction();

interceptor.setSession(session);
interceptor.setUserId( currentUser.getId() );

session.save(newItem); // Triggers onSave() of the Interceptor

tx.commit();
session.close();
```

The interceptor is active for the `Session` you open it with.

If you work with `sessionFactory.getCurrentSession()`, you don't control the opening of a `Session`; it's handled transparently by one of Hibernate's built-in implementations of `CurrentSessionContext`. You can write your own (or extend an existing) `CurrentSessionContext` implementation and supply your own routine for opening the current `Session` and assigning an interceptor to it.

Another way to enable an interceptor is to set it globally on the `Configuration` with `setInterceptor()` before building the `SessionFactory`. However, any interceptor that is set on a `Configuration` and active for all `Sessions` must be implemented thread-safe! The single `Interceptor` instance is shared by concurrently running `Sessions`. The `AuditLogInterceptor` implementation isn't thread-safe: It uses member variables (the `inserts` and `updates` queues).

You can also set a shared thread-safe interceptor that has a no-argument constructor for all `EntityManager` instances in JPA with the following configuration option in persistence.xml:

```
<persistence-unit name="...">
  <properties>
      <property name="hibernate.ejb.interceptor"
                value="my.ThreadSafeInterceptorImpl"/>
      ...
  </properties>
</persistence-unit>
```

Let's get back to that interesting `Session`-handling code in the interceptor and find out why you pass the `connection()` of the current `Session` to `AuditLog.logEvent()`.

Using a temporary Session

It should be clear why you require a Session inside the AuditLogInterceptor. The interceptor has to create and persist AuditLogRecord objects, so a first attempt for the onSave() method could be the following routine:

```
if (entity instanceof Auditable) {

    AuditLogRecord logRecord = new AuditLogRecord(...);
    // set the log information

    session.save(logRecord);
}
```

This seems straightforward: Create a new AuditLogRecord instance and save it, using the currently running Session. This doesn't work.

It's illegal to invoke the original Hibernate Session from an Interceptor callback. The Session is in a fragile state during interceptor calls. You can't save() a new object during the saving of other objects! A nice trick that avoids this issue is opening a new Session only for the purpose of saving a single AuditLogRecord object. You reuse the JDBC connection from the original Session.

This *temporary* Session handling is encapsulated in the AuditLog class, shown in listing 12.2.

Listing 12.2 The AuditLog helper class uses a temporary Session

```
public class AuditLog {

    public static void logEvent(
        String message,
        Auditable entity,
        Long userId,
        Connection connection) {

        Session tempSession =
                getSessionFactory().openSession(connection);

        try {
            AuditLogRecord record =
                new AuditLogRecord(message,
                                   entity.getId(),
                                   entity.getClass(),
                                   userId );

            tempSession.save(record);
            tempSession.flush();

        } finally {
            tempSession.close();
```

```
            }
        }
    }
```

The logEvent() method uses a new Session on the same JDBC connection, but it never starts or commits any database transaction. All it does is execute a single SQL statement during flushing.

This trick with a temporary Session for some operations on the same JDBC connection and transaction is sometimes useful in other situations. All you have to remember is that a Session is nothing more than a cache of persistent objects (the persistence context) and a queue of SQL operations that synchronize this cache with the database.

We encourage you to experiment and try different interceptor design patterns. For example, you could redesign the auditing mechanism to log any entity, not only Auditable. The Hibernate website also has examples using nested interceptors or even for logging a complete history (including updated property and collection information) for an entity.

The org.hibernate.Interceptor interface also has many more methods that you can use to hook into Hibernate's processing. Most of them let you influence the outcome of the intercepted operation; for example, you can veto the saving of an object. We think that interception is almost always sufficient to implement any orthogonal concern.

Having said that, Hibernate allows you to hook deeper into its core with the extendable event system it's based on.

12.3.3 *The core event system*

Hibernate 3.x was a major redesign of the implementation of the core persistence engine compared to Hibernate 2.x. The new core engine is based on a model of events and listeners. For example, if Hibernate needs to save an object, an event is triggered. Whoever listens to this kind of event can catch it and handle the saving of the object. All Hibernate core functionalities are therefore implemented as a set of default listeners, which can handle all Hibernate events.

This has been designed as an open system: You can write and enable your own listeners for Hibernate events. You can either replace the existing default listeners or extend them and execute a side effect or additional procedure. Replacing the event listeners is rare; doing so implies that your own listener implementation can take care of a piece of Hibernate core functionality.

Essentially, all the methods of the `Session` interface correlate to an event. The `load()` method triggers a `LoadEvent`, and by default this event is processed with the `DefaultLoadEventListener`.

A custom listener should implement the appropriate interface for the event it wants to process and/or extend one of the convenience base classes provided by Hibernate, or any of the default event listeners. Here's an example of a custom load event listener:

```
public class SecurityLoadListener extends DefaultLoadEventListener {

    public void onLoad(LoadEvent event,
                       LoadEventListener.LoadType loadType)
        throws HibernateException {

        if ( !MySecurity.isAuthorized(
            event.getEntityClassName(), event.getEntityId()
            )
        ) {
            throw MySecurityException("Unauthorized access");
        }

        super.onLoad(event, loadType);

    }
}
```

This listener calls the static method `isAuthorized()` with the entity name of the instance that has to be loaded and the database identifier of that instance. A custom runtime exception is thrown if access to that instance is denied. If no exception is thrown, the processing is passed on to the default implementation in the superclass.

Listeners should be considered effectively singletons, meaning they're shared between requests and thus shouldn't save any transaction related state as instance variables. For a list of all events and listener interfaces in native Hibernate, see the API Javadoc of the `org.hibernate.event` package. A listener implementation can also implement multiple event-listener interfaces.

Custom listeners can either be registered programmatically through a Hibernate `Configuration` object or specified in the Hibernate configuration XML (declarative configuration through the properties file isn't supported). You also need a configuration entry telling Hibernate to use the listener in addition to the default listener:

```
<session-factory>
    ...
    <event type="load">
```

```
        <listener class="auction.persistence.MyLoadListener"/>
    </event>

</session-factory>
```

Listeners are registered in the same order they're listed in your configuration file. You can create a stack of listeners. In this example, because you're extending the built-in `DefaultLoadEventListener`, there is only one. If you didn't extend the `DefaultLoadEventListener`, you'd have to name the built-in `DefaultLoad-EventListener` as the first listener in your stack—otherwise you'd disable loading in Hibernate!

Alternatively you may register your listener stack programmatically:

```
Configuration cfg = new Configuration();

LoadEventListener[] listenerStack =
    { new MyLoadListener(), … };

cfg.getEventListeners().setLoadEventListeners(listenerStack);
```

Listeners registered declaratively can't share instances. If the same class name is used in multiple `<listener/>` elements, each reference results in a separate instance of that class. If you need the capability to share listener instances between listener types, you must use the programmatic registration approach.

Hibernate `EntityManager` also supports customization of listeners. You can configure shared event listeners in your `persistence.xml` configuration as follows:

```
<persistence-unit name="...">
  <properties>
      <property name="hibernate.ejb.event.load"
                value="auction.persistence.MyLoadListener, …"/>
      ...
  </properties>
</persistence-unit>
```

The property name of the configuration option changes for each event type you want to listen to (`load` in the previous example).

If you replace the built-in listeners, as `MyLoadListener` does, you need to extend the correct default listeners. At the time of writing, Hibernate `EntityMan-ager` doesn't bundle its own `LoadEventListener`, so the listener that extends `org.hibernate.event.DefaultLoadEventListener` still works fine. You can find a complete and up-to-date list of Hibernate `EntityManager` default listeners in the reference documentation and the Javadoc of the `org.hibernate.ejb.event` package. Extend any of these listeners if you want to keep the basic behavior of the Hibernate `EntityManager` engine.

You rarely have to extend the Hibernate core event system with your own functionality. Most of the time, an `org.hibernate.Interceptor` is flexible enough. It helps to have more options and to be able to replace any piece of the Hibernate core engine in a modular fashion.

The EJB 3.0 standard includes several interception options, for session beans and entities. You can wrap any custom interceptor around a session bean method call, intercept any modification to an entity instance, or let the Java Persistence service call methods on your bean on particular lifecycle events.

12.3.4 *Entity listeners and callbacks*

EJB 3.0 entity listeners are classes that intercept entity callback events, such as the loading and storing of an entity instance. This is similar to native Hibernate interceptors. You can write custom listeners, and attach them to entities through annotations or a binding in your XML deployment descriptor.

Look at the following trivial entity listener:

```
import javax.persistence.*;

public class MailNotifyListener {

    @PostPersist
    @PostLoad
    public void notifyAdmin(Object entity) {
        mail.send("Somebody saved or loaded: " + entity);
    }

}
```

An entity listener doesn't implement any particular interface; it needs a no-argument constructor (in the previous example, this is the default constructor). You apply callback annotations to any methods that need to be notified of a particular event; you can combine several callbacks on a single method. You aren't allowed to duplicate the same callback on several methods.

The listener class is bound to a particular entity class through an annotation:

```
import javax.persistence.*;

@Entity
@EntityListeners(MailNotifyListener.class)
public class Item {
    ...

    @PreRemove
    private void cleanup() {
        ...
    }
}
```

The @EntityListeners annotation takes an array of classes, if you need to bind several listeners. You can also place callback annotations on the entity class itself, but again, you can't duplicate callbacks on methods in a single class. However, you can implement the same callback in several listener classes or in the listener and entity class.

You can also apply listeners to superclasses for the whole hierarchy and define default listeners in your persistence.xml configuration file. Finally, you can exclude superclass listeners or default listeners for a particular entity with the @ExcludeSuperclassListeners and @ExcludeDefaultListeners annotations.

All callback methods can have any visibility, must return void, and aren't allowed to throw any checked exceptions. If an unchecked exception is thrown, and a JTA transaction is in progress, this transaction is rolled back.

A list of available JPA callbacks is shown in Table 12.2.

Table 12.2 JPA event callbacks and annotations

Callback annotation	Description
@PostLoad	Triggered after an entity instance has been loaded with find() or getReference(), or when a Java Persistence query is executed. Also called after the refresh() method is invoked.
@PrePersist, @PostPersist	Occurs immediately when persist() is called on an entity, and after the database insert.
@PreUpdate, @PostUpdate	Executed before and after the persistence context is synchronized with the database—that is, before and after flushing. Triggered only when the state of the entity requires synchronization (for example, because it's considered dirty).
@PreRemove, @PostRemove	Triggered when remove() is called or the entity instance is removed by cascading, and after the database delete.

Unlike Hibernate interceptors, entity listeners are stateless classes. You therefore can't rewrite the previous Hibernate audit-logging example with entity listeners, because you'd need to hold the state of modified objects in local queues. Another problem is that an entity listener class isn't allowed to use the EntityManager. Certain JPA implementations, such as Hibernate, let you again apply the trick with a temporary second persistence context, but you should look at EJB 3.0 interceptors for session beans and probably code this audit-logging at a higher layer in your application stack.

12.4 *Summary*

In this chapter, you learned how to work with large and complex datasets efficiently. We first looked at Hibernate's cascading options and how transitive persistence can be enabled with Java Persistence and annotations. Then we covered the bulk operations in HQL and JPA QL and how you write batch procedures that work on a subset of data to avoid memory exhaustion.

In the last section, you learned how to enable Hibernate data filtering and how you can create dynamic data views at the application level. Finally, we introduced the Hibernate `Interceptor` extension point, the Hibernate core event system, and the standard Java Persistence entity callback mechanism.

Table 12.3 shows a summary you can use to compare native Hibernate features and Java Persistence.

In the next chapter, we switch perspective and discuss how you retrieve objects from the database with the best-performing fetching and caching strategy.

Table 12.3   Hibernate and JPA comparison chart for chapter 12

Hibernate Core	Java Persistence and EJB 3.0
Hibernate supports transitive persistence with cascading options for all operations.	Transitive persistence model with cascading options equivalent to Hibernate. Use Hibernate annotations for special cases.
Hibernate supports bulk `UPDATE`, `DELETE`, and `INSERT ... SELECT` operations in polymorphic HQL, which are executed directly in the database.	JPA QL supports direct bulk `UPDATE` and `DELETE`.
Hibernate supports query result cursors for batch updates.	Java Persistence does not standardize querying with cursors, fall back to the Hibernate API.
Powerful data filtering is available for the creation of dynamic data views.	Use Hibernate extension annotations for the mapping of data filters.
Extension points are available for interception and event listeners.	Provides standardized entity lifecycle callback handlers.

Optimizing fetching and caching

This chapter covers

- Global fetching strategies
- Caching in theory
- Caching in practice

In this chapter, we'll show you how to retrieve objects from the database and how you can optimize the loading of object networks when you navigate from object to object in your application.

We then enable caching; you'll learn how to speed up data retrieval in local and distributed applications.

13.1 Defining the global fetch plan

Retrieving persistent objects from the database is one of the most interesting parts of working with Hibernate.

13.1.1 The object-retrieval options

Hibernate provides the following ways to get objects out of the database:

- Navigating the object graph, starting from an already loaded object, by accessing the associated objects through property accessor methods such as `aUser.getAddress().getCity()`, and so on. Hibernate automatically loads (and preloads) nodes of the graph while you call accessor methods, if the persistence context is still open.

- Retrieval by identifier, the most convenient method when the unique identifier value of an object is known.

- The Hibernate Query Language (HQL), which is a full object-oriented query language. The Java Persistence query language (JPA QL) is a standardized subset of the Hibernate query language.

- The Hibernate `Criteria` interface, which provides a type-safe and object-oriented way to perform queries without the need for string manipulation. This facility includes queries based on example objects.

- Native SQL queries, including stored procedure calls, where Hibernate still takes care of mapping the JDBC result sets to graphs of persistent objects.

In your Hibernate or JPA application, you use a combination of these techniques.

We won't discuss each retrieval method in much detail in this chapter. We're more interested in the so-called default *fetch plan* and *fetching strategies*. The default fetch plan and fetching strategy is the plan and strategy that applies to a particular entity association or collection. In other words, it defines *if* and *how* an associated object or a collection should be loaded, when the owning entity object is loaded, and when you access an associated object or collection. Each retrieval method may use a different plan and strategy—that is, a plan that defines what part of the persistent object network should be retrieved and how it should be retrieved. Your goal is to find the best retrieval method and fetching strategy for every use case in your application; at the same time, you also want to minimize the number of SQL queries for best performance.

Before we look at the fetch plan options and fetching strategies, we'll give you an overview of the retrieval methods. (We also mention the Hibernate caching system sometimes, but we fully explore it later in this chapter.)

You saw how objects are retrieved by identifier earlier in the previous chapter, so we won't repeat it here. Let's go straight to the more flexible query options, HQL (equivalent to JPA QL) and `Criteria`. Both allow you to create arbitrary queries.

The Hibernate Query Language and JPA QL

The Hibernate Query Language is an object-oriented dialect of the familiar database query language SQL. HQL bears some close resemblance to ODMG OQL, but unlike OQL, it's adapted for use with SQL databases and is easier to learn (thanks to its close resemblance to SQL) and fully implemented (we don't know of any OQL implementation that is complete).

The EJB 3.0 standard defines the Java Persistence query language. This new JPA QL and the HQL have been aligned so that JPA QL is a *subset* of HQL. A valid JPA QL query is always also a valid HQL query; HQL has more options that should be considered vendor extensions of the standardized subset.

HQL is commonly used for object retrieval, not for updating, inserting, or deleting data. Object state synchronization is the job of the persistence manager, not the developer. But, as we've shown in the previous chapter, HQL and JPA QL support direct bulk operations for updating, deleting, and inserting, if required by the use case (mass data operations).

Most of the time, you only need to retrieve objects of a particular class and restrict by the properties of that class. For example, the following query retrieves a user by first name.

```
Query q = session.createQuery(
    "from User as u where u.firstname = :fname"
);
q.setString("fname", "John");
List result = q.list();
```

After preparing query q, you bind a value to the named parameter :fname. The result is returned as a `List` of `User` objects.

HQL is powerful, and even though you may not use the more advanced features all the time, they're needed for more difficult problems. For example, HQL supports

- The ability to apply restrictions to properties of associated objects related by reference or held in collections (to navigate the object graph using query language).

- The ability to retrieve only properties of an entity or entities, without the overhead of loading the entity itself into the persistence context. This is sometimes called a report query; it is more correctly called *projection*.

- The ability to order the results of the query.

- The ability to paginate the results.

- Aggregation with `group by`, `having`, and aggregate functions like `sum`, `min`, and `max`/`min`.

- Outer joins when retrieving multiple objects per row.

- The ability to call standard and user-defined SQL functions.

- Subqueries (nested queries).

We discuss all these features in chapters 14 and 15, together with the optional native SQL query mechanism.

Querying with a criteria

The Hibernate *query by criteria* (QBC) API allows a query to be built by manipulation of criteria objects at runtime. This lets you specify constraints dynamically without direct string manipulations, but you don't lose much of the flexibility or power of HQL. On the other hand, queries expressed as criteria are often much less readable than queries expressed in HQL.

Retrieving a user by first name is easy with a `Criteria` object:

```
Criteria criteria = session.createCriteria(User.class);
criteria.add( Restrictions.like("firstname", "John") );
List result = criteria.list();
```

A `Criteria` is a tree of `Criterion` instances. The `Restrictions` class provides static factory methods that return `Criterion` instances. Once the desired criteria tree is build, it's executed against the database.

Many developers prefer query by criteria, considering it a more object-oriented approach. They also like the fact that the query syntax may be parsed and validated at compile time, whereas HQL expressions aren't parsed until runtime (or startup, if externalized named queries are used).

The nice thing about the Hibernate `Criteria` API is the `Criterion` framework. This framework allows extension by the user, which is more difficult in the case of a query language like HQL.

Note that the `Criteria` API is native to Hibernate; it isn't part of the Java Persistence standard. In practice, `Criteria` will be the most common Hibernate extension you utilize in your JPA application. We expect that a future version of the JPA or EJB standard will include a similar programmatic query interface.

Querying by example

As part of the `Criteria` facility, Hibernate supports *query by example* (QBE). The idea behind query by example is that the application supplies an instance of the queried class, with certain property values set (to nondefault values). The query returns all persistent instances with matching property values. Query by example isn't a particularly powerful approach. However, it can be convenient for some applications, especially if it's used in combination with `Criteria`:

```
Criteria criteria = session.createCriteria(User.class);

User exampleUser = new User();
exampleUser.setFirstname("John");
criteria.add( Example.create(exampleUser) );

criteria.add( Restrictions.isNotNull("homeAddress.city") );

List result = criteria.list();
```

This example first creates a new `Criteria` that queries for `User` objects. Then you add an `Example` object, a `User` instance with only the `firstname` property set. Finally, a `Restriction` criterion is added before executing the query.

A typical use case for query by example is a search screen that allows users to specify a range of different property values to be matched by the returned result set. This kind of functionality can be difficult to express cleanly in a query language; string manipulations are required to specify a dynamic set of constraints.

The `Criteria` API and the example query mechanism are discussed in more detail in chapter 15.

You now know the basic retrieval options in Hibernate. We focus on the object-fetching plans and strategies for the rest of this section.

Let's start with the definition of *what* should be loaded into memory.

13.1.2 *The lazy default fetch plan*

Hibernate defaults to a *lazy* fetching strategy for all entities and collections. This means that Hibernate by default loads only the objects you're querying for. Let's explore this with a few examples.

If you query for an Item object (let's say you load it by its identifier), exactly this Item and nothing else is loaded into memory:

```
Item item = (Item) session.load(Item.class, new Long(123));
```

This retrieval by identifier results in a single (or possibly several, if inheritance or secondary tables are mapped) SQL statement that retrieves an Item instance. In the persistence context, in memory, you now have this item object available in persistent state, as shown in figure 13.1.

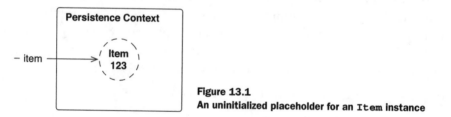

Figure 13.1
An uninitialized placeholder for an Item instance

We've lied to you. What is available in memory after the load() operation isn't a persistent item object. Even the SQL that loads an Item isn't executed. Hibernate created a *proxy* that looks like the real thing.

13.1.3 *Understanding proxies*

Proxies are placeholders that are generated at runtime. Whenever Hibernate returns an instance of an entity class, it checks whether it can return a proxy instead and avoid a database hit. A proxy is a placeholder that triggers the loading of the real object when it's accessed for the first time:

```
Item item = (Item) session.load(Item.class, new Long(123));
item.getId();
item.getDescription(); // Initialize the proxy
```

The third line in this example triggers the execution of the SQL that retrieves an Item into memory. As long as you access only the database identifier property, no initialization of the proxy is necessary. (Note that this isn't true if you map the identifier property with direct field access; Hibernate then doesn't even know that the getId() method exists. If you call it, the proxy has to be initialized.)

A proxy is useful if you need the Item only to create a reference, for example:

```
Item item = (Item) session.load(Item.class, new Long(123));
User user = (User) session.load(User.class, new Long(1234));

Bid newBid = new Bid("99.99");
newBid.setItem(item);
newBid.setBidder(user);

session.save(newBid);
```

You first load two objects, an Item and a User. Hibernate doesn't hit the database to do this: It returns two proxies. This is all you need, because you only require the Item and User to create a new Bid. The save(newBid) call executes an INSERT statement to save the row in the BID table with the foreign key value of an Item and a User—this is all the proxies can and have to provide. The previous code snippet doesn't execute any SELECT!

If you call get() instead of load() you trigger a database hit and no proxy is returned. The get() operation always hits the database (if the instance isn't already in the persistence context and if no transparent second-level cache is active) and returns null if the object can't be found.

A JPA provider can implement lazy loading with proxies. The method names of the operations that are equivalent to load() and get() on the EntityManager API are find() and getReference():

```
Item item = em.find(Item.class, new Long(123));

Item itemRef = em.getReference(Item.class, new Long(1234));
```

The first call, find(), has to hit the database to initialize an Item instance. No proxies are allowed—it's the equivalent of the Hibernate get() operation. The second call, getReference(), *may* return a proxy, but it doesn't have to—which translates to load() in Hibernate.

Because Hibernate proxies are instances of runtime generated subclasses of your entity classes, you can't get the class of an object with the usual operators. This is where the helper method HibernateProxyHelper.getClassWithoutInitializingProxy(o) is useful.

Let's assume you have an Item instance into memory, either by getting it explicitly or by calling one of its properties and forcing initialization of a proxy. Your persistence context now contains a fully loaded object, as shown in figure 13.2.

Again, you can see proxies in the picture. This time, these are proxies that have been generated for all *-to-one* associations. Associated entity objects are *not* loaded right away; the proxies carry the identifier values only. From a different

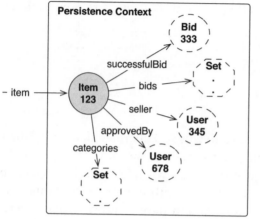

Figure 13.2
Proxies and collection wrappers represent the boundary of the loaded graph.

perspective: the identifier values are all foreign key columns in the item's row. Collections also aren't loaded right away, but we use the term *collection wrapper* to describe this kind of placeholder. Internally, Hibernate has a set of smart collections that can initialize themselves on demand. Hibernate replaces your collections with these; that is why you should use collection interfaces only in your domain model. By default, Hibernate creates placeholders for all associations and collections, and only retrieves value-typed properties and components right away. (This is unfortunately not the default fetch plan standardized by Java Persistence; we'll get back to the differences later.)

> **FAQ** *Does lazy loading of one-to-one associations work?* Lazy loading for one-to-one associations is sometimes confusing for new Hibernate users. If you consider one-to-one associations based on shared primary keys (chapter 7, section 7.1.1, "Shared primary key associations"), an association can be proxied only if it's `constrained="true"`. For example, an `Address` always has a reference to a `User`. If this association is nullable and optional, Hibernate first would have to hit the database to find out whether a proxy or a `null` should be applied—the purpose of lazy loading is to not hit the database at all. You can enable lazy loading through bytecode instrumentation and interception, which we'll discuss later.

A proxy is initialized if you call any method that is not the identifier getter method, a collection is initialized if you start iterating through its elements or if you call any of the collection-management operations, such as `size()` and `contains()`. Hibernate provides an additional setting that is mostly useful for large collections; they can be mapped as *extra* lazy. For example, consider the collection of bids of an Item:

```
<class name="Item" table="ITEM">
    ...

    <set name="bids"
         lazy="extra"
         inverse="true">
        <key column="ITEM_ID"/>
        <one-to-many class="Bid"/>
    </set>

</class>
```

The collection wrapper is now smarter than before. The collection is no longer initialized if you call `size()`, `contains()`, or `isEmpty()`—the database is queried to retrieve the necessary information. If it's a `Map` or a `List`, the operations `containsKey()` and `get()` also query the database directly. A Hibernate extension annotation enables the same optimization:

```
@OneToMany
@org.hibernate.annotations.LazyCollection(
    org.hibernate.annotations.LazyCollectionOption.EXTRA
)
private Set<Bid> bids = new HashSet<Bid>();
```

Let's define a fetch plan that isn't completely lazy. First, you can disable proxy generation for entity classes.

13.1.4 Disabling proxy generation

Proxies are a good thing: They allow you to load only the data that is really needed. They even let you create associations between objects without hitting the database unnecessarily. Sometimes you need a different plan—for example, you want to express that a `User` object should *always* be loaded into memory and no placeholder should be returned instead.

You can disable proxy generation for a particular entity class with the `lazy="false"` attribute in XML mapping metadata:

```
<class name="User"
       table="USERS"
       lazy="false">
    ...
</class>
```

The JPA standard doesn't require an implementation with proxies; the word proxy doesn't even appear in the specification. Hibernate *is* a JPA provider that relies on proxies by default, so the switch that disables Hibernate proxies is available as a vendor extension:

```
@Entity
@Table(name = "USERS")
@org.hibernate.annotations.Proxy(lazy = false)
public class User { ... }
```

Disabling proxy generation for an entity has serious consequences. All of these operations require a database hit:

```
User user = (User) session.load(User.class, new Long(123));
User user = em.getReference(User.class, new Long(123));
```

A `load()` of a `User` object can't return a proxy. The JPA operation `getReference()` can no longer return a proxy reference. This may be what you desired to achieve. However, disabling proxies also has consequences for all associations that reference the entity. For example, the `Item` entity has a `seller` association to a `User`. Consider the following operations that retrieve an `Item`:

```
Item item = (Item) session.get(Item.class, new Long(123));
Item item = em.find(Item.class, new Long(123));
```

In addition to retrieving the `Item` instance, the `get()` operation now also loads the linked `seller` of the `Item`; no `User` proxy is returned for this association. The same is true for JPA: The `Item` that has been loaded with `find()` doesn't reference a `seller` proxy. The `User` who is selling the `Item` must be loaded right away. (We answer the question *how* this is fetched later.)

Disabling proxy generation on a global level is often too coarse-grained. Usually, you only want to disable the lazy loading behavior of a particular entity association or collection to define a fine-grained fetch plan. You want the opposite: eager loading of a particular association or collection.

13.1.5 *Eager loading of associations and collections*

You've seen that Hibernate is lazy by default. All associated entities and collections aren't initialized if you load an entity object. Naturally, you often want the opposite: to specify that a particular entity association or collection should *always* be loaded. You want the guarantee that this data is available in memory without an additional database hit. More important, you want a guarantee that, for example, you can access the `seller` of an `Item` if the `Item` instance is in detached state. You have to define this fetch plan, the part of your object network that you want to always load into memory.

Let's assume that you always require the seller of an Item. In Hibernate XML mapping metadata you'd map the association from Item to User as lazy="false":

```
<class name="Item" table="ITEM">
    ...

    <many-to-one name="seller"
                 class="User"
                 column="SELLER_ID"
                 update="false"
                 not-null="true"
                 lazy="false"/>
    ...
</class>
```

The same "always load" guarantee can be applied to collections—for example, all bids of an Item:

```
<class name="Item" table="ITEM">
    ...

    <many-to-one name="seller" lazy="false" .../>
    <set name="bids"
         lazy="false"
         inverse="true">
      <key column="ITEM_ID"/>
      <one-to-many class="Bid"/>
    </set>

    ...
</class>
```

If you now get() an Item (or force the initialization of a proxied Item), both the seller object and all the bids are loaded as persistent instances into your persistence context:

```
Item item = (Item) session.get(Item.class, new Long(123));
```

The persistence context after this call is shown graphically in figure 13.3.

Other lazy mapped associations and collections (the bidder of each Bid instance, for example) are again uninitialized and are loaded as soon as you access them. Imagine that you close the persistence context after loading an Item. You can now navigate, in detached state, to the seller of the Item and iterate through all the bids for that Item. If you navigate to the categories this Item is assigned to, you get a LazyInitializationException! Obviously, this collection

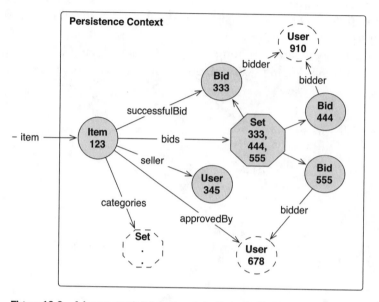

Figure 13.3   A larger graph fetched eagerly through disabled lazy associations and collections

wasn't part of your fetch plan and wasn't initialized before the persistence context was closed. This also happens if you try to access a proxy—for example, the User that approved the item. (Note that you can access this proxy two ways: through the approvedBy and bidder references.)

With annotations, you switch the FetchType of an entity association or a collection to get the same result:

```
@Entity
public class Item {

    ...

    @ManyToOne(fetch = FetchType.EAGER)
    private User seller;

    @OneToMany(fetch = FetchType.EAGER)
    private Set<Bid> bids = new HashSet<Bid>();

    ...
}
```

The FetchType.EAGER provides the same guarantees as lazy="false" in Hibernate: the associated entity instance must be fetched eagerly, not lazily. We already mentioned that Java Persistence has a different default fetch plan than Hibernate. Although all associations in Hibernate are completely lazy, all @ManyToOne and

`@OneToOne` associations default to `FetchType.EAGER`! This default was standardized to allow Java Persistence provider implementations without lazy loading (in practice, such a persistence provider wouldn't be very useful). We recommend that you default to the Hibernate lazy loading fetch plan by setting `FetchType.LAZY` in your to-one association mappings and only override it when necessary:

```
@Entity
public class Item {

    ...

    @ManyToOne(fetch = FetchType.LAZY)
    private User seller;

    ...

}
```

You now know how to create a fetch plan; that is, how you define what part of the persistent object network should be retrieved into memory. Before we show you how to define *how* these objects should be loaded and how you can optimize the SQL that will be executed, we'd like to demonstrate an alternative lazy loading strategy that doesn't rely on proxies.

13.1.6 *Lazy loading with interception*

Runtime proxy generation as provided by Hibernate is an excellent choice for transparent lazy loading. The only requirement that this implementation exposes is a package or public visible no-argument constructor in classes that must be proxied and nonfinal methods and class declarations. At runtime, Hibernate generates a subclass that acts as the proxy class; this isn't possible with a private constructor or a final entity class.

On the other hand, many other persistence tools don't use runtime proxies: They use *interception*. We don't know of many good reasons why you'd use interception instead of runtime proxy generation in Hibernate. The nonprivate constructor requirement certainly isn't a big deal. However, in two cases, you may not want to work with proxies:

- The only cases where runtime proxies aren't completely transparent are polymorphic associations that are tested with `instanceof`. Or, you may want to typecast an object but can't, because the proxy is an instance of a runtime-generated subclass. We show how to avoid this issue and how to work around the problem in chapter 7, section 7.3.1, "Polymorphic many-to-one associations." Interception instead of proxies also makes these issues disappear.

- Proxies and collection wrappers can only be used to lazy load entity associations and collections. They can't be used to lazy load individual scalar properties or components. We consider this kind of optimization to be rarely useful. For example, you usually don't want to lazy load the initialPrice of an Item. Optimizing at the level of individual columns that are selected in SQL is unnecessary if you aren't working with (a) a significant number of optional columns or (b) with optional columns containing large values that have to be retrieved on-demand. Large values are best represented with *locator objects* (LOBs); they provide lazy loading by definition without the need for interception. However, interception (in addition to proxies, usually) can help you to optimize column reads.

Let's discuss interception for lazy loading with a few examples.

Imagine that you don't want to utilize a proxy of User entity class, but you still want the benefit of lazy loading an association to User—for example, as seller of an Item. You map the association with no-proxy:

```
<class name="Item" table="ITEM">
    ...

    <many-to-one name="seller"
                 class="User"
                 column="SELLER_ID"
                 update="false"
                 not-null="true"
                 lazy="no-proxy"/>
    ...
</class>
```

The default of the lazy attribute is proxy. By setting no-proxy, you're telling Hibernate to apply interception to this association:

```
Item item = (Item) session.get(Item.class, new Long(123));
User seller = item.getSeller();
```

The first line retrieves an Item object into persistent state. The second line accesses the seller of that Item. This call to getSeller() is intercepted by Hibernate and triggers the loading of the User in question. Note how proxies are more lazy than interception: You can call item.getSeller().getId() without forcing initialization of the proxy. This makes interception less useful if you only want to set references, as we discussed earlier.

You can also lazy load properties that are mapped with <property> or <component>; here the attribute that enables interception is lazy="true", in Hibernate XML mappings. With annotations, @Basic(fetch = FetchType.LAZY) is a hint for Hibernate that a property or component should be lazy loaded through interception.

To disable proxies and enable interception for associations with annotations, you have to rely on a Hibernate extension:

```
@ManyToOne
@JoinColumn(name="SELLER_ID", nullable = false, updatable = false)
@org.hibernate.annotations.LazyToOne(
    org.hibernate.annotations.LazyToOneOption.NO_PROXY

)
private User seller;
```

To enable interception, the bytecode of your classes must be instrumented after compilation, before runtime. Hibernate provides an Ant task for that purpose:

```
<target name="instrument" depends="compile">

    <taskdef name="instrument"
            classname=
    "org.hibernate.tool.instrument.cglib.InstrumentTask"
            classpathref="project.classpath"/>

    <instrument verbose="true">
        <fileset dir="${build.dir}/my/entity/package/">
            <include name="*.class"/>
        </fileset>
    </instrument>

</target>
```

We leave it up to you if you want to utilize interception for lazy loading—in our experience, good use cases are rare.

Naturally, you not only want to define *what* part of your persistent object network must be loaded, but also *how* these objects are retrieved. In addition to creating a fetch plan, you want to optimize it with the right fetching strategies.

13.2 Selecting a fetch strategy

Hibernate executes SQL SELECT statements to load objects into memory. If you load an object, a single or several SELECTs are executed, depending on the number of tables which are involved and the *fetching strategy* you've applied.

Your goal is to minimize the number of SQL statements and to simplify the SQL statements, so that querying can be as efficient as possible. You do this by applying the best fetching strategy for each collection or association. Let's walk through the different options step by step.

By default, Hibernate fetches associated objects and collections lazily whenever you access them (we assume that you map all to-one associations as `FetchType.LAZY` if you use Java Persistence). Look at the following trivial code example:

```
Item item = (Item) session.get(Item.class, new Long(123));
```

You didn't configure any association or collection to be nonlazy, and that proxies can be generated for all associations. Hence, this operation results in the following SQL SELECT:

```
select item.* from ITEM item where item.ITEM_ID = ?
```

(Note that the real SQL Hibernate produces contains automatically generated aliases; we've removed them for readability reasons in all the following examples.) You can see that the SELECT queries only the ITEM table and retrieves a particular row. All entity associations and collections aren't retrieved. If you access any proxied association or uninitialized collection, a second SELECT is executed to retrieve the data on demand.

Your first optimization step is to reduce the number of additional on-demand SELECTs you necessarily see with the default lazy behavior—for example, by prefetching data.

13.2.1 *Prefetching data in batches*

If every entity association and collection is fetched only on demand, many additional SQL SELECT statements may be necessary to complete a particular procedure. For example, consider the following query that retrieves all Item objects and accesses the data of each items seller:

```
List allItems = session.createQuery("from Item").list();

processSeller( (Item)allItems.get(0) );
processSeller( (Item)allItems.get(1) );
processSeller( (Item)allItems.get(2) );
```

Naturally, you use a loop here and iterate through the results, but the problem this code exposes is the same. You see one SQL SELECT to retrieve all the Item objects, and an additional SELECT for *every* seller of an Item as soon as you process it. All associated User objects are proxies. This is one of the worst-case scenarios we'll describe later in more detail: the *n+1 selects problem*. This is what the SQL looks like:

```
select items...

select u.* from USERS u where u.USER_ID = ?
select u.* from USERS u where u.USER_ID = ?
```

```
select u.* from USERS u where u.USER_ID = ?
...
```

Hibernate offers some algorithms that can prefetch User objects. The first optimization we now discuss is called *batch fetching*, and it works as follows: If one proxy of a User must be initialized, go ahead and initialize several in the same SELECT. In other words, if you already know that there are three Item instances in the persistence context, and that they all have a proxy applied to their seller association, you may as well initialize all the proxies instead of just one.

Batch fetching is often called a *blind-guess optimization*, because you don't know how many uninitialized User proxies may be in a particular persistence context. In the previous example, this number depends on the number of Item objects returned. You make a guess and apply a *batch-size* fetching strategy to your User class mapping:

```
<class name="User"
        table="USERS"
        batch-size="10">
...
</class>
```

You're telling Hibernate to prefetch up to 10 uninitialized proxies in a single SQL SELECT, if one proxy must be initialized. The resulting SQL for the earlier query and procedure may now look as follows:

```
select items...

select u.* from USERS u where u.USER_ID in (?, ?, ?)
```

The first statement that retrieves all Item objects is executed when you list() the query. The next statement, retrieving three User objects, is triggered as soon as you initialize the first proxy returned by allItems.get(0).getSeller(). This query loads three sellers at once—because this is how many items the initial query returned and how many proxies are uninitialized in the current persistence context. You defined the batch size as "up to 10." If more than 10 items are returned, you see how the second query retrieves 10 sellers in one batch. If the application hits another proxy that hasn't been initialized, a batch of another 10 is retrieved—and so on, until no more uninitialized proxies are left in the persistence context or the application stops accessing proxied objects.

FAQ   *What is the real batch-fetching algorithm?* You can think about batch fetching as explained earlier, but you may see a slightly different algorithm if you experiment with it in practice. It's up to you if you want to know and understand this algorithm, or if you trust Hibernate to do the right thing. As an example, imagine a batch size of 20 and a total number of 119 uninitialized proxies that have to be loaded in batches. At startup time, Hibernate reads the mapping metadata and creates 11 batch loaders internally. Each loader knows how many proxies it can initialize: 20, 10, 9, 8, 7, 6, 5, 4, 3, 2, 1. The goal is to minimize the memory consumption for loader creation and to create enough loaders that every possible batch fetch can be produced. Another goal is to minimize the number of SQL SELECTs, obviously. To initialize 119 proxies Hibernate executes seven batches (you probably expected six, because 6 x 20 > 119). The batch loaders that are applied are five times 20, one time 10, and one time 9, automatically selected by Hibernate.

Batch fetching is also available for collections:

```
<class name="Item" table="ITEM">
    ...
    <set name="bids"
         inverse="true"
         batch-size="10">
        <key column="ITEM_ID"/>
        <one-to-many class="Bid"/>
    </set>

</class>
```

If you now force the initialization of one bids collection, up to 10 more collections of the same type, if they're uninitialized in the current persistence context, are loaded right away:

```
select items...

select b.* from BID b where b.ITEM_ID in (?, ?, ?)
```

In this case, you again have three Item objects in persistent state, and touching one of the unloaded bids collections. Now all three Item objects have their bids loaded in a single SELECT.

Batch-size settings for entity proxies and collections are also available with annotations, but only as Hibernate extensions:

```
@Entity
@Table(name = "USERS")
@org.hibernate.annotations.BatchSize(size = 10)
public class User { ... }

@Entity
public class Item {

    ...

    @OneToMany
```

```
@org.hibernate.annotations.BatchSize(size = 10)
private Set<Bid> bids = new HashSet<Bid>();

...

}
```

Prefetching proxies and collections with a batch strategy is really a blind guess. It's a smart optimization that can significantly reduce the number of SQL statements that are otherwise necessary to initialize all the objects you're working with. The only downside of prefetching is, of course, that you may prefetch data you won't need in the end. The trade-off is possibly higher memory consumption, with fewer SQL statements. The latter is often much more important: Memory is cheap, but scaling database servers isn't.

Another prefetching algorithm that isn't a blind guess uses *subselects* to initialize many collections with a single statement.

13.2.2 *Prefetching collections with subselects*

Let's take the last example and apply a (probably) better prefetch optimization:

```
List allItems = session.createQuery("from Item").list();

processBids( (Item)allItems.get(0) );
processBids( (Item)allItems.get(1) );
processBids( (Item)allItems.get(2) );
```

You get one initial SQL SELECT to retrieve all Item objects, and one additional SELECT for each bids collection, when it's accessed. One possibility to improve this would be batch fetching; however, you'd need to figure out an optimum batch size by trial. A much better optimization is *subselect fetching* for this collection mapping:

```
<class name="Item" table="ITEM">
    ...
    <set name="bids"
         inverse="true"
         fetch="subselect">
        <key column="ITEM_ID"/>
        <one-to-many class="Bid"/>
    </set>

</class>
```

Hibernate now initializes *all* bids collections for all loaded Item objects, as soon as you force the initialization of one bids collection. It does that by rerunning the first initial query (slightly modified) in a subselect:

```
select i.* from ITEM i

select b.* from BID b
    where b.ITEM_ID in (select i.ITEM_ID from ITEM i)
```

In annotations, you again have to use a Hibernate extension to enable this optimization:

```
@OneToMany
@org.hibernate.annotations.Fetch(
    org.hibernate.annotations.FetchMode.SUBSELECT
)
private Set<Bid> bids = new HashSet<Bid>();}
```

Prefetching using a subselect is a powerful optimization; we'll show you a few more details about it later, when we walk through a typical scenario. Subselect fetching is, at the time of writing, available only for collections, not for entity proxies. Also note that the original query that is rerun as a subselect is only remembered by Hibernate for a particular `Session`. If you detach an `Item` instance without initializing the collection of `bids`, and then reattach it and start iterating through the collection, no prefetching of other collections occurs.

All the previous fetching strategies are helpful if you try to reduce the number of additional `SELECT`s that are natural if you work with lazy loading and retrieve objects and collections on demand. The final fetching strategy is the opposite of on-demand retrieval. Often you want to retrieve associated objects or collections in the same initial `SELECT` with a `JOIN`.

13.2.3 *Eager fetching with joins*

Lazy loading is an excellent default strategy. On other hand, you can often look at your domain and data model and say, "Every time I need an `Item`, I also need the `seller` of that `Item`." If you can make that statement, you should go into your mapping metadata, enable *eager fetching* for the `seller` association, and utilize SQL joins:

```
<class name="Item" table="ITEM">
    ...
    <many-to-one name="seller"
                 class="User"
                 column="SELLER_ID"
                 update="false"
                 fetch="join"/>

</class>
```

Hibernate now loads both an `Item` and its `seller` in a single SQL statement. For example:

```
Item item = (Item) session.get(Item.class, new Long(123));
```

This operation triggers the following SQL SELECT:

```
select i.*, u.*
from ITEM i
    left outer join USERS u on i.SELLER_ID = u.USER_ID
where i.ITEM_ID = ?
```

Obviously, the seller is no longer lazily loaded on demand, but immediately. Hence, a fetch="join" disables lazy loading. If you only enable eager fetching with lazy="false", you see an immediate second SELECT. With fetch="join", you get the seller loaded in the same single SELECT. Look at the resultset from this query shown in figure 13.4.

select i.*, u.* from ITEM i
left outer join USERS u on i.SELLER_ID = u.USER_ID
where i.ITEM_ID = ?

ITEM_ID	DESCRIPTION	SELLER_ID	...	USER_ID	USERNAME	...
1	Item Nr. One	2	...	2	johndoe	...

Figure 13.4   Two tables are joined to eagerly fetch associated rows.

Hibernate reads this row and marshals two objects from the result. It connects them with a reference from Item to User, the seller association. If an Item doesn't have a seller all u.* columns are filled with NULL. This is why Hibernate uses an *outer* join, so it can retrieve not only Item objects with sellers, but all of them. But you know that an Item has to have a seller in CaveatEmptor. If you enable <many-to-one not-null="true"/>, Hibernate executes an inner join instead of an outer join.

You can also set the eager join fetching strategy on a collection:

```
<class name="Item" table="ITEM">
    ...
    <set name="bids"
         inverse="true"
         fetch="join">
        <key column="ITEM_ID"/>
        <one-to-many class="Bid"/>
    </set>

</class>
```

If you now load many Item objects, for example with createCriteria(Item. class).list(), this is how the resulting SQL statement looks:

```
select i.*, b.*
from ITEM i
    left outer join BID b on i.ITEM_ID = b.ITEM_ID
```

The resultset now contains *many* rows, with duplicate data for each Item that has many bids, and NULL fillers for all Item objects that don't have bids. Look at the resultset in figure 13.5.

Hibernate creates three persistent Item instances, as well as four Bid instances, and links them all together in the persistence context so that you can navigate this graph and iterate through collections—even when the persistence context is closed and all objects are detached.

Eager-fetching collections using *inner* joins is conceptually possible, and we'll do this later in HQL queries. However, it wouldn't make sense to cut off all the Item objects without bids in a global fetching strategy in mapping metadata, so there is no option for global inner join eager fetching of collections.

With Java Persistence annotations, you enable eager fetching with a FetchType annotation attribute:

```
@Entity
public class Item {

    ...

    @ManyToOne(fetch = FetchType.EAGER)
    private User seller;

    @OneToMany(fetch = FetchType.EAGER)
    private Set<Bid> bids = new HashSet<Bid>();

    ...
}
```

This mapping example should look familiar: You used it to disable lazy loading of an association and a collection earlier. Hibernate by default interprets this as an

select i.* , b.* from ITEM i
left outer join BID b on i.ITEM_ID = b.ITEM_ID

ITEM_ID	DESCRIPTION	...	BID_ID	ITEM_ID	AMOUNT
1	Item Nr. One	...	1	1	99.00
1	Item Nr. One	...	2	1	100.00
1	Item Nr. One	...	3	1	101.00
2	Item Nr. Two	...	4	2	4.99
3	Item Nr. Three	...	NULL	NULL	NULL

Figure 13.5
Outer join fetching of associated collection elements

eager fetch that shouldn't be executed with an immediate second SELECT, but with a JOIN in the initial query.

You can keep the FetchType.EAGER Java Persistence annotation but switch from join fetching to an immediate second select explicitly by adding a Hibernate extension annotation:

```
@Entity
public class Item {

    ...

    @ManyToOne(fetch = FetchType.EAGER)
    @org.hibernate.annotations.Fetch(
        org.hibernate.annotations.FetchMode.SELECT
    )
    private User seller;

}
```

If an Item instance is loaded, Hibernate will eagerly load the seller of this item with an immediate second SELECT.

Finally, we have to introduce a global Hibernate configuration setting that you can use to control the maximum number of joined entity associations (not collections). Consider all many-to-one and one-to-one association mappings you've set to fetch="join" (or FetchType.EAGER) in your mapping metadata. Let's assume that Item has a successfulBid association, that Bid has a bidder, and that User has a shippingAddress. If all these associations are mapped with fetch="join", how many tables are joined and how much data is retrieved when you load an Item?

The number of tables joined in this case depends on the global hibernate. max_fetch_depth configuration property. By default, no limit is set, so loading an Item also retrieves a Bid, a User, and an Address in a single select. Reasonable settings are small, usually between 1 and 5. You may even *disable* join fetching for many-to-one and one-to-one associations by setting the property to 0! (Note that some database dialects may preset this property: For example, MySQLDialect sets it to 2.)

SQL queries also get more complex if inheritance or joined mappings are involved. You need to consider a few extra optimization options whenever secondary tables are mapped for a particular entity class.

13.2.4 *Optimizing fetching for secondary tables*

If you query for objects that are of a class which is part of an inheritance hierarchy, the SQL statements get more complex:

```
List result = session.createQuery("from BillingDetails").list();
```

This operation retrieves all `BillingDetails` instances. The SQL `SELECT` now depends on the inheritance mapping strategy you've chosen for `BillingDetails` and its subclasses `CreditCard` and `BankAccount`. Assuming that you've mapped them all to one table (a *table-per-hierarchy*), the query isn't any different than the one shown in the previous section. However, if you've mapped them with implicit polymorphism, this single HQL operation may result in *several* SQL `SELECT`s against each table of each subclass.

Outer joins for a table-per-subclass hierarchy

If you map the hierarchy in a normalized fashion (see the tables and mapping in chapter 5, section 5.1.4, "Table per subclass"), all subclass tables are `OUTER JOIN`ed in the initial statement:

```
select
    b1.BILLING_DETAILS_ID,
    b1.OWNER,
    b1.USER_ID,
    b2.NUMBER,
    b2.EXP_MONTH,
    b2.EXP_YEAR,
    b3.ACCOUNT,
    b3.BANKNAME,
    b3.SWIFT,
    case
        when b2.CREDIT_CARD_ID is not null then 1
        when b3.BANK_ACCOUNT_ID is not null then 2
        when b1.BILLING_DETAILS_ID is not null then 0
    end as clazz
from
        BILLING_DETAILS b1
    left outer join
        CREDIT_CARD b2
            on b1.BILLING_DETAILS_ID = b2.CREDIT_CARD_ID
    left outer join
        BANK_ACCOUNT b3
            on b1.BILLING_DETAILS_ID = b3.BANK_ACCOUNT_ID
```

This is already a interesting query. It joins three tables and utilizes a `CASE` ... `WHEN` ... `END` expression to fill in the `clazz` column with a number between 0 and 2. Hibernate can then read the resultset and decide on the basis of this number what class each of the returned rows represents an instance of.

Many database-management systems limit the maximum number of tables that can be combined with an `OUTER JOIN`. You'll possibly hit that limit if you have a wide and deep inheritance hierarchy mapped with a normalized strategy (we're talking about inheritance hierarchies that should be reconsidered to accommodate the fact that after all, you're working with an SQL database).

Switching to additional selects

In mapping metadata, you can then tell Hibernate to switch to a different fetching strategy. You want some parts of your inheritance hierarchy to be fetched with immediate additional SELECT statements, not with an OUTER JOIN in the initial query.

The only way to enable this fetching strategy is to refactor the mapping slightly, as a mix of *table-per-hierarchy* (with a discriminator column) and *table-per-subclass* with the <join> mapping:

```
<class name="BillingDetails"
       table="BILLING_DETAILS"
       abstract="true">

    <id name="id"
        column="BILLING_DETAILS_ID"
        .../>

    <discriminator
        column="BILLING_DETAILS_TYPE"
          type="string"/>

    ...
    <subclass name="CreditCard" discriminator-value="CC">
        <join table="CREDIT_CARD" fetch="select">
            <key column="CREDIT_CARD_ID"/>
            ...
        </join>
    </subclass>

    <subclass name="BankAccount" discriminator-value="BA">
        <join table="BANK_ACCOUNT" fetch="join">
            <key column="BANK_ACCOUNT_ID"/>
            ...

        </join>
    </subclass>

</class>
```

This mapping breaks out the CreditCard and BankAccount classes each into its own table but preserves the discriminator column in the superclass table. The fetching strategy for CreditCard objects is select, whereas the strategy for BankAccount is the default, join. Now, if you query for all BillingDetails, the following SQL is produced:

```
select
    b1.BILLING_DETAILS_ID,
    b1.OWNER,
    b1.USER_ID,
    b2.ACCOUNT,
    b2.BANKNAME,
    b2.SWIFT,
    b1.BILLING_DETAILS_TYPE as clazz
from
    BILLING_DETAILS b1
    left outer join
        BANK_ACCOUNT b2
            on b1.BILLING_DETAILS_ID = b2.BANK_ACCOUNT_ID

select cc.NUMBER, cc.EXP_MONTH, cc.EXP_YEAR
from CREDIT_CARD cc where cc.CREDIT_CARD_ID = ?

select cc.NUMBER, cc.EXP_MONTH, cc.EXP_YEAR
from CREDIT_CARD cc where cc.CREDIT_CARD_ID = ?
```

The first SQL SELECT retrieves all rows from the superclass table and all rows from
the BANK_ACCOUNT table. It also returns discriminator values for each row as the
clazz column. Hibernate now executes an additional select against the CREDIT_
CARD table for each row of the first result that had the right discriminator for a
CreditCard. In other words, two queries mean that two rows in the BILLING_
DETAILS superclass table represent (part of) a CreditCard object.

This kind of optimization is rarely necessary, but you now also know that you
can switch from a default join fetching strategy to an additional immediate
select whenever you deal with a <join> mapping.

We've now completed our journey through all options you can set in mapping
metadata to influence the default fetch plan and fetching strategy. You learned
how to define *what* should be loaded by manipulating the lazy attribute, and *how*
it should be loaded by setting the fetch attribute. In annotations, you use
FetchType.LAZY and FetchType.EAGER, and you use Hibernate extensions for
more fine-grained control of the fetch plan and strategy.

Knowing all the available options is only one step toward an optimized and
efficient Hibernate or Java Persistence application. You also need to know when
and when not to apply a particular strategy.

13.2.5 *Optimization guidelines*

By default, Hibernate never loads data that you didn't ask for, which reduces
the memory consumption of your persistence context. However, it also exposes
you to the so-called n+1 selects problem. If every association and collection is

initialized only on demand, and you have no other strategy configured, a particular procedure may well execute dozens or even hundreds of queries to get all the data you require. You need the right strategy to avoid executing too many SQL statements.

If you switch from the default strategy to queries that eagerly fetch data with joins, you may run into another problem, the *Cartesian product* issue. Instead of executing too many SQL statements, you may now (often as a side effect) create statements that retrieve too much data.

You need to find the middle ground between the two extremes: the correct fetching strategy for each procedure and use case in your application. You need to know which global fetch plan and strategy you should set in your mapping metadata, and which fetching strategy you apply only for a particular query (with HQL or `Criteria`).

We now introduce the basic problems of too many selects and Cartesian products and then walk you through optimization step by step.

The n+1 selects problem

The n+1 selects problem is easy to understand with some example code. Let's assume that you don't configure any fetch plan or fetching strategy in your mapping metadata: Everything is lazy and loaded on demand. The following example code tries to find the highest `Bids` for all `Items` (there are many other ways to do this more easily, of course):

```
List<Item> allItems = session.createQuery("from Item").list();
// List<Item> allItems = session.createCriteria(Item.class).list();

Map<Item, Bid> highestBids = new HashMap<Item, Bid>();

for (Item item : allItems) {
    Bid highestBid = null;
    for (Bid bid : item.getBids() ) { // Initialize the collection
        if (highestBid == null)
            highestBid = bid;
        if (bid.getAmount() > highestBid.getAmount())
            highestBid = bid;
    }
    highestBids.put(item, highestBid);
}
```

First you retrieve all `Item` instances; there is no difference between HQL and `Criteria` queries. This query triggers one SQL `SELECT` that retrieves all rows of the `ITEM` table and returns *n* persistent objects. Next, you iterate through this result and access each `Item` object.

What you access is the `bids` collection of each `Item`. This collection isn't initialized so far, the `Bid` objects for each item have to be loaded with an additional query. This whole code snippet therefore produces n+1 selects.

You always want to avoid n+1 selects.

A first solution could be a change of your global mapping metadata for the collection, enabling prefetching in batches:

```
<set name="bids"
    inverse="true"
    batch-size="10">
    <key column="ITEM_ID"/>
    <one-to-many class="Bid"/>
</set>
```

Instead of n+1 selects, you now see n/10+1 selects to retrieve the required collections into memory. This optimization seems reasonable for an auction application: "Only load the bids for an item when they're needed, on demand. But if one collection of bids must be loaded for a particular item, assume that other item objects in the persistence context also need their bids collections initialized. Do this in batches, because it's somewhat likely that *not all* item objects need their bids."

With a subselect-based prefetch, you can reduce the number of selects to exactly two:

```
<set name="bids"
    inverse="true"
    fetch="subselect">
    <key column="ITEM_ID"/>
    <one-to-many class="Bid"/>
</set>
```

The first query in the procedure now executes a single SQL SELECT to retrieve all `Item` instances. Hibernate remembers this statement and applies it again when you hit the first uninitialized collection. All collections are initialized with the second query. The reasoning for this optimization is slightly different: "Only load the bids for an item when they're needed, on demand. But if one collection of bids must be loaded, for a particular item, assume that *all* other item objects in the persistence context also need their bids collection initialized."

Finally, you can effectively turn off lazy loading of the `bids` collection and switch to an eager fetching strategy that results in only a single SQL SELECT:

```
<set name="bids"
    inverse="true"
    fetch="join">
```

```
        <key column="ITEM_ID"/>
        <one-to-many class="Bid"/>
    </set>
```

This seems to be an optimization you shouldn't make. Can you really say that "whenever an item is needed, all its bids are needed as well"? Fetching strategies in mapping metadata work on a global level. We don't consider fetch="join" a common optimization for collection mappings; you rarely need a fully initialized collection *all the time.* In addition to resulting in higher memory consumption, every OUTER JOINed collection is a step toward a more serious Cartesian product problem, which we'll explore in more detail soon.

In practice, you'll most likely enable a batch or subselect strategy in your mapping metadata for the bids collection. If a particular procedure, such as this, requires all the bids for each Item in-memory, you modify the initial HQL or Criteria query and apply a dynamic fetching strategy:

```
List<Item> allItems =
    session.createQuery("from Item i left join fetch i.bids")
           .list();

List<Item> allItems =
    session.createCriteria(Item.class)
        .setFetchMode("bids", FetchMode.JOIN)
        .list();

// Iterate through the collections...
```

Both queries result in a single SELECT that retrieves the bids for all Item instances with an OUTER JOIN (as it would if you have mapped the collection with join="fetch").

This is likely the first time you've seen how to define a fetching strategy that isn't global. The global fetch plan and fetching strategy settings you put in your mapping metadata are just that: global defaults that always apply. Any optimization process also needs more fine-grained rules, fetching strategies and fetch plans that are applicable for only a particular procedure or use case. We'll have much more to say about fetching with HQL and Criteria in the next chapter. All you need to know now is that these options exist.

The n+1 selects problem appears in more situations than just when you work with lazy collections. Uninitialized proxies expose the same behavior: You may need many SELECTs to initialize all the objects you're working with in a particular procedure. The optimization guidelines we've shown are the same, but there is one exception: The fetch="join" setting on <many-to-one> or <one-to-one> associations is a common optimization, as is a @ManyToOne(fetch = FetchType.EAGER) annotation (which is the default in Java Persistence). Eager join fetching of single-ended associations, unlike eager outer-join fetching of collections, doesn't create a Cartesian product problem.

The Cartesian product problem

The opposite of the n+1 selects problem are SELECT statements that fetch *too much* data. This Cartesian product problem always appears if you try to fetch several "parallel" collections.

Let's assume you've made the decision to apply a global fetch="join" setting to the bids collection of an Item (despite our recommendation to use global prefetching and a dynamic join-fetching strategy only when necessary). The Item class has other collections: for example, the images. Let's also assume that you decide that all images for each item have to be loaded all the time, eagerly with a fetch="join" strategy:

```
<class name="Item">
    ...

    <set name="bids"
         inverse="true"
         fetch="join">
        <key column="ITEM_ID"/>
        <one-to-many class="Bid"/>
    </set>

    <set name="images"
         fetch="join">
        <key column="ITEM_ID"/>
        <composite-element class="Image">...
    </set>

</class>
```

If you map two parallel collections (their owning entity is the same) with an eager outer-join fetching strategy, and load all Item objects, Hibernate executes an SQL SELECT that creates a product of the two collections:

```
select item.*, bid.*, image.*
    from ITEM item
        left outer join BID bid on item.ITEM_ID = bid.ITEM_ID
        left outer join ITEM_IMAGE image on item.ITEM_ID = image.ITEM_ID
```

Look at the resultset of that query, shown in figure 13.6.

This resultset contains lots of redundant data. Item 1 has three bids and two images, item 2 has one bid and one image, and item 3 has no bids and no images. The size of the product depends on the size of the collections you're retrieving: 3 times 2, 1 times 1, plus 1, total 8 result rows. Now imagine that you have 1,000

```
select item.*, bid.*, image.* from ITEM item
left outer join BID bid on item.ITEM_ID = bid.ITEM_ID
left outer join ITEM_IMAGE image on item.ITEM_ID = image.ITEM_ID
```

ITEM_ID	DESCRIPTION	...	BID_ID	ITEM_ID	AMOUNT	...	IMAGE_NAME
1	Item Nr. One	...	1	1	99.00	...	foo.jpg
1	Item Nr. One	...	1	1	99.00	...	bar.jpg
1	Item Nr. One	...	2	1	100.00	...	foo.jpg
1	Item Nr. One	...	2	1	100.00	...	bar.jpg
1	Item Nr. One	...	3	1	101.00	...	foo.jpg
1	Item Nr. One	...	3	1	101.00	...	bar.jpg
2	Item Nr. Two	...	4	2	4.99	...	baz.jpg
3	Item Nr. Three	...	NULL	NULL	NULL	...	NULL

Figure 13.6 A product is the result of two outer joins with many rows.

items in the database, and each item has 20 bids and 5 images—you'll see a result-set with possibly 100,000 rows! The size of this result may well be several megabytes. Considerable processing time and memory are required on the database server to create this resultset. All the data must be transferred across the network. Hibernate immediately removes all the duplicates when it marshals the resultset into persistent objects and collections—redundant information is skipped. Three queries are certainly faster!

You get three queries if you map the parallel collections with fetch="subselect"; this is the recommended optimization for parallel collections. However, for every rule there is an exception. As long as the collections are small, a product may be an acceptable fetching strategy. Note that parallel single-valued associations that are eagerly fetched with outer-join SELECTs don't create a product, by nature.

Finally, although Hibernate lets you create Cartesian products with fetch="join" on two (or even more) parallel collections, it throws an exception if you try to enable fetch="join" on parallel <bag> collections. The result-set of a product can't be converted into bag collections, because Hibernate can't know which rows contain duplicates that are valid (bags allow duplicates) and which aren't. If you use bag collections (they are the default @OneToMany collection in Java Persistence), don't enable a fetching strategy that results in products. Use subselects or immediate secondary-select fetching for parallel eager fetching of bag collections.

Global and dynamic fetching strategies help you to solve the n+1 selects and Cartesian product problems. Hibernate offers another option to initialize a proxy or a collection that is sometimes useful.

Forcing proxy and collection initialization

A proxy or collection wrapper is automatically initialized whenever any of its methods are invoked (except for the identifier property getter, which may return the identifier value without fetching the underlying persistent object). Prefetching and eager join fetching are possible solutions to retrieve all the data you'd need.

You sometimes want to work with a network of objects in detached state. You retrieve all objects and collections that should be detached and then close the persistence context.

In this scenario, it's sometimes useful to explicitly initialize an object before closing the persistence context, without resorting to a change in the global fetching strategy or a different query (which we consider the solution you should always prefer).

You can use the static method `Hibernate.initialize()` for manual initialization of a proxy:

```
Session session = sessionFactory.openSession();
Transaction tx = session.beginTransaction();

Item item = (Item) session.get(Item.class, new Long(1234));

Hibernate.initialize( item.getSeller() );

tx.commit();
session.close();

processDetached( item.getSeller() );
...
```

`Hibernate.initialize()` may be passed a collection wrapper or a proxy. Note that if you pass a collection wrapper to `initialize()`, it doesn't initialize the target entity objects that are referenced by this collection. In the previous example, `Hibernate.initalize( item.getBids() )` wouldn't load all the `Bid` objects inside that collection. It initializes the collection with proxies of `Bid` objects!

Explicit initialization with this static helper method is rarely necessary; you should always prefer a dynamic fetch with HQL or `Criteria`.

Now that you know all the options, problems, and possibilities, let's walk through a typical application optimization procedure.

Optimization step by step

First, enable the Hibernate SQL log. You should also be prepared to read, understand, and evaluate SQL queries and their performance characteristics for your specific database schema: Will a single outer-join operation be faster than two selects? Are all the indexes used properly, and what is the cache hit-ratio inside the database? Get your DBA to help you with that performance evaluation; only he has the knowledge to decide what SQL execution plan is the best. (If you want to become an expert in this area, we recommend the book *SQL Tuning* by Dan Tow, [Tow, 2003].)

The two configuration properties `hibernate.format_sql` and `hibernate.use_sql_comments` make it a lot easier to read and categorize SQL statements in your log files. Enable both during optimization.

Next, execute use case by use case of your application and note how many and what SQL statements are executed by Hibernate. A use case can be a single screen in your web application or a sequence of user dialogs. This step also involves collecting the object retrieval methods you use in each use case: walking the object links, retrieval by identifier, HQL, and `Criteria` queries. Your goal is to bring down the number (and complexity) of SQL statements for each use case by tuning the default fetch plan and fetching strategy in metadata.

It's time to define your fetch plan. Everything is lazy loaded by default. Consider switching to `lazy="false"` (or `FetchType.EAGER`) on many-to-one, one-to-one, and (sometimes) collection mappings. The global fetch plan defines the objects that are always eagerly loaded. Optimize your queries and enable eager fetching if you need eagerly loaded objects not globally, but in a particular procedure—a use case only.

Once the fetch plan is defined and the amount of data required by a particular use case is known, optimize *how* this data is retrieved. You may encounter two common issues:

- *The SQL statements use join operations that are too complex and slow.* First optimize the SQL execution plan with your DBA. If this doesn't solve the problem, remove `fetch="join"` on collection mappings (or don't set it in the first place). Optimize all your many-to-one and one-to-one associations by considering if they really need a `fetch="join"` strategy or if the associated object should be loaded with a secondary select. Also try to tune with the global `hibernate.max_fetch_depth` configuration option, but keep in mind that this is best left at a value between 1 and 5.

■ *Too many SQL statements may be executed.* Set fetch="join" on many-to-one and one-to-one association mappings. In rare cases, if you're absolutely sure, enable fetch="join" to disable lazy loading for particular collections. Keep in mind that more than one eagerly fetched collection per persistent class creates a product. Evaluate whether your use case can benefit from prefetching of collections, with batches or subselects. Use batch sizes between 3 and 15.

After setting a new fetching strategy, rerun the use case and check the generated SQL again. Note the SQL statements and go to the next use case. After optimizing all use cases, check every one again and see whether any global optimization had side effects for others. With some experience, you'll easily be able to avoid any negative effects and get it right the first time.

This optimization technique is practical for more than the default fetching strategies; you may also use it to tune HQL and Criteria queries, which can define the fetch plan and the fetching strategy dynamically. You often can replace a global fetch setting with a new dynamic query or a change of an existing query—we'll have much more to say about these options in the next chapter.

In the next section, we introduce the Hibernate caching system. Caching data on the application tier is a complementary optimization that you can utilize in any sophisticated multiuser application.

13.3 *Caching fundamentals*

A major justification for our claim that applications using an object/relational persistence layer are expected to outperform applications built using direct JDBC is the potential for caching. Although we'll argue passionately that most applications should be designed so that it's possible to achieve acceptable performance *without* the use of a cache, there is no doubt that for some kinds of applications, especially read-mostly applications or applications that keep significant metadata in the database, caching can have an enormous impact on performance. Furthermore, scaling a highly concurrent application to thousands of online transactions usually requires some caching to reduce the load on the database server(s).

We start our exploration of caching with some background information. This includes an explanation of the different caching and identity scopes and the impact of caching on transaction isolation. This information and these rules can be applied to caching in general and are valid for more than just Hibernate applications. This discussion gives you the background to understand why the

Hibernate caching system is the way it is. We then introduce the Hibernate caching system and show you how to enable, tune, and manage the first- and second-level Hibernate cache. We recommend that you carefully study the fundamentals laid out in this section before you start using the cache. Without the basics, you may quickly run into hard to debug concurrency problems and risk the integrity of your data.

Caching is all about performance optimization, so naturally it isn't part of the Java Persistence or EJB 3.0 specification. Every vendor provides different solutions for optimization, in particular any second-level caching. All strategies and options we present in this section work for a native Hibernate application or an application that depends on Java Persistence interfaces and uses Hibernate as a persistence provider.

A cache keeps a representation of current database state close to the application, either in memory or on disk of the application server machine. The cache is a local copy of the data. The cache sits between your application and the database. The cache may be used to avoid a database hit whenever

- The application performs a lookup by identifier (primary key).
- The persistence layer resolves an association or collection lazily.

It's also possible to cache the results of queries. As you'll see in the chapter 15, the performance gain of caching query results is minimal in many cases, so this functionality is used much less often.

Before we look at how Hibernate's cache works, let's walk through the different caching options and see how they're related to identity and concurrency.

13.3.1 *Caching strategies and scopes*

Caching is such a fundamental concept in object/relational persistence that you can't understand the performance, scalability, or transactional semantics of an ORM implementation without first knowing what kind of caching strategy (or strategies) it uses. There are three main types of cache:

- *Transaction scope cache*—Attached to the current unit of work, which may be a database transaction or even a conversation. It's valid and used only as long as the unit of work runs. Every unit of work has its own cache. Data in this cache isn't accessed concurrently.

- *Process scope cache*—Shared between many (possibly concurrent) units of work or transactions. This means that data in the process scope cache is accessed by concurrently running threads, obviously with implications on transaction isolation.

- *Cluster scope cache*—Shared between multiple processes on the same machine or between multiple machines in a cluster. Here, network communication is an important point worth consideration.

A process scope cache may store the persistent instances themselves in the cache, or it may store just their persistent state in a disassembled format. Every unit of work that accesses the shared cache then reassembles a persistent instance from the cached data.

A cluster scope cache requires some kind of *remote process communication* to maintain consistency. Caching information must be replicated to all nodes in the cluster. For many (not all) applications, cluster scope caching is of dubious value, because reading and updating the cache may be only marginally faster than going straight to the database.

Persistence layers may provide multiple levels of caching. For example, a *cache miss* (a cache lookup for an item that isn't contained in the cache) at the transaction scope may be followed by a lookup at the process scope. A database request is the last resort.

The type of cache used by a persistence layer affects the scope of object identity (the relationship between Java object identity and database identity).

Caching and object identity

Consider a transaction-scoped cache. It seems natural that this cache is also used as the identity scope of objects. This means the cache implements identity handling: Two lookups for objects using the same database identifier return the same actual Java instance. A transaction scope cache is therefore ideal if a persistence mechanism also provides unit of work-scoped object identity.

Persistence mechanisms with a process scope cache may choose to implement process-scoped identity. In this case, object identity is equivalent to database identity for the whole process. Two lookups using the same database identifier in two concurrently running units of work result in the same Java instance. Alternatively, objects retrieved from the process scope cache may be returned *by value*. In this case, each unit of work retrieves its own copy of the state (think about raw data), and resulting persistent instances aren't identical. The scope of the cache and the scope of object identity are no longer the same.

A cluster scope cache always needs remote communication, and in the case of POJO-oriented persistence solutions like Hibernate, objects are always passed remotely by value. A cluster scope cache therefore can't guarantee identity across a cluster.

For typical web or enterprise application architectures, it's most convenient that the scope of object identity be limited to a single unit of work. In other words, it's neither necessary nor desirable to have identical objects in two concurrent threads. In other kinds of applications (including some desktop or fat-client architectures), it may be appropriate to use process scoped object identity. This is particularly true where memory is extremely limited—the memory consumption of a unit of work scoped cache is proportional to the number of concurrent threads.

However, the real downside to process-scoped identity is the need to synchronize access to persistent instances in the cache, which results in a high likelihood of deadlocks and reduced scalability due to lock contention.

Caching and concurrency

Any ORM implementation that allows multiple units of work to share the same persistent instances must provide some form of object-level locking to ensure synchronization of concurrent access. Usually this is implemented using read and write locks (held in memory) together with deadlock detection. Implementations like Hibernate that maintain a distinct set of instances for each unit of work (unit of work-scoped identity) avoid these issues to a great extent.

It's our opinion that locks held in memory should be avoided, at least for web and enterprise applications where multiuser scalability is an overriding concern. In these applications, it usually isn't required to compare object identity across *concurrent* units of work; each user should be completely isolated from other users.

There is a particularly strong case for this view when the underlying relational database implements a multiversion concurrency model (Oracle or PostgreSQL, for example). It's somewhat undesirable for the object/relational persistence cache to redefine the transactional semantics or concurrency model of the underlying database.

Let's consider the options again. A transaction/unit of work-scoped cache is preferred if you also use unit of work-scoped object identity and if it's the best strategy for highly concurrent multiuser systems. This first-level cache is mandatory, because it also guarantees identical objects. However, this isn't the only cache you can use. For some data, a second-level cache scoped to the process (or cluster) that returns data by value can be a useful. This scenario therefore has two cache layers; you'll later see that Hibernate uses this approach.

Let's discuss which data benefits from second-level caching—in other words, when to turn on the process (or cluster) scope second-level cache in addition to the mandatory first-level transaction scope cache.

Caching and transaction isolation

A process or cluster scope cache makes data retrieved from the database in one unit of work visible to another unit of work. This may have some nasty side effects on transaction isolation.

First, if an application has nonexclusive access to the database, process scope caching shouldn't be used, except for data which changes rarely and may be safely refreshed by a cache expiry. This type of data occurs frequently in content management-type applications but rarely in EIS or financial applications.

There are two main scenarios for nonexclusive access to look out for:

- Clustered applications
- Shared legacy data

Any application that is designed to scale must support clustered operation. A process scope cache doesn't maintain consistency between the different caches on different machines in the cluster. In this case, a cluster scope (distributed) second-level cache should be used instead of the process scope cache.

Many Java applications share access to their database with other applications. In this case, you shouldn't use any kind of cache beyond a unit of work scoped first-level cache. There is no way for a cache system to know when the legacy application updated the shared data. Actually, it's *possible* to implement application-level functionality to trigger an invalidation of the process (or cluster) scope cache when changes are made to the database, but we don't know of any standard or best way to achieve this. Certainly, it will never be a built-in feature of Hibernate. If you implement such a solution, you'll most likely be on your own, because it's specific to the environment and products used.

After considering nonexclusive data access, you should establish what isolation level is required for the application data. Not every cache implementation respects all transaction isolation levels and it's critical to find out what is required. Let's look at data that benefits most from a process- (or cluster-) scoped cache. In practice, we find it useful to rely on a data model diagram (or class diagram) when we make this evaluation. Take notes on the diagram that express whether a particular entity (or class) is a good or bad candidate for second-level caching.

A full ORM solution lets you configure second-level caching separately for each class. Good candidate classes for caching are classes that represent

- Data that changes rarely
- Noncritical data (for example, content-management data)
- Data that is local to the application and not shared

Bad candidates for second-level caching are

- Data that is updated often
- Financial data
- Data that is shared with a legacy application

These aren't the only rules we usually apply. Many applications have a number of classes with the following properties:

- A small number of instances
- Each instance referenced by many instances of another class or classes
- Instances that are rarely (or never) updated

This kind of data is sometimes called *reference data*. Examples of reference data are ZIP codes, reference addresses, office locations, static text messages, and so on. Reference data is an excellent candidate for caching with a process or cluster scope, and any application that uses reference data heavily will benefit greatly if that data is cached. You allow the data to be refreshed when the cache timeout period expires.

We shaped a picture of a dual layer caching system in the previous sections, with a unit of work-scoped first-level and an optional second-level process or cluster scope cache. This is close to the Hibernate caching system.

13.3.2 *The Hibernate cache architecture*

As we hinted earlier, Hibernate has a two-level cache architecture. The various elements of this system can be seen in figure 13.7:

- The first-level cache is the persistence context cache. A Hibernate `Session` lifespan corresponds to either a single request (usually implemented with one database transaction) or a conversation. This is a mandatory first-level cache that also guarantees the scope of object and database identity (the exception being the `StatelessSession`, which doesn't have a persistence context).
- The second-level cache in Hibernate is pluggable and may be scoped to the process or cluster. This is a cache of state (returned by value), not of actual

persistent instances. A cache concurrency strategy defines the transaction isolation details for a particular item of data, whereas the cache provider represents the physical cache implementation. Use of the second-level cache is optional and can be configured on a per-class and per-collection basis—each such cache utilizes its own physical cache region.

- Hibernate also implements a cache for query resultsets that integrates closely with the second-level cache. This is an optional feature; it requires two additional physical cache regions that hold the cached query results and the timestamps when a table was last updated. We discuss the query cache in the next chapters because its usage is closely tied to the query being executed.

We've already discussed the first-level cache, the persistence context, in detail. Let's go straight to the optional second-level cache

The Hibernate second-level cache

The Hibernate second-level cache has process or cluster scope: All persistence contexts that have been started from a particular `SessionFactory` (or are associ-

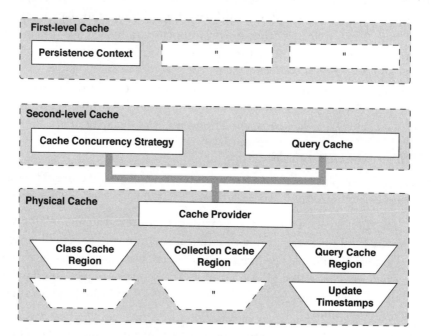

Figure 13.7   Hibernate's two-level cache architecture

ated with `EntityManagers` of a particular persistence unit) share the same second-level cache.

Persistent instances are stored in the second-level cache in a disassembled form. Think of disassembly as a process a bit like serialization (the algorithm is much, much faster than Java serialization, however).

The internal implementation of this process/cluster scope cache isn't of much interest. More important is the correct usage of the *cache policies*—caching strategies and physical cache providers.

Different kinds of data require different cache policies: The ratio of reads to writes varies, the size of the database tables varies, and some tables are shared with other external applications. The second-level cache is configurable at the granularity of an individual class or collection role. This lets you, for example, enable the second-level cache for reference data classes and disable it for classes that represent financial records. The cache policy involves setting the following:

- Whether the second-level cache is enabled
- The Hibernate concurrency strategy
- The cache expiration policies (such as timeout, LRU, and memory-sensitive)
- The physical format of the cache (memory, indexed files, cluster-replicated)

Not all classes benefit from caching, so it's important to be able to disable the second-level cache. To repeat, the cache is usually useful only for read-mostly classes. If you have data that is updated much more often than it's read, don't enable the second-level cache, even if all other conditions for caching are true! The price of maintaining the cache during updates can possibly outweigh the performance benefit of faster reads. Furthermore, the second-level cache can be dangerous in systems that share the database with other writing applications. As explained in earlier sections, you must exercise careful judgment here for each class and collection you want to enable caching for.

The Hibernate second-level cache is set up in two steps. First, you have to decide which *concurrency strategy* to use. After that, you configure cache expiration and physical cache attributes using the *cache provider.*

Built-in concurrency strategies

A concurrency strategy is a mediator: It's responsible for storing items of data in the cache and retrieving them from the cache. This is an important role, because it also defines the transaction isolation semantics for that particular item. You'll have to decide, for each persistent class and collection, which cache concurrency strategy to use if you want to enable the second-level cache.

The four built-in concurrency strategies represent decreasing levels of strictness in terms of transaction isolation:

- *Transactional*—Available in a managed environment only, it guarantees full transactional isolation up to *repeatable read*, if required. Use this strategy for read-mostly data where it's critical to prevent stale data in concurrent transactions, in the rare case of an update.

- *Read-write*—This strategy maintains *read committed* isolation, using a timestamping mechanism and is available only in nonclustered environments. Again, use this strategy for read-mostly data where it's critical to prevent stale data in concurrent transactions, in the rare case of an update.

- *Nonstrict-read-write*—Makes no guarantee of consistency between the cache and the database. If there is a possibility of concurrent access to the same entity, you should configure a sufficiently short expiry timeout. Otherwise, you may read stale data from the cache. Use this strategy if data hardly ever changes (many hours, days, or even a week) and a small likelihood of stale data isn't of critical concern.

- *Read-only*—A concurrency strategy suitable for data which never changes. Use it for reference data only.

Note that with decreasing strictness comes increasing performance. You have to carefully evaluate the performance of a clustered cache with full transaction isolation before using it in production. In many cases, you may be better off disabling the second-level cache for a particular class if stale data isn't an option! First benchmark your application with the second-level cache disabled. Enable it for good candidate classes, one at a time, while continuously testing the scalability of your system and evaluating concurrency strategies.

It's possible to define your own concurrency strategy by implementing `org.hibernate.cache.CacheConcurrencyStrategy`, but this is a relatively difficult task and appropriate only for rare cases of optimization.

Your next step after considering the concurrency strategies you'll use for your cache candidate classes is to pick a *cache provider*. The provider is a plug-in, the physical implementation of a cache system.

Choosing a cache provider

For now, Hibernate forces you to choose a single cache provider for the whole application. Providers for the following open source products are built into Hibernate:

- *EHCache* is a cache provider intended for a simple process scope cache in a single JVM. It can cache in memory or on disk, and it supports the optional Hibernate query result cache. (The latest version of EHCache now supports clustered caching, but we haven't tested this yet.)

- *OpenSymphony OSCache* is a service that supports caching to memory and disk in a single JVM, with a rich set of expiration policies and query cache support.

- *SwarmCache* is a cluster cache based on JGroups. It uses clustered invalidation but doesn't support the Hibernate query cache.

- *JBoss Cache* is a fully transactional replicated clustered cache also based on the JGroups multicast library. It supports replication or invalidation, synchronous or asynchronous communication, and optimistic and pessimistic locking. The Hibernate query cache is supported, assuming that clocks are synchronized in the cluster.

It's easy to write an adaptor for other products by implementing `org.hibernate.cache.CacheProvider`. Many commercial caching systems are pluggable into Hibernate with this interface.

Not every cache provider is compatible with every concurrency strategy! The compatibility matrix in table 13.1 will help you choose an appropriate combination.

Setting up caching involves two steps: First, you look at the mapping metadata for your persistent classes and collections and decide which cache concurrency

Table 13.1   Cache concurrency strategy support

Concurrency strategy cache provider	Read-only	Nonstrict-read-write	Read-write	Transactional
EHCache	X	X	X	
OSCache	X	X	X	
SwarmCache	X	X		
JBoss Cache	X			X

strategy you'd like to use for each class and each collection. In the second step, you enable your preferred cache provider in the global Hibernate configuration and customize the provider-specific settings and physical cache regions. For example, if you're using OSCache, you edit oscache.properties, or for EHCache, ehcache.xml in your classpath.

Let's enable caching for the CaveatEmptor Category, Item, and Bid classes.

13.4 Caching in practice

First we'll consider each entity class and collection and find out what cache concurrency strategy may be appropriate. After we select a cache provider for local and clustered caching, we'll write their configuration file(s).

13.4.1 Selecting a concurrency control strategy

The Category has a small number of instances and is updated rarely, and instances are shared between many users. It's a great candidate for use of the second-level cache.

Start by adding the mapping element required to tell Hibernate to cache Category instances.

```
<class name="auction.model.Category"
       table="CATEGORY">

    <cache usage="read-write"/>

    <id ...

</class>
```

The usage="read-write" attribute tells Hibernate to use a read-write concurrency strategy for the auction.model.Category cache. Hibernate now hits the second-level cache whenever you navigate to a Category or when you load a Category by identifier.

If you use annotations, you need a Hibernate extension:

```
@Entity
@Table(name = "CATEGORY")
@org.hibernate.annotations.Cache(usage =
    org.hibernate.annotations.CacheConcurrencyStrategy.READ_WRITE
)
public class Category { ... }
```

You use read-write instead of nonstrict-read-write because Category is a highly concurrent class, shared between many concurrent transactions. (It's clear that a read committed isolation level is good enough.) A nonstrict-read-write would rely only on cache expiration (timeout), but you prefer changes to categories to be visible immediately.

The class caches are always enabled for a whole hierarchy of persistent classes. You can't only cache instances of a particular subclass.

This mapping is enough to tell Hibernate to cache all simple `Category` property values, but not the state of associated entities or collections. Collections require their own `<cache>` region. For the `items` collection you use a `read-write` concurrency strategy:

```
<class name="auction.model.Category"
        table="CATEGORY">

    <cache usage="read-write"/>

    <id ...

    <set name="items">
        <cache usage="read-write"/>
        <key ...
    </set>

</class>
```

The region name of the collection cache is the fully qualified class name plus the collection property name, `auction.model.Category.items`. The `@org.hibernate.annotations.Cache` annotation can also be declared on a collection field or getter method.

This cache setting is effective when you call `aCategory.getItems()`—in other words, a collection cache is a region that contains "which items are in which category." It's a cache of identifiers only; there is no actual `Category` or `Item` data in that region.

If you require the `Item` instances themselves to be cached, you must enable caching of the `Item` class. A *read-write* strategy is especially appropriate. Your users don't want to make decisions (placing a bid, for example) based on possibly stale `Item` data. Let's go a step further and consider the collection of bids: A particular `Bid` in the `bids` collection is immutable, but the *collection* of `bids` is mutable, and concurrent units of work need to see any addition or removal of a collection element without delay:

```
<class name="Item"
        table="ITEM">

    <cache usage="read-write"/>

    <id ...

    <set name="bids">
```

```
        <cache usage="read-write"/>
        <key ...
    </set>
</class>
```

You apply a *read-only* strategy for the Bid class:

```
<class name="Bid"
       table="BID" mutable="false">

    <cache usage="read-only"/>

    <id ...

</class>
```

Bid data is therefore never expired from the cache, because it can only be created and never updated. (Bids may of course be expired by the cache provider—for example, if the maximum number of objects in the cache is reached.) Hibernate also removes the data from the cache if a Bid instance is deleted, but it doesn't provide any transactional guarantees in doing so.

User is an example of a class that could be cached with the *nonstrict-read-write* strategy, but we aren't certain that it makes sense to cache users.

Let's set the cache provider, its expiration policies, and the physical regions of your cache. You use *cache regions* to configure class and collection caching individually.

13.4.2 *Understanding cache regions*

Hibernate keeps different classes/collections in different *cache regions*. A region is a named cache: a handle by which you may reference classes and collections in the cache provider configuration and set the expiration policies applicable to that region. A more graphical description is that regions are buckets of data, of which there are two types: One type of region contains the disassembled data of entity instances, and the other type contains only identifiers of entities that are linked through a collection.

The name of the region is the class name in the case of a class cache, or the class name together with the property name in the case of a collection cache. Category instances are cached in a region named auction.model.Category, whereas the items collection is cached in a region named auction.model.Category.items.

The Hibernate configuration property named hibernate.cache.region_prefix may be used to specify a region name prefix for a particular SessionFactory or persistence unit. For example, if the prefix is set to db1, Category is cached in a region named `db1.auction.model.Category`. This setting is necessary if your application works with multiple `SessionFactory` instances or persistence units. Without it, cache region names of different persistence units may conflict.

Now that you know about cache regions, you can configure the physical properties of the `auction.model.Category` cache. First let's choose a cache provider. Suppose you're running your auction application in a single JVM, so you don't need a cluster-aware provider.

13.4.3 *Setting up a local cache provider*

You need to set the configuration property that selects a cache provider:

```
hibernate.cache.provider_class = org.hibernate.cache.EhCacheProvider
```

You choose EHCache as your second-level cache in this case.

Now, you need to specify the properties of the cache regions. EHCache has its own configuration file, ehcache.xml, in the classpath of the application. The Hibernate distribution comes bundled with example configuration files for all bundled cache providers, so we recommend that you read the usage comments in those files for detailed configuration and assume the defaults for all options we don't mention explicitly.

A cache configuration in ehcache.xml for the `Category` class may look like this:

```
<cache name="auction.model.Category"
       maxElementsInMemory="500"
       eternal="true"
       timeToIdleSeconds="0"
       timeToLiveSeconds="0"
       overflowToDisk="false"
/>
```

There are a small number of `Category` instances. You therefore disable eviction by choosing a cache size limit greater than the number of categories in the system and setting `eternal="true"`, disabling eviction by timeout. There is no need to expire cached data by timeout because the `Category` cache concurrency strategy is *read-write* and because there are no other applications changing category data directly in the database. You also disable disk-based cache overflow, because you know there are few instances of `Category` and so memory consumption won't be a problem.

`Bids`, on the other hand, are small and immutable, but there are many of them, so you must configure EHCache to carefully manage the cache memory consumption. You use both an expiry timeout and a maximum cache size limit:

```
<cache name="auction.model.Bid"
       maxElementsInMemory="50000"
       eternal="false"
       timeToIdleSeconds="1800"
       timeToLiveSeconds="100000"
       overflowToDisk="false"
/>
```

The `timeToIdleSeconds` attribute defines the expiry time in seconds since an element was last accessed in the cache. You must set a sensible value here, because you don't want unused bids to consume memory. The `timeToLiveSeconds` attribute defines the maximum expiry time in seconds since the element was added to the cache. Because bids are immutable, you don't need them to be removed from the cache if they're being accessed regularly. Hence, `timeToLiveSeconds` is set to a high number.

The result is that cached bids are removed from the cache if they haven't been used in the past 30 minutes or if they're the least recently used item when the total size of the cache has reached its maximum limit of 50,000 elements.

You disable the disk-based cache in this example because you anticipate that the application server will be deployed to the same machine as the database. If the expected physical architecture was different, you might enable the disk-based cache to reduce network traffic. Accessing data on the local disk is faster than accessing the database across a network.

Optimal cache eviction policies are, as you can see, specific to the data and application. You must consider many external factors, including available memory on the application server machine, expected load on the database machine, network latency, existence of legacy applications, and so on. Some of these factors can't be known at development time, so you often need to iteratively test the performance impact of different settings in the production environment or a simulation. We consider optimization with the second-level cache something you won't do during development, because testing without real datasets and concurrency doesn't show the final performance and scalability of the system. This is especially true in a more complex scenario, with a replicated cache in a cluster of machines.

13.4.4 Setting up a replicated cache

EHCache is an excellent cache provider if your application is deployed on a single virtual machine. However, enterprise applications supporting thousands of concurrent users may require more computing power, and scaling your application may be critical to the success of your project. Hibernate applications are naturally scalable: No Hibernate aspect limits the nodes on which your application is deployed. With a few changes to your cache setup, you may even use a clustered caching system.

We recommend JBoss Cache, a cluster-safe caching system based on TreeCache and the JGroups multicast library. JBoss Cache is extremely scalable and cluster communication can be tuned in any way imaginable.

We now step through a setup of JBoss Cache for CaveatEmptor for a small cluster of two nodes, called node *A* and node *B*. However, we only scratch the surface of the topic, cluster configurations are by nature complex and many settings depend on the particular scenario.

First, you have to check that all the mapping files use *read-only* or *transactional* as a cache concurrency strategy. These are the only strategies supported by the JBoss Cache provider. There is a nice trick that helps avoiding this search and replace problem in the future. Instead of placing <cache> elements in your mapping files, you can centralize cache configuration in your `hibernate.cfg.xml`:

```
<hibernate-configuration>
<session-factory>

    <property .../>
    <mapping .../>

    <class-cache
            class="org.hibernate.auction.model.Item"
            usage="transactional"/>

    <collection-cache
            collection="org.hibernate.auction.model.Item.bids"
            usage="transactional"/>

</session-factory>

</hibernate-configuration>
```

You enabled transactional caching for `Item` and the `bids` collection in this example. However, there is one important caveat: At the time of writing, Hibernate runs into a conflict if you also have <cache> elements in the mapping file for `Item`. You therefore can't use the global configuration to override the mapping file settings. We recommend using the centralized cache configuration right from the start, especially if you aren't sure how your application may be deployed. It's also easier to tune cache settings with a single configuration location.

The next step to the cluster setup is the configuration of the JBoss Cache provider. First, you enable it in the Hibernate configuration—for example, if you aren't using properties, in `hibernate.cfg.xml`:

```
<property name="cache.provider_class">
    org.hibernate.cache.TreeCacheProvider
</property>
```

JBoss Cache has its own configuration file, `treecache.xml`, expected in the classpath of your application. In some scenarios, you need a different configuration for each node in your cluster, and you must make sure the correct file is copied to the classpath on deployment. Let's look at a typical configuration file. In the two-node cluster (named `MyCluster`), this file is used on node *A*:

```
<server>

  <classpath codebase="./lib"
              archives="jboss-cache.jar, jgroups.jar"/>

  <mbean code="org.jboss.cache.TreeCache"
      name="jboss.cache:service=TreeCache">

   <depends>jboss:service=Naming</depends>
   <depends>jboss:service=TransactionManager</depends>

   <attribute name="TransactionManagerLookupClass">
       org.jboss.cache.GenericTransactionManagerLookup
   </attribute>

   <attribute name="ClusterName">MyCluster</attribute>

   <attribute name="NodeLockingScheme">PESSIMISTIC</attribute>
   <attribute name="CacheMode">REPL_SYNC</attribute>
   <attribute name="IsolationLevel">REPEATABLE_READ</attribute>

   <attribute name="FetchInMemoryState">false</attribute>
   <attribute name="InitialStateRetrievalTimeout">20000</attribute>
   <attribute name="SyncReplTimeout">20000</attribute>
   <attribute name="LockAcquisitionTimeout">15000</attribute>

   <attribute name="ClusterConfig">
       <config>
         <UDP loopback="false"/>

         <PING timeout="2000"
               num_initial_members="3"
               up_thread="false"
               down_thread="false"/>

         <FD_SOCK/>

         <pbcast.NAKACK gc_lag="50"
                     retransmit_timeout="600,1200,2400,4800"
                     max_xmit_size="8192"
                     up_thread="false" down_thread="false"/>

           <UNICAST timeout="600,1200,2400"
                     window_size="100"
                     min_threshold="10"
```

```
                    down_thread="false"/>
            <pbcast.STABLE desired_avg_gossip="20000"
                           up_thread="false"
                           down_thread="false"/>

            <FRAG frag_size="8192"
                  down_thread="false"
                  up_thread="false"/>

            <pbcast.GMS join_timeout="5000"
                        join_retry_timeout="2000"
                        shun="true" print_local_addr="true"/>

            <pbcast.STATE_TRANSFER up_thread="true"
                                   down_thread="true"/>
          </config>
      </attribute>

    </mbean>
  </server>
```

Granted, this configuration file may look scary at first, but it's easy to understand. You have to know that it's not only a configuration file for JBoss Cache, it's many things in one: a JMX service configuration for JBoss AS deployment, a configuration file for TreeCache, and a fine-grained configuration of JGroups, the communication library.

Ignore the JBoss-deployment related first lines and look at the first attribute, `TransactionManagerLookupClass`. The `GenericTransactionManagerLookup` tries to find the transaction manager in most popular application servers, but it also works in a stand-alone environment without JTA (clustered caching without a transaction manager is a rare scenario). If JBoss Cache throws an exception on startup, telling you that it can't find the transaction manager, you'll have to create such a lookup class yourself for your JTA provider/application server.

Next are the configuration attributes for a replicated cache that uses *synchronized* communication. This means that a node sending a synchronization message waits until all nodes in the group acknowledge the message. This is a good choice for a real replicated cache; asynchronous nonblocking communication would be more appropriate if the node *B* was a *hot standby* (a node that immediately takes over if node *A* fails) instead of a live partner. This is a question of failover versus computing capacity, both good reasons to set up a cluster. Most of the configuration attributes should be self-explanatory, such as timeouts and the fetching of state when a node comes into a cluster.

JBoss Cache can also evict elements, to prevent memory exhaustion. In this example, you don't set up an eviction policy, so the cache slowly starts to fill all available memory. You'll have to consult the JBoss Cache documentation for eviction policy configuration; the usage of Hibernate region names and eviction settings is similar to EHCache.

JBoss Cache also supports invalidation instead of replication of modified data in a cluster, a potentially better performing choice. The Hibernate query cache, however, requires replication. You can also switch to OPTIMISTIC locking instead of pessimistic, again boosting scalability of the clustered cache. Doing so requires a different Hibernate cache provider plug-in, `org.hibernte.cache.OptimisticTreeCacheProvider`.

Finally, let's look at the JGroups cluster communication configuration. The order of communication protocols is extremely important, so don't change or add lines randomly. Most interesting is the first protocol, `<UDP>`. The `loopback` attribute must be set to true if node *A* is a Microsoft Windows machine (it isn't in this case).

The other JGroups attributes are more complex and can be found in the JGroups documentation. They deal with the discovery algorithms used to detect new nodes in a group, failure detection, and, in general, the management of the group communication.

After changing the cache concurrency strategy of your persistent classes to *transactional* (or *read-only*) and creating a treecache.xml file for node *A*, you can start up your application and look at the log output. We recommend enabling DEBUG logging for the `org.jboss.cache` package; you'll then see how JBoss Cache reads the configuration and reports node *A* as the first node in the cluster. To deploy node *B*, deploy the application on that node; no configuration file needs to be changed (if the second node also isn't a Microsoft Windows machine). If you start this second node, you should see join messages on both nodes. Your Hibernate application now uses fully transactional caching in a cluster.

There is one final optional setting to consider. For cluster cache providers, it may be better to set the Hibernate configuration option `hibernate.cache.use_minimal_puts` to true. When this setting is enabled, Hibernate adds an item to the cache only after checking to ensure that the item isn't already cached. This strategy performs better if cache writes (puts) are much more expensive than cache reads (gets). This is the case for a replicated cache in a cluster, but not for a local cache or a cache provider that relies on invalidation instead of replication.

No matter if you're using a cluster or a local cache, you sometimes need to control it programmatically, either for testing or tuning purposes.

13.4.5 *Controlling the second-level cache*

Hibernate has some useful methods that can help you test and tune your cache. Consider the global configuration switch for the second-level cache, hibernate.cache.use_second_level_cache. By default, any <cache> element in your mapping files (or in hibernate.cfg.xml, or an annotation) triggers the second-level cache and loads the cache provider at startup. If you want to disable the second-level cache globally without removing the cache mapping elements or annotations, set this configuration property to false.

Just as the Session and EntityManager provide methods for controlling the persistence context first-level cache programmatically, so does the SessionFactory for the second-level cache. In a JPA application, you have to get access to the underlying internal SessionFactory, as described in chapter 2, section 2.2.4, "Switching to Hibernate interfaces."

You can call evict() to remove an element from the second-level cache by specifying the class and the object identifier value:

```
SessionFactory.evict( Category.class, new Long(123) );
```

You may also evict all elements of a certain class or only evict a particular collection role by specifying a region name:

```
SessionFactory.evict("auction.model.Category");
```

You'll rarely need these control mechanisms. Also note that eviction of the second-level cache is nontransactional, that is, the cache region isn't locked during eviction.

Hibernate also offers CacheMode options that can be activated for a particular Session. Imagine that you want to insert many objects into the database in one Session. You need to do this in batches, to avoid memory exhaustion—every object is added to the first-level cache. However, it's also added to the second-level cache, if enabled for the entity class. A CacheMode controls the interaction of Hibernate with the second-level cache:

```
Session session = sessionFactory.openSession();
Transaction tx = session.beginTransaction();

session.setCacheMode(CacheMode.IGNORE);

for ( int i=0; i<100000; i++ ) {
    Item item = new Item(...);
    session.save(item);
    if ( i % 100 == 0 ) {
        session.flush();
        session.clear();
```

```
      }
   }
   tx.commit();
   session.close();
```

Setting `CacheMode.IGNORE` tells Hibernate not to interact with the second-level cache, in this particular `Session`. The available options are as follows:

- `CacheMode.NORMAL`—The default behavior.

- `CacheMode.IGNORE`—Hibernate never interacts with the second-level cache except to invalidate cached items when updates occur.

- `CacheMode.GET`—Hibernate may read items from the second-level cache, but it won't add items except to invalidate items when updates occur.

- `CacheMode.PUT`—Hibernate never reads items from the second-level cache, but it adds items to the cache as it reads them from the database.

- `CacheMode.REFRESH`—Hibernate never reads items from the second-level cache, but it adds items to the cache as it reads them from the database. In this mode, the effect of `hibernate.cache.use_minimal_puts` is bypassed, in order to *force* a cache refresh in a replicated cluster cache.

Good use cases for any cache modes except `NORMAL` and `IGNORE` are rare.

This completes our discussion of the first- and second-level caches in a Hibernate application. We'd like to repeat a statement we made at the beginning of this section: Your application should perform satisfactorily without the second-level cache. You've only cured the symptoms, not the actual problem if a particular procedure in your application is running in 2 instead of 50 seconds with the second-level cache enabled. Customization of the fetch plan and fetching strategy is always your first optimization step; then, use the second-level cache to make your application snappier and to scale it to the concurrent transaction load it will have to handle in production.

13.5 Summary

In this chapter, you created a global fetch plan and defined which objects and collections should be loaded into memory at all times. You defined the fetch plan based on your use cases and how you want to access associated entities and iterate through collections in your application.

Next, you selected the right fetching strategy for your fetch plan. Your goal is to minimize the number of SQL statements and the complexity of each SQL statement that must be executed. You especially want to avoid the n+1 selects and Cartesian product issues we examined in detail, using various optimization strategies.

The second half of this chapter introduced caching with the theory behind caching and a checklist you can apply to find out which classes and collections are good candidates for Hibernate's optional second-level cache. You then configured and enabled second-level caching for a few classes and collections with the local EHCache provider, and a cluster-enabled JBoss Cache.

Table 13.2 shows a summary you can use to compare native Hibernate features and Java Persistence.

Table 13.2 Hibernate and JPA comparison chart for chapter 13

Hibernate Core	Java Persistence and EJB 3.0
Hibernate supports fetch-plan definition with lazy loading through proxies or based on interception.	Hibernate implements a Java Persistence provider with proxy or interception-based lazy loading.
Hibernate allows fine-grained control over fetch-plan and fetching strategies.	Java Persistence standardizes annotations for fetch plan declaration, Hibernate extensions are used for fine-grained fetching strategy optimization.
Hibernate provides an optional second-level class and collection data cache, configured in a Hibernate configuration file or XML mapping files.	Use Hibernate annotations for declaration of the cache concurrency strategy on entities and collections.

The next chapters deal exclusively with querying and how to write and execute HQL, JPA QL, SQL, and `Criteria` queries with all Hibernate and Java Persistence interfaces.

Querying with HQL and JPA QL

14

This chapter covers

- Understanding the various query options
- Writing HQL and JPA QL queries
- Joins, reporting queries, subselects

Queries are the most interesting part of writing good data access code. A complex query may require a long time to get right, and its impact on the performance of the application can be tremendous. On the other hand, writing queries becomes much easier with more experience, and what seemed difficult at first is only a matter of knowing some of the more advanced features.

If you've been using handwritten SQL for a number of years, you may be concerned that ORM will take away some of the expressiveness and flexibility that you're used to. This isn't the case with Hibernate and Java Persistence.

Hibernate's powerful query facilities allow you to express almost everything you commonly (or even uncommonly) need to express in SQL, but in object-oriented terms—using classes and properties of classes.

We'll show you the differences between native Hibernate queries and the standardized subset in Java Persistence. You may also use this chapter as a reference; hence some sections are written in a less verbose style but show many small code examples for different use cases. We also sometimes skip optimizations in the CaveatEmptor application for better readability. For example, instead of referring to the `MonetaryAmount` value type, we use a `BigDecimal` amount in comparisons.

First, we show you how queries are executed. Don't let yourself be distracted by the queries; we discuss them soon.

14.1 Creating and running queries

Let's start with a few examples so you understand the basic usage. In earlier chapters, we mentioned that there are three ways to express queries in Hibernate:

- Hibernate Query Language (HQL), and the subset standardized as JPA QL:
  ```
  session.createQuery("from Category c where c.name like 'Laptop%'");
  entityManager.createQuery(
      "select c from Category c where c.name like 'Laptop%'"
  );
  ```

- Criteria API for *query by criteria* (QBC) and *query by example* (QBE):
  ```
  session.createCriteria(Category.class)
          .add( Restrictions.like("name", "Laptop%") );
  ```

- Direct SQL with or without automatic mapping of resultsets to objects:
  ```
  session.createSQLQuery(
      "select {c.*} from CATEGORY {c} where NAME like 'Laptop%'"
  ).addEntity("c", Category.class);
  ```

A query must be prepared in application code before execution. So, querying involves several distinct steps:

1 Create the query, with any arbitrary restriction or projection of data that you want to retrieve.

2 Bind runtime arguments to query parameters; the query can be reused with changing settings.

3 Execute the prepared query against the database and retrieval of data. You can control how the query is executed and how data should be retrieved into memory (all at once or piecemeal, for example).

Hibernate and Java Persistence offer query interfaces and methods on these interfaces to prepare and execute arbitrary data retrieval operations.

14.1.1 *Preparing a query*

The `org.hibernate.Query` and `org.hibernate.Criteria` interfaces both define several methods for controlling execution of a query. In addition, `Query` provides methods for binding concrete values to query parameters. To execute a query in your application, you need to obtain an instance of one of these interfaces, using the `Session`.

Java Persistence specifies the `javax.persistence.Query` interface. The standardized interface isn't as rich as the native Hibernate API, but offers all necessary methods to execute a query in different ways and to bind arguments to query parameters. Unfortunately, the useful Hibernate `Criteria` API has no equivalent in Java Persistence, although it's highly likely that a similar query interface will be added in a future version of the standard.

Creating a query object

To create a new Hibernate `Query` instance, call either `createQuery()` or `create-SQLQuery()` on a `Session`. The `createQuery()` method prepares an HQL query:

```
Query hqlQuery = session.createQuery("from User");
```

`createSQLQuery()` is used to create an SQL query using the native syntax of the underlying database:

```
Query sqlQuery =
        session.createSQLQuery(
            "select {user.*} from USERS {user}"
        ).addEntity("user", User.class);
```

In both cases, Hibernate returns a newly instantiated `Query` object that may be used to specify exactly how a particular query should be executed and to allow execution of the query. So far, no SQL has been sent to the database.

To obtain a `Criteria` instance, call `createCriteria()`, passing the class of the objects you want the query to return. This is also called the *root entity* of the criteria query, the `User` in this example:

```
Criteria crit = session.createCriteria(User.class);
```

The `Criteria` instance may be used in the same way as a `Query` object—but it's also used to construct the object-oriented representation of the query, by adding `Criterion` instances and navigating associations to new `Criterias`.

With the Java Persistence API, your starting point for queries is the `EntityManager`. To create a `javax.persistence.Query` instance for JPA QL, call `createQuery()`:

```
Query ejbQuery = em.createQuery("select u from User u");
```

To create a native SQL query, use `createNativeQuery()`:

```
Query sqlQuery =
        session.createNativeQuery(
        "select u.USER_ID, u.FIRSTNAME, u.LASTNAME from USERS u",
        User.class
        );
```

The way you define the returned objects from a native query is slightly different than in Hibernate (there are no placeholders in the query here).

After you've created the query, you prepare it for execution by setting various options.

Paging the result

A commonly used technique is *pagination*. Users may see the result of their search request (for example, for specific `Items`) as a page. This page shows a limited subset (say, 10 `Items`) at a time, and users can navigate to the next and previous pages manually. In Hibernate, `Query` and `Criteria` interfaces support this pagination of the query result:

```
Query query =
        session.createQuery("from User u order by u.name asc");
query.setMaxResults(10);
```

The call to `setMaxResults(10)` limits the query resultset to the first 10 objects (rows) returned by the database. In this `Criteria` query, the requested page starts in the middle of the resultset:

```
Criteria crit = session.createCriteria(User.class);
crit.addOrder( Order.asc("name") );
crit.setFirstResult(40);
crit.setMaxResults(20);
```

Starting from the fortieth object, you retrieve the next 20 objects. Note that there is no standard way to express pagination in SQL—Hibernate knows the tricks to make this work efficiently on your particular database. You can even *add* this flexible pagination option to an SQL query. Hibernate will rewrite your SQL for pagination:

```
Query sqlQuery =
        session.createSQLQuery("select {u.*} from USERS {u}")
                .addEntity("u", User.class);
sqlQuery.setFirstResult(40);
sqlQuery.setMaxResults(20);
```

You may use the method-chaining coding style (methods return the receiving object instead of `void`) with the `Query` and `Criteria` interfaces, rewriting the two previous examples as follows:

```
Query query =
        session.createQuery("from User u order by u.name asc")
                .setMaxResults(10);
Criteria crit =
        session.createCriteria(User.class)
                .addOrder( Order.asc("name") )
                .setFirstResult(40)
                .setMaxResults(20);
```

Chaining method calls is less verbose and is supported by many Hibernate APIs. The Java Persistence query interfaces also support pagination and method chaining for JPA QL and native SQL queries with the `javax.persistence.Query` interface:

```
Query query =
        em.createQuery("select u from User u order by u.name asc")
          .setFirstResult(40)
          .setMaxResults(20);
```

Next in preparing your query is the setting of any runtime parameters.

Considering parameter binding

Without runtime parameter binding, you have to write bad code:

```
String queryString =
        "from Item i where i.description like '" + search + "'";
List result = session.createQuery(queryString).list();
```

You should never write this code because a malicious user could search for the following item description—that is, by entering the value of `search` in a search dialog box as

```
foo' and callSomeStoredProcedure() and 'bar' = 'bar
```

As you can see, the original `queryString` is no longer a simple search for a string but also executes a stored procedure in the database! The quote characters aren't escaped; hence the call to the stored procedure is another valid expression in the query. If you write a query like this, you open up a major security hole in your application by allowing the execution of arbitrary code on your database. This is known as an *SQL injection* security issue. Never pass unchecked values from user input to the database! Fortunately, a simple mechanism prevents this mistake.

The JDBC driver includes functionality for safely binding values to SQL parameters. It knows exactly what characters in the parameter value to escape, so that the previous vulnerability doesn't exist. For example, the quote characters in the given `search` are escaped and are no longer treated as control characters but as a part of the search string value. Furthermore, when you use parameters, the database is able to efficiently cache precompiled prepared statements, improving performance significantly.

There are two approaches to *parameter binding*: using positional or using named parameters. Hibernate and Java Persistence support both options, but you can't use both at the same time for a particular query.

With named parameters, you can rewrite the query as

```
String queryString =
    "from Item item where item.description like :search";
```

The colon followed by a parameter name indicates a named parameter. Then, bind a value to the `search` parameter:

```
Query q = session.createQuery(queryString)
                .setString("search", searchString);
```

Because `searchString` is a user-supplied string variable, you call the `setString()` method of the `Query` interface to bind it to the named parameter (`:search`). This code is cleaner, much safer, and performs better, because a single compiled SQL statement can be reused if only bind parameters change.

Often, you'll need multiple parameters:

```
String queryString = "from Item item"
            + " where item.description like :search"
            + " and item.date > :minDate";

Query q = session.createQuery(queryString)
            .setString("search", searchString)
            .setDate("minDate", mDate);
```

The same query and code looks slightly different in Java Persistence:

```
Query q = em.createQuery(queryString)
            .setParameter("search", searchString)
            .setParameter("minDate", mDate, TemporalType.DATE);
```

The `setParameter()` method is a generic operation that can bind all types of arguments, it only needs a little help for temporal types (the engine needs to know if you want only the date, time, or a full timestamp bound). Java Persistence supports only this method for binding of parameters (Hibernate, by the way, has it too).

Hibernate, on the other hand, offers many other methods, some of them for completeness, others for convenience, that you can use to bind arguments to query parameters.

Using Hibernate parameter binding

You've called `setString()` and `setDate()` to bind arguments to query parameters. The native Hibernate `Query` interface provides similar convenience methods for binding arguments of most of the Hibernate built-in types: everything from `setInteger()` to `setTimestamp()` and `setLocale()`. They're mostly optional; you can rely on the `setParameter()` method to figure out the right type automatically (except for temporal types).

A particularly useful method is `setEntity()`, which lets you bind a persistent entity (note that `setParameter()` is smart enough to understand even that automatically):

```
session.createQuery("from Item item where item.seller = :seller")
        .setEntity("seller", theSeller);
```

However, there is also a generic method that allows you to bind an argument of any Hibernate type:

```
String queryString = "from Item item"
                    + " where item.seller = :seller and"
                    + " item.description like :desc";

session.createQuery(queryString)
        .setParameter( "seller",
                       theSeller,
                       Hibernate.entity(User.class) )
        .setParameter( "desc", description, Hibernate.STRING );
```

This works even for custom user-defined types, like `MonetaryAmount`:

```
Query q = session.createQuery("from Bid where amount > :amount");
q.setParameter( "amount", givenAmount,
                Hibernate.custom(MonetaryAmountUserType.class) );
```

If you have a JavaBean with `seller` and `description` properties, you can call the `setProperties()` method to bind the query parameters. For example, you can pass query parameters in an instance of the `Item` class itself:

```
Item item = new Item();
item.setSeller(seller);
item.setDescription(description);

String queryString = "from Item item"
                    + " where item.seller = :seller and"
                    + " item.description like :desccription";

session.createQuery(queryString).setProperties(item);
```

The `setProperties()` binding matches names of JavaBean properties to named parameters in the query string, internally calling `setParameter()` to guess the Hibernate type and bind the value. In practice, this turns out to be less useful than it sounds, because some common Hibernate types aren't guessable (temporal types, in particular).

The parameter binding methods of `Query` are null-safe. So the following code is legal:

```
session.createQuery("from User as u where u.username = :name")
        .setString("name", null);
```

However, the result of this code is almost certainly not what you intended! The resulting SQL will contain a comparison like `USERNAME` = null, which *always* evaluates to null in SQL ternary logic. Instead, you must use the `is null` operator:

```
session.createQuery("from User as u where u.username is null");
```

Using positional parameters

If you prefer, you can use positional parameters instead in Hibernate and Java Persistence:

```
String queryString = "from Item item"
                    + " where item.description like ?"
                    + " and item.date > ?";

Query q = session.createQuery(queryString)
                .setString(0, searchString)
                .setDate(1, minDate);
```

Java Persistence also supports positional parameters:

```
String queryString = "from Item item"
                    + " where item.description like ?1"
                    + " and item.date > ?2";

Query q = em.createQuery(queryString)
```

```
.setParameter(1, searchString)
.setParameter(2, minDate, TemporalType.DATE);
```

Not only is this code much less self-documenting than the alternative with named parameters, it's also much more vulnerable to easy breakage if you change the query string slightly:

```
String queryString = "from Item item"
                   + " where item.date > ?"
                   + " and item.description like ?";
```

Every change of the position of the bind parameters requires a change to the parameter binding code. This leads to fragile and maintenance-intensive code. Our recommendation is to avoid positional parameters. They may be more convenient if you build complex queries programmatically, but the `Criteria` API is a much better alternative for that purpose.

If you have to use positional parameters, remember that Hibernate starts counting at 0, but Java Persistence starts at 1, and that you have to add a number to each question mark in a JPA QL query string. They have different legacy roots: Hibernate in JDBC, Java Persistence in older versions of EJB QL.

In addition to bind parameters, you often want to apply other *hints* that influence how a query is executed.

Setting query hints

Let's assume that you make modifications to persistent objects before executing a query. These modifications are only present in memory, so Hibernate (and Java Persistence providers) *flushes* the persistence context and all changes to the database before executing your query. This guarantees that the query runs on current data and that no conflict between the query result and the in-memory objects can occur.

This is sometimes impractical: for example, if you execute a sequence that consists of many query-modify-query-modify operations, and each query is retrieving a different dataset than the one before. In other words, you don't need to flush your modifications to the database before executing a query, because conflicting results aren't a problem. Note that the persistence context provides repeatable read for entity objects, so only scalar results of a query are a problem anyway.

You can disable flushing of the persistence context with `setFlushMode()` on a `Session` or `EntityManager`. Or, if you want to disable flushing only before a particular query, you can set a `FlushMode` on the `Query` (Hibernate and JPA) object:

```
Query q = session.createQuery(queryString)
          .setFlushMode(FlushMode.COMMIT);
```

```
Criteria criteria = session.createCriteria(Item.class)
                            .setFlushMode(FlushMode.COMMIT);

Query q = em.createQuery(queryString)
            .setFlushMode(FlushModeType.COMMIT);
```

Hibernate won't flush the persistence context before executing any of these queries.

Another optimization is a fine-grained `org.hibernate.CacheMode` for a particular query result. You used a cache mode in chapter 13, section 13.4.5, "Controlling the second-level cache," to control how Hibernate interacts with the second-level cache. If Hibernate retrieves an object by identifier, it looks it up in the first-level persistence context cache and, if enabled, the second-level cache region for this entity. The same happens when you execute a query that returns entity instances: During marshaling of the query result, Hibernate tries to resolve all entity instances by looking them up from the persistence context cache first—it ignores the entity data of the query result if the entity instance is in the persistence context cache. And, if the retrieved entity instance wasn't in any cache, Hibernate puts it there after the query completes. You can control this behavior with a `CacheMode` on a query:

```
Query q = session.createQuery("from Item")
                 .setCacheMode(CacheMode.IGNORE);

Criteria criteria = session.createCriteria(Item.class)
                           .setCacheMode(CacheMode.IGNORE);

Query q = em.createQuery(queryString)
            .setHint("org.hibernate.cacheMode",
                     org.hibernate.CacheMode.IGNORE);
```

A `CacheMode.IGNORE`, for example, tells Hibernate not to interact with the second-level cache for any entity returned by this query. In other words, any `Item` retrieved by this query isn't put in the second-level cache. Setting this cache mode is useful if you execute a query that shouldn't update the second-level cache, maybe because the data you're retrieving is only relevant for a particular situation, and shouldn't exhaust the available space in the cache region.

In "Controlling the persistence context cache" in chapter 9, section 9.3.3, we talked about the control of the persistence context and how you can reduce memory consumption and prevent long dirty checking cycles. One way to disable dirty checking for a particular persistent object is to set `session.setRead-Only(object, true)` (the `EntityManager` doesn't support this API).

You can tell Hibernate that all entity objects returned by a query should be considered read-only (although not detached):

```
Query q = session.createQuery("from Item")
                    .setReadOnly(true);

Criteria criteria = session.createCriteria(Item.class)
                            .setReadOnly(true);

Query q = em.createQuery("select i from Item i")
                .setHint("org.hibernate.readOnly", true);
```

All Item objects returned by this query are in persistent state, but no snapshot for automatic dirty checking is enabled in the persistence context. Hibernate doesn't persist any modifications automatically, unless you disable read-only mode with session.setReadOnly(object, false).

You can control how long a query is allowed to run by setting a *timeout*:

```
Query q = session.createQuery("from Item")
                    .setTimeout(60); // 1 minute

Criteria criteria = session.createCriteria(Item.class)
                            .setTimeout(60);
Query q = em.createQuery("select i from Item i")
                .setHint("org.hibernate.timeout", 60);
```

This method has the same semantics and consequences as the setQueryTimeout() method on a JDBC Statement. Also related to the underlying JDBC is the *fetch size*:

```
Query q = session.createQuery("from Item")
                    .setFetchSize(50);

Criteria criteria = session.createCriteria(Item.class)
                            .setFetchSize(50);

Query q = em.createQuery("select i from Item i")
                .setHint("org.hibernate.fetchSize", 50);
```

The JDBC fetch size is an optimization hint for the database driver; it may not result in any performance improvement if the driver doesn't implement this functionality. If it does, it can improve the communication between the JDBC client and the database, by retrieving many rows in one batch when the client operates on a query result (that is, on a ResultSet). Because Hibernate is working with the ResultSet behind the scenes, this hint can improve data retrieval if you execute a query with list()—which you'll do soon.

When you optimize an application you often have to read complex SQL logs. We highly recommend that you enable hibernate.use_sql_comments; Hibernate will then add a comment to each SQL statement it writes to the logs. You can set a custom comment for a particular query with setComment():

```
Query q = session.createQuery("from Item")
                 .setComment("My Comment...");

Criteria criteria = session.createCriteria(Item.class)
                          .setComment("My Comment...");

Query q = em.createQuery("select i from Item i")
              .setHint("org.hibernate.comment", "My Comment...");
```

The hints you've been setting so far are all related to Hibernate or JDBC handling. Many developers (and DBAs) consider a query hint to be something completely different. In SQL, a query hint is a comment in the SQL statement that contains an instruction for the SQL optimizer of the database management system. For example, if the developer or DBA thinks that the execution plan selected by the database optimizer for a particular SQL statement isn't the fastest, they use a hint to force a different execution plan. Hibernate and Java Persistence don't support arbitrary SQL hints with an API; you'll have to fall back to native SQL and write your own SQL statement—you can of course execute that statement with the provided APIs.

(With some database-management systems you can control the optimizer with an SQL comment at the beginning of an SQL statement; in that case, use `Query.setComment()` to add the hint. In other scenarios, you may be able to write an `org.hibernate.Interceptor` and manipulate an SQL statement in the `onPrepareStatement(sql)` method before it's sent to the database.)

Finally, you can control whether a query should force a pessimistic lock in the database management system—a lock that is held until the end of the database transaction:

```
Query q = session.createQuery("from Item item")
                 .setLockMode("item", LockMode.UPGRADE);

Criteria criteria = session.createCriteria(Item.class)
                          .setLockMode(LockMode.UPGRADE);
```

Both queries, if supported by your database dialect, result in an SQL statement that includes a ... FOR UPDATE operation (or the equivalent, if supported by the database system and dialect). Currently, pessimistic locking isn't available (but it's planned as a Hibernate extension hint) on the Java Persistence query interface.

Let's assume that queries are now prepared, so you can run them.

14.1.2 *Executing a query*

Once you've created and prepared a `Query` or `Criteria` object, you're ready to execute it and retrieve the result into memory. Retrieving the whole result into memory in one turn is the most common way to execute a query; we call this *listing*. Some other options are available that we also discuss next:, iterating and scrolling. Scrolling is about as useful as iteration: You rarely need one of these options. We'd guess that more than 90 percent of all query execution relies on the `list()` and `getResultList()` methods in a regular application.

First, the most common case.

Listing all results

In Hibernate, the `list()` method executes the query and returns the results as a `java.util.List`:

```
List result = myQuery.list();
```

The `Criteria` interface also supports this operation:

```
List result = myCriteria.list();
```

In both cases, one or several SELECTs statements are executing immediately, depending on your fetch plan. If you map any associations or collections as non-lazy, they must be fetched in addition to the data you want retrieved with your query. All these objects are loaded into memory, and any entity objects that are retrieved are in persistent state and added to the persistence context.

Java Persistence offers a method with the same semantics, but a different name:

```
List result = myJPAQuery.getResultList();
```

With some queries you know that the result is only a single instance—for example, if you want only the highest bid. In this case, you can read it from the result list by index, `result.get(0)`. Or, you can limit the number of returned rows with `setMaxResult(1)`. Then you may execute the query with the `uniqueResult()` method, because you know only one object will be returned:

```
Bid maxBid =
    (Bid) session.createQuery("from Bid b order by b.amount desc")
            .setMaxResults(1)
            .uniqueResult();
Bid bid = (Bid) session.createCriteria(Bid.class)
            .add( Restrictions.eq("id", id) )
            .uniqueResult();
```

If the query returns more than one object, an exception is thrown. If the query result is empty, a `null` is returned. This also works in Java Persistence, again with a different method name (and, unfortunately, an exception is thrown if the result is empty):

```
Bid maxBid = (Bid) em.createQuery(
                    "select b from Bid b order by b.amount desc"
                ).setMaxResults(1)
                .getSingleResult();
```

Retrieving all results into memory is the most common way to execute a query. Hibernate supports some other methods that you may find interesting if you want to optimize the memory consumption and execution behavior of a query.

Iterating through the results

The Hibernate `Query` interface also provides the `iterate()` method to execute a query. It returns the same data as `list()`, but relies on a different strategy for retrieving the results.

When you call `iterate()` to execute a query, Hibernate retrieves only the primary key (identifier) values of entity objects in a first SQL `SELECT`, and then tries to find the rest of the state of the objects in the persistence context cache, and (if enabled) the second-level cache. Consider the following code:

```
Query categoryByName =
    session.createQuery("from Category c where c.name like :name");
categoryByName.setString("name", categoryNamePattern);
List categories = categoryByName.list();
```

This query results in execution of at least one SQL `SELECT`, with all columns of the `CATEGORY` table included in the `SELECT` clause:

```
select CATEGORY_ID, NAME, PARENT_ID from CATEGORY where NAME like ?
```

If you expect that categories are already cached in the persistence context or the second-level cache, then you need only the identifier value (the key to the cache). This therefore reduces the amount of data fetched from the database. The following SQL is slightly more efficient:

```
select CATEGORY_ID from CATEGORY where NAME like ?
```

You can use the `iterate()` method for this:

```
Query categoryByName =
    session.createQuery("from Category c where c.name like :name");
categoryByName.setString("name", categoryNamePattern);
Iterator categories = categoryByName.iterate();
```

The initial query retrieves only `Category` primary key values. You then iterate through the result; Hibernate looks up each `Category` object in the current persistence context and, if enabled, in the second-level cache. If a cache miss occurs,

Hibernate executes an additional SELECT for each turn, retrieving the full Category object by its primary key from the database.

In most cases, this is a minor optimization. It's usually much more important to minimize *row* reads than to minimize *column* reads. Still, if your object has large string fields, this technique may be useful to minimize data packets on the network and therefore latency. It should be clear that it's really effective only if the second-level cache region for the iterated entity is enabled. Otherwise it produces n+1 selects!

Hibernate keeps the iterator open until you finish iteration through all results or until the Session is closed. You can also close it explicitly with org.hibernate.Hibernate.close(iterator).

Also note that Hibernate Criteria and Java Persistence, at the time of writing, don't support this optimization.

Another optimized way to execute a query is *scrolling* through the result.

Scrolling with database cursors

Plain JDBC provides a feature called *scrollable resultsets.* This technique uses a cursor that is held on the database management system. The cursor points to a particular row in the result of a query, and the application can move the cursor forward and backward. You can even jump to a particular row with the cursor.

One of the situations where you should scroll through the results of a query instead of loading them all into memory involves resultsets that are too large to fit into memory. Usually you try to further restrict the result by tightening the conditions in the query. Sometimes this isn't possible, maybe because you need all of the data, but want to retrieve it in several steps.

You've already seen scrolling in "Writing a procedure with batch updates" chapter 12, section 12.2.2 and how to implement procedures that work on batches of data, because this is where it's most useful. The following example shows an overview of other interesting options on the ScrollableResults interface:

```
ScrollableResults itemCursor =
    session.createQuery("from Item").scroll();

itemCursor.first();
itemCursor.last();
itemCursor.get();

itemCursor.next();
itemCursor.scroll(3);
itemCursor.getRowNumber();
itemCursor.setRowNumber(5);
itemCursor.previous();
```

```
itemCursor.scroll(-3);

itemCursor.close();
```

This code doesn't make much sense; it displays the most interesting methods on the `ScrollableResults` interface. You can set the cursor to the first and last `Item` object in the result, or get the `Item` the cursor is currently pointing to with `get()`. You can go to a particular `Item` by jumping to a position with `setRowNumber()` or scroll backward and forward with `next()` and `previous()`. Another option is scrolling forward and backward by an offset, with `scroll()`.

Hibernate `Criteria` queries can also be executed with scrolling instead of `list()`; the returned `ScrollableResults` cursor works the same. Note that you absolutely must close the cursor when you're done working with it, before you end the database transaction. Here is a `Criteria` example that shows the opening of a cursor:

```
ScrollableResults itemCursor =
    session.createCriteria(Item.class)
            .scroll(ScrollMode.FORWARD_ONLY);

... // Scroll only forward

itemCursor.close()
```

The `ScrollMode` constants of the Hibernate API are equivalent to the constants in plain JDBC. In this case, the constant ensures that your cursor can only move forward. This may be required as a precaution; some JDBC drivers don't support scrolling backward. Other available modes are `ScrollMode.SCROLL_INSENSITIVE` and `ScrollMode.SCROLL_SENSITIVE`. An insensitive cursor won't expose you to modified data while the cursor is open (effectively guaranteeing that no dirty reads, unrepeatable reads, or phantom reads can slip into your resultset). On the other hand, a sensitive cursor exposes newly committed data and committed modifications to you while you work on your resultset. Note that the Hibernate persistence context cache still provides repeatable read for entity instances, so only modified scalar values you project in the resultset can be affected by this setting.

So far, the code examples we've shown all embed query string literals in Java code. This isn't unreasonable for simple queries, but once you begin considering complex queries that must be split over multiple lines, this gets a bit unwieldy.

14.1.3 *Using named queries*

We don't like to see HQL or JPA QL string literals scattered all over the Java code, unless really necessary. Hibernate lets you externalize query strings to the mapping metadata, a technique that is called *named queries*. This lets you store all queries related to a particular persistent class (or a set of classes) encapsulated with the other metadata of that class in an XML mapping file. Or, if you use annotations, you can create named queries as metadata of a particular entity class or put them into an XML deployment descriptor. The name of the query is used to call it from application code.

Calling a named query

In Hibernate, the getNamedQuery() method obtains a Query instance for a named query:

```
session.getNamedQuery("findItemsByDescription")
        .setString("desc", description);
```

In this example, you call the named query findItemsByDescription and bind a string argument to the named parameter desc.

Java Persistence also supports named queries:

```
em.createNamedQuery("findItemsByDescription")
    .setParameter("desc", description);
```

Named queries are global—that is, the name of a query is considered to be a unique identifier for a particular SessionFactory or persistence unit. How and where they're defined, in XML mapping files or annotations, is no concern of your application code. Even the query language doesn't matter.

Defining a named query in XML metadata

You can place a named query inside any <hibernate-mapping> element in your XML metadata. In larger applications, we recommend isolating and separating all named queries into their own file. Or, you may want some queries to be defined in the same XML mapping file as a particular class.

The <query> defines a named HQL or JPA QL query:

```
<query name="findItemsByDescription"><![CDATA[
        from Item item where item.description like :desc
]]></query>
```

You should wrap the query text into a CDATA instruction so the XML parser doesn't get confused by any characters in your query string that may accidentally be considered XML (such as the *less than* operator).

If you place a named query definition inside a <class> element, instead of the root, it's prefixed with the name of the entity class; for example, findItemsByDescription is then callable as auction.model.Item.findItemsByDescription. Otherwise, you need to make sure the name of the query is globally unique.

All query hints that you set earlier with an API can also be set declaratively:

```
<query name="findItemsByDescription"
       cache-mode="ignore"
       comment="My Comment..."
       fetch-size="50"
       read-only="true"
       timeout="60"><![CDATA[
    from Item item where item.description like :desc
]]></query>
```

Named queries don't have to be HQL or JPA QL strings; they may even be native SQL queries—and your Java code doesn't need to know the difference:

```
<sql-query name="findItemsByDescription">
    <return alias="item" class="Item"/>
    <![CDATA[
        select {item.*} from item where description like :desc
    ]]>
</sql-query>
```

This is useful if you think you may want to optimize your queries later by fine-tuning the SQL. It's also a good solution if you have to port a legacy application to Hibernate, where SQL code was isolated from the hand-coded JDBC routines. With named queries, you can easily port the queries one-by-one to mapping files. We'll have much more to say about native SQL queries in the next chapter.

Defining a named query with annotations

The Java Persistence standard specifies the @NamedQuery and @NamedNativeQuery annotations. You can either place these annotations into the metadata of a particular class or into JPA XML descriptor file. Note that the query name must be globally unique in all cases; no class or package name is automatically prefixed.

Let's assume you consider a particular named query to belong to a particular entity class:

```
package auction.model;

import ...;

@NamedQueries({
    @NamedQuery(
      name = "findItemsByDescription",
      query = "select i from Item i where i.description like :desc"
      ),
    ...
})
@Entity
@Table(name = "ITEM")
public class Item { ... }
```

A much more common solution is the encapsulation of queries in the `orm.xml` deployment descriptor:

```
<entity-mappings ...>
    ...
    <named-query name="findAllItems">
        <query>select i from Item i</query>
    </named-query>

    <entity class="Item">
        ...
        <named-query name="findItemsByDescription">
          <query>
              select i from Item i where i.description like :desc
          </query>
          <hint name="org.hibernate.comment" value="My Comment"/>
          <hint name="org.hibernate.fetchSize" value="50"/>
          <hint name="org.hibernate.readOnly" value="true"/>
          <hint name="org.hibernate.timeout" value="60"/>
        </named-query>

    </entity>

</entity-mappings>
```

You can see that the Java Persistence descriptor supports an extension point: the `hints` element of a `named-query` definition. You can use it to set Hibernate-specific hints, as you did earlier programmatically with the `Query` interface.

Native SQL queries have their own element and can also be either defined inside or outside an entity mapping:

```
<named-native-query name="findItemsByDescription"
                    result-set-mapping="myItemResult">
    <query>select i.NAME from ITEM i where i.DESC = :desc</query>
    <hint name="org.hibernate.timeout" value="200"/>
</named-native-query>
```

Embedding native SQL is much more powerful than we've shown so far (you can define arbitrary resultset mappings). We'll get back to other SQL emedding options in the next chapter.

We leave it up to you if you want to utilize the named query feature. However, we consider query strings in the application code (except if they're in annotations) to be the second choice; you should always externalize query strings if possible.

You now know how to create, prepare, and execute a query with the Hibernate and Java Persistence APIs and metadata. It's time to learn the query languages and options in more detail. We start with HQL and JPA QL.

14.2 Basic HQL and JPA QL queries

Let's start with some simple queries to get familiar with the HQL syntax and semantics. We apply *selection* to name the data source, *restriction* to match records to the criteria, and *projection* to select the data you want returned from a query.

> **TRY IT** *Testing Hibernate queries*—The *Hibernate Tools* for the Eclipse IDE support a Hibernate Console view. You can test your queries in the console window, and see the generated SQL and the result immediately.

You'll also learn JPA QL in this section, because it's a subset of the functionality of HQL—we'll mention the differences when necessary.

When we talk about queries in this section, we usually mean SELECT statements, operations that retrieve data from the database. HQL also supports UPDATE, DELETE, and even INSERT .. SELECT statements, as we discussed in chapter 12, section 12.2.1, "Bulk statements with HQL and JPA QL." JPA QL includes UPDATE and DELETE. We won't repeat these bulk operations here and will focus on SELECT statements. However, keep in mind that some differences between HQL and JPA QL may also apply to bulk operations—for example, whether a particular function is portable.

SELECT statements in HQL work even without a SELECT clause; only FROM is required. This isn't the case in JPA QL, where the SELECT clause isn't optional. This isn't a big difference in practice; almost all queries require a SELECT clause, whether you write JPA QL or HQL. However, we start our exploration of queries with the FROM clause, because in our experience it's easier to understand. Keep in mind that to translate these queries to JPA QL, you must theoretically add a SELECT clause to complete the statement, but Hibernate lets you execute the query anyway if you forget it (assuming SELECT *).

14.2.1 Selection

The simplest query in HQL is a selection (note that we don't mean SELECT clause or statement here, but from where data is selected) of a single persistent class:

```
from Item
```

This query generates the following SQL:

```
select i.ITEM_ID, i.NAME, i.DESCRIPTION, ... from ITEM i
```

Using aliases

Usually, when you select a class to query from using HQL or JPA QL, you need to assign an *alias* to the queried class to use as a reference in other parts of the query:

```
from Item as item
```

The as keyword is always optional. The following is equivalent:

```
from Item item
```

Think of this as being a bit like the temporary variable declaration in the following Java code:

```
for ( Iterator i = allQueriedItems.iterator(); i.hasNext(); ) {
    Item item = (Item) i.next();
    ...
}
```

You assign the alias item to queried instances of the Item class, allowing you to refer to their property values later in the code (or query). To remind yourself of the similarity, we recommend that you use the same naming convention for aliases that you use for temporary variables (camelCase, usually). However, we may use shorter aliases in some of the examples in this book, such as i instead of item, to keep the printed code readable.

FAQ *Are HQL and JPA QL case sensitive?* We never write HQL and JPA QL keywords in uppercase; we never write SQL keywords in uppercase either. It looks ugly and antiquated—most modern terminals can display both uppercase and lowercase characters. However, HQL and JPA QL aren't case-sensitive for keywords, so you can write FROM Item AS item if you like shouting.

Polymorphic queries

HQL and JPA QL, as object-oriented query languages, support *polymorphic queries*—queries for instances of a class and all instances of its subclasses, respectively. You already know enough HQL and JPA QL to be able to demonstrate this. Consider the following query:

```
from BillingDetails
```

This returns objects of the type BillingDetails, which is an abstract class. In this case, the concrete objects are of the subtypes of BillingDetails: CreditCard and BankAccount. If you want only instances of a particular subclass, you may use

```
from CreditCard
```

The class named in the from clause doesn't even need to be a mapped persistent class; any class will do! The following query returns all persistent objects:

```
from java.lang.Object
```

Of course, this also works for interfaces—this query returns all serializable persistent objects:

```
from java.io.Serializable
```

Likewise, the following criteria query returns all persistent objects (yes, you can select all the tables of your database with such a query):

```
from java.lang.Object
```

Note that Java Persistence doesn't standardize polymorphic queries that use non-mapped interfaces. However, this works with Hibernate EntityManager.

Polymorphism applies not only to classes named explicitly in the FROM clause, but also to polymorphic associations, as you'll see later in this chapter.

We've discussed the FROM clause, now let's move on to the other parts of HQL and JPA QL.

14.2.2 Restriction

Usually, you don't want to retrieve all instances of a class. You must be able express constraints on the property values of objects returned by the query. This is called *restriction*. The WHERE clause is used to express a restriction in SQL, HQL, and JPA QL. These expressions may be as complex as you need to narrow down the piece of data you're looking for. Note that restriction doesn't only apply to SELECT statements; you also use a restriction to limit the scope of an UPDATE or DELETE operation.

This is a typical WHERE clause that restricts the results to all User objects with the given email address:

```
from User u where u.email = 'foo@hibernate.org'
```

Notice that the constraint is expressed in terms of a property, email, of the User class, and that you use an object-oriented notion for this.

The SQL generated by this query is

```
select u.USER_ID, u.FIRSTNAME, u.LASTNAME, u.USERNAME, u.EMAIL
  from USER u
  where u.EMAIL = 'foo@hibernate.org'
```

You can include literals in your statements and conditions, with single quotes. Other commonly used literals in HQL and JPA QL are TRUE and FALSE:

```
from Item i where i.isActive = true
```

A restriction is expressed using ternary logic. The WHERE clause is a logical expression that evaluates to true, false, or null for each tuple of objects. You construct logical expressions by comparing properties of objects to other properties or literal values using the built-in comparison operators.

FAQ   *What is ternary logic?*   A row is included in an SQL resultset if and only if the WHERE clause evaluates to true. In Java, notNullObject==null evaluates to false and null==null evaluates to true. In SQL, NOT_NULL_COL-UMN=null and null=null both evaluate to null, not true. Thus, SQL needs a special operator, IS NULL, to test whether a value is null. This *ternary logic* is a way of handling expressions that may be applied to null column values. Treating null not as a special marker but as a regular value is an SQL extension to the familiar binary logic of the relational model. HQL and JPA QL have to support this ternary logic with ternary operators.

Let's walk through the most common comparison operators.

Comparison expressions

HQL and JPA QL support the same basic comparison operators as SQL. Here are a few examples that should look familiar if you know SQL:

```
from Bid bid where bid.amount between 1 and 10
from Bid bid where bid.amount > 100
from User u where u.email in ('foo@bar', 'bar@foo')
```

Because the underlying database implements ternary logic, testing for null values requires some care. Remember that null = null doesn't evaluate to true in SQL, but to null. All comparisons that use a null operand evaluate to null. (That's why you usually don't see the null literal in queries.) HQL and JPA QL provide an SQL-style IS [NOT] NULL operator:

```
from User u where u.email is null
from Item i where i.successfulBid is not null
```

This query returns all users with no email address and items which are sold.

The LIKE operator allows wildcard searches, where the wildcard symbols are % and _, as in SQL:

```
from User u where u.firstname like 'G%'
```

This expression restricts the result to users with a firstname starting with a capital G. You may also negate the LIKE operator, for example, in a substring match expression:

```
from User u where u.firstname not like '%Foo B%'
```

The percentage symbol stands for any sequence of characters; the underscore can be used to wildcard a single character. You can define an escape character if you want a literal percentage or underscore:

```
from User u where u.firstname not like '\%Foo%' escape='\'
```

This query returns all users with a firstname that starts with *%Foo.*

HQL and JPA QL support arithmetic expressions:

```
from Bid bid where ( bid.amount / 0.71 ) - 100.0 > 0.0
```

Logical operators (and parentheses for grouping) are used to combine expressions:

```
from User user
        where user.firstname like 'G%' and user.lastname like 'K%'
from User u
        where ( u.firstname like 'G%' and u.lastname like 'K%' )
        or u.email in ('foo@hibernate.org', 'bar@hibernate.org' )
```

You can see the precedence of operators in table 14.1, from top to bottom.

The listed operators and their precedence are the same in HQL *and* JPA QL. The arithmetic operators, for example multiplication and addition, are self-explanatory. You've already seen how binary comparison expressions have the same semantics as their SQL counterpart and how to group and combine them with logical operators. Let's discuss collection handling.

Table 14.1 HQL and JPA QL operator precedence

Operator	Description
.	Navigation path expression operator
+, −	Unary positive or negative signing (all unsigned numeric values are considered positive)
*, /	Regular multiplication and division of numeric values
+, −	Regular addition and subtraction of numeric values
=, <>, <, >, >=, <=, [NOT] BETWEEN, [NOT] LIKE, [NOT] IN, IS [NOT] NULL,	Binary comparison operators with SQL semantics
IS [NOT] EMPTY, [NOT] MEMBER [OF]	Binary operators for collections in HQL and JPA QL
NOT, AND, OR	Logical operators for ordering of expression evaluation

Expressions with collections

All expressions in the previous sections included only single-valued path expressions: `user.email`, `bid.amount`, and so on. You can also use path expressions that end in collections in the `WHERE` clause of a query, with the right operators.

For example, let's assume you want to restrict your query result by the size of a collection:

```
from Item i where i.bids is not empty
```

This query returns all `Item` instances that have an element in their `bids` collection. You can also express that you require a particular element to be present in a collection:

```
from Item i, Category c where i.id = '123' and i member of c.items
```

This query returns `Item` and `Category` instances—usually you add a `SELECT` clause and project only one of the two entity types. It returns an `Item` instance with the primary key `'123'` (a literal in single quotes) and all `Category` instances this `Item` instance is associated with. (Another trick you use here is the special `.id` path; this field always refers to the database identifier of an entity, no matter what the name of the identifier property is.)

There are many other ways to work with collections in HQL and JPA QL. For example, you can use them in function calls.

Calling functions

An extremely powerful feature of HQL is the ability to call SQL functions in the `WHERE` clause. If your database supports user-defined functions (most do), you can put this to all sorts of uses, good or evil. For the moment, let's consider the usefulness of the standard ANSI SQL functions `UPPER()` and `LOWER()`. These can be used for case-insensitive searching:

```
from User u where lower(u.email) = 'foo@hibernate.org'
```

Another common expression is concatenation—although SQL dialects are different here, HQL and JPA QL support a portable `concat()` function:

```
from User user
        where concat(user.firstname, user.lastname) like 'G% K%'
```

Also typical is an expression that requires the size of a collection:

```
from Item i where size(i.bids) > 3
```

JPA QL standardizes the most common functions, as summarized in table 14.2.

Table 14.2 Standardized JPA QL functions

Function	Applicability
UPPER(s), LOWER(s)	String values; returns a string value
CONCAT(s1, s2)	String values; returns a string value
SUBSTRING(s, offset, length)	String values (offset starts at 1); returns a string value
TRIM([[BOTH|LEADING|TRAILING] char [FROM]] s)	Trims spaces on BOTH sides of s if no char or other specification is given; returns a string value
LENGTH(s)	String value; returns a numeric value
LOCATE(search, s, offset)	Searches for position of ss in s starting at offset; returns a numeric value
ABS(n), SQRT(n), MOD(dividend, divisor)	Numeric values; returns an absolute of same type as input, square root as double, and the remainder of a division as an integer
SIZE(c)	Collection expressions; returns an integer, or 0 if empty

All the standardized JPA QL functions may be used in the WHERE and HAVING clauses of a query (the latter you'll see soon). The native HQL is a bit more flexible. First, it offers additional portable functions, as shown in table 14.3.

Table 14.3 Additional HQL functions

Function	Applicability
BIT_LENGTH(s)	Returns the number of bits in s
CURRENT_DATE(), CURRENT_TIME(), CURRENT_TIMESTAMP()	Returns the date and/or time of the database management system machine
SECOND(d), MINUTE(d), HOUR(d), DAY(d), MONTH(d), YEAR(d)	Extracts the time and date from a temporal argument
CAST(t as Type)	Casts a given type t to a Hibernate Type
INDEX(joinedCollection)	Returns the index of joined collection element
MINELEMENT(c), MAXELEMENT(c), MININDEX(c), MAXINDEX(c), ELEMENTS(c), INDICES(c)	Returns an element or index of indexed collections (maps, lists, arrays)
Registered in org.hibernate.Dialect	Extends HQL with other functions in a dialect

Most of these HQL functions translate into a counterpart in SQL you've probably used before. This translation table is customizable and extendable with an `org.hibernate.Dialect`. Check the source code of the dialect you're using for your database; you'll probably find many other SQL functions already registered there for immediate use in HQL. Keep in mind that every function that isn't included in the `org.hibernate.Dialect` superclass may not be portable to other database management systems!

Another recent addition to the Hibernate API is the `addSqlFunction()` method on the Hibernate `Configuration` API:

```
Configuration cfg = new Configuration();
cfg.addSqlFunction(
    "lpad",
    new StandardSQLFunction("lpad", Hibernate.STRING)
);
... cfg.buildSessionFactory();
```

This operation adds the SQL function `lpad` to HQL. See the Javadoc of `Standard-SQLFunction` and its subclasses for more information.

HQL even tries to be smart when you call a function that wasn't registered for your SQL dialect: Any function that is called in the `WHERE` clause of an HQL statement, and that isn't known to Hibernate, is passed directly to the database, as an SQL function call. This works great if you don't care about database portability, but it requires that you keep your eyes open for nonportable functions if you do care.

Finally, before we move on to the `SELECT` clause in HQL and JPA QL, let's see how results can be ordered.

Ordering query results

All query languages provide some mechanism for ordering query results. HQL and JPA QL provide an `ORDER BY` clause, similar to SQL.

This query returns all users, ordered by username:

```
from User u order by u.username
```

You specify ascending and descending order using `asc` or `desc`:

```
from User u order by u.username desc
```

You may order by multiple properties:

```
from User u order by u.lastname asc, u.firstname asc
```

You now know how to write a `FROM`, `WHERE`, and `ORDER BY` clause. You know how to select the entities you want to retrieve instances of and the necessary expressions and operations to restrict and order the result. All you need now is the ability to project the data of this result to what you need in your application.

14.2.3 Projection

The SELECT clause performs projection in HQL and JPA QL. It allows you to specify exactly which objects or properties of objects you need in the query result.

Simple projection of entities and scalar values

For example, consider the following HQL query:

```
from Item i, Bid b
```

This is a valid HQL query, but it's invalid in JPA QL—the standard requires that you use a SELECT clause. Still, the same result that is implicit from this *product* of Item and Bid can also be produced with an explicit SELECT clause. This query returns ordered pairs of Item and Bid instances:

```
Query q = session.createQuery("from Item i, Bid b");
// Query q = em.createQuery("select i, b from Item i, Bid b");

Iterator pairs = q.list().iterator();
// Iterator pairs = q.getResultList().iterator();

while ( pairs.hasNext() ) {
    Object[] pair = (Object[]) pairs.next();
    Item item = (Item) pair[0];
    Bid bid = (Bid) pair[1];
}
```

This query returns a List of Object[]. At index 0 is the Item, and at index 1 is the Bid. Because this is a product, the result contains every possible combination of Item and Bid rows found in the two underlying tables. Obviously, this query isn't useful, but you shouldn't be surprised to receive a collection of Object[] as a query result.

The following explicit SELECT clause also returns a collection of Object[]s:

```
select i.id, i.description, i.initialPrice
    from Item i where i.endDate > current_date()
```

The Object[]s returned by this query contain a Long at index 0, a String at index 1, and a BigDecimal or MonetaryAmount at index 2. These are scalar values, not entity instances. Therefore, they aren't in any persistent state, like an entity instance would be. They aren't transactional and obviously aren't checked automatically for dirty state. We call this kind of query a *scalar query*.

Getting distinct results

When you use a SELECT clause, the elements of the result are no longer guaranteed to be unique. For example, item descriptions aren't unique, so the following query may return the same description more than once:

```
select item.description from Item item
```

It's difficult to see how it could be meaningful to have two identical rows in a query result, so if you think duplicates are likely, you normally use the DISTINCT keyword:

```
select distinct item.description from Item item
```

This eliminates duplicates from the returned list of Item descriptions.

Calling functions

It's also (for some Hibernate SQL dialects) possible to call database specific SQL functions from the SELECT clause. For example, the following query retrieves the current date and time from the database server (Oracle syntax), together with a property of Item:

```
select item.startDate, current_date() from Item item
```

The technique of database functions in the SELECT clause isn't limited to database-dependent functions. it works with other more generic (or standardized) SQL functions as well:

```
select item.startDate, item.endDate, upper(item.name)
    from Item item
```

This query returns Object[]s with the starting and ending date of an item auction, and the name of the item all in uppercase.

In particular, it's possible to call SQL *aggregate functions*, which we'll cover later in this chapter. Note, however, that the Java Persistence standard and JPA QL don't guarantee that any function that isn't an aggregation function can be called in the SELECT clause. Hibernate and HQL allow more flexibility, and we think other products that support JPA QL will provide the same freedom to a certain extent. Also note that functions that are unknown to Hibernate aren't passed on to the database as an SQL function call, as they are in the WHERE clause. You have to register a function in your org.hibernate.Dialect to enable it for the SELECT clause in HQL.

The previous sections should get you started with basic HQL and JPA QL. It's time to look at the more complex query options, such as *joins, dynamic fetching, subselects,* and *reporting queries.*

14.3 Joins, reporting queries, and subselects

It's difficult to categorize some queries as advanced and others as basic. Clearly, the queries we've shown you in the previous sections of this chapter aren't going to get you far.

At the least you also need to know how *joins* work. The ability to arbitrarily join data is one of the fundamental strengths of relational data access. Joining data is also the basic operation that enables you to fetch several associated objects and collections in a single query. We now show you how basic join operations work and how you use them to write a *dynamic fetching* strategy.

Other techniques we'd consider advanced include nesting of statements with *subselects* and *report queries* that aggregate and group results efficiently.

Let's start with joins and how they can be used for dynamic fetching.

14.3.1 Joining relations and associations

You use a *join* to combine data in two (or more) relations. For example, you may join the data in the ITEM and BID tables, as shown in figure 14.1. (Note that not all columns and possible rows are shown; hence the dotted lines.)

What most people think of when they hear the word *join* in the context of SQL databases is an *inner join*. An inner join is the most important of several types of joins and the easiest to understand. Consider the SQL statement and result in figure 14.2. This SQL statement is an *ANSI-style inner join* in the FROM clause.

If you join tables ITEM and BID with an inner join, using their common attributes (the ITEM_ID column), you get all items and their bids in a new result table. Note that the result of this operation contains only items that *have* bids. If you want *all* items, and NULL values instead of bid data when there is no corresponding bid, you use a *(left) outer join*, as shown in figure 14.3.

You can think of a table join as working as follows. First, you take a product of the two tables, by taking all possible combinations of ITEM rows with BID rows.

ITEM

ITEM_ID	DESCRIPTION	...
1	Item Nr. One	...
2	Item Nr. Two	...
3	Item Nr. Three	...

BID

BID_ID	ITEM_ID	AMOUNT
1	1	99.00
2	1	100.00
3	1	101.00
4	2	4.99

Figure 14.1   The ITEM and BID tables are obvious candidates for a join operation.

```
select i.*, b.* from ITEM i
inner join BID b on i.ITEM_ID = b.ITEM_ID
```

ITEM_ID	DESCRIPTION	...	BID_ID	ITEM_ID	AMOUNT
1	Item Nr. One	...	1	1	99.00
1	Item Nr. One	...	2	1	100.00
1	Item Nr. One	...	3	1	101.00
2	Item Nr. Two	...	4	2	4.99

Figure 14.2
The result table of an ANSI-style inner join of two tables

Second, you filter these joined rows using a *join condition*. (Any good database engine has much more sophisticated algorithms to evaluate a join; it usually doesn't build a memory-consuming product and then filters all rows.) The join condition is a boolean expression that evaluates to true if the joined row is to be included in the result. In case of the left outer join, each row in the (left) ITEM table that *never* satisfies the join condition is also included in the result, with NULL values returned for all columns of BID.

A *right* outer join retrieves all bids and null if a bid has no item—not a sensible query in this situation. Right outer joins are rarely used; developers always think from left to right and put the driving table first.

In SQL, the join condition is usually specified explicitly. (Unfortunately, it isn't possible to use the name of a foreign key constraint to specify how two tables are to be joined.) You specify the join condition in the ON clause for an ANSI-style join or in the WHERE clause for a so-called *theta-style join*, where I.ITEM_ID = B.ITEM_ID.

We now discuss the HQL and JPA QL join options. Remember that both are based on and translated into SQL, so even if the syntax is slightly different you should always refer to the two examples shown earlier and verify that you understood what the resulting SQL and resultset looks like.

```
select i.*, b.* from ITEM i
left outer join BID b on i.ITEM_ID = b.ITEM_ID
```

ITEM_ID	DESCRIPTION	...	BID_ID	ITEM_ID	AMOUNT
1	Item Nr. One	...	1	1	99.00
1	Item Nr. One	...	2	1	100.00
1	Item Nr. One	...	3	1	101.00
2	Item Nr. Two	...	4	2	4.99
3	Item Nr. Three	...	NULL	NULL	NULL

Figure 14.3
The result of an ANSI-style left outer join of two tables

HQL and JPA QL join options

In Hibernate queries, you don't usually specify a join condition explicitly. Rather, you specify the name of a mapped Java class association. This is basically the same feature we'd prefer to have in SQL, a join condition expressed with a foreign key constraint name. Because you've mapped most, if not all, foreign key relationships of your database schema in Hibernate, you can use the names of these mapped associations in the query language. This is really syntactical sugar, but it's convenient.

For example, the `Item` class has an association named `bids` with the `Bid` class. If you name this association in a query, Hibernate has enough information in the mapping document to then deduce the table join expression. This helps make queries less verbose and more readable.

In fact, HQL and JPA QL provide four ways of expressing (inner and outer) joins:

- An *implicit* association join
- An *ordinary* join in the `FROM` clause
- A *fetch* join in the `FROM` clause
- A *theta-style* join in the `WHERE` clause

Later we show you how to write a join between two classes that don't have an association defined (a theta-style join) and how to write ordinary and fetch joins in the `FROM` clause of a query.

Implicit association joins are common abbreviations. (Note that we decided to make the following examples easier to read and understand by often omitting the `SELECT` clause—valid in HQL, invalid in JPA QL.)

Implicit association joins

So far, you've used simple qualified property names like `bid.amount` and `item.description` in queries. HQL and JPA QL support multipart property path expressions with a dot notation for two different purposes:

- Querying components
- Expressing implicit association joins

The first use is straightforward:

```
from User u where u.homeAddress.city = 'Bangkok'
```

You reference parts of the mapped component `Address` with a dot notation. No tables are joined in this query; the properties of the `homeAddress` component are all mapped to the same table together with the `User` data. You can also write a path expression in the `SELECT` clause:

```
select distinct u.homeAddress.city from User u
```

This query returns a `List` of `Strings`. Because duplicates don't make much sense, you eliminate them with `DISTINCT`.

The second usage of multipart path expressions is implicit association joining:

```
from Bid bid where bid.item.description like '%Foo%'
```

This results in an implicit join on the many-to-one associations from `Bid` to `Item`—the name of this association is `item`. Hibernate knows that you mapped this association with the `ITEM_ID` foreign key in the `BID` table and generates the SQL join condition accordingly. Implicit joins are always directed along many-to-one or one-to-one associations, never through a collection-valued association (you can't write `item.bids.amount`).

Multiple joins are possible in a single path expression. If the association from `Item` to `Category` is many-to-one (instead of the current many-to-many), you can write

```
from Bid bid where bid.item.category.name like 'Laptop%'
```

We frown on the use of this syntactic sugar for more complex queries. SQL joins are important, and especially when optimizing queries, you need to be able to see at a glance exactly how many of them there are. Consider the following query (again, using a many-to-one from `Item` to `Category`):

```
from Bid bid
    where bid.item.category.name like 'Laptop%'
    and bid.item.successfulBid.amount > 100
```

How many joins are required to express this in SQL? Even if you get the answer right, it takes more than a few seconds to figure out. The answer is three; the generated SQL looks something like this:

```
select ...
from BID B
inner join ITEM I on B.ITEM_ID = I.ITEM_ID
inner join CATEGORY C on I.CATEGORY_ID = C.CATEGORY_ID
inner join BID SB on I.SUCCESSFUL_BID_ID = SB.BID_ID
where C.NAME like 'Laptop%'
and SB.AMOUNT > 100
```

It's more obvious if you express this query with explicit HQL and JPA QL joins in the `FROM` clause.

Joins expressed in the FROM clause

Hibernate differentiates between the purposes for joining. Suppose you're querying Items. There are two possible reasons why you may be interested in joining them with Bids.

You may want to limit the item returned by the query on the basis of some criterion that should be applied to their Bids. For example, you may want all Items that have a bid of more than $100; hence this requires an *inner join*. You aren't interested in items that have no bids so far.

On the other hand, you may be primarily interested in the Items, but you may want to execute an outer join just because you want to retrieve all the Bids for the queried Items in the same single SQL statement, something we called eager join fetching earlier. Remember that you prefer to map all associations *lazy* by default, so an eager, outer-join fetch query is used to override the default fetching strategy at runtime for a particular use case.

Let's first write some queries that use inner joins for the purpose of restriction. If you want to retrieve Item instances and restrict the result to items that have bids with a certain amount, you have to assign an alias to a joined association:

```
from Item i
    join i.bids b
        where i.description like '%Foo%'
        and b.amount > 100
```

This query assigns the alias i to the entity Item and the alias b to the joined Items bids. You then use both aliases to express restriction criteria in the WHERE clause.

The resulting SQL is:

```
select i.DESCRIPTION, i.INITIAL_PRICE, ...
        b.BID_ID, b.AMOUNT, b.ITEM_ID, b.CREATED_ON
from ITEM i
inner join BID b on i.ITEM_ID = b.ITEM_ID
where i.DESCRIPTION like '%Foo%'
and b.AMOUNT > 100
```

The query returns all combinations of associated Bids and Items as ordered pairs:

```
Query q = session.createQuery("from Item i join i.bids b");
Iterator pairs = q.list().iterator();
while ( pairs.hasNext() ) {
    Object[] pair = (Object[]) pairs.next();
    Item item = (Item) pair[0];
    Bid bid = (Bid) pair[1];
}
```

Instead of a List of Items, this query returns a List of Object[] arrays. At index 0 is the Item, and at index 1 is the Bid. A particular Item may appear multiple times, once for each associated Bid. These duplicate items are duplicate in-memory references, not duplicate instances!

If you don't want the Bids in the query result, you may specify a SELECT clause in HQL (it's mandatory anyway for JPA QL). You use the alias in a SELECT clause to project only the objects you want:

```
select i
from Item i join i.bids b
where i.description like '%Foo%'
and b.amount > 100
```

Now the generated SQL looks like this:

```
select i.DESCRIPTION, i.INITIAL_PRICE, ...
from ITEM i
inner join BID b on i.ITEM_ID = b.ITEM_ID
where i.DESCRIPTION like '%Foo%'
and b.AMOUNT > 100
```

The query result contains just Items, and because it's an *inner join*, only Items that have Bids:

```
Query q = session.createQuery("select i from Item i join i.bids b");
Iterator items = q.list().iterator();
while ( items.hasNext() ) {
    Item item = (Item) items.next();
}
```

As you can see, using aliases in HQL and JPA QL is the same for both direct classes and joined associations. You used a collection in the previous examples, but the syntax and semantics are the same for single-valued associations, such as many-to-one and one-to-one. You assign aliases in the FROM clause by naming the association and then use the aliases in the WHERE and possibly SELECT clause.

HQL and JPA QL offer an alternative syntax for joining a collection in the FROM clause and to assign it an alias. This IN() operator has its history in an older version of EJB QL. It's semantics are the same as those of a regular collection join. You can rewrite the last query as follows:

```
select i
from Item i in(i.bids) b
where i.description like '%Foo%'
and b.amount > 100
```

The from Item i in(i.bids) b results in the same inner join as the earlier example with from Item i join i.bids b.

So far, you've only written inner joins. Outer joins are mostly used for dynamic fetching, which we'll discuss soon. Sometimes you want to write a simple query with an outer join without applying a dynamic fetching strategy. For example, the following query is a variation of the first query and retrieves items and bids with a minimum amount:

```
from Item i
    left join i.bids b
        with b.amount > 100
        where i.description like '%Foo%'
```

The first thing that is new in this statement is the LEFT keyword. Optionally you can write LEFT OUTER JOIN and RIGHT OUTER JOIN, but we usually prefer the short form. The second change is the additional join condition following the WITH keyword. If you place the b.amount > 100 expression into the WHERE clause you'd restrict the result to Item instances that have bids. This isn't what you want here: You want to retrieve items and bids, and even items that don't have bids. By adding an additional join condition in the FROM clause, you can restrict the Bid instances and still retrieve all Item objects. This query again returns ordered pairs of Item and Bid objects. Finally, note that additional join conditions with the WITH keyword are available only in HQL; JPA QL supports only the basic outer join condition represented by the mapped foreign key association.

A much more common scenario in which outer joins play an important role is eager dynamic fetching.

Dynamic fetching strategies with joins

All queries you saw in the previous section have one thing in common: The returned Item instances have a collection named bids. This collection, if mapped as lazy="true" (default), isn't initialized, and an additional SQL statement is triggered as soon as you access it. The same is true for all single-ended associations, like the seller of each Item. By default, Hibernate generates a proxy and loads the associated User instance lazily and only on-demand.

What options do you have to change this behavior? First, you can change the fetch plan in your mapping metadata and declare a collection or single-valued association as lazy="false". Hibernate then executes the necessary SQL to guarantee that the desired network of objects is loaded at all times. This also means that a single HQL or JPA QL statement may result in several SQL operations!

On the other hand, you usually don't modify the fetch plan in mapping metadata unless you're absolutely sure that it should apply globally. You usually write a new fetch plan for a particular use case. This is what you already did by writing HQL and JPA QL statements; you defined a fetch plan with selection, restriction, and projection. The only thing that will make it more efficient is the right *dynamic fetching strategy.* For example, there is no reason why you need several SQL statements to fetch all `Item` instances and to initialize their `bids` collections, or to retrieve the `seller` for each `Item`. This can be done at the same time, with a join operation.

In HQL and JPA QL you can specify that an associated entity instance or a collection should be eagerly fetched with the `FETCH` keyword in the `FROM` clause:

```
from Item i
    left join fetch i.bids
        where i.description like '%Foo%'
```

This query returns all items with a description that contains the string `"Foo"` and all their bids collections in a single SQL operation. When executed, it returns a list of `Item` instances, with their `bids` collections fully initialized. This is quite different if you compare it to the ordered pairs returned by the queries in the previous section!

The purpose of a fetch join is performance optimization: You use this syntax only because you want eager initialization of the `bids` collections in a single SQL operation:

```
select i.DESCRIPTION, i.INITIAL_PRICE, ...
        b.BID_ID, b.AMOUNT, b.ITEM_ID, b.CREATED_ON
from ITEM i
left outer join BID b on i.ITEM_ID = b.ITEM_ID
where i.DESCRIPTION like '%Foo%'
```

An additional `WITH` clause wouldn't make sense here. You can't restrict the `Bid` instances: All the collections must be fully initialized.

You can also prefetch many-to-one or one-to-one associations, using the same syntax:

```
from Bid bid
    left join fetch bid.item
    left join fetch bid.bidder
        where bid.amount > 100
```

This query executes the following SQL:

```
select b.BID_ID, b.AMOUNT, b.ITEM_ID, b.CREATED_ON
        i.DESCRIPTION, i.INITIAL_PRICE, ...
        u.USERNAME, u.FIRSTNAME, u.LASTNAME, ...
from BID b
left outer join ITEM i on i.ITEM_ID = b.ITEM_ID
left outer join USER u on u.USER_ID = b.BIDDER_ID
where b.AMOUNT > 100
```

If you write JOIN FETCH. without LEFT, you get eager loading with an inner join (also if you use INNER JOIN FETCH); a prefetch with an inner join, for example, returns Item objects with their bids collection fully initialized, but no Item objects that don't have bids. Such a query is rarely useful for collections but can be used for a many-to-one association that isn't nullable; for example, join fetch item.seller works fine.

Dynamic fetching in HQL and JPA QL is straightforward; however, you should remember the following caveats:

- You never assign an alias to any fetch-joined association or collection for further restriction or projection. So left join fetch i.bids b where b = ... is invalid, whereas left join fetch i.bids b join fetch b.bidder is valid.

- You shouldn't fetch more than one collection in parallel; otherwise you create a Cartesian product. You can fetch as many single-valued associated objects as you like without creating a product. This is basically the same problem we discussed in chapter 13, section 13.2.5, "The Cartesian product problem."

- HQL and JPA QL ignore any fetching strategy you've defined in mapping metadata. For example, mapping the bids collection in XML with fetch="join", has no effect on any HQL or JPA QL statement. A dynamic fetching strategy ignores the global fetching strategy (on the other hand, the global fetch plan isn't ignored—every nonlazy association or collection is guaranteed to be loaded, even if several SQL queries are needed).

- If you eager-fetch a collection, duplicates may be returned. Look at figure 14.3: This is exactly the SQL operation that is executed for a select i from Item i join fetch i.bids HQL or JPA QL query. Each Item is duplicated on the left side of the result table as many times as related Bid data is present. The List returned by the HQL or JPA QL query preserves these duplicates as references. If you prefer to filter out these duplicates you need to either wrap the List in a Set (for example, with Set noDupes = new LinkedHashSet(resultList)) or use the DISTINCT keyword: select distinct i from Item i join fetch i.bids —note that in this case the DIS-TINCT doesn't operate at the SQL level, but forces Hibernate to filter out duplicates in memory when marshaling the result into objects. Clearly, duplicates can't be avoided in the SQL result.

- Query execution options that are based on the SQL result rows, such as pagination with `setMaxResults()`/`setFirstResult()`, are semantically incorrect if a collection is eagerly fetched. If you have an eager fetched collection in your query, at the time of writing, Hibernate falls back to limiting the result in-memory, instead of using SQL. This may be less efficient, so we don't recommend the use of `JOIN FETCH` with `setMaxResults()`/`setFirstResult()`. Future versions of Hibernate may fall back to a different SQL query strategy (such as two queries and subselect fetching) if `setMaxResults()`/`setFirstResult()` is used in combination with a `JOIN FETCH`.

This is how Hibernate implements dynamic association fetching, a powerful feature that is essential for achieving high performance in any application. As explained in chapter 13, section 13.2.5, "Optimization step by step," tuning the fetch plan and fetching strategy with queries is your first optimization, followed by global settings in mapping metadata when it becomes obvious that more and more queries have equal requirements.

The last join option on the list is the theta-style join.

Theta-style joins

A product lets you retrieve all possible combinations of instances of two or more classes. This query returns all ordered pairs of `Users` and `Category` objects:

```
from User, Category
```

Obviously, this isn't usually useful. There is one case where it's commonly used: theta-style joins.

In traditional SQL, a theta-style join is a Cartesian product together with a join condition in the `WHERE` clause, which is applied on the product to restrict the result.

In HQL and JPA QL, the theta-style syntax is useful when your join condition isn't a foreign key relationship mapped to a class association. For example, suppose you store the `User`'s name in log records, instead of mapping an association from `LogRecord` to `User`. The classes don't know anything about each other, because they aren't associated. You can then find all the `Users` and their `LogRecords` with the following theta-style join:

```
from User user, LogRecord log where user.username = log.username
```

The join condition here is a comparison of `username`, present as an attribute in both classes. If both rows have the same `username`, they're joined (with an inner join) in the result. The query result consists of ordered pairs:

```
Iterator i =
    session.createQuery("from User user, LogRecord log" +
                        " where user.username = log.username")
              .list().iterator ();
while ( i.hasNext() ) {
    Object[] pair = (Object[]) i.next();
    User user = (User) pair[0];
    LogRecord log = (LogRecord) pair[1];
}
```

You can of course apply a SELECT clause to project only the data you're interested in.

You probably won't need to use the theta-style joins often. Note that it's currently not possible in HQL or JPA QL to outer join two tables that don't have a mapped association—theta-style joins are inner joins.

Finally, it's extremely common to perform queries that compare primary key or foreign key values to either query parameters or other primary or foreign key values.

Comparing identifiers

If you think about identifier comparison in more object-oriented terms, what you're really doing is comparing object references. HQL and JPA QL support the following:

```
from Item i, User u
    where i.seller = u and u.username = 'steve'
```

In this query, i.seller refers to the foreign key to the USER table in the ITEM table (on the SELLER_ID column), and user refers to the primary key of the USER table (on the USER_ID column). This query uses a theta-style join and is equivalent to the much preferred

```
from Item i join i.seller u
    where u.username = 'steve'
```

On the other hand, the following theta-style join *can't* be re-expressed as a FROM clause join:

```
from Item i, Bid b
    where i.seller = b.bidder
```

In this case, i.seller and b.bidder are both foreign keys of the USER table. Note that this is an important query in the application; you use it to identify people bidding for their own items.

You may also want to compare a foreign key value to a query parameter, perhaps to find all Comments from a User:

```
User givenUser = ...
Query q = session.createQuery(
                    "from Comment c where c.fromUser = :user"
                    );
q.setEntity("user", givenUser);
List result = q.list();
```

Alternatively, sometimes you prefer to express these kinds of queries in terms of identifier values rather than object references. An identifier value may be referred to by either the name of the identifier property (if there is one) or the special property name id. (Note that only HQL guarantees that id always refers to any arbitrarily named identifier property; JPA QL doesn't.)

These queries are equivalent to the earlier queries:

```
from Item i, User u
    where i.seller.id = u.id and u.username = 'steve'

from Item i, Bid b
    where i.seller.id = b.bidder.id
```

However, you may now use the identifier value as a query parameter:

```
Long userId = ...
Query q = session.createQuery(
                    "from Comment c where c.fromUser.id = :userId"
                    );
q.setLong("userId", userId);
List result = q.list();
```

Considering identifier attributes, there is a world of difference between the following queries:

```
from Bid b where b.item.id = 1

from Bid b where b.item.description like '%Foo%'
```

The second query uses an implicit table join; the first has no joins at all!

This completes our discussion of queries that involve joins. You learned how to write a simple implicit inner join with dot notation and how to write an explicit inner or outer join with aliases in the FROM clause. We also looked at dynamic fetching strategies with outer and inner join SQL operations.

Our next topic is advanced queries that we consider to be mostly useful for *reporting*.

14.3.2 *Reporting queries*

Reporting queries take advantage of the database's ability to perform efficient grouping and aggregation of data. They're more relational in nature; they don't always return entities. For example, instead of retrieving `Item` entities that are in persistent state (and automatically dirty checked), a report query may only retrieve the `Item` names and initial auction prices. If this is the only information you need (maybe even aggregated, the highest initial price in a category, and so on.) for a report screen, you don't need transactional entity instances and can save the overhead of automatic dirty checking and caching in the persistence context.

HQL and JPA QL allow you to use several features of SQL that are most commonly used for reporting—although they're also used for other things. In reporting queries, you use the `SELECT` clause for projection and the `GROUP BY` and `HAVING` clauses for aggregation.

Because we've already discussed the basic `SELECT` clause, we'll go straight to aggregation and grouping.

Projection with aggregation functions

The aggregate functions that are recognized by HQL and standardized in JPA QL are `count()`, `min()`, `max()`, `sum()` and `avg()`.

This query counts all the `Item`s:

```
select count(i) from Item i
```

The result is returned as a `Long`:

```
Long count =
    (Long) session.createQuery("select count(i) from Item i")
                    .uniqueResult();
```

The next variation of the query counts all `Item`s which have a `successfulBid` (null values are eliminated):

```
select count(i.successfulBid) from Item i
```

This query calculates the total of all the successful `Bid`s:

```
select sum(i.successfulBid.amount) from Item i
```

The query returns a `BigDecimal`, because the `amount` property is of type `BigDecimal`. The `SUM()` function also recognizes `BigInteger` property types and returns `Long` for all other numeric property types. Notice the use of an implicit join in the `SELECT` clause: You navigate the association (`successfulBid`) from `Item` to `Bid` by referencing it with a dot.

The next query returns the minimum and maximum bid amounts for a particular Item:

```
select min(bid.amount), max(bid.amount)
        from Bid bid where bid.item.id = 1
```

The result is an ordered pair of BigDecimals (two instances of BigDecimals, in an Object[] array).

The special COUNT(DISTINCT) function ignores duplicates:

```
select count(distinct i.description) from Item i
```

When you call an aggregate function in the SELECT clause, without specifying any grouping in a GROUP BY clause, you collapse the result down to a single row, containing the aggregated value(s). This means that (in the absence of a GROUP BY clause) any SELECT clause that contains an aggregate function must contain *only* aggregate functions.

For more advanced statistics and reporting, you need to be able to perform *grouping*.

Grouping aggregated results

Just like in SQL, any property or alias that appears in HQL or JPA QL outside of an aggregate function in the SELECT clause must also appear in the GROUP BY clause. Consider the next query, which counts the number of users with each last name:

```
select u.lastname, count(u) from User u
group by u.lastname
```

Look at the generated SQL:

```
select u.LAST_NAME, count(u.USER_ID)
from USER u
group by u.LAST_NAME
```

In this example, the u.lastname isn't inside an aggregate function; you use it to group the result. You also don't need to specify the property you like to count. The generated SQL automatically uses the primary key, if you use an alias that has been set in the FROM clause.

The next query finds the average bid amount for each item:

```
select bid.item.id, avg(bid.amount) from Bid bid
group by bid.item.id
```

This query returns ordered pairs of Item identifier and average bid amount values. Notice how you use the id special property to refer to the identifier of a persistent class, no matter what the real property name of the identifier is. (Again, this special property isn't standardized in JPA QL.)

The next query counts the number of bids and calculates the average bid per unsold item:

```
select bid.item.id, count(bid), avg(bid.amount)
from Bid bid
where bid.item.successfulBid is null
group by bid.item.id
```

That query uses an implicit association join. For an explicit ordinary join in the FROM clause (not a fetch join), you can re-express it as follows:

```
select bidItem.id, count(bid), avg(bid.amount)
from Bid bid
    join bid.item bidItem
where bidItem.successfulBid is null
group by bidItem.id
```

Sometimes, you want to further restrict the result by selecting only particular values of a group.

Restricting groups with having

The WHERE clause is used to perform the relational operation of restriction upon rows. The HAVING clause performs restriction upon groups.

For example, the next query counts users with each last name that begins with "A":

```
select user.lastname, count(user)
from User user
group by user.lastname
    having user.lastname like 'A%'
```

The same rules govern the SELECT and HAVING clauses: Only grouped properties may appear outside of an aggregate function. The next query counts the number of bids per unsold item, returning results for only those items that have more than 10 bids:

```
select item.id, count(bid), avg(bid.amount)
from Item item
    join item.bids bid
where item.successfulBid is null
group by item.id
    having count(bid) > 10
```

Most report queries use a SELECT clause to choose a list of projected or aggregated properties. You've seen that when there is more than one property or alias listed in the SELECT clause, Hibernate returns the query results as tuples—each row of the query result list is an instance of Object[].

Utilizing dynamic instantiation

Tuples, especially common with report queries, are inconvenient, so HQL and JPA QL provide a SELECT NEW constructor call. In addition to creating new objects dynamically with this technique, you can also use it in combination with aggregation and grouping.

If you define a class called ItemBidSummary with a constructor that takes a Long, a Long, and a BigDecimal, the following query may be used:

```
select new ItemBidSummary(
            bid.item.id, count(bid), avg(bid.amount)
            )
from Bid bid
where bid.item.successfulBid is null
group by bid.item.id
```

In the result of this query, each element is an instance of ItemBidSummary, which is a summary of an Item, the number of bids for that item, and the average bid amount. Note that you have to write a fully qualified classname here, with a package name. unless the class has been imported into the HQL namespace (see chapter 4, section 4.3.3, "Naming entities for querying"). This approach is type-safe, and a data transfer class such as ItemBidSummary can easily be extended for special formatted printing of values in reports.

The ItemBidSummary class is a Java bean, it doesn't have to be a mapped persistent entity class. On the other hand, if you use the SELECT NEW technique with a mapped entity class, all instances returned by your query are in *transient* state—so you can use this feature to populate several new objects and then save them.

Report queries can have an impact on the performance of your application. Let's explore this issue some more.

Improving performance with report queries

The only time we have ever seen any significant overhead in Hibernate code compared to direct JDBC queries—and then only for unrealistically simple toy test cases—is in the special case of read-only queries against a local database. In this case, it's possible for a database to completely cache query results in memory and respond quickly, so benchmarks are generally useless if the dataset is small: Plain SQL and JDBC are always the fastest option.

Hibernate, on the other hand, even with a small dataset, must still do the work of adding the resulting objects of a query to the persistence context cache (perhaps also the second-level cache) and manage uniqueness, and so on. If you ever wish to avoid the overhead of managing the persistence context cache, report queries give you a way to do this. The overhead of a Hibernate report query compared to direct SQL/JDBC isn't usually measurable, even in unrealistic extreme cases, like loading one million objects from a local database without network latency.

Report queries using projection in HQL and JPA QL let you specify which properties you wish to retrieve. For report queries, you aren't selecting entities in managed state, but only properties or aggregated values:

```
select user.lastname, count(user) from User user
group by user.lastname
```

This query doesn't return persistent entity instances, so Hibernate doesn't add any persistent object to the persistence context cache. This means that no object must be watched for dirty state either.

Therefore, reporting queries result in faster release of allocated memory, because objects aren't kept in the persistence context cache until the context is closed—they may be garbage collected as soon as they're dereferenced by the application, after executing the report.

Almost always, these considerations are extremely minor, so don't go out and rewrite all your read-only transactions to use report queries instead of transactional, cached, and managed objects. Report queries are more verbose and (arguably) less object-oriented. They also make less efficient use of Hibernate's caches, which is much more important once you consider the overhead of remote communication with the database in production systems. You should wait until you find a case where you have a real performance problem before using this optimization.

You can already create really complex HQL and JPA QL queries with what you've seen so far. Even more advanced queries may include nested statements, known as *subselects*.

14.3.3 Using subselects

An important and powerful feature of SQL is *subselects*. A subselect is a select query embedded in another query, usually in the SELECT, FROM, or WHERE clauses.

HQL and JPA QL support subqueries in the WHERE clause. Subselects in the FROM clause aren't supported by HQL and JPA QL (although the specification lists them as a possible future extension) because both languages have no *transitive closure*. The result of a query may not be tabular, so it can't be reused for selection in a

FROM clause. Subselects in the SELECT clause are also not supported in the query language, but can be mapped to properties with a *formula*, as shown in "Inverse joined properties" in chapter 8, section 8.1.3.

(Some platforms supported by Hibernate don't implement SQL subselects. Hibernate supports subselects only if the SQL database management system provides this feature.)

Correlated and uncorrelated nesting

The result of a subquery may contain either a single row or multiple rows. Typically, subqueries that return single rows perform aggregation. The following subquery returns the total number of items sold by a user; the outer query returns all users who have sold more than 10 items:

```
from User u where 10 < (
    select count(i) from u.items i where i.successfulBid is not null
)
```

This is a *correlated subquery*—it refers to an alias (u) from the outer query The next subquery is an *uncorrelated subquery*:

```
from Bid bid where bid.amount + 1 >= (
    select max(b.amount) from Bid b
)
```

The subquery in this example returns the maximum bid amount in the entire system; the outer query returns all bids whose amount is within one (dollar) of that amount.

Note that in both cases, the subquery is enclosed in parentheses. This is always required.

Uncorrelated subqueries are harmless, and there is no reason to not use them when convenient, although they can always be rewritten as two queries (they don't reference each other). You should think more carefully about the performance impact of correlated subqueries. On a mature database, the performance cost of a simple correlated subquery is similar to the cost of a join. However, it isn't necessarily possible to rewrite a correlated subquery using several separate queries.

Quantification

If a subquery returns multiple rows, it's combined with *quantification*. ANSI SQL, HQL, and JPA QL define the following quantifiers:

- ALL—The expression evaluates to true if the comparison is true for all values in the result of the subquery. It evaluates to false if a single value of the subquery result fails the comparison test.

- ANY—The expression evaluates to `true` if the comparison is true for some (any) value in the result of the subquery. If the subquery result is empty or no value satisfies the comparison, it evaluates to `false`. The keyword `SOME` is a synonym for `ANY`.

- IN—This binary comparison operator can compare a list of values against the result of a subquery and evaluates to `true` if all values are found in the result.

For example, this query returns items where all bids are less than 100:

```
from Item i where 100 > all ( select b.amount from i.bids b )
```

The next query returns all the others, items with bids greater than 100:

```
from Item i where 100 <= any ( select b.amount from i.bids b )
```

This query returns items with a bid of exactly 100:

```
from Item i where 100 = some ( select b.amount from i.bids b )
```

So does this one:

```
from Item i where 100 in ( select b.amount from i.bids b )
```

HQL supports a shortcut syntax for subqueries that operate on elements or indices of a collection. The following query uses the special HQL `elements()` function:

```
List result =
    session.createQuery("from Category c" +
                        " where :givenItem in elements(c.items)")
            .setEntity("givenItem", item)
            .list()
```

The query returns all categories to which the item belongs and is equivalent to the following HQL (and valid JPA QL), where the subquery is more explicit:

```
List result =
 session.createQuery(
 "from Category c where :givenItem in (select i from c.items i)"
 )
 .setEntity("item", item)
 .list();
```

Along with `elements()`, HQL provides `indices()`, `maxelement()`, `minelement()`, `maxindex()`, `minindex()`, and `size()`, each of which is equivalent to a certain correlated subquery against the passed collection. Refer to the Hibernate documentation for more information about these special functions; they're rarely used.

Subqueries are an advanced technique; you should question frequent use of subqueries because queries with subqueries can often be rewritten using only joins and aggregation. However, they're powerful and useful from time to time.

14.4 Summary

You're now able to write a wide variety of queries in HQL and JPA QL. You learned in this chapter how to prepare and execute queries, and how to bind parameters. We've shown you restriction, projection, joins, subselects, and many other options that you probably already know from SQL.

Table 14.4 shows a summary you can use to compare native Hibernate features and Java Persistence.

Table 14.4 Hibernate and JPA comparison chart for chapter 14

Hibernate Core	Java Persistence and EJB 3.0
Hibernate APIs support query execution with listing, iteration, and scrolling.	Java Persistence standardizes query execution with listing.
Hibernate supports named and positional query bind parameters.	Java Persistence standardizes named and positional bind parameter options.
Hibernate query APIs support application-level query hints.	Java Persistence allows developers to supply arbitrary vendor-specific (Hibernate) query hints.
HQL supports SQL-like restriction, projection, joins, subselects, and function calls.	JPA QL supports SQL-like restriction, projection, joins, subselects, and function calls—subset of HQL.

In the next chapter we focus on more advanced query techniques, such as programmatic generation of complex queries with the `Criteria` API and embedding of native SQL queries. We'll also talk about the query cache and when you should enable it.

Advanced query options

This chapter covers

- Querying with Criteria and Example APIs
- Embedding native SQL queries
- Collection filters
- The optional query result cache

This chapter explains all query options that you may consider optional or advanced. You'll need the first subject of this chapter, the Criteria query interface, whenever you create more complex queries programmatically. This API is much more convenient and elegant than programmatic generation of query strings for HQL and JPA QL. Unfortunately, it's also only available as a native Hibernate API; Java Persistence doesn't (yet) standardize a programmatic query interface.

Both Hibernate and Java Persistence support queries written in native SQL. You can embed SQL and stored procedure calls in your Java source code or externalize them to mapping metadata. Hibernate can execute your SQL and convert the resultset into more convenient objects, depending on your mapping.

Filtering of collections is a simple convenience feature of Hibernate—you won't use it often. It helps you to replace a more elaborate query with a simple API call and a query fragment, for example, if you want to obtain a subset of the objects in a collection.

Finally, we'll discuss the optional query result cache—we've already mentioned that it's not useful in all situations, so we'll take a closer look at the benefits of caching results of a query and when you'd ideally enable this feature.

Let's start with query by criteria and query by example.

15.1 Querying with criteria and example

The Criteria and Example APIs are available in Hibernate only; Java Persistence doesn't standardize these interfaces. As mentioned earlier, it seems likely that other vendors, not only Hibernate, support a similar extension interface and that a future version of the standard will include this functionality.

Querying with programmatically generated criteria and example objects is often the preferred solution when queries get more complex. This is especially true if you have to create a query at runtime. Imagine that you have to implement a search mask in your application, with many check boxes, input fields, and switches the user can enable. You must create a database query from the user's selection. The traditional way to do this is to create a query string through concatenation, or maybe to write a *query builder* that can construct the SQL query string for you. You'd run into the same problem if you'd try to use HQL or JPA QL in this scenario.

The Criteria and Example interfaces allow you to build queries programmatically by creating and combining objects in the right order. We now show you how to work with these APIs, and how to express selection, restriction, joins, and projection. We assume that you've read the previous chapter and that you know how these operations are translated into SQL. Even if you decide to use the `Criteria` and `Example` APIs as your primary way to write queries, keep in mind that HQL and JPA QL are always more flexible due to their string-based nature.

Let's start with some basic selection and restriction examples.

15.1.1 *Basic criteria queries*

The simplest criteria query looks like this:

```
session.createCriteria(Item.class);
```

It retrieves all persistent instances of the `Item` class. This is also called the *root entity* of the criteria query.

Criteria queries also support polymorphism:

```
session.createCriteria(BillingDetails.class);
```

This query returns instances of `BillingDetails` and its subclasses. Likewise, the following criteria query returns all persistent objects:

```
session.createCriteria(java.lang.Object.class);
```

The `Criteria` interface also supports ordering of results with the `addOrder()` method and the `Order` criterion:

```
session.createCriteria(User.class)
        .addOrder( Order.asc("lastname") )
        .addOrder( Order.asc("firstname") );
```

You don't need to have an open `Session` to create a criteria object; a `Detached-Criteria` can be instantiated and later attached to a `Session` for execution (or to another `Criteria` as a subquery):

```
DetachedCriteria crit =
  DetachedCriteria.forClass(User.class)
          .addOrder( Order.asc("lastname") )
          .addOrder( Order.asc("firstname") );

List result = crit.getExecutableCriteria(session).list();
```

Usually you want to restrict the result and don't retrieve all instances of a class.

Applying restrictions

For a criteria query, you must construct a `Criterion` object to express a constraint. The `Restrictions` class provides factory methods for built-in `Criterion` types. Let's search for `User` objects with a particular email address:

```
Criterion emailEq = Restrictions.eq("email", "foo@hibernate.org");
Criteria crit = session.createCriteria(User.class);
crit.add(emailEq);
User user = (User) crit.uniqueResult();
```

You create a `Criterion` that represents the restriction for an equality comparison and add it to the `Criteria`. This `eq()` method has two arguments: first the name of the property, and then the value that should be compared. The property name is always given as a string; keep in mind that this name may change during a refactoring of your domain model and that you must update any predefined criteria queries manually. Also note that the criteria interfaces don't support explicit parameter binding, because it's not needed. In the previous example you bound the string `"foo@hibernate.org"` to the query; you can bind any `java.lang.Object` and let Hibernate figure out what to do with it. The `uniqueResult()` method executes the query and returns exactly one object as a result—you have to cast it correctly.

Usually, you write this a bit less verbosely, using method chaining:

```
User user =
   (User) session.createCriteria(User.class)
                 .add(Restrictions.eq("email", "foo@hibernate.org"))
                 .uniqueResult();
```

Obviously, criteria queries are more difficult to read if they get more complex—a good reason to prefer them for dynamic and programmatic query generation, but to use externalized HQL and JPA QL for predefined queries. A new feature of JDK 5.0 is *static imports*; it helps making criteria queries more readable. For example, by adding

```
import static org.hibernate.criterion.Restrictions.*;
```

you're able to abbreviate the criteria query restriction code to

```
User user =
   (User) session.createCriteria(User.class)
                 .add( eq("email", "foo@hibernate.org") )
                 .uniqueResult();
```

An alternative to obtaining a `Criterion` is a `Property` object—this will be more useful later in this section when we discuss projection:

```
session.createCriteria(User.class)
        .add( Property.forName("email").eq("foo@hibernate.org") );
```

You can also name a property of a component with the usual dot notation:

```
session.createCriteria(User.class)
        .add( Restrictions.eq("homeAddress.street", "Foo"));
```

The `Criteria` API and the `org.hibernate.criterion` package offer many other operators besides `eq()` you can use to construct more complex expressions.

Creating comparison expressions

All regular SQL (and HQL, JPA QL) comparison operators are also available via the `Restrictions` class:

```
Criterion restriction =
  Restrictions.between("amount",
                new BigDecimal(100),
                new BigDecimal(200) );
session.createCriteria(Bid.class).add(restriction);

session.createCriteria(Bid.class)
        .add( Restrictions.gt("amount", new BigDecimal(100) ) );

String[] emails = { "foo@hibernate.org", "bar@hibernate.org" };
session.createCriteria(User.class)
        .add( Restrictions.in("email", emails) );
```

A ternary logic operator is also available; this query returns all users with no email address:

```
session.createCriteria(User.class)
        .add( Restrictions.isNull("email") );
```

You also need to be able to find users who *do* have an email address:

```
session.createCriteria(User.class)
        .add( Restrictions.isNotNull("email") );
```

You can also test a collection with `isEmpty()`, `isNotEmpty()`, or its actual size:

```
session.createCriteria(Item.class)
        .add( Restrictions.isEmpty("bids"));

session.createCriteria(Item.class)
        .add( Restrictions.sizeGt("bids", 3));
```

Or you can compare two properties:

```
session.createCriteria(User.class)
        .add( Restrictions.eqProperty("firstname", "username") );
```

The criteria query interfaces also have special support for string matching.

String matching

For criteria queries, wildcarded searches may use either the same wildcard symbols as HQL and JPA QL (percentage sign and underscore) or specify a `MatchMode`. The `MatchMode` is a convenient way to express a substring match without string manipulation. These two queries are equivalent:

```
session.createCriteria(User.class)
        .add( Restrictions.like("username", "G%") );

session.createCriteria(User.class)
        .add( Restrictions.like("username", "G", MatchMode.START) );
```

The allowed MatchModes are START, END, ANYWHERE, and EXACT.

You often also want to perform case-insensitive string matching. Where you'd resort to a function such as LOWER() in HQL or JPA QL, you can rely on a method of the Criteria API:

```
session.createCriteria(User.class)
        .add( Restrictions.eq("username", "foo").ignoreCase() );
```

You can combine expressions with logical operators.

Combining expressions with logical operators

If you add multiple Criterion instances to the one Criteria instance, they're applied conjunctively (using and):

```
session.createCriteria(User.class)
        .add( Restrictions.like("firstname", "G%") )
        .add( Restrictions.like("lastname", "K%") );
```

If you need disjunction (or), there are two options. The first is to use Restrictions.or() together with Restrictions.and():

```
session.createCriteria(User.class)
        .add(
            Restrictions.or(
                Restrictions.and(
                    Restrictions.like("firstname", "G%"),
                    Restrictions.like("lastname", "K%")
                ),
                Restrictions.in("email", emails)
            )
        );
```

The second option is to use Restrictions.disjunction() together with Restrictions.conjunction():

```
session.createCriteria(User.class)
        .add( Restrictions.disjunction()
            .add( Restrictions.conjunction()
                .add( Restrictions.like("firstname", "G%") )
                .add( Restrictions.like("lastname", "K%") )
            )
            .add( Restrictions.in("email", emails) )
        );
```

We think both these options are ugly, even after spending five minutes trying to format them for maximum readability. JDK 5.0 static imports can help improve readability considerably, but even so, unless you're constructing a query on the fly, the HQL or JPA QL string is much easier to understand.

You may have noticed that many standard comparison operators (less than, greater than, equals, and so on) are built into the `Criteria` API, but certain operators are missing. For example, any arithmetic operators such as addition and division aren't supported directly.

Another issue is function calls. `Criteria` has built-in functions only for the most common cases such as string case-insensitive matching. HQL, on the other hand, allows you to call arbitrary SQL functions in the `WHERE` clause.

The `Criteria` API has a similar facility: You can add an arbitrary SQL expression as a `Criterion`.

Adding arbitrary SQL expressions

Let's assume you want to test a string for its length and restrict your query result accordingly. The `Criteria` API has no equivalent to the `LENGTH()` function in SQL, HQL, or JPA QL.

You can, however, add a plain SQL function expression to your `Criteria`:

```
session.createCriteria(User.class)
    .add( Restrictions.sqlRestriction(
            "length({alias}.PASSWORD) < ?",
            5,
            Hibernate.INTEGER
        )
    );
```

This query returns all `User` objects that have a password with less than 5 characters. The `{alias}` placeholder is needed to prefix any table alias in the final SQL; it always refers to the table the root entity is mapped to (`USERS` in this case). You also use a position parameter (named parameters aren't supported by this API) and specify its type as `Hibernate.INTEGER`. Instead of a single bind argument and type, you can also use an overloaded version of the `sqlRestriction()` method that supports arrays of arguments and types.

This facility is powerful—for example, you can add an SQL `WHERE` clause subselect with quantification:

```
session.createCriteria(Item.class)
    .add( Restrictions.sqlRestriction(
            "'100' > all" +
            " ( select b.AMOUNT from BID b" +
```

```
     "      where b.ITEM_ID = {alias}.ITEM_ID )"
         )
     );
```

This query returns all Item objects which have no bids greater than 100. (The Hibernate criteria query system is extensible: You could also wrap the LENGTH() SQL function in your own implementation of the Criterion interface.)

Finally, you can write criteria queries that include subqueries.

Writing subqueries

A subquery in a criteria query is a WHERE clause subselect. Just like in HQL, JPA QL, and SQL, the result of a subquery may contain either a single row or multiple rows. Typically, subqueries that return single rows perform aggregation.

The following subquery returns the total number of items sold by a user; the outer query returns all users who have sold more than 10 items:

```
DetachedCriteria subquery =
                    DetachedCriteria.forClass(Item.class, "i");

subquery.add( Restrictions.eqProperty("i.seller.id", "u.id"))
        .add( Restrictions.isNotNull("i.successfulBid") )
        .setProjection( Property.forName("i.id").count() );

Criteria criteria = session.createCriteria(User.class, "u")
                    .add( Subqueries.lt(10, subquery) );
```

This is a correlated subquery. The DetachedCriteria refers to the u alias; this alias is declared in the outer query. Note that the outer query uses a *less than* operator because the subquery is the right operand. Also note that i.seller.id does not result in a join, because SELLER_ID is a column in the ITEM table, which is the root entity for that detached criteria.

Let's move on to the next topic about criteria queries: joins and dynamic fetching.

15.1.2 Joins and dynamic fetching

Just like in HQL and JPA QL, you may have different reasons why you want to express a join. First, you may want to use a join to restrict the result by some property of a joined class. For example, you may want to retrieve all Item instances that are sold by a particular User.

Of course, you also want to use joins to dynamically fetch associated objects or collections, as you'd do with the fetch keyword in HQL and JPA QL. In criteria queries you have the same options available, with a FetchMode.

We first look at regular joins and how you can express restrictions that involve associated classes.

Joining associations for restriction

There are two ways to express a join in the Criteria API; hence there are two ways in which you can use aliases for restriction. The first is the createCriteria() method of the Criteria interface. This basically means you can nest calls to createCriteria():

```
Criteria itemCriteria = session.createCriteria(Item.class);
itemCriteria.add(
    Restrictions.like("description",
                      "Foo",
                      MatchMode.ANYWHERE)
);

Criteria bidCriteria = itemCriteria.createCriteria("bids");
bidCriteria.add( Restrictions.gt( "amount", new BigDecimal(99) ) );

List result = itemCriteria.list();
```

You usually write the query as follows (method chaining):

```
List result =
  session.createCriteria(Item.class)
    .add( Restrictions.like("description",
                            "Foo",
                            MatchMode.ANYWHERE)
    )
    .createCriteria("bids")
     .add( Restrictions.gt("amount", new BigDecimal(99) ) )
    .list();
```

The creation of a Criteria for the bids of the Item results in an inner join between the tables of the two classes. Note that you may call list() on either Criteria instance without changing the query result. Nesting criteria works not only for collections (such as bids), but also for single-valued associations (such as seller):

```
List result =
  session.createCriteria(Item.class)
    .createCriteria("seller")
     .add( Restrictions.like("email", "%@hibernate.org") )
    .list();
```

This query returns all items that are sold by users with a particular email address pattern.

The second way to express inner joins with the `Criteria` API is to assign an alias to the joined entity:

```
session.createCriteria(Item.class)
        .createAlias("bids", "b")
        .add( Restrictions.like("description", "%Foo%") )
        .add( Restrictions.gt("b.amount", new BigDecimal(99) ) );
```

And the same for a restriction on a single-valued association, the `seller`:

```
session.createCriteria(Item.class)
        .createAlias("seller", "s")
        .add( Restrictions.like("s.email", "%hibernate.org" ) );
```

This approach doesn't use a second instance of `Criteria`; it's basically the same alias assignment mechanism you'd write in the `FROM` clause of an HQL/JPA QL statement. Properties of the joined entity must then be qualified by the alias assigned in `createAlias()` method, such as `s.email`. Properties of the root entity of the criteria query (`Item`) may be referred to without the qualifying alias, or with the alias `"this"`:

```
session.createCriteria(Item.class)
        .createAlias("bids", "b")
        .add( Restrictions.like("this.description", "%Foo%") )
        .add( Restrictions.gt("b.amount", new BigDecimal(99) ) );
```

Finally, note that at the time of writing only joining of associated entities or collections that contain references to entities (one-to-many and many-to-many) is supported in Hibernate with the `Criteria` API. The following example tries to join a collection of components:

```
session.createCriteria(Item.class)
        .createAlias("images", "img")
        .add( Restrictions.gt("img.sizeX", 320 ) );
```

Hibernate fails with an exception and tells you that the property you want to alias doesn't represent an entity association. We think this feature will likely be implemented by the time you read this book.

Another syntax that is also invalid, but that you may be tempted to try, is an implicit join of a single-valued association with the dot notation:

```
session.createCriteria(Item.class)
        .add( Restrictions.like("seller.email", "%hibernate.org") );
```

The `"seller.email"` string isn't a property or a component's property path. Create an alias or a nested `Criteria` object to join this entity association.

Let's discuss dynamic fetching of associated objects and collections.

Dynamic fetching with criteria queries

In HQL and JPA QL, you use the `join fetch` operation to eagerly fill a collection or to initialize an object that is mapped as lazy and would otherwise be proxied. You can do the same using the `Criteria` API:

```
session.createCriteria(Item.class)
        .setFetchMode("bids", FetchMode.JOIN)
        .add( Restrictions.like("description", "%Foo%") );
```

This query returns all `Item` instance with a particular collection and eagerly loads the `bids` collection for each `Item`.

A `FetchMode.JOIN` enables eager fetching through an SQL outer join. If you want to use an inner join instead (rare, because it wouldn't return items that don't have bids), you can force it:

```
session.createCriteria(Item.class)
        .createAlias("bids", "b", CriteriaSpecification.INNER_JOIN)
        .setFetchMode("b", FetchMode.JOIN)
        .add( Restrictions.like("description", "%Foo%") );
```

You can also prefetch many-to-one and one-to-one associations:

```
session.createCriteria(Item.class)
        .setFetchMode("bids", FetchMode.JOIN)
        .setFetchMode("seller", FetchMode.JOIN)
        .add( Restrictions.like("description", "%Foo%") );
```

Be careful, though. The same caveats as in HQL and JPA QL apply here: Eager fetching more than one collection in parallel (such as bids *and* images) results in an SQL Cartesian product that is probably slower than two separate queries. Limiting the resultset for pagination, if you use eager fetching for collections, is also done in-memory.

However, dynamic fetching with `Criteria` and `FetchMode` is slightly different than in HQL and JPA QL: A `Criteria` query doesn't ignore the global fetching strategies as defined in the mapping metadata. For example, if the bids collection is mapped with `fetch="join"` or `FetchType.EAGER`, the following query results in an outer join of the ITEM and BID table:

```
session.createCriteria(Item.class)
        .add( Restrictions.like("description", "%Foo%") );
```

The returned `Item` instances have their bids collections initialized and fully loaded. This doesn't happen with HQL or JPA QL unless you manually query with LEFT JOIN FETCH (or, of course, map the collection as `lazy="false"`, which results in a second SQL query).

As a consequence, criteria queries may return duplicate references to distinct instances of the root entity, even if you don't apply `FetchMode.JOIN` for a collection in your query. The last query example may return hundreds of `Item` references, even if you have only a dozen in the database. Remember our discussion in "Dynamic fetching strategies with joins," in chapter 14, section 14.3.1 and look again at the SQL statement and resultset in figure 14.3.

You can remove the duplicate references in the result `List` by wrapping it in a `LinkedHashSet` (a regular `HashSet` wouldn't keep the order or the query result). In HQL and JPA QL, you can also use the `DISTINCT` keyword; however, there is no direct equivalent of this in `Criteria`. This is where the `ResultTransformer` becomes useful.

Applying a result transformer

A result transformer can be applied to a query result so that you can filter or marshal the result with your own procedure instead of the Hibernate default behavior. Hibernate's default behavior is a set of default transformers that you can replace and/or customize.

All criteria queries return only instances of the root entity, by default:

```
List result = session.createCriteria(Item.class)
                     .setFetchMode("bids", FetchMode.JOIN)
                     .setResultTransformer(Criteria.ROOT_ENTITY)
                     .list();

Set distinctResult = new LinkedHashSet(result);
```

The `Criteria.ROOT_ENTITY` is the default implementation of the `org.hibernate.transform.ResultTransformer` interface. The previous query produces the same result, with or without this transformer set. It returns all `Item` instances and initializes their `bids` collections. The `List` probably (depending on the number of `Bids` for each `Item`) contains duplicate `Item` references.

Alternatively, you can apply a different transformer:

```
List distinctResult =
    session.createCriteria(Item.class)
           .setFetchMode("bids", FetchMode.JOIN)
           .setResultTransformer(Criteria.DISTINCT_ROOT_ENTITY)
           .list();
```

Hibernate now filters out duplicate root entity references before returning the result—this is effectively the same filtering that occurs in HQL or JPA QL if you use the `DISTINCT` keyword.

Result transformers are also useful if you want to retrieve aliased entities in a join query:

```
Criteria crit =
        session.createCriteria(Item.class)
                .createAlias("bids", "b")
                .createAlias("seller", "s")
                .setResultTransformer(Criteria.ALIAS_TO_ENTITY_MAP);

List result = crit.list();
for (Object aResult : result) {
    Map map = (Map) aResult;
    Item item   = (Item) map.get(Criteria.ROOT_ALIAS);
    Bid  bid    = (Bid)  map.get("b");
    User seller = (User) map.get("s");
    ...
}
```

First, a criteria query is created that joins `Item` with its `bids` and `seller` associations. This is an SQL inner join across three tables. The result of this query, in SQL, is a table where each result row contains item, bid, and user data—almost the same as shown in figure 14.2. With the default transformer, Hibernate returns only `Item` instances. And, with the `DISTINCT_ROOT_ENTITY` transformer, it filters out the duplicate `Item` references. Neither option seems sensible—what you really want is to return all information in a map. The `ALIAS_TO_ENTITY_MAP` transformer can marshal the SQL result into a collection of `Map` instances. Each `Map` has three entries: an `Item`, a `Bid`, and a `User`. All result data is preserved and can be accessed in the application. (The `Criteria.ROOT_ALIAS` is a shortcut for `"this"`.)

Good use cases for this last transformer are rare. Note that you can also implement your own `org.hibernate.transform.ResultTransformer`. Furthermore, HQL and native SQL queries also support a `ResultTransformer`:

```
Query q = session.createQuery(
    "select i.id as itemId," +
    "       i.description as desc," +
    "       i.initialPrice as price from Item i");
q.setResultTransformer( Transformers.aliasToBean(ItemDTO.class) );
```

This query now returns a collection of `ItemDTO` instances, and the attributes of this bean are populated through the setter methods `setItemId()`, `setDesc()`, and `setPrice()`.

A much more common way to define what data is to be returned from a query is projection. The Hibernate criteria supports the equivalent of a `SELECT` clause for simple projection, aggregation, and grouping.

15.1.3 Projection and report queries

In HQL, JPA QL, and SQL, you write a SELECT clause to define the projection for a particular query. The Criteria API also supports projection, of course programmatically and not string-based. You can select exactly which objects or properties of objects you need in the query result and how you possibly want to aggregate and group results for a report.

Simple projection lists

The following criteria query returns only the identifier values of Item instances which are still on auction:

```
session.createCriteria(Item.class)
        .add( Restrictions.gt("endDate", new Date()) )
        .setProjection( Projections.id() );
```

The setProjection() method on a Criteria accepts either a single projected attribute, as in the previous example, or a list of several properties that are to be included in the result:

```
session.createCriteria(Item.class)
        .setProjection( Projections.projectionList()
            .add( Projections.id() )
            .add( Projections.property("description") )
            .add( Projections.property("initialPrice") )
        );
```

This query returns a List of Object[], just like HQL or JPA QL would with an equivalent SELECT clause. An alternative way to specify a property for projection is the Property class:

```
session.createCriteria(Item.class)
        .setProjection( Projections.projectionList()
            .add( Property.forName("id") )
            .add( Property.forName("description") )
            .add( Property.forName("initialPrice") )
        );
```

In HQL and JPA QL, you can use dynamic instantiation with the SELECT NEW operation and return a collection of custom objects instead of Object[]. Hibernate bundles a ResultTransformer for criteria queries that can do almost the same (in fact, it's more flexible). The following query returns the same result as the previous one, but wrapped in data transfer objects:

```
session.createCriteria(Item.class)
        .setProjection( Projections.projectionList()
            .add( Projections.id()
```

```
                            .as("itemId") )
        .add( Projections.property("description")
                            .as("itemDescription") )
        .add( Projections.property("initialPrice")
                            .as("itemInitialPrice") )
    ).setResultTransformer(
        new AliasToBeanResultTransformer(ItemPriceSummary.class)
    );
```

The `ItemPriceSummary` is a simple Java bean with setter methods or public fields named `itemId`, `itemDescription`, and `itemInitialPrice`. It doesn't have to be a mapped persistent class; only the property/field names must match with the aliases assigned to the projected properties in the criteria query. Aliases are assigned with the `as()` method (which you can think of as the equivalent of the `AS` keyword in an SQL `SELECT`). The result transformer calls the setter methods or populates the fields directly and returns a collection of `ItemPriceSummary` objects.

Let's do more complex projection with criteria, involving aggregation and grouping.

Aggregation and grouping

The usual aggregation functions and grouping options are also available in criteria queries. A straightforward method counts the number of rows in the result:

```
session.createCriteria(Item.class)
        .setProjection( Projections.rowCount() );
```

TIP *Getting the total count for pagination*—In real applications, you often must allow users to page through lists and at the same time inform them how many total items are in the list. One way to get the total number is a `Criteria` query that executes a `rowCount()`. Instead of writing this additional query, you can execute the same `Criteria` that retrieves the data for the list with `scroll()`. Then call `last()` and `getRowNumber()` to jump and get the number of the last row. This plus one is the total number of objects you list. Don't forget to close the cursor. This technique is especially useful if you're working with an existing `DetachedCriteria` object and you don't want to duplicate and manipulate its projection to execute a `rowCount()`. It also works with HQL or SQL queries.

More complex aggregations use aggregation functions. The following query finds the number of bids and average bid amount each user made:

```
session.createCriteria(Bid.class)
        .createAlias("bidder", "u")
        .setProjection( Projections.projectionList()
```

```
            .add( Property.forName("u.id").group() )
            .add( Property.forName("u.username").group() )
            .add( Property.forName("id").count())
            .add( Property.forName("amount").avg() )
        );
```

This query returns a collection of Object[]s with four fields: the user's identifier, login name, number of bids, and the average bid amount. Remember that you can again use a result transformer for dynamic instantiation and have data transfer objects returned, instead of Object[]s. An alternative version that produces the same result is as follows:

```
session.createCriteria(Bid.class)
        .createAlias("bidder", "u")
        .setProjection( Projections.projectionList()
          .add( Projections.groupProperty("u.id") )
          .add( Projections.groupProperty("u.username") )
          .add( Projections.count("id") )
          .add( Projections.avg("amount") )
        );
```

The syntax you prefer is mostly a matter of taste. A more complex example applies aliases to the aggregated and grouped properties, for ordering of the result:

```
session.createCriteria(Bid.class)
        .createAlias("bidder", "u")
        .setProjection( Projections.projectionList()
          .add( Projections.groupProperty("u.id") )
          .add( Projections.groupProperty("u.username").as("uname") )
          .add( Projections.count("id") )
          .add( Projections.avg("amount") )
        )
        .addOrder( Order.asc("uname") );
```

At the time of writing, support for HAVING and restriction on aggregated results isn't available in Hibernate criteria queries. This will probably be added in the near future.

You can add native SQL expressions to restrictions in a criteria query; the same feature is available for projection.

Using SQL projections

An SQL projection is an arbitrary fragment that is added to the generated SQL SELECT clause. The following query produces the aggregation and grouping as in the previous examples but also adds an additional value to the result (the number of items):

```
String sqlFragment =
    "(select count(*) from ITEM i where i.ITEM_ID = ITEM_ID)" +
    " as numOfItems";

session.createCriteria(Bid.class)
        .createAlias("bidder", "u")
        .setProjection( Projections.projectionList()
            .add( Projections.groupProperty("u.id") )
            .add( Projections.groupProperty("u.username") )
            .add( Projections.count("id") )
            .add( Projections.avg("amount) )
            .add( Projections.sqlProjection(
                    sqlFragment,
                    new String[] { "numOfItems" },
                    new Type[] { Hibernate.LONG }
                )
            )
        );
```

The generated SQL is as follows:

```
select
        u.USER_ID,
        u.USERNAME,
        count(BID_ID),
        avg(BID_AMOUNT),
        (select
            count(*)
        from
            ITEM i
        where
            i.ITEM_ID = ITEM_ID) as numOfItems
    from
        BID
    inner join
        USERS u
            on BIDDER_ID = u.USER_ID
    group by
        u.USER_ID,
        u.USERNAME
```

The SQL fragment is embedded in the SELECT clause. It can contain any arbitrary expression and function call supported by the database management system. Any unqualified column name (such as ITEM_ID) refers to the table of the criteria root entity (BID). You must tell Hibernate the returned alias of the SQL projection, numOfItems, and its Hibernate value mapping type, Hibernate.LONG.

The real power of the Criteria API is the possibility to combine arbitrary Criterions with *example objects*. This feature is known as query by example.

15.1.4 *Query by example*

It's common for criteria queries to be built programmatically by combining several optional criterions depending on user input. For example, a system administrator may wish to search for users by any combination of first name or last name and retrieve the result ordered by username.

Using HQL or JPA QL, you can build the query using string manipulations:

```
public List findUsers(String firstname,
                      String lastname) {

    StringBuffer queryString = new StringBuffer();
    boolean conditionFound = false;

    if (firstname != null) {
        queryString.append("lower(u.firstname) like :firstname ");
        conditionFound=true;
    }
    if (lastname != null) {
        if (conditionFound) queryString.append("and ");
        queryString.append("lower(u.lastname) like :lastname ");
        conditionFound=true;
    }

    String fromClause = conditionFound ?
                            "from User u where " :
                            "from User u ";

    queryString.insert(0, fromClause).append("order by u.username");

    Query query = getSession()
                        .createQuery( queryString.toString() );

    if (firstname != null)
        query.setString( "firstName",
                            '%' + firstname.toLowerCase() + '%' );
    if (lastname != null)
        query.setString( "lastName",
                            '%' + lastname.toLowerCase() + '%' );

    return query.list();
}
```

This code is pretty tedious and noisy, so let's try a different approach. The `Criteria` API with what you've learned so far looks promising:

```
public List findUsers(String firstname,
                      String lastname) {

    Criteria crit = getSession().createCriteria(User.class);

    if (firstname != null) {
        crit.add( Restrictions.ilike("firstname",
```

```
                                firstname,
                                MatchMode.ANYWHERE) );
    }
    if (lastname != null) {
        crit.add( Restrictions.ilike("lastname",
                                lastname,
                                MatchMode.ANYWHERE) );
    }

    crit.addOrder( Order.asc("username") );

    return crit.list();
}
```

This code is much shorter. Note that the ilike() operator performs a case-insensitive match. There seems to be no doubt that this is a better approach. However, for search screens with many optional search criteria, there is an even better way.

As you add new search criteria, the parameter list of findUsers() grows. It would be better to capture the searchable properties as an object. Because all the search properties belong to the User class, why not use an instance of User for that purpose?

Query by example (QBE) relies on this idea. You provide an instance of the queried class with some properties initialized, and the query returns all persistent instances with matching property values. Hibernate implements QBE as part of the Criteria query API:

```
public List findUsersByExample(User u) throws {

    Example exampleUser =
        Example.create(u)
                .ignoreCase()
                .enableLike(MatchMode.ANYWHERE)
                .excludeProperty("password");

    return getSession().createCriteria(User.class)
                    .add(exampleUser)
                    .list();

}
```

The call to create() returns a new instance of Example for the given instance of User. The ignoreCase() method puts the example query into a case-insensitive mode for all string-valued properties. The call to enableLike() specifies that the SQL like operator should be used for all string-valued properties, and specifies a MatchMode. Finally, you can exclude particular properties from the search with excludeProperty(). By default, all value-typed properties, excluding the identifier property, are used in the comparison.

You've significantly simplified the code *again*. The nicest thing about Hibernate `Example` queries is that an `Example` is just an ordinary `Criterion`. You can freely mix and match query by example with query by criteria.

Let's see how this works by further restricting the search results to users with unsold `Items`. For this purpose, you may add a `Criteria` to the example user, constraining the result using its `items` collection of `Items`:

```
public List findUsersByExample(User u){

    Example exampleUser =
      Example.create(u)
             .ignoreCase()
             .enableLike(MatchMode.ANYWHERE);

    return getSession().createCriteria(User.class)
            .add( exampleUser )
            .createCriteria("items")
                .add( Restrictions.isNull("successfulBid") )
            .list();
}
```

Even better, you can combine `User` properties and `Item` properties in the same search:

```
public List findUsersByExample(User u, Item i) {

    Example exampleUser =
      Example.create(u).ignoreCase().enableLike(MatchMode.ANYWHERE);

    Example exampleItem =
      Example.create(i).ignoreCase().enableLike(MatchMode.ANYWHERE);

    return getSession().createCriteria(User.class)
            .add( exampleUser )
            .createCriteria("items")
                .add( exampleItem )
            .list();
}
```

At this point, we invite you to take a step back and consider how much code would be required to implement *this* search screen using hand-coded SQL/JDBC. We won't reproduce it here; it would stretch for pages. Also note that the client of the `findUsersByExample()` method doesn't need to know anything about Hibernate, and it can still create complex criteria for searching.

If HQL, JPA QL, and even `Criteria` and `Example` aren't powerful enough to express a particular query, you must fall back to native SQL.

15.2 *Using native SQL queries*

HQL, JPA QL, or criteria queries should be flexible enough to execute almost any query you like. They refer to the mapped object schema; hence, if your mapping works as expected, Hibernate's queries should give you the power you need to retrieve data any way you like. There are a few exceptions. If you want to include a native SQL hint to instruct the database management systems query optimizer, for example, you need to write the SQL yourself. HQL, JPA QL, and criteria queries don't have keywords for this.

On the other hand, instead of falling back to a manual SQL query, you can always try to *extend* the built-in query mechanisms and include support for your special operation. This is more difficult to do with HQL and JPA QL, because you have to modify the grammar of these string-based languages. It's easy to extend the `Criteria` API and add new methods or new `Criterion` classes. Look at the Hibernate source code in the `org.hibernate.criterion` package; it's well designed and documented.

When you can't extend the built-in query facilities or prevent nonportable manually written SQL, you should first consider using Hibernate's native SQL query options, which we now present. Keep in mind that you can always fall back to a plain JDBC `Connection` and prepare any SQL statement yourself. Hibernate's SQL options allow you to *embed* SQL statements in a Hibernate API and to benefit from extra services that make your life easier.

Most important, Hibernate can handle the resultset of your SQL query.

15.2.1 *Automatic resultset handling*

The biggest advantage of executing an SQL statement with the Hibernate API is automatic marshaling of the tabular resultset into business objects. The following SQL query returns a collection of `Category` objects:

```
List result = session.createSQLQuery("select * from CATEGORY")
                     .addEntity(Category.class)
                     .list();
```

Hibernate reads the resultset of the SQL query and tries to discover the column names and types as defined in your mapping metadata. If the column `CATEGORY_NAME` is returned, and it's mapped to the `name` property of the `Category` class, Hibernate knows how to populate that property and finally returns fully loaded business objects.

The * in the SQL query projects all selected columns in the resultset. The automatic discovery mechanism therefore works only for trivial queries; more complex queries need an explicit projection. The next query returns a collection of Item objects:

```
session.createSQLQuery("select {i.*} from ITEM i" +
                       " join USERS u on i.SELLER_ID = u.USER_ID" +
                       " where u.USERNAME = :uname")
        .addEntity("i", Item.class)
        .setParameter("uname", "johndoe");
```

The SQL SELECT clause includes a placeholder which names the table alias i and projects all columns of this table into the result. Any other table alias, such as the joined USERS table, which is only relevant for the restriction, isn't included in the resultset. You now tell Hibernate with addEntity() that the placeholder for alias i refers to all columns that are needed to populate the Item entity class. The column names and types are again automatically guessed by Hibernate during query execution and result marshaling.

You can even eagerly fetch associated objects and collections in a native SQL query:

```
session.createSQLQuery("select {i.*}, {u.*} from ITEM i" +
                       " join USERS u on i.SELLER_ID = u.USER_ID" +
                       " where u.USERNAME = :uname")
        .addEntity("i", Item.class)
        .addJoin("u", "i.seller")
        .setParameter("uname", "johndoe");
```

This SQL query projects two sets of columns from two table aliases, and you use two placeholders. The i placeholder again refers to the columns that populate the Item entity objects returned by this query. The addJoin() method tells Hibernate that the u alias refers to columns that can be used to immediately populate the associated seller of each Item.

Automatic marshaling of resultsets into business objects isn't the only benefit of the native SQL query feature in Hibernate. You can even use it if all you want to retrieve is a simple scalar value.

15.2.2 Retrieving scalar values

A scalar value may be any Hibernate value type. Most common are strings, numbers, or timestamps. The following SQL query returns item data:

```
List result = session.createSQLQuery("select * from ITEM").list();
```

The `result` of this query is a `List` of `Object[]`s, effectively a table. Each field in each array is of scalar type—that is, a string, a number, or a timestamp. Except for the wrapping in an `Object[]`, the result is exactly the same as that of a similar plain JDBC query. This is obviously not too useful, but one benefit of the Hibernate API is that it throws unchecked exceptions so you don't have to wrap the query in `try`/`catch` block as you have to if you call the JDBC API.

If you aren't projecting everything with `*`, you need to tell Hibernate what scalar values you want to return from your result:

```
session.createSQLQuery("select u.FIRSTNAME as fname from USERS u")
        .addScalar("fname");
```

The `addScalar()` method tells Hibernate that your `fname` SQL alias should be returned as a scalar value and that the type should be automatically guessed. The query returns a collection of strings. This automatic type discovery works fine in most cases, but you may want to specify the type explicitly sometimes—for example, when you want to convert a value with a `UserType`:

```
Properties params = new Properties();
params.put("enumClassname", "auction.model.Rating");

session.createSQLQuery(
        "select c.RATING as rating from COMMENTS c" +
        " where c.FROM_USER_ID = :uid"
    )
    .addScalar("rating",
                Hibernate.custom(StringEnumUserType.class, params) )
    .setParameter("uid", new Long(123));
```

First, look at the SQL query. It selects the `RATING` column of the `COMMENTS` table and restricts the result to comments made by a particular user. Let's assume that this field in the database contains string values, such as `EXCELLENT`, `OK`, or `BAD`. Hence, the result of the SQL query is string values.

You'd naturally map this not as a simple string in Java but using an enumeration and probably a custom Hibernate `UserType`. We did this in chapter 5, section 5.3.7, "Mapping enumerations," and created a `StringEnumUserType` that can translate from strings in the SQL database to instances of any enumeration in Java. It must be parameterized with the `enumClassname` you want it to convert values to—`auction.model.Rating` in this example. By setting the prepared custom type with the `addScalar()` method on the query, you enable it as a converter that handles the result, and you get back a collection of `Rating` objects instead of simple strings.

Finally, you can mix scalar results and entity objects in the same native SQL query:

```
session.createSQLQuery(
        "select {i.*}, u.FIRSTNAME as fname from ITEM i" +
        " join USERS u on i.SELLER_ID = u.USER_ID" +
        " where u.USERNAME = :uname"
    )
    .addEntity("i", Item.class)
    .addScalar("fname")
    .setParameter("uname", "johndoe");
```

The result of this query is again a collection of `Object[]`s. Each array has two fields: an `Item` instance and a string.

You probably agree that native SQL queries are even harder to read than HQL or JPA QL statements and that it seems much more attractive to isolate and externalize them into mapping metadata. You did this in chapter 8, section 8.2.2, "Integrating stored procedures and functions," for stored procedure queries. We won't repeat this here, because the only difference between stored procedure queries and plain SQL queries is the syntax of the call or statement—the marshaling and resultset mapping options are the same.

Java Persistence standardizes JPA QL and also allows the fallback to native SQL.

15.2.3 Native SQL in Java Persistence

Java Persistence supports native SQL queries with the `createNativeQuery()` method on an `EntityManager`. A native SQL query may return entity instances, scalar values, or a mix of both. However, unlike Hibernate, the API in Java Persistence utilizes mapping metadata to define the resultset handling. Let's walk through some examples.

A simple SQL query doesn't need an explicit resultset mapping:

```
em.createNativeQuery("select * from CATEGORY", Category.class);
```

The resultset is automatically marshaled into a collection of `Category` instances. Note that the persistence engine expects all columns required to create an instance of `Category` to be returned by the query, including all property, component, and foreign key columns—otherwise an exception is thrown. Columns are searched in the resultset by name. You may have to use aliases in SQL to return the same column names as defined in your entity mapping metadata.

If your native SQL query returns multiple entity types or scalar types, you need to apply an explicit resultset mapping. For example, a query that returns a collection of `Object[]`s, where in each array index 0 is an `Item` instance and index 1 is a `User` instance, can be written as follows:

```
em.createNativeQuery("select " +
    "i.ITEM_ID, i.ITEM_PRICE, u.USERNAME, u.EMAIL " +
    "from ITEM i join USERS u where i.SELLER_ID = u.USER_ID",
    "ItemSellerResult");
```

The last argument, `ItemSellerResult`, is the name of a result mapping you define in metadata (at the class or global JPA XML level):

```
@SqlResultSetMappings({
    @SqlResultSetMapping(
        name = "ItemSellerResult",
        entities = {
            @EntityResult(entityClass = auction.model.Item.class),
            @EntityResult(entityClass = auction.model.User.class)
        }
    )
})
```

This resultset mapping likely doesn't work for the query we've shown—remember that for automatic mapping, all columns that are required to instantiate `Item` and `User` objects must be returned in the SQL query. It's unlikely that the four columns you return represent the only persistent properties. For the sake of the example, let's assume that they are and that your actual problem is the names of the columns in the resultset, which don't match the names of the mapped columns. First, add aliases to the SQL statement:

```
em.createNativeQuery("select " +
    "i.ITEM_ID as ITEM_ID, i.ITEM_PRICE as ITEM_PRICE, " +
    "u.USERNAME as USER_NAME, u.EMAIL as USER_EMAIL " +
    "from ITEM i join USERS u on i.SELLER_ID = u.USER_ID",
    "ItemSellerResult");
```

Next, use `@FieldResult` in the resultset mapping to map aliases to fields of the entity instances:

```
@SqlResultSetMapping(
name = "ItemSellerResult",
entities = {
    @EntityResult(
        entityClass = auction.model.Item.class,
        fields = {
            @FieldResult(name = "id", column = "ITEM_ID"),
            @FieldResult(name = "initialPrice", column = "ITEM_PRICE")
        }),
    @EntityResult(
```

```
        entityClass = auction.model.User.class,
        fields = {
          @FieldResult(name = "username", column = "USER_NAME"),
          @FieldResult(name = "email", column = "USER_EMAIL")
        })
    })
```

You can also return scalar typed results. The following query returns auction item identifiers and the number of bids for each item:

```
em.createNativeQuery("select " +
    "i.ITEM_ID as ITEM_ID, count(b.*) as NUM_OF_BIDS " +
    "from ITEM i join BIDS b on i.ITEM_ID = b.ITEM_ID " +
    "group by ITEM_ID",
    "ItemBidResult");
```

The resultset mapping doesn't contain entity result mappings this time, only columns:

```
@SqlResultSetMapping(
name = "ItemBidResult",
columns = {
    @ColumnResult(name = "ITEM_ID"),
    @ColumnResult(name = "NUM_OF_BIDS")
})
```

The result of this query is a collection of `Object[]`s, with two fields, both of some numeric type (most likely `long`). If you want to mix entities and scalar types as a query result, combine the `entities` and `columns` attributes in a `@Sql-ResultSetMapping`.

Finally, note that the JPA specification doesn't require that named parameter binding is supported for native SQL queries. Hibernate supports this.

Next, we discuss another more exotic but convenient Hibernate feature (Java Persistence doesn't have an equivalent): *collection filters.*

15.3 *Filtering collections*

You may wish to execute a query against all elements of a collection. For instance, you may have an `Item` and wish to retrieve all bids for that particular item, ordered by the time that the bid was created. You can map a sorted or ordered collection for that purpose, but there is an easier choice. You can write a query, and you should already know how:

```
session.createQuery("from Bid b where b.item = :givenItem" +
                " order by b.created asc")
    .setEntity("givenItem", item);
```

This query works because the association between bids and items is bidirectional and each `Bid` knows its `Item`. There is no join in this query; `b.item` refers to the `ITEM_ID` column in the `BID` table, and you set the value for the comparison directly. Imagine that this association is unidirectional—`Item` has a collection of `Bids`, but no inverse association exists from `Bid` to `Item`. You can try the following query:

```
select b from Item i join i.bids b
    where i = :givenItem order by b.amount asc
```

This query is inefficient—it uses an entirely unnecessary join. A better, more elegant solution is to use a *collection filter*—a special query that can be applied to a persistent collection (or array). It's commonly used to further restrict or order a result. You apply it on an already loaded `Item` and its collection of bids:

```
List filteredCollection =
        session.createFilter( item.getBids(),
                            "order by this.created asc" ).list();
```

This filter is equivalent to the first query of this section and results in identical SQL. The `createFilter()` method on the `Session` takes two arguments: a persistent collection (it doesn't have to be initialized) and an HQL query string. Collection filter queries have an implicit FROM clause and an implicit WHERE condition. The alias `this` refers implicitly to elements of the collection of bids.

Hibernate collection filters aren't executed in memory. The collection of bids may be uninitialized when the filter is called and, if so, remains uninitialized. Furthermore, filters don't apply to transient collections or query results. They may be applied only to a persistent collection currently referenced by an entity instance attached to the Hibernate persistence context. The term filter is somewhat misleading, because the result of filtering is a completely new and different collection; the original collection isn't touched.

The only required clause of a HQL query is the FROM clause. Because a collection filter has an implicit FROM clause, the following is a valid filter:

```
List filteredCollection =
        session.createFilter( item.getBids(), "" ).list();
```

To the great surprise of everyone, including the designer of this feature, this *trivial filter* turns out to be useful. You may use it to paginate collection elements:

```
List filteredCollection =
        session.createFilter( item.getBids(), "" )
                .setFirstResult(50)
                .setMaxResults(100)
                .list();
```

Usually, you use an ORDER BY with paginated queries, however.

Even though you don't need a FROM clause in a collection filter, you may have one if you like. A collection filter doesn't even need to return elements of the collection being filtered. The next query returns any Category with the same name as a category in the given collection:

```
String filterString =
    "select other from Category other where this.name = other.name";

List result =
    session.createFilter( cat.getChildCategories(), filterString )
            .list();
```

The following query returns a collection of Users who have bid on the item:

```
List result =
    session.createFilter( item.getBids(),
                            "select this.bidder" )
            .list();
```

The next query returns all these users' bids (including those for other items):

```
List result =
    session.createFilter(
        item.getBids(),
        "select elements(this.bidder.bids)"
    ).list();
```

Note that the query uses the special HQL elements() function to project all elements of a collection.

All this is a lot of fun, but the most important reason for the existence of collection filters is to allow the application to retrieve some elements of a collection without initializing the whole collection. In the case of large collections, this is important to achieve acceptable performance. The following query retrieves all bids made by a user in the past week:

```
List result =
    session.createFilter( user.getBids(),
                            "where this.created > :oneWeekAgo" )
            .setTimestamp("oneWeekAgo", oneWeekAgo)
            .list();
```

Again, this doesn't initialize the bids collection of the User.

Queries, no matter in what language and what API they're written, should always be tuned to perform as expected before you decide to speed them up with the optional *query cache*.

15.4 *Caching query results*

We talked about the second-level cache and Hibernate's general cache architecture in chapter 13, section 13.3, "Caching fundamentals." You know that the second-level cache is a shared cache of data, and that Hibernate tries to resolve data through a lookup in this cache whenever you access an unloaded proxy or collection or when you load an object by identifier (these are all identifier lookups, from the point of view of the second-level cache). Query results, on the other hand, are by default not cached.

Some queries still use the second-level cache, depending on how you execute a query. For example, if you decide to execute a query with iterate(), as we showed in the previous chapter, only the primary keys of entities are retrieved from the database, and entity data is looked up through the first-level and, if enabled for a particular entity, second-level cache. We also concluded that this option makes sense only if the second-level cache is enabled, because an optimization of column reads usually doesn't influence performance.

Caching query results is a completely different issue. The query result cache is by default disabled, and every HQL, JPA QL, SQL, and Criteria query always hits the database first. We first show you how to enable the query result cache and how it works. We then discuss why it's disabled and why few queries benefit from result caching.

15.4.1 *Enabling the query result cache*

The query cache must be enabled using a Hibernate configuration property:

```
hibernate.cache.use_query_cache = true
```

However, this setting alone isn't enough for Hibernate to cache query results. By default, all queries always ignore the cache. To enable query caching for a particular query (to allow its results to be added to the cache, and to allow it to draw its results *from* the cache), you use the org.hibernate.Query interface.

```
Query categoryByName =
    session.createQuery("from Category c where c.name = :name");
categoryByName.setString("name", categoryName);
categoryByName.setCacheable(true);
```

The setCachable() method enables the result cache. It's also available on the Criteria API. If you want to enable result caching for a javax.persistence.Query, use setHint("org.hibernate.cacheable", true).

15.4.2 *Understanding the query cache*

When a query is executed for the first time, its results are cached in a cache region—this region is different from any other entity or collection cache region you may already have configured. The name of the region is by default `org.hibernate.cache.QueryCache`.

You can change the cache region for a particular query with the `setCache-Region()` method:

```
Query categoryByName =
    session.createQuery("from Category c where c.name = :name");
categoryByName.setString("name", categoryName);
categoryByName.setCacheable(true);
categoryByName.setCacheRegion("my.Region");
```

This is rarely necessary; you use a different cache region for some queries only if you need a different region configuration—for example, to limit memory consumption of the query cache on a more fine-grained level.

The standard query result cache region holds the SQL statements (including all bound parameters) and the resultset of each SQL statement. This isn't the complete SQL resultset, however. If the resultset contains entity instances (the previous example queries return `Category` instances), only the identifier values are held in the resultset cache. The data columns of each entity are discarded from the resultset when it's put into the cache region. So, hitting the query result cache means that Hibernate will, for the previous queries, find some `Category` identifier values.

It's the responsibility of the second-level cache region `auction.model.Category` (in conjunction with the persistence context) to cache the state of entities. This is similar to the lookup strategy of `iterate()`, as explained earlier. In other words, if you query for entities and decide to enable caching, make sure you also enabled regular second-level caching for these entities. If you don't, you may end up with *more* database hits after enabling the query cache.

If you cache the result of a query that doesn't return entity instances, but returns only the same scalar values (e.g., item names and prices), these values are held in the query result cache directly.

If the query result cache is enabled in Hibernate, another always required cache region is also present: `org.hibernate.cache.UpdateTimestampsCache`. This is a cache region used by Hibernate internally.

Hibernate uses the timestamp region to decide whether a cached query resultset is stale. When you re-execute a query that has caching enabled, Hibernate looks in the timestamp cache for the timestamp of the most recent insert, update, or delete made to the queried table(s). If the found timestamp is later than the timestamp of the cached query results, the cached results are discarded and a new query is issued. This effectively guarantees that Hibernate won't use the cached query result if any table that may be involved in the query contains updated data; hence, the cached result may be stale. For best results, you should configure the timestamp region so that the update timestamp for a table doesn't expire from the cache while query results from these tables are still cached in one of the other regions. The easiest way is to turn off expiry for the timestamp cache region in your second-level cache provider's configuration.

15.4.3 *When to use the query cache*

The majority of queries don't benefit from result caching. This may come as a surprise. After all, it sounds like avoiding a database hit is always a good thing. There are two good reasons why this doesn't always work for arbitrary queries, compared to object navigation or retrieval by identifier.

First, you must ask how often you're going to execute the same query repeatedly. Granted, you may have a few queries in your application that are executed over and over again, with exactly the same arguments bound to parameters, and the same automatically generated SQL statement. We consider this a rare case, but when you're certain a query is executed repeatedly, it becomes a good candidate for result caching.

Second, for applications that perform many queries and few inserts, deletes, or updates, caching queries can improve performance and scalability. On the other hand if the application performs many writes, the query cache won't be utilized efficiently. Hibernate expires a cached query resultset when there is *any* insert, update, or delete of *any* row of a table that appeared in the cached query result. This means cached results may have a short lifetime, and even if a query is executed repeatedly, no cached result can be used due to concurrent modifications of the same data (same tables).

For many queries, the benefit of the query result cache is nonexistent or, at least, doesn't have the impact you'd expect. But one special kind of query can greatly benefit from result caching.

15.4.4 *Natural identifier cache lookups*

Let's assume that you have an entity that has a natural key. We aren't talking about a natural primary key, but about a *business key* that applies to a single or compound attributes of your entity. For example, the login name of a user can be a unique business key, if it's immutable. This is the key we already isolated as perfect for the implementation of a good `equals()` object equality routine. You can find examples of such keys in "Implementing equality with a business key," in chapter 9, section 9.2.3.

Usually, you map the attributes that form your natural key as regular properties in Hibernate. You may enable a `unique` constraint at the database level to represent this key. For example, if you consider the `User` class, you may decide that `username` and `emailAddress` form the entity's business key:

```
<class name="User">
    <id name="id".../>

    <property name="username" unique-key="UNQ_USERKEY"/>
    <property name="emailAddress" unique-key="UNQ_USERKEY"/>
    ...

</class>
```

This mapping enables a unique key constraint at the database level that spans two columns. Let's also assume that the business key properties are immutable. This is unlikely, because you probably allow users to update their email addresses, but the functionality we're presenting now makes sense only if you're dealing with an immutable business key. You map immutability as follows:

```
<class name="User">
    <id name="id".../>

    <property name="username"
                unique-key="UNQ_USERKEY"
                update="false"/>

    <property name="emailAddress"
                unique-key="UNQ_USERKEY"
                update="false"/>
    ...

</class>
```

Or, to utilize cache lookups by business key, you can map it with `<natural-id>`:

```
<class name="User">
    <id name="id".../>

    <cache usage="read-write"/>

    <natural-id mutable="false">
        <property name="username"/>
        <property name="emailAddress"/>
    </natural-id>
    ...

</class>
```

This grouping automatically enables the generation of a unique key SQL constraint that spans all grouped properties. If the `mutable` attribute is set to `false`, it also prevents updating of the mapped columns. You can now use this business key for cache lookups:

```
Criteria crit = session.createCriteria(User.class);

crit.add( Restrictions.naturalId()
            .set("username", "johndoe")
            .set("emailAddress", "jd@hibernate.org")
        );
crit.setCacheable(true);

User result = (User) crit.uniqueResult();
```

This criteria query finds a particular user object based on the business key. It results in a second-level cache lookup by business key—remember that this is usually a lookup by primary key and is possible only for retrieval by primary identifier. The business key mapping and `Criteria` API allow you to express this special second-level cache lookup by business key.

At the time of writing, no Hibernate extension annotation for a natural identifier mapping is available, and HQL doesn't support an equivalent keyword for lookup by business key.

From our point of view, caching at the second-level is an important feature, but it's not the first option when optimizing performance. Errors in the design of queries or an unnecessarily complex part of your object model can't be improved with a "cache it all" approach. If an application performs at an acceptable level only with a hot cache—that is, a full cache after several hours or days runtime—it should be checked for serious design mistakes, unperformant queries, and n+1 select problems. Before you decide to enable any of the query cache options explained here, first review and tune your application following the guidelines presented in "Optimization step by step," in chapter 13, section 13.2.5.

15.5 Summary

In this chapter, you've generated queries programmatically with the Hibernate `Criteria` and `Example` APIs. We also looked at embedded and externalized SQL queries and how you can map the resultset of an SQL query to more convenient business objects automatically. Java Persistence also supports native SQL and standardizes how you can map the resultset of externalized SQL queries.

Finally, we covered the query result cache and discussed why it's useful only in certain situations.

Table 15.1 shows a summary you can use to compare native Hibernate features and Java Persistence.

Table 15.1 Hibernate and JPA comparison chart for chapter 15

Hibernate Core	Java Persistence and EJB 3.0
Hibernate supports a powerful `Criteria` and `Example` API for programmatic query generation.	Some QBC and QBE API is expected in an upcoming version of the standard.
Hibernate has flexible mapping options for embedded and externalized SQL queries, with automatic marshaling of resultsets.	Java Persistence standardizes SQL embedding and mapping and supports resultset marshaling.
Hibernate supports a collection filter API.	Java Persistence doesn't standardize a collection filter API.
Hibernate can cache query results.	A Hibernate-specific query hint can be used to cache query results.

In the next chapter, we'll bring all the pieces together and focus on the design and architecture of applications with Hibernate, Java Persistence, and EJB 3.0 components. We'll also unit test a Hibernate application.

Creating and testing
layered applications

Hibernate is intended to be used in just about any architectural scenario imaginable. Hibernate may run inside a servlet container; you can use it with web application framework like Struts, WebWork, or Tapestry, or inside an EJB container, or to manage persistent data in a Java Swing application.

Even—perhaps *especially*—with all these options, it's often difficult to see exactly how Hibernate should be integrated into a particular Java-based architecture. Inevitably, you'll need to write infrastructural code to support your own application design. In this chapter, we describe common Java architectures and show how Hibernate can be integrated into each scenario.

We discuss how you design and create layers in a typical request/response based web application, and how you separate code by functionality. After this, we introduce Java EE services and EJBs and show how managed components can make your life easier and reduce the infrastructure coding that would otherwise be necessary.

Finally, we assume that you're also interested in testing your layered application, with or without managed components. Today, testing is one of the most important activities in a developer's work, and applying the right tools and strategies is essential for quick turnaround times and productivity (not to mention the quality of the software). We'll look at unit, functional, and integration testing with our current favorite testing framework, *TestNG*.

Let's start with a typical web application example.

16.1 Hibernate in a web application

We emphasized the importance of disciplined application layering in chapter 1. Layering helps achieve separation of concerns, making code more readable by grouping code that does similar things. Layering, however, carries a price. Each extra layer increases the amount of code it takes to implement a simple piece of functionality—and more code makes the functionality more difficult to change.

In this section, we show you how to integrate Hibernate in a typical layered application. We assume that you want to write a simple web application with Java servlets. We need a simple use case of the CaveatEmptor application to demonstrate these ideas.

16.1.1 Introducing the use case

When a user places a bid on an item, CaveatEmptor must perform the following tasks, all in a single request:

1 Check that the amount entered by the user is greater than the maximum amount of existing bids for the item.

2 Check that the auction hasn't yet ended.

3 Create a bid for the item.

4 Inform the user of the outcome of the tasks.

If either checks fail, the user should be informed of the reason; if both checks are successful, the user should be informed that the bid has been placed. These checks are the business rules. If a failure occurs while accessing the database, users should be informed that the system is currently unavailable (an infrastructure concern).

Let's see how you can implement this in a web application.

16.1.2 *Writing a controller*

Most Java web applications use some kind of *Model/View/Controller* (MVC) application framework; even many that use plain servlets follow the MVC pattern by using templating to implement the presentation code, separating application control logic into a servlet or multiple servlets.

You'll now write such a controller servlet that implements the previously introduced use case. With an MVC approach, you write the code that implements the "place bid" use case in an execute() method of an action named PlaceBidAction. Assuming some kind of web framework, we don't show how to read request parameters or how to forward to the next page. The code shown may even be the implementation of a doPost() method of a plain servlet.

The first attempt at writing such a controller, shown in listing 16.1, mixes all concerns in one place—there are no layers.

Listing 16.1 Implementing a use case in one execute() method

```
public void execute() {

    Long itemId = ...          // Get value from request
    Long userId = ...          // Get value from request
    BigDecimal bidAmount = ...  // Get value from request
    Transaction tx = null;

    try {
                        ❶
        Session session =   ↵
            HibernateUtil.getSessionFactory().getCurrentSession();

        tx = session.beginTransaction();

        // Load requested Item
```

```
                Item item = (Item) session.load(Item.class, itemId);    ◁┐
                                                                          2
                // Check auction still valid
                if ( item.getEndDate().before( new Date() ) ) {    ◁┐
                    ...       // Forward to error page                    3
                }

                // Check amount of Bid      4
                Query q =                      ◁┘
                    session.createQuery("select max(b.amount)" +
                                        " from Bid b where b.item = :item");
                q.setEntity("item", item);
                BigDecimal maxBidAmount = (BigDecimal) q.uniqueResult();
                if (maxBidAmount.compareTo(bidAmount) > 0) {
                    ...       // Forward to error page
                }

                // Add new Bid to Item                                    5
                User bidder = (User) session.load(User.class, userId);   ◁┘
                Bid newBid = new Bid(bidAmount, item, bidder);
                item.addBid(newBid);
                                                                          6
                ...       // Place new Bid into request context    ◁┘

                tx.commit();                                       ◁┐
                                                                   7
                ...       // Forward to success page
        } catch (RuntimeException ex) {    ◁┐
            if (tx != null) tx.rollback();   8
            throw ex;
        }
    }
```

① You get a `Session` using the current persistence context and then start a database transaction. We introduced the `HibernateUtil` class in "Building a SessionFactory" in chapter 2, section 2.1.3, and we discussed persistence context scoping in chapter 11, section 11.1, "Propagating the Hibernate Session." A new database transaction is started on the current Session.

② You load the `Item` from the database, using its identifier value.

③ If the ending date of the auction is before the current date, you forward to an error page. Usually you want a more sophisticated error handling for this exception, with a qualified error message.

④ Using an HQL query, you check whether there is a higher bid for the current item in the database. If there is one, you forward to an error message.

⑤ If all checks are successful, you place the new bid by adding it to the item. You don't have to save it manually—it's saved using transitive persistence (cascading from the Item to Bid).

⑥ The new Bid instance needs to be stored in some variable that is accessible by the following page, so you can display it to the user. You can use an attribute in the servlet request context for this.

⑦ Committing the database transaction flushes the current state of the Session to the database and closes the current Session automatically.

⑧ If any RuntimeException is thrown, either by Hibernate or by other services, you roll back the transaction and rethrow the exception to be handled appropriately outside the controller.

The first thing wrong with this code is the clutter caused by all the transaction and exception-handling code. Because this code is typically identical for all actions, you would like to centralize it somewhere. One option is to place it in the execute() method of some abstract superclass of your actions. You also have a problem with *lazy initialization*, if you access the new bid on the success page, pulling it out of the request context for rendering: The Hibernate persistence context is closed and you can no longer load lazy collections or proxies.

Let's start cleaning up this design and introduce layers. The first step is to enable lazy loading on the success page by implementing the *Open Session in View* pattern.

16.1.3 *The Open Session in View pattern*

The motivation behind the *Open Session in View* (OSIV) pattern is that the view pulls information from business objects by navigating the object network beginning at some detached object—for example, the newly created Bid instance that was placed in the request context by your action. The view—that is, the page that must be rendered and displayed—accesses this detached object to get the content data for the page.

In a Hibernate application, there may be uninitialized associations (proxies or collections) that must be traversed while rendering the view. In this example, the view may list all items sold by the bidder (as part of an overview screen) by calling newBid.getBidder().getItems().iterator(). This is a rare case but certainly a valid access. Because the items collection of the User is loaded only on demand (Hibernate's lazy association and collection default behavior), it isn't initialized at this point. You can not load uninitialized proxies and collections of an entity instance that is in detached state.

If the Hibernate `Session` and therefore the persistence context is always closed at the end of the action's `execute()` method, Hibernate throws a `LazyInitializationException` when this unloaded association (or collection) is accessed. The persistence context is no longer available, so Hibernate can't load the lazy collection on access.

> **FAQ**   *Why can't Hibernate open a new Session if it has to lazy load objects?* The Hibernate `Session` is the persistence context, the scope of object identity. Hibernate guarantees that there is at most one in-memory representation of a particular database row, in one persistence context. Opening a `Session` on-demand, behind the scenes, would also create a new persistence context, and all objects loaded in this identity scope would potentially conflict with objects loaded in the original persistence context. You can't load data on-demand when an object is out of the guaranteed scope of object identity—when it's detached. On the other hand, you can load data as long as the objects are in persistent state, managed by a `Session`, even when the original transaction has been committed. In such a scenario, you have to enable the autocommit mode, as discussed in chapter 10, section 10.3, "Nontransactional data access." We recommend that you don't use the autocommit mode in a web application; it's much easier to extend the original `Session` *and* transaction to span the whole request. In systems where you can't easily begin and end a transaction when objects have to be loaded on-demand inside a `Session`, such as Swing desktop applications that use Hibernate, the autocommit mode is useful.

A first solution would be to ensure that all needed associations and collections are fully initialized before forwarding to the view (we discuss this later), but a more convenient approach in a two-tiered architecture with a colocated presentation and persistence layer is to leave the persistence context open until the view is completely rendered.

The OSIV pattern allows you to have a single Hibernate persistence context per request, spanning the rendering of the view and potentially multiple action `execute()`s. It can also be implemented easily—for example, with a servlet filter:

```
public class HibernateSessionRequestFilter implements Filter {

    private SessionFactory sf;
    private static Log log = ...;

    public void doFilter(ServletRequest request,
```

```
                  ServletResponse response,
                  FilterChain chain)
        throws IOException, ServletException {

    try {
        // Starting a database transaction
        sf.getCurrentSession().beginTransaction();

        // Call the next filter (continue request processing)
        chain.doFilter(request, response);

        // Commit the database transaction
        sf.getCurrentSession().getTransaction().commit();

    } catch (Throwable ex) {
        // Rollback only
        try {
            if (sf.getCurrentSession().getTransaction().isActive())
                sf.getCurrentSession().getTransaction().rollback();
        } catch (Throwable rbEx) {
            log.error("Could not rollback after exception!", rbEx);
            rbEx.printStackTrace();
        }

        // Let others handle it...
        throw new ServletException(ex);
    }

}

public void init(FilterConfig filterConfig)
            throws ServletException {
    sf = HibernateUtil.getSessionFactory();
}

public void destroy() {}

}
```

This filter acts as an interceptor for servlet requests. It runs every time a request hits the server and must be processed. It needs the `SessionFactory` on startup, and it gets it from the `HibernateUtil` helper class. When the request arrives, you start a database transaction and open a new persistence context. After the controller has executed and the view has been rendered, you commit the database transaction. Thanks to Hibernate's auomatic `Session` binding and propagation, this is also automatically the scope of the persistence context.

Exception handling has also been centralized and encapsulated in this interceptor. It's up to you what exception you'd like to catch for a rollback of the database transaction; `Throwable` is the catch-all variation, which means that even thrown `Errors`, not only `Exceptions` and `RuntimeExceptions`, trigger a rollback. Note that the actual rollback can also throw an error or exception—always make sure (for example, by printing out the stack trace) that this secondary exception doesn't hide or swallow the original problem that led to the rollback.

The controller code is now free from transaction and exception handling and already looks much better:

```
public void execute() {

    // Get values from request

    Session session =
        HibernateUtil.getSessionFactory().getCurrentSession();

    // Load requested Item
    // Check auction still valid
    // Check amount of Bid
    // Add new Bid to Item
    // Place new Bid in scope for next page
    // Forward to success page

}
```

The current `Session` returned by the `SessionFactory` is the same persistence context that is now scoped to the interceptor wrapping this method (and the rendering of the result page).

Refer to your web container's documentation to see how you can enable this filter class as an interceptor for particular URLs; we recommend that you apply it only to URLs that require database access during execution. Otherwise, a database transaction and Hibernate `Session` is started for every HTTP request on your server. This can potentially exhaust your database connection pool, even if no SQL statements are sent to the database server.

You can implement this pattern any way you like, as long as you have the ability to intercept requests and to wrap code around your controller. Many web frameworks offer native interceptors; you should use whatever you find most appealing. The implementation shown here with a servlet filter isn't free of problems.

Changes made to objects in the `Session` are flushed to the database at irregular intervals and finally when the transaction is committed. The transaction commit may occur after the view has been rendered. The problem is the buffer size of the servlet engine: If the contents of the view exceed the buffer size, the buffer may get flushed and the contents sent to the client. The buffer may be flushed many times when the content is rendered, but the first flush also sends the HTTP protocol status code. If the SQL statements on Hibernate flush/commit trigger a constraint violation in the database, the user may already have seen a successful output! You can't change the status code (for example, use a `500  Internal Server Error`); it's already been sent to the client (as `200 OK`).

There are several ways to prevent this rare exception: Adjust the buffer size of your servlets, or flush the `Session` before forwarding/redirecting to the view. Some web frameworks don't immediately fill the response buffer with rendered content—they use their own buffer and flush it only with the response after the view has been completely rendered, so we consider this a problem with plain Java servlet programming.

Let's continue with the cleanup of the controller and extract the business logic into the business layer.

16.1.4 Designing smart domain models

The idea behind the MVC pattern is that control logic (in the example application, this is pageflow logic), view definitions, and business logic should be cleanly separated. Currently, the controller contains some business logic—code that you may be able to reuse in the admittedly unlikely event that your application gains a new user interface—and the domain model consists of dumb data-holding objects. The persistent classes define state, but no behavior.

We suggest you migrate the business logic into the domain model, creating a business layer. The API of this layer is the domain model API. This adds a couple of lines of code, but it also increases the potential for later reuse and is more object-oriented and therefore offers various ways to extend the business logic (for example, using a *strategy pattern* for different bid strategies if suddenly you need to implement "lowest bid wins"). You can also test business logic independently from pageflow or any other concern.

First, add the new method placeBid() to the Item class:

```
public class Item {
    ...

    public Bid placeBid(User bidder, BigDecimal bidAmount,
                        Bid currentMaxBid, Bid currentMinBid)
    throws BusinessException {

    // Check highest bid (TODO:Strategy pattern?)
    if (currentMaxBid != null &&
        currentMaxBid.getAmount().compareTo(bidAmount) > 0) {
        throw new BusinessException("Bid too low.");
    }

    // Auction still valid
    if ( this.getEndDate().before( new Date() ) )
        throw new BusinessException("Auction already ended");

    // Create new Bid
    Bid newBid = new Bid(bidAmount, this, bidder);
```

```
        // Place bid for this Item
        this.addBid(newBid);

        return newBid;
    }

}
```

This code basically performs all checks that need the state of the business objects but don't execute data-access code. The motivation is to encapsulate business logic in classes of the domain model without any dependency on persistent data access or any other infrastructure. Keep in mind that these classes should know nothing about persistence, because you may need them outside of the persistence context (for example, in the presentation tier or in a logic unit test).

You moved code from the controller to the domain model, with one noteworthy exception. This code from the old controller couldn't be moved as is:

```
// Check amount of Bid
Query q = session.createQuery("select max(b.amount)" +
                             " from Bid b where b.item = :item");
q.setEntity("item", item);
BigDecimal maxBidAmount = (BigDecimal) q.uniqueResult();

if (maxBidAmount.compareTo(bidAmount) > 0) {
...        // Forward to error page
}
```

You'll frequently face the same situation in real applications: Business logic is mixed with data-access code and even pageflow logic. It's sometimes difficult to extract only the business logic without any dependencies. If you now look at the solution, the introduction of currentMaxBid and currentMinBid parameters on the Item.placeBid() method, you can see how to solve this kind of problem. Pageflow and data-access code remains in the controller but supplies the required data for the business logic:

```
public void execute() {

    Long itemId = ...              // Get value from request
    Long userId = ...              // Get value from request
    BigDecimal bidAmount = ...     // Get value from request

    Session session =
        HibernateUtil.getSessionFactory().getCurrentSession();

    // Load requested Item
    Item item = (Item) session.load(Item.class, itemId);

    // Get maximum and minimum bids for this Item
    Query q = session.getNamedQuery(QUERY_MAXBID);
    q.setParameter("itemid", itemId);
```

```
Bid currentMaxBid = (Bid) q.uniqueResult();

q = session.getNamedQuery(QUERY_MINBID);
q.setParameter("itemid", itemId);
Bid currentMinBid = (Bid) q.uniqueResult();

// Load bidder
User bidder = (User) session.load(User.class, userId);

try {

    Bid newBid = item.placeBid(bidder,
                               bidAmount,
                               currentMaxBid,
                               currentMinBid);

    ...       // Place new Bid into request context

    ...       // Forward to success page

} catch (BusinessException e) {
    ...       // Forward to appropriate error page
}

}
```

The controller is now completely unaware of any business logic—it doesn't even know whether the new bid must be higher or lower than the last one. You have encapsulated all business logic in the domain model and can now test the business logic as an isolated unit without any dependency on actions, pageflow, persistence, or other infrastructure code (by calling the `Item.placeBid()` in a unit test).

You can even design a different pageflow by catching and forwarding specific exceptions. The `BusinessException` is a declared and checked exception, so you have to handle it in the controller in some way. It's up to you if you want to roll back the transaction in this case, or if you have a chance to recover in some way. However, always consider the state of your persistence context when handling exceptions: There may be unflushed modifications from a previous attempt present when you reuse the same `Session` after an application exception. (Of course, you can never reuse a `Session` that has thrown a fatal runtime exception.) The safe way is to always roll back the database transaction on any exception and to retry with a fresh `Session`.

The action code looks good already. You should try to keep your architecture simple; isolating exception and transaction handling and extracting business logic can make a significant difference. However, the action code is now bound to Hibernate, because it uses the `Session` API to access the database. The MVC pattern doesn't say much about where the P for Persistence should go.

16.2 Creating a persistence layer

Mixing data-access code with application logic violates the emphasis on separation of concerns. There are several reasons why you should consider hiding the Hibernate calls behind a facade, the so-called persistence layer:

- The persistence layer can provide a higher level of abstraction for data-access operations. Instead of basic CRUD and query operations, you can expose higher-level operations, such as a getMaximumBid() method. This abstraction is the primary reason why you want to create a persistence layer in larger applications: to support reuse of the same non-CRUD operations.

- The persistence layer can have a generic interface without exposing actual implementation details. In other words, you can hide the fact that you're using Hibernate (or Java Persistence) to implement the data-access operations from any client of the persistence layer. We consider persistence layer portability an unimportant concern, because full object/relational mapping solutions like Hibernate already provide database portability. It's highly unlikely that you'll rewrite your persistence layer with different software in the future and still not want to change any client code. Furthermore, consider Java Persistence as a standardized and fully portable API.

- The persistence layer can unify data-access operations. This concern is related to portability, but from a slightly different angle. Imagine that you have to deal with mixed data-access code, such as Hibernate and JDBC operations. By unifying the facade that clients see and use, you can hide this implementation detail from the client.

If you consider portability and unification to be side effects of creating a persistence layer, your primary motivation is achieving a higher level of abstraction and the improved maintainability and reuse of data-access code. These are good reasons, and we encourage you to create a persistence layer with a generic facade in all but the simplest applications. It's again important that you don't overengineer your system and that you first consider using Hibernate (or Java Persistence APIs) directly without any additional layering. Let's assume you want to create a persistence layer and design a facade that clients will call.

There is more than one way to design a persistence layer facade—some small applications may use a single PersistenceManager object; some may use some kind of command-oriented design, and others mix data-access operations into domain classes (active record)—but we prefer the DAO pattern.

16.2.1 *A generic data-access object pattern*

The DAO design pattern originated in Sun's Java Blueprints. It's even used in the infamous Java Petstore demo application. A DAO defines an interface to persistence operations (CRUD and finder methods) relating to a particular persistent entity; it advises you to group together code that relates to persistence of that entity.

Using JDK 5.0 features such as generics and variable arguments, you can design a nice DAO persistence layer easily. The basic structure of the pattern we're proposing here is shown in figure 16.1.

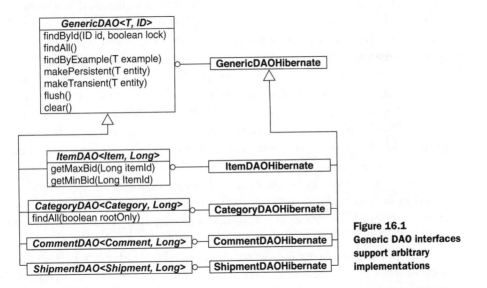

**Figure 16.1
Generic DAO interfaces
support arbitrary
implementations**

We designed the persistence layer with two parallel hierarchies: interfaces on one side, implementations on the other side. The basic object-storage and -retrieval operations are grouped in a generic superinterface and a superclass that implements these operations with a particular persistence solution (we'll use Hibernate). The generic interface is extended by interfaces for particular entities that require additional business-related data-access operations. Again, you may have one or several implementations of an entity DAO interface.

Let's first consider the basic CRUD operations that every entity shares and needs; you group these in the generic superinterface:

```
public interface GenericDAO<T, ID extends Serializable> {

    T findById(ID id, boolean lock);
```

```
        List<T> findAll();

        List<T> findByExample(T exampleInstance,
                              String... excludeProperty);

        T makePersistent(T entity);

        void makeTransient(T entity);

        void flush();

        void clear();

    }
```

The `GenericDAO` is an interface that requires type arguments if you want to implement it. The first parameter, `T`, is the entity instance for which you're implementing a DAO. Many of the DAO methods use this argument to return objects in a type-safe manner. The second parameter defines the type of the database identifier—not all entities may use the same type for their identifier property. The second thing that is interesting here is the variable argument in the `findByExample()` method; you'll soon see how that improves the API for a client.

Finally, this is clearly the foundation for a persistence layer that works *state-oriented*. Methods such as `makePersistent()` and `makeTransient()` change an object's state (or many objects at once with cascading enabled). The `flush()` and `clear()` operations can be used by a client to manage the persistence context. You'd write a completely different DAO interface if your persistence layer were *statement-oriented*; for example if you weren't using Hibernate to implement it but only plain JDBC.

The persistence layer facade we introduced here doesn't expose any Hibernate or Java Persistence interface to the client, so theoretically you can implement it with any software without making any changes to client code. You may not want or need persistence layer portability, as explained earlier. In that case, you should consider exposing Hibernate or Java Peristence interfaces—for example, a `findByCriteria(DetachedCriteria)` method that clients can use to execute arbitrary Hibernate `Criteria` queries. This decision is up to you; you may decide that exposing Java Persistence interfaces is a safer choice than exposing Hibernate interfaces. However, you should know that while it's possible to change the implementation of the persistence layer from Hibernate to Java Persistence or to any other fully featured state-oriented object/relational mapping software, it's almost impossible to rewrite a persistence layer that is state-oriented with plain JDBC statements.

Next, you implement the DAO interfaces.

16.2.2 *Implementing the generic CRUD interface*

Let's continue with a possible implementation of the generic interface, using Hibernate APIs:

```
public abstract class
        GenericHibernateDAO<T, ID extends Serializable>
            implements GenericDAO<T, ID> {

    private Class<T> persistentClass;
    private Session session;

    public GenericHibernateDAO() {
        this.persistentClass = (Class<T>)
            ( (ParameterizedType) getClass().getGenericSuperclass() )
                .getActualTypeArguments()[0];
     }

    public void setSession(Session s) {
        this.session = s;
    }

    protected Session getSession() {
        if (session == null)
            session = HibernateUtil.getSessionFactory()
                                    .getCurrentSession();
        return session;
    }

    public Class<T> getPersistentClass() {
        return persistentClass;
    }

    . . .
```

So far this is the internal plumbing of the implementation with Hibernate. In the implementation, you need access to a Hibernate `Session`, so you require that the client of the DAO injects the current `Session` it wants to use with a setter method. This is mostly useful in integration testing. If the client didn't set a `Session` before using the DAO, you look up the current `Session` when it's needed by the DAO code.

The DAO implementation must also know what persistent entity class it's for; you use Java Reflection in the constructor to find the class of the `T` generic argument and store it in a local member.

If you write a generic DAO implementation with Java Persistence, the code looks almost the same. The only change is that an `EntityManager` is required by the DAO, not a `Session`.

You can now implement the actual CRUD operations, again with Hibernate:

```java
@SuppressWarnings("unchecked")
public T findById(ID id, boolean lock) {
    T entity;
    if (lock)
        entity = (T) getSession()
            .load(getPersistentClass(), id, LockMode.UPGRADE);
    else
        entity = (T) getSession()
            .load(getPersistentClass(), id);

    return entity;
}

@SuppressWarnings("unchecked")
public List<T> findAll() {
    return findByCriteria();
}

@SuppressWarnings("unchecked")
public List<T> findByExample(T exampleInstance,
                             String... excludeProperty) {
    Criteria crit =
        getSession().createCriteria(getPersistentClass());
    Example example =  Example.create(exampleInstance);
    for (String exclude : excludeProperty) {
        example.excludeProperty(exclude);
    }
    crit.add(example);
    return crit.list();
}

@SuppressWarnings("unchecked")
public T makePersistent(T entity) {
    getSession().saveOrUpdate(entity);
    return entity;
}

public void makeTransient(T entity) {
    getSession().delete(entity);
}

public void flush() {
    getSession().flush();
}

public void clear() {
    getSession().clear();
}

/**
 * Use this inside subclasses as a convenience method.
 */
@SuppressWarnings("unchecked")
protected List<T> findByCriteria(Criterion... criterion) {
```

```
    Criteria crit =
        getSession().createCriteria(getPersistentClass());
    for (Criterion c : criterion) {
        crit.add(c);
    }
    return crit.list();
    }

}
```

All the data-access operations use `getSession()` to get the `Session` that is assigned to this DAO. Most of these methods are straightforward, and you shouldn't have any problem understanding them after reading the previous chapters of this book. The `@SurpressWarning` annotations are optional—Hibernate interfaces are written for JDKs before 5.0, so all casts are unchecked and the JDK 5.0 compiler generates a warning for each otherwise. Look at the protected `find-ByCriteria()` method: We consider this a convenience method that makes the implementation of other data-access operations easier. It takes zero or more `Criterion` arguments and adds them to a `Criteria` that is then executed. This is an example of JDK 5.0 variable arguments. Note that we decided not to expose this method on the public generic DAO interface; it's an implementation detail (you may come to a different conclusion).

An implementation with Java Persistence is straightforward, although it doesn't support a `Criteria` API. Instead of `saveOrUpdate()`, you use `merge()` to make any transient or detached object persistent, and return the merged result.

You've now completed the basic machinery of the persistence layer and the generic interface it exposes to the upper layer of the system. In the next step, you create entity-related DAO interfaces and implement them by extending the generic interface and implementation.

16.2.3 *Implementing entity DAOs*

Let's assume that you want to implement non-CRUD data-access operations for the `Item` business entity. First, write an interface:

```
public interface ItemDAO extends GenericDAO<Item, Long> {

    Bid getMaxBid(Long itemId);
    Bid getMinBid(Long itemId);

}
```

The `ItemDAO` interface extends the generic super interface and parameterizes it with an `Item` entity type and a `Long` as the database identifier type. Two data-access operations are relevant for the `Item` entity: `getMaxBid()` and `getMinBid()`.

An implementation of this interface with Hibernate extends the generic CRUD implementation:

```
public class ItemDAOHibernate
        extends     GenericHibernateDAO<Item, Long>
        implements  ItemDAO {

    public Bid getMaxBid(Long itemId) {
        Query q = getSession().getNamedQuery("getItemMaxBid");
        q.setParameter("itemid", itemId);
        return (Bid) q.uniqueResult();
    }

    public Bid getMinBid(Long itemId) {
        Query q = getSession().getNamedQuery("getItemMinBid");
        q.setParameter("itemid", itemId);
        return (Bid) q.uniqueResult();
    }

}
```

You can see how easy this implementation was, thanks to the functionality provided by the superclass. The queries have been externalized to mapping metadata and are called by name, which avoids cluttering the code.

We recommend that you create an interface even for entities that don't have any non-CRUD data-access operations:

```
public interface CommentDAO extends GenericDAO<Comment, Long> {
    // Empty
}
```

The implementation is equally straightforward:

```
public static class CommentDAOHibernate
        extends GenericHibernateDAO<Comment, Long>
        implements CommentDAO {}
```

We recommend this empty interface and implementation because you can't instantiate the generic abstract implementation. Furthermore, a client should rely on an interface that is specific for a particular entity, thus avoiding costly refactoring in the future if additional data-access operations are introduced. You might not follow our recommendation, however, and make `GenericHibernateDAO` nonabstract. This decision depends on the application you're writing and what changes you expect in the future.

Let's bring this all together and see how clients instantiate and use DAOs.

16.2.4 *Using data-access objects*

If a client wishes to utilize the persistence layer, it has to instantiate the DAOs it needs and then call methods on these DAOs. In the previously introduced Hibernate web application use case, the controller and action code look like this:

```
public void execute() {

    Long itemId = ...           // Get value from request
    Long userId = ...           // Get value from request
    BigDecimal bidAmount = ...   // Get value from request

    // Prepare DAOs
    ItemDAO itemDAO = new ItemDAOHibernate();
    UserDAO userDAO = new UserDAOHibernate();

    // Load requested Item
    Item item = itemDAO.findById(itemId, true);

    // Get maximum and minimum bids for this Item
    Bid currentMaxBid = itemDAO.getMaxBid(itemId);
    Bid currentMinBid = itemDAO.getMinBid(itemId);

    // Load bidder
    User bidder = userDAO.findById(userId, false);

    try {

        Bid newBid = item.placeBid(bidder,
                                   bidAmount,
                                   currentMaxBid,
                                   currentMinBid);

        ...     // Place new Bid into request context

        ...     // Forward to success page

    } catch (BusinessException e) {
        ...     // Forward to appropriate error page
    }

}
```

You almost manage to avoid any dependency of controller code on Hibernate, except for one thing: You still need to instantiate a specific DAO implementation in the controller. One (not very sophisticated) way to avoid this dependency is the traditional abstract factory pattern.

First, create an abstract factory for data-access objects:

```
public abstract class DAOFactory {

    /**
     * Factory method for instantiation of concrete factories.
     */
```

```
    public static DAOFactory instance(Class factory) {
        try {
            return (DAOFactory)factory.newInstance();
        } catch (Exception ex) {
            throw new RuntimeException(
                    "Couldn't create DAOFactory: " + factory
                    );
        }
    }

    // Add your DAO interfaces here
    public abstract ItemDAO getItemDAO();
    public abstract CategoryDAO getCategoryDAO();
    public abstract CommentDAO getCommentDAO();
    public abstract UserDAO getUserDAO();
    public abstract BillingDetailsDAO getBillingDetailsDAO();
    public abstract ShipmentDAO getShipmentDAO();

}
```

This abstract factory can build and return any DAO. Now implement this factory for your Hibernate DAOs:

```
public class HibernateDAOFactory extends DAOFactory {

    public ItemDAO getItemDAO() {
        return (ItemDAO) instantiateDAO(ItemDAOHibernate.class);
    }

    ...

    private GenericHibernateDAO instantiateDAO(Class daoClass) {
        try {
            GenericHibernateDAO dao = (GenericHibernateDAO)
                                    daoClass.newInstance();
            return dao;
        } catch (Exception ex) {
            throw new RuntimeException(
                    "Can not instantiate DAO: " + daoClass, ex
                    );
        }
    }

    // Inline all empty DAO implementations

    public static class CommentDAOHibernate
            extends GenericHibernateDAO<Comment, Long>
            implements CommentDAO {}

    public static class ShipmentDAOHibernate
            extends GenericHibernateDAO<Shipment, Long>
            implements ShipmentDAO {}

    ...

}
```

Several interesting things happen here. First, the implementation of the factory encapsulates how the DAO is instantiated. You can customize this method and set a Session manually before returning the DAO instance.

Second, you move the implementation of CommentDAOHibernate into the factory as a public static class. Remember that you need this implementation, even if it's empty, to let clients work with interfaces related to an entity. However, nobody forces you to create dozens of empty implementation classes in separate files; you can group all the empty implementations in the factory. If in the future you have to introduce more data-access operations for the Comment entity, move the implementation from the factory to its own file. No other code needs to be changed—clients rely only on the CommentDAO interface.

With this factory pattern, you can further simplify how DAOs are used in the web application controller:

```
public void execute() {

    Long itemId = ...              // Get value from request
    Long userId = ...              // Get value from request
    BigDecimal bidAmount = ...     // Get value from request

    // Prepare DAOs
    DAOFactory factory = DAOFactory.instance(DAOFactory.HIBERNATE);
    ItemDAO itemDAO = factory.getItemDAO();
    UserDAO userDAO = factory.getUserDAO();

    // Load requested Item
    Item item = itemDAO.findById(itemId, true);

    // Get maximum and minimum bids for this Item
    Bid currentMaxBid = itemDAO.getMaxBid(itemId);
    Bid currentMinBid = itemDAO.getMinBid(itemId);

    // Load bidder
    User bidder = userDAO.findById(userId, false);

    try {
        ...
    }

}
```

The only dependency on Hibernate, and the only line of code that exposes the true implementation of the persistence layer to client code, is the retrieval of the DAOFactory. You may want to consider moving this parameter into your application's external configuration so that you can possibly switch DAOFactory implementations without changing any code.

> **TIP**   *Mixing Hibernate and JDBC code in a DAO*—Rarely do you have to use plain
> JDBC when you have Hibernate available. Remember that if you need a
> JDBC `Connection` to execute a statement that Hibernate can't produce
> automatically, you can always fall back with `session.connection()`. So,
> we don't think you need different and separate DAOs for a few JDBC calls.
> The issue with mixing Hibernate and plain JDBC isn't the fact that you
> sometimes may have to do it (and you should definitely expect that
> Hibernate won't solve 100 percent of all your problems) but that devel-
> opers often try to hide what they did. There is no problem with mixed
> data-access code as long as it's properly documented. Also remember
> that Hibernate supports almost all SQL operations with native APIs, so
> you don't necessarily have to fall back to plain JDBC.

You've now created a clean, flexible, and powerful persistence layer that hides the
details of data access from any client code. The following questions are likely still
on your mind:

- *Do you have to write factories?*   The factory pattern is traditional and is used in
  applications that mostly rely on lookup of stateless services. An alternative
  (or sometimes complementary) strategy is *dependency injection*. The EJB 3.0
  specification standardizes dependency injection for managed components,
  so we'll look at an alternative DAO wiring strategy later in this chapter.

- *Do you have to create one DAO interface per domain entity?*   Our proposal
  doesn't cover all possible situations. In larger applications, you may want to
  group DAOs by domain package or create deeper hierarchies of DAOs that
  provide more fine-grained specialization for particular subentities. There
  are many variations of the DAO pattern, and you shouldn't restrict your
  options with our recommended generic solution. Feel free to experiment,
  and consider this pattern a good starting point.

You now know how to integrate Hibernate in a traditional web application and
how to create a persistence layer following best practices patterns. If you have
to design and write a three-tier application, you need to consider a quite different architecture.

16.3   *Introducing the Command pattern*

The patterns and strategies introduced in the previous sections are perfect if you
have to write a small to medium sized web application with Hibernate and Java Persistence. The OSIV pattern works in any two-tiered architecture, where the presentation, business, and persistence layers are colocated on the same virtual machine.

However, as soon as you introduce a third tier and move the presentation layer to a separate virtual machine, the current persistence context can't be held open anymore until the view has been rendered. This is typically the case in three-tiered EJB application, or in an architecture with a rich client in a separate process.

If the presentation layer runs in a different process, you need to minimize the requests between this process and the tier that runs the business and persistence layers of the application. This means that you can't use the previous lazy approach, where the view is allowed to pull data from the domain model objects as needed. Instead, the business tier must accept responsibility for fetching all data that is needed subsequently for rendering the view.

Although certain patterns that can minimize remote communication, such as the *session facade* and *data transfer object* (DTO) patterns, have been widely used in the Java developer community, we want to discuss a slightly different approach. The *Command* pattern (often also called *EJB Command*) is a sophisticated solution that combines the advantages of other strategies.

Let's write a three-tiered application that utilizes this pattern.

16.3.1 *The basic interfaces*

The *Command* pattern is based on the idea of a hierarchy of command classes, all of which implement a simple Command interface. Look at this hierarchy in figure 16.2.

A particular Command is an implementation of an action, an event, or anything that can fit a similar description. Client code creates command objects and prepares them for execution. The CommandHandler is an interface that can execute Command objects. The client passes a Command object to a handler on the server tier, and the handler executes it. The Command object is then returned to the client.

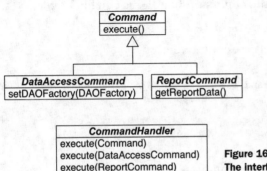

Figure 16.2
The interfaces of the Command pattern

The Command interface has an execute() method; any concrete command must implement this method. Any subinterface may add additional methods that are called before (setters) or after (getter) the Command is executed. A Command is therefore combining *input, controller,* and *output* for a particular event.

Executing Command objects—that is, calling their execute() method—is the job of a CommandHandler implementation. Execution of commands is dispatched polymorphically.

The implementation of these interfaces (and abstract classes) can look as follows:

```
public interface Command {
    public void execute() throws CommandException;
}
```

Commands also encapsulate exception handling, so that any exception thrown during execution is wrapped in a CommandException that can then be handled accordingly by the client.

The DataAccessCommand is an abstract class:

```
public abstract class DataAccessCommand implements Command {
    protected DAOFactory daoFactory;

    public void setDAOFactory(DAOFactory daoFactory) {
        this.daoFactory = daoFactory;
    }

}
```

Any Command that needs to access the database must use a data-access object, so a DAOFactory must be set before a DataAccessCommand can be executed. This is usually the job of the CommandHandler implementation, because the persistence layer is on the server tier.

The remote interface of the command handler is equally simple:

```
public interface CommandHandler {

    public Command executeCommand(Command c)
                throws CommandException;

    public DataAccessCommand executeCommand(DataAccessCommand c)
                throws CommandException;

    public Reportcommand executeCommand(ReportCommand c)
                throws CommandException;
}
```

Let's write some concrete implementations and use commands.

16.3.2 *Executing command objects*

A client that wishes to execute a command needs to instantiate and prepare a `Command` object. For example, placing a bid for an auction requires a `BidForAuctionCommand` on the client:

```
BidForItemCommand bidForItem =
            new BidForItemCommand(userId, itemId, bidAmount);

try {
    CommandHandler handler = getCommandHandler();

    bidForItem = (BidForItemCommand)handler.execute(bidForItem);

    // Extract new bid for rendering
    newBid = bidForItem.getNewBid();

    // Forward to success page

} catch (CommandException ex) {
    // Forward to error page
    // ex.getCause();

}
```

A `BidForItemCommand` needs all input values for this action as constructor arguments. The client then looks up a command handler and passes the `BidForItemCommand` object for execution. The handler returns the instance after execution, and the client extracts any output values from the returned object. (If you work with JDK 5.0, use generics to avoid unsafe typecasts.)

How the command handler is looked up or instantiated depends on the implementation of the command handler and how remote communication occurs. You don't even have to call a remote command handler—it can be a local object.

Let's look at the implementation of the command and the command handler.

Implementing business commands

The `BidForItemCommand` extends the abstract class `DataAccessCommand` and implements the `execute()` method:

```
public class BidForItemCommand extends DataAccessCommand
                               implements Serializable {

    // Input
    private Long userId;
    private Long itemId;
    private BigDecimal bidAmount;

    // Output
    private Bid newBid;

    public BidForItemCommand(Long userId,
```

```
                              Long itemId,
                              BigDecimal bidAmount) {
        this.userId = userId;
        this.itemId = itemId;
        this.bidAmount = bidAmount;
    }

    public Bid getNewBid() {
        return newBid;
    }

    public void execute() throws CommandException {

        ItemDAO itemDAO = daoFactory.getItemDAO();
        UserDAO userDAO = daoFactory.getUserDAO();

        try {

            Bid currentMaxBid = itemDAO.getMaxBid(itemId);
            Bid currentMinBid = itemDAO.getMinBid(itemId);

            Item item = itemDAO.findById(itemId, false);
            newBid = item.placeBid(userDAO.findById(userId, false),
                                   bidAmount,
                                   currentMaxBid,
                                   currentMinBid);

        } catch (BusinessException ex) {
            throw new CommandException(ex);
        }
    }

}
```

This is basically the same code you wrote in the last stage of the web application refinement earlier in this chapter. However, with this approach, you have a clear contract for required input and returned output of an action.

Because Command instances are sent across the wire, you need to implement Serializable (this marker should be in the concrete class, not the superclasses or interfaces).

Let's implement the command handler.

Implementing a command handler

The command handler can be implemented in any way you like; its responsibilities are simple. Many systems need only a single command handler, such as the following:

```
@Stateless
public class CommandHandlerBean implements CommandHandler {

    // The persistence layer we want to call
```

```
DAOFactory daoFactory =
    DAOFactory.instance(DAOFactory.HIBERNATE);

@TransactionAttribute(TransactionAttributeType.NEVER)
public Command executeCommand(Command c)
        throws CommandException {
    c.execute();
    return c;
}

@TransactionAttribute(TransactionAttributeType.REQUIRED)
public Command executeCommand(DataAccessCommand c)
        throws CommandException {
    c.setDAOFactory(daoFactory);
    c.execute();
    return c;
}
}
```

This is a command handler implemented as a stateless EJB 3.0 session bean. You use an EJB lookup on the client to get a reference to this (local or remote) bean and then pass Command objects to it for execution. The handler knows how to prepare a particular type of command—for example, by setting a reference to the persistence layer before execution.

Thanks to container-managed and declarative transactions, this command handler contains no Hibernate code. Of course, you can also implement this command handler as a POJO without EJB 3.0 annotations and manage transaction boundaries programmatically. One the other hand, because EJBs support remote communication out of the box, they're the best choice for command handlers in three-tier architectures.

There are many more variations of this basic Command pattern.

16.3.3 Variations of the Command pattern

First, not everything is perfect with the Command pattern. Probably the most important issue with this pattern is the requirement for nonpresentation interfaces on the client classpath. Because the BidForItemCommand needs the DAOs, you have to include the persistence layer interface on the client's classpath (even if the command is executed only on the middle tier). There is no real solution, so the severity of this problem depends on your deployment scenario and how easily you can package your application accordingly. Note that the client needs the DAO interfaces only to instantiate a DataAccessCommand, so you may be able to stabilize the interfaces before you work on the implementation of your persistence layer.

Also, because you have just one command, the Command pattern seems like more work then the traditional session facade pattern. However, as the system grows, addition of new commands is made simpler because crosscutting concerns like exception handling and authorization checking may be implemented in the command handler. Commands are easy to implement and extremely reusable. You shouldn't feel restricted by our proposed command interface hierarchy; feel free to design more complex and sophisticated command interfaces and abstract commands. You can also group commands together using delegation—for example, a `DataAccessCommand` can instantiate and call a `ReportCommand`.

A command is a great assembler for data that is required for rendering of a particular view. Instead of having the view pull the information from lazy loaded business objects (which requires colocation of the presentation and persistence layer, so you can stay inside the same persistence context), a client can prepare and execute the commands that are needed to render a particular screen—each command transports data to the presentation layer in its output properties. In a way, a command is a kind of data-transfer object with a built-in assembling routine.

Furthermore, the Command pattern enables you to implement any *Undo* functionality easily. Each command can have an `undo()` method that can negate any permanent changes that have been made by the `execute()` method. Or, you can queue several command objects on the client and send them to the command handler only when a particular conversation completes.

The Command pattern is also great if you have to implement a desktop application. You can, for example, implement a command that fires events when data is changed. All dialogs that need to be refreshed listen to this event, by registering a listener on the command handler.

You can wrap the commands with EJB 3.0 interceptors. For example, you can write an interceptor for your command handler session bean that can transparently inject a particular service on command objects of a particular type. You can combine and stack these interceptors on your command handler. You can even implement a client-local command handler which, thanks to EJB interceptors, can transparently decide whether a command needs to be routed to the server (to another command handler) or if the command can be executed disconnected on the client.

The stateless session bean need not be the only command handler. It's easy to implement a JMS-based command handler that executes commands asynchronously. You can even store a command in the database for scheduled execution. Commands may be used outside of the server environment—in a batch process or unit test case, for example.

In practice, an architecture that relies on the Command pattern works nicely.

In the next section, we discuss how EJB 3.0 components can further simplify a layered application architecture.

16.4 Designing applications with EJB 3.0

We've focused on the Java Persistence standard in this book and discussed only a few examples of other EJB 3.0 programming constructs. We wrote some EJB session beans, enabled container-managed transactions, and used container injection to get an `EntityManager`.

There is much more to be discovered in the EJB 3.0 programming model. In the following sections, we show you how to simplify some of the previous patterns with EJB 3.0 components. However, we again only look at features that are relevant for a database application, so you need to refer to other documentation if you want to know more about timers, EJB interceptors, or message-driven EJBs.

First you'll implement an action in a web application with a stateful session bean, a conversational controller. Then you'll simplify data-access objects by turning them into EJBs to get container-managed transactions and injection of dependencies. You'll also switch from any Hibernate interfaces to Java Persistence, to stay fully compatible with EJB 3.0.

You start by implementing a conversation with EJB 3.0 components in a web application.

16.4.1 Implementing a conversation with stateful beans

A stateful session bean (SFSB) is the perfect controller for a potentially long-running conversation between the application and the user. You can write an SFSB that implements all the steps in a conversation—for example, a *PlaceItem* conversation:

1. User enters item information
2. User can add images for an item
3. User submits the completed form

Step 2 of this conversation can be executed repeatedly, if more than one image must be added. Let's implement this with an SFSB that uses Java Persistence and the `EntityManager` directly.

A single SFSB instance is responsible for the whole conversation. First, here's the business interface:

```
public interface PlaceItem {

    public Item createItem(Long userId, Map itemData);

    public void addImage(String filename);

    public void submit();
}
```

In the first step of the conversation, the user enters the basic item details and supplies a user identifier. From this, an `Item` instance is created and stored in the conversation. The user can then execute `addImage()` events several times. Finally, the user completes the form, and the `submit()` method is called to end the conversation. Note how you can read the interface like a story of your conversation.

This is a possible implementation:

```
@Stateful
@TransactionAttribute(TransactionAttributeType.NEVER)
public class PlaceItemBean implements PlaceItem {

    @PersistenceContext(type = PersistenceContextType.EXTENDED)
    private EntityManager em;

    private Item item;
    private User seller;

    public Item createItem(Long userId, Map itemData) {

        // Load seller into conversation
        seller = em.find(User.class, userId);

        // Create item for conversation
        item = new Item(itemData, seller);
        user.addItem(item);

        return item;
    }

    public void addImage(String filename) {
        item.getImages().add(filename);
    }

    @Remove
    @TransactionAttribute(TransactionAttributeType.REQUIRED)
    public void submit() {
        em.persist(item);
    }
}
```

An instance of this stateful session bean is bound to a particular EJB client, so it also acts as a cache during the conversation. You use an extended persistence context that is flushed only when `submit()` returns, because this is the only method that executes inside a transaction. All data access in other methods runs in auto-commit mode. So `em.find(User.class, userId)` executes nontransactional, whereas `em.persist(item)` is transactional. Because the `submit()` method is also marked with `@Remove`, the persistence context is closed automatically when this method returns, and the stateful session bean is destroyed.

A variation of this implementation doesn't call the `EntityManager` directly, but data-access objects.

16.4.2 *Writing DAOs with EJBs*

A data-access object is the perfect stateless session bean. Each data-access method doesn't require any state; it only needs an `EntityManager`. So, when you implement a `GenericDAO` with Java Persistence, you require an `EntityManager` to be set:

```
public abstract class GenericEJB3DAO<T,ID extends Serializable>
        implements GenericDAO<T, ID> {

    private Class<T> entityBeanType;

    private EntityManager em;

    public GenericEJB3DAO() {
        this.entityBeanType = (Class<T>)
            ( (ParameterizedType) getClass().getGenericSuperclass() )
                .getActualTypeArguments()[0];
    }

    @PersistenceContext
    public void setEntityManager(EntityManager em) {
        this.em = em;
    }

    protected EntityManager getEntityManager() {
        return em;
    }

    public Class<T> getEntityBeanType() {
        return entityBeanType;
    }

    ...
}
```

This is really the same implementation you created earlier for Hibernate in section 16.2.2, "Implementing the generic CRUD interface." However, you mark the `setEntityManager()` method with `@PersistenceContext`, so you get automatic injection of the right `EntityManager` when this bean executes inside a container. If it's executed outside of an EJB 3.0 runtime container, you can set the Entity-Manager manually.

We won't show you the implementation of all CRUD operations with JPA; you should be able to implement `findById()`, and so on, on your own.

Next, here's the implementation of a concrete DAO with business data-access methods:

```
@Stateless
@TransactionAttribute(TransactionAttributeType.REQUIRED)
public class ItemDAOBean extends GenericEJB3DAO<Item, Long>
                    implements ItemDAO {

    public Bid getMaxBid(Long itemId) {
        Query q = getEntityManager()
                    .createNamedQuery("getItemMaxBid");
        q.setParameter("itemid", itemId);
        return (Bid) q.getSingleResult();
    }

    public Bid getMinBid(Long itemId) {
        Query q = getEntityManager()
                    .createNamedQuery("getItemMinBid");
        q.setParameter("itemid", itemId);
        return (Bid) q.getSingleResult();
    }
    ...
}
```

This concrete subclass is the stateless EJB session bean, and all methods that are called, included those inherited from the `GenericDAO` superclass, require a transaction context. If a client of this DAO calls a method with no active transaction, a transaction is started for this DAO method.

You no longer need any DAO factories. The conversation controller you wrote earlier is wired with the DAOs automatically through dependency injection.

16.4.3 *Utilizing dependency injection*

You now refactor the `PlaceItem` conversation controller and add a persistence layer. Instead of accessing JPA directly, you call DAOs that are injected into the conversation controller by the container at runtime:

```
@Stateful
public class PlaceItemWithDAOsBean implements PlaceItem {

    @PersistenceContext(
        type = PersistenceContextType.EXTENDED,
        properties =
            @PersistenceProperty(
                name="org.hibernate.flushMode",
                value="MANUAL"
            )
```

```
    )
    private EntityManager em;

    @EJB ItemDAO itemDAO;
    @EJB UserDAO userDAO;

    private Item item;
    private User seller;

    public Item createItem(Long userId, Map itemData) {

        // Load seller into conversation
        seller = userDAO.findById(userId);

        // Create item for conversation
        item = new Item(itemData, seller);

        return item;
    }

    public void addImage(String filename) {
        item.getImages().add(filename);
    }

    @Remove
    public void submit() {
        itemDAO.makePersistent(item);
        em.flush();
    }
}
```

The @EJB annotation marks the itemDAO and userDAO fields for automatic dependency injection. The container looks up an implementation (which implementation is vendor-dependent, but in this case there is only one for each interface) of the given interface and sets it on the field.

You haven't disabled transactions in this implementation, but only disabled automatic flushing with the Hibernate org.hibernate.flushmode extension property. You then flush the persistence context once, when the @Remove method of the SFSB completes and before the transaction of this method commits.

There are two reasons for this:

- All DAO methods you're calling require a transaction context. If you don't start a transaction for each method in the conversation controller, the transaction boundary is a call on one of the data-access objects. However, you want the createItem(), addImages(), and submit() methods to be the scope of the transaction, in case you execute several DAO operations.

- You have an extended persistence context that is automatically scoped and bound to the stateful session bean. Because the DAOs are stateless session beans, this single persistence context can be propagated into all DAOs only when a transaction context is active and propagated as well. If the DAOs are stateful session beans, you can propagate the current persistence context through instantiation even when there is no transaction context for a DAO call, but that also means the conversation controller must destroy any stateful DAOs manually.

Without the Hibernate extension property, you'd have to make your DAOs stateful session beans to allow propagation of the persistence context between nontransactional method calls. It would then be the responsibility of the controller to call the `@Remove` method of each DAO in its own `@Remove` method—you don't want either. You want to disable flushing without writing any nontransactional methods.

EJB 3.0 includes many more injection features, and they extend to other Java EE 5.0 specifications. For example, you can use `@EJB` injection in a Java servlet container, or `@Resource` to get any named resource from JNDI injected automatically. However, these features are outside the scope of this book.

Now that you've created application layers, you need a way to test them for correctness.

16.5 Testing

Testing is probably the single most important activity in which a Java developer engages during a day of work. Testing determines the correctness of the system from a functional standpoint as well as from a performance and scalability perspective. Successfully executing tests means that all application components and layers interact correctly and work together smoothly and as specified.

You can test and proof a software system many different ways. In the context of persistence and data management, you're naturally most interested in automated tests. In the following sections, you create many kinds of tests that you can run repeatedly to check the correct behavior of your application.

First we look at different categories of tests. Functional, integration, and standalone unit testing all have a different goal and purpose, and you need to know when each strategy is appropriate. We then write tests and introduce the *TestNG* framework (http://www.testng.org). Finally, we consider stress and load testing and how you can find out whether your system will scale to a high number of concurrent transactions.

16.5.1 *Understanding different kinds of tests*

We categorize software testing as follows:

- *Acceptance testing*—This kind of test isn't necessarily automated and usually isn't the job of the application developer and system designers. Acceptance testing is the final stage of testing of a system, conducted by the customer (or any other party) who is deciding whether the system meets the project requirements. These tests can include any metric, from functionality, to performance, to usability.

- *Performance testing*—A stress or load test exercises the system with a high number of concurrent users, ideally an equal or a higher load than is expected once the software runs in production. Because this is such an important facet of testing for any application with online transactional data processing, we look at performance testing later in more detail.

- *Logic unit testing*—These tests consider a single piece of functionality, often only a business method (for example, whether the highest bid really wins in the auction system). If a component is tested as a single unit, it's tested independently from any other component. Logic unit testing doesn't involve any subsystems like databases.

- *Integration unit testing*—An integration test determines whether the interaction between software components, services, and subsystems works as expected. In the context of transaction processing and data management, this can mean that you want to test whether the application works correctly with the database (for example, whether a newly made bid for an auction item is correctly saved in the database).

- *Functional unit testing*—A functional test exercises a whole use case and the public interface in all application components that are needed to complete this particular use case. A functional test can include application workflow and the user interface (for example, by simulating how a user must be logged in before placing a new bid for an auction item).

In the following sections, we focus on integration unit testing because it's the most relevant kind of test when persistent data and transaction processing are your primary concerns. That doesn't mean other kinds of tests aren't equally important, and we'll provide hints along the way. If you want to get the full picture, we recommend *JUnit in Action* ([Massol, 2003]).

We don't use JUnit, but TestNG. This shouldn't bother you too much, because the fundamentals we present are applicable with any testing framework. We think TestNG makes integration and functional unit testing easier than JUnit, and we especially like its JDK 5.0 features and annotation-based configuration of test assemblies.

Let's write a simple isolated logic unit test first, so you can see how TestNG works.

16.5.2 *Introducing TestNG*

TestNG is a testing framework that has some unique functionality, which makes it especially useful for unit testing that involves complex test setups such as integration or functional testing. Some of TestNG's features are JDK 5.0 annotations for the declaration of test assemblies, support for configuration parameters and flexible grouping of tests into test suites, support for a variety of plug-ins for IDEs and Ant, and the ability to execute tests in a specific order by following dependencies.

We want to approach these features step by step, so you first write a simple logic unit test without any integration of a subsystem.

A unit test in TestNG

A logic unit test validates a single piece of functionality and checks whether all business rules are followed by a particular component or method. If you followed our discussion earlier in this chapter about smart domain models (section 16.1.4, "Designing 'smart' domain models"), you know that we prefer to encapsulate unit-testable business logic in the domain model implementation. A logic unit test executes a test of methods in the business layer and domain model:

```
public class AuctionLogic {

    @org.testng.annotations.Test(groups = "logic")
    public void highestBidWins() {

        // A user is needed
        User user = new User(...);

        // Create an Item instance
        Item auction = new Item(...);

        // Place a bid
        BigDecimal bidAmount = new BigDecimal("100.00");
        auction.placeBid(user, bidAmount,
                        new BigDecimal(0), new BigDecimal(0) );

        // Place another higher bid
        BigDecimal higherBidAmount = new BigDecimal("101.00");
        auction.placeBid(user, higherBidAmount,
```

```
                    bidAmount, bidAmount );

          // Assert state
          assert auction.getBids().size() == 2;
      }

  }
```

The class `AuctionLogic` is an arbitrary class with so-called test methods. A *test method* is any method marked with the `@Test` annotation. Optionally, you can assign group names to test methods so that you can assemble a test suite dynamically by combining groups later on.

The test method `highestBidWins()` executes part of the logic for the "Placing a bid" use case. First, an instance of `User` is needed for placing bids—that this, is the same user isn't a concern for this test.

This test can fail several ways, indicating that a business rule has been violated. The first bid gets the auction started (the current maximum and minimum bids are both zero), so you don't expect any failure here. Placing a second bid is the step that must succeed without throwing a `BusinessException`, because the new bid amount is higher than the previous bid amount. Finally, you assert the state of the auction with the Java `assert` keyword and a comparison operation.

You often want to test business logic for failure and expect an exception.

Expecting failures in a test

The auction system has a pretty serious bug. If you look at the implementation of `Item.placeBid()` in section 16.1.4, "Designing 'smart' domain models," you can see that you check whether the given new bid amount is higher than any existing bid amount. However, you never check it against the initial starting price of an auction. That means a user can place any bid, even if it's lower than the initial price.

You test this by testing for failure. The following procedure expects an exception:

```java
public class AuctionLogic {

    @Test(groups = "logic")
    public void highestBidWins() { ... }

    @Test(groups = "logic")
    @ExpectedExceptions(BusinessException.class)
    public void initialPriceConsidered() {

        // A user is needed
        User user = new User(...);

        // Create an Item instance
        Item auction = new Item(..., new BigDecimal("200.00") );
```

```
        // Place a bid
        BigDecimal bidAmount = new BigDecimal("100.00");
        auction.placeBid(user, bidAmount,
                        new BigDecimal(0), new BigDecimal(0) );
    }

}
```

Now, placing a bid with a value of 100 has to fail, because the initial starting price of the auction is 200. TestNG requires that this method throws a `BusinessException`—otherwise the test fails. More fine-grained business exception types let you test failures for core parts of the business logic more accurately.

In the end, how many execution paths of your domain model are considered defines your overall business logic test coverage. You can use tools such as *cenqua clover* (http://www.cenqua.com/clover/), which can extract the code coverage percentage of your test suite and provide many other interesting details about the quality of your system.

Let's execute these previous test methods with TestNG and Ant.

Creating and running a test suite

You can create a test suite dozens of ways with TestNG and start the tests. You can call test methods directly with a click of a button in your IDE (after installing the TestNG plug-in), or you can integrate unit testing in your regular build with an Ant task and an XML description of the test suite.

An XML test suite description for the unit tests from the last sections looks as follows:

```
<!DOCTYPE suite SYSTEM "http://testng.org/testng-1.0.dtd" >

<suite name="CaveatEmptor" verbose="2">

    <test name="BusinessLogic">
        <run><include name="logic.*"/></run>

        <packages>
            <package name="auction.test"/>
        </packages>

        <!-- Or just the class...
        <classes>
            <class name="auction.test.AuctionLogic"/>
        </classes>
            -->
    </test>

</suite>
```

A test suite is an assembly of several logical tests—don't confuse this with test methods. A logical test is determined at runtime by TestNG. For example, the logical test with the name BusinessLogic includes all test methods (that is, methods marked with @Test) in classes of the auction.test package. These test methods must belong to a group that starts with the name logic; note that .* is a regular expression meaning "any number of arbitrary characters." Alternatively, you can list the test classes you'd like to consider part of this logical test explicitly, instead of the whole package (or several packages).

You can write some test classes and methods, arrange them in any way that is convenient, and then create arbitrary test assemblies by mixing and matching classes, packages, and named groups. This assembly of logical tests from arbitrary classes and packages and the separation into groups with wildcard matching make TestNG more powerful than many other testing frameworks.

Save the suite description XML file as test-logic.xml in the base directory of your project. Now, run this test suite with Ant and the following target in your build.xml:

```
<taskdef resource="testngtasks" classpathref="project.classpath"/>

<target name="unittest.logic" depends="compile, copymetafiles">
      description="Run logic unit tests with TestNG">

    <delete dir="${basedir}/test-output"/>
    <mkdir  dir="${basedir}/test-output"/>

    <testng outputDir="${basedir}/test-output"
            classpathref="project.classpath">
        <xmlfileset dir="${basedir}">
            <include name="test-logic.xml"/>
        </xmlfileset>
    </testng>

</target>
```

First, the TestNG Ant tasks are imported into the build. Then, the unittest.logic target starts a TestNG run with the suite description file test-logic.xml in the base directory of your project. TestNG creates an HTML report in the outputDir, so you clean this directory every time before running a test.

Call this Ant target and experiment with your first TestNG assembly. Next we discuss integration testing, and how TestNG can support you with flexible configuration of the runtime environment.

16.5.3 *Testing the persistence layer*

Testing the persistence layer means several components have to be exercised and checked to see whether they interact correctly. This means:

- *Testing mappings*—You want to test mappings for syntactical correctness (whether all columns and tables that are mapped match the properties and classes).

- *Testing object state transitions*—You want to test whether an object transitions correctly from transient to persistent to detached state. In other words, you want to ensure that data is saved correctly in the database, that it can be loaded correctly, and that all potential cascading rules for transitive state changes work as expected.

- *Testing queries*—Any nontrivial HQL, `Criteria`, and (possibly) SQL query should be tested for correctness of the returned data.

All these tests require that the persistence layer isn't tested stand-alone but is integrated with a running database-management system. Furthermore, all other infrastructure, such as a Hibernate `SessionFactory` or a JPA `EntityManagerFactory`, must be available; you need a runtime environment that enables any services you want to include in the integration test.

Consider the database-management system on which you want to run these tests. Ideally, this should be the same DBMS product you'll deploy in production for your application. On the other hand, in some cases you may run integration tests on a different system in development—for example, the lightweight HSQL DB. Note that object-state transitions can be tested transparently, thanks to Hibernate's database portability features. Any sophisticated application has mappings and queries that are often tailored for a particular database-management system (with formulas and native SQL statements), so any integration test with a nonproduction database product won't be meaningful. Many DBMS vendors offer free licenses or even lightweight versions of their major database products for development purposes. Consider these before switching to a different database-management system during development.

You must first prepare the test environment and enable the runtime infrastructure before you write any integration unit tests.

Writing a DBUnit superclass

An environment for integration testing of a persistence layer requires that the database-management system is installed and active—we expect that this is taken care of in your case. Next, you need to consider your integration test assembly and how you can execute configuration and tests in the right order.

First, to use your data-access objects you have to start Hibernate—building a `SessionFactory` is the easiest part. More difficult is defining the sequence of configuration operations that are required before and after you run a test. A common sequence is this:

1. Reset the database content to a well-known state. The easiest way to do this is through an automatic export of a database schema with the Hibernate toolset. You then start testing with an empty, clean database.

2. Create any base data for the test by importing the data into the database. This can be done in various ways, such as programmatically in Java code or with tools such as DBUnit (http://www.dbunit.org).

3. Create objects, and execute whatever state transition you want to test, such as saving or loading an object by calling your DAOs in a TestNG test method.

4. Assert the state after a transition by checking the objects in Java code and/ or by executing SQL statements and verifying the state of the database.

Consider several such integration tests. Should you always start from step 1 and export a fresh database schema after every test method, and then import all base data again? If you execute a large number of tests, this can be time consuming. On the other hand, this approach is much easier than deleting and cleaning up after every test method, which would be an additional step.

A tool that can help you with these configuration and preparation steps for each test is DBUnit. You can import and manage data sets easily—for example, a data set that must be reset into a known state for each test run.

Even though TestNG allows you to combine and assemble test suites in any way imaginable, a superclass that encapsulates all configuration and DBUnit setup operations is convenient. Look at a superclass appropriate for integration testing of Hibernate data-access objects in listing 16.2.

Listing 16.2   A superclass for Hibernate integration testing

```
public abstract class HibernateIntegrationTest {

    protected SessionFactory sessionFactory;         ❶

    protected String dataSetLocation;                ❷
    protected List<DatabaseOperation> beforeTestOperations
            = new ArrayList<DatabaseOperation>();
    protected List<DatabaseOperation> afterTestOperations
            = new ArrayList<DatabaseOperation>();
```

```
private ReplacementDataSet dataSet;                    ③

@BeforeTest(groups = "integration-hibernate")          ④
void startHibernate() throws Exception {
    sessionFactory = HibernateUtil.getSessionFactory();
}

@BeforeClass(groups = "integration-hibernate")         ⑤
void prepareDataSet() throws Exception {

    // Check if subclass has prepared everything
    prepareSettings();
    if (dataSetLocation == null)
        throw new RuntimeException(
            "Test subclass needs to prepare a dataset location"
        );

    // Load the base dataset file
    InputStream input =
            Thread.currentThread().getContextClassLoader()
                .getResourceAsStream(dataSetLocation);

    dataSet = new ReplacementDataSet(
                  new FlatXmlDataSet(input)
              );
    dataSet.addReplacementObject("[NULL]", null);
}

@BeforeMethod(groups = "integration-hibernate")        ⑥
void beforeTestMethod() throws Exception {
    for (DatabaseOperation op : beforeTestOperations ) {
        op.execute(getConnection(), dataSet);
    }
}

  @AfterMethod(groups = "integration-hibernate")       ⑦
void afterTestMethod() throws Exception {
    for (DatabaseOperation op : afterTestOperations ) {
        op.execute(getConnection(), dataSet);
    }
}

// Subclasses can/have to override the following methods

protected IDatabaseConnection getConnection() throws Exception {  ⑧

    // Get a JDBC connection from Hibernate
    Connection con =
        ((SessionFactoryImpl)sessionFactory).getSettings()
                .getConnectionProvider().getConnection();

    // Disable foreign key constraint checking
    con.prepareStatement("set referential_integrity FALSE")
        .execute();
```

```
        return new DatabaseConnection( con);
    }
    protected abstract void prepareSettings();
```

```
}
```

---

❶ All tests in a particular suite use the same Hibernate `SessionFactory`.

❷ A subclass can customize the DBUnit database operations that are executed before and after every test method.

❸ A subclass can customize which DBUnit data set should be used for all its test methods.

❹ Hibernate is started before a logical test of the test assembly runs—again, note that `@BeforeTest` doesn't mean before each test method.

❺ For each test (sub)class, a DBUnit data set must be loaded from an XML file, and all null markers have to be replaced with real NULLs.

❻ Before each test method, you execute the required database operations with DBUnit.

❼ After each test method, you execute the required database operations with DBUnit.

❽ By default, you obtain a plain JDBC connection from Hibernate's `Connection-Provider` and wrap it in a DBUnit `DatabaseConnection`. You also disable foreign key constraint checking for this connection.

❾ A subclass must override this method and prepare the data-set file location and operations that are supposed to run before and after each test method.

This superclass takes care of many things at once, and writing integration tests as subclasses is easy. Each subclass can customize which DBUnit data set it wants to work with (we'll discuss these data sets soon) and what operations on that data set (for example, `INSERT` and `DELETE`) have to run before and after a particular test method executes.

Note that this superclass assumes the database is active and a valid schema has been created. If you want to re-create and automatically export the database schema for each test suite, enable the `hibernate.hbm2ddl.auto` configuration option by setting it to `create`. Hibernate then drops the old and exports a fresh database schema when the `SessionFactory` is built.

Next, let's look at the DBUnit data sets.

Preparing the data sets

With the proposed testing strategy, each test (sub)class works with a particular data set. This is merely a decision we made to simplify the superclass; you can use a data set per test method or a single data set for the whole logical test, if you like.

A data set is a collection of data that DBUnit can maintain for you. There are a great many ways to create and work with data sets in DBUnit. We'd like to introduce one of the easiest scenarios, which is often sufficient. First, write a data set into an XML file, in the syntax as required by DBUnit:

```
<?xml version="1.0"?>

<dataset>
    <USERS      USER_ID          ="1"
                OBJ_VERSION      ="0"
                FIRSTNAME        ="John"
                LASTNAME         ="Doe"
                USERNAME         ="johndoe"
                PASSWORD         ="secret"
                EMAIL            ="jd@mail.tld"
                RANK             ="0"
                IS_ADMIN         ="false"
                CREATED          ="2006-09-23 13:45:00"
                HOME_STREET      ="[NULL]"
                HOME_ZIPCODE     ="[NULL]"
                HOME_CITY        ="[NULL]"
                DEFAULT_BILLING_DETAILS_ID ="[NULL]"
    />

    <ITEM />
</dataset>
```

You don't need a DTD for this file, although specifying a DTD lets you verify the syntactical correctness of the data set (it also means that you must convert part of your database schema into a DTD). Each row of data has its own element with the name of the table. For example, one <USERS> element declares the data for one row in the USERS table. Note that you use [NULL] as the token that is replaced by the integration testing superclass with a real SQL NULL. Also note that you can add an empty row for each table that you'd like DBUnit to maintain. In the data set shown here, the ITEM table is part of the data set, and DBUnit can delete any data in that table (which comes in handy later).

Let's assume that this data set is saved in an XML file basedata.xml in the auction.test.dbunit package. Next you'll write a test class that utilizes this data set.

Writing a test class

A *test class* groups test methods that rely on a particular data set. Look at the following example:

```
public class PersistentStateTransitions
                extends HibernateIntegrationTest {

    protected void prepareSettings() {
        dataSetLocation = "auction/test/dbunit/basedata.xml";
        beforeTestOperations.add(DatabaseOperation.CLEAN_INSERT);
    }

    ...

}
```

This is a subclass of `HibernateIntegrationTest`, and it prepares the location of the data set it requires. It also requires that a `CLEAN_INSERT` operation runs before any test method. This DBUnit database operation deletes all rows (effectively cleans the `USERS` and `ITEM` tables) and then inserts the rows as defined in the data set. You have a clean database state for each test method.

DBUnit includes many built-in `DatabaseOperations`, such as `INSERT`, `DELETE`, `DELETE_ALL`, and even `REFRESH`. Check the DBUnit reference documentation for a complete list; we won't repeat it here. Note that you can stack operations:

```
public class PersistentStateTransitions
                extends HibernateIntegrationTest {

    protected void prepareSettings() {
        dataSetLocation = "auction/test/dbunit/basedata.xml";
        beforeTestOperations.add(DatabaseOperation.DELETE_ALL);
        beforeTestOperations.add(DatabaseOperation.INSERT);
        afterTestOperations.add(DatabaseOperation.DELETE_ALL);
    }

    ...

}
```

Before each test method, all content in the data set tables is deleted and then inserted. After each test method, all database content in the data set tables is deleted again. This stack guarantees a clean database state before and after each test method.

You can now write the actual test methods in this test class. The name of the class, `PersistentStateTransition`, hints at what you want to do:

```
@Test(groups = "integration-hibernate")
public void storeAndLoadItem() {

    // Start a unit of work
```

```
sessionFactory.getCurrentSession().beginTransaction();

// Prepare the DAOs
ItemDAOHibernate itemDAO = new ItemDAOHibernate();
itemDAO.setSession( sessionFactory.getCurrentSession() );

UserDAOHibernate userDAO = new UserDAOHibernate();
userDAO.setSession( sessionFactory.getCurrentSession() );

// Prepare a user object
User user = userDAO.findById(11, false);

// Make a new auction item persistent
Calendar startDate = GregorianCalendar.getInstance();
Calendar endDate = GregorianCalendar.getInstance();
endDate.add(Calendar.DAY_OF_YEAR, 3);

Item newItem =
    new Item( "Testitem", "Test Description", user,
              new BigDecimal(123), new BigDecimal(333),
              startDate.getTime(), endDate.getTime() );

itemDAO.makePersistent(newItem);

// End the unit of work
sessionFactory.getCurrentSession()
              .getTransaction().commit();

// Direct SQL query for database state in auto-commit mode
StatelessSession s = sessionFactory.openStatelessSession();
Object[] result = (Object[])
        s.createSQLQuery("select INITIAL_PRICE ip," +
                         "SELLER_ID sid from ITEM")
          .addScalar("ip",  Hibernate.BIG_DECIMAL)
          .addScalar("sid", Hibernate.LONG)
          .uniqueResult();
s.close();

// Assert correctness of state
assert result[0].getClass() == BigDecimal.class;
assert result[0].equals( newItem.getInitialPrice().getValue() );
assert result[1].equals( 11 );

}
```

This test method makes an `Item` instance persistent. Although this looks like a lot of code, there are only a few interesting parts.

A `User` instance is required for this state transition, so the user data you define in the data set is loaded through Hibernate. You have to provide the same identifier value (`11` in the example) you wrote into the data set as the primary key.

When the unit of work commits, all state transitions are completed and the state of the `Session` is synchronized with the database. The final step is the real test, asserting that the database content is in the expected state.

You can test the database state many ways. Obviously, you don't use a Hibernate query or `Session` operation for this purpose, because Hibernate is an additional layer between your test and the real database content. To ensure that you're really hitting the database and that you're seeing the state as is, we recommend that you use an SQL query.

Hibernate makes it easy to execute an SQL query and to check the returned values. In the example, you open a Hibernate `StatelessSession` to create this SQL query. The database connection used in this query is in autocommit mode (`hibernate.connection.autocommit` set to `true`), because you don't start a transaction. This is the perfect use case for `StatelessSession`, because it deactivates any cache, any cascading, any interceptors, or anything that could interfere with your view on the database.

Let's bring this all together in a TestNG test suite and an Ant target.

Running the integration tests

This is the XML test suite descriptor:

```
<!DOCTYPE suite SYSTEM "http://testng.org/testng-1.0.dtd" >

<suite name="CaveatEmptor" verbose="2">

    <test name="PersistenceLayer">
        <groups>
            <run><include name="integration-hibernate.*"/></run>
        </groups>

        <packages>
            <package name="auction.test.dbunit"/>
        </packages>
    </test>

</suite>
```

The logical test `PersistenceLayer` includes all test classes and test methods found in the package `auction.test.dbunit`, if their group name starts with `integration-hibernate`. This is also true for any TestNG configuration methods (those marked with `@BeforeClass` and so on), so you need to place any classes (the superclass, too) with configuration methods in the same package and add them to the same group.

To run this test suite with Ant, replace the name of the XML suite descriptor in the Ant target you wrote in section 16.5.2, "Creating and running a test suite."

We've only scratched the surface of TestNG and DBUnit in the previous examples. There are many more useful options; for example, you can parameterize test methods in TestNG with arbitrary settings in your suite descriptor. You can create a test assembly that starts an EJB 3.0 container server (see the code in chapter 2, section 2.2.3, "Running the application" and the `EJB3IntegrationTest` super-class in the CaveatEmptor download) and then test your EJB layers. We recommend the documentation of TestNG and DBUnit, respectively, as you start building out your testing environment from the base classes and with the strategies we've shown.

You may wonder how you can test mappings and queries, because we've only discussed testing of object-state transitions. First, you can test mappings easily by setting `hibernate.hbm2ddl.auto` to `validate`. Hibernate then verifies the mappings by checking them against database catalog metadata when the `SessionFactory` is built. Second, testing queries is the same as testing object state transitions: Write integration test methods, and assert the state of the returned data.

Finally, we consider load and stress testing, and which aspects you have to focus on if you want to test the performance of your system.

16.5.4 *Considering performance benchmarks*

One of the most difficult things in enterprise application development is guaranteeing performance and scalability of an application. Let's define these terms first.

Performance is usually considered to be the reaction time of a request/response-based application. If you click a button, you expect a response in half a second. Or, depending on the use case, you expect that a particular event (or batch operation) can be executed in a reasonable time frame. Naturally, reasonable depends on the case and usage patterns of some application functionality.

Scalability is the ability of a system to perform reasonably under higher load. Imagine that instead of 1 person clicking 1 button, 5,000 people click a lot of buttons. The better the scalability of a system, the more concurrent users you can pack on it without performance degradation.

We already had much to say about performance. Creating a system that performs well is, in our opinion, synonymous to creating a Hibernate/database application that has no obvious performance bottlenecks. A performance bottleneck can be anything you consider a programming mistake or bad design—for example, the wrong fetching strategy, a wrong query, or bad handling of the `Session` and persistence context. Testing a system for reasonable performance is usually part of the acceptance tests. In practice, performance testing is often done by a dedicated group of end user testers in a lab environment, or with a closed user group in real-world conditions. Pure automated performance tests are rare.

You can also find performance bottlenecks with an automated scalability test; this is the ultimate goal. However, we've seen many stress and load tests in our careers, and most of them didn't consider one or several of the following rules:

- *Test scalability with real-world data sets.* Don't test with a data set that can fit completely into the cache of a hard disk on the database server. Use data that already exists, or use a test data generator to produce test data (for example, TurboData: http://www.turbodata.ca/). Make sure the test data is as close as possible to the data the system will work on in production, with the same amount, distribution, and selectivity.

- *Test scalability with concurrency.* An automated performance test that measures the time it takes to do a single query with a single active user doesn't tell you anything about the scalability of the system in production. Persistence services like Hibernate are designed for high concurrency, so a test without concurrency may even show an overhead you don't expect! As soon as you enable more concurrent units of work and transactions, you'll see how features such as the second-level cache help you to keep up performance.

- *Test scalability with real use cases.* If your application has to process complex transactions (for example, calculating stock market values based on sophisticated statistical models), you should test the scalability of the system by executing these use cases. Analyze your use cases, and pick the scenarios that are prevalent—many applications have only a handful of use cases that are most critical. Avoid writing microbenchmarks that randomly store and load a few thousand objects; the numbers from these kinds of tests are meaningless.

Creating a test environment for the automatic execution of scalability tests is an involved effort. If you follow all our rules, you need to spend some time analyzing your data, your use cases, and your expected system load first. Once you have this information, it's time to set up automated tests.

Typically, a scalability test of a client/server application requires the simulation of concurrently running clients and the collection of statistics for each executed operation. You should consider existing testing solutions, either commercial (such as LoadRunner, http://www.mercury.com/) or open source (such as The Grinder [http://grinder.sourceforge.net/] or JMeter [http://jakarta.apache.org/jmeter/]). Creating tests usually involves writing control scripts for the simulated clients as well as configuring the agents that run on the server processes (for example, for direct execution of particular transactions or the collection of statistics).

Finally, testing performance and (especially) scalability of a system is naturally a separate stage in the lifecycle of a software application. You shouldn't test the scalability of system in the early stages of development. You shouldn't enable the second-level cache of Hibernate until you have a testing environment that was built following the rules we've mentioned.

At a later stage in your project, you may add automated scalability tests to the nightly integration tests. You should test the scalability of your system before going into production, as part of the regular test cycle. On the other hand, we don't recommend delaying any kind of performance and scalability testing until the last minute. Don't try to fix your performance bottlenecks one day before you go into production by tweaking the Hibernate second-level cache. You probably won't succeed.

Consider performance and load testing to be an essential part of your development process, with well-defined stages, metrics, and requirements.

16.6 *Summary*

In this chapter, we looked at layered applications and some important patterns and best practices. We discussed how you can design a web application with Hibernate and implement the Open Session in View pattern. You now know how to create smart domain models and how to separate business logic from controller code. The flexible Command pattern is a major asset in your software design arsenal. We looked at EJB 3.0 components and how you can further simplify a POJO application by adding a few annotations.

Finally, we discussed the persistence layer extensively; you wrote data-access objects and integration tests with TestNG that exercise the persistence layer.

Introducing JBoss Seam

17

This chapter covers

- Web application development with JSF and EJB 3.0
- Improving web applications with Seam
- Integrating Seam with Hibernate Validator
- Managing persistence contexts with Seam

In this last chapter, we show you the *JBoss Seam* framework. Seam is an innovative new framework for web application development with the Java EE 5.0 platform. Seam brings two new standards, JavaServer Faces (JSF) and EJB 3.0, much closer together, by unifying their component and programming models. Most attractive for developers who rely on Hibernate (or any Java Persistence provider in EJB 3.0) is Seam's automatic persistence context management and the first-class constructs it provides for the definition of conversations in the application flow. If you've ever seen a `LazyInitializationException` in your Hibernate application, Seam has the right solutions.

There is much more to be said about Seam, and we encourage you to read this chapter even if you already made a decision for a different framework or if you aren't writing a web application. Although Seam currently targets web applications and also relies on JSF as a presentation framework, other options should be available in the future (you can already use Ajax calls to access Seam components, for example). Furthermore, many central concepts of Seam are currently being standardized and brought back into the Java EE 5.0 platform with the Web Beans JSR 299 (http://www.jcp.org/en/jsr/detail?id=299).

There are many ways to explain Seam and equally many ways to learn Seam. In this chapter, we first look at the problems Seam promises to solve; then, we discuss various solutions and highlight the features that are most appealing to you as a Hibernate user.

17.1 The Java EE 5.0 programming model

Java EE 5.0 is significantly easier to use and much more powerful than its predecessors. Two specifications of the Java EE 5.0 platform that are most relevant for web application developers are JSF and EJB 3.0.

What's so great about JSF and EJB 3.0? We first highlight major concepts and features in each specification. You'll then write a small example with JSF and EJB 3.0 and compare it to the old way of writing web applications in Java (think Struts and EJB 2.x). After that, we'll focus on the issues that are still present and how Seam can make JSF and EJB 3.0 an even more powerful and convenient combination.

Note that it's impossible to cover all of JSF and EJB 3.0 in this chapter. We recommend that you read this chapter together with the Sun Java EE 5.0 tutorial (http://java.sun.com/javaee/5/docs/tutorial/doc/) and browse through the tutorial if you want to know more about a particular subject. On the other hand, if you've already had some contact with JSF or EJB 3.0 (or even Hibernate), you'll likely find learning Seam easy.

17.1.1 Considering JavaServer Faces

JSF simplifies building web user interfaces in Java. As a presentation framework, JSF provides the following high-level features:

- JSF defines an extensible component model for visual components, often called *widgets*.

- JSF defines a component programming model for *backing beans*, or *managed* beans, which contain the application logic.

- JSF defines the interaction between the user interface and the application logic and allows you to bind both together in a flexible fashion.

- JSF allows you to define navigation rules declaratively in XML—that is, which page is displayed for a particular outcome in your application logic.

Let's spend a little more time on each of these features and what makes them useful.

JSF defines a set of built-in visual components that every JSF implementation has to support (such as buttons and input text fields). These visual components are rendered on pages as HTML (and Javascript). At the time of writing, several high-quality open source and commercial JSF widget libraries are available. Ready-made visual components are great for you as a developer; you don't have to code them by hand, and, most important, you don't have to maintain them or make them work on different browsers (which is especially painful if you need more sophisticated visual components that use Javascript).

Pages are created with any HTML templating engine that understands JSF widgets. Although JSP seems like an obvious choice, in our experience it isn't the best. We found that *JavaServer Facelets* (https://facelets.dev.java.net/) is a perfect fit for building JSF views and creating HTML templates that contain JSF widgets. (Another nice bonus of using Facelets is that you get the new unified expression language for free, even without a JSP 2.1-capable servlet container.) We'll use Facelets in all JSF examples in this chapter.

JSF-managed application components, called *backing beans*, make your web application interface work; they contain the application code. These are regular POJOs, and they're defined and wired together in JSF XML configuration files. This wiring supports basic dependency injection, as well as lifecycle management of backing bean instances. The available scopes for a backing bean (where it lives) are the current HTTP request context, the current HTTP session context, and the global application context. You write application logic by creating beans and letting JSF manage their lifecycle in one of these contexts.

You can bind model values from a backing bean to a visual component with an expression language. For example, you create a page with a text input field and bind it to a named backing bean field or getter/setter method pair. This backing bean name is then mapped in JSF configuration to an actual backing bean class, along with a declaration of how an instance of that class should be handled by JSF (in the request, in the HTTP session, or in the application context). The JSF engine automatically keeps the backing bean field (or property) synchronized with the state of the widget as seen (or manipulated) by the user.

JSF is an event-driven presentation framework. If you click a button, a JSF `ActionEvent` is fired and passed to registered listeners. A listener for an action event is again a backing bean you name in your JSF configuration. The backing bean can then react to this event—for example, by saving the current value of a backing bean field (which is bound to a text input widget) into the database. This is a simplified explanation of what JSF does. Internally, each request from the web browser passes through several phases of processing.

A typical request-processing sequence on the server, when you click a button on a JSF page, is as follows (this process is illustrated in figure 17.7):

1 *Restore View* of all widgets (JSF can store the widget state on the server or on the client).

2 *Apply Request Parameters* to update the state of widgets.

3 *Process Validations* that are necessary to validate user input.

4 *Update Model Values* that back the widget by calling the bound fields and setter methods of a backing bean.

5 *Invoke Application*, and pass the action event to listeners.

6 *Render Response* page the user sees.

Obviously a request can take different routes; for example, Render Response may occur after Process Validations, if a validation fails.

A nice illustration of the JSF lifecycle and the processing phases can be found in the already mentioned Sun Java EE 5 tutorial in chapter 9, "The Life Cycle of a JavaServer Faces Page." We'll also get back to the JSF processing model later in this chapter.

Which response is rendered and what page is shown to the user depends on the defined navigation rules and what the outcome of an action event is. Outcomes in JSF are simple strings, like "success" or "failure." These strings are produced by your backing beans and then mapped in a JSF XML configuration file to pages. This is also called *free navigation flow*, for example, you can click the *Back* button in your browser or jump directly to a page by entering its URL.

JSF, combined with Facelets, is a great solution if you're looking for a web framework. On the other hand, the backing beans of your web application—the components that implement the application logic—usually need to access transactional resources (databases, most of the time). This is where EJB 3.0 comes into the picture.

17.1.2 *Considering EJB 3.0*

EJB 3.0 is a Java EE 5.0 standard that defines a programming model for transactional components. For you, as a web application developer, the following features of EJB 3.0 are most interesting:

- EJB 3.0 defines a component programming model that is primarily based on annotations on plain Java classes.

- EJB 3.0 defines stateless, stateful, and message-driven components, and how the runtime environment manages the lifecycle of component instances.

- EJB 3.0 defines how components are wired together, how you can obtain references to components, and how components can call each other.

- EJB 3.0 defines how crosscutting concerns are handled, such as transactions and security. You can also write custom interceptors and wrap them around your components.

- EJB 3.0 standardizes Java Persistence and how you can access an SQL database with automatic and transparent object/relational mapping.

If you want to access an SQL database, you create your domain model entity classes (such as Item, User, Category) and map them with annotations from the Java Persistence specification to a database schema. The EJB 3.0 persistence manager API, the EntityManager, is now your gateway for database operations.

You execute database operations in EJB 3.0 components—for example, stateful or stateless session beans. These beans are plain Java classes, which you enable as EJBs with a few annotations. You then get the container's services, such as automatic dependency injection (you get the EntityManager when you need it) and declarative transaction demarcation on component methods. Stateful session beans help you to keep state for a particular client, for example, if a user has to go through several pages in a conversation with the application.

Can you use EJB 3.0 components and entities as backing beans for JSF actions and widgets? Can you bind a JSF text field widget to a field in your Item entity class? Can a JSF button-click be directly routed to a session bean method?

Let's try this with an example.

17.1.3 *Writing a web application with JSF and EJB 3.0*

The web application you'll create is simple; it has a search screen where users can enter an identifier for a particular item, and a detail screen that appears when the item is found in the database. On this detail screen, users can edit the item's data and save the changes to the database.

(We don't think you should necessarily code this application while reading the examples; later, we make significant improvements by introducing Seam. That's the time to start coding.)

Start with the data model for the entity: an Item.

Creating the entity class and mapping

The Item entity class comes from CaveatEmptor. It's also already annotated and mapped to the SQL database (listing 17.1).

Listing 17.1   An annotated and mapped entity class

```
package auction.model;
import ...;

@Entity
@Table(name = "ITEM")
public class Item implements Serializable {

    @Id @GeneratedValue
    @Column(name = "ITEM_ID")
    private Long id = null;

    @Column(name = "ITEM_NAME", length = 255,
            nullable = false, updatable = false)
    private String name;

    @ManyToOne(fetch = FetchType.LAZY)
    @JoinColumn(name="SELLER_ID",
                nullable = false, updatable = false)
    private User seller;

    @Column(name = "DESCRIPTION", length = 4000, nullable = false)
    private String description;

    @Column( name="INITIAL_PRICE", nullable = false)
```

```
    private BigDecimal initialPrice;

    Item() {}

    // Getter and setter methods...
}
```

This is a simplified version of the CaveatEmptor Item entity, without any collections. Next is the search page that allows users to search for item objects.

Writing the search page with Facelets and JSF

The search page of the application is a page written with Facelets as the templating engine, and it's valid XML. JSF widgets are embedded in that page to create the search form with its input fields and buttons (listing 17.2).

Listing 17.2 The search.xhtml page in XHTML with Facelets

```
<!DOCTYPE html PUBLIC        <——❶
        "-//W3C//DTD XHTML 1.0 Transitional//EN"
        "http://www.w3.org/TR/xhtml1/DTD/xhtml1-transitional.dtd">

<html xmlns="http://www.w3.org/1999/xhtml"         <——┐
      xmlns:ui="http://java.sun.com/jsf/facelets"    ❷
      xmlns:h="http://java.sun.com/jsf/html"
      xmlns:f="http://java.sun.com/jsf/core">

<head>                                                        ❸
    <title>CaveatEmptor - Search items</title>
    <link href="screen.css" rel="stylesheet" type="text/css"/>   <——┘
</head>

<body>                              ❹
<ui:include src="header.xhtml"/>    <——┘

<h:form>   <——❺                                                            ❻
        <span class="errors"><h:message for="itemSearchField"/></span>    <——
                                                                   <——┐
        <div class="entry">                                          ❼
            <div class="label">Enter item identifier:</div>
                                                        ❽
            <div class="input">
                <h:inputText id="itemSearchField"    <——┘
                             size="3" required="true"
                             value="#{itemEditor.itemId}">    ❾
                    <f:validateLongRange minimum="0"/>    <——
                </h:inputText>
            </div>
        </div>

        <div class="entry">
```

```
        <div class="label"> </div>

        <div class="input">
            <h:commandButton value="Search" styleClass="button"
                             action="#{itemEditor.doSearch}"/>
        </div>
    </div>

  </h:form>

  </body>
  </html>
```

❿

❶ Every valid XHTML file needs the right document type declaration.

❷ In addition to the regular XHTML namespace, you import the Facelets and two JSF namespaces for visual HTML components and core JSF components (for example, for input validation).

❸ The page layout is handled with cascading stylesheets (CSS) externalized to a separate file.

❹ A common page header template is imported with <ui:import> from Facelets.

❺ A JSF form (note the h namespace) is an HTML form that, if submitted, is processed by the JSF servlet.

❻ JSF can output messages, such as validation errors.

❼ Each <div> is a label or a form field, styled with the CSS class label or input.

❽ The JSF input text component that renders an HTML input field. The identifier is useful to bind it to error-message output, the size defines the visual size of the input field, and user input is required when this form is submitted. The most interesting part is the *value binding* of the input field to a backing bean (named itemEditor) and a getter/setter method pair (named getItemId()/setItemId()) on that backing bean. This is the data model this input field is bound to, and JSF synchronizes changes automatically.

❾ JSF also supports input validation and comes with a range of built-in validators. Here you declare that user input can't be negative (item identifiers are positive integers).

❿ The submit button of the form has an *action binding* to the method doSearch() of the backing bean named itemEditor. What happens after the action executes depends on the outcome of that method.

This is how the page looks rendered in the browser (figure 17.1).

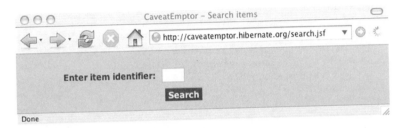

Figure 17.1 The search page with JSF widgets

If you look at the URL, you see that the page has been called with the suffix .jsf; you probably expected to see search.xhtml. The .jsf suffix is a servlet mapping; the JSF servlet runs whenever you call a URL that ends in .jsf, and after installation of Facelets, you configured it in web.xml to use .xhtml internally. In other words, the search.xhtml page is rendered by the JSF servlet.

If you click the Search button without entering a search value, an error message is shown on the page. This also happens if you try to enter a noninteger or nonpositive integer value, and it's all handled by JSF automatically.

If you enter a valid item identifier value, and the backing bean finds the item in the database, you're forwarded to the item-editing screen. (Let's finish the user interface before focusing on the application logic in the backing bean.)

Writing the edit page

The edit page shows the details of the item that has been found in the search and allows the user to edit these details. When the user decides to save his changes, and after all validation is successful, the application shows the search page again.

The source code for the edit page is shown in listing 17.3.

Listing 17.3 The edit.xhtml page with a detail form

```
<!DOCTYPE html PUBLIC
...
<html xmlns=
...
<head>
...
<body>
...
<h2>Editing item: #{itemEditor.itemId}</h2>         ❶

<h:form>

    <span class="errors"><h:messages/></span>
```

```
        <div class="entry">
            <div class="label">Name:</div>
            <div class="input">
                <h:inputText required="true" size="25"
                             value="#{itemEditor.itemName}">
                    <f:validateLength minimum="5" maximum="255"/>
                </h:inputText>
            </div>
        </div>
        <div class="entry">
            <div class="label">Description:</div>
            <div class="input">
                <h:inputTextarea cols="40" rows="4" required="true"
                                 value="#{itemEditor.itemDescription}">
                    <f:validateLength minimum="10" maximum="4000"/>
                </h:inputTextarea>
            </div>
        </div>
        <div class="entry">
            <div class="label">Initial price (USD):</div>
            <div class="input">
                <h:inputText size="6" required="true"
                             value="#{itemEditor.itemInitialPrice}" >
                    <f:converter converterId="javax.faces.BigDecimal"/>
                </h:inputText>
            </div>
        </div>
        <div class="entry">
            <div class="label"> </div>
            <div class="input">
                <h:commandButton value="Save" styleClass="button"
                                 action="#{itemEditor.doSave}"/>
            </div>
        </div>

    </h:form>

</body>
</html>
```

❶ You can place a value-binding expression outside of any component. In this case, the getItemId() method on the itemEditor backing bean is called, and the return value ends up in the HTML page.

❷ Again, a value binding is used to bind the input text field to a getter/setter method pair (or field) in the backing bean.

❸ This action binding references the doSave() method in the itemEditor backing bean. Depending on the outcome of that method, either the page is displayed again (with error messages) or the user is forwarded to the search page.

Figure 17.2 shows the rendered page.

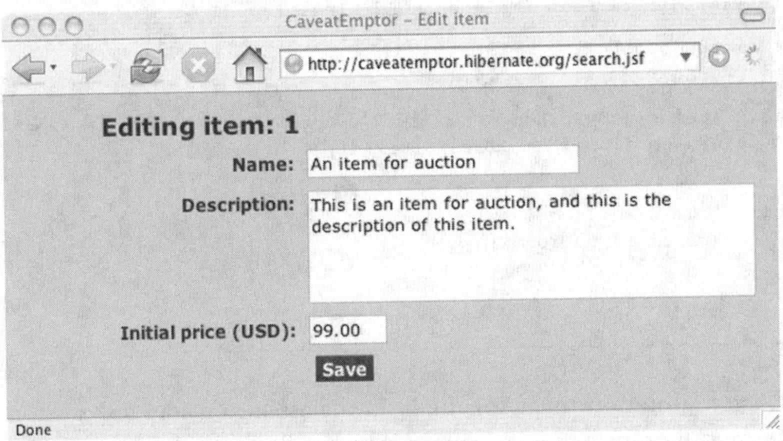

Figure 17.2 The edit page with loaded item details

Why is the URL showing search.jsf? Shouldn't it be edit.jsf? Consider the request processing of the JSF servlet. If the user clicks the Search button on the search.jsf page, the backing bean's doSearch() method runs after input validation. If the outcome of that method triggers a forward to the edit.xhtml page, this document is rendered by the JSF servlet, and the HTML is sent to the browser. The URL doesn't change! Users can't bookmark the edit page, which in this simple application is desirable.

Now that you've completed the top layer of the application, the view, consider the layer that accesses the database (you might call this the business layer). Because accessing an SQL database is a transactional operation, you write an EJB.

Accessing the database in an EJB
If you've worked with EJB 2.x (and Struts) before, the code that accesses the database is most likely procedural code in a stateless session bean. Let's do that in EJB 3.0 (listing 17.4).

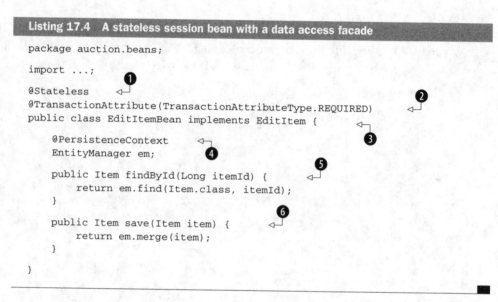

Listing 17.4   A stateless session bean with a data access facade

```
package auction.beans;

import ...;

@Stateless
@TransactionAttribute(TransactionAttributeType.REQUIRED)
public class EditItemBean implements EditItem {

    @PersistenceContext
    EntityManager em;

    public Item findById(Long itemId) {
        return em.find(Item.class, itemId);
    }

    public Item save(Item item) {
        return em.merge(item);
    }

}
```

❶ A @Stateless annotation turns this plain Java class into a stateless session bean. At runtime, a pool of instances is prepared, and each client that requests a session bean gets an instance from the pool to execute a method.

❷ All methods that are called on this session bean are wrapped in a system transaction, which enlists all transactional resources that may be used during that procedure. This is also the default if you don't annotate the bean.

❸ A session bean needs an interface. Usually you implement this interface directly. The EditItem interface has two methods.

❹ When the runtime container hands out a session bean instance from the pool, it injects an EntityManager with a (fresh) persistence context scoped to the transaction.

❺ If a client calls findById(), a system transaction starts. The EntityManager operation executes an SQL query in that transaction; the persistence context is flushed and closed when the transaction commits (when the method returns). The returned Item entity instance is in detached state.

❻ If a client calls save(), a system transaction starts. The given detached instance is merged into a (new) persistence context. Any changes made on the detached Item instance are flushed and committed to the database. A new handle to the now up-to-date Item instance is returned. This new Item instance is again in detached state when the method returns, and the persistence context is closed.

You can call the session bean shown in listing 17.4 a *data access object* (DAO). It can also be a *session facade*. The application isn't complex enough to make a clear distinction; if more nondata access methods were added to its interface, the session bean would represent part of the business layer interface with a traditional (mostly procedural) session facade.

A piece is still missing from the puzzle: The JSF input widgets and buttons have value and action bindings to a backing bean. Is the backing bean the same as the session bean, or do you have to write another class?

Connecting the layers with a backing bean

Without Seam, you have to write a backing bean that connects your JSF widget state and actions to the transactional stateless session bean. This backing bean has the getter and setter methods that are referenced with expressions in the pages. It can also talk to the session bean and execute transactional operations. The code for the backing bean is shown in listing 17.5.

Listing 17.5 A JSF backing bean component connects the layers.

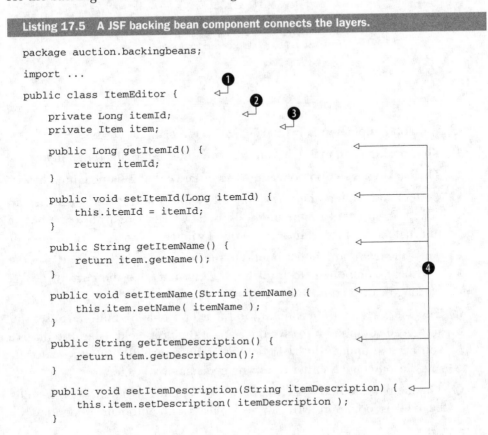

```
package auction.backingbeans;

import ...

public class ItemEditor {          1

    private Long itemId;           2
    private Item item;             3

    public Long getItemId() {
        return itemId;
    }

    public void setItemId(Long itemId) {
        this.itemId = itemId;
    }

    public String getItemName() {
        return item.getName();
    }                                               4

    public void setItemName(String itemName) {
        this.item.setName( itemName );
    }

    public String getItemDescription() {
        return item.getDescription();
    }

    public void setItemDescription(String itemDescription) {
        this.item.setDescription( itemDescription );
    }
```

```
public BigDecimal getItemInitialPrice() {
    return item.getInitialPrice();
}
public void setItemInitialPrice(BigDecimal itemInitialPrice) {
    this.item.setInitialPrice( itemInitialPrice );
}

public String doSearch() {
    item = getEditItemEJB().findById(itemId);
    return item != null ? "found" : null;
}

public String doSave() {
    item = getEditItemEJB().save(item);
    return "success";
}

private EditItem getEditItemEJB() {
    try {
        return (EditItem)
                new InitialContext()
                    .lookup("caveatemptor/EditItemBean/local");
    } catch (NamingException ex) {
        throw new RuntimeException(ex);
    }
}
}
```

❶ You don't implement any interfaces; this is a plain Java class.

❷ The backing bean maintains an item identifier internally with a field.

❸ The backing bean also holds the `Item` instance that is being edited by a user.

❹ Getter and setter methods for all value bindings in `search.xhtml` and `edit.xhtml`. These are the methods used by JSF to synchronize the backing beans internal model state with the state of UI widgets.

❺ The `doSearch()` method is bound to the action of a JSF button. It uses the EJB session bean component to find the `Item` instance for the current `itemId` in the backing bean. Its outcome is either the string `found` or `null`.

❻ The `doSave()` method is bound to the action of a JSF button. It uses the EJB session bean component to save the state of the `item` field. (Because this is a merge, you have to update the `item` field with the returned value, the state after merging.) Its outcome is either the string `success` or an exception.

❼ The helper method `getEditItemEJB()` obtains a handle on the EJB session bean. This lookup in JNDI can be replaced with automatic dependency injection if the runtime environment supports the Java Servlet 2.5 specification. (At the time of writing, Tomcat 5.5 implements only Java Servlets 2.4, and Tomcat 6 is in alpha stage.)

The backing bean is a component that is managed by the JSF runtime. The expressions you use in the pages refer to a backing bean by name, itemEditor. In the JSF XML configuration file (WEB-INF/faces-config.xml usually), you map this name to the backing bean class (listing 17.6).

Listing 17.6   A JSF configuration describes the backing bean and navigation flow.

```
<?xml version="1.0"?>
<!DOCTYPE faces-config PUBLIC
    "-//Sun Microsystems, Inc.//DTD JavaServer Faces Config 1.0//EN"
    "http://java.sun.com/dtd/web-facesconfig_1_1.dtd" >

<faces-config>

    <managed-bean>
        <managed-bean-name>itemEditor</managed-bean-name>
        <managed-bean-class>
            auction.backingbeans.ItemEditor
        </managed-bean-class>
        <managed-bean-scope>session</managed-bean-scope>
    </managed-bean>

    <navigation-rule>
        <from-view-id>/search.xhtml</from-view-id>
        <navigation-case>
            <from-outcome>found</from-outcome>
            <to-view-id>/edit.xhtml</to-view-id>
        </navigation-case>
    </navigation-rule>

    <navigation-rule>
        <from-view-id>/edit.xhtml</from-view-id>
        <navigation-case>
            <from-outcome>success</from-outcome>
            <to-view-id>/search.xhtml</to-view-id>
        </navigation-case>
    </navigation-rule>

</faces-config>
```

This application has one backing bean and two navigation rules. The backing bean is declared with the name itemEditor and implemented by auction.backingBeans.ItemEditor. Expressions in JSF pages can now reference methods and fields of that backing bean in a loosely coupled fashion, by name. The JSF servlet manages instances of the backing bean, one instance for each HTTP session.

Let's take this one step further: An expression in a JSF page is a string, such as #{itemEditor.itemId}. This expression basically results in a search for a variable named itemEditor. Searched, in that order, are the current request, the current HTTP session, and the current application context. If a JSF page renders and this expression has to be evaluated, then either a variable with that name is found in the HTTP session context, or the JSF servlet creates a new backing bean instance and binds it into the HTTP session context.

The navigation rules declare which page is rendered after an action outcome. This is a mapping from strings, returned by actions, to pages.

Your application is now complete; it's time to analyze it in more detail.

17.1.4 Analyzing the application

Possibly you look at the code in the previous sections and think, "This was a lot of code to write to put four form fields onto web pages and connect them to four columns in the database." Or, if you've spent a lot of time with EJB 2.x and Struts, you'll probably say, "This is great: I don't have to manage the HTTP session myself anymore, and all the EJB boilerplate code is gone."

You're right either way. Java EE 5.0 and especially JSF and EJB 3.0 are a significant step forward for Java web applications, but not everything is perfect. We'll now look at the advantages of Java EE 5.0 and compare it to J2EE 1.4 and web frameworks before JSF. But we'll also try to find things that can be improved, code that can be avoided, and strategies that can be simplified. This is where Seam comes in later.

Comparing the code to J2EE

If you have a J2EE 1.4/Struts background, this JSF and EJB 3.0 application already looks much more appealing. There are fewer artifacts than in a traditional Java web application—for example, you can detach an Item instance from the session bean facade and transfer it into the JSF backing bean. With EJB 2.x entity beans, you needed a data transfer object (DTO) to do this.

The code is much more compact. With EJB 2.x, the session bean must implement the SessionBean interface with all its maintenance methods. In EJB 3.0, this is resolved with a simple @Stateless annotation. There is also no Struts ActionForm code that manually binds the state of an HTML form field to an instance variable in the action listener.

Overall, the application is transparent, with no obscure calls that maintain values in the HTTP session or in the HTTP request. JSF transparently puts and looks up values in these contexts.

If you consider the object/relational mapping of the Item class, you'll probably agree that a few annotations on a POJO are simpler than a deployment descriptor for an EJB 2.x entity bean. Furthermore, object/relational mapping as defined by Java Persistence is not only much more powerful and feature-rich than EJB 2.x. entity beans, but also a lot easier to use (even compared to native Hibernate).

What we couldn't show in a simple application is the power behind JSF and EJB 3.0. JSF is amazingly flexible and extensible; you can write your own HTML widgets, you can hook into the processing phases of a JSF request, and you can even create your own view layer (if Facelets isn't what you want) without much effort. EJB 3.0 is much easier to tame than EJB 2.x, and it also has features (such as interceptors and dependency injection) that have never before been available in a standardized Java programming model.

The application can easily be tested with a testing framework like JUnit or TestNG. All classes are plain Java classes; you can instantiate them, set (mock) dependencies manually, and run a test procedure.

However, there is room for improvement.

Improving the application

The first thing that stands out in this JSF/EJB 3.0 application is the JSF backing bean. What's the purpose of this class? It's required by JSF, because you need to bind values and actions to its fields and methods. But the code doesn't do anything useful: It passes any action to an EJB, one to one. Worse, it's the artifact with the most lines of code.

You might argue that it decouples the view from the business layer. That seems reasonable, if you use your EJB with a different view layer (say, a rich client). Still, if the application is a simple web application, the backing bean results in tighter coupling between the layers. Any change you make to either the view or the business layer requires changes to the component with the most lines of code. If you want to improve the code, get rid of the artificial layering and remove the backing bean. There is no reason why an EJB shouldn't be the backing bean. A programming model shouldn't force you to layer your application (it shouldn't restrict you, either). To improve the application, you need to collapse artificial layers.

The application doesn't work in several browser windows. Imagine that you open the search page in two browser windows. In the first, you search for item 1;

in the second, you search for item 2. Both browser windows show you an edit screen with the details of item 1 and item 2. What happens if you make changes to item 1 and click Save? The changes are made on item 2! If you click Save in the first browser window, you work on the state that is present in the HTTP session, where the backing bean lives. However, the backing bean no longer holds item 1—the current state is now the state of the second browser window, editing item 2. In other words, you started two conversations with the application, but the conversations weren't isolated from each other. The HTTP session isn't the right context for concurrent conversation state; it's shared between browser windows. You can't fix this easily. Making this (trivial) application work in several browser windows requires major architectural changes. Today, users expect web applications to work in several browser windows.

The application leaks memory. When a JSF page first tries to resolve the `item-Editor` variable, a new instance of `ItemEditor` is bound to the variable in the HTTP session context. This value is never cleaned up. Even if the user clicks Save on the edit screen, the backing bean instance stays in the HTTP session until the user logs out or the HTTP session times out. Imagine that a much more sophisticated application has many forms and many backing beans. The HTTP session grows as the user clicks through the application, and replicating the HTTP session to other nodes in a cluster gets more expensive with every click. If a user comes back to the item search screen, after working with another module of the application, old data is shown in the forms. One solution for this problem would be manual cleanup of the HTTP session at the end of a conversation, but there is no easy way to do this. With JSF and EJB 3.0, you must code this manually. In our experience, handling variables and values in the HTTP session manually is a common source of issues that are incredibly difficult to track down.

The flow of the application is difficult to visualize and control. How do you know where clicking the Search button will take you? At a minimum, you have to look into two files: the backing bean, which returns string outcomes, and the JSF XML configuration file, which defines the page shown for a particular outcome. There is also the ever-present problem of the Back button in the browser, a nasty problem in any conversation that has more than two screens.

Think also about the *business process*. How can you define that your flow of pages is part of a larger business process? Imagine that searching and editing an item is only one task in a business process that involves many more steps—for example, as part of a review process. No tools or strategies help you integrate business process management in your application. Today, you can no longer afford to ignore the business processes of which your applications is a part; you need a programming model that supports business-process management.

Finally, this application includes too much XML. There is no way around metadata in the application, but not all of it has to be in an XML file. Metadata in XML files is great if it changes independently from code. This may be true for navigation rules, but it probably isn't true for the declaration of backing beans and the context they live in. This kind of metadata grows linearly with the size of your application—every backing bean must be declared in XML. Instead, you should put an annotation on your class that says, "I'm a backing bean for JSF, and I live inside the HTTP session (or any other) context." It's unlikely that your class will suddenly change its role without any changes to the class code.

If you agree with this analysis, you'll like Seam.

17.2 *Improving the application with Seam*

The web application you've written to search and edit web items can be improved if you add Seam into the mix. You start with basic Seam features:

- Seam makes the JSF backing bean unnecessary. You can bind JSF widget values and actions directly to EJB stateful and stateless session beans. Seam introduces a unified component model: All your classes can be turned into Seam components with annotations. Components are wired together in a loosely coupled fashion, with string expressions.

- Seam introduces new contexts and manages component scope automatically. This rich context model includes logical contexts that are meaningful to the application, such as a *conversation* or *business-process* context.

- Seam introduces a stateful programming model, which is great for conversations. A stateful application with Seam-managed conversations works in multiple browser windows with no extra effort.

This is a short list of what Seam can do; there is much more that you'll put to use later. Let's first create a basic conversational, stateful, simple Seam application. Your first step is Seam setup and configuration.

If you want to follow the examples with code, download the CaveatEmptor package for Seam from http://caveatemptor.hibernate.org, and open it in your IDE. This is also a good starting point if you want to code your own Seam project later.

17.2.1 Configuring Seam

Figure 17.3 shows the files before and after the changes you make to the web application in the following sections.

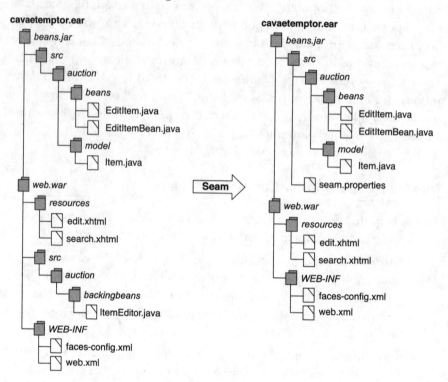

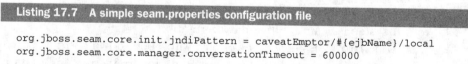

Figure 17.3   The application archive before and after Seam was introduced

Two major changes are made: The JSF backing bean is no longer necessary, and the beans.jar archive has a new file, seam.properties. This file contains two Seam configuration options for this simple application (listing 17.7).

Listing 17.7   A simple seam.properties configuration file

```
org.jboss.seam.core.init.jndiPattern = caveatEmptor/#{ejbName}/local
org.jboss.seam.core.manager.conversationTimeout = 600000
```

The first setting is necessary for Seam to integrate with an EJB 3.0 container. Because Seam is now responsible for wiring component instances at runtime, it needs to know how to obtain EJBs through lookup. The JNDI pattern shown here is for JBoss application server. (Seam runs on any Java EE 5.0 server and even with and without EJB 3.0 in regular Tomcat. We think it's most convenient if you start with JBoss application server, because you don't need to install any extra services.)

To completely integrate Seam with EJB 3.0, Seam also needs to intercept all calls to your EJBs. This is easy to do, thanks to EJB 3.0 support for custom interceptors. You won't see any interceptors in the code of your classes, because they're usually defined with a global wildcard that matches all EJBs in META-INF/ejb-jar.xml (not shown here). If you download a Seam example, it will have this file.

The second setting in seam.properties defines that Seam can destroy an inactive user conversation after 600,000 milliseconds (10 minutes). This setting frees up memory in the HTTP session when a user decides to go to lunch.

The seam.properties file is not only a configuration file for Seam—it's also a marker. When Seam starts up, it scans the classpath and all archives for Seam components (classes with the right annotation). However, scanning all JARs would be too expensive, so Seam only scans JAR files and directories recursively that have a seam.properties file in the root path. Even if you don't have any configuration settings, you need an empty seam.properties file in the archive with your Seam component classes.

You can find more Seam configuration options, and the integration with JSF and the servlet container, in web.xml and faces-config.xml. We'll get back to faces-config.xml later; web.xml isn't interesting (see the commented file in the CaveatEmptor package).

Seam can also be configured with a components.xml file in the WARs WEB-INF directory. You'll use that later when more complex configuration of components is required. (Much of Seam is written as Seam components. The string `org.jboss.seam.core.manager` is a component name, and `conversationTimeout` is a property you can access like any other component property.)

Your next step is replacing the JSF backing bean with a Seam component.

17.2.2 *Binding pages to stateful Seam components*

The search.xhtml page doesn't change at all; review the code in listing 17.2. This page has a value binding to `itemEditor.itemId` and an action binding to `itemEditor.doSearch`. When the page is rendered by the JSF servlet, these expressions are evaluated, and the widgets are bound to the respective methods in the `itemEditor` bean.

The EJB component interface

The itemEditor bean is now an EJB. The interface of this EJB is EditItem.java (listing 17.8).

Listing 17.8   The interface of a stateful component

```
package auction.beans;

import ...

public interface EditItem {

    // Value binding methods
    public Long getItemId();
    public void setItemId(Long itemId);

    public Item getItem();

    // Action binding methods
    public String doSearch();
    public String doSave();

    // Cleanup routine
    public void destroy();

}
```

The first two methods are the getter and setter for the value binding of the search input text field of the page. The getItem() method (you don't need a setter here) will be used later by the edit page. The doSearch() method is bound to the Search button, doSave() will be bound to a button on the edit page.

This is an interface for a stateful component. A stateful component is instantiated when it's first requested—for example, because a page is rendered for the first time. Every stateful component needs a method that the runtime environment can call when the component is destroyed. You could use the doSave() method and say that the component's lifecycle ends when this method completes, but you'll see in a minute why a separate method is cleaner.

Next, let's look at the implementation of this interface.

The EJB component implementation

The standard stateful component in EJB 3.0 is a stateful session bean. The implementation in EditItemBean.java is a POJO class with a few extra annotations. In listing 17.9, all Seam annotations are shown in bold.

Listing 17.9 The implementation of a stateful component

```
package auction.beans;

import ...                              ❶

@Name("itemEditor")                        ❷
@Scope(ScopeType.CONVERSATION)

@Stateful         ❸
public class EditItemBean implements EditItem {

    @PersistenceContext      ❹
    EntityManager em;
                             ❺
    private Long itemId;
    public Long getItemId() { return itemId; }
    public void setItemId(Long itemId) { this.itemId = itemId; }

    private Item item;
    public Item getItem() { return item; }      ❻

    @Begin
    public String doSearch() {
        item = em.find(Item.class, itemId);

        if (item == null)
            FacesMessages.instance().add(
                "itemSearchField",
                new FacesMessage("No item found.")
            );

        return item != null ? "found" : null;
    }
                  ❼
    @End
    public String doSave() {                    •
        item = em.merge(item);
        return "success";
    }
                    ❽
    @Destroy
    @Remove
    public void destroy() {}

}
```

❶ The Seam @Name annotation declares the name for this Seam component. It also turns this EJB into a Seam component. You can now reference this component anywhere under this name.

❷ When an instance of this component is required, Seam instantiates it for you. Seam puts the instance into a context under its name. Here's a formal description:

An instance of `EditItem` is managed by Seam in the conversation context, as a value of the contextual variable `itemEditor`.

❸ A POJO needs the EJB 3.0 `@Stateful` annotation to become a stateful session bean.

❹ The EJB 3.0 container injects an `EntityManager` with a fresh persistence context into this bean, before a method is called by any client of the bean. The persistence context is closed when the method returns (assuming this method call is also the scope of a system transaction, which is the default here).

❺ This stateful component holds state internally, in the fields `itemId` and `item`. The state is exposed with property accessor methods.

❻ A Seam `@Begin` annotation marks a method that begins a long-running conversation. If a JSF action triggers a call to this method, Seam maintains the state of this component across HTTP requests. The `doSearch()` method returns a string outcome (or `null`) and generates a JSF message that can be rendered on a page. The Seam `FacesMessages` helper makes this message-passing easy.

❼ A Seam `@End` annotation marks a method that ends a long-running conversation. If a JSF action triggers a call to this method, and the method returns, Seam will destroy the component's state and no longer maintain it across HTTP requests.

❽ The Seam `@Destroy` annotation marks the method that is called by Seam when the component state has to be destroyed (when the end of the conversation has been reached). This is useful for internal cleanup (there is nothing to do in this case). The EJB 3.0 `@Remove` annotation marks the method that a client (Seam, in this case) has to call to remove the stateful session bean instance. These two annotations usually appear on the same method.

Why don't you mark the `doSave()` method with `@End`, `@Destroy`, and `@Remove`? The `doSave()` method might throw an exception, and this exception has to roll back any system transaction. Seam, however, logs and swallows any exception thrown by its `@Destroy` method, so you frequently see empty destroy methods in stateful Seam components. Furthermore, the component instance is needed for a little while after the saving of an item, to render a response.

This EJB implementation encapsulates all application logic; there is no more Java code anywhere else (well, there is the `Item` entity class). If you ignore trivial code, the application logic is only four lines in the two action methods.

Two more changes are necessary to make the application work. Some value bindings in edit.xhtml need to be modified, and the block of XML that defined the old JSF backing bean can be removed from faces-config.xml.

Binding values and actions

Open edit.xhtml, and change the value bindings of the JSF input widgets as shown in listing 17.10.

```
...
<h2>Editing item: #{itemEditor.itemId}</h2>

<h:form>

    <span class="errors"><h:messages/></span>

    <div class="entry">
        <div class="label">Name:</div>
        <div class="input">
            <h:inputText required="true" size="25"
                         value="#{itemEditor.item.name}">
                <f:validateLength minimum="5" maximum="255"/>
            </h:inputText>
        </div>
    </div>
    <div class="entry">
        <div class="label">Description:</div>
        <div class="input">
            <h:inputTextarea cols="40" rows="4" required="true"
                             value="#{itemEditor.item.description}">
                <f:validateLength minimum="10" maximum="4000"/>
            </h:inputTextarea>
        </div>
    </div>

    <div class="entry">
        <div class="label">Initial price (USD):</div>
        <div class="input">
            <h:inputText size="6" required="true"
                         value="#{itemEditor.item.initialPrice}" >
                <f:converter converterId="javax.faces.BigDecimal"/>
            </h:inputText>
        </div>
    </div>

    <div class="entry">
        <div class="label"> </div>
        <div class="input">
            <h:commandButton value="Save" styleClass="button"
                             action="#{itemEditor.doSave}"/>
        </div>
    </div>

</h:form>
...
```

The bindings that changed are the expressions for the name, description, and initial price input fields. They now reference `itemEditor.item`, which can be resolved to the Seam component's `getItem()` method. JSF calls `getName()` and `setName()` on the returned `Item` entity to synchronize the state of the widget. The same technique is used to bind and synchronize the description and initial price of the item. When the user enters a new price, the `initialPrice` of the `Item` instance that is held by the `itemEditor` component is automatically updated.

The action binding for the Save button doesn't change—the method `doSave()` of the `itemEditor` component is still the right listener. You can see how logical component names and the expression language allow you to couple the view and the business layer easily and not too tightly.

Finally, update faces-config.xml as shown in listing 17.11.

Listing 17.11   The JSF configuration file without backing beans

```
...

<faces-config>

    <navigation-rule>
        <from-view-id>/search.xhtml</from-view-id>
        <navigation-case>
            <from-outcome>found</from-outcome>
            <to-view-id>/edit.xhtml</to-view-id>
        </navigation-case>
    </navigation-rule>
    <navigation-rule>
        <from-view-id>/edit.xhtml</from-view-id>
        <navigation-case>
            <from-outcome>success</from-outcome>
            <to-view-id>/search.xhtml</to-view-id>
        </navigation-case>
    </navigation-rule>

    <!-- Integrate Seam with the JSF request processing model -->
    <lifecycle>
        <phase-listener>
            org.jboss.seam.jsf.SeamPhaseListener
        </phase-listener>
    </lifecycle>

</faces-config>
```

Compare this to the previous JSF configuration in listing 17.6. The backing bean declaration is gone (moved to two Seam annotations on the EJB). The phase listener is new: Seam has to hook into the JSF servlet and listen to the processing of every HTTP request. A custom JSF phase listener integrates Seam with JSF.

We presented quite a few new concepts, which you probably have never seen if this is your first contact with Seam. Let's analyze the application in more detail and find out whether the issues we identified earlier for the plain JSF and EJB 3.0 application have been resolved.

17.2.3 *Analyzing the Seam application*

The interface of the web application hasn't changed; it looks the same. The only thing your users will probably notice is that they can search and edit items in several browser windows without overlapping state and data modifications.

Seam promotes a strong and well-defined stateful application programming model. Let's follow the flow of the application (figure 17.4) and find out how this works internally.

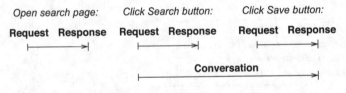

Figure 17.4 The request/response flow of the application

Opening the search page

When you open a browser window and enter the /search.jsf URL, an HTTP GET request is sent to the JSF servlet. The JSF processing lifecycle begins (figure 17.5).

Nothing really interesting happens until the JSF servlet enters the Render Response phase of the request processing. There is no view to restore and no HTTP request parameters that must be applied to the view components (the widgets).

When the response, the search.xhtml file, is rendered, JSF uses a variable resolver to evaluate the #{itemEditor.itemId} value binding. The Seam variable resolver is smarter than the standard JSF variable resolver. It searches for `item-Editor` not in the HTTP request, the HTTP session, and the global application context, but in Seams logical contexts. You're right if you think these logical contexts are the same—we'll have much more to say about this in a moment. For now, think about Seam contexts as variable holders that are searched hierarchically, from the context with the narrowest scope (the current *event*) to the context with the widest scope (the current *application*).

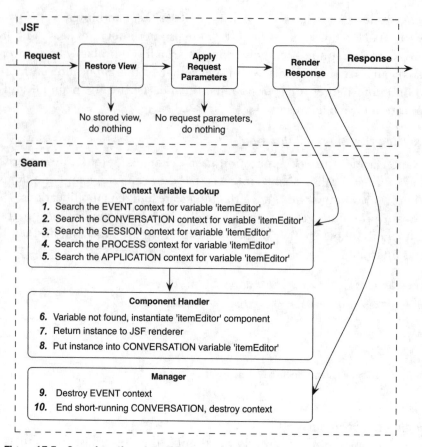

Figure 17.5   Seam is active when JSF renders the response, the search page.

The variable `itemEditor` can't be found. So, Seam's component handler starts looking for a Seam component with that name. It finds the stateful session bean you've written and creates an instance. This EJB instance is then given to the JSF page renderer, and the renderer puts the return value of `getItemId()` into the search input text field. The method returns `null`, so the field is empty when you open the page for the first time.

The Seam component handler also realizes that the stateful session bean had an `@Scope(CONVERSATION)` annotation. The instance is therefore put into the conversation context, as a value of the contextual variable `itemEditor`, the name of the component.

When the page is rendered completely, Seam is invoked again (through the Seam phase listener). The Seam *event* context has a small scope: It's able to hold variables only during a single HTTP request. Seam destroys this context and everything inside (nothing you currently need).

Seam also destroys the current conversation context and with it the `itemEdi-tor` variable that was just created. This may surprise you—you probably expected the stateful session bean to be good for several requests. However, the scope of the conversation context is a single HTTP request, if nobody promotes it to a long-running conversation during that request. You promote a short single-request conversation to a long-running conversation by calling a component method that has been marked with `@Begin`. This didn't happen in this request.

The search page is now displayed by the browser, and the application waits for user input and a click of the Search button.

Searching for an item

When a user clicks the Search button, an HTTP POST request is send to the server and processed by JSF (figure 17.6). You have to look at the source code of search.xhtml and `EditItemBean` to understand this illustration.

Stored in the previous request (usually in the HTTP session on the server), JSF now finds a widget tree that represents the view (search.xhtml) and re-creates it internally. This widget tree is small: It has a form, an input text field and a submit button. In *Apply Request Parameters*, all user input is taken from the HTTP request and synchronized with the state of the widgets. The input text field widget now holds the search string entered by the user.

> **TIP** *Debugging the JSF widget tree*—Facelets can show you the JSF widget tree. Put `<ui:debug hotkey="D"/>` anywhere in your page, and open the page in your browser (as a JSF URL, of course). Now press Ctrl+Shift+d, and a pop-up window with the JSF widget/component tree opens. If you click Scoped Variables, you can see where Seam internally stores its contexts and managers (this probably isn't very interesting if you are not a Seam developer).

During Process Validations, the JSF validator ensures that the search string entered by the user is a nonnegative integer and that the input value is present. If validation fails, the JSF servlet jumps to the Render Response phase and renders the search.xhtml page again with error messages (the processing of this phase looks like in figure 17.6).

After validation, JSF synchronizes the values of the model objects that have been bound to widgets. It calls `itemEditor.setItemId()`. This variable is resolved by Seam, with a lookup in all Seam contexts. Because no `itemEditor` variable is found in any context, a new instance of `EditItemBean` is created and placed into

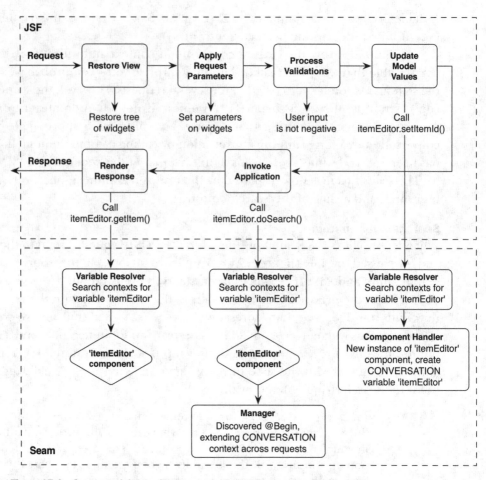

Figure 17.6 **Seam participates in the processing of the search action.**

the conversation context. The `setItemId()` method is called on this stateful session bean instance.

JSF now executes the action of the request by calling the bound method `item-Editor.doSearch`. Seam resolves the `itemEditor` variable and finds it in the conversation context. The `doSearch()` method is called on the `EditItemBean` instance, and the EJB 3.0 container handles transaction and persistence context during that call. Two things happen during the call: The `item` member variable of the `itemEditor` now holds an `Item` instance found in the database (or `null`, if nothing was found), and the `@Begin` annotation promotes the current conversation to a long-running conversation. The conversation context is held by Seam until a method with an @End annotation is called.

The doSearch() method returns the string found, or null. This outcome is evaluated by JSF, and the navigation rules from faces-config.xml apply. If the outcome is null, the search.xhtml page is rendered with the *Item not found* error message. If the outcome is found, the navigation rules declare that the edit.xhtml page is rendered.

During rendering of the edit.xhtml page, the variable itemEditor must be resolved again by JSF. Seam finds the itemEditor context variable in the conversation context, and JSF binds values of widgets on the page (text output, text input) to the properties of the item instance returned by itemEditor.getItem().

> **TIP** *Browsing the Seam contexts*—You can debug a Seam application more easily if you use the Seam debugging screen. This screen must be enabled. To do so, edit your seam.properties file and add org.jboss. seam.core.init.debug = true. Now, access the URL /debug.jsf to browse the Seam contexts for this browser window. You can see all the variables and the values that are in the current conversation, *session*, *process*, and *application* contexts.

At the end of the request, Seam destroys its event context. The conversation context isn't destroyed; the user of the application started a long-running conversation by executing a search. The application waits for user input while showing the edit page. If the user searches again in another browser window, a second, concurrently running conversation is started and promoted to a long-running conversation. The two conversations and their contexts are isolated automatically by Seam.

Editing an item

When the user clicks Save, the edit form is submitted to the server with an HTTP POST request (figure 17.7).

The view that is restored in this request is edit.xhtml, JSF recreates an internal widget tree of the form and all its fields and applies the HTTP request values. Validation is slightly more complex; you've defined a few more JSF validators on the edit.xhtml page.

After successful validation, JSF updates the bound model values by calling the setter methods on the Item instance returned by itemEditor.getItem(). The itemEditor binding resolves (through Seam) to a contextual variable in the current conversation context. Seam extended the conversation context into the

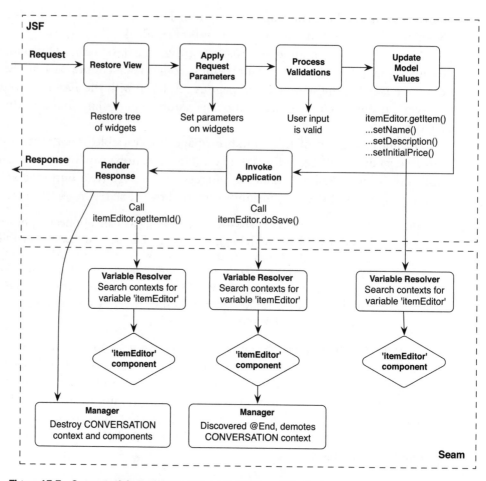

Figure 17.7   Seam participates in the processing of the edit action.

current request, because it was promoted to a long-running conversation in the previous request.

Next, `itemEditor.doSave()` is called; the variable is again resolved in the *conversation* context. The code in `EditItemBean` either throws an exception (if the EJB 3.0 container or the `EntityManager` throw an exception) or returns the string outcome `success`. The method is marked as `@End`, so the Seam manager marks the current conversation for cleanup after the Render Response phase.

The string outcome `success` is mapped to /search.xhtml in the JSF navigation rules. During Render Response, the value bindings on the search.xhtml page must be resolved. The only value binding is `#{itemEditor.itemId}`, so Seam again tries to find the `itemEditor` component in all contexts. The `itemEditor` from the (demoted but still active) conversation context is used, and `getItemId()` returns a value. The user therefore sees the input field not empty, but showing the same search value that was entered at the beginning of the conversation.

When Render Response completes, Seam removes the demoted conversation context and destroys all stateful components instances that live in that context. The `destroy()` method is called on the `EditItemBean`. Because it's marked with `@Remove`, the EJB 3.0 container also cleans up the stateful session bean internally. The user now sees the search page and can begin another conversation.

If you've never used JSF, this is a lot of new information to digest. On the other hand, if you're familiar with JSF, you can see that Seam is basically listening to the processing phases of the JSF servlet and replacing the variable resolver for value and action bindings with a more powerful variation.

We've barely scratched the surface of Seam with this trivial application. Let's discuss some more interesting and advanced features of Seam that make creating complex web applications with a database back end just as easy.

17.3 *Understanding contextual components*

In the previous sections, you've turned the basic JSF and EJB 3.0 web application into a stateful, conversational Seam application. Doing so resulted in less code and improved the application's functionality. You shouldn't stop there—Seam has more to offer.

You can wire Seam components together in a contextual fashion. This is a powerful concept that can have a deep impact on how you design a stateful application. In our experience, it's one of the major reasons why Seam applications have few lines of compact code. To demonstrate, we discuss how you can create new application functionality.

Almost all web application have a login/logout feature and the concept of a logged-in user. We assume that a user must log in to CaveatEmptor as soon as the first page of the application appears (which you'll enforce to be the login screen). A login screen and the application logic to support it are a perfect scenario to learn how Seam components can be wired together contextually.

17.3.1 *Writing the login page*

The user sees the login screen as shown in figure 17.8.

This is a JSF page called login.xhtml, written with Facelets (listing 17.12).

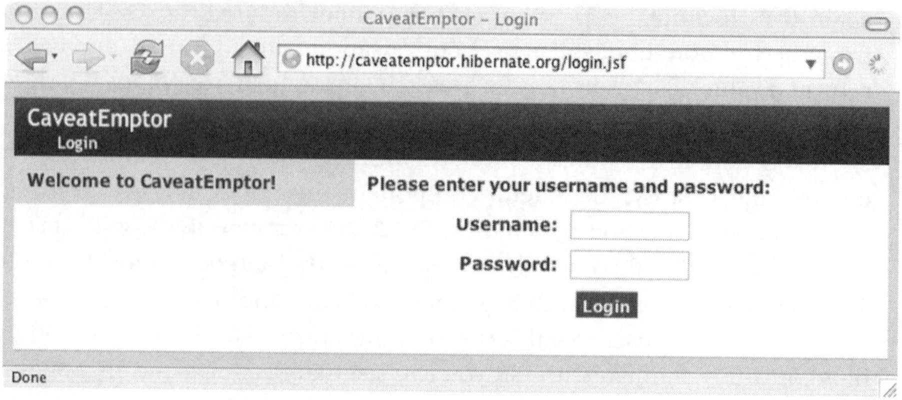

Figure 17.8   The login screen of CaveatEmptor

Listing 17.12   The `login.xhtml` page source code

```
...
<ui:composition xmlns="http://www.w3.org/1999/xhtml"
                xmlns:ui="http://java.sun.com/jsf/facelets"
                xmlns:h="http://java.sun.com/jsf/html"
                xmlns:f="http://java.sun.com/jsf/core"
                template="template.xhtml">

    <ui:define name="screen">Login</ui:define>

    <ui:define name="sidebar">

        <h1>Welcome to CaveatEmptor!</h1>

    </ui:define>

    <ui:define name="content">
    <div class="section">

        <h1>Please enter your username and password:</h1>

        <h:form>

        <span class="errors"><h:messages/></span>

        <div class="entry">
            <div class="label">Username:</div>
            <div class="input">
                <h:inputText required="true" size="10"
                            value="#{currentUser.username}">
                    <f:validateLength minimum="3" maximum="255"/>
                </h:inputText>
            </div>
        </div>
    </div>
```

```
            <div class="entry">
                <div class="label">Password:</div>
                <div class="input">
                    <h:inputSecret required="true" size="10"
                                 value="#{currentUser.password}"/>
                </div>
            </div>

            <div class="entry">
                <div class="label"> </div>
                <div class="input">
                    <h:commandButton value="Login" styleClass="button"
                                     action="#{login.doLogin}"/>
                </div>
            </div>

            </h:form>

        </div>
        </ui:define>

    </ui:composition>
```

You can see a bit more of Facelets in this source: how a global page template is referenced (in the <ui:composition> tag) and how snippets supported by this template (screen, sidebar, content) are defined.

The content of the page is a regular JSF form, with value and action bindings to named components. The input fields of the login form are bound to attributes of the currentUser, and the Login button is bound to the doLogin() method of the login component.

When the login page is rendered for the first time, JSF tries to resolve the value and action bindings. It uses the Seam variable resolver to find the referenced objects. The Seam variable resolver doesn't find the objects in any Seam context, so instances of currentUser and login are created.

Let's look at the source of these components.

17.3.2 *Creating the components*

The first component is currentUser. This is a class you already have in CaveatEmptor: the User entity class. You can turn it into a component that can be handled by Seam with annotations:

```
package auction.model;

import ...

@Name("user")
```

```
@Role(name = "currentUser", scope = ScopeType.SESSION)
@Entity
public class User implements Serializable {

    @Id @GeneratedValue
    private Long id = null;

    private String firstname;
    private String lastname;
    private String username;
    private String password;

    ...

    public User() {}

}
```

The first Seam annotation, @Name, turns this POJO into a Seam component. Whenever Seam now looks for a component with the name user, and no Seam context holds a variable of that name, a new empty instance of User is created by Seam and put into the event context under the variable name user. The event context is the default context for entity Seam components (stateful and stateless beans have a different default context).

For the login functionality, you don't need a User instance in the *event* context, so you define an additional role for this component. Whenever Seam looks for a component with the name currentUser, and no Seam context has a variable with that name, Seam instantiates a User and puts it into the *session* context (the HTTP session). You can easily refer to currentUser anywhere in your code and metadata and get a reference to the current User object back from Seam.

When login.xhtml is rendered, Seam creates a fresh User object and binds it into the session context. This user isn't logged in yet; you need to enter a username and a password and click the Login button.

Doing so executes, in another request, the doLogin() method on the login component. An implementation of this component as a stateless session bean is shown in listing 17.13.

> **Listing 17.13   A stateless Seam component implements login and logout procedures.**

```
package auction.beans;

import ...

@Name("login")

@Stateless
public class LoginBean implements Login {
```

```
@In @Out
private User currentUser;

@PersistenceContext
EntityManager em;

@In
private Context sessionContext;

public String doLogin() {
  User validatedUser = null;

  Query loginQuery = em.createQuery(
                      "select u from User u where" +
                      " u.username = :uname" +
                      " and u.password = :pword"
                    );
  loginQuery.setParameter("uname", currentUser.getUsername());
  loginQuery.setParameter("pword", currentUser.getPassword());

  List result = loginQuery.getResultList();
  if (result.size() == 1) validatedUser = (User) result.get(0);

  if (validatedUser == null) {
     FacesMessages.instance().add(
       new FacesMessage("Invalid username or password!")
     );
     return null;
  } else {
     currentUser = validatedUser;

     sessionContext.set(LoggedIn.LOGIN_TOKEN, true);
     // or:
     Contexts.getSessionContext()
             .set(LoggedIn.LOGIN_TOKEN, true);

     return "start";
  }
}

public String doLogout() {
    Seam.invalidateSession();
    return "login";
}

}
```

This code has two new Seam annotations: @In and @Out. These are variable aliasing hints you use for component wiring. Let's discuss the rest of the code first before we focus on these tags.

The doLogin() method takes the username and password of the member variable currentUser and tries to find this user in the database. If no user is found, a JSF error message is queued, and a `null` outcome results in redisplay of the login page. If a user is found, it's assigned to the member variable `current-User`, replacing the old value of that variable (nothing changes in the HTTP session so far).

You also put a token (a simple boolean) into the session context, to indicate that the current `User` is logged in. This token will be useful later when you need to test whether the current user is logged in. We also discuss the `doLogout()` method later; it invalidates the current HTTP session.

Let's figure out what `@In` and `@Out` do.

17.3.3 *Aliasing contextual variables*

Aliasing a contextual variable sounds complex. However, it's the formal description of what's going on when you use `@In` and `@Out` in the code of a Seam component. Look at figure 17.9, which shows what happens in the Invoke Application request-processing phase after the user clicks Login.

The `@In` annotation tells Seam that you want a value assigned to a member variable of this component. The value is assigned by Seam before a method of the component is called (Seam intercepts every call).

Where does the value come from? Seam reads the name of the member variable, the field name `currentUser` in the previous example, and starts looking for a contextual variable with the same name in all its contexts. At the time `doLogin()` is called, Seam finds a `currentUser` variable in the session context. It takes

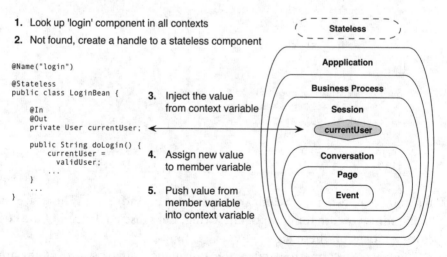

Figure 17.9 Seam synchronizes a member alias with a contextual variable.

this value and assigns it to the member variable of the component. This is a reference to the same `User` instance that is in the session context; you create an *alias* in the scope of the component. You can then call methods on the `current-User` member variable, like `getUsername()` and `getPassword()`.

The `@Out` annotation tells Seam that you want a value assigned to a contextual variable when (any) method of the component returns. The name of the contextual variable is `currentUser`, the same as the field name. The context of the variable is the default context of the `currentUser` Seam component (in the previous example, the session context). (Remember the role you assigned in the `User` class?) Seam takes the value of the member variable and puts it into a contextual variable.

Read the `doLogin()` method again.

Before the method executes, Seam injects the value of the contextual variable `currentUser` (found in the session context) into the member variable with the same name. The method then executes and works with the member variable. After a successful login (database query), the value of the member variable is replaced. This new value must be pushed back into the contextual variable. After the method executes, Seam pushes the value of the member variable `current-User` into the default context defined for this component, the session.

Instead of fields, you can also use getter and setter method pairs for aliasing. For example, `@In` can be on `setCurrentUser()` and `@Out` on `getCurrentUser()`. In both cases, the name of the aliased contextual variable will be `currentUser`.

The `@In` and `@Out` annotations are extremely powerful. You'll see a few more examples later in this chapter, but we'd need many more pages to describe all the things you can do with these annotations. Please also read the tutorials in the Seam reference documentation.

You can also work with contextual variables directly, without aliasing them as member variables. In listing 17.13, the `doLogin()` method calls the `Contexts` directly to set a variable value.

Finally, Seam contexts form a hierarchy (except the pseudocontext *stateless*) that is searched from narrowest to widest scope whenever a contextual variable needs to be looked up (and when you don't declare explicitly which context should be searched). The Seam reference documentation has a list of contexts and their scopes in chapter 2; we won't repeat it here.

Let's finish the login/logout feature and add the missing pieces in configuration and code.

17.3.4 *Completing the login/logout feature*

The navigation rules for the login/logout feature are missing. These are in faces-config.xml for JSF:

```
<navigation-rule>

    <navigation-case>
        <from-outcome>login</from-outcome>
        <to-view-id>/login.xhtml</to-view-id>
        <redirect/>
    </navigation-case>

    <navigation-case>
        <from-outcome>start</from-outcome>
        <to-view-id>/catalog.xhtml</to-view-id>
    </navigation-case>

</navigation-rule>
```

When a user successfully logs in, the `start` outcome of the action takes the browser to the start page of the application, which in CaveatEmptor is the catalog of auction items.

When a user logs out (by clicking a button that is bound to the `login.doLogout()` method), the `login` outcome is returned, and /login.xhtml is rendered. The rule you define here also says that this is done via browser redirect. This approach has two consequences: First, the user sees /login.jsf as the URL in the browser; and second, the redirect is done immediately after the Invoke Application phase, after `doLogout()` executes. You need this redirect to start a fresh HTTP session in the following Render Response phase. The old HTTP session is marked invalid by `doLogout()` and is discarded after the Invoke Application phase.

The application isn't really secure. Although users end up on the login page when they open the application, they can bookmark other pages (like the auction item catalog) and jump directly to a URL. You need to protect the pages and redirect the user to the login page, if no logged-in token is present.

You also need to protect component bean methods directly, in case the user finds a way to execute an action without rendering the page first. (This is possible with Seam components that are exposed through JavaScript.) You protect component methods with an EJB 3.0 interceptor (listing 17.14).

Listing 17.14 An EJB 3.0 interceptor that checks the logged-in token

```
package auction.interceptors;

import ...

@Name("loginInterceptor")
```

```
@Interceptor(around={BijectionInterceptor.class,
                     ValidationInterceptor.class,
                     ConversationInterceptor.class,
                     BusinessProcessInterceptor.class},
             within= RemoveInterceptor.class)
public class LoggedInInterceptor {

    @AroundInvoke
    public Object checkLoggedIn(InvocationContext invocation)
                    throws Exception {

        String loggedInOutcome = checkLoggedIn();

        if (loggedInOutcome == null) {
            return invocation.proceed();
        } else {
            return loggedInOutcome;
        }
    }

    public String checkLoggedIn() {
        boolean isLoggedIn =
                Contexts.getSessionContext()
                        .get(LoggedIn.LOGIN_TOKEN) != null;
        if (isLoggedIn) {
            return null;
        } else {
            return "login";
        }
    }

}
```

This interceptor has two uses. First, it's an EJB 3.0 `@Interceptor` that is executed in the middle of other EJB 3.0 interceptors. These other interceptors are all from Seam, and you need to place your own interceptors in the right position of the stack. The EJB 3.0 annotation `@AroundInvoke` marks the method that is called before and after any method on your protected components is called. If the `checkLoggedIn()` method doesn't return anything (null outcome), the invocation of the intercepted component call can proceed. If the outcome isn't null, this outcome is passed on to the JSF navigation handler, and the intercepted component call doesn't proceed.

The interceptor class is also a Seam plain Java component (Seam components don't have to be EJBs) with the name `loginInterceptor`. The default context for a JavaBean component is the *event*. You can now use this component name in expressions—for example, with the expression `#{loginInterceptor.check-LoggedIn}`—without going through EJB interception. This is useful to protect the pages from direct access. In Seam. you can define actions that run before a page is rendered. These declarations are in WEB-INF/pages.xml:

```
<pages>

    <page view-id="/catalog.xhtml"
            action="#{loginInterceptor.checkLoggedIn}"/>

</pages>
```

When a user hits the /catalog.jsf URL directly, the `loginInterceptor.check-LoggedIn()` action runs. If this action has a non-null outcome, Seam treats the outcome as a regular JSF outcome and the navigation rules apply.

Finally, you protect your component methods by applying the interceptor to an EJB class. This can be done in XML (META-INF/ejb-jar.xml), which is great if you want to use wildcards and protect all beans in a particular package. Or, you can write a helper annotation that encapsulates the interceptor:

```
package auction.interceptors;

import ...

@Target(TYPE)
@Retention(RUNTIME)
@Documented
@Interceptors(LoggedInInterceptor.class)
public @interface LoggedIn {
    public static final String LOGIN_TOKEN  = "loggedIn";
}
```

This annotation also contains the string constant to which all the other code refers, which is convenient. Now, apply this annotation on an EJB class:

```
package auction.beans;

import ...

@Name("catalog")

@LoggedIn

@Stateful
public class CatalogBean implements Catalog { ... }
```

Whenever any method of this EJB is called, the `LoggedInInterceptor` runs and validates that the user is logged in. If the user isn't logged in, the interceptor returns the `login` outcome to JSF.

You can also check for the logged-in token on a page—for example, if you have to decide whether the Logout button should be rendered:

```
<h:form>
    <h:panelGroup rendered="#{loggedIn}">
        Current user: <b>#{currentUser.username}</b>
        (<h:commandLink value="Logout" action="#{login.doLogout}"/>)
    </h:panelGroup>
</h:form>
```

The expression #{loggedIn} resolves to the boolean context variable loggedIn that is either present in the session context or not.

The login/logout functionality of the application is now complete. Pages and component methods are secured; only a logged-in user can open and call them.

How do people get user accounts? They have to fill out a registration form. You must validate the form data and create the account in the database.

17.4 *Validating user input*

In the previous example, the login screen and login/logout code, you rely on standard JSF validators and your own code in the doLogin() method to validate user input. When a user submits the login form, JSF runs the declared validators (in login.xhtml) in the Process Validations phase. If the user enters a username and a password, validation is successful, and the login.doLogin() method executes. The given username and password are bound to the database query. User input is validated twice:

- JSF validates the HTML form input before it synchronizes the value of each input field with the bound model, the currentUser in the Seam session context. If you access currentUser later in an action method, you have the guarantee that the validation rules of your pages have been checked.

- The JDBC driver validates the user input when you bind the username and password to the JPA QL query. Internally, this is a binding to a regular JDBC PreparedStatement, so the JDBC driver escapes any dangerous characters that the user may have entered.

Validating user input in the presentation layer and ensuring that no SQL injection attacks are possible is good enough for a simple login screen. But what if you need to validate a User object before it's *saved* in the database—for example, during an account registration procedure?

You need more complex validation: You have to check the length of the entered username and see whether any illegal characters have been used, and you also need to validate the quality of the password. All this can be solved with more and possibly custom validation in the JSF presentation layer, but the database schema also must validate the integrity of stored data. For example, you create database constraints that limit the length of the value stored in the USERNAME column or require a successful string-pattern match.

In any sophisticated application, input validation is a concern that needs to be handled not only in the presentation layer, but in several layers and even in different tiers. It's a crosscutting concern that can affect all your code. With *Hibernate Validator*, you can isolate and encapsulate validation and data integrity rules easily, for all application layers.

17.4.1 *Introducing Hibernate Validator*

Hibernate Validator is a module of Hibernate Annotations. You can use Hibernate Validator even without Hibernate and Seam, with only hibernate3.jar and hibernate-annotations.jar on your classpath, in any Java application. (It's likely that Hibernate Validator will be forked into its own stand-alone module in the future. This depends on the work done in JSR 303, "Bean Validation"; see http://jcp.org/en/jsr/detail?id=303.)

Hibernate Validator is a set of annotations you apply to your domain model to define data validation and integrity rules declaratively. You can extend Hibernate Validator with your own constraints, by writing your own annotations.

These applied integrity and validation rules can be used with the following:

- *Plain Java*—You can call the ClassValidator API anywhere in Java code and supply objects that need to be checked. The validator either completes validation or returns an array of InvalidValue objects. Each InvalidValue contains the details about the validation failure, such as the property name and error message.

- *Hibernate*—In native Hibernate, you can register Hibernate Validator events that hook into the internal processing of Hibernate persistence operations. With these events, Hibernate can validate any object you're inserting or updating in the database automatically and transparently. An Invalid-StateException that contains the details is thrown when validation fails.

- *Hibernate EntityManager*—If you use the Java Persistence API with Hibernate EntityManager, the Hibernate Validator events are activated by default, and all entity instances are checked against the validation annotations when you insert or update an object in the database.

- *SchemaExport*—Hibernate's database schema-generation feature can create database constraints that reflect your integrity rules in SQL DDL. The

SchemaExport (hbm2ddl) tool reads the validation annotations on your domain model and renders them in SQL DDL. Each annotation knows how the SQL should look (or if no equivalent constraint exists in SQL). This is especially powerful if you write your own validation annotations based on custom procedural SQL constraints (triggers, and so on). You can encapsulate a custom database-integrity rule in a single Java annotation and use Hibernate Validator to check instances of an annotated class at runtime.

- *Seam*—With Seam, you can integrate Hibernate Validator with the presentation layer and logic of your application. Seam can automatically call the validation API when a JSF form is submitted and decorate the form with any validation error messages.

You've already used Seam and Hibernate EntityManager in the previous sections. As soon as you add Hibernate Validator annotations to your entity classes, these integrity rules are validated by Hibernate when the persistence context is flushed to the database.

Let's tie Hibernate Validator into the JSF user interface and implement an account registration feature for CaveatEmptor.

17.4.2 *Creating the registration page*

We'll begin with the user interface. You need a new page, register.xhtml, with a JSF form. To get to that page, you must provide a link on the login.xhtml page, so users know they can register:

```
<ui:define name="sidebar">

    <h1>Welcome to CaveatEmptor!</h1>

    <div>
        <h:form>
            If you don't have an account, please
            <h:commandLink action="register" immediate="true">
                register...
            </h:commandLink>
        </h:form>
    </div>

</ui:define>
```

Submitting this form immediately jumps to the Render Response phase in the request processing (no validation, model binding, or action execution is necessary). The register string is a simple navigation outcome, defined in the navigation rules in faces-config.xml:

```
<navigation-rule>
    <navigation-case>
        <from-outcome>login</from-outcome>
        <to-view-id>/login.xhtml</to-view-id>
        <redirect/>
    </navigation-case>

    <navigation-case>
        <from-outcome>register</from-outcome>
        <to-view-id>/register.xhtml</to-view-id>
        <redirect/> <!-- Make this bookmark-able -->
    </navigation-case>
    ...
</navigation-rule>
```

See the screenshot of the registration page in figure 17.10.

The code for the JSF form on register.xhtml uses some visual Seam components for JSF (these can be found in the jboss-seam-ui.jar file).

Decorating the page with Seam tags

The Seam components you now use integrate the page with Hibernate Validator (listing 17.15). We've left out the basic HTML of the page; the only interesting part is the form and how validation of that form works. You also need to declare the namespace for the Seam taglib to use the components in Facelets templates; the prefix used in all the following examples is s.

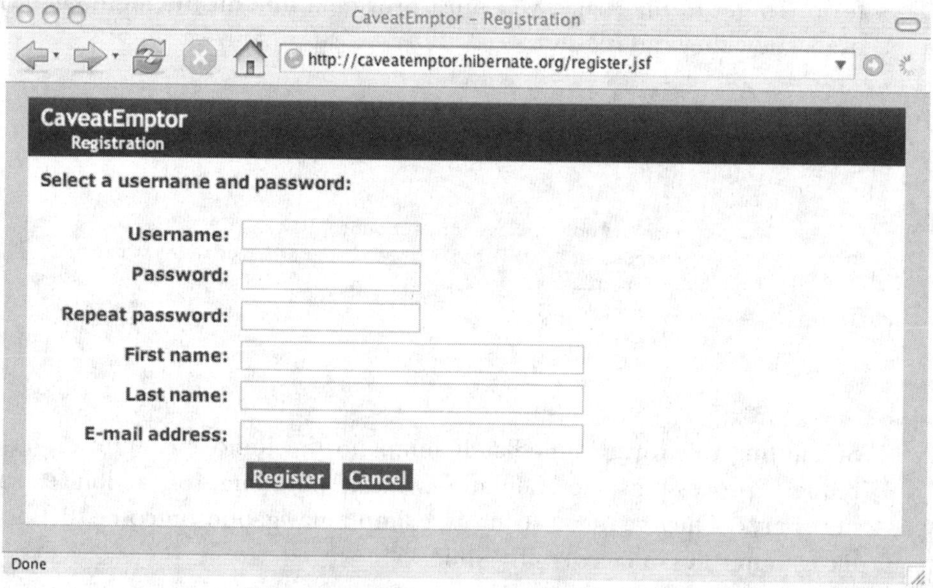

Figure 17.10 The register.xhtml page

Listing 17.15   The `registration.xhtml` source with validation

```
<ui:composition ...
                xmlns:s="http://jboss.com/products/seam/taglib"
                ...>
<h:form>

    <f:facet name="beforeInvalidField">        ①
        <h:graphicImage value="/img/attention.gif"
                        width="18" height="18"
                        styleClass="attentionImage"/>
    </f:facet>
    <f:facet name="afterInvalidField">         ②
        <s:message/>
    </f:facet>

    <div class="errors" align="center">        ③
        <h:messages globalOnly="true"/>
    </div>

    <s:validateAll>        ④

        <div class="entry">
            <div class="label">Username:</div>        ⑤
            <div class="input"><s:decorate>              ⑥
                <h:inputText size="16" required="true"
                             value="#{currentUser.username}"/>
            </s:decorate></div>
        </div>

        <div class="entry">
            <div class="label">Password:</div>
            <div class="input"><s:decorate>
                <h:inputSecret size="16" required="true"
                               value="#{currentUser.password}"/>
            </s:decorate></div>
        </div>

        <div class="entry">
            <div class="label">Repeat password:</div>
            <div class="input"><s:decorate>
                <h:inputSecret size="16" required="true"
                               value="#{register.verifyPassword}"/>
            </s:decorate></div>
        </div>

        <div class="entry">
            <div class="label">Firstname:</div>
            <div class="input"><s:decorate>
                <h:inputText size="32" required="true"
                             value="#{currentUser.firstname}"/>
            </s:decorate></div>
        </div>
```

```
    . . .

  </s:validateAll>

  <div class="entry">
     <div class="label"> </div>

     <div class="input">
        <h:commandButton value="Register" styleClass="button"
                         action="#{register.doRegister}"/>

        <h:commandButton value="Cancel" styleClass="button"
                         action="login" immediate="true"/>
     </div>
  </div>

  </h:form>
```

❶ This component facet is used by the Seam decorator for error display. You'll see it before any input field that has an invalid value.

❷ The Seam decorator places the error message after the invalid field.

❸ Global error messages that aren't assigned to any field are displayed at the top of the form.

❹ The <s:validateAll/> Seam tag enables Hibernate Validator for all child tags—that is, all input fields that are encapsulated in this form. You can also enable Hibernate Validator for only a single field by wrapping the input field with <s:validate/>.

❺ The <s:decorate> Seam tag handles the validation error messages. It wraps the beforeInvalidField and afterInvalidField facets around the input field if an error occurs.

❻ The JSF input widget has a visible size of 16 characters. Note that JSF doesn't limit the string size the user can enter, but it requires that the user enters a value. This "not null" validation is still the job of JSF, not Hibernate Validator.

❼ The Register button has an action binding to register.doRegister, a Seam component.

❽ You need a Cancel button that redirects the user to the login page. You again skip processing of the form with immediate="true".

When the registration form is submitted, Seam participates in the JSF Process Validations phase and calls Hibernate Validator for every entity object to which you bound an input field. In this case, only a single entity instance must be validated, currentUser, which Seam looks up in its contexts.

If the Process Validations phase completes, `register.doRegister` executes in Invoke Application. This is a stateful session bean that lives in the event context.

The registration Seam component

The registration form has two bindings to the `register` Seam component. The first binding is a value binding, with `register.verifyPassword`. JSF and Seam now synchronize the user input from this field with the `register.setVerify-Password()` and `register.getVerifyPassword()` methods.

The second binding is an action binding of the Register button to the `register.doRegister()` method. This method must implement additional checks after JSF and Hibernate Validator input validation, before the `currentUser` can be stored as a new account in the database. See the code in listing 17.16.

Listing 17.16   A stateful session bean implements the registration logic.

```
package auction.beans;

import ...
                                    ❶
@Name("register")               ◁─
@Scope(ScopeType.EVENT)

@Stateful
public class RegisterBean implements Register {        ❷
                                                      ◁─
    @In
    private User currentUser;

    @PersistenceContext
    private EntityManager em;            ❸
                                        ◁─
    @In(create=true)
    private transient FacesMessages facesMessages;       ❹
                                                        ◁─
    private String verifyPassword;
    public String getVerifyPassword() {
        return verifyPassword;
    }
    public void setVerifyPassword(String verifyPassword) {
        this.verifyPassword = verifyPassword;
    }
                                 ❺
    public String doRegister() {    ◁─

        if (!currentUser.getPassword().equals(verifyPassword)) {       ❻
            facesMessages.add("Passwords didn't match!")              ◁─
            verifyPassword = null;
            return null;
        }
                          ❼
        List existing =      ◁─
```

```
                em.createQuery("select u.username from User u" +
                             " where u.username = :uname")
                    .setParameter("uname", currentUser.getUsername())
                    .getResultList();

          if (existing.size() != 0) {
              facesMessages.add("User exists!");
              return null;
          } else {                                  ❽
              em.persist(currentUser);           ⏎
              facesMessages.add("Registration complete.");
              return "login";
          }
      }

      @Remove @Destroy                           ❾
      public void destroy() {}                 ⏎

  }
```

❶ The register Seam component is created by Seam and destroyed when the event context is destroyed, which is the scope of a single JSF request.

❷ Seam injects the currentUser, aliased from the contextual variable in the session context.

❸ Seam injects (or creates, if the variable can't be found in any context) an instance of FacesMessages. This is a convenient helper if you need to send messages to a JSF page; you used it before without injection but through manual lookup.

❹ The verifyPassword field of this component is synchronized with the JSF form.

❺ This method implements the main logic for registration of a new account. It's called after Hibernate Validator checks the currentUser.

❻ The two passwords entered by the user have to match; otherwise an error message is shown above the form. The null outcome triggers a redisplay of the login form with the error message.

❼ Usernames are unique in the database. This multirow constraint can't be checked in-memory by Hibernate Validator. You need to execute a database query and validate the username.

❽ If all validations pass, you persist() the currentUser object; the persistence context is flushed, and the transaction is committed when the doRegister() method returns. The outcome login redirects the user back to the login page, where the *Registration complete* message is rendered above the login form.

❾ Seam calls the component's destroy() method at the end of the JSF request, when the event context is destroyed. The EJB 3.0 container removes the stateful session bean because the method is marked with @Remove.

User input validation is often more complex than checking a single value on a single object. Seam calls Hibernate Validator for all bound entity instance of the registration form. However, a duplicate check of the entered username requires database access. You could write your own Hibernate Validator extension for this purpose, but it seems unreasonable to always check the database for a duplicate username when a User object must be validated. On the other hand, it's natural that business logic is implemented with procedural code, not completely declaratively.

So far, Hibernate Validator does nothing. If you submit the registration form without entering any values, only the built-in JSF validator for required="true" runs. You get a built-in JSF error message on each input field that says that a value is required.

Annotating the entity class

Hibernate Validator isn't active because there are no integrity rules on the User entity class, so all objects pass the validation test. You can add validation annotations on the fields or on the getter methods of the entity class:

```
package auction.model;

import ...

@Name("user")
@Role(name = "currentUser", scope = ScopeType.SESSION)

@Entity
@Table(name = "USERS")
public class User implements Serializable {

    @Id @GeneratedValue
    @Column(name = "USER_ID")
    private Long id = null;

    @Column(name = "USERNAME", nullable = false, unique = true)
    @org.hibernate.validator.Length(
        min = 3, max = 16,
        message = "Minimum {min}, maximum {max} characters."
    )
    @org.hibernate.validator.Pattern(
        regex="^\\w*$",
        message = "Invalid username!"
    )
    private String username;
```

```
@Column(name = "`PASSWORD`", length = 12, nullable = false)
private String password;

@Column(name = "FIRSTNAME", length = 255, nullable = false)
private String firstname;

@Column(name = "LASTNAME", length = 255, nullable = false)
private String lastname;

...}
```

You apply only two Hibernate Validator annotations: the `@Length` and `@Pattern` validators. These validators have attributes such as the maximum and minimum length, or a regular expression pattern (see `java.util.regex.Pattern`). A list of all built-in validation annotations can be found in the Hibernate Validator reference documentation in the Hibernate Annotations package. You can also easily write your own annotations.

All validation annotations have a `message` attribute. This message is displayed next to the form field if a validation failure occurs.

You can add more validation annotations that also check the password, the first name, and the last name of the `User`. Note that the `length` attribute of the USER-NAME `@Column` annotation has been removed. Thanks to the length validation annotation, Hibernate's schema export tool now knows that a `VARCHAR(16)` must be created in the database schema. On the other hand, the `nullable = false` attribute stays, for the generation of a `NOT NULL` database column constraint. (You could use a `@NotNull` validation annotation from Hibernate Validator, but JSF already checks that field for you: The form field is `required="true"`.)

After you add the validation annotations to `User`, submitting the registration form with incomplete values displays error messages, as shown in figure 17.11.

The registration feature is now complete; users can create new accounts. What doesn't seem to be perfect are the error messages. If you try the code, you'll see that the error messages aren't as nice as the ones shown in figure 17.11. The fields that require input have an ugly *_id23: Field input is required* message, instead. Also, is it a good idea to put English error messages into your entity classes, even if they're in annotation metadata?

Instead of replacing only the default JSF error messages (which include the automatically generated widget identifiers), let's isolate all user interface messages and also allow users to switch languages.

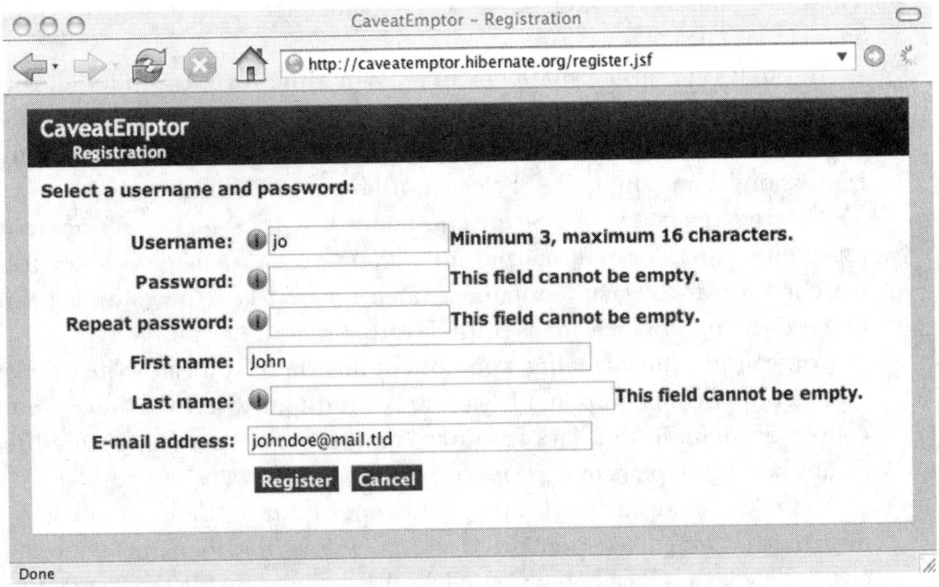

Figure 17.11 Seam decorates the input fields with validation error messages.

17.4.3 *Internationalization with Seam*

The first step toward a multilanguage application is a language switcher—let's say, a link the user can click in the top menu of the application. Seam has a `locale-Selector` component (it lives in the session context) that makes this easy:

```
<h:form>
    <h:panelGroup>
        <h:outputText value="#{messages['SelectLanguage']}"/>:
        <h:commandLink
            value="EN"
            action="#{localeSelector.selectLanguage('en')}"/>
        |
        <h:commandLink
            value="DE"
            action="#{localeSelector.selectLanguage('de')}"/>
    </h:panelGroup>
</h:form>
```

This little form has two hyperlinks, EN and DE. Users can click the links to switch the application's interface between English and German. The link actions are bound to the `localeSelector.selectLanguage()` method, with literal arguments.

These arguments, en and de, are ISO language codes; see the Javadoc for java.util.Locale.

But that isn't all that happens here. When the form is rendered, the #{messages['SelectLanguage']} expression is evaluated, and the output of that expression is rendered as text, before the comand links. The output of this expression is something like "Select your language:". Where does it come from?

Clearly, messages is a Seam component; it lives in the session context. It represents a map of externalized messages; SelectLanguage is a key this map is searched for. If the map contains a value for that key, the value is printed out. Otherwise, SelectLanguage is printed verbatim.

You can use the messages component anywhere you can write an expression that resolves Seam components (which is almost anywhere). This component is a convenient handle to a Java resource bundle, which is a complicated term that means key/value pairs in a .properties file.

Seam automatically reads messages.properties from the root of your classpath into the messages component. However, the actual filename depends on the currently selected locale. If a user clicks the DE link, the file that is searched in the classpath is named messages_de.properties. If English is the active language (which is the default, depending on the JSF configuration and browser), the file that is loaded is messages_en.properties.

Here is a snippet of messages_en.properties:

```
SelectLanguage = Select language:
PleaseRegisterHint = Create a new account...
SelectUsernameAndPassword = Select a username and password
PasswordVerify = Repeat password
PasswordVerifyField = Controlpassword
Firstname = First name
Lastname = Last name
Email = E-mail address
TooShortOrLongUsername = Minimum 3, maximum 16 characters.
NotValidUsername = Invalid name! {TooShortOrLongUsername}
PasswordVerifyFailed = Passwords didn't match, try again.
UserAlreadyExists = A user with this name already exists.
SuccessfulRegistration = Registration complete, please log in:
DoRegister = Register
Cancel = Cancel

# Override JSF defaults
javax.faces.component.UIInput.REQUIRED = This field cannot be empty.
```

The last line overrides the default JSF validation error message for the input field widget. The syntax {Key} is useful if you want to combine message; the TooShortOrLongUsername message is appended to the NotValidUsername message.

You can now replace all the strings in your XHTML files with expressions that look up keys in the `messages` Seam component. You can also use keys from resource bundles in your `RegistrationBean` component, in Java code:

```
public String doRegister() {
    if (!currentUser.getPassword().equals(verifyPassword)) {
        facesMessages
            .addFromResourceBundle("PasswordVerifyFailed");
        verifyPassword = null;
        return null;
    }

    List existing =
        em.createQuery("select u.username from User u" +
                       " where u.username = :uname")
            .setParameter("uname", currentUser.getUsername())
            .getResultList();

    if (existing.size() != 0) {
        facesMessages
            .addFromResourceBundle("UserAlreadyExists");
        return null;
    } else {
        em.persist(currentUser);
        facesMessages
            .addFromResourceBundle("SuccessfulRegistration");
        return "login";
    }
}
```

And finally, you can use resource bundle keys in the messages of Hibernate Validator (this isn't a Seam feature—it works without Seam as well):

```
@Entity
public class User implements Serializable {

...
    @Column(name = "USERNAME", nullable = false, unique = true)
    @org.hibernate.validator.Length(
        min = 3, max = 16,
        message = "{TooShortOrLongUsername}"
    )
    @org.hibernate.validator.Pattern(
        regex="^\\w*$",
        message = "{NotValidUsername}"
    )
    private String username;

...}
```

Let's translate the resource bundle and save it as message_de.properties:

```
SelectLanguage = Sprache:
PleaseRegisterHint = Neuen Account anlegen...
SelectUsernameAndPassword = Benutzername und Passwort w\u00e4hlen
PasswordVerify = Passwort (Wiederholung)
PasswordVerifyField = Kontrollpasswort
Firstname = Vorname
Lastname = Nachname
Email = E-mail Adresse
TooShortOrLongUsername = Minimum 3, maximal 16 Zeichen.
NotValidUsername = Ung\u00fcltiger name! {TooShortOrLongUsername}
PasswordVerifyFailed = Passworte nicht gleich, bitte wiederholen.
UserAlreadyExists = Ein Benutzer mit diesem Namen existiert bereits.
SuccessfulRegistration = Registrierung komplett, bitte einloggen:
DoRegister = Registrieren
Cancel = Abbrechen

# Override JSF defaults
javax.faces.component.UIInput.REQUIRED = Eingabe erforderlich.
```

Note that you use UTF sequences to express characters which are not ASCII. If the user selects German in the application and tries to register without completing the form, all messages appear in German (figure 17.12).

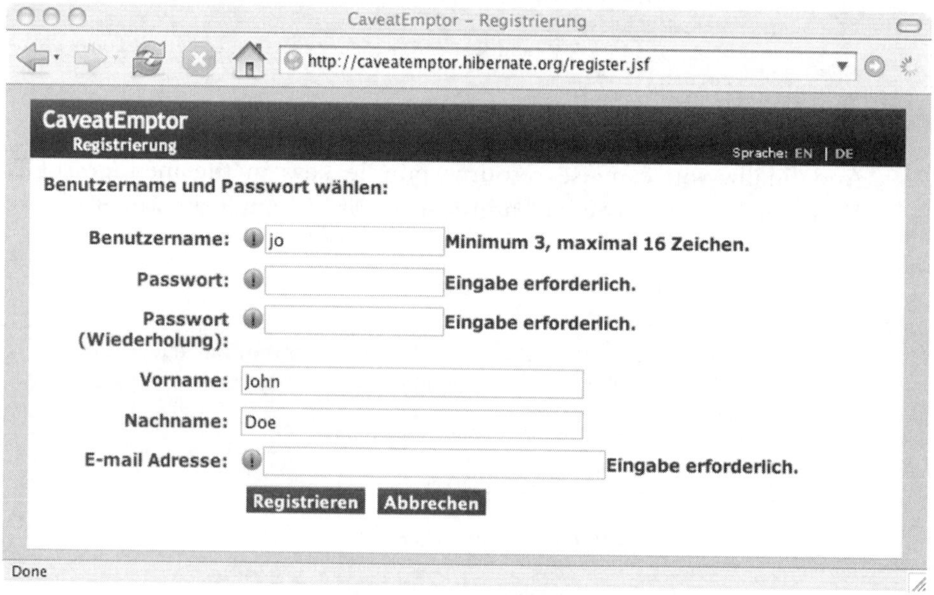

Figure 17.12 The user interface has been translated to German.

The selected language is a session-scoped setting. It's now active until the user logs out (which invalidates the HTTP session). If you also set the `localeSelector.cookieEnabled=true` switch in seam.properties, the users language selection will be stored as a cookie in the web browser.

The last but not least important Seam feature we want to demonstrate is automatic persistence context handling through Seam. If you've ever seen a `LazyInitializationException` in a Hibernate application (and who hasn't?), this is the perfect solution.

17.5 *Simplifying persistence with Seam*

All the previous examples in this chapter use the `EntityManager` that was injected by the EJB 3.0 container. A member field in an EJB is annotated with `@PersistenceContext`, and the scope of the persistence context is always the transaction started and committed for a particular action method. In Hibernate terms, a Hibernate `Session` is opened, flushed, and closed for every method called on a session bean.

When a session bean method returns and the persistence context is closed, all entity instances you loaded from the database in that bean method are in detached state. You can render these instances on a JSF page by accessing their initialized properties and collections, but you get a `LazyInitializationException` if you try to access an uninitialized association or collection. You also have to reattach (or merge, with the Java Persistence API) a detached instance if you want to have it in persistent state again. Furthermore, you have to carefully code the `equals()` and `hashCode()` methods of your entity classes, because the guaranteed identity scope is only the transaction, the same as the (relatively short) persistence context scope.

We've discussed the consequences of the detached object state several times before in this book. Almost always, we've concluded that avoiding the detached state by *extending* the persistence context and identity scope beyond a transaction is a preferable solution. You've seen the Open Session in View pattern that extends the persistence context to span a whole request. Although this pattern is a pragmatic solution for applications that are built in a stateless fashion, where the most important scope is the request, you need a more powerful variation if you write a stateful Seam application with conversations.

If you let Seam inject an `EntityManager` into your session beans, and if you let Seam manage the persistence context, you'll get the following:

- *Automatic binding and scoping of an extended persistence context to the conversation*—You have a guaranteed identity scope that spans your conversation. A particular conversation has at most one in-memory representation of a particular database row. There are no detached objects, and you can easily compare entity instances with double equals (a==b). You don't have to implement `equals()` and `hashCode()` and compare entity instances by business key.

- *No more `LazyInitializationExceptions` when you access an uninitalized proxy or collection in a conversation*—The persistence context is active for the whole conversation, and the persistence engine can fetch data on demand at all times. Seam provides a much more powerful and convenient implementation of the Open Session in View pattern, which avoids detached objects not only during a single request but also during a whole conversation.

- *Automatic wrapping of the JSF request in several system transactions*—Seam uses several transactions to encapsulate the phases in the JSF request lifecycle. We'll discuss this transaction assembly later; one of its benefits is that you have an optimized assembly that keeps database lock times as short as possible, without any coding.

Let's demonstrate this with an example by rewriting the registration procedure from the previous section as a conversation with an extended persistence context. The previous implementation was basically stateless: The `RegisterBean` was only scoped to a single event.

17.5.1 *Implementing a conversation*

Go back and read the code shown in listing 17.16. This stateful session bean is the backing bean for the account registration page in CaveatEmptor. When a user opens or submits the registration page, an instance of that bean is created and active while the event is being processed. JSF binds the form values into the bean (through `verifyPassword` and the Seam-injected `currentUser`) and calls the action listener methods when necessary.

This is a stateless design. Although you use a stateful session bean, its scope is a single request, the event context in Seam. This approach works fine because the conversation the user goes through is trivial—only a single page with a single form

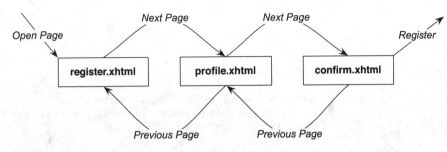

Figure 17.13   The CaveatEmptor registration wizard

has to be filled in and submitted. Figure 17.13 shows a more sophisticated registration procedure.

The user opens register.xhtml and enters the desired username and password. After the user clicks Next Page, a second form with the profile data (first name, email address, and so on) is presented and must be filled out. The last page shows all the account and profile data again, so the user can confirm it (or step back and correct it).

This registration procedure is a wizard-style conversation, with the usual Next Page and Previous Page buttons that allow the user to step through the conversation. Many applications need this kind of dialog. Without Seam, implementing multipage conversations is still difficult for web application developers. (Note that there are many other good use cases for conversations; the wizard dialog is common.)

Let's write the pages and Seam components for this conversation.

The registration page

The register.xhtml page looks almost like the one shown in listing 17.15. You remove the profile form fields (first name, last name, email address) and replace the Register button with a Next Page button:

```
...

<s:validateAll>

    <div class="entry">
        <div class="label">Username:</div>
        <div class="input">
            <s:decorate>
                <h:inputText size="16" required="true"
                             value="#{register.user.username}"/>
            </s:decorate>
        </div>
```

```
        </div>

        <div class="entry">
            <div class="label">Password:</div>

            <div class="input">
                <s:decorate>
                    <h:inputSecret size="16" required="true"
                                   value="#{register.user.password}"/>
                </s:decorate>
            </div>
        </div>

        <div class="entry">
            <div class="label">Repeat password:</div>
            <div class="input">
                <s:decorate>
                    <h:inputSecret size="16" required="true"
                                   value="#{register.verifyPassword}"/>
                </s:decorate>
            </div>
        </div>

    </s:validateAll>

    <div class="entry">
        <div class="label"> </div>
        <div class="input">
            <h:commandButton value="Next Page"
                             styleClass="button"
                             action="#{register.enterAccount}"/>
        </div>
    </div>
</div>
```

You're still referring to the `register` component to bind values and actions; you'll see that class in a moment. You bind the form values to the `User` object returned by `register.getUser()`. The `currentUser` is gone. You now have a conversation context and no longer need to use the HTTP session context (the previous implementation didn't work if the user tried to register two accounts in two browser windows at the same time). The `register` component now holds the state of the `User` that is bound to all form fields during the conversation.

The outcome of the `enterAccount()` method forwards the user to the next page, the profile form. Note that you still rely on Hibernate Validator for input validation, called by Seam (`<s:validateAll/>`) in the Process Validations phase of the request. If input validation fails, the page is redisplayed.

The profile page

The profile.xhtml page is almost the same as the register.xhtml page. The profile form includes the profile fields, and the buttons at the bottom of the page allow a user to step back or forward in the conversation:

```
...
<div class="entry">
    <div class="label">E-mail address:</div>
    <div class="input">
        <s:decorate>
            <h:inputText size="32" required="true"
                         value="#{register.user.email}"/>
        </s:decorate>
    </div>
</div>

<div class="entry">
    <div class="label"> </div>

    <div class="input">
        <h:commandButton value="Previous Page"
                         styleClass="button"
                         action="register"/>

        <h:commandButton value="Next Page"
                         styleClass="button"
                         action="#{register.enterProfile}"/>
    </div>
</div>
```

Any form field filled out by the user is applied to the register.user model when the form is submitted. The Previous Page button skips the Invoke Application phase and results in the register outcome—the previous page is displayed. Note that there is no <s:validateAll/> around this form; you don't want to Process Validations when the user clicks the Previous Page button. Calling Hibernate Validator is now delegated to the register.enterProfile action. You should validate the form input only when the user clicks Next Page. However, you keep the decoration on the form fields to display any validation error messages.

The next page shows a summary of the account and profile.

The summary page

On confirm.xhtml, all input is presented in a summary, allowing the user to review the account and profile details before finally submitting them for registration:

```
...
<div class="entry">
    <div class="label">Last name:</div>
    <div class="output">#{register.user.lastname}</div>
</div>

<div class="entry">
    <div class="label">E-mail address:</div>
    <div class="output">#{register.user.email}</div>
</div>

<div class="entry">
    <div class="label"> </div>

    <div class="input">
        <h:commandButton value="Previous Page"
                         styleClass="button"
                         action="profile"/>

        <h:commandButton value="Register"
                         styleClass="button"
                         action="#{register.confirm}"/>
    </div>
</div>
```

The Previous Page button renders the response defined by the `profile` outcome, which is the previous page. The `register.confirm` method is called when the user clicks Register. This action method ends the conversation.

Finally, you write the Seam component that backs this conversation.

Writing a conversational Seam component

The `RegisterBean` shown in listing 17.16 must be scoped to the conversation. First, here's the interface:

```
public interface Register {

    // Value binding methods
    public User getUser();
    public void setUser(User user);

    public String getVerifyPassword();
    public void setVerifyPassword(String verifyPassword);

    // Action binding methods
    public String enterAccount();
    public String enterProfile();
    public String confirm();

    // Cleanup routine
    public void destroy();
}
```

One of the advantages of the Seam conversation model is that you can read your interface like a story of your conversation. The user enters account data and then the profile data. Finally, the input is confirmed and stored.

The implementation of the bean is shown in listing 17.17.

Listing 17.17 A conversation-scoped Seam component

```
package auction.beans;

import ...

@Name("register")                                    ❶
@Scope(ScopeType.CONVERSATION)          ⟵

@Stateful
public class RegisterBean implements Register {
                                                    ❷
    @PersistenceContext                     ⟵
    private EntityManager em;

    @In(create=true)
    private transient FacesMessages facesMessages;
                                                    ❸
    private User user;                      ⟵
    public User getUser() {
        if (user == null) user = new User();
        return user;
    }
    public void setUser(User user) {
        this.user = user;
    }
                                           ❹
    private String verifyPassword;      ⟵
    public String getVerifyPassword() {
        return verifyPassword;
    }
    public void setVerifyPassword(String verifyPassword) {
        this.verifyPassword = verifyPassword;
    }
                                 ❺
    @Begin(join = true)         ⟵
    public String enterAccount() {
        if ( verifyPasswordMismatch() || usernameExists() ) {
            return null; // Redisplay page
        } else {
            return "profile";
        }
    }
                                                      ❻
    @IfInvalid(outcome = Outcome.REDISPLAY)    ⟵
    public String enterProfile() {
        return "confirm";
    }
```

```
@End(ifOutcome = "login")              ⬅  ⑦
public String confirm() {
    if ( usernameExists() ) return "register"; // Safety check
    em.persist(user);
    facesMessages.add("Registration successful!");
    return "login";
}

@Remove @Destroy
public void destroy() {}

private boolean usernameExists() {
    List existing =
        em.createQuery("select u.username from User u" +
                           " where u.username = :uname")
             .setParameter("uname",
                                 user.getUsername())
             .getResultList();

    if (existing.size() != 0) {
        facesMessages.add("Username exists");
        return true;
    }
    return false;
}

private boolean verifyPasswordMismatch() {
    if (!user.getPassword().equals(verifyPassword)) {
        facesMessages.add("Passwords do not match");
        verifyPassword = null;
        return true;
    }
    return false;
}
}
```

❶ When Seam instantiates this component, an instance is bound into the conversation context under the variable name register.

❷ The EJB 3.0 container injects a transaction-scoped persistence context. You'll use Seam here later to inject a conversation-scoped persistence context.

❸ The user member variable is exposed with accessor methods so that JSF input widgets can be bound to individual User properties. The state of the user is held during the conversation by the register component.

❹ The verifyPassword member variable is also exposed with accessor methods for value binding in forms, and the state is held during the conversation.

❺ When the user clicks Next Page on the first screen, the enterAccount() method is called. The current conversation is promoted to a long-running conversation with @Begin, when this method returns, so it spans future requests until an @End marked method returns. Because users may step back to the first page and resubmit the form, you need to join an existing conversation if it's already in progress.

❻ When the user clicks Next Page on the second screen, the enterProfile() method is called. Because it's marked with @IfInvalid, Seam executes Hibernate Validator for input validation. If an error occurs, the page is redisplayed (Outcome.REDISPLAY is a convenient constant shortcut) with error messages from Hibernate Validator. If there are no errors, the outcome is the final page of the conversation.

❼ When the user clicks Register on the last screen, the confirm() method is called. When the method returns the login outcome, Seam ends the long-running conversation and destroys the component by calling the method marked with @Destroy. Meanwhile, if some other person picks the same username, you redirect the user back to the first page of the conversation; the conversation context stays intact and active.

You've seen most of the annotations earlier in this chapter. The only new annotation is @IfInvalid, which triggers Hibernate Validator when the enterProfile() method is called. The registration conversation is now complete, and everything works as expected. The persistence context is handled by the EJB container, and a fresh persistence context is assigned to each action method when the method is called.

You haven't run into any problems because the code and pages don't load data on demand by pulling data in the view from the detached domain objects. However, almost any conversation more complex than the registration process will trigger a LazyInitializationException.

17.5.2 *Letting Seam manage the persistence context*

Let's provoke a LazyInitializationException. When the user enters the final screen of the conversation, the confirmation dialog, you present a list of auction categories. The user can select the default category for their account: the auction category they want to browse and sell items in by default. The list of categories is loaded from the database and exposed with a getter method.

Triggering a LazyInitializationException

Edit the `RegisterBean` component and expose a list of auction categories, loaded from the database:

```
public class RegisterBean implements Register {
    ...

    private List<Category> categories;
    public List<Category> getCategories() {
        return categories;
    }
    ...

    @IfInvalid(outcome = Outcome.REDISPLAY)
    public String enterProfile() {
        categories =
                em.createQuery("select c from Category c" +
                                " where c.parentCategory is null")
                        .getResultList();
        return "confirm";
    }

}
```

You also add the `getCategories()` method to the interface of the component. In the confirm.xhtml view, you can now bind to this getter method to show the categories:

```
...
<div class="entry">
    <div class="label">E-mail address:</div>
    <div class="output">#{register.user.email}</div>
</div>

<div class="entry">
    <div class="label">Default category:</div>
    <div class="input">
        <tr:tree var="cat"
                value="#{registrationCategoryAdapter.treeModel}">
            <f:facet name="nodeStamp">
                <h:outputText value="#{cat.name}"/>
            </f:facet>
        </tr:tree>
    </div>
</div>
...
```

To display categories, you use a different widget, which isn't in the standard JSF set. It's a visual tree data component from the Apache MyFaces Trinidad project. It also needs an adapter that converts the list of categories into a tree data model.

But this isn't important (you can find the libraries and configuration for this in the CaveatEmptor download).

What *is* important is that if the tree of categories is rendered, the persistence context was closed already in the Render Response phase, after `enterProfile()` was invoked. Which categories are now fully available in detached state? Only the root categories, categories with no parent category, have been loaded from the database. If the user clicks the tree display and wants to see whether a category has any children, the application fails with a `LazyInitializationException`.

With Seam, you can easily extend the persistence context to span the whole conversation, not only a single method or a single event. On-demand loading of data is then possible anywhere in the conversation and in any JSF processing phase.

Injecting a Seam persistence context

First, configure a Seam managed persistence context. Edit (or create) the file components.xml in your WEB-INF directory:

```
<components>

    <component name="org.jboss.seam.core.init">

        <!-- Enable seam.debug page -->
        <property name="debug">false</property>

        <!-- How does Seam lookup EJBs in JNDI -->
        <property name="jndiPattern">
            caveatemptor/#{ejbName}/local
        </property>
    </component>

    <component name="org.jboss.seam.core.manager">

        <!-- 10 minute inactive conversation timeout -->
        <property name="conversationTimeout">600000</property>

    </component>

    <component
        name="caveatEmptorEM"
        class="org.jboss.seam.core.ManagedPersistenceContext">
        <property name="persistenceUnitJndiName">
            java:/EntityManagerFactories/caveatEmptorEMF
        </property>
    </component>

</components>
```

You also move all other Seam configuration options into this file, so seam.properties is now empty (but still required as a marker for the component scanner).

When Seam starts up, it configures the class `ManagedPersistenceContext` as a Seam component. This is like putting Seam annotations onto that class (there are also annotations on this Seam-bundled class). The name of the component is `caveatEmptorEM`, and it implements the `EntityManager` interface. Whenever you now need an `EntityManager`, let Seam inject the `caveatEmptorEM`.

(The `ManagedPersistenceContext` class needs to know how to get a real `EntityManager`, so you have to provide the name of the `EntityManagerFactory` in JNDI. How you get the `EntityManagerFactory` into JDNI depends on your Java Persistence provider. In Hibernate, you can configure this binding with `jboss.entity.manager.factory.jndi.name` in persistence.xml.)

Modify the `RegisterBean` again, and use the Seam persistence context:

```
@Name("register")
@Scope(ScopeType.CONVERSATION)

@Stateful
public class RegisterBean implements Register {

    @In(create = true, value = "caveatEmptorEM")
    private EntityManager em;

    ...
```

When a method on this component is called for the first time, Seam creates an instance of `ManagedPersistenceContext`, binds it into the variable `caveatEmptorEM` in the conversation context, and injects it into the member field `em` right before the method is executed. When the conversation context is destroyed, Seam destroys the `ManagedPersistenceContext` instance, which closes the persistence context.

When is the persistence context flushed?

Integrating the persistence context lifecycle

The Seam-managed persistence context is flushed whenever a transaction commits. Instead of wrapping transactions (with annotations) around your action methods, let Seam also manage transactions. This is the job of a different Seam phase listener for JSF, replacing the basic one in faces-config.xml:

```
<lifecycle>
 <phase-listener>
   org.jboss.seam.jsf.TransactionalSeamPhaseListener
 </phase-listener>
</lifecycle>
```

This listener uses two system transactions to handle one JSF request. One transaction is started in the Restore View phase and committed after the Invoke

Application phase. Any system exceptions in these phases trigger an automatic rollback of the transaction. A different response can be prepared with an exception handler (this is weak point in JSF—you have to use a servlet exception handler in web.xml to do this). By committing the first transaction after the action method execution is complete, you keep any database locks created by SQL DML in the action methods as short as possible.

A second transaction spans the Render Response phase of a JSF request. Any view that pulls data on demand (and triggers initialization of lazy loaded associations and collections) runs in this second transaction. This is a transaction in which data is only read, so no database locks (if your database isn't running in repeatable read mode, or if it has a multiversion concurrency control system) are created during that phase.

Finally, note that the persistence context spans the conversation, but that flushing and commits may occur during the conversation. Hence, the whole conversation isn't atomic. You can disable automatic flushing with `@Begin(flush-Mode = FlushModeType.MANUAL)` when a conversation is promoted to be long-running; you then have to call `flush()` manually when the conversation ends (usually in the method marked with `@End`).

The persistence context is now available through Seam injection in any component, stateless or stateful. It's always the same persistence context in a conversation; it acts as a cache and identity map for all entity objects that have been loaded from the database.

An extended persistence context that spans a whole conversation has other benefits that may not be obvious at first. For example, the persistence context is not only the identity map, but also the cache of all entity objects that have been loaded from the database during a conversation.

Imagine that you don't hold conversational state between requests, but push every piece of information either into the database or into the HTTP session (or into hidden form fields, or cookies, or request parameters...) at the end of each request. When the next request hits the server, you assemble state again by accessing the database, the HTTP session, and so on. Because you have no other useful contexts and no conversational programming model, you must reassemble and disassemble the application state for every request. This stateless application design doesn't scale—you can't hit the database (the tier that is most expensive to scale) for every client request!

Developers try to solve this problem by enabling the Hibernate second-level cache. However, scaling an application with a conversational cache is much more interesting than scaling it with a dumb second-level data cache. Especially in a cluster, a second-level cache forces an update of the caches on all cluster nodes whenever any piece of data is modified by any node. With the conversational cache, only the nodes required for load balancing or failover of this particular conversation have to participate in replication of the current conversation data (which is in this case stateful session bean replication). Replication can be significantly reduced, because no global shared cache needs to be synchronized.

We'd like to talk about Seam much more and show you other examples, but we're running out of paper.

17.6 Summary

In this chapter, we looked at JSF, EJB 3.0, and how a web application that utilizes these standards can be improved with the JBoss Seam framework. We discussed Seam's contexts and how components can be wired together in a contextual fashion. We talked about integration of Seam with Hibernate Validator, and you saw why a Seam-managed persistence context is the perfect solution for `LazyInitializationExceptions`.

If you found this excourse into the Seam world interesting, much more is waiting to be discovered:

- The Seam component model also supports an event/listener concept, which allows components to call each other with a loosely coupled (wired through expressions) observer/observable pattern.

- You can enable a stateful navigation flow for a conversation with a pageflow descriptor, replacing the stateless JSF navigation model. This solves any problems you may have with the user clicking the Back button in the browser during a conversation.

- Seam has a sophisticated concurrency model for asynchronous processing on the server (integrated with JMS), as well as concurrency handling in conversations (Seam protects conversations from double-submits).

- Seam allows you to tie conversations and business process management tasks together easily. It integrates the workflows and business process context of JBoss jBPM (http://www.jboss.com/products/jbpm).

- Seam integrates JBoss Rules (http://www.jboss.com/products/rules). You can access policies in Seam components and Seam components from rules.

- A JavaScript library is bundled with Seam. With this Remoting framework, you can call Seam components from client-side code easily. Seam can handle any Ajax requests to your server.

- The Seam Application Framework provides out-of-the-box components that enable you to write an easily extendable CRUD database application in minutes.

- Seam components are easily testable, with or without an (embeddable) container. Seam makes integration and functional testing extremely easy with the `SeamTest` superclass for TestNG; this class allows you to script interactions that simulate a web browser.

If you want to continue with Seam and explore other features that didn't make it into this list, continue with the tutorials in the Seam reference documentation.

appendix A:
SQL fundamentals

A table, with its rows and columns, is a familiar sight to anyone who has worked with an SQL database. Sometimes you'll see tables referred to as *relations*, rows as *tuples*, and columns as *attributes*. This is the language of the *relational data model*, the mathematical model that SQL databases (imperfectly) implement.

The relational model allows you to define data structures and constraints that guarantee the integrity of your data (for example, by disallowing values that don't accord with your business rules). The relational model also defines the relational operations of restriction, projection, Cartesian product, and relational join [Codd, 1970]. These operations let you do useful things with your data, such as summarizing or navigating it.

Each of the operations produces a new table from a given table or combination of tables. SQL is a language for expressing these operations in your application (therefore called a *data language*) and for defining the base tables on which the operations are performed.

You write SQL *data definition language* (DDL) statements to create and manage the tables. We say that DDL defines the *database schema*. Statements such as CREATE TABLE, ALTER TABLE, and CREATE SEQUENCE belong to DDL.

You write SQL *data manipulation language* (DML) statements to work with your data at runtime. Let's describe these DML operations in the context of some tables of the CaveatEmptor application.

In CaveatEmptor, you naturally have entities like *item*, *user*, and *bid*. We assume that the SQL database schema for this application includes an ITEM table and a BID table, as shown in figure A.1. The datatypes, tables, and constraints for this schema are created with SQL DDL (CREATE and ALTER operations).

Insertion is the operation of creating a new table from an old table by adding a row. SQL databases perform this operation in place, so the new row is added to the existing table:

```
insert into ITEM values (4, 'Fum', 45.0)
```

ITEM

ITEM_ID	DESCRIPTION	
1	Item Nr. One	...
2	Item Nr. Two	...
3	Item Nr. Three	...

BID

BID_ID	ITEM_ID	AMOUNT
1	1	99.00
2	1	100.00
3	1	101.00
4	2	4.99

Figure A.1
Example tables with example data

An SQL *update* modifies an existing row:

```
update ITEM set PRICE = 47.0 where ITEM_ID = 4
```

A *deletion* removes a row:

```
delete from ITEM where ITEM_ID = 4
```

The real power of SQL lies in querying data. A single query may perform many relational operations on several tables. Let's look at the basic operations.

Restriction is the operation of choosing rows of a table that match a particular criterion. In SQL, this criterion is the expression that occurs in the where clause:

```
select * from ITEM where NAME like 'F%'
```

Projection is the operation of choosing columns of a table and eliminating duplicate rows from the result. In SQL, the columns to be included are listed in the select clause. You can eliminate duplicate rows by specifying the distinct keyword:

```
select distinct NAME from ITEM
```

A *Cartesian product* (also called *cross join*) produces a new table consisting of all possible combinations of rows of two existing tables. In SQL, you express a Cartesian product by listing tables in the from clause:

```
select * from ITEM i, BID b
```

A relational *join* produces a new table by combining the rows of two tables. For each pair of rows for which a *join condition* is true, the new table contains a row with all field values from both joined rows. In ANSI SQL, the join clause specifies a table join; the join condition follows the on keyword. For example, to retrieve all items that have bids, you join the ITEM and the BID table on their common ITEM_ID attribute:

```
select * from ITEM i inner join BID b on i.ITEM_ID = b.ITEM_ID
```

A join is equivalent to a Cartesian product followed by a restriction. So, joins are often instead expressed in theta style, with a product in the from clause and the join condition in the where clause. This SQL theta-style join is equivalent to the previous ANSI-style join:

```
select * from ITEM i, BID b where i.ITEM_ID = b.ITEM_ID
```

Along with these basic operations, relational databases define operations for aggregating rows (GROUP BY) and ordering rows (ORDER BY):

```
select b.ITEM_ID, max(b.AMOUNT)
from BID b
group by b.ITEM_ID
having max(b.AMOUNT) > 15
order by b.ITEM_ID asc
```

SQL was called a *structured* query language in reference to a feature called *subselects*. Because each relational operation produces a new table from an existing table or tables, an SQL query may operate on the result table of a previous query. SQL lets you express this using a single query, by nesting the first query inside the second:

```
select *
from (
    select b.ITEM_ID as ITEM, max(b.AMOUNT) as AMOUNT
    from BID b
    group by b.ITEM_ID
)
where AMOUNT > 15
order by ITEM asc
```

The result of this query is equivalent to the previous one.

A subselect may appear anywhere in an SQL statement; the case of a subselect in the where clause is the most interesting:

```
select * from BID b
    where b.AMOUNT >= (select max(c.AMOUNT) from BID c)
```

This query returns the largest bids in the database. Where clause subselects are often combined with *quantification*. The following query is equivalent:

```
select * from BID b
    where b.AMOUNT >= all(select c.AMOUNT from BID c)
```

An SQL restriction criterion is expressed in a sophisticated expression language that supports mathematical expressions, function calls, string matching, and perhaps even more sophisticated features such as full-text search:

```
select * from ITEM i
    where lower(i.DESCRIPTION) like '%gc%'
        or lower(i.DESCRIPTION) like '%excellent%'
```

appendix B:
Mapping quick reference

Many Hibernate books list all possible XML mapping elements and mapping annotations in an appendix. The usefulness of doing so is questionable. First, this information is already available in a convenient form; you only need to know how to get it. Second, any reference we might add here would be outdated in a matter of months, maybe even weeks. The core Hibernate mapping strategies don't change that often, but little details, options, and attributes are always modified in the process of improving Hibernate.

And isn't the main reason you want a mapping reference—so you have an up-to-date list of all options?

- You can get a list of all XML mapping elements and attributes bundled with Hibernate in hibernate-mapping-3.0.dtd. Open this file in any text editor, and you'll see that it's fully documented and very readable. You can print it out as a quick reference if you work with XML mapping files. If the syntax of the DTD bothers you, do a few quick search/replace operations on a copy of this file to replace the DTD tags with something you prefer in your printed output.

- You can get a list of all mapping annotations by reading the Javadoc for the `javax.persistence` and `org.hibernate.annotations` packages. The Javadoc is bundled with the Hibernate Annotations package. For example, to get a clickable, up-to-date reference for all Hibernate extension annotations, open api/org/hibernate/annotations/package-summary.html.

references

Ambler, Scott W. 2002. "Data Modeling 101." http://www.agiledata.org/essays/dataModeling101.html.

Booch, Grady, James Rumbaugh, and Ivar Jacobson. 2005. *The Unified Modeling Language User Guide,* second edition. Boston: Addison-Wesley Professional.

Codd, E.F. 1970. "A Relational Model of Data for Large Shared Data Banks." *Communications of the ACM* 13 (6): 377-87. http://www.acm.org/classics/nov95/toc.html.

Date, C.J. 2003. *An Introduction to Database Systems,* eighth edition. Boston: Addison Wesley.

Evans, Eric. 2003. *Domain-Driven Design: Tackling Complexity in the Heart of Software.* Boston: Addison-Wesley Professional.

Fowler, Martin. 1999. *Refactoring: Improving the Design of Existing Code.* Boston: Addison-Wesley Professional.

Fowler, Martin. 2003. *Patterns of Enterprise Application Architecture.* Boston: Addison-Wesley Professional.

Fussel, Mark L. 1997. *Foundations of Object-Relational Mapping.* http://www.chimu.com/publications/objectRelational/.

Gamma, E., R. Helm, R. Johnson, and J. Vlissides. 1995. *Design Patterns: Elements of Reusable Object-Oriented Software.* Boston: Addison-Wesley Professional.

Laddad, Ramnivas. 2003. *AspectJ in Action: Practical Aspect-Oriented Programming.* New York: Manning Publications.

Marinescu, Floyd. 2002. *EJB Design Patterns: Advanced Patterns, Processes and Idioms.* New York: John Wiley and Sons.

Massol, Vincent, and Ted Husted. 2003. *JUnit in Action.* New York: Manning Publications.

Pascal, Fabian. 2000. *Practical Issues in Database Management: A Reference for the Thinking Practitioner.* Boston: Addison-Wesley Professional.

Tow, Dan. 2003. *SQL Tuning.* Sebastopol, CA: O'Reilly and Associates.

Walls, Craig, and Norman Richards. 2004. *XDoclet in Action.* New York: Manning Publications.

index

MORE JAVA TITLES FROM MANNING

iText in Action:
Creating and Manipulating PDF
> by Bruno Lowagie
> ISBN: 1-932394-79-6
> 688 pages
> $49.99
> November 2006

Groovy in Action
> by Dierk Koenig with Andrew Glover,
> Paul King, Buillaume Laforge,
> and Jon Skeet
> Foreword by James Gosling
> ISBN: 1-932394-84-2
> 420 pages
> $44.99
> December 2006

For ordering information on these and other Manning titles,
please visit www.manning.com

MORE JAVA TITLES FROM MANNING

Ajax in Practice
  by David Crane, Jord Sonneveld,
    and Bear Bibeault
  ISBN: 1-932394-99-0
  450 pages
  $44.99
  February 2007

Prototype and Scriptaculous Quickly
  by David Crane and Bear Bibeault
    with Tom Locke
    Foreword by Thomas Fuchs
  ISBN: 1-933988-03-7
  350 pages
  $44.99
  March 2007

For ordering information on these and other Manning titles,
please visit www.manning.com

MORE JAVA TITLES FROM MANNING

MORE JAVA TITLES FROM MANNING

Hibernate Quickly
> by Patrick Peak and Nick Heudecker
> ISBN: 1-932394-41-9
> 456 pages
> $44.95
> August 2005

wxPython in Action
> by Noel Rappin and Robin Dunn
> ISBN: 1-932394-62-1
> 620 pages
> $44.95
> March 2006

For ordering information on these and other Manning titles,
please visit www.manning.com